MAX BECKMANN

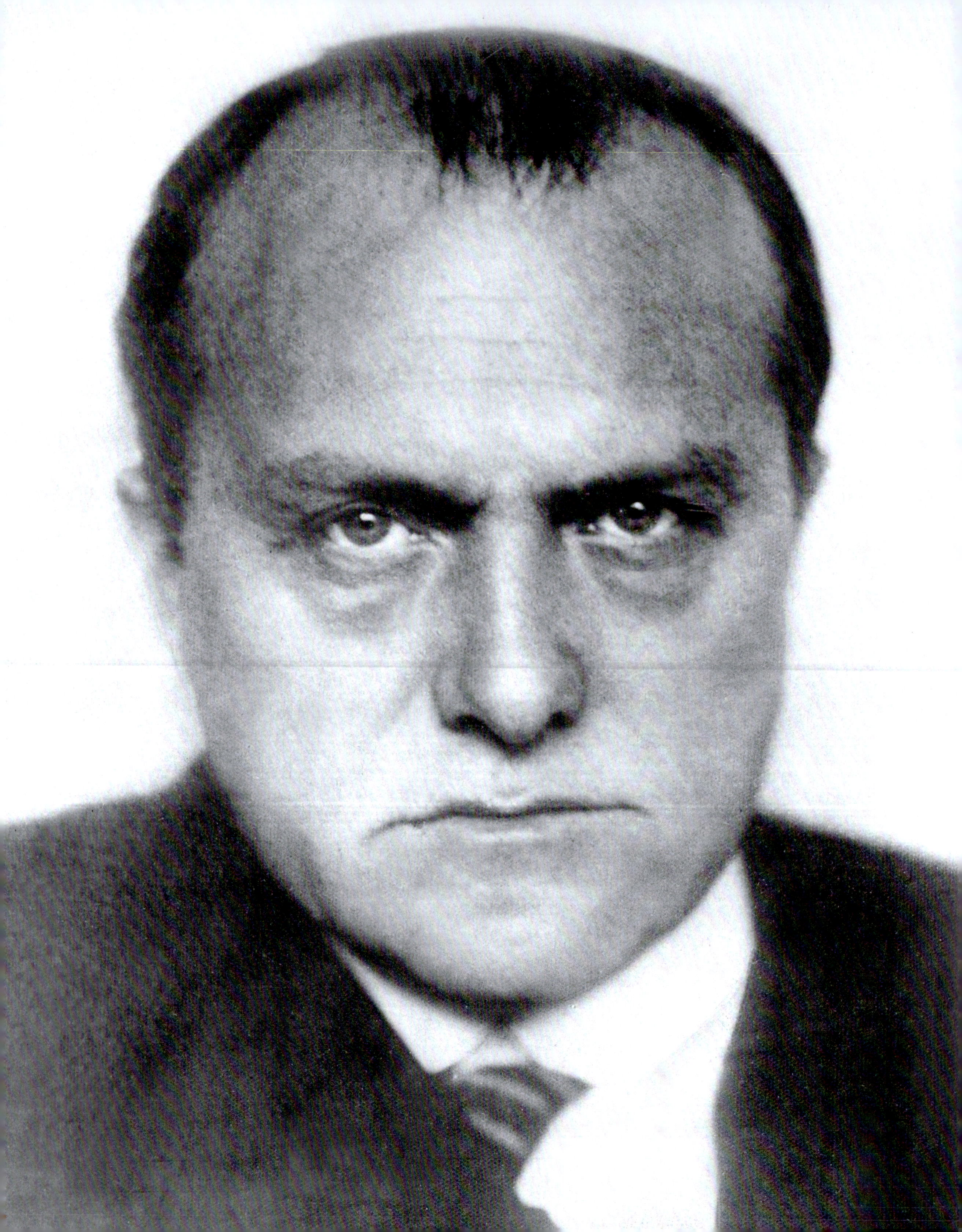

MAX BECKMANN
THE FORMATIVE YEARS 1915–1925

Edited by Olaf Peters
Preface by Ronald S. Lauder, foreword by Renée Price

With contributions by

Anna Maria Heckmann
Jürgen Müller
Olaf Peters
Dietrich Schubert
Elisa Tamaschke
Christiane Zeiller

With translated texts by

Max Beckmann and Heinrich Simon

RONALD S. LAUDER
NEUE GALERIE
MUSEUM FOR GERMAN AND AUSTRIAN ART
NEW YORK

PRESTEL
MUNICH • LONDON • NEW YORK

This catalogue has been published in conjunction with the exhibition

MAX BECKMANN: THE FORMATIVE YEARS, 1915–1925

Neue Galerie New York
October 5, 2023 – January 15, 2024

Curator
Olaf Peters

Exhibition Design
Richard Pandiscio,
William Loccisano / Pandiscio Green

Director of Publications
Scott Gutterman

Managing Editor
Janis Staggs

Editorial Assistant
Liesbet Van Leemput

Book Design
Richard Pandiscio,
William Loccisano / Pandiscio Green

Translation
Steven Lindberg

Project Coordinator
Cornelia Hübler

Production
Andrea Cobré

Origination
Schnieber Graphik, Munich

Printing and Binding
Longo AG, Bozen

Prestel Verlag, Munich
A member of Penguin Random House
Verlagsgruppe GmbH
Neumarkter Strasse 28
81673 Munich

A CIP catalogue record for this book is available from the British Library.

Library of Congress Control Number:
2023941002

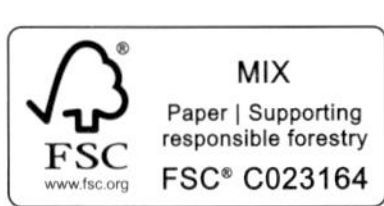

Penguin Random House Verlagsgruppe
FSC® N001967

Printed in Italy

ISBN 978-3-7913-7994-4

www.prestel.com

PAGE 2: Max Beckmann. Photo: ullstein bild / ullstein bild via Getty Images

PAGE 7: Paul Weller, Max Beckmann painting at an easel. Photo: Tate Images © Reserved

PAGE 9: Marie-Louise von Motesiczky and Mathilde Beckmann in fancy dress with Max Beckmann, 1920–30s. Photo: Tate Images

ACKNOWLEDGMENTS

Alexander Adler, New York
Selini Andres, Mannheim
Art Installation Design, New York
Mary Ellen Banisch, New York
Vivian Endicott Barnett, New York
Frances Beatty, New York
Mayen Beckmann, Berlin/Cologne
Tanja Borghardt, Bremen
Emily Braun, New York
Antonia Bryan, New York
Hendrik Bündge, Stuttgart
Matti Bunzl, New York
Sam Cameron, New York
Carla Caputo, New York
Andrea Cobré, Munich
Rosa Corral, Minneapolis
Tina Dähn, Berlin
Alexander Eiling, Frankfurt am Main
Fred Elghanayan, New York
Adina Ferber, New York
Anna-Lena Goltz, Halle (Saale)
Scott Hankins, Chapel Hill
Isabelle Harnoncourt, New York
Anna Maria Heckmann, Stuttgart
Kay Heymer, Düsseldorf
Max Hollein, New York
Cornelia Hübler, Munich
Joachim Jäger, Berlin
Oliver Kase, München
Evelyn Kelley, New York
Cait Kennedy, Saint Louis
Hulya Kolabas, New York
Hannah Korm, New York
Anna Kovacs, Waltham
Jennifer Lim, New York
Steven Lindberg, Berlin
Jill Lloyd, London
Bill Loccisano, Sarasota
Sirena Maxfield, New York
Cassie Mazzucco, New York
Janet Moore, Boston
Jürgen Müller, Dresden
Pia Müller-Tamm, Karlsruhe
Hannah Murray, London
Vlasta Odell, New York
Richard Pandiscio, New York
Natasha Perine, Chicago
Olaf Peters, Halle (Saale)
Katja Plankenhorn, Karlsruhe
Carina Plath, Hannover
Ernst Ploil, Vienna
Sami Rama, Branford
Mark Ramirez, Toledo
Esther-Maria Rittwagen, Lübeck
Jerry Rivera, New York
Stella Rollig, Vienna
Bridget Rymer, New York
Puppa Sayn-Wittgenstein, New York
Andreas Schalhorn, Berlin
Jackie Scalisi, New York
Mark Schlesinger, San Antonio
Dieter Scholz, Berlin
Rachel Schumann, Cologne
Antje Seeger, Halle (Saale)
Luise Seppeler, Berlin
Elizabeth Szancer, New York
Elisa Tamaschke, Berlin
Michele Tayler, Houston
Christina Végh, Bielefeld
Nara Wood, Cobb
Yagna Yass-Alston, New York
Christiane Zeiller, Munich
Jack Zinterhofer, New York
Will Zinterhofer, New York
Tom Zoufaly, New York

CONTENTS

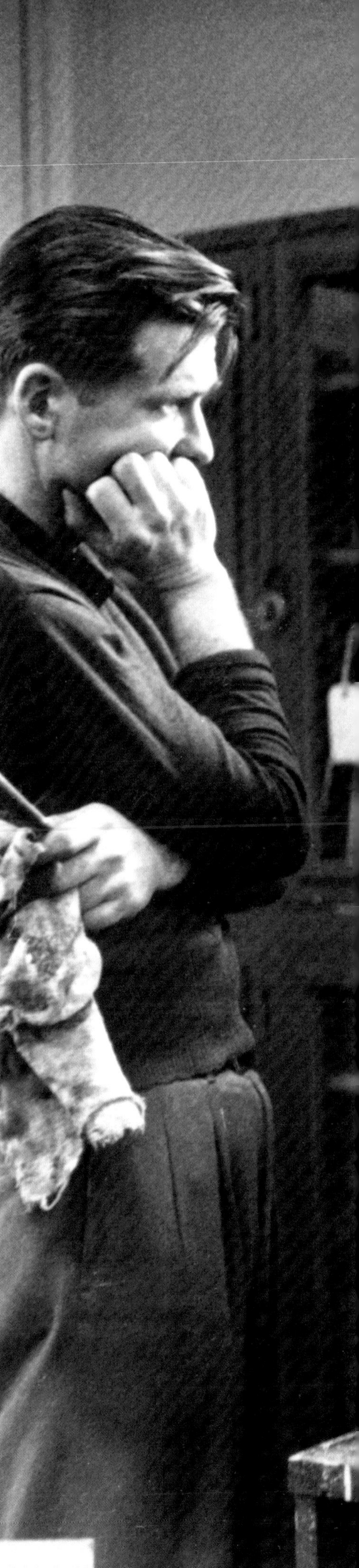

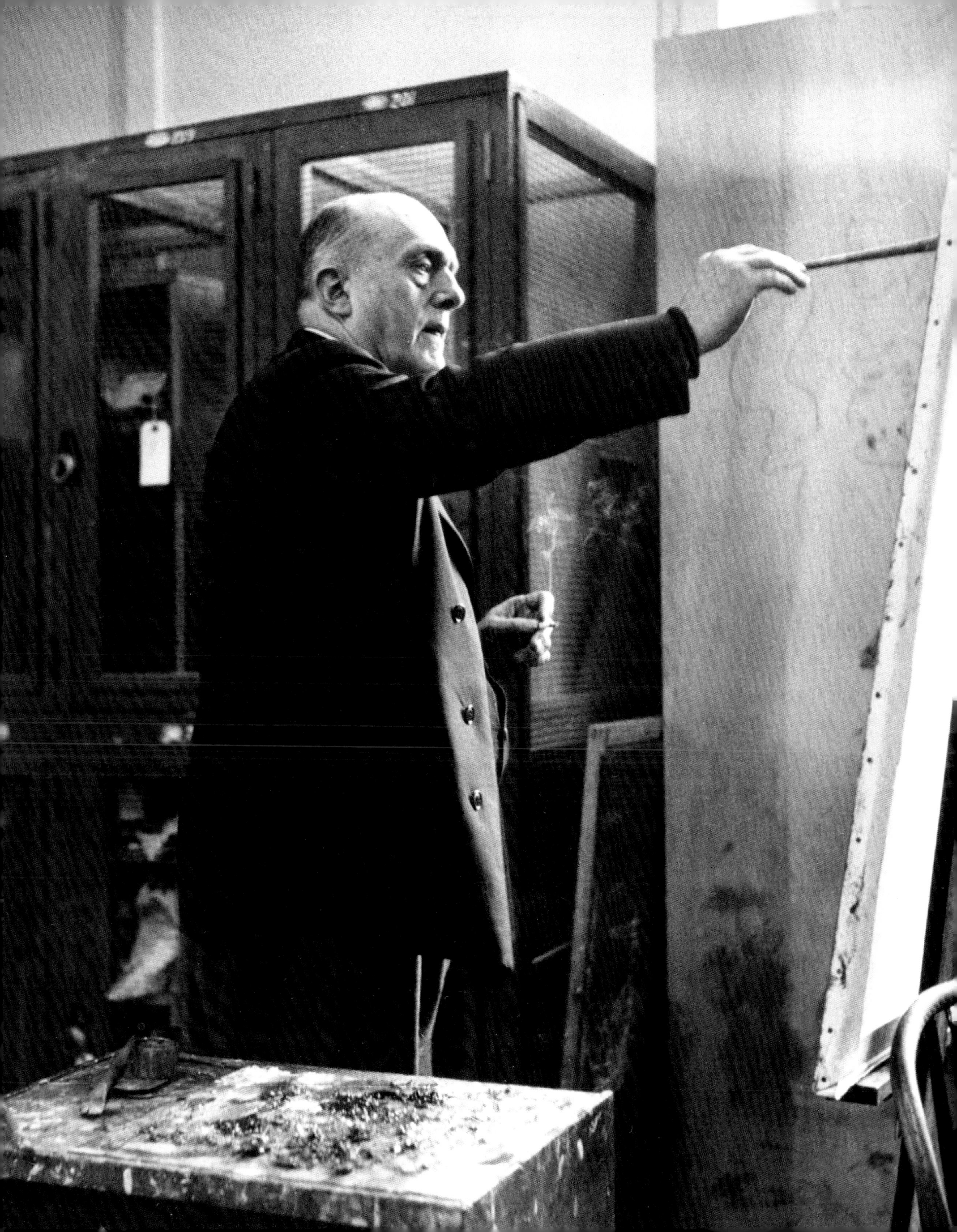

PREFACE

Max Beckmann is truly a giant of modern German art, someone who stands outside of any single category. He was a visionary, a man who captured not only the times he lived in, but someone who could see the future—see what *could* happen and what *would* happen.

I still remember the first time I encountered a work by Beckmann as a teenager in a midtown gallery here in New York. It was a triptych and I instantly saw the power and the strength of this extraordinary artist. I went right out and purchased every book I could find on Beckmann because I was so curious and wanted to learn more about him. This coincided with my growing interest in German and Austrian art.

It has been my good fortune to acquire a number of works by the artist over the years. The first extraordinary Beckmann painting to enter my collection was *Galleria Umberto* (1925). This work is incredibly prophetic in that it contains imagery of things to come. We see an Italian flag sinking into the water as if it is drowning; we see a dismembered figure, suggesting the torture during the Fascist era; there is a crystal ball offering a glimpse into the future and bugle sounding a warning. Think about this for a moment. In 1925, Mussolini had been in power for just three years and it would be another 20 years, two full decades of chaos, before the Italian dictator would meet his ignoble demise. Yet the painting anticipates both the rise and the downfall of Fascism in Italy along with all the turmoil in between. It is a mesmerizing picture, with a bizarre, dreamlike quality that makes it unforgettable.

The highlight for me, though, was the opportunity to acquire, with a fellow collector, the incredible *Self-Portrait with Horn* (1938), which Beckmann painted while he was living in exile in Amsterdam. It's interesting to note that Beckmann left Germany in 1937 on the day after Hitler's radio address on what he called degenerate art. This painting, which had once been in the collection of the artist's friend Stephan Lackner, seems to sum up so much about the experience of refugees, torn from their homeland and forced to establish himself in a new, unfamiliar environment. The horn also announces a warning about the rise of Nazism and intolerance. Because of the clarity and power of this painting, we can still hear that warning today.

I have been pleased to support exhibitions of Beckmann's work over the years, whether at the temporary branch of The Museum of Modern Art in Queens (2003) or in a pairing with Otto Dix at the Neue Galerie (2005). The current exhibition explores the early years of Beckmann's career, from the time of his traumatic experiences during World War I through his success during the Weimar Republic, and finally to the period in which he was driven into exile. All have shown important facets of an individual who gathered the tumultuous events taking place around him and converted them into extraordinary works of art.

The curator for this exhibition is Olaf Peters, who has organized several critically acclaimed shows for the Neue Galerie, including "Degenerate Art: The Attack on Modern Art in Nazi Germany, 1937" (2014) and "Berlin Metropolis: 1918–1933" (2015–16). He has been aided by Richard Pandiscio and Bill Loccisano, who designed the exhibition, and by my longtime associate Tom Zoufaly, who oversaw the installation. Together, they bring to light the gifts of an artist who seemed to sum up, and to transcend, the times he lived in. Museums and individuals in the United States and Europe generously provided key loans, helping to create a full representation of this singular artist. I trust our guests will enjoy experiencing Beckmann as much as I have since first encountering his work more than 50 years ago.

Ronald S. Lauder
President, Neue Galerie New York

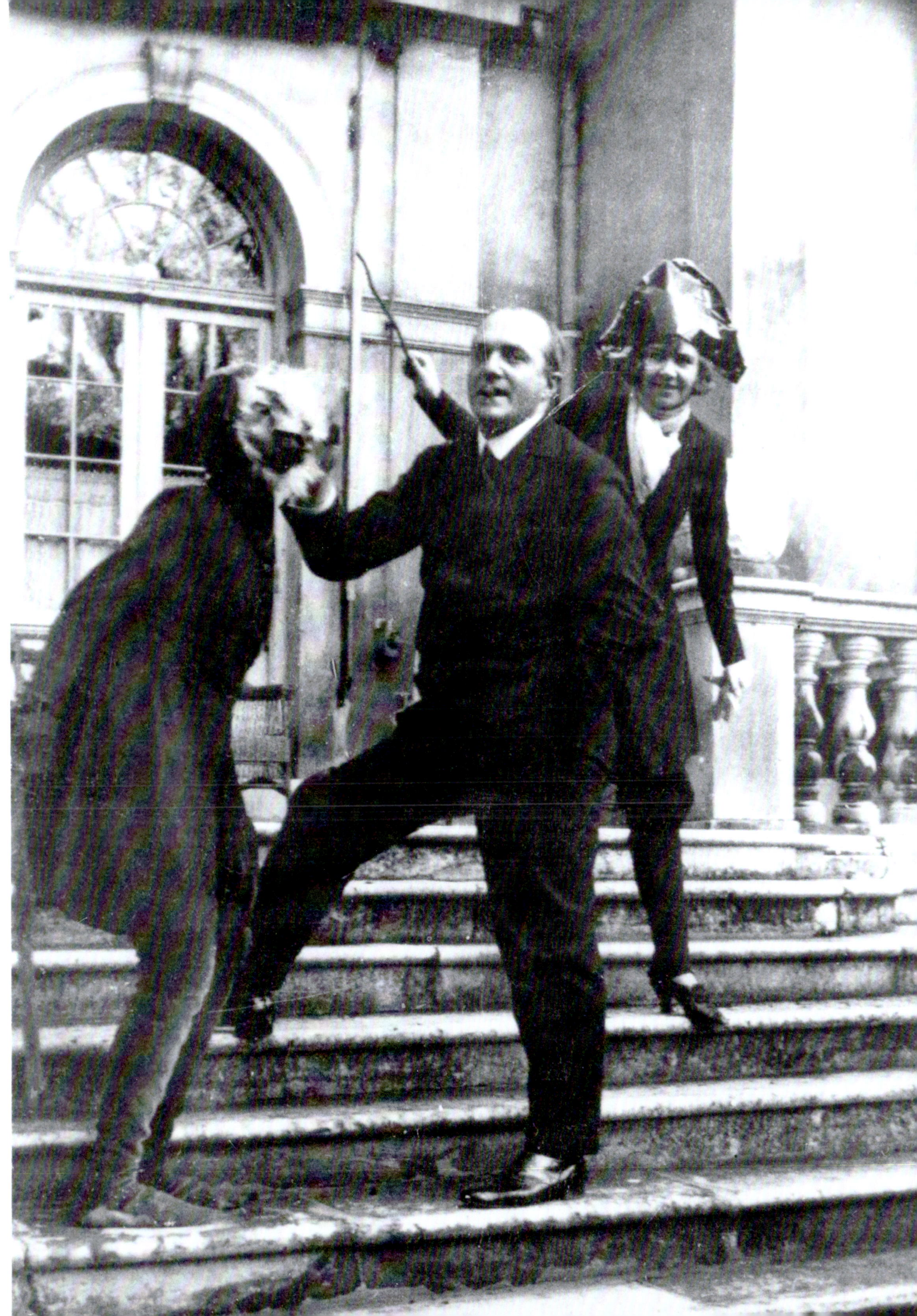

FOREWORD

Max Beckmann is one of the outstanding painters of the twentieth century. By presenting a monographic exhibition of his work, the Neue Galerie New York is fulfilling a longstanding goal. The museum's extended collection includes central works by Beckmann, such as the major portfolio of prints *Die Hölle* (Hell, 1919) and the early political allegory *Galleria Umberto* (1925). These works represent the point of departure for this project. The basic thesis of the exhibition is that Beckmann, after the profoundly disturbing experience of World War I, managed to advance to a new pictorial conception. The painter both assimilated his experiences and connected to concurrent developments in art. Indeed, our exhibition offers an in-depth look and invites a close reading of key works of these formative years.

There have been several exhibitions on Beckmann in the last couple of years. Ours is different, however, in focusing on this particular time period and his artistic approach. For many of his contemporaries, Beckmann came to epitomize the latest evolution of representational painting. In 1925, when he was 41 years old, Beckmann emerged as the crucial figure in the exhibition "Die Neue Sachlichkeit: Deutsche Malerie nach dem Expressionismus" (New Objectivity: German Painting after Expressionism) in Mannheim, even though he would later distance himself from that term. This turning point marks the endpoint of our exhibition and explains its restriction to the years from 1915 to 1925.

The exhibition gathers together some of the masterpieces of Beckmann's art including the outstanding paintings *Fastnacht* (Carnival, 1920, Tate, London), *Der Traum* (The Dream, 1921, Saint Louis Art Museum), and *Die Barke* (The Bark, 1926, Private Collection). Our show offers the unique opportunity to experience these works together and to reflect on the genesis of Beckmann's mature style of painting.

A key step to Beckmann's transformation was his focus on religious topics in paintings around 1917-18. They are centrally important in this context and we are proud to display three key examples from major public collections. They reveal his stylistic development but also outline the painter's horizon of interpretation as he sought to portray his own era using the pictorial formulas of the Passion of Christ and other biblical themes.

Around 1920, Beckmann was intensely preoccupied by the social and political fault lines of the era. That is why his work of this phase was considered verism and associated with the leftist wing of the *Neue Sachlichkeit*—something that is often forgotten today. Beckmann himself spoke of his art in terms of "transcendental objectivity." The subjects of these works prepare the ground, in terms of both form and content, for Beckmann's later paintings.

The Neue Galerie exhibition and the catalogue are not just about the bolstering of his stature as an artist from 1915 to 1925, but also about the seminal energy he brought to his work at the time; the artist himself repeatedly returned to this phase over the course of his career. The self-referential aspect of Beckmann's work thus comes clearly into view. It is our aspiration to contribute to a deeper understanding of Beckmann's artistic productivity.

The exhibition was conceived and has been organized by Prof. Dr. Olaf Peters, who has taught art history in Halle an der Saale University since 2006 and is an esteemed Member of the Board of Trustees of the Neue Galerie. He also has organized the exhibitions "Otto Dix" (2010), and the trilogy "Degenerate Art: The Attack on Modern Art in Nazi Germany, 1937" (2014), "Berlin Metropolis: 1918-1933" (2015-16), and "Before the Fall: German and Austrian Art of the 1930s" (2018) for the Neue Galerie. His thesis at the University of Bonn was a broad monograph on Beckmann, and he is one of the leading experts on the artist. Prof. Dr. Peters, together with his fellow authors Ms. Anna Maria Heckmann, Prof. Dr. Jürgen Müller,

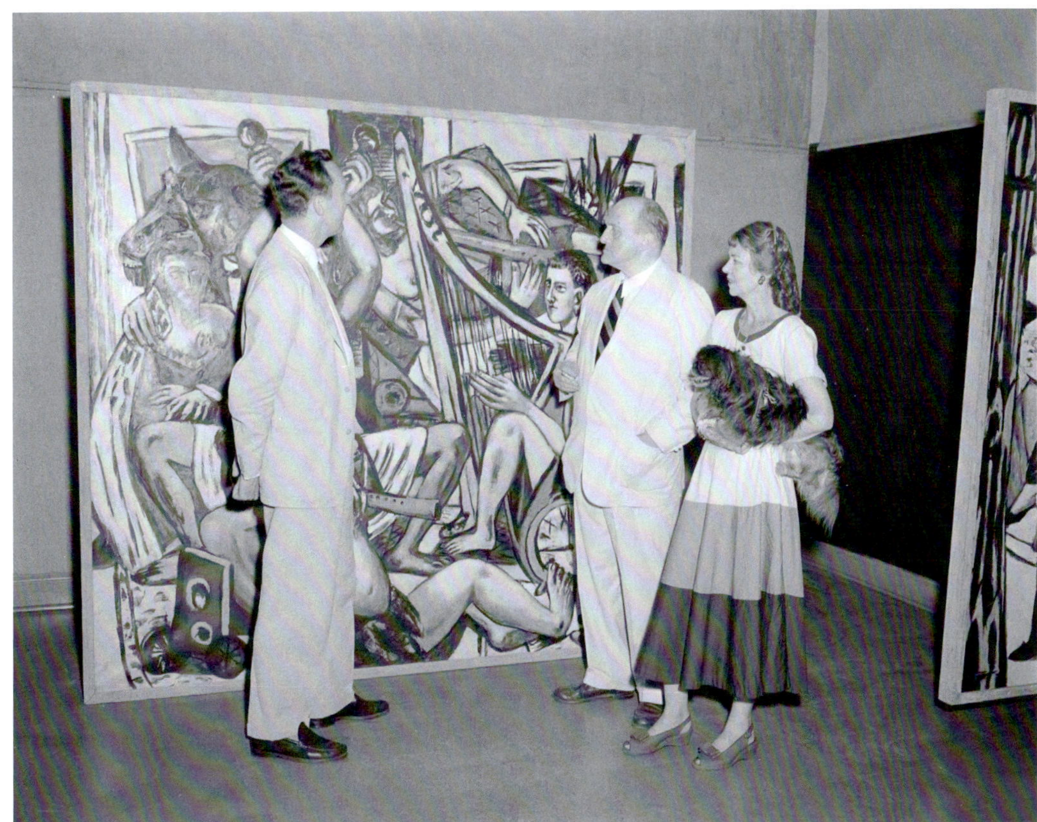

Max Beckmann, his wife Quappi, and his dog Butschy in front of *Blind Man's Buff* with Perry Rathbone, director of the City Art Museum of St. Louis, 1948. University of Colorado Photolab Collection, no. 1975, Art Department, Max Beckmann Show. Archives, University of Colorado at Boulder Libraries

Prof. Dr. Dietrich Schubert, Dr. Elisa Tamaschke, and Dr. Christiane Zeiller, brings fresh perspectives to Beckmann's complex, sometimes difficult, and multilayered art. All of these contributors deserve our sincere thanks.

We are most grateful to the host of institutional and private lenders who made our exhibition possible, including Ms. Katie Ziglar, Ackland Art Museum; Mr. James Rondeau, The Art Institute of Chicago; Dr. Bernhard Maaz, Bayerische Staatsgemäldesammlungen Pinakothek der Moderne; Mr. Richard Armstrong, Solomon R. Guggenheim Museum; Prof. Dr. Christoph Grunenberg, Kunsthalle Bremen; Dr. Johan Holten, Kunsthalle Mannheim; Dr. Dagmar Korbacher, Kupferstichkabinett Staatliche Museen zu Berlin; Mr. Matthew Teitelbaum, Museum of Fine Arts Boston; Dr. Glenn D. Lowry, The Museum of Modern Art, New York; Dr. Alexander Bastek, Museum Behnhaus Drägerhaus; Dr. Yilmaz Dziewior, Museum Ludwig; Ms. Josefa Simon; the Acacia Corporation; Dr. Christiane Zeiller; Ms. Mayen Beckmann; Dr. Gannit Ankori, Rose Art Museum; Dr. Min Jung Kim, Saint Louis Art Museum; Mr. Klaus Biesenbach and Dr. Joachim Jäger, Staatliche Museen zu Berlin, Neue Nationalgalerie; Dr. Maria Balshaw, CBE and Ms. Frances Morris, Tate Modern; Dr. Adam M. Levine, Toledo Museum of Art; and Ms. Alejandra Peña-Gutiérrez, Weisman Art Museum. We also offer our thanks to those lenders who wish to remain anonymous.

Every major loan exhibition needs the support of friends and trusted advisors. Among these for the Neue Galerie were Frances Beatty, Mayen Beckmann, Isabelle Harnoncourt, Lukas Minssen, Puppa Sayn Wittgenstein, and Wilfried Utermann. We offer them our gratitude.

I wish to thank Richard Pandiscio and Bill Loccisano of Pandiscio Green for their wonderful contributions to the design of our exhibition and of this catalogue. The tireless staff of the Neue Galerie deserves to be acknowledged as well, including Deputy Director and Chief Operating Officer Scott Gutterman, Director of Curatorial and Managing Editor of Publications Janis Staggs, Manager of Curatorial Liesbet Van Leemput, Chief Registrar and Director of Exhibitions Stacey Traunfeld, Associate Registrar Julie Jung, and Director of Communications Michelle Perlin.

And once again, we must express our deepest gratitude to Ronald S. Lauder, the co-founder of our museum, whose enthusiasm, vision, and generosity for the arts is boundless. He has been a collector of work by Max Beckmann for several decades. The Neue Galerie is his gift to the world, and bringing this museum to life is our great privilege.

Renée Price
Director, Neue Galerie New York

BECOMING BECKMANN

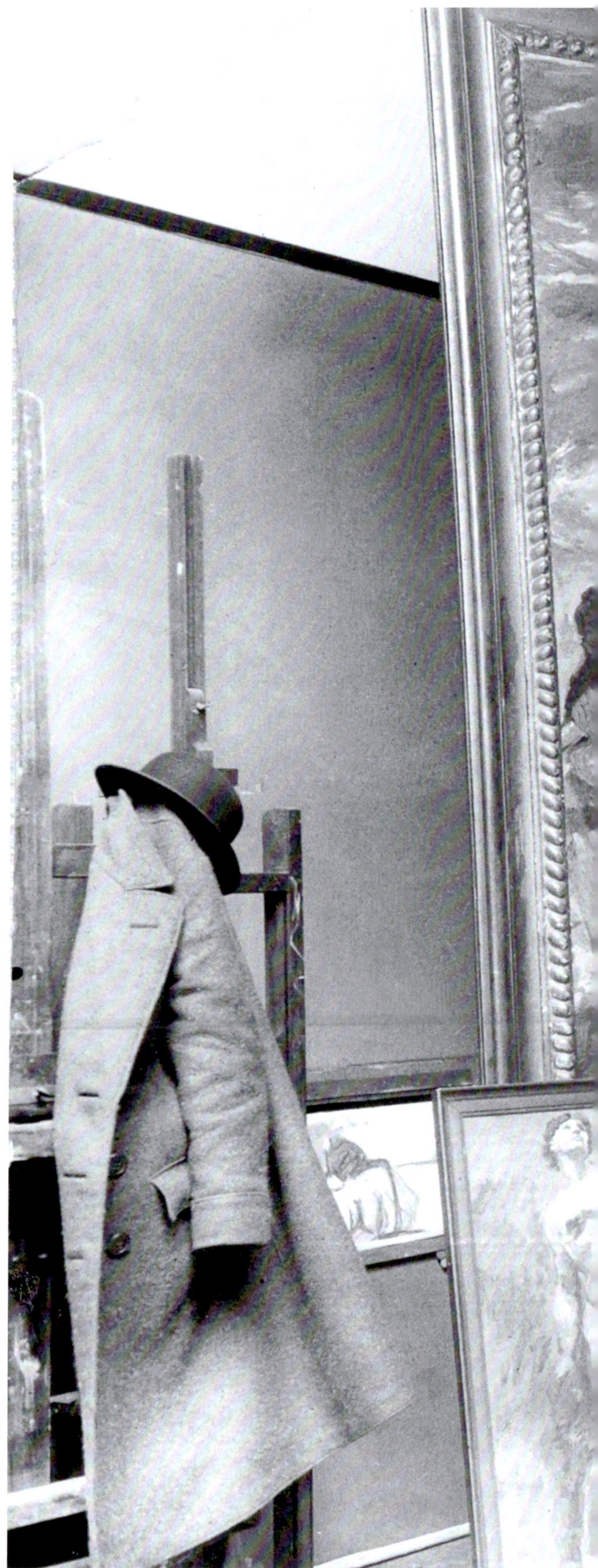

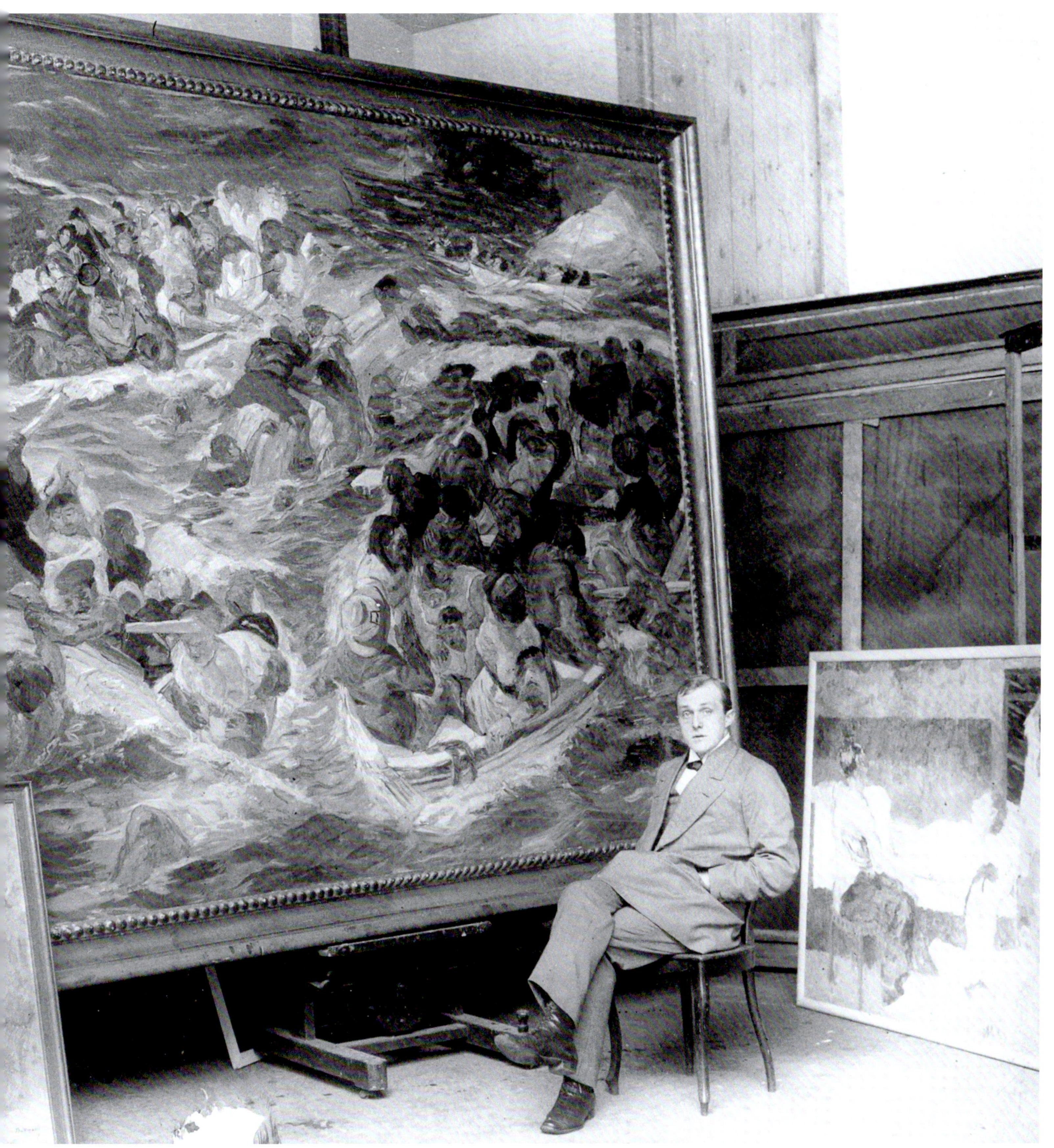

Max Beckmann in his Berlin studio in front of *Sinking of the Titanic*, 1912. © Oliver Baker, Germanisches Nationalmuseum, Deutsches Kunstarchiv, Nürnberg, NL Schmidt, Doris

TRANSCENDENTAL OBJECTIVITY

MAX BECKMANN'S MODERNITY

Olaf Peters

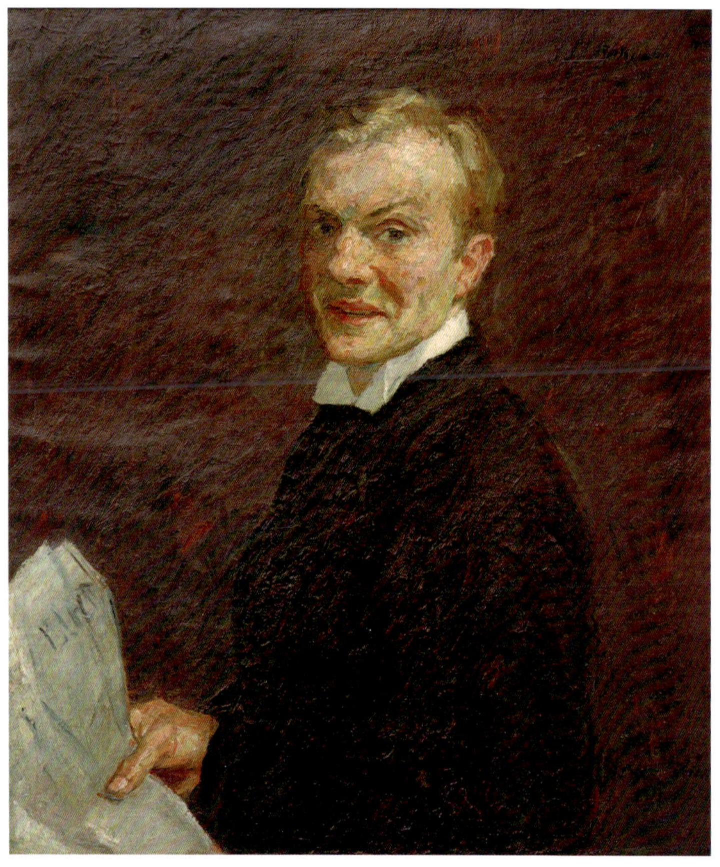

TURNS AGAINST AVANT-GARDE

Max Beckmann adopted early on a position against the artistic avant-garde and did not shy away from public controversy when doing so. In 1912 he had a public dispute with Franz Marc of the Blauer Reiter (Blue Rider).[1] What artistic concept—which Beckmann was already associating with the term *Sachlichkeit* (objectivity) at this point—was the artist trying to realize in opposition to the avant-garde that was advancing toward abstraction? How did the painter define himself in relation to the latest developments in modern art? In the context of the famous so-called "Bremen Art Dispute" of 1911 led by Carl Vinnen,[2] Beckmann rashly dismissed Henri Matisse as one of the "untalented persons" and recommended instead painters of the late nineteenth century such as Wilhelm Leibl, Max Liebermann, and Adolf Menzel as "instructive artists"[3] [Fig. 1]. Beckmann did so, however, without siding with Vinnen, a Worspweder painter who adopted a conservative, *völkisch* (racist-populist) position.[4] How did Beckmann integrate into his own creations artistic concepts that he had publicly rejected and then transform them into order to develop them? These questions will be addressed in what follows and in the other essays in this catalogue in order to explain the growing rift as well as the continuity that are manifest in his oeuvre. It distinguishes the early work from the work from 1915 onward and then also characterizes the later development after 1925. The decade between 1915 and 1925 mediates between two larger blocks of pictures and itself represents such a block, one that is without question a summit in German painting of the twentieth century.[5]

The famous controversy between Beckmann and Marc flared up already in 1912.[6] In the journal *Pan*, Beckmann argued for "*Sachlichkeit*,"[7] and polemicized against Fauvism, Primitivism, and Expressionism. Above all, Beckmann took aim at the increasingly clear trend to abandon the representational image: "What is feeble and overly aesthetic about this so-called new painting is its failure to distinguish between the idea of a wallpaper or poster and that of a 'picture.'"[8] The fundamental artistic conflict between, on the one hand, his own Impressionist painting style, which was ill-suited to mastering the large, sometimes sublime subjects (Crucifixion, shipwreck, earthquake) he chose and, on the other, his dismissive reaction toward the contemporaneous trends of the avant-garde, made it necessary for the artist to thoroughly rethink his own position. The literary scholar and theorist of the avant-garde Peter Bürger rightly called him a "thinking artist," because he was trying to fathom the problems of painting not just in practice but also in theory.[9]

Beckmann had reached a dead end and had to reformulate his approach to painting[10] if he wanted to assert himself in the continual battles of the artistic field.[11] Following his encounter with the latest European painting at the "Herbstsalon" (Autumn Salon) in Berlin in 1913[12], and the fundamental criticism of Beckmann's earlier oeuvre as "geriatric"[13], and the outbreak of World War I in 1914, which was like a catalyst for the fundamental stylistic transformation of his work.[14] He had to react to this and tried to situate his own concept on the threshold between a planar, stylishly decorative and a spatial one, which he understood as a dichotomy. Influenced by Rembrandt van Rijn, Francisco Goya, and the early Paul Cézanne, he emphasized spatial depth in his art: "As for myself, I paint and try to develop my style exclusively in terms of deep space, something that in contrast to superficially decorative art penetrates as far as possible into the very core of nature and the spirit of things."[15] That did not, however, keep Beckmann from productively reworking the so-called decorative art he loathed and integrating it into his visual cosmos, for example, by making use of the achievements of Cubism in pictorial autonomy.

World War I, in which Beckmann volunteered as a medical orderly, prompted the painter to find a new form of objective perception and representation. Initially, Beckmann proudly reported to his wife, Minna Beckmann-Tube, on his daily experiences in the war.[16] He soon abandoned that. The experience of combat radicalized modern artists in their manner of aesthetic expression and techniques in both form and content, and so too Beckmann.[17] That meant a break with his early painted work; Beckmann only achieved a unique artistic style because of the war. The process of transforming and breaking away from his early monumental Impressionist paintings can indeed be followed in a sometimes-oppressive way in his paintings, his drawings, and his letters from the field.[18] It is not so much the personal existential threat—Beckmann was hardly at great risk in his activities as a medical orderly—as it was the experience of horror in the face of death and mutilation that

1. Max Beckmann, *Self-Portrait (Laughing)*, 1910, oil on canvas. Stiftung Stadtmuseum Berlin. Photo: akg-images

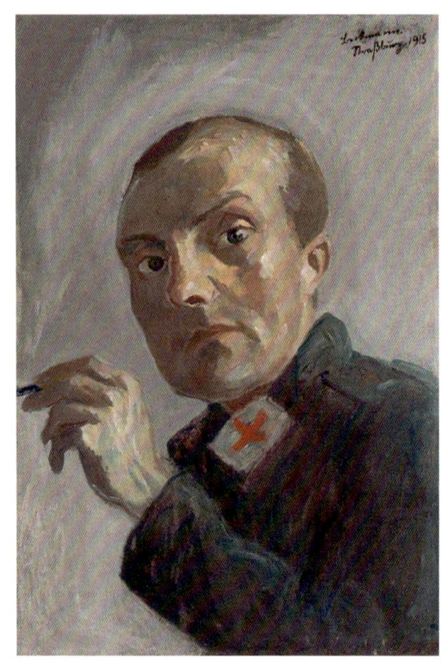

2. Max Beckmann, *Self-Portrait as Medical Orderly,* 1915, oil on canvas. Kunst- und Museumsverein im Von der Heydt-Museum Wuppertal. Photo: Antje Zeis-Loi, Medienzentrum Wuppertal

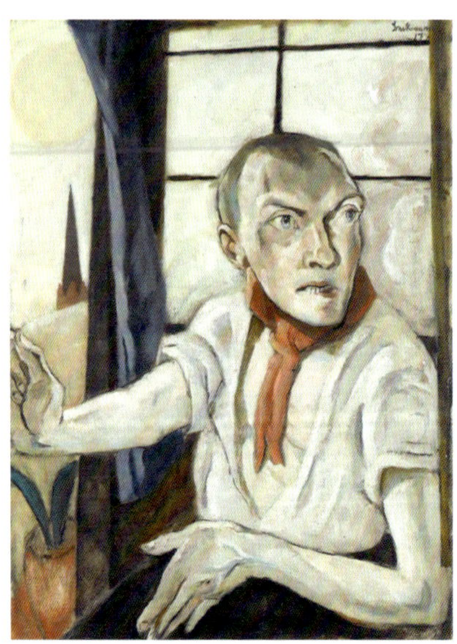

3. Max Beckmann, *Self-Portrait with Red Scarf,* 1917, oil on canvas. Staatsgalerie Stuttgart. Photo: © Staatsgalerie Stuttgart

provoked an almost obligatory artistic reinvention. The artist experienced "horrible things" and drew because it seemed to offer protection from "death and danger," as he reported to his wife in an oft-cited letter from October 3, 1914.[19] Seeing the wartime drawings and prints, one senses that he was trying to keep the horrors he had observed and captured at a distance and used his sketches to try to ward off misfortune. Beckmann transposed the pain and violence of the war into Christian iconography of the Passion: "I saw some remarkable things. In the semidarkness of the shelter, half-naked, blood-covered men that were having white bandages applied. Grand and painful in expression. New visions of scourgings of Christ. Then a first lieutenant was brought in who had just received a bad chest wound. A handsome face, already very pallid, with reddish hair and a grayish pink skin tone. He was absolutely calm and very feeble."[20]

His enthusiasm over being able to render what he had witnessed in a manner that was artistically adequate still seems strange, but nightmares would soon haunt the painter. The drawn and etched self-portraits made between 1915 and 1917 clearly reveal the artist's nervous strain, compounded by the separation from his family that soon followed. During the period in Frankfurt am Main thereafter, Beckmann found acceptance, stability, and support from his friends Fridel and Ugi Battenberg, and it marks a sharp turning point in his life and work.[21] The existential crisis could not be overcome immediately and reverberated for a long time. It can be seen during the war in his *Selbstbildnis beim Zeichnen* (Self-Portrait while Drawing) [see ill. on p. 116].[22] His *Selbstbildnis als Krankenpfleger* (Self-Portrait as Medical Orderly) [Fig. 2], in which he is almost too awake, with his eyes widening in panic, belongs here as well. This small-format painting demonstrates that he is on the way to a new form of perception, and it stands at the breaking point of a stylistic transformation. One can sense in it the reorientation, a turn to objectivity, that Beckmann himself described as a turning point: "For the first time it becomes evident what I had meanwhile gone through in the war."[23] The diagnostic gaze depicted in this painting gives way in 1917 to a resigned gaze turned inward in *Selbstbildnis mit rotem Schal* (Self-Portrait with Red Scarf) [Fig. 3]. Beckmann introduces an existential symbol in the form of a scarf painted in an alarming red.[24] Our exhibition begins with the paintings of this phase.

This is the period when Beckmann's ambitious attempt to grapple with the confusion and fault lines of the epoch in the traditional interpretive schema of Christian iconography failed, and yet he continued to refer to it. This has been well documented by scholars using the example of the large *Auferstehung* (Resurrection) of 1916–18.[25] He broke off work on this powerful and monumental painting and left it unfinished, and then rolled it out again in the 1940s, in the middle of World War II. Ultimately, Beckmann abandoned the canvas for good.[26] Beckmann's significant paintings of the late 1910s and early 1920s continue to synthesize Christian iconography and contemporaneous reality. *Die Nacht* (The Night) [Fig. 4], an early major work of the postwar period, is such an aesthetic concentration. It depicts the brutal massacre of an entire family,[27] It is a Triumph of Death for its time, the negation of life in a cramped, angular attic room, and can be read as an iconographic quotation of the famous *Triumph of Death* in Pisa, a fresco from Trecento on the Camposanto.[28] Beckmann's painting marks a rupture in civilization; it reveals the questioning and breakdown of the traditional bourgeois order after World War I in the face of defeat and revolution. He continued to see himself as a modern painter who was at once conscious of the tradition and an eminent contemporary. Beckmann includes his family in *The Night,* even though they were living apart at the time, and he traces the separation to external causes. The people depicted are victims of a quotidian civil war whose boundless brutality threatens to hollow out civil society, to make life a daily martyrdom, and destroys one's own family.[29] Contemporary history and biography cannot be separated from each other.

TRANSCENDENTAL OBJECTIVITY AS "VIOLENT VERISM"

In 1918 with an eye to his concept of art, Beckmann coined the seemingly paradoxical term "transcendental objectivity." With this phrase he attempted to summarize the new development in his painting.[30] Stylistically, he was creating an amalgamation of Expressionism, Cubism, and late medieval art. But the term goes beyond that to consider the representation of his own time that

4. Max Beckmann, *The Night*, 1918–19, oil on canvas. Kunstsammlung Nordrhein-Westfalen, Düsseldorf. Photo: bpk Bildagentur / Kunstsammlung Nordrhein-Westfalen / Walter Klein / Art Resource, NY

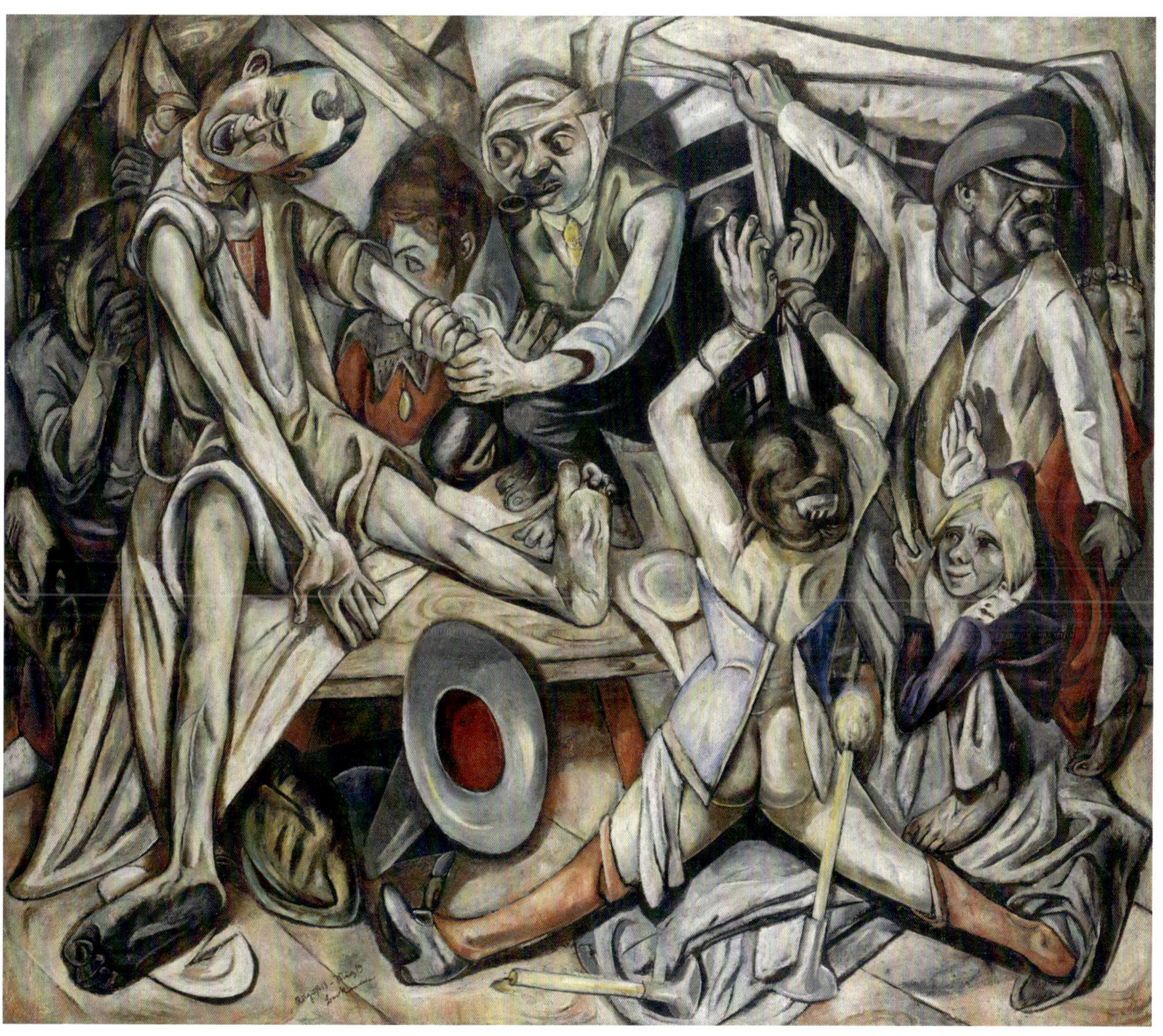

sought to be objective and realistic together with a metaphysical claim to the interpretation of the world. Beckmann would subscribe to the latter all of his life. Around 1918–20, he tried to achieve that through an interpretive return to the national art tradition of early German and Netherlandish art, which Jürgen Müller address elsewhere in this catalogue. Beckmann experienced the crucial Northern influences that would be so important for his later reception and his understanding of himself as an artist in the nationalistically stoked climate of World War I. They are referenced in a letter he wrote to his wife, Minna, on April 17, 1915, in which he reported on a trip to Brussels:

> *I saw wonderful Brueghels, some remarkable Rogier van der Weyden, who among the Belgian primitives appeals to me most of all. But certainly a wonderful portrait by Cranach made the most intense impression on me. A man with slanted eyes, beard and wearing fur seen against a bare wall, and some unknown German primitives, who seemed remarkable to me in their almost brutal, raw sincerity, their robust, almost peasantlike strength. These paintings once again inspired me immensely and confirmed me in my convictions. I felt myself to be near to all of them and felt at home while in enemy country.*[31]

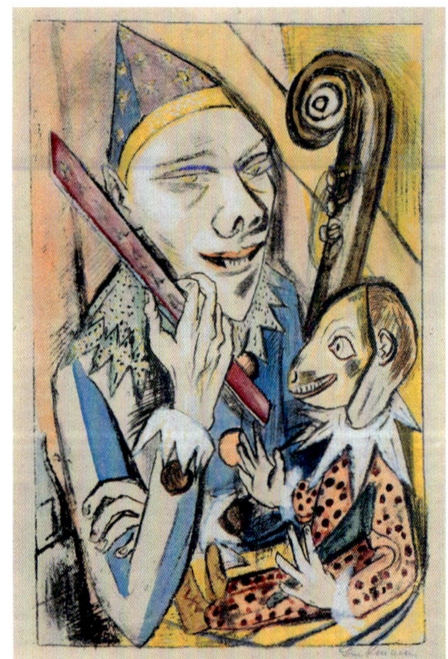

5. Max Beckmann, *Pierrot and Mask,* 1920, colored lithograph. Private Collection

Beckmann could make an intellectual connection that offered him a place of refuge.

In his "*Bekenntnis*" (Confession) from 1918, he complemented this national turn with sideswipes at Impressionism, abstraction in the works of the successors to the Blauer Reiter, and late Expressionism, which he regarded as increasingly flat.[32] By associating the medieval Gothic, which was considered authentically German, with Expressionism—which by then had acquired German connotations—and aiming this synthesis against the abstract, expressive tendencies of the avant garde, Beckmann's "transcendental objectivity" satisfied the concept of a "German art" that both artists and art critics demanded at the time.[33]

Stylistically, Beckmann was abreast with his times with his reception of Cubism and Expressionism, while seemingly paradoxically, he rejected Expressionism and abstraction in equal measure and transcended them while moving toward the *Neue Sachlichkeit.* This artistic process was crucial for his future. For Beckmann, engaging with Cubism proved to be necessary to break free of one of the core conceptual problems of his art before World War I.[34] In the view of the liberal critic Max Osborn, this was a "lack of an internal framework" and the absence of a "solid construction of the whole" of the composition. This made the drifting apart of Beckmann's large-format, Impressionist history paintings of the time inevitable.[35] Osborn thus anticipated the critic Carl Einstein's fundamental criticism of Impressionism, who later claimed that Impressionism had overcome—indeed, even dissolved and broke down—history painting of the nineteenth century by discovering and thematizing light.[36]

In this view, the problems with Beckmann's prewar painting resulted, on the one hand, from the painter attempting to cling to the grand subject of history while using modern premises of Impressionist painting that were paradoxical in that context. On the other hand, this contrasted with the new drawing-like quality in Beckmann's painting.[37] Gustav Friedrich Hartlaub succinctly remarked of this development "that the 'painter' becomes a 'draftsman'; the broadly flowing substance of the paint solidifies into a linear frame."[38] Beckmann was

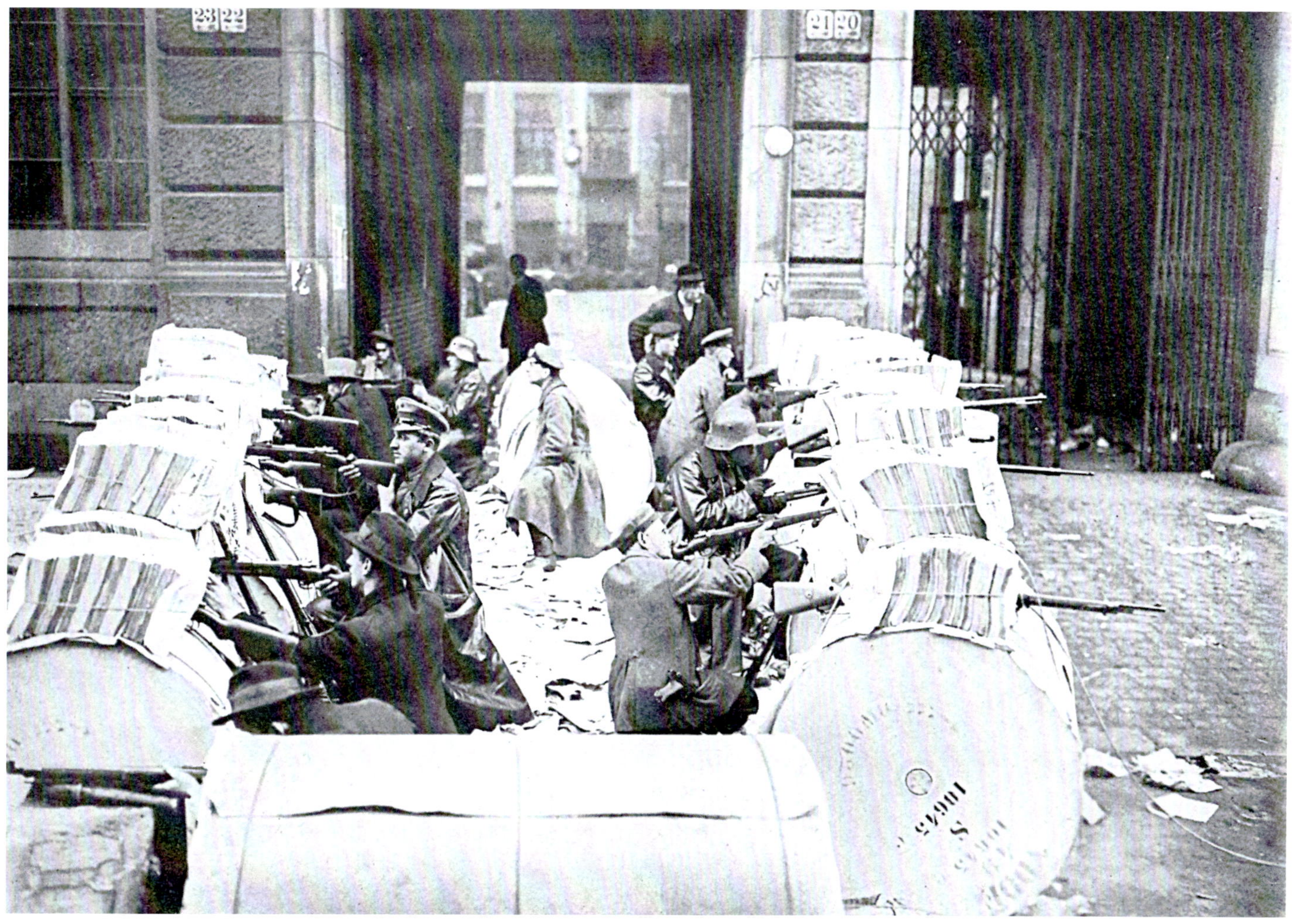

6. Street battle during the Revolution in Berlin, 1919

able to use this to resolve his artistic dilemma for a time and was accepted into a tradition that was perceived as decidedly German [Fig. 5]. In Paul Westheim's *Kunstblatt*, one of the leading art journals of the Weimar Republic, the Frankfurt-based journalist and Beckmann collector Heinrich Simon remarked unequivocally in 1919: "This unnatural art, that is to say, art that has not clung to the pleasing but instead advanced to the spiritual, this ugly art, i.e., truth-seeking, raw and violent art, i.e., courageous art that does not shrink from the most difficult problems, is and will always be the true German art. [...] Beckmann is a German painter in that sense."[39] Years later, when Beckmann was encountering the first hostilities from the National Socialists, he asked his art dealer Günther Franke to emphasize precisely this fact to the National Socialists to protect him from future attacks.[40] This turned out to be an illusion, and Beckmann became a prominent victim of National Socialism's anti-modernist art policy after 1933.

That Beckmann unsparingly confronted reality in his art after World War I was perceived as "German" and at the same time contemporary. Updating the link to the Christian tradition in a stylistic idiom with national connotations of early German or Netherlandish painting was in Beckmann's case a way of making the wide-ranging dubiousness of the present his theme. By appropriating and even mocking the tradition, Beckmann was emphatically culminating the turn away from the Christian religion and faith that he had described to his Munich publisher Reinhard Piper. The painter had explained it to him already in July 1919 in Frankfurt am Main: "A new mystical feeling will form. Humility before God is over. My

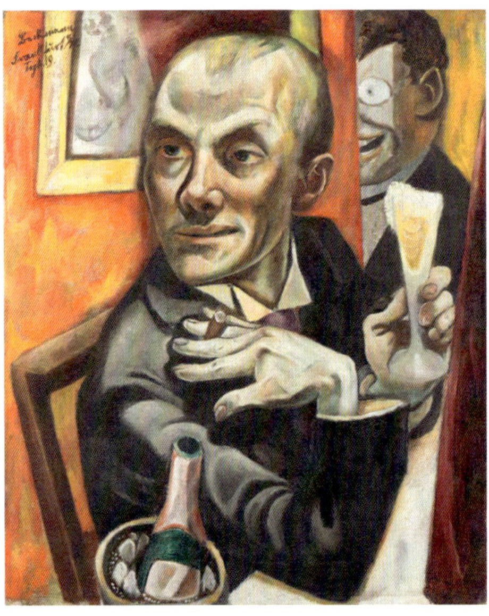

7. Max Beckmann, *Self-Portrait with Champagne Glass,* 1919, oil on canvas. Städel Museum Frankfurt. Photo: bpk Bildagentur / Städel Museum Frankfurt / Art Resource, NY

religion is arrogance before God, defiance of God. Defiance that he has created us so that we cannot love one another. In my paintings I accused God of everything he has done wrong."[41] This is a harbinger of the late work of Beckmann, who will systematically build up these suggestions of a new mystical feeling that he shared with many of his contemporaries and had been systematically building up in his metaphysically grounded works since the late 1920s. The "swindle" of the world of the Greek gods, about which the artist also complained to Piper, and a number of Beckmann's other pictorial and intellectual sources were syncretistically adapted, creatively instrumentalized, dynamically synthesized, and amalgamated in his painted work. But that is a later development, beginning around 1930.

First, bitter mockery became Beckmann's means for articulating his outrage. Its iconography is rooted in Christian culture, against which it turns and whose loss of meaning it reveals by means of inversion. The art critic Paul Westheim observed at the time: "It could be said that today, if not the Christian faith as a whole, at least its mythology and dogma, its physical relationships and spiritual fixations have lost their meaning."[42] Beckmann makes that clear using the artistic idiom of the Christian faith. The painter appears to have lost his faith in general and yet continues to express a metaphysical need: Beckmann's goal was a "metaphysics of representationalism. [...] In my *The Night*, too, the metaphysical should make one forget the representational. It should be overcome by the metaphysical. One should only see the beauty the way a funeral march is also beautiful."[43] That must be seen as a direct consequence of the experiences of World War I and the civil-war-like phase of the formation of the Weimar Republic, which had an almost violent effect on Beckmann's work [Fig. 6].

The contemporaneous art critic Wilhelm Hausenstein tried to express Beckmann's effort, which he saw as a rigorously metaphysical element, in the following words:

> *The interlocking of immoderation and construction is obviously, all too obviously, a German virtue—a German necessity. At this interlocking, however, a next step was taken and is still being taken. A violent verism occurred—an excessive, penetrating, tormenting perception of things, a naturalism without equal. And another next step was taken: the transformation of things into chimeras. This metamorphosis, too, is only logical. It corresponds to the constructive sense of the imaginary. Verism has suddenly turned into the metaphysical. That is what produces the chimerical quality of German Gothic that gives this Gothic its particular note; is what produces the chimerical quality of Beckmann's art.*[44]

Beckmann had honored his program of transcendental objectivity, but his paintings and prints did often depict the world as a bleak "chimera" [Fig. 7; p. 49].[45] His contemporaries regarded the paintings of the years from 1917 to around 1925 as "incredibly sober and cold, of an unrelenting alertness and sharpness, that replaces lyric pathos with an almost cynical objectivity."[46] His work clearly articulated to his contemporaries that they were placed in a void, that they were transcendentally homeless (Georg Lukács).[47] They were thus articulating a widespread feeling of the time. It was founded on the comprehensive critique of metaphysics of the nineteenth century,[48] and in Beckmann's case had developed during the war, but at the same time he was fighting it. The "new church" he projected in his creative "*Bekenntnis*" (Confession) became a church of nihilism, despite his intention to the contrary [Fig. 8]. "That is my crazy hope which I can't give up, which in spite of everything is stronger in me than ever before. And someday I want to make buildings along with my pictures. To build a tower in which humanity can shriek out its rage and despair and all its poor hopes and joys and wild yearning. A new church. Perhaps this age may help me."[49] The program he formulated and pursued in his paintings failed in terms of its subject matter insofar as it was not able to produce a new sense of community. He remarked to the publisher Reinhard Piper on January 9, 1917: "I am managing gradually to express myself more substantially and that provides me with stability and calm in

8. Max Beckmann, *Resurrection,* 1916–18 (unfinished), oil and charcoal on canvas. Staatsgalerie Stuttgart. Photo: © Staatsgalerie Stuttgart

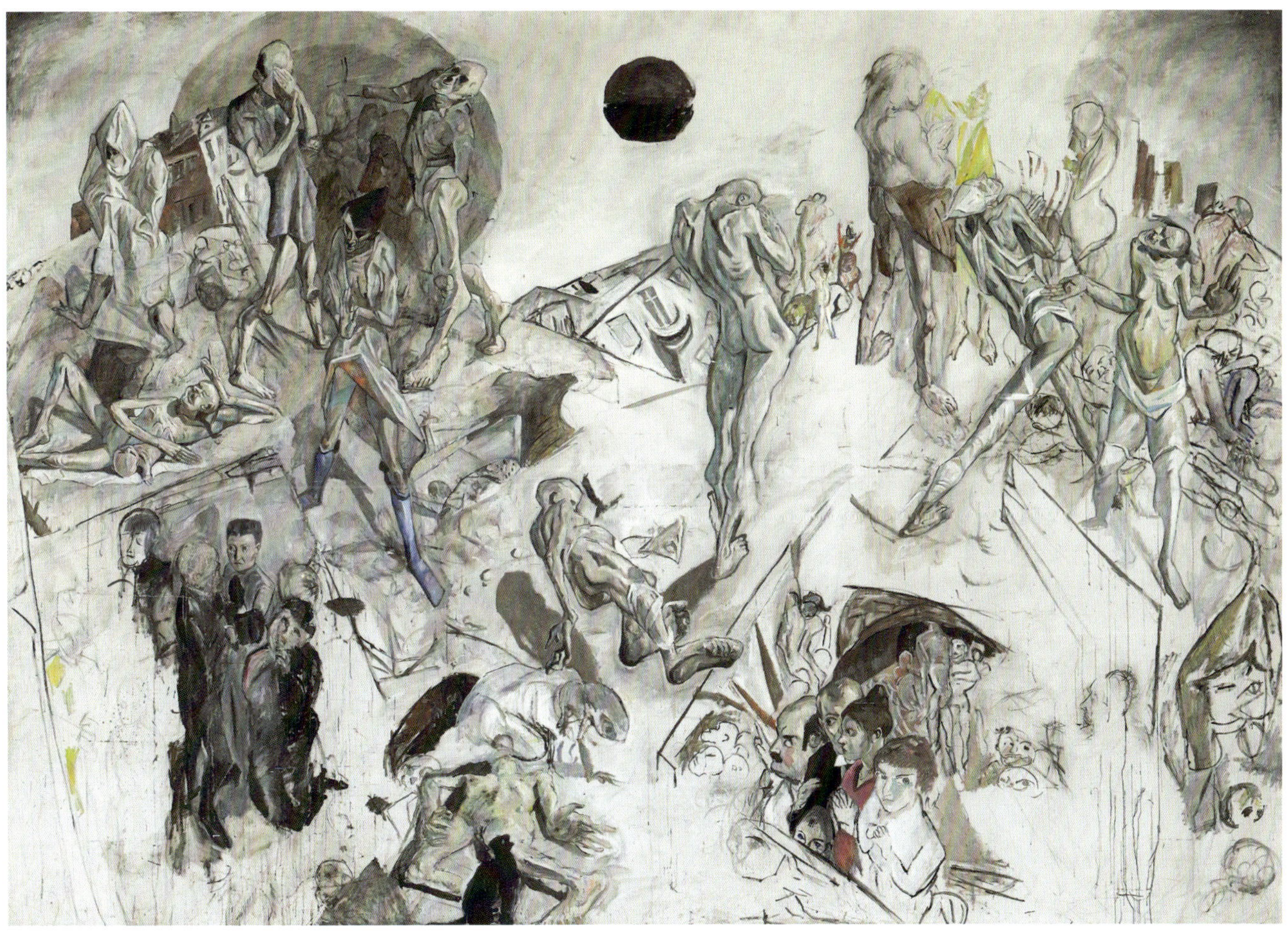

this great madness in which we are now living more than before."[50] In May of that year he wrote to Piper again: "Yes, the war. Hopefully, you are still doing fine, by the way. In that respect. The only thing that is still possible is art and for me painting. In these times when all concepts are turned upside down you can only live in this mixture of somnambulism and dreadful awareness unless you want to be just as dull as an animal."[51]

The artist described the goal of his painting: "to confine [reality], to beat it down and to strangle it."[52] External reality is forced into an abstract formal framework on the canvas, thus literally subjecting it to the reality of the painting. Beckmann urgently expressed this in his "Confession," or, "Creative Credo," which was written during the final phase of the war but not published until two years later. Because it is so important, we reproduce it in full in this catalogue (see pp. 48–50). He writes there regarding the production of the picture: "I don't cry. I hate tears, they are a sign of slavery. I keep my mind on my business—on a leg, on an arm, on the penetration of the surface thanks to the wonderful effects of foreshortening, on the partitioning of space, on the relationship of straight and curved lines. [...] Most important for me is volume, trapped in height and width; volume on the plane, depth without losing the awareness of the plane, the architecture of the picture."[53]

The passage powerfully demonstrates Beckmann's existential despair in the face of devastating historical events. The painter imposed on himself a stoic, almost fatalistic stance that was intended to immunize him against such historical events. He fled into the picture, where he could and did do violence to the external reality that could not be controlled. There he could impose his aesthetic, form-controlling, Old Master, and Cubist stylistic principles. This passage confirms the sharp observation of Alfred Neumeyer, which still deserves to be underscored, that the paintings of the *Neue Sachlichkeit*—to which Beckmann's work of this period certainly belonged, in the form of critical verism[54]—had lost an "awareness of reality," despite its ostentatiously displayed "cult of the object."[55] It is therefore incorrect when referring to paintings from around 1920 to speak of space in the classical sense of the optically consistent organization of three-dimensionality. A space in the literal sense is shown: for example, you can see the planks of a floor, the walls, and the boards of a wooden ceiling. But this space, which appears to be organized according to one-point perspective, soon proves to be an illusion that is in the process of dissociating. Paintings of the *Neue Sachlichkeit* do not offer a naturalistic depiction of visible reality; rather, they transfer reality into the painted image. In doing so, they break it up by unsettling traditional ways of seeing by means of perspectival rifts and leaps or overly sharp, unreal depictions—for example, views from up close and from afar that are equally sharp—and so it does lose an awareness of reality in Neumeyer's sense. The "continuous surface cohesiveness"[56] of the paintings that Beckmann produced as if by force conflicts with a traditional perspectival rendering of the pictorial space to which he had been largely indebted, despite several exceptions, before the war. Beckmann's unconventional and productive synthesis of the art of the Old Masters and that of Cubism is manifested here.

Beckmann addressed these connections in a letter to Reinhard Piper of February 8, 1918, with a clearly anti-Expressionist thrust. He was reflecting on the aforementioned crisis of Expressionism, which would soon be replaced by Dadaism and the verism of the *Neue Sachlichkeit*: "It is truly interesting for me to be here just now, because Frankfurt is a bastion of Expressionism. Nevertheless, I have succeeded here of all places to persuade a large number of people with my paintings, which unfortunately you do not know yet, that the Expressionist concern was indeed just a decoratively literary one, which has nothing to do with a vital sense of art. Now I can prove to you with my paintings and prints that one can be new without doing Expressionism or Impressionism. New based on the old law of art: roundness in the plane."[57]

One of the most powerful effects of Beckmann's paintings from the early Weimar Republic doubtless results, in addition to the aspect of "roundness," from his coloring. If one closely examines the paintings made of a reduced palette of shades of red, yellow, green, gray, and a little blue and violet, one often senses a gleaming and glowing, despite a certain frigidness that the paintings can exude. They are in essence grisaille paintings with very few color values scattered across the canvas as if in a patchwork quilt. Black, gray, and white sometimes play a strong role as contrast, and a painting such as *Christus und die Sünderin* (Christ and the Sinner) of 1917 [Plate 22] radiates a coldness that is only increased by the few color tones that flare up. The impression is quite different in the case of *Der Traum* (The Dream) of 1921 [Fig. 9; Plate 72], in which the figures and objects are fused as if cast in molten lava, without conveying the impression of glazing. Beckmann produces a disturbing effect with his coloration. Looking back in 1928, the critic Hausenstein rightly connected it with the illuminated manuscripts of the Middle Ages: "In the early paintings Beckmann's color touches on the style of medieval miniatures (and, by the way, not just the color): this Beckmann was doing what is called 'illuminating.'"[58] In the upper part of the painting in particular, where

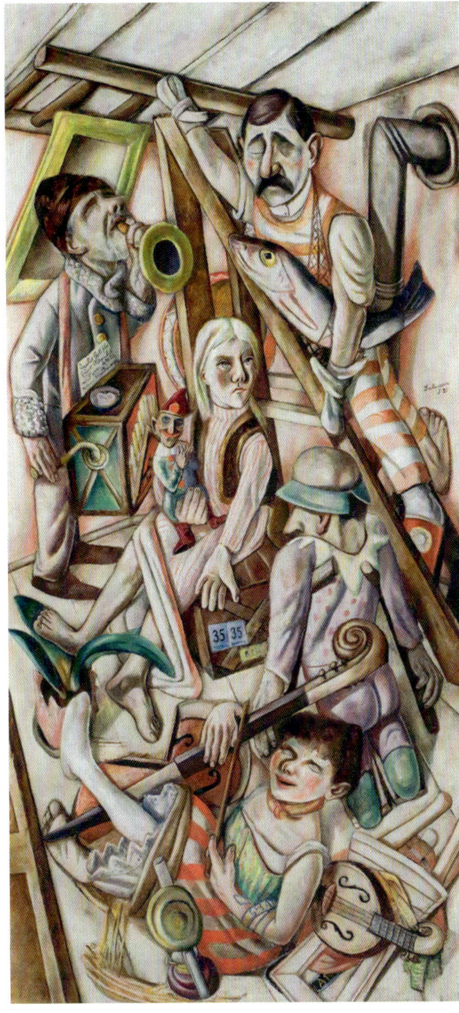

9. Max Beckmann, *The Dream*, 1921, oil on canvas. Saint Louis Art Museum, Bequest Morton D. May

the walls of the room that serve as background for the action, an almost pathological note of suffering enters the work. Surrounded by a feverish aura, all of the people and objects glow pink here. Any touch or movement must cause them unbelievable pain. Like hardly any other picture by this painter, *The Dream* possesses a quality of the ignited, the vulnerable, which interprets existence as torment. It occurs again in compressed form and is referred back to itself in the captivating and dismaying *Selbstbildnis vor rotem Vorhang* (Self-Portrait in front of Red Curtain) of 1923 [see Plate 91].

A FORCED PICTORIAL ORDER TO OVERCOME CONTINGENCY

In his brilliant analysis of the 1921 painting *The Dream*, the Heidelberg art historian Wilhelm Franger worked out perspectives on Beckmann's painting of this period that can be generalized.[59] He writes, for example, that the relief character of the painting that is repeatedly visibly interrupted is supported by the overall pale coloration of the picture. It grants wide space to the formal aspect, to the drawing, and one senses "a very sharp, especially and painfully sharp, fixation of the object by means of form."[60] The canvas confronts the viewer in this way as a self-contained tectonic framework. It is unshakeable, even though everything has become jumbled up, and so the relationship of form and content seems problematic. Fraenger pointed to this antagonistic structure and recognized it as the painting's true set of problems: "If we try to define Beckmann's idea of form in terms of his ethical character, we observe an earnest striving for pictorial clarity and regularity, for discipline and rule and verse meter. This ordering tendency of the sense of form runs strictly counter to Beckmann's will to express himself. Because he aims straight for ugliness, arbitrariness, and violence, disfiguring and deforming, in a word: for the anarchy of the grotesque that explodes all norms."[61]

Fraenger sees in Beckmann's work an irresolvable conflict between a constructive, objective will to order and a subjective will to express himself. The work produces an ambivalent sensation of order and compulsion, of norm and arbitrariness. In Fraenger's view, the artist painted to combat solipsistic isolation and the individualistic-atomist structure of life today. He ordered, tamed, and disciplined the disorder of life. He was painting the world as it should be,[62] even when it meant doing violence to it. Fraenger is getting at the afore-mentioned central matter that the painter was trying to record and control via his art—the chaos of his time. The painter's will to form, modeled on the early German masters, was to capture and order a senseless world and an almost unbearable randomness.[63] In late 1922, Beckmann emphasized to his publisher Reinhard Piper the role of the early German artists: "It is very nice that you are publishing something about the early German painters. Right now, especially, it is a matter of struggling to keep from falling back into an archaizing time, but only, with an awareness of our own insane and yet strong time, become lovingly conscious of our ancestors. And the proper selection under the proper light can contribute a great deal to that."[64]

Seemingly paradoxically, the attempt to create order could culminate in an impression of the mechanically determined and of "fatality." Hausenstein expresses that view: "Beckmann possesses more and in a stronger way than any other painter today (or any day) the sense of the mechanical quality of our age." And he goes on to speak of transitions from the human into the technical, of the organic into the mechanical, and of the soulful into the material-constructive, and then continues: "Beckmann is the protagonist of such insightful perception. That accounts for the mechanical connection and machine-like functioning of his paintings, especially of the terrible period from 1920 to 1925: from *Fastnacht* (Carnival) [Plate 67] to *Galleria Umberto* [Plate 101] (which should really be called arcade)."[65] We are able to show both paintings in our exhibition and hence present major works that impressively mark the timespan emphasized by his contemporaries.

Carnival a very personal painting for the artist and stands at the beginning of the sometimes-eccentric vertical formats that

Beckmann will later select for major works and the individual panels of the triptychs of 1932–33.[66] In the center we see Fridel Battenberg. Beckmann was able to stay at her home at the beginning of his Frankfurt period. She is standing precisely on the central axis of the painting with her legs casually crossed. She is flanked not by her husband, Ugi, but by Beckmann's Berlin-based art-dealer Jsrael Ber Neumann.[67] A figure in a grotesque animal mask is lying curled up on the floor: it is generally thought to be Beckmann himself, whose masked mouth outlined in red touches Fridel Battenberg's red shoes, whose color takes up the eye and hue of the mask. This eye is directed frontally at the viewer, but artificially; Fridel, by contrast, gazes with her blue eyes into a vague distance; and Neumann appears to be looking at Fridel but scarcely reaches her. The entire scene takes place in a cramped space overfilled with objects and beings (candles, mirror, gramophone, horn, champagne bucket, dog, and cat). Beckmann skillfully harmonizes the forms and colors. Directions are indicated and adopted, and yet it all plays out within the narrow, vertical, rectangle of the painting without really crossing the edge of the painting. It suggests comparison with late medieval carved altarpieces, as if their compression of figures has been transferred to canvas. The indications of the space and its volumes being partially splintered and faceted reflect Beckmann's grappling with Cubism, whose lack of color is, however, ostentatiously outdone in this comparatively colorful painting. The theme of carnival justifies the garish and grotesque qualities of this overture "of the terrible period from 1920 to 1925" (Wilhelm Hausenstein). Beckmann's *The Dream* of the following year, 1921, transports this into the immediate present day of Berlin, which Beckmann visited at the beginning of the Weimar Republic and addressed in the *Berliner Reise* (Trip to Berlin) series of prints [see p. 158].[68] In the painting, the costumed cripples and a blind hurdy-gurdy man evoke the misery of the postwar era.

Das Trapez (The Trapeze) [Plate 73] of 1923 takes up one central theme in Beckmann's art—alongside the café, the dancehall, and the variety theater:[69] the iconography of carnies and the circus.[70] Beckmann compresses the seven artists into a tight space: they interlock, touch, and sometimes hold one another, and yet they also move past one another in a strangely disconnected way. The lowest figure, with his legs in an extreme split, almost appears to have been trampled down. The female figure at lower left combines eroticism with compulsion in that her nipple is visible, while her closed eyes and slender red mouth suggest a certain forbearance. Moving relatively freely, by contrast, the large female figure on the right and the young man in a striped leotard, who looks like a mixture of Beckmann and his son, Peter, move comparatively freely. The man in the white leotard stuck under the ceiling holding an iron chain in his mouth completes the scene and corresponds, like one part of a bracket, to the figure pressed to the floor.

Hard black contours frame the colors, and Beckmann has created a wonderful chord of lemony green, reddish pink, and indigo. The ropes holding the trapeze bar make the figures look like a heap of marionettes that have been carelessly tossed aside but take on a certain life of their own, even as they appear rigid and transfixed. Their large, dark eyes underscore that interpretation in an almost melancholy way. Only the crouching figure on the right, whom Beckmann has given another mask—this one fiery red and fleshy—stands apart somewhat. He is facing out of the structure, while one white-gloved hand seems to be raised at the edge of the painting, as if to

10. Max Beckmann, *Portrait of Fridel Battenberg*, 1920, oil on canvas. Sprengel Museum Hannover. Photo: bpk Bildagentur / Sprengel Museum Hannover / Michael Herling / Aline Gwose / Art Resource, NY

cross this aesthetic boundary into the viewer's space, tentatively at first. It is left uncertain whether he will ever straighten up.

Beckmann was trying to articulate here the position he had already outlined in an exemplary way during the final phase of World War I. On the occasion of the exhibition of prints organized in Berlin by Neumann in 1917, the author wrote in the foreword to the catalogue: "Be the child of one's time. Naturalism against one's own self. Objectivity of the inner vision."[71] The term "objectivity" (*Sachlichkeit*) is used here to mean the phenomenon of establishing distance. The writer Stefan George

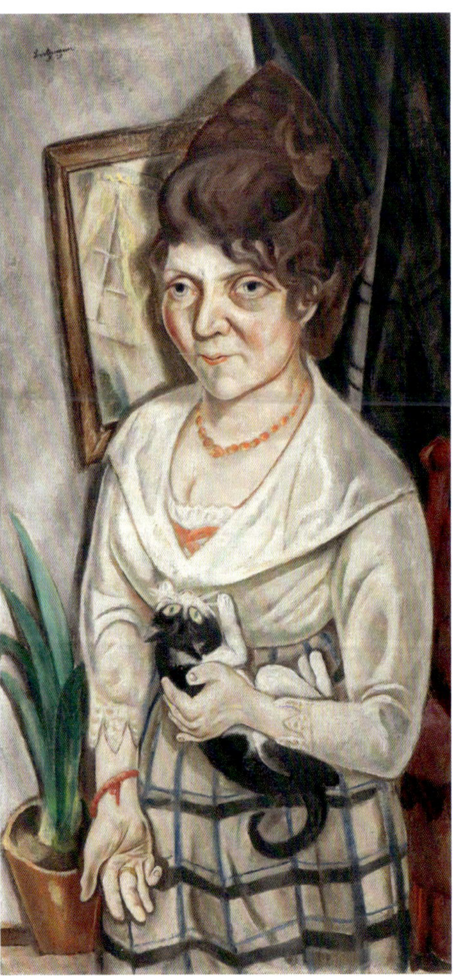

expressed himself similarly when describing his living in Switzerland and his critical distance from the wartime actions in the sentences: "A fine objectivity! And I cry out to all of you: whether it ends badly or well: the most difficult thing comes ONLY AFTERWARD!!"[72] Beckmann decisively adopted a position opposite to utopian, nonobjective Expressionism;[73] he did not, however, cling to a negative polemic and attitude but rather, under the influence of the war and the stylistic hodgepodge of early German art, Expressionism, Cubo-Futurism, and Dadaism in the form of a veristic *Neue Sachlichkeit*, created a genuine style and prevailed with it.[74] *The Night*, *Carnival*, *The Dream*, and *The Trapeze* emphatically honored this program and left behind the religious themes of 1917. Beckmann became "contemporary," and in that sense also modern, precisely because he had recourse to the past and thus in a certain way dovetailed the contemporary with the timeless. Beckmann is a painter of modern life with all its tragedy and violence.

NEW OBJECTIVITY AND BEYOND

One controversial question is whether Beckmann should be categorized as a proponent of the *Neue Sachlichkeit*—a style of the era that can, admittedly, scarcely be defined.[75] The director of the Kunsthalle Mannheim at the time, Gustav Friedrich Hartlaub, used the term "Die Neue Sachlichkeit" for this movement as early as 1923. In his now-famous brochure in the runup to the exhibition of that name in 1925, Hartlaub explained his goal of providing a survey of the artistic production of the past ten years, which he said had explicitly dedicated itself to a "positively tangible reality" and whose approach had been "neither Impressionistically dissolved nor Expressionistically abstract."[76] That precisely defines Beckmann's formulation of the artistic problem as described above, though without identifying it. Under a title that would lend the movement its name—"Die Neue Sachlichkeit: Deutsche Malerei seit dem Expressionismus" (The New Objectivity: German Painting since Expressionism)—this epochal exhibition was held from June 14 to September 18, 1925, in Mannheim and was shown in several German cities thereafter.[77] According to the catalogue, five paintings by Beckmann were exhibited when the exhibition opened. They were: *Christus und die Sünderin* (Christ and the Sinner) [Plate 22] and *Strasse mit Luftballon* (Landscape with Balloon) [Plate 18], both of 1917, *Doppelbildnis* (a double portrait of Käthe and Walter Carl) of 1918, *Bildnis mit alter Dame/Frau Tube* (Portrait with an Old Lady/Mrs. Tube) of 1919, and finally the 1923 *Doppelporträt Zwei Frauen* (a double portrait of Marie Swarzenski and Carla Netter). The artist was thus represented in this programmatic exhibition with crucial works after his significant stylistic change around 1915–17. Despite the information in the exhibition catalogue, however, there were more works than the five named above, which ultimately made Beckmann figure as a significant proponent of the *Neue Sachlichkeit*. No fewer than nine paintings arrived in mid-July, by way of Beckmann's Frankfurt gallery Zinglers Kabinett from a presentation at the Hamburger Kunstverein, and were shown at the exhibition in Mannheim. The delivery note, dated July 17, 1925, has been preserved in the archives of the Kunsthalle Mannheim and lists such important works as the 1920 *Porträt Frau Battenberg* [Fig. 10], *Bar in Baden-Baden* of 1923, and the 1924 painting *Am Lido* [Plate 102], based on impressions from an Italian journey. With a total of fourteen paintings on view, Beckmann was one of the most important artists in this significant exhibition venue of the modern era; in Dresden, one of the venues where this traveling exhibition was shown next, he was represented by fifteen paintings. Against this backdrop, it makes no sense to remove Beckmann from the context of the *Neue Sachlichkeit*. Including him should, of course, not diminish his artistic independence either. He was a protagonist and hence one outstanding figure among many.

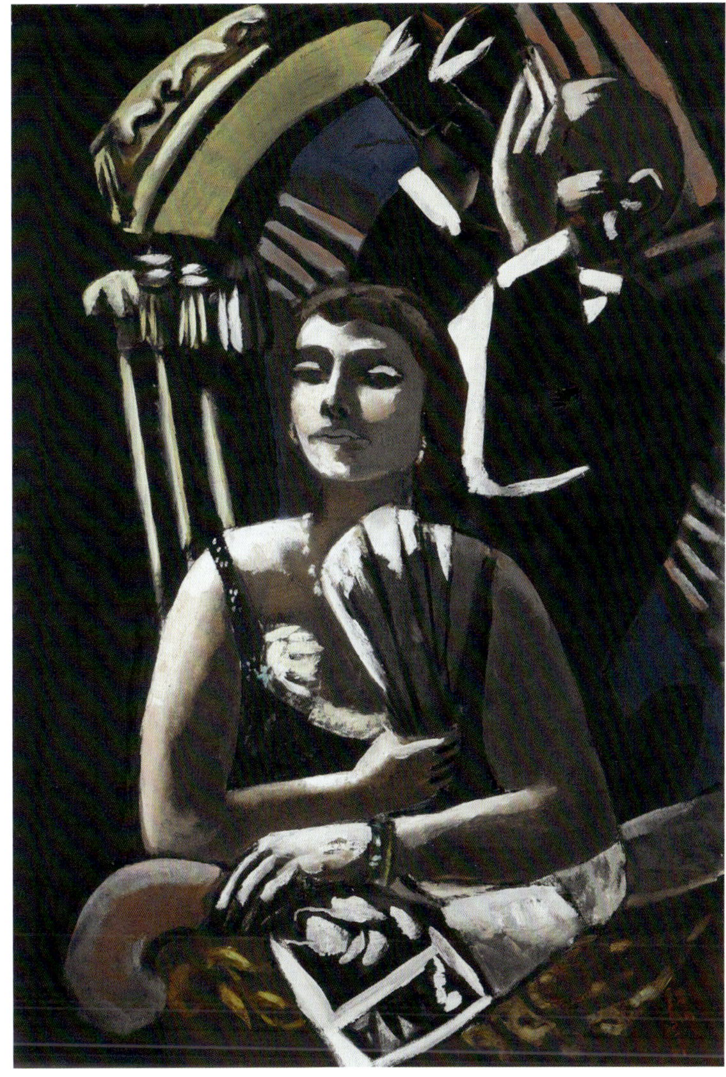

11. Max Beckmann, *The Loge*, 1928, oil on canvas. Staatsgalerie Stuttgart. Photo: © Staatsgalerie Stuttgart

In 1928, on the occasion of a presentation of Beckmann's paintings at the Munich gallery of the dealer Günther Franke, Hausenstein pointed to the difficulty of categorizing his work and demanded: "Let us refrain from placing Beckmann in a contemporary category! He is no 'Expressionist'; nor does he have anything to do with the galvanic arts with which the 'Neue Sachlichkeit' is trying to conjure the corpses of our epoch back to an artificial life in artificial clarity, to a sterilized life in germ-free atmospheres."[78] The critic was, however, following here the painter's own attempt to distance himself,[79] making himself the latter's mouthpiece, but this is untenable from today's perspective. In the first half of the 1920s, Beckmann was one proponent of the *Neue Sachlichkeit*, perhaps even the main one. His work is associated with an emphatically representational painting that polemically distinguished itself from Expressionism and yet was still related to it.

For Hartlaub, Beckmann was the "greatest living artist," and in 1928 he became the first museum director in Germany to organize a survey of his works.[80] The Kunsthalle came close to acquiring Beckmann's 1918-19 magnum opus *The Night*. Hartlaub's predecessor Fritz Wichert had brought the painting to the museum for viewing. It appeared, however, that the acquisition could not get past the committee responsible, however, so it was never even presented to it. The Kunsthalle did purchase *Christ and the Sinner* and *Portrait with an Old Lady/Mrs. Tube*. The museum's director tied his hopes for a future artistic evolution in Germany to Beckmann personally. Hartlaub expected a productive synthesis from him. It was supposed to overcome from the outset the "two-wing" separation of the *Neue Sachlichkeit* he had himself made in 1922, which remains problematic today: "perhaps tomorrow or the day after the two currents will be unified and a broad riverbed created in the process. We await a future, redeemed Max Beckmann"[81] [Fig. 11].

Then in 1928 it seemed to Hartlaub "as if the long, arduous climb has only now ended, as if the high route is only now really beginning."[82] For him, the painter was the "protagonist of the epoch," whose oeuvre reflected Germany's evolution after World War I. The art historian saw in Beckmann's paintings from 1924–25 onward a new, unfamiliar composure and asked: "Does this relative assuagement of Beckmann's latest art reflect a recovery of our age, a purification, stabilization of our entire being after so much boundless destruction?"[83] Our exhibition attempts to make precisely this artistic process and this expectation of the time clearly understandable. In the early 1920s Beckmann was working out a position as a painter that he gradually changed and rewrote. But it remained the prerequisite for a late work that, while probably never revealing a "redeemed Beckmann" (Gustav F. Hartlaub), continues to draw attention, to seem topical, and to challenge our seeing and understanding in a productive way.

Translated from the German by Steven Lindberg

Acknowledgments

This exhibition and publication have been a labor of love. In 2010 I had the pleasure of organizing a monographic exhibition on Otto Dix for the Neue Galerie, which was to be supplemented by a similar exhibition on Max Beckmann. I thank Ronald S. Lauder, Renée Price, and the Neue Galerie team for their enduring trust and support.

The concept for the exhibition and my arguments in the essays and work descriptions had their foundation in my extensive and detailed monograph *Vom schwarzen Seiltänzer: Max Beckmann zwischen Weimarer Republik und Exil* (Berlin: Reimer, 2005), and have been taken up, updated, and reexamined here.

1 On this fundamental Marc-Beckmann controversy, see Dietrich Schubert, "Die Beckmann-Marc-Kontroverse von 1912: "Sachlichkeit" versus "Innerer Klang," in *Expressionismus und Kulturkrise*, ed. Bernd Hüppauf (Heidelberg: Carl Winter, 1983), 207–44; Christoph Engels, *Auf der Suche nach einer "deutschen Kunst": Max Beckmann in der Wilhelminischen Kunstkritik* (Weimar: VDG, 1997), 142–54; and Cathrin Klingsöhr-Leroy, "Controversial Positions: Franz Marc and Max Beckmann," trans. Michael Wolfson, in *Max Beckmann and Berlin*, ed. Thomas Köhler and Stefanie Heckmann, exh. cat. Berlinische Galerie (Bielefeld: Kerber, 2015), 76–83.

2 Cf. *Ein Protest deutscher Künstler, mit Einleitung von Carl Vinnen* (Jena: Eugen Diederichs, 1911).

3 Max Beckmann, "Response to *In Battle for Art: The Answer to the 'Protest of German Artists,'*" in Beckmann, *Self-Portrait in Words: Collected Writings and Statements, 1903–1950*, ed. Barbara Copeland Buenger, trans. Barbara Copeland Buenger and Reinhold Heller with David Britt (Chicago, IL: University of Chicago Press, 1997), 110–12, esp. 112. Buenger's essential collection of translation and commentaries on Beckmann's texts has recently been completed in German: Petra Kipphoff, *Max Beckmann: Der Maler als Schreiber* (Springe: zu Klampen, 2021).

4 On the controversy in general, see *Van Gogh: Fields; the Field with Poppies and the Artists' Dispute*, ed. Wulf Herzogenrath and Dorothee Hansen, exh. cat. Kunsthalle Bremen (Ostfildern: Hatje Cantz, 2002).

5 On this phase of his work in general, see Carla Schulz-Hoffmann, *Max Beckmann: Der Maler* (Munich: Bruckmann, 1991), 31–64; Reinhard Spieler, *Max Beckmann, 1884–1950: The Path to Myth*, trans. Charity Scott Stokes (Cologne: Taschen, 1994), 25–73; Olaf Peters, *Vom schwarzen Seiltänzer: Max Beckmann zwischen Weimarer Republik und Exil* (Berlin: Reimer, 2005), 21–75; Uwe M. Schneede, *Max Beckmann: Der Maler seiner Zeit* (Munich: C. H. Beck, 2009), 47–106; and, most recently, Dietrich Schubert, *Max Beckmann: Vom Vietzker Strand zur Departure; Die Kristallation seiner Werturteile und seine bildnerische Praxis 1904–1936* (Petersberg: Michael Imhof, 2021), 63–169; and Christian Lenz, *Max Beckmann* (Münster: Rhema, 2022), 47–121.

6 See Schubert, "Die Beckmann-Marc-Kontroverse von 1912" (see note 1); Engels, *Auf der Suche nach einer "deutschen Kunst"* (see note 1); *Max Beckmann: Die frühen Bilder*, exh. cat. (Bielefeld: Kunsthalle; Frankfurt am Main: Städelsches Kunstinstitut, 1982); and Karen Lang, "Max Beckmann's Inconceivable Modernism," in *Of "Truths Impossible to Put in Words": Max Beckmann Contextualized*, ed. Rose-Carol Washton Long and Maria Makela (Bern: Peter Lang, 2008), 81–101, esp. 91–7.

7 As early as 1906, the art critic Willy Pastor had already certified an almost "perverse objectivity" in view of his Impressionist-naturalist engagement with sociocritical themes. See Engels, *Auf der Suche nach einer "deutschen Kunst"* (see note 1), 97.

8 Max Beckmann, "Thoughts on Timely and Untimely Art," in Beckmann, *Self-Portrait in Words* (see note 3), 113–17, esp. 116.

9 See Peter Bürger, "'Transzendentale Sachlichkeit': Das künstlerische Programm von Max Beckmann, wie es in seinen Schriften zum Ausdruck kommt," *Neue Züricher Zeitung*, no. 237 (October 12, 2013): 29.

10 On the immanent opposition—that is, the one formulated from the foundation of the avant-garde outward—versus a formalist modernism that was gaining broad acceptance, see the ambitious, sometimes somewhat simplistic overview in Bernard Smith, *Modernism's History: A Study in Twentieth-Century Art and Ideas* (New Haven, CT: Yale University Press, 1998), which rightly questions the one-sided model of evolution of twentieth-century art developed on the paradigm of French modernism. For details, see also Olaf Peters, "The Struggle for Artistic Modernity: Max Beckmann in the Crisis Year of 1913," trans. Steven Lindberg, in Köhler and Heckmann, *Max Beckmann and Berlin* (see note 1), 84–92.

11 I borrow this term from Pierre Bourdieu. See esp. Pierre Bourdieu, *The Rules of Art: Genesis and Structure of the Literary Field*, trans. Susan Emanuel (Stanford, CA: Stanford University Press, 1995), and, as an exemplary, unfinished study, Pierre Bourdieu, *Manet: A Symbolic Revolution*, ed. Pascale Casanova et al., trans. Peter Collier and Margaret Rigaud-Drayton (Cambridge: Polity, 2017).

12 On the exhibition, see *Stationen der Moderne: Die bedeutenden Kunstausstellungen der Moderne in Deutschland*, exh. cat. (Berlin: Berlinische Galerie, 1988), 130–53, and Peter Selz, "Der 'Erste Deutsche Herbstsalon,' Berlin 1913," in *Die Kunst der Ausstellung: Eine Dokumentation dreissig exemplarischer Kunstausstellungen dieses Jahrhunderts*, ed. Bernd Klüser and Katharina Hegewisch (Frankfurt am Main: Insel, 1991), 56–63.

13 "*The paintings* that Beckmann is showing this time seem almost geriatric." See Adolf Behne, "Die erste Ausstellung der Freien Sezession," *Die Gegenwart* 85, no. 17 (April 25, 1914): 261–64, esp. 263, quoted in Engels, *Auf der Suche nach einer "deutschen Kunst"* (see note 1), 178.

14 On this process, see also the profound essay by Jay A. Clarke, "Space as Metaphor: Beckmann and the Conflicts of Secessionist Style in Berlin," in Washton Long and Makela, *Of "Truths Impossible to Put in Words"* (see note 6), 49–80.

15 Max Beckmann, "The New Program," in Beckmann, *Self-Portrait in Words* (see note 3), 130–32, esp. 132. On the criticism, see Engels, *Auf der Suche nach einer "deutschen Kunst"* (see note 1), 176–79.

16 Max Beckmann to Minna Beckmann-Tube, September 24, 1914, in Beckmann, *Self-Portrait in Words* (see note 3), 138–39.

17 For a good introductory sketch, see Corona Hepp, *Avantgarde: Moderne Kunst, Kulturkritik und Reformbewegung nach der Jahrhundertwende* (Munich: Deutscher Taschenbuch-Verlag, 1987), 148–59. In addition to numerous exhibition catalogues, two comprehensive discussions should be mentioned: Annegret Jürgens-Kirchhoff, *Schreckensbilder: Krieg und Kunst im 20. Jahrhundert* (Berlin: Reimer, 1993), esp. 151–204; and Dietrich Schubert, *Künstler im Trommelfeuer des Krieges, 1914–1918* (Heidelberg: Wunderhorn, 2013), esp. 279–301.

18 On the drawings and their context, see Stephan von Wiese, *Max Beckmanns zeichnerisches Werk, 1903–1925* (Düsseldorf: Droste, 1978); Carla Schulz-Hoffmann, "Max Beckmann im 1. Weltkrieg: Die Bilder, die Briefe," in *Max Beckmann: Vorträge, 1996–1998* (Munich: Max Beckmann Archiv, 2000), 49–61; Alexander Dückers, "Vom Welttheater und der Sachlichkeit: Zu den Zeichnungen von Beckmann und Dix," in *Aspekte deutscher Zeichenkunst*, ed. Iris Lauterbach and Margret Stuffmann (Munich: Zentralinstitut für Kunstgeschichte, [2006]), 175–84; and the essays by Christian Lenz and Christiane Zeiller in *Max Beckmann: Beiträge, 2004–2005* (Munich: Max Beckmann Archiv, 2006), 75–94 and 95–107; an edition of letters was published as early as 1916: Max Beckmann, *Briefe im Kriege* (Berlin: Bruno Cassirer, 1916); cf. Max Beckmann, *Briefe*, ed. Klaus Gallwitz et al., 3 vols. (Munich: Piper, 1993–96), 1:90–153.

19 See Max Beckmann to Minna Beckmann-Tube, October 3, 1914, in Beckmann, *Self-Portrait in Words* (see note 3), 140–41, esp. 140.

20 Max Beckmann to Minna Beckmann-Tube, May 5, 1915, in Beckmann, *Self-Portrait in Words* (see note 3), 165–68, esp. 167.

21 On his Frankfurt period, see *Max Beckmann: Frankfurt, 1915–1933: Eine Ausstellung zum 100. Geburtstag*, exh. cat. (Frankfurt am Main: Städtische Galerie im Städelschen Kunstinstitut, 1983); *Max Beckmann in Frankfurt*, ed. Klaus Gallwitz (Frankfurt am Main: Insel, 1984); *Max Beckmann: Die Frankfurter Jahre*, ed. W. A. Nagel, text by Ewald Rathke (Hanau: Peters, 1991); Schneede, *Max Beckmann* (see note 5), 46–153; Schubert, *Max Beckmann* (see note 5); and Lenz, *Max Beckmann* (see note 5), 63–154.

22 See Max Beckmann, *Self-Portrait while Drawing*, 1915, pen and black ink, 31.7 × 24.3 cm (12 1/2 x 9 1/2 in.), Graphische Sammlung, Staatsgalerie Stuttgart, W 280. On this sheet, see Wiese 1978 (see note 18), 62–67.

23 Quoted in *Max Beckmann: Retrospective*, ed. Carla Schulz-Hoffmann and Judith C. Weiss, exh. cat. Saint Louis Art Museum et. al. (Munich: Prestel; New York: W. W. Norton, 1984), 200. Beckmann himself remarked in a letter to his wife: "It's good for me that there's war now. Everything I did previously was no more than an apprenticeship. I'm still learning and growing." Max Beckmann to Minna Beckmann-Tube, May 11, 1915, in Beckmann, *Self-Portrait in Words* (see note 3), 169.

24 On this work, see especially Kurt Soiné, "Christus Beckmann? Zu Max Beckmanns Selbstbildnis mit rotem Schal," *Jahrbuch der Staatlichen Kunstsammlungen in Baden-Württemberg* 39 (2002): 95–116.

25 See, fundamentally, Dietrich Schubert, *Max Beckmann: Auferstehung und Erscheinung der Toten* (Worms: Werner, 1985); Stephan von Wiese, "'Somnambulismus' und 'Bewusstseinshelle': Zu Max Beckmanns 'Auferstehung' (1916/18)," in *Max Beckmann: Symposium, 15./16. Mai 1984* (Cologne: Josef-Haubrich-Kunsthalle, 1987), 79–95; Schneede, *Max Beckmann* (see note 5), 54–61, and, most recently, Lenz, *Max Beckmann* (see note 5), 66–70.

26 See the diary entries on February 24, 1944; October 5, 1948; and October 14, 1948, in Max Beckmann, *Tagebücher 1940–1950*, 2nd ed. (Munich: Piper,1987), 82 and 291–92.

27 See, fundamentally, Matthias Eberle, *Max Beckmann: Die Nacht; Passion ohne Erlösung* (Frankfurt am Main: Fischer Taschenbuchverlag, 1984); Jürgens-Kirchhoff, *Schreckensbilder* (see note 17), 176–98; *Max Beckmann: Die Nacht*, ed. Anette Kruszynski, exh. cat. (Düsseldorf: Kunstsammlung Nordrhein-Westfalen, 1997); Schneede, *Max Beckmann* (see note 5), 69–75.

28 See Christian Lenz, *Max Beckmann und die Alten Meister: "Eine ganz nette Reihe von Freunden* (Munich: Braus, 2000), 138–44, and Jürgen Müller in the present volume.

29 On this, with a summary of earlier research, see Benjamin Ziemann, "Germany after the First World War—A Violent Society? Results and Implications of Recent Research on Weimar Germany," *Journal of Modern European History* 1 (2003): 80–94.

30 See Max Beckmann, "Creative Credo," in Beckmann, *Self-Portrait in Words* (see note 3), 181–85, esp. 185.

31 Max Beckmann to Minna Beckmann-Tube, April 17, 1915, in Beckmann, *Self-Portrait in Words* (see note 3), 158–59, esp. 158.

32 See Beckmann, "Creative Credo" (see note 30). Zur 'Krise' des Expressionismus um 1920, see, fundamentally, Richard Brinkmann, *Expressionismus:*

Internationale Forschung zu einem internationalen Phänomen (Stuttgart: J. B. Metzler, 1980), 217–23, and Jenns E. Howoldt, "Krise des Expressionismus: Anmerkungen zu vier Briefen Wilhelm Worringes an Carl Georg Heise," *IDEA: Jahrbuch der Hamburger Kunsthalle* 8 (1989): 159–73; *The Ideological Crisis of Expressionism: The Literary and Artistic German War Colony in Belgium, 1914–1918*, ed. Rainer Rumold and O. K. Werckmeister (Columbia, SC: Camden House, 1990), and Joan Weinstein, *The End of Expressionism: Art and the November Revolution in Germany* (Chicago: University of Chicago Press, 1990).

33 See, fundamentally, Magdalena Bushart, *Der Geist der Gotik und die expressionistische Kunst: Kunstgeschichte und Kunsttheorie, 1911–1925* (Munich: Silke Schreiber, 1990). For a discussion of Beckmann's work in this context, see Engels, *Auf der Suche nach einer "deutschen Kunst"* (see note 1), 179–87, and Charles W. Haxthausen, "'Das Gegenwärtige zeitlos machen und das Zeitlose gegenwärtig': Max Beckmann zwischen Formalismus und Mythos," in Kruszynski, *Max Beckmann* (see note 27), 35–52, and Schneede, *Max Beckmann* (see note 5), 62–8.

34 See, for example, Alexander Dückers, *Max Beckmann: Die Hölle, 1919*, exh. cat. (Berlin: Kupferstichkabinett, 1983); Jörn Pabst, "Anmerkungen zur Genese der Mappe *Die Hölle* von Max Beckmann," in *Max Beckmann: Aufsätze* (Munich: Max Beckmann Archiv, 2002), 9–19; Schneede, *Max Beckmann* (see note 5), 75–80; Lenz, *Max Beckmann* (see note 5), 90–5; and Elisa Tamaschke in the present volume.

35 See Max Osborn, "Berliner Ausstellungen," *Kunstchronik*, n.s. 21 (1909–10): cols. 403–7, esp. 404, quoted in Engels, *Auf der Suche nach einer "deutschen Kunst"* (see note 1), 133–34.

36 See Carl Einstein, *Die Kunst des 20. Jahrhunderts*, 3rd ed. (1931), ed. Uwe Fleckner and Thomas W. Gaehtgens (Berlin: Fannei & Walz, 1996; orig. pub. 1926), 39–48.

37 See especially Wilhelm Fraenger, "Max Beckmann, 'Der Traum': Ein Beitrag zu Physiognomik des Grotesken," in Curt Glaser et. al., *Max Beckmann* (Munich: Piper, 1924), 35–58. For an early emphasis on and analysis of the content, see also Paul-Ferdinand Schmidt, "Max Beckmann," *Der Cicerone* 11, no. 21 (1919): 675–84, esp. 678–79.

38 *Max Beckmann: Das gesammelte Werk; Gemälde, Graphik, Handzeichnungen aus den Jahren 1905 bis 1927*, exh. cat. (Mannheim: Städtische Kunsthalle, 1928), 7.

39 Heinrich Simon, "Max Beckmann," *Das Kunstblatt* 3 (1919): 257–64, esp. 264. See also Schmidt, "Max Beckmann" (see note 37), and Gustav Friedrich Hartlaub, *Kunst und Religion: Ein Versuch über die Möglichkeit neuer religiöser Kunst* (Leipzig: Kurt Wolff, 1919), 84. Hartlaub's assessment of this phase of work was even greater in 1928: "For a time one felt reminded of the late Gothic, and in any case this new grammar, as opposed to the Impressionism or Naturalism of his early period, should be seen as national-German." *Max Beckmann: Das gesammelte Werk* (see note 38), 7.

40 See Max Beckmann to Günther Franke, October 23, 1930, in Beckmann, *Briefe* (see note 18), 2:178: "When you have an opportunity to do so, do not forget to teach the Nazis that I am a *German* painter. On Wednesday, there was already an attack on me in the *Völkischer Beobachter*. Do not forget.—It may be important one day."

41 Max Beckmann, *Die Realität der Träume in den Bildern: Schriften und Gespräche, 1911 bis 1950* (Munich: Piper, 1990), 28; see also Reinhard Piper, *Mein Leben als Verleger: Vormittag, Nachmittag* (Munich: Piper, 1991); orig. pub. 1947–50), 331. Cf. the contemporaneous view of Hartlaub, *Kunst und Religion* (see note 39), 83–85. On the gnostic background that several authors see reflected in it, see Friedhelm W. Fischer, *Max Beckmann: Symbol und Weltbild; Grundriss zu einer Deutung des Gesamtwerks* (Munich: Wilhelm Fink, 1972), 18–19 and 53–57; and Karoline Hille, *Spuren der Moderne: Die Mannheimer Kunsthalle von 1918–1933* (Berlin: Akademie, 1994), 231–49. See also the essay Gustav Friedrich Hartlaub, "Die Kunst und die neue Gnosis," *Das Kunstblatt* 1 (1917): 166–79, which Beckmann may have known because he was in contact with Hartlaub, who published about him in 1919. See also V. Curt Habicht, "Die Kunst im Lichte der Gnosis," *Das Kunstblatt* 7 (1923): 109–12.

42 Paul Westheim, "Das Religiöse in der Kunst der Gegenwart," *Das Kunstblatt* 2 (1918): 180–91, esp. 181.

43 Beckmann in conversation with his publisher Reinhard Piper in 1919, quoted in Piper, *Mein Leben als Verleger* (see note 41), 327.

44 Wilhelm Hausenstein, "Max Beckmann," in Glaser, *Max Beckmann* (see note 37), 59–72, esp. 70. On the central complex of the Gothic rection in Expressionism addressed by Hausenstein, see Bushart, *Der Geist der Gotik* (see note 33).

45 See Fraenger, "Max Beckmann" (see note 37), 55.

46 Hartlaub in his introductory essay on the retrospective in Mannheim; *Max Beckmann: Das gesammelte Werk* (see note 38), 6.

47 Georg Lukács, *The Theory of the Novel: A Historico-philosophical Essay on the Forms of Great Epic*, trans. Anna Bostock (Cambridge, MA: MIT Press, 1971), 41.

48 On the background in the history of science and philosophy, see Herbert Schnädelbach, *Philosophie*

in Deutschland, 1831–1933 (Frankfurt am Main: Suhrkamp, 1983), and *Krise des Historismus—Krise der Wirklichkeit: Wissenschaft, Kunst und Literatur, 1880–1932*, ed. Otto Gerhard Oexle (Göttingen: Vandenhoeck & Ruprecht, 2007).

49 Beckmann, "Creative Credo" (see note 30), 185.

50 Max Beckmann to Reinhard Piper, January 9, 1917, in Beckmann, *Briefe* (see note 18), 1:152–53, esp. 153.

51 Max Beckmann to Reinhard Piper, May 1917, in Beckmann, *Briefe* (see note 18), 1:161–62, esp. 162.

52 Beckmann, "Creative Credo" (see note 30), 184.

53 Ibid. Beckmann expressed something similar to Julius Meier-Graefe, mid-March 1919, in Beckmann, *Briefe* (see note 18), 1:177.

54 See Olaf Peters, *Nach-Krieg: Reflexionen in der Kunstkritik der Weimarer Republik am Beispiel des Verismus*, in, "Künstlerischer Ausdruck und die Narben des Ersten Weltkriegs: Kontinuitäten und Zäsuren (1919–2019); Deutsch-französische Perspektiven," special issue, *Symposium Culture@Kultur* 3 (2021) 17–26. See also, exemplarily, Christian Lenz, "George Grosz und Max Beckmann," in *Max Beckmann: Beiträge, 2002* (Munich: Max Beckmann Archiv, 2003), 9–22.

55 See Alfred Neumeyer, "Zur Raumpsychologie der Neuen Sachlichkeit," *Zeitschrift für bildende Kunst* 61, no. 1 (1927–28): 66–72. On Beckmann's formal means, see also the important contemporaneous reflection of Schmidt, "Max Beckmann" (see note 37).

56 On this term, and an approach that is very helpful to a formal description of Beckmann's painting, see Otto Pächt, "Design Principles of Fifteenth-Century Northern Painting," in *The Vienna School Reader: Politics and Art Historical Method in the 1930s*, ed. Christopher S. Wood (New York: Zone, 2000), 243–321, esp. 253.

57 Max Beckmann to Reinhold Piper, February 8, 1918, in Beckmann, *Briefe* (see note 18), 1:164–65, 165. See also Piper, *Mein Leben als Verleger* (see note 41), 335–36. Frankfurt, the metropolis on the Main River, could indeed be called a "bastion of Expressionism" in the 1920s, because of the outstanding collections of Expressionism of Ludwig and Rosy Fischer and of Carl Hagemann, in both of which Beckmann was represented only marginally, but also because of the activities of the museums there. See the essays by Thomas W. Gaehtgens and Tanja Baensch in *Museum im Widerspruch: Das Städel und der Nationalsozialismus*, ed. Uwe Fleckner and Max Hollein (Berlin: Akademie, 2011).

58 Wilhelm Hausenstein, "Vorrede," in *Max Beckmann: Gemälde aus den Jahren 1920–28; Illustriertes Verzeichnis*, exh. cat. (Munich: Graphisches Kabinett Günther Franke, 1928), n.p.

59 Fraenger, "Max Beckmann" (see note 37); for a detailed discussion of the painting, see Peters, *Vom schwarzen Seiltänzer* (see note 5), 21–43, and Lynette Roth, *Max Beckmann at the Saint Louis Art Museum: The Paintings* (Munich: Prestel, 2015), 84–9.

60 Fraenger, "Max Beckmann" (see note 37), 59.

61 Ibid., 51.

62 See ibid., 56.

63 Elsewhere, I have connected Fraenger's interpretation to the contemporaneous discussion of the crisis of historicism. See Olaf Peters, "Max Beckmann, die Neue Sachlichkeit und der Werterelativismus in der Weimarer Republik," *Wallraf-Richartz-Jahrbuch* 61 (2000): 237–61; Peters, *Vom schwarzen Seiltänzer* (see note 5), 21–75, and Olaf Peters, "New Objectivity Painting and the Weimar Republic's Modernity Crisis," in *Reinterpreting the Past: Traditionalist Artistic Trends in Central and Eastern Europe of the 1920s and 1930s*, ed. Irena Kossowska (Warsaw: Institute of Art of the Polish Academy of Sciences, 2010), 47–64.

64 Piper, *Mein Leben als Verleger* (see note 41), 336.

65 Hausenstein, "Vorrede" (see note 57), n.p.

66 See, fundamentally, Sarah O'Brien-Twohig, *Beckmann Carnival* (London: Tate Gallery, 1984).

67 On their friendship, see Ursula Harter and Stephan von Wiese, ed., *Max Beckmann und J. B. Neumann: Der Künstler und sein Händler in Briefen und Dokumenten, 1917–1950* (Cologne: DuMont, 2011).

68 On the *Berliner Reise* series, see *Max Beckmann: Druckgraphik, 1914–1924*, exh. cat. Staatliche Kunsthalle, Karlsruhe (Heidelberg: Kehrer, 2005), 142–51; Rose-Carol Washton Long, "Ambivalence: Personal and Political," in Washton Long and Makela, *Of "Truths Impossible to Put in Words"* (see note 6), 103–34, esp. 123–28, and Barbara Werr, 'A Good and Actually Quite Amusing Thing': Max Beckmann's *Trip to Berlin*," trans. Michael Wolfson, in Köhler and Heckmann, *Max Beckmann and Berlin* (see note 1), 128–35.

69 On this, see Astrid Becker, *Max Beckmann: Selbst- und Weltbild in den Themen "Caféhaus" und "Tanz"* (Marburg: Tectum, 2010). See also the painting *Varieté* (Variety Show) of 1921.

70 See also Cornelia Homburg, "Circus Beckmann," in *Max Beckmann: A Dream of Life*, ed. Tilman Osterwold, exh. cat. Zentrum Paul Klee, Bern (Ostfildern: Hatje Cantz, 2006), 35–49.

71 Max Beckmann, "Catalogue Foreword for Exhibition at I. B. Neumann Graphisches Kabinett, Berlin, *Max Beckmann Graphik*," in Beckmann, *Self-Portrait in Words* (see note 3), 178–80, esp. 180.

72 Quoted in Stefan Breuer, *Ästhetischer Fundamentalismus: Stefan George und der deutsche*

Antimodernismus (Darmstadt: Primus, 1996), 74. See also Robert E. Norton, *Secret Germany: Stefan George and His Circle* (Ithaca, NY: Cornell University Press, 2002).

73 See also Max Beckmann to Reinhard Piper, February 8, 1918, in Beckmann, *Briefe* (see note 18), 1:164–65. Beckmann also chose the term "*Sachlichkeit*" in Max Beckmann to Minna Beckmann-Tube, June 8, 1915, in Beckmann, *Briefe* (see note 18), 1:140–41. Looking at Beckmann's literary production of the early 1920s, which survives only in part, Thomas Schober developed the persuasive thesis that Beckmann expressly distanced himself from Expressionism here too and was close to the literature of the *Neue Sachlichkeit*. See Thomas Schober, *Das Theater der Maler: Studien zur Theatermoderne anhand dramatischer Werke von Kokoschka, Kandinsky, Barlach, Beckmann, Schwitters und Schlemmer* (Stuttgart: M und P, 1994), 279–84. See also Sebastian Karnatz, *Eine Szene im Theater der Unendlichkeit: Max Beckmanns Dramen und ihre Bedeutung für seine Bildrhetorik* (Göttingen: V&R unipress, 2011), esp. part E, "Bildwelt – Allegorie, Welttheater, Mythos," which is important for an overall interpretation.

74 With regard to the -isms of the avant-garde, the critic Willi Wolfradt spoke of a true "stylistic conflict" in the art of the time. See Willi Wolfradt, "Der Stilkonflikt in der Kunst der Gegenwart," *Das Kunstblatt* 5 (1921): 38–48.

75 See Janina Nentwig, "A Question of Perspective: Max Beckmann and New Objectivity," trans. Steven Lindberg, in Köhler and Heckmann, *Max Beckmann and Berlin* (see note 1), 156–63.

76 *Der Querschnitt* 3, nos. 3–4 (1923): 200.

77 See *Die Neue Sachlichkeit: Deutsche Malerei seit dem Expressionismus*, exh. cat. (Mannheim: Städtische Kunsthalle, 1925), and the summary in Hille, *Spuren der Moderne* (see note 41), 82–155.

78 *Max Beckmann: Gemälde aus den Jahren 1920–28* (see note 57), n.p.

79 In this context, see Beckmann's important letter to Wilhelm Hausenstein of March 12, 1926, in which he reacted to Franz Roh's book *Nach-Expressionismus* and noted: "My impetus was to open up representationalism to debate in a new art form." Beckmann is thus clearly identifying with the new representationalism/objectivity while at the same time distancing himself from a seemingly popular, massive, and diluted movement. Max Beckmann to Wilhelm Hausenstein, March 12, 1926, in Beckmann, *Briefe* (see note 18), 2:33–4, esp. 34. Beckmann is referring to Roh, *Nach-Expressionismus: Magischer Realismus; Probleme der neuesten europäischen Malerei* (Leipzig: Klinkhardt & Biermann, 1925), a key publication of the time.

80 See *Max Beckmann: Das gesammelte Werk* (see note 38), and Hille, *Spuren der Moderne* (see note 41), 220–73.

81 On this, see Hartlaub's contribution to the questionnaire "Ein neuer Naturalismus??," *Das Kunstblatt* 6 (1922): 369–414, esp. 389–93, 390.

82 *Max Beckmann: Das gesammelte Werk* (see note 38), 5.

83 Ibid., 8.

FROM SECESSIONIST TO INDIVIDUALIST

MAX BECKMANN'S CAREER AND RECEPTION, 1913 TO 1925

Anna Maria Heckmann

KÜNSTLER UNSERER ZEIT

I.

MAX BECKMANN

VON

HANS KAISER

VERLEGT BEI PAUL CASSIRER IN BERLIN
1 9 1 3

In the years from 1913 to 1925, Max Beckmann's style transformed fundamentally, and he reinvented himself. In this formative phase of his life and career, the artist evolved from the leading Berlin Secessionist recognized early on as the great individualist who set a course for the international art market while always distinguishing himself from the dominant fashions in art. This essay will first elaborate on the ambiguous position that Beckmann adopted in the Berlin art world until 1914 in the tension between the Secession and the avant-garde. Then it will explicate why Beckmann had to be freed from his Berlin milieu "violently"[1] before finding his own, alternative path to modernity as a "new Beckmann." As his approach to the *Neue Sachlichkeit* (New Objectivity), for which he essentially prepared the way, shows, the experience of the crisis of an overly close connection to an art movement and group also shaped Beckmann's later stubborn self-portrayal as a loner and unique phenomenon of German modernism.

BETWEEN SECESSION AND AVANT-GARDE

First, a look at the year 1913, which began spectacularly for the young Beckmann. Forty-seven of Beckmann's works were included in a monographic survey at the Kunstsalon Paul Cassirer at Viktoriastrasse 35 in Berlin.[2] The exhibition presented a master who commandingly addressed the entire repertoire of classical art history and shied from none of the great subjects. Cassirer's publishing house released a monograph on Beckmann, who was only twenty-nine, to accompany the presentation. Authored by the young journalist Hans Kaiser, Beckmann was celebrated as a paradigmatic Berlin artist [Fig. 1].[3] Cassirer was one of the most important German art dealers for modern and contemporary art and had played a crucial role in the establishment of Impressionism in particular. He was also the publisher of the Pan-Presse, the long-standing managing director of the Berlin Secession, and immensely influential. This was not the first time Beckmann had experienced the honor of an exhibition in Cassirer's Kunstsalon.[4] Since arriving in Berlin in 1904, the ambitious artist had made a name for himself in the contested art world of the capital. After only a few years, he became the youngest full member of the Berlin Secession and joined its board and jury. On enormous canvases, he depicted great subjects such as *Sintflut* (The Flood),[5] *Auferstehung* (Resurrection),[6] and *Untergang der Titanic* (Sinking of the Titanic)[7] [Fig. 2], and with them he dominated the walls of the exhibition venue of the Berlin Secession. Nearly all of the noted critics regarded his honor with a monograph by Hans Kaiser to be premature, overly ambitious, or even counterproductive for Beckmann's further development as an artist.[8] Nevertheless, numerous observers considered Beckmann to be one of the most promising talents of the younger generation of the Secession, who aimed for a genesis of the new using the means and subjects of the history of art and of Impressionism.

In the summer of 1913 and a few months after the exhibition at Cassirer ended, the Berlin art scene was up in arms, resulting in a promising opportunity for Beckmann. The Berlin Secession was splitting up as a result of various conflicts and power struggles, and the rising generation of young artists in the capital experienced a temporary loss of orientation and homeland.[9] The choice of the right exhibition platform in Berlin, the undisputed center of contemporary art in Germany, was a crucial tactical choice but also an ideological decision of principles that led to a war of ideas that sometimes became quite polemical. Two prominent opposing positions resulted from it. On the one hand, there was Herwarth Walden with his Sturm-Galerie; Walden in 1913 was preparing for the "Erster Deutscher Herbstsalon" (First German Autumn Salon).[10] Walden stood for the international avant-garde and cosmopolitanism, for trends to artistic abstraction, for politically leftist, antibourgeois activism, and avant-garde pathos. Under the then still undifferentiated umbrella term "Expressionism," the Cubists, Italian Futurists, and for a time also the artists of the Blaue Reiter (Blue Rider) found their way to him in these years. His antipode was Cassirer, who planned the "Herbstausstellung 1913" (Autumn Exhibition 1913) as a direct competition for Walden's autumn salon. Cassirer also tried to win over the young generation of artists for that project and later for a re-establishment of the dissolved Secession.[11] The former Berlin Secession—Cassirer's immediate milieu—was the voice of a moderate, indeed almost anti-avant-garde contemporary art. It stood for adherence to representationalism and tradition, for reference to the artistic models of Symbolism, Realism, Impressionism, and, last but not least, proximity to collectors and the bourgeoisie.

When the choice of their future exhibition venue in Berlin—Walden or Cassirer, "Herbstsalon" or "Herbstausstellung"—

1. Title page of *Max Beckmann* by Hans Kaiser, 1913 (Paul Cassirer Verlag: Berlin, 1913).

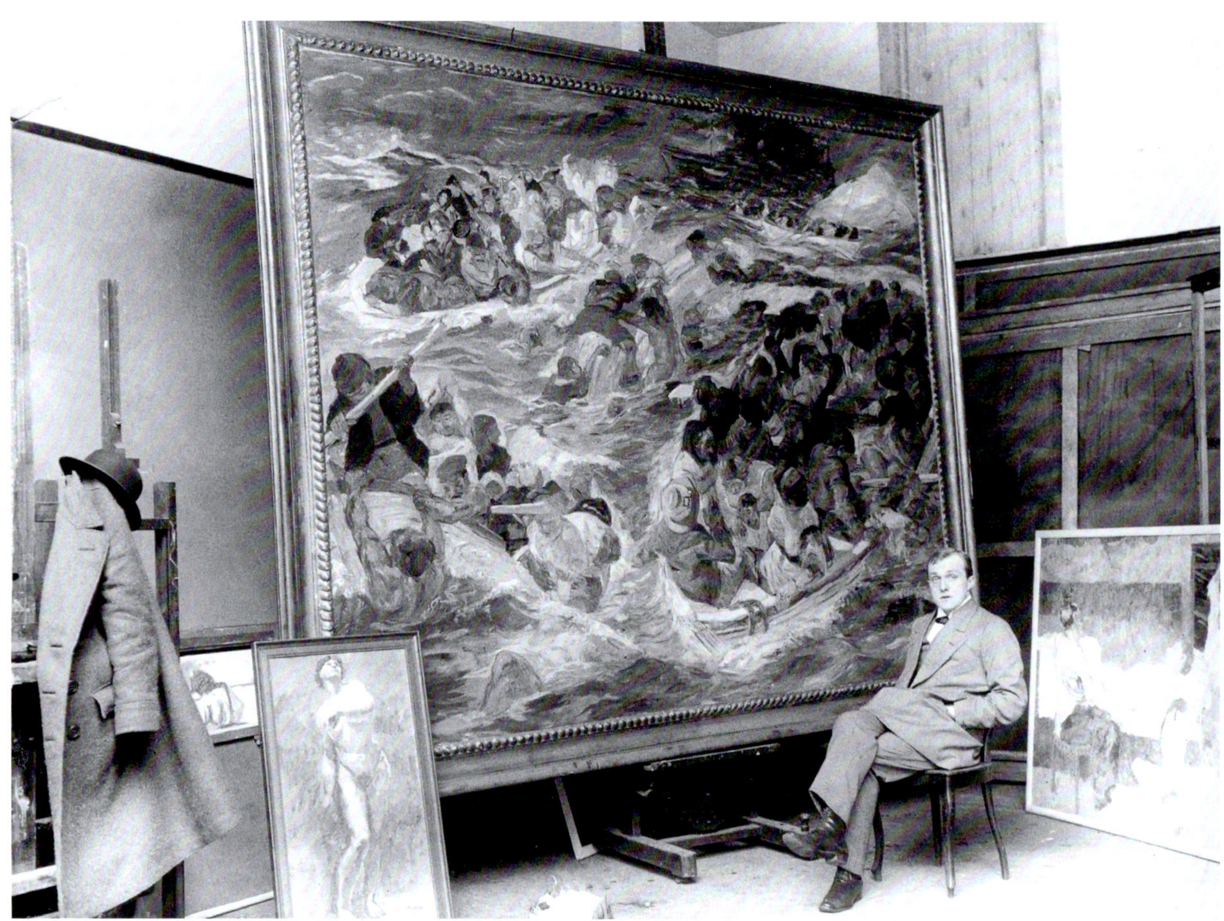

2. Max Beckmann in his Berlin studio in front of *Sinking of the Titanic*, 1912. © Oliver Baker, Germanisches Nationalmuseum, Deutsches Kunstarchiv, Nürnberg, NL Schmidt, Doris

became more critical for young artists in the autumn of 1913, the Secession was closer to Beckmann's goals than Walden's Sturm-Galerie, because Beckmann was at odds with the artistic paradigms of fellow artists of his age in the avant-garde of the time. With regard to Expressionism, which had begun its parade of success in 1913, Beckmann had shown himself to be ready for a fight. As a member of the board of the former Berlin Secession in the years leading up to this, he had been one of those responsible for rejecting numerous Expressionist works. In 1912, moreover, he had exchanged blows with the Munich Expressionist Franz Marc in articles in an ambitious public opposition to that avant-garde movement, which at the time had overwhelming numbers in Berlin.[12] Very much in the jargon of contemporaneous critics, Beckmann accused Marc's Expressionism and the Fauvist Matisse school of an inability to distinguish posters and wallpaper patterns from real art and denigrated their art as "applied art," that is, decorative, formalistic, and superficial.[13] Differentiating himself from their aesthetic trend of "flatness" and abstraction, Beckmann identified the goals of his art as the construction of spatial depth and a "conjunction of artistic sensuality with the artistic objectivity and actuality of the things to be represented."[14] At the same time, Beckmann saw himself as an heir to the Impressionists and the illuminaries of art history such as Rembrandt van Rijn, Jacopo Tintoretto, and Eugène Delacroix, whose mastery and great subject matter he wanted to harness for contemporary themes. His understanding of himself as an artist thus contrasted sharply with the developments of the contemporaneous avant-garde, who proclaimed a radical disavowal of established traditions and institutions.[15] Moreover, the professional ethos of the avant-garde, including a self-commitment to an antibourgeois, bohemian lifestyle, made it

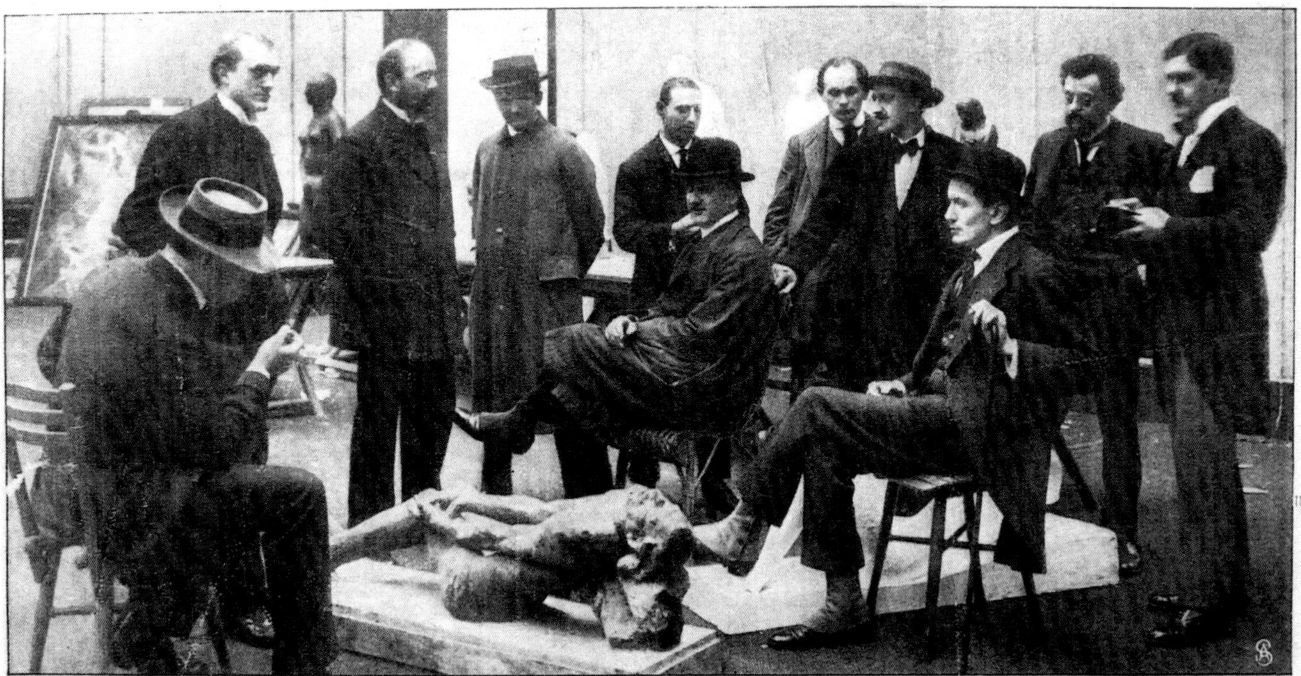

impossible to achieve social status or financial success.[16] Beckmann was far from adopting such a role model. He was searching for a different place in the art world of the time, with respect to both his work and society.

Together with the personalities of the Berlin Secession and the young representatives of a moderate, representational modernism, Beckmann found himself not on the side of Walden in 1913 but on that of his supporter Cassirer. He had reason to hope that a Secession exhibition under the new flag of Cassirer would result in a complete Beckmann room in its exhibition venue, the Ausstellungshaus am Kurfürstendamm.[17] In an association with many members, that honor was usually reserved for the greats of the Secession, such as Max Liebermann, or for special anniversaries. Beckmann was accordingly engaged in the founding of the new artists' association: the Freie Secession (Free Secession).[18] It opened its first summer exhibition on April 12, 1914. Beckmann was a member of the board and of the jury [Fig. 3]; he shaped its new beginning, and its first exhibition clearly bore his signature.[19] The association's new emblem featured the roots of a felled tree out of whose stump a plant was growing: symbolizing a fresh beginning and continuity at the same time [Fig. 4]. In keeping with this institutional self-image, the first summer exhibition of the Freie Secession was curated in a way to show that developments in contemporaneous art derived from French and German Impressionism and the great role models of the Secession such as Ferdinand Hodler, Liebermann, and Hans Thoma. One special success for Beckmann with regards to its content was that he was able to oust the French School of Matisse, which had been prominently represented in the 1913 summer exhibition of the Berlin Secession before its split and which he had discredited publicly, entirely from the rooms of the Freie Secession.[20]

Because the post of the president of the Freie Secession remained unfilled for its first months, Beckmann gave the speech for the opening of the exhibition himself. In it, very much in the tradition of Secessionism, he identified an awareness of quality and stylistic

3. Jury of the Freie Secession during the installation of the summer exhibition, 1914

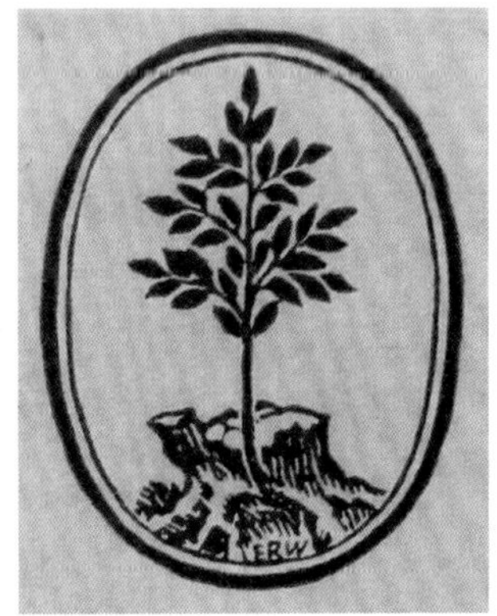

4. Emblem of the Freie Secession, 1914

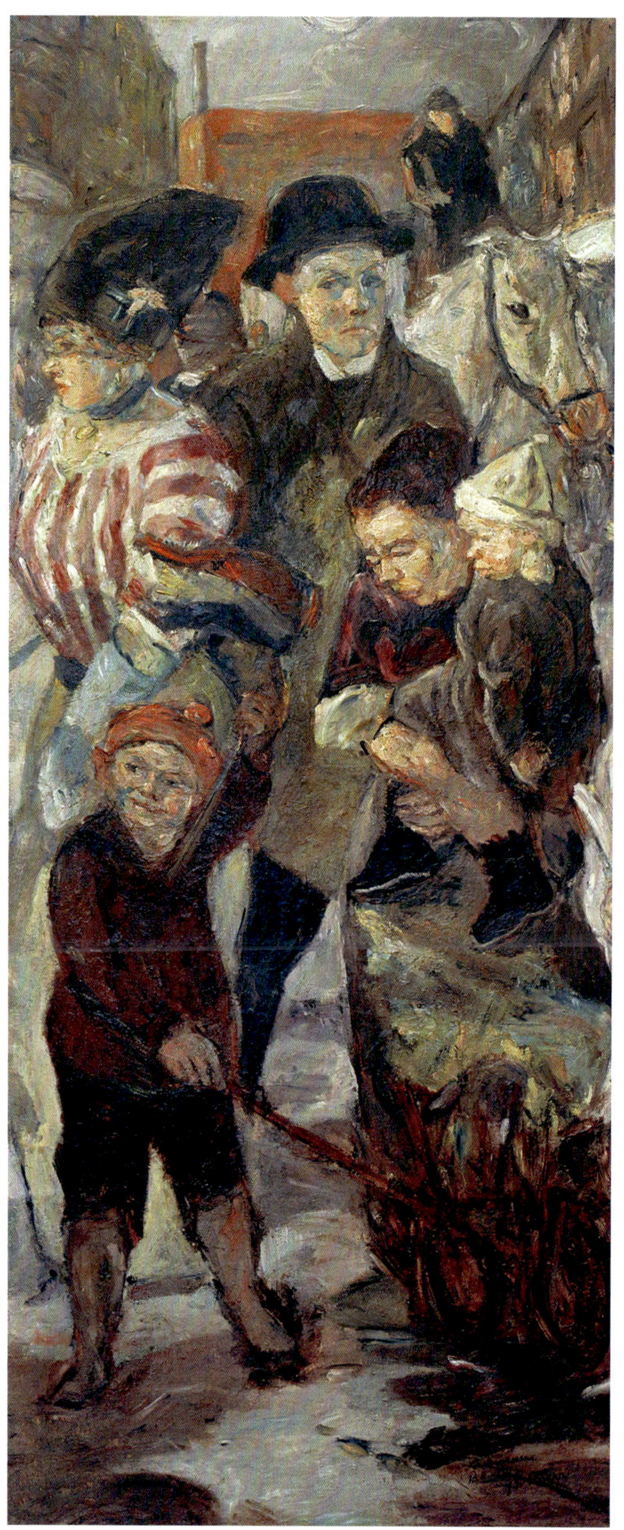

liberalism as the association's most important values. Nevertheless, in his remarks he also took a position on his own very personal artistic intentions: "We hope that our steely self-cultivation will enable us to successfully lead art out of the atmosphere of sentimental anarchy in which it now finds itself back to a clearer and more objective state."[21] He was thus sending a clear signal of a new beginning and at the same time establishing himself as a key figure of a newly assembled representational modernism with an awareness of tradition. After this speech, Lovis Corinth believed him capable of anything: "Beckmann will presumably be the man of the future, possibly shutting out P. Cassirer."[22] In 1914, therefore, Beckmann cultivated the bearing of an established artist and Secessionist who could already point to a monograph on his "lifework." He occupied a position of power in the most important exhibition venue of the capital managed by the artists themselves, and could claim for himself with a grand gesture his own place in contemporary art that rose above all the dominant -isms of art.

But for Beckmann, his influential new position in the Freie Secession was associated not only with his interest in artistic politics but above all with the hope of shoring up his own distinctive artistic standpoint. Whereas in the earlier exhibitions of the old Secession Beckmann had come on strong with enormous history paintings in the manner of Romanticism, he now switched to more modest formats and contemporary subjects. For example, at the exhibition of the Freie Secession in 1914 he showed three works with motifs of the metropolis [Fig. 5] and of sports, which enabled him to open up to contemporaneous art at least on an iconographic level.[23] Just how much Beckmann was on the defensive with regard to style, however, was demonstrated by the direct comparison with the few Expressionist works that had been accepted into the exhibition. Various works by the Brücke artists, including August Macke, Ludwig Meidner, and others, were combined in a single "room of the wild ones" and clearly revealed Beckmann's conservatism to the Berlin audience. There was a torrent of criticism. The discrepancy between the grand theses that Beckmann had formulated about his art and his antiquated-looking methods was abundantly obvious. The architect and journalist Adolf Behne wrote of Beckmann's superficially brilliant appearance at the Freie Secession: "It was presumably meant to be a profession of rejuvenation that *Max Beckmann* was the speaker at the exhibition opening. But his youth is truly only one of numbers. *The paintings* that Beckmann is showing this time seem almost geriatric."[24]

In this exhibition Meidner showed one of his now famous apocalyptic visions of the metropolis and another magnum opus, *Revolution (Barrikadenkampf)* (Revolution [Fighting on the Barricades]) [Fig. 6]. Unlike Beckmann, by this point, Meidner had long since left behind the visual language of Impressionism and developed a stylistic drama and expressivity that did justice to the nervous atmosphere of a modern technological metropolis.[25] In an essay titled "Das neue Programm" (The New Program) in 1914, Meidner clearly summed up how radically new aesthetic means were also necessary to address contemporary issues: "The sweet and fluffy quality of these agriculturalists [the Impressionists—AMH] is also found in the paintings of cities. But should monstrosities of buildings be painted with the same dots and transparency as brooks or boulevards like flowerbeds?! It is not possible to solve our problem with Impressionist technique."[26] Beckmann, too, failed in this way in his street scenes. *Der Cicerone* judged them thus: "Beckmann, too, was not fortunate this time. He addressed his favorite problem once

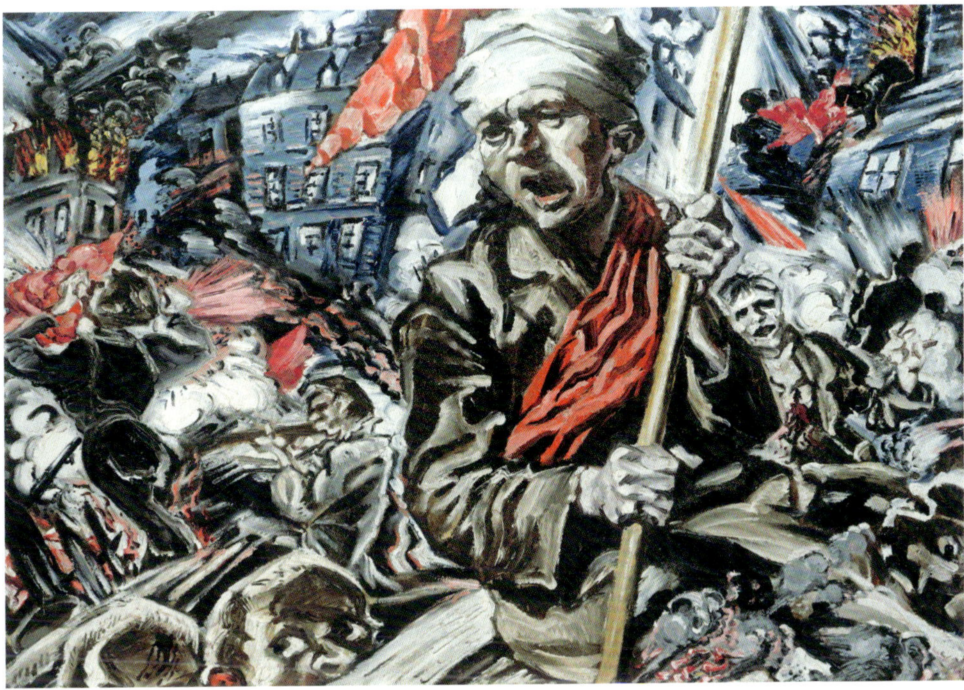

5. Opposite: Max Beckmann, *The Street*, 1914, oil on canvas. Berlinische Galerie. Photo: akg-images

6. Ludwig Meidner, *Revolution (Fighting on the Barricades)*, 1912-13, oil on canvas. Nationalgalerie, Staatliche Museen zu Berlin. Photo: bpk Bildagentur / Nationalgalerie, Staatliche Museen zu Berlin / Jörg P. Anders / Art Resource, NY

again and tried to discipline moving masses with color, but he did not succeed. His street falls apart. One is forced to read out details without feeling the overall rhythm."[27]

Marc's "Anti-Beckmann," his second article in the dispute between the two artists fought in journals in 1912, shows that Beckmann's artistic intensions were misunderstood because of his aesthetic at the time, his insistence on representationalism, and his polarizing statements against Expressionism. He was regarded by many as a defender of a traditional art oriented around representational skill, which is why a reputation as a reactionary clung to him from the perspective of his avant-garde colleagues.[28] Much the same is true in general of the other young members of the Freie Secession, who were dismissed by their colleagues from the Sturm group as traitors to the common cause of revolution in art.[29]

With his intention of providing a new, contemporary perspective on Impressionism and Naturalism, however, Beckmann often met with a lack of understanding in the prewar years even within his "own" Secessionist camp. For example, Karl Scheffler, an influential art critic from Cassirer's circle, devoted a detailed monographic article to him in March 1913.[30] He respected Beckmann's great artistic ambitions but he accused him of a lack of creative power for which he tried to compensate by an even greater bluster in the subject matter: "One sees museum paintings of large format with swirling ascensions to heaven, tumultuous battles of Amazons, crucifixions full of the horror and screeching of death, earthquakes, rapes, and scenes of dying. [...] This painter can take on whatever he likes: he ends up more or less in the catastrophic."[31] From Scheffler's perspective, Beckmann's cardinal error was not that of clinging to representationalism but rather insisting on the great pictorial subject, on heroic and metaphorical content. Even eight years later, when Beckmann was able to realize his goals much more clearly after making a fundamental stylistic transformation, Scheffler did not warm to Beckmann's "probing intellectuality.[32] The art historical paradigm that a subject worthy of painting determines the quality of the work of art had been swept away by the Impressionists in France and the Berlin and Munich Secessionists in Germany with their focus on the formal qualities of art. Two decades later that was still regarded as the crucial liberating coup of modern art. Even in the second decade of the twentieth century, Liebermann's oft-cited conviction that the content of a painting is that much greater the less focus there is on its subject was still the only conceivable guiding principle among art theorists, in the Secession, and even among the avant-garde arists.[33]

Instead of flower gardens, Beckmann painted biblical and historical scenes in a monumental Impressionist style and sought to imbue even the benign genre of the still-life with enough metaphor to elevate it to an eternal parable. At the same time, he strove for spatial depth and a classical pictorial construction, a broken, earthy color palette in the manner of German Impressionism, and his paintings radiated the spirit of the history of art. It makes sense that with this approach Beckmann was unable to connect either to the devoted Secessionists on Kurfürstendamm or the circles of the Expressionists and Cubists. Contrary to what his hard-fought influential position in the Freie Secession would suggest, Beckmann was artistically isolated before the war. In the painting *Ringkämpfer* (Wrestlers) [Fig. 7], which was presented on the entrance wall in the Freie Secession exhibition, the artist had portrayed himself. The painting reflects Beckmann's fundamental artistic crisis and proves that he was completely aware of his situation at the time. His alter ego in the painting has been brought to the floor in the crazy exertion of his metaphorical struggle for recognition, the art market, and modernity and risks succumbing to his opponent.

THE CAESURA OF WORLD WAR I AND LIBERATION FROM THE SECESSIONIST MILIEU

A little later, Beckmann's "wrestling" at the time was suddenly interrupted by his military service in World War I. In the autumn of 1915, his traumatic experiences in the war caused a nervous breakdown and he was granted "leave for special treatment in Frankfurt."[34] This transfer was probably initiated by a physician who was a friend of Beckmann and thus presumably coordinated with the artist. After his experience of an artistic crisis before the war, the painter was aware that in addition to recovering his mental energies he needed to find himself as an artist in a fundamental way.[35] That project necessitated that he retreat from the nerve-racking art world of the capital where Beckmann had sided with the Secession camp as described above and was therefore trapped in a role as Impressionist and traditionalist in many ways: in terms of style, ideology, and artistic politics. His search for recognition in the Berlin art world, the testing of his energies, and the distinguishing himself from the paths of colleagues his own age in Berlin had so preoccupied Beckmann "for many years that he was unable to find himself as a painter."[36] In "provincial" Frankfurt, by contrast, Beckmann could work on developing his own suitable visual language while uninfluenced and unobserved by the sharp-tongued critics of the capital. In retrospect, Beckmann described his breaking free of the network he had built up in Berlin and his self-imposed isolation in Frankfurt to the art critic Julius Meier-Graefe as an act of artistic liberation. "As you know, I regard that period [in Berlin—AMH] as years of apprenticeship in which I grappled with everything that was there as intensely as possible. Artistic as well as human. By being violently pulled out of a milieu that was beginning to become dangerous for me, I had the good fortune to fend for myself completely,

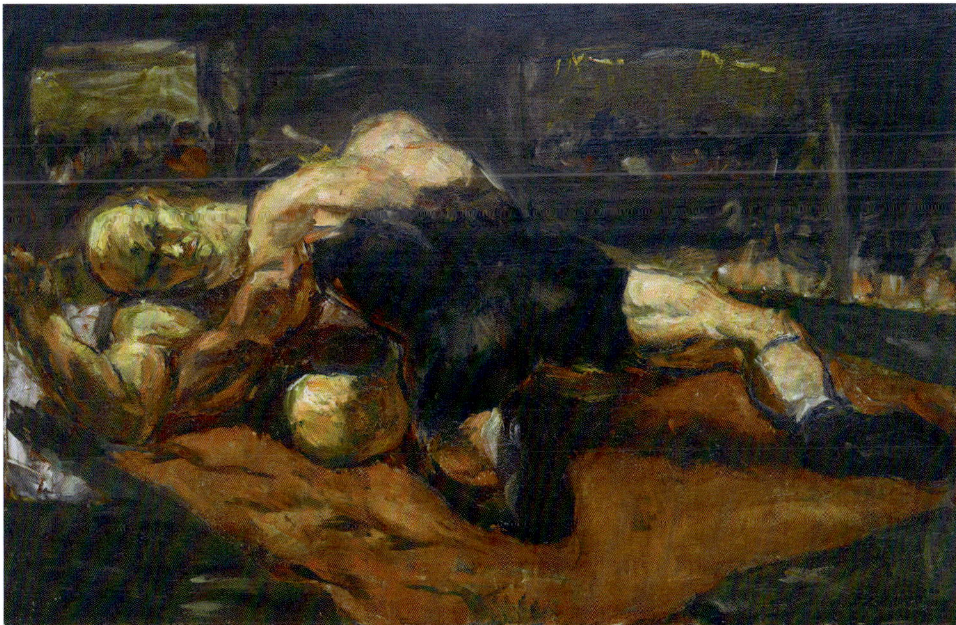

7. Max Beckmann, *Wrestlers*, 1913, oil on canvas. Museum Pfalzgalerie Kaiserslautern. Photo: Andreas Kusch © mpk

and in that way I gained a great deal of calm and concentration so that now in the stillness I perhaps have the energy to realize what I previously imagined, sometimes more clearly and sometimes more vaguely."[37]

In keeping with that insight, in 1916 and 1917 Beckmann also thoroughly repositioned himself in the Berlin art market. He distanced himself from the institution of the Freie Secession and its milieu, which was associated with the Impressionism he needed to overcome, on the one hand, but also increasingly from 1917 onward with the figurative Expressionism he rejected. He also withdrew from Cassirer's Kunstsalon at this time. Instead, he found in Jsrael Ber Neumann a young art dealer who was still untainted by the complicated networks and groupings of the prewar years [Fig. 8].[38] Neumann wanted to establish himself as an opposite pole to Cassirer, but neither did he exhibit the antibourgeois, revolutionary attitude of the Sturm-Galerie.[39] By signing a contract with Neumann in July 1916 for sole distribution of his graphic works, the artist wanted to reposition himself within the avant-garde of the capital.[40] Beckmann's business and personal partnership with Neumann turned out to be a very fortunate move, despite many disputes and a sometimes brusque tone. As an admirer of Beckmann's art and willing supporter of the artist's ambitious plans, the gallerist accompanied Beckmann's career until 1932.[41] In February 1924, Neumann opened an American branch of his gallery on Fifty-seventh Street in New York, which prepared the ground for Beckmann's later success on the international art market.[42]

BECKMANN AS A PROTAGONIST OF NEW OBJECTIVITY

The paintings of his early Frankfurt period demonstrate that Beckmann had acknowledged the criticism of his previous works. By synthesizing Cubist and Expressionist stylistic means, he addressed earlier deficits such as the lack of coherence in the composition and a lack of harmony between the subject and the style. In a transitional phase from 1917 onward, one clearly observes a brightening of the palette of Beckmann's works; the use of impasto disappeared, as did his earlier Impressionist style in general, in favor of clear contours and intricate, solid compositions. The works of 1917 and 1918 are characterized by a favoring of subjects from the tradition of medieval art to contemporaneous reality, as can be seen in works such as *Adam und Eva* (Adam and Eve),[43] *Kreuzabnahme* (Descent from the Cross),[44] and *Christus und die Sünderin* (Christ and the Sinner)[45] [see Plates 21–23]. In his choice of themes and stylistic means during this phase of reinvention, Beckmann oriented himself around the Gothic, a tradition that at the time was seen as specifically German.

With *Die Nacht* (The Night) [Fig. 4, p. 17],[46] Beckmann managed his definitive turn away from Impressionism in early 1919, while at the same time pointedly employing his new stylistic means.[47] In splintered, tightly nested forms, the painting depicts a claustrophobic scene of violence in an attic. A Cubist formal rigor with "glass-clear lines"[48] and a supernatural light meet objective, realistic rendering and the gesture of pain of the Old Masters. Form and content are closely related and reinforce each other. Beckmann's visual language was now so mature that he no longer had to have recourse to early German or Netherlandish subjects but could achieve his intended expression using a theme taken from the present. His depiction of a horrible attack on and murdering of a family was immediately recognized by contemporary viewers as a metaphor for current conditions.[49]

After Beckmann had considerably scaled back on exhibition activity for several years, he now resumed public showings of his paintings: first in 1919 at the Vereinigung für Neue Kunst e. V. in Frankfurt am Main and finally in 1921, after long years of absence, in the capital again at the Kunstsalon J. B. Neumann in Berlin, where a number of his paintings completed after 1915 were shown. Because of Beckmann's fundamental stylistic transformation, but also because of the works' novelty, this presentation astonished viewers.[50] In the postwar years, Expressionism had declined in quality and become a fashionable phenomenon. Even apologists of the movement, such as Wilhelm Worringer and Wilhelm Hausenstein, regarded it as outdated.[51] Art critics saw only empty epigonism in exhibitions of contemporary art everywhere and had for some time been waiting for new, inspiring ideas. Now the "new Beckmann" appeared with what he had formulated in 1912 as his true goal—at a time when he was still widely misunderstood: "My impetus had been to open up representationalism to debate in a new art form," Beckmann wrote to Hausenstein retrospectively in 1926.[52] The journal *Das Kunstblatt* reported that even after the first exhibitions of his new paintings that representationalism was still the greatest challenge and provocation for most of his contemporaries. At the same time, however, it was acknowledged that with his new works Beckmann had moved to the front of the newly emergent contemporary art.[53]

The assessment of Gustav Friedrich Hartlaub, director of the Städtische Kunsthalle in Mannheim, would be especially consequential: As early as 1922, in a questionnaire in *Das Kunstblatt*, he cited Beckmann's art in relation to the "New Naturalism" emerging in contemporary art.[54] Hartlaub sketched for the first time the rising trend of representational art that he would later be the first to call "*Neue Sachlichkeit*" (New Objectivity), which was beginning to be seen in the work of several artists such as Otto Dix, George Grosz, Alexander Kanoldt, and Georg Schrimpf. Based on Beckmann's new style, Hartlaub assigned him a prominent position as the great hope and figure of integration for this new German modernism. He divided the movement into two major directions, the conservative classicists and the leftist verists, and he saw Beckmann, who could not be clearly assigned to either direction, as a possible mediator between those two poles: "We are waiting for a future, a redeemed Max Beckmann."[55] In 1925, Hartlaub organized the epochal exhibition "Die Neue Sachlichkeit: Deutsche Malerei seit dem Expressionismus" (The New Objectivity: German Painting since Expressionism) at the Städtische Kunsthalle in Mannheim on the art movement he had discussed previously in 1922 and that had now reached the apex of its success [Fig. 9].[56] Beckmann was represented by fourteen of his works post-1917; his paintings were thus one focus of the show, along with the "classicist" Kanoldt.[57] The exhibition was a resounding success. It was shown in modified form in Dresden, Chemnitz, Erfurt, and Dessau, and gradually it elevated

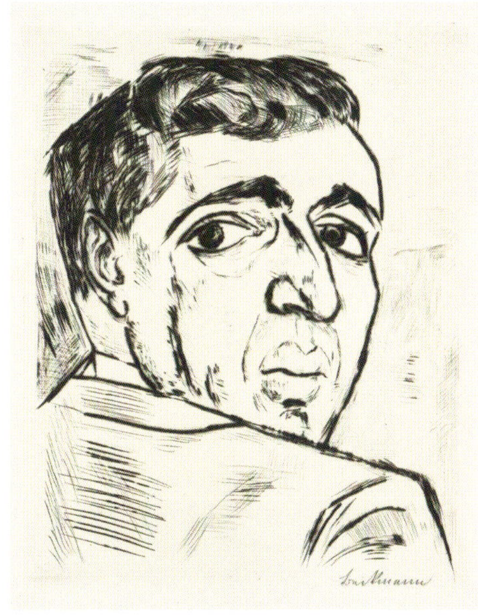

8. Max Beckmann, *Portrait of J.B. Neumann*, 1919, drypoint on cream wove paper. Art Institute of Chicago. Gift of the Print and Drawing Club. Photo: Art Institute of Chicago / Art Resource, NY

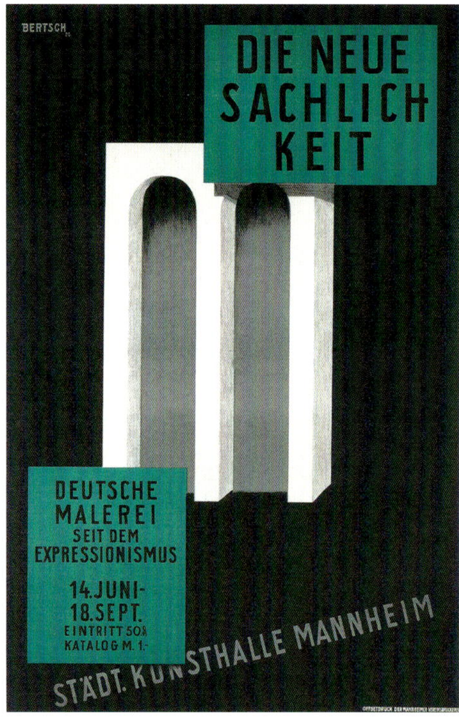

9. Karl Bertsch, poster for the "Die Neue Sachlichkeit: Deutsche Malerei seit dem Expressionismus" exhibition, Städtische Kunsthalle Mannheim, 1925, colored lithograph

Beckmann to being appreciated as a key figure of German postwar modernism. Even if with his effort to transcend the object represented—in his "Creative Credo" of 1918 he had coined the term "transcendental objectivity" for this[58]—he was pursuing a different goal than most painters of the *Neue Sachlichkeit*, who deliberately remained within the limits of the visible, Beckmann happily accepted the position assigned to him as a pioneer and leader of the movement.[59] When the exhibition at the Kunsthalle was finally shown, after several years in preparation, Beckmann had already set off for new intellectual shores.[60]

DISTINGUISHING HIMSELF FROM NEW OBJECTIVITY AND GERMAN PROVINCIALISM

Soon after the exhibition in Mannheim opened, Beckmann sensed that his art was again about to be tied to a movement. Beckmann still vividly recalled his prewar experience that being associated too closely, both personally and stylistically, with a group of artists, with all the expectations and attributions of roles that go along with it, could be a disadvantage both for his independent development and for his reputation and career. When it appeared in the mid-1920s that the *Neue Sachlichkeit* would become the dominant style of the Weimar Republic, Beckmann wrote to his fiancée, Mathilde von Kaulbach: "that is becoming a fashion now, and I have to do everything to escape the bustle that will now grow more and more."[61] The association of the *Neue Sachlichkeit* as a specifically German art phenomenon was inopportune for Beckmann, who as his success grew found the identification as a German artist he had initially sought increasingly unattractive as it seemed to him limiting and provincial.[62]

Beckmann's individualism and need to distinguish himself were already obvious in his early years in Berlin, but in his phase of finding himself he had sought or at least permitted an artistic and social contextualization. Although he had personally struggled to reach the position of spokesman for the Secessionists, the role of pioneer of the *Neue Sachlichkeit* was stylistically justified but had been assigned to him by others. Over the course of his later career, Beckmann was painstakingly concerned with conveying the image of an artistic "one-horse carriage"[63] and clearly distinguishing himself from the art activity around him.[64] His works from 1925 onward, such as *Italienische Fantasie* (Italian Fantasy)[65] and *Die Barke* (The Bark)[66] [see Plates 100 and 104], heralded a turn away from the mass phenomenon of the *Neue Sachlichkeit* and a new change in style. Beckmann was no longer looking to Berlin but rather to Paris, and from that time forward he positioned himself in the international art market as a European artist.[67]

Translated from the German by Steven Lindberg

1 Max Beckmann to Julius Meier-Graefe, mid-March 1919, in Max Beckmann, *Briefe*, ed. Klaus Gallwitz, Uwe M. Schneede, and Stephan von Wiese with Barbara Golz, vol. 1 (1899–1925) (Munich: Piper, 1993), 176–77.

2 Dates: January 23 to mid-February 1913; see Bernhard Echte and Walter Feilchenfeldt, eds., *Kunstsalon Paul Cassirer: Die Ausstellungen*, vol. 6, *Eine neue Klassik* (1912–1914) (Wädenswil: Nimbus, 2016), 255–98.

3 Hans Kaiser, *Max Beckmann* (Berlin: Paul Cassirer, 1913). Kaiser was rather unknown in Berlin; this monograph was his first book. Beckmann was very satisfied with it. See Christoph Engels, *Auf der Suche nach einer "deutschen" Kunst: Max Beckmann in der Wilhelminischen Kunstkritik* (Kromsdorf: VDG Weimar, 1997), 169–70.

4 He had done so previously in 1907 and 1910; see Bernhard Echte and Walter Feilchenfeldt, eds., *Kunstsalon Paul Cassirer: Die Ausstellungen*, vol. 3, *Den Sinnen ein magischer Rausch* 1905-1908 (Wädenswil: Nimbus, 2013), 336–60, and Bernhard Echte and Walter Feilchenfeldt, eds., *Kunstsalon Paul Cassirer: Die Ausstellungen*, vol. 4, *Ganz eigenartige neue Werke* (1908–10) (Wädenswil: Nimbus, 2013), 360–82.

5 *Max Beckmann: Katalog der Gemälde*, comp. Erhard Göpel and Barbara Göpel, ed. Hans Martin von Erffa for the Max Beckmann Gesellschaft (Bern: Kornfeld, 1976) (cited hereafter as Göpel). Göpel 97, *Sintflut* (The Flood), 1908, 221 × 216 cm (87 x 85 in.).

6 Göpel 104, *Auferstehung* (Resurrection), 1908, 395 × 250 cm (155 1/2 x 98 3/8 in.).

7 Göpel 159, *Untergang der Titanic* (Sinking of the Titanic), 1912, 264.8 × 330.2 cm (104 1/4 x 130 in.).

8 For example, Curt Glaser, "Berliner Ausstellungen," *Die Kunst für Alle* 28, no. 11 (March 1, 1913): 264; Paul Fechter, "Max Beckmann. Zur Ausstellung bei Cassirer," *Vossische Zeitung*, no. 54 (January 30, 1913): 5; and Fritz Stahl, "Berliner Ausstellungschronik," *Berliner Tageblatt*, no. 55 (January 31, 1913): 2.

9 For details, see Peter Paret, *The Berlin Secession: Modernism and Its Enemies in Imperial Germany* (Cambridge, MA: Belknap Press of Harvard University Press, 1981), 230–32; Anke Matelowski, *Berliner Secession, 1899–1937: Chronik, Kontext, Schicksal* (Wädenswil: Nimbus, 2017), 75–85; Rudolf Pfefferkorn, *Die Berliner Sezession: Eine Epoche deutscher Kunstgeschichte* (Berlin: Haude & Spener, 1972), 52.

10 Georg Brühl, *Herwarth Walden und "Der Sturm,"* (Cologne: DuMont, 1983); Mario-Andreas von Lüttichau, "Erster Deutscher Herbstsalon," *Stationen der Moderne: Die bedeutenden Kunstausstellungen des 20. Jahrhunderts in Deutschland*, exh. cat. Berlinische Galerie (Berlin: Nicolai, 1988), 131–140; Mario-Andreas von Lüttichau, "'Uns ist nicht das Leben die Kunst. Aber die Kunst das Leben' (Herwarth Walden): Der Erste Deutsche Herbstsalon im Spiegel der zeitgenössischen Kritik," *Der Sturm: Zentrum der Avantgarde*, vol. 2, *Aufsätze*, ed. Andrea von Hülsen-Esch and Gerhard Finck, exh. cat. (Wuppertal: Von-der-Heydt-Museum, 2012), 243–50.

11 Christian Kennert, *Paul Cassirer und sein Kreis: Ein Berliner Wegbereiter der Moderne* (Frankfurt am Main: Peter Lang, 1996); Georg Brühl, *Die Cassirers: Streiter für den Impressionismus* (Leipzig: Edition Leipzig, 1991).

12 Cathrin Klingsöhr-Leroy, "Controversial Positions: Franz Marc and Max Beckmann," trans. Michael Wolfson, in *Max Beckmann and Berlin*, ed. Thomas Köhler and Stefanie Heckmann, exh. cat. Berlinische Galerie (Bielefeld: Kerber, 2015), 76–83; Nina Peter, "Franz Marc und Max Beckmann: Die Kontroverse von 1912," in *Max Beckmann: Kleine Stillleben*, ed. Cathrin Klingsöhr-Leroy und Nina Peter, exh. cat. Franz Marc Museum, Kochel a. See (Berlin: Deutscher Kunstverlag, 2013), 101–5.

13 Max Beckmann, "Gedanken über zeitgemässe und unzeitgemässe Kunst: Eine Erwiderung," *PAN* 2, no. 17 (March 14, 1912): 499–502.

14 Max Beckmann, "Thoughts on Timely and Untimely Art," in Beckmann, *Self-Portrait in Words: Collected Writings and Statements, 1903–1950*, ed. Barbara Copeland Buenger, trans. Barbara Copeland Buenger and Reinhold Heller with David Britt (Chicago, IL: University of Chicago Press, 1997), 113–17, esp. 116–17.

15 On this, see, among others, Peter Bürger, *Theory of the Avant-Garde*, trans. Michael Shaw (Minneapolis: University of Minnesota Press, 1984), and Klaus von Beyme, *Das Zeitalter der Avantgarden: Kunst und Gesellschaft 1905–1955* (Munich: C. H. Beck, 2005).

16 Wolfgang Ruppert, *Der moderne Künstler: Zur Sozial- und Kulturgeschichte der kreativen Individualität in der kulturellen Moderne im 19. und frühen 20. Jahrhundert* (Frankfurt am Main: Suhrkamp, 1998).

17 Cassirer had motivated the former Secessionist to participate but made it a condition that a room in the Secession's Ausstellungshaus am Kurfürstendamm be dedicated to Beckmann, a move that many of his fellow artists regarded critically. See Georg Kolbe to Curt Herrmann, July 11, 1913, in *Curt Herrmann, 1854–1929: Ein Maler der Moderne in Berlin*, vol. 2, *Die Briefe*, ed. Rolf Bothe, exh. cat. Berlin Museum (Berlin: Arenhövel, 1989), letter 88, p. 386.

18 My dissertation on the Freie Secession is forthcoming.

19 Dates: April 11–September 20, 1914. *Erste Ausstellung der Freien Secession*, exh. cat. (Berlin: Ausstellungshaus am Kurfürstendamm, 1914).

20 Henri Matisse's *La danse* (1910) was presented as a key work at the twenty-sixth exhibition of the Berlin Secession. Moreover, Paul Cassirer, who was president of the Secession at the time, showed numerous other French artists of the Fauvist movement that Beckmann rejected; see *Katalog der XXVI. Ausstellung der Berliner Secession*, exh. cat. (Berlin: Ausstellungshaus am Kurfürstendamm, 1913).

21 "Eröffnung der Freien Sezession," *Berliner Volkszeitung*, no. 170 (April 11, 1914): 2.

22 Lovis Corinth to Hermann Struck, in *Lovis Corinth: Eine Dokumentation*, ed. Thomas Corinth (Tübingen: Wasmuth, 1979), 187.

23 On Beckmann's artistic crisis in 1913, see Olaf Peters, "The Struggle for Modernity in Art: Max Beckmann in the Crisis Year of 1913," trans. Steven Lindberg, in Köhler and Heckmann, *Max Beckmann and Berlin* (see note 12), 84–91. The exhibition included Göpel 177, *Ringkämpfer* (Wrestlers), 1913, 56 × 86.5 cm (22 x 34 in.); Göpel 180 and Göpel 181, *Die Strasse* (The Street), 1914, ca. 171 × 200 cm (67 3/8 x 78 3/4 in. and later cut in two). The third painting was perhaps Göpel 151, *Die Strasse*, which Göpel indicates was dated 1914, 168 × 118 cm (66 1/8 x 46 1/2 in.). On Beckmann's street scenes, see Nina Peter, "The Painter as Eyewitness: Max Beckmann's Early Berlin Street Scenes Series," trans. Michael Wolfson, in *Max Beckmann and Berlin*, ed. Thomas Köhler and Stefanie Heckmann, exh. cat. Berlinische Galerie (Bielefeld: Kerber, 2015), 118–26.

24 Adolf Behne, "Die erste Ausstellung der Freien Sezession," *Die Gegenwart* 85, no. 17 (April 25, 1914): 261–64, esp. 263 (emphasis original).

25 For a stylistic comparison of the two painters in the years 1912–14, see Sarah O'Brien-Twohig, "Beckmann and the City," in *Max Beckmann: Retrospective*, ed. Carla Schulz-Hoffmann and Judith C. Weiss, exh. cat. Saint Louis Art Museum et. al. (Munich: Prestel; New York: W. W. Norton, 1984), 91–109, esp. 94–96.

26 Felix Meidner, "Anleitung zum Malen von Grossstadtbildern," text for "Das neue Programm," *Kunst und Künstler* 12, no. 6 (1914): 312–14, esp. 312. The article was published as part of the journal's questionnaire concerning the ambitions of various contemporaneous artists. Max Beckmann also took a position in which he went to battle against "modern painting" much as he had in 1912.

27 Hans Friedeberger, "Die Ausstellung der Freien Sezession," *Der Cicerone*, no. 8 (1914): 290–92.

28 Peter, "Franz Marc and Max Beckmann" (see note 12), 103.

29 For example, Carl Einstein after *Herbstausstellung 1913*: Carl Einstein, "Herbstausstellung am Kurfürstendamm," *Die Aktion* 3, no. 51 (1913): cols. 1186–89, esp. col. 1187.

30 Karl Scheffler, "Max Beckmann," *Kunst und Künstler* 11, no. 6 (1913): 297–305.

31 Ibid., 297.

32 Karl Scheffler, "Kunstausstellungen. Berlin," *Kunst und Künstler* 19, no. 3 (1921): 112–13. And even more pointedly several years later: Karl Scheffler, "Max Beckmann," *Kunst und Künstler* 22, no. 5 (1924): 107–10.

33 See Charles W. Haxthausen, "Das Gegenwärtige zeitlos machen und das Zeitlose gegenwärtig: Max Beckmann zwischen Formalismus und Mythos," in *Max Beckmann: Die Nacht*, ed. Anette Kruszynski, exh. cat. Kunstsammlung Nordrhein-Westfalen, Düsseldorf (Ostfildern-Ruit: Hatje, 1997), 35–52, esp. 35.

34 Max Beckmann to Ugi and Fridel Battenberg, quoted in Stephan von Wiese, *Max Beckmanns zeichnerisches Werk, 1903–1925* (Düsseldorf: Droste, 1978), 172 n. 126. On Beckmann's time in Frankfurt am Main, see Klaus Gallwitz, ed., *Max Beckmann in Frankfurt* (Frankfurt am Main: Insel, 1984); relativized by Dietrich Schubert, *Max Beckmann vom Vietzker-Strand zur Departure: Die Kristallisation seiner Werturteile und seine bildnerische Praxis, 1904–1939* (Petersberg: Michael Imhof, 2021), 78.

35 The beginnings of Beckmann's artistic orientation can be seen in a number of drawings from 1914 and 1915; see von Wiese, *Max Beckmanns zeichnerisches Werk* (see note 34), 45–108.

36 J. B. Neumann, "Sorrow and Champagne," in *Max Beckmann und J. B: Neumann: Der Künstler und sein Händler in Briefen und Dokumenten, 1917–1950*, ed. Ursula Harter and Stephan von Wiese (Cologne: Walther König, 2011), 285–323, esp. 289.

37 Max Beckmann to Julius Meier-Graefe, mid-March 1919, in Beckmann, *Briefe* (see note 1), 176–77.

38 Harter and von Wiese, *Max Beckmann und J. B. Neumann* (see note 36).

39 Neumann, "Sorrow and Champagne" (see note 36), 286.

40 Graphisches Kabinett J. B. Neumann to Max Beckmann, July 12, 1916, in Harter and von Wiese, *Max Beckmann und J. B. Neumann* (see note 36), 39 (Letter 1). According to Neumann's autobiographical account, Max Beckmann had previously tried to win him over as his Berlin dealer in 1912. At the time, however, Neumann did not understand Beckmann's art, so they did not end up working together. Neumann, "Sorrow and Champagne" (see note 36), 286.

41 Ursula Harter and Stephan von Wiese, "J.B. Neumann und der 'Beckmann Concern,'" in Harter and von Wiese, *Max Beckmann und J. B. Neumann* (see note 36), 19–31, esp. 28.

42 Ibid., 26.

43 Göpel 196, *Adam und Eva* (Adam and Eve), 1917.

44 Göpel 192, *Kreuzabnahme* (Descent from the Cross), 1917.

45 Göpel 197, *Christus und die Sünderin* (Christ and the Sinner), 1917.

46 Göpel 200, *Die Nacht* (The Night), 1918–19.

47 On this magnum opus, see Matthias Eberle, *Die Nacht: Passion ohne Erlösung* (Frankfurt am Main: Fischer Taschenbuch Verlag, 1984), and Kruszynski, *Max Beckmann: Die Nacht* (see note 33).

48 Max Beckmann to Julius Meier-Graefe, mid-March 1919, in Beckmann, *Briefe* (see note 1), 176–77, esp. 177.

49 Haxthausen, "Das Gegenwärtige zeitlos machen und das Zeitlose gegenwärtig" (see note 33), 39. As an example of his contemporaneous reception, see Dr. Paul Ferdinand Schmidt, "Max Beckmann," *Vossische Zeitung*, no. 360 (July 18, 1919): 3.

50 Heinrich Simon, "Max Beckmann," *Das Kunstblatt* 3 (1919): 257–64; Haxthausen, "Das Gegenwärtige zeitlos machen und das Zeitlose gegenwärtig" (see note 33), 38.

51 Wilhelm Worringer, *Künstlerische Zeitfragen: Lesung vor der Deutschen Goethegesellschaft. München Nov. 1920* (Munich: H. Bruckmann, 1921), reprinted in Wilhelm Worringer, *Schriften*, vol. 1, ed. Hannes Böhringer, Helga Grebing and Beate Söntgen (Munich: Wilhelm Fink, 2004), 895–909; Wilhelm Hausenstein, *Die Kunst in diesem Augenblick* (Munich: Hyperion, 1920), reprinted in Wilhelm Hausenstein, *Die Kunst in diesem Augenblick: Aufsätze und Tagebuchblätter aus 50 Jahren*, ed. Hans Melchers (Munich: Prestel, 1960), 262–71
and 279–83.

52 Max Beckmann to Wilhelm Hausenstein, March 12, 1926, in Max Beckmann, *Briefe*, ed. Klaus Gallwitz, Uwe M. Schneede, and Stephan von Wiese with Barbara Golz, vol. 2 (1925–37) (Munich: Piper, 1993), 33–34, esp. 34.

53 W. Sch., "Ausstellungen. Frankfurt," in: *Das Kunstblatt* 5, no. 6 (1921): 190–91, esp. 190; Schmidt, "Max Beckmann" (see note 49); Paul F. Schmidt, "Max Beckmann: Zur Ausstellung seiner neuesten Arbeiten in Frankfurt a.M.," *Der Cicerone* 11, no 12 (1919): 380–81; L. Moser, "Mannheim. Kunsthalle-Ausstellung: Die neue Sachlichkeit," *Kunst und Künstler* 23, no. 12 (1925): 474.

54 G. F. Hartlaub, "Ein neuer Naturalismus?? Eine Rundfrage des Kunstblatts," *Das Kunstblatt* 6, no. 9 (1922): 389–93.

55 Ibid., 393.

56 Dates: June 14–September 13, 1925. *Ausstellung Neue Sachlichkeit. Deutsche Malerei seit dem Expressionismus*, exh. cat. (Mannheim: Städtische Kunsthalle, 1925).

57 The exhibition catalogue lists only five works, but nine additional paintings by Beckmann were delivered to the exhibition a little later; see Olaf Peters, *Vom Schwarzen Seiltänzer: Max Beckmann zwischen Weimarer Republik und Exil* (Berlin: Reimer, 2005), 68.

58 The reference is the epistemological paradox of a metaphysical transcendence of things by art that clings to visual appearance. Max Beckmann, "Creative Credo," in Beckmann, *Self-Portrait in Words: Collected Writings and Statements, 1903–1950*, ed. Barbara Copeland Buenger, trans. Barbara Copeland Buenger and Reinhold Heller with David Britt (Chicago, IL: University of Chicago Press, 1997), 181–85.

59 On Beckmann's position within the *Neue Sachlichkeit* movement, see Peters, *Vom Schwarzen Seiltänzer* (see note 57), 61–94; Janina Nentwig, "A Question of Perspective: Max Beckmann and New Objectivity," trans. Steven Lindberg, in Köhler and Heckmann, *Max Beckmann and Berlin* (see note 12), 156–63.

60 On the history of this exhibition, see Karoline Hille, *Spuren der Moderne: Die Mannheimer Kunsthalle von 1918–1933* (Berlin: Akademie, 1994); Hans-Jürgen Buderer and Manfred Fath, *Neue Sachlichkeit: Bilder auf der Suche nach der Wirklichkeit; Figurative Malerei der zwanziger Jahre*, exh. cat. Städtische Kunsthalle, Mannheim (Munich: Prestel, 1994), 11–37.

61 Max Beckmann to Mathilde von Kaulbach, July 21, [1925], in Beckmann, *Briefe* (see note 1), 343.

62 Even years later, Beckmann was struggling to avoid being identified as a German painter because he hoped it would improve his success in the international market. See, for example, Max Beckmann to J. B. Neumann, November 24, 1928, in Harter and von Wiese, *Max Beckmann und J. B. Neumann* (see note 36), 185 (Letter 75).

63 Hans Belting, *Max Beckmann: Tradition as a Problem in Modern Art*, trans. Peter Wortsman (New York: Timken, 1989), 13.

64 Anna Maria Heckmann, "The 'Beckmann Corporation': Max Beckmann as Strategist of His Career," trans. Steven Lindberg, in Köhler und Heckmann, *Max Beckmann and Berlin* (see note 12), 164–73.

65 Göpel 238, *Italienische Fantasie* (Italian Fantasy), 1925.

66 Göpel 253, *Die Barke (Spiel der Wellen)* (The Bark [Play of Waves]), 1926.

67 See, for example, Max Beckmann to J. B. Neumann, October 10, 1927, in in Harter and von Wiese, *Max Beckmann und J. B. Neumann* (see note 36), 177 (Letter 69).

CREATIVE CREDO, 1918–20

Max Beckmann

I paint and I'm satisfied to let it go at that, since I'm by nature tongue-tied and only a terrific interest in something can squeeze a few words out of me.

Nowadays whenever I listen to painters who have a way with words, frequently with real astonishment, I become a little uneasy about whether I can find language beautiful and spirited enough to convey my enthusiasm and passion for the objects of the visible world. However, I've finally calmed myself about this. I'm now satisfied to tell myself: "You are a painter, do your job and let those who can, talk." I believe that essentially I love painting so much because it forces me to be objective. There is nothing I hate more than sentimentality. The stronger my determination grows to grasp the unutterable things of this world, the deeper and more powerful the emotion burning inside me about our existence, the tighter I keep my mouth shut and the harder I try to capture the terrible, thrilling monster of life's vitality and to confine it, to beat it down and to strangle it with crystal-clear, razor-sharp lines and planes.

I don't cry. I hate tears, they are a sign of slavery. I keep my mind on my business—on a leg, on an arm, on the penetration of the surface thanks to the wonderful effects of foreshortening, on the partitioning of space, on the relationship of straight and curved lines, on the interesting placement of small, variously and curiously shaped round forms next to straight and flat surfaces, walls, tabletops, wooden crosses, or house façades. Most important for me is volume, trapped in height and width; volume on the plane, depth without losing the awareness of the plane, the architecture of the picture.

Piety? God? O beautiful, much misused words. I'm both when I have done my work in such a way that I can finally die. A painted or drawn hand, a grinning or weeping face, that is my confession of faith; if I have felt anything at all about life it can be found there.

The war has now dragged to a miserable end. But it hasn't changed my ideas about life in the least, it has only confirmed them. We are on our way to very difficult times. But right now, perhaps more than before the war, I need to be with people. In the city. That is just where we belong these days. We must be a part of all the misery that is coming. We have to surrender our heart and our nerves, we must

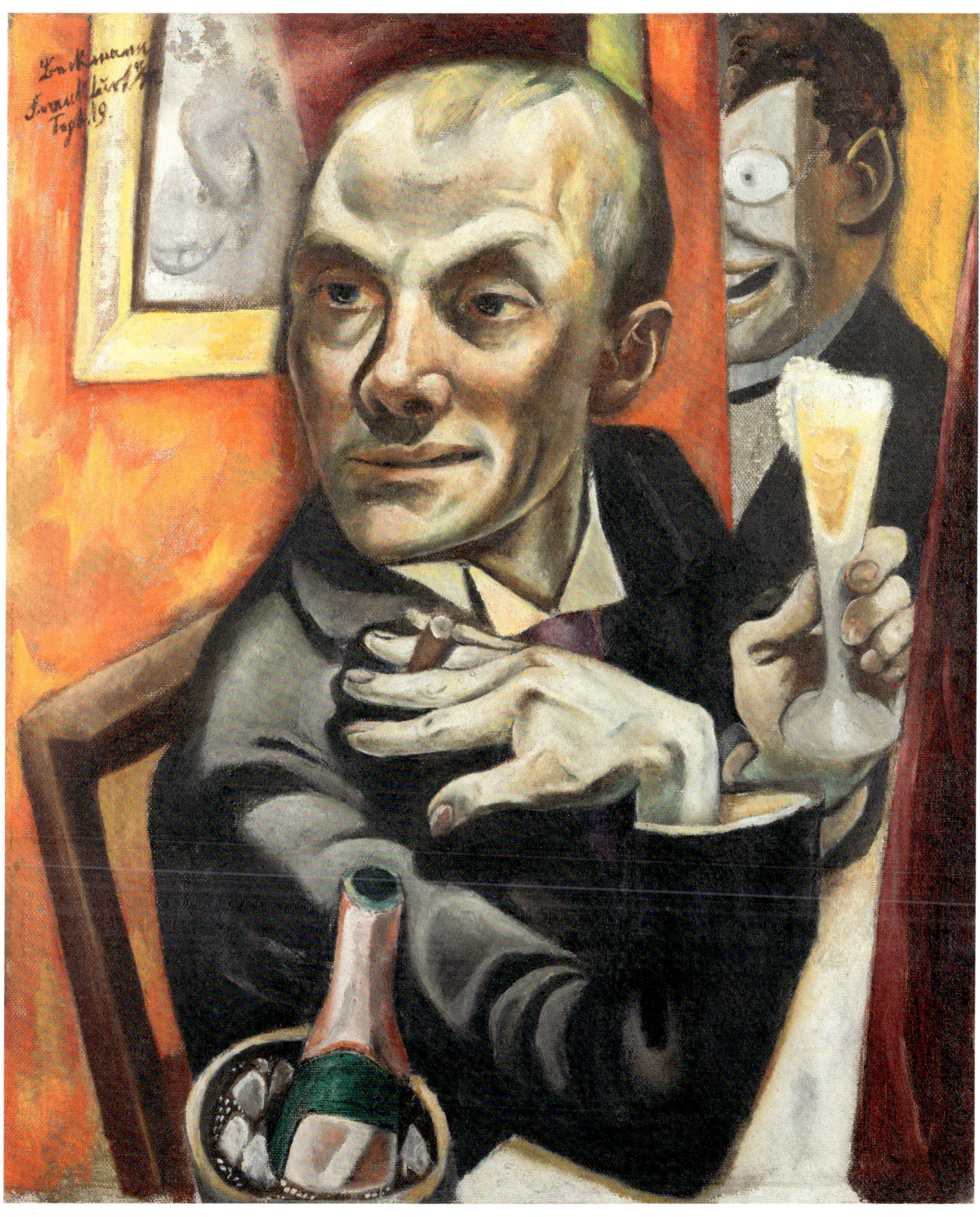

Max Beckmann, *Self-Portrait with Champagne Glass,* 1919, oil on canvas. Städel Museum Frankfurt.
Photo: bpk Bildagentur / Städel Museum Frankfurt / Art Resource, NY

abandon ourselves to the horrible cries of pain of deluded people. Right now we have to get as close to the people as possible. It's the only course of action that might give some purpose to our superfluous and selfish existence—that we give people a picture of their fate. And we can do that only if we love humanity.

Actually it's stupid to love humanity, nothing but a heap of egoism (and we are a part of it too). But I love it anyway. I love its meanness, its banality, its dullness, its cheap contentment, and its oh-so-very-rare heroism. But in spite of this, every single person is a unique event, as if he had just fallen from Orion. And isn't the city the best place to experience this? They say that the air in the country is cleaner and that there are fewer temptations. But I believe that dirt is the same wherever you are. Cleanliness is a matter of the will. Farmers and landscapes are all very beautiful and occasionally even refreshing. But the great orchestra of humanity is still in the city.

What was really unhealthy and disgusting before the war was that business interests and a mania for success and influence had infected all of us in one form or another. Well, we have had four years of staring straight into the stupid face of horror. Perhaps a few people were really impressed. Assuming, of course, anyone had the slightest inclination to be impressed.

Complete withdrawal in order to achieve that famous purity people talk about as well as the loss of self in God, right now all that is too bloodless and also loveless for me. You don't dare do that kind of thing until your work is finished, and our work is painting.

I certainly hope we are finished with much of the past. Finished with the mindless imitation of visible reality; finished with feeble, archaistic, and empty decoration, and finished with that false, sentimental, and swooning mysticism! I hope we will achieve a transcendental objectivity out of a deep love for nature and humanity. The sort of thing you can see in the art of Mäleßkircher, Grünewald, Brueghel, Cézanne, and Van Gogh.

Perhaps with the decline of business, perhaps (something I hardly dare hope) with the development of the communistic principle, the love of objects for their own sake will become stronger. I believe this is the only possibility open to us for achieving a great universal style.

That is my crazy hope which I can't give up, which in spite of everything is stronger in me than ever before. And someday I want to make buildings along with my pictures. To build a tower in which humanity can shriek out its rage and despair and all its poor hopes and joys and wild yearning. A new church. Perhaps this age may help me.

Max Beckmann

Self-Portrait in Words: Collected Writings and Statements, 1903–1950, ed. Barbara Copeland Buenger, trans. Barbara Copeland Buenger and Reinhold Heller with David Britt (Chicago, IL: University of Chicago Press, 1997), 181–85.

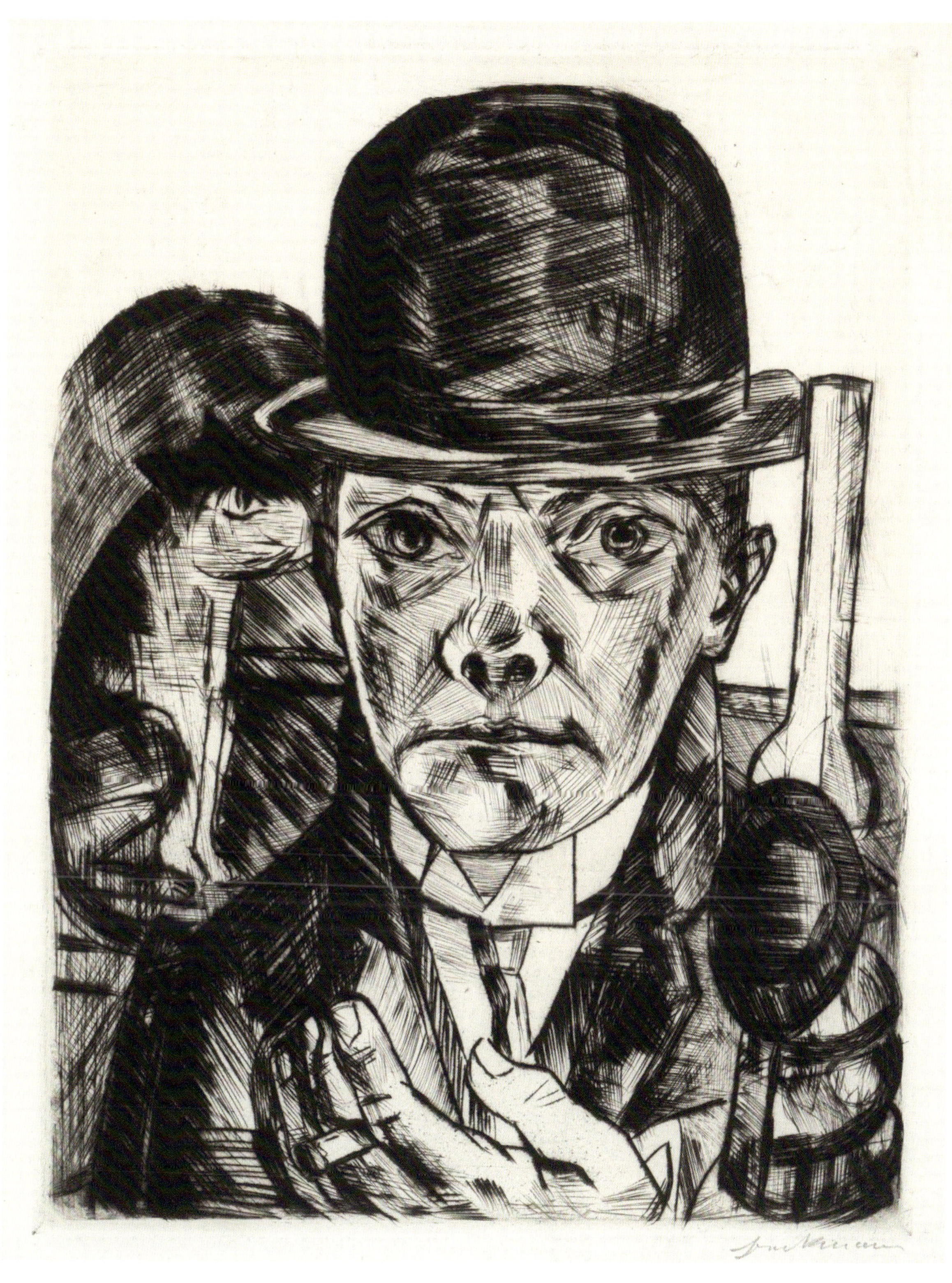

1. SELF-PORTRAIT IN BOWLER HAT, 1921

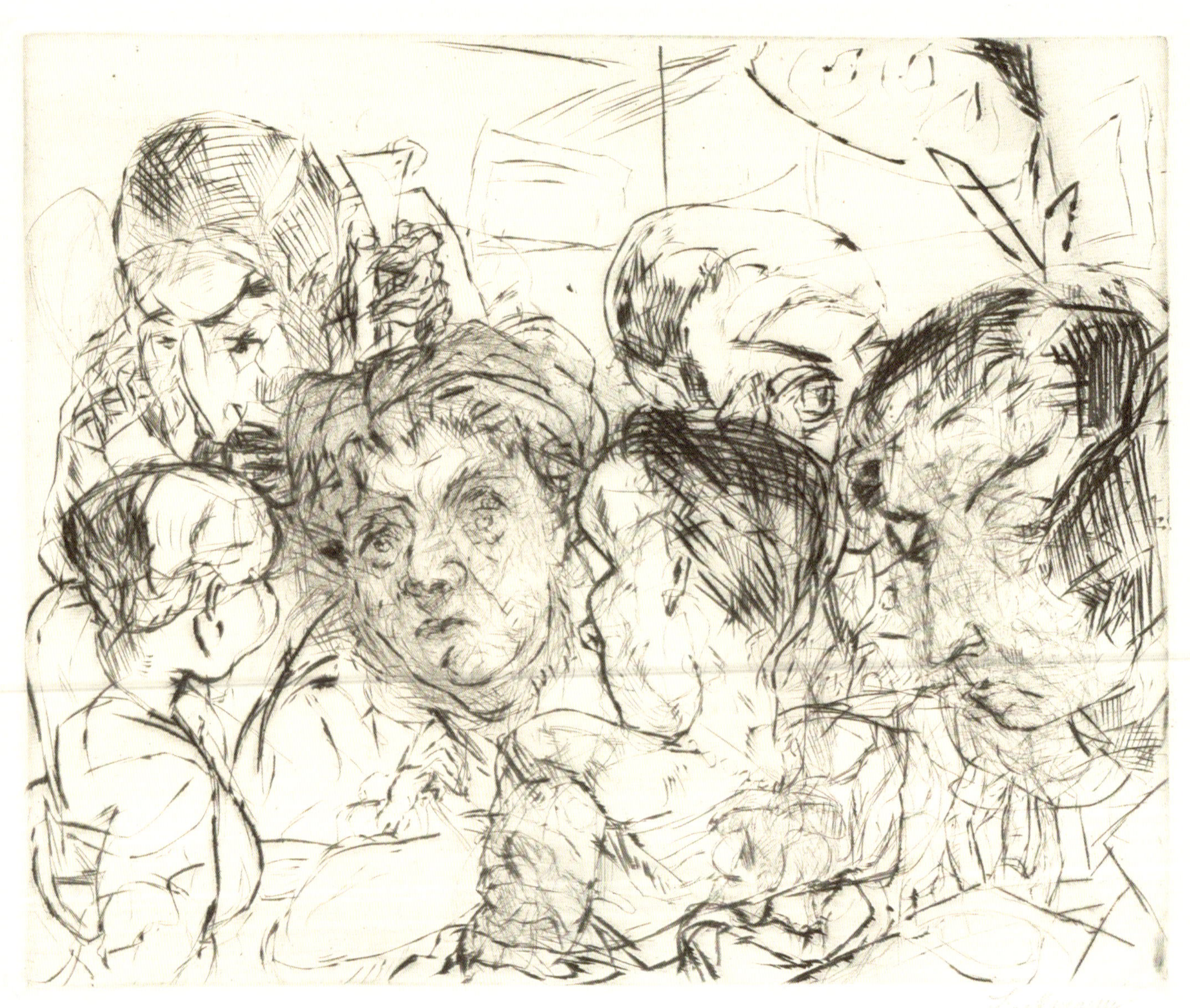

2. SOCIETY, 1915

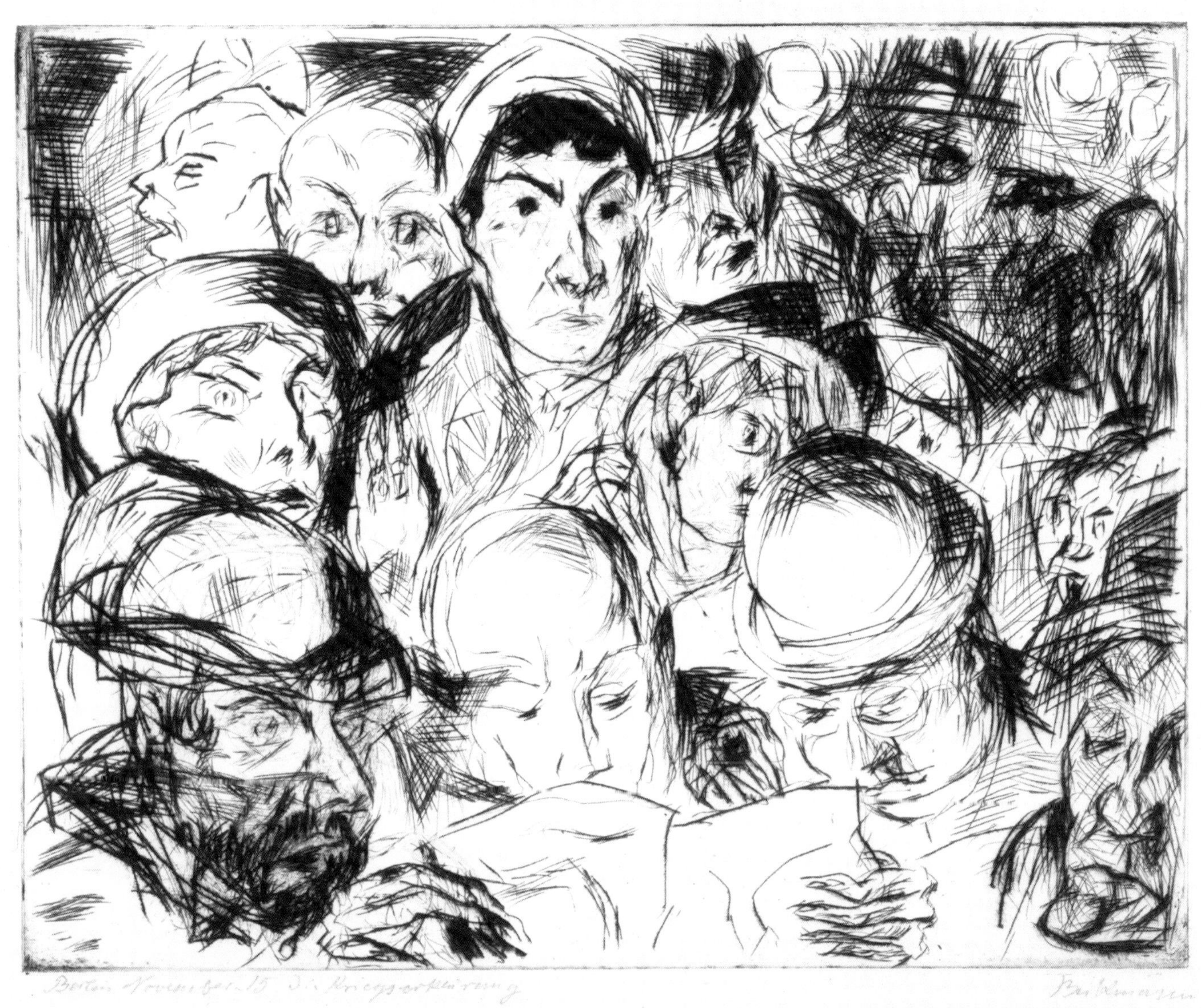

3. DECLARATION OF WAR, PLATE 3, ANNUAL FAIR PORTFOLIO, 1914

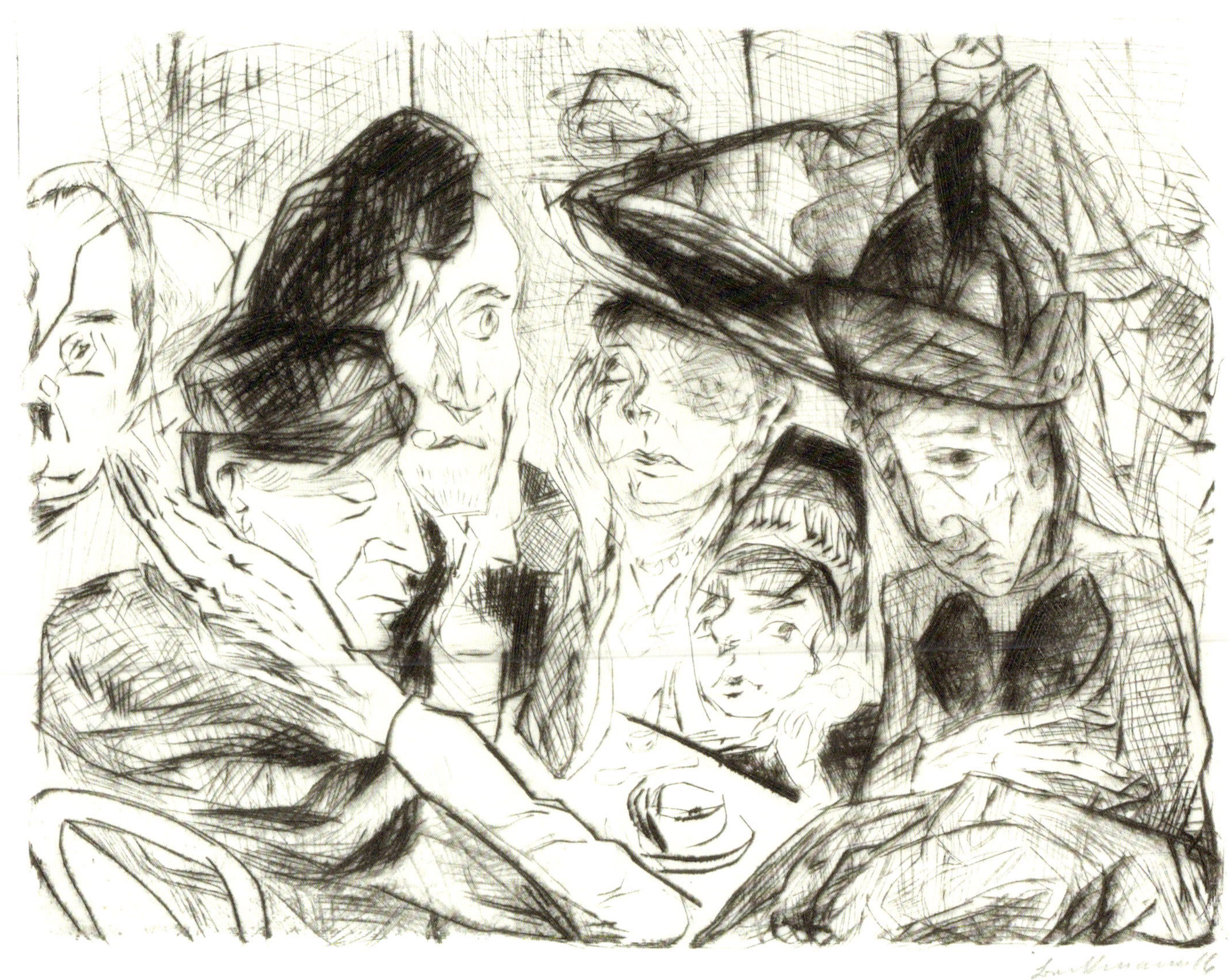

4. CAFÉ (TWO OLD WOMEN IN FOREGROUND), PRINTED 1916, PUBLISHED 1918

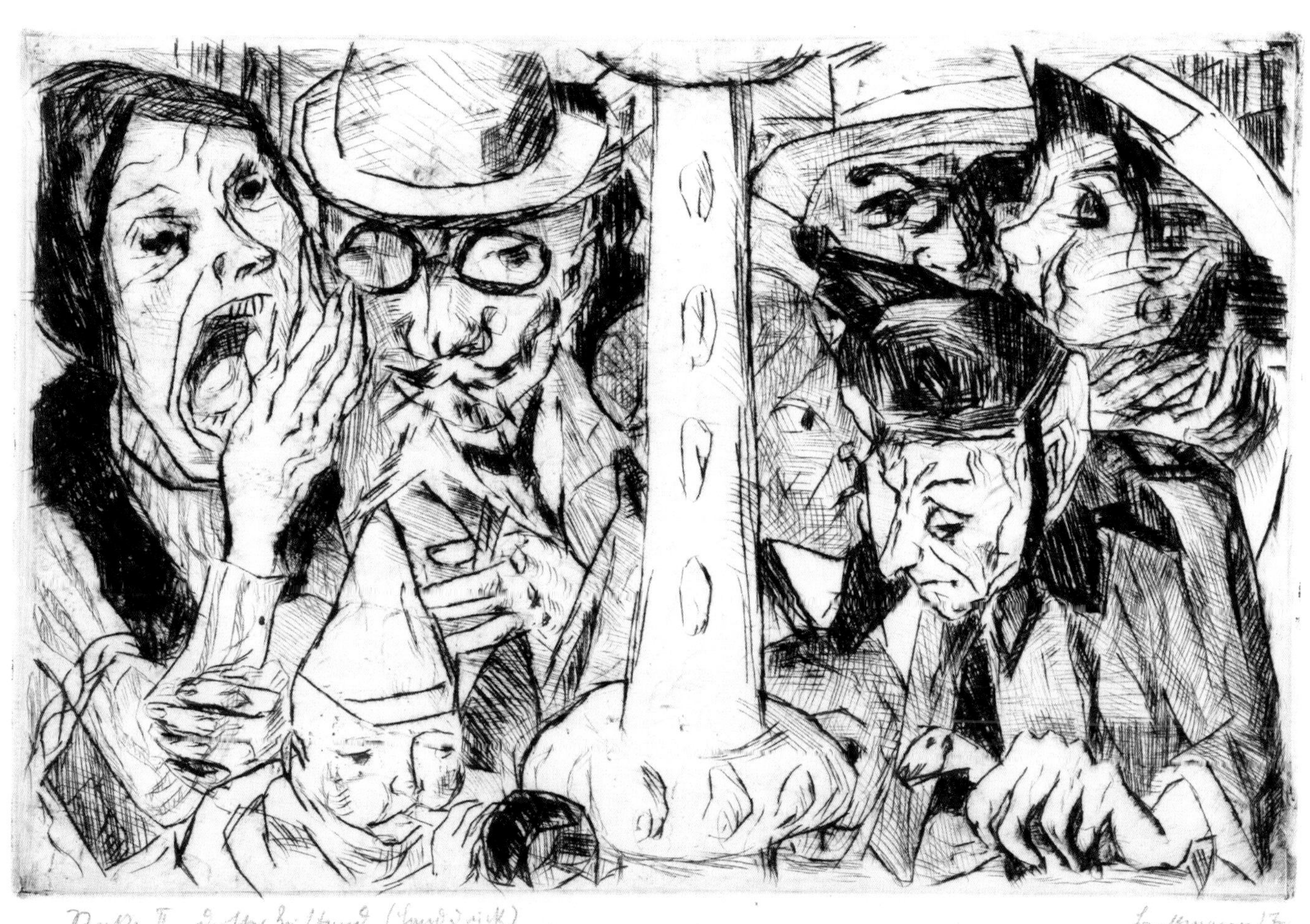

5. STREET II, 1916–17, DATED 1917

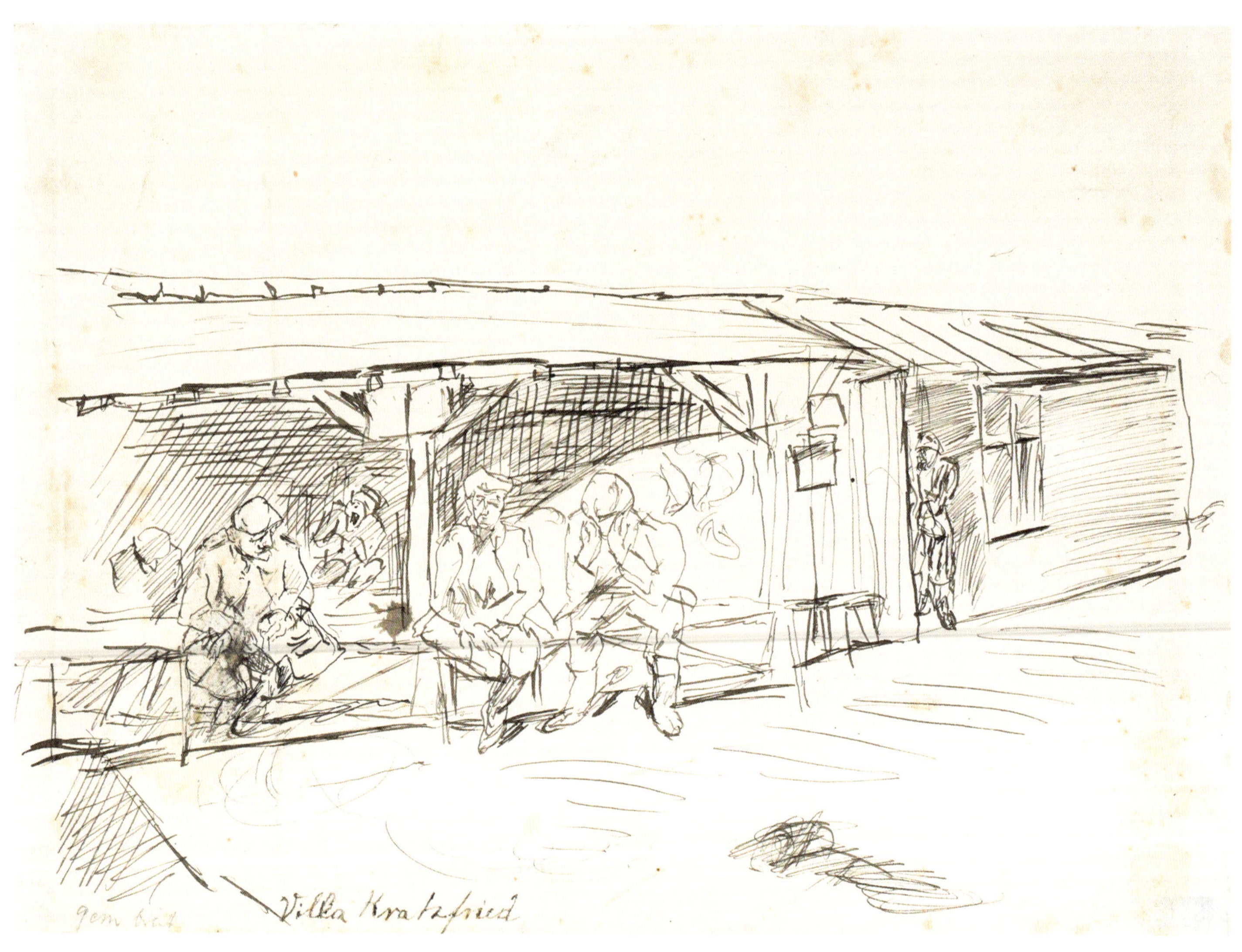

6. OPEN LATRINE HOUSE (VILLA KRATZFRIED), 1915

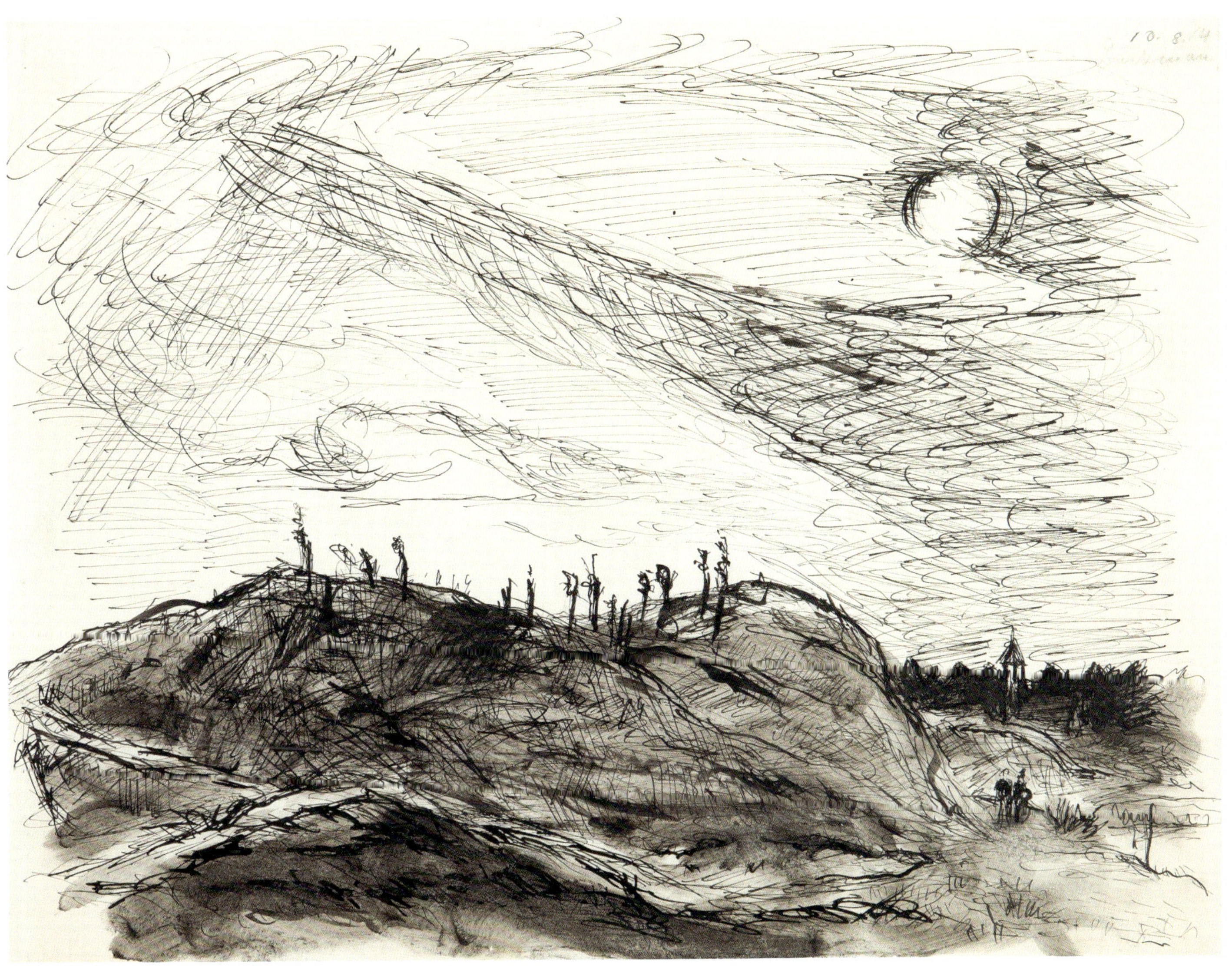

7. HILLY LANDSCAPE AGAINST THE SUN, 1915

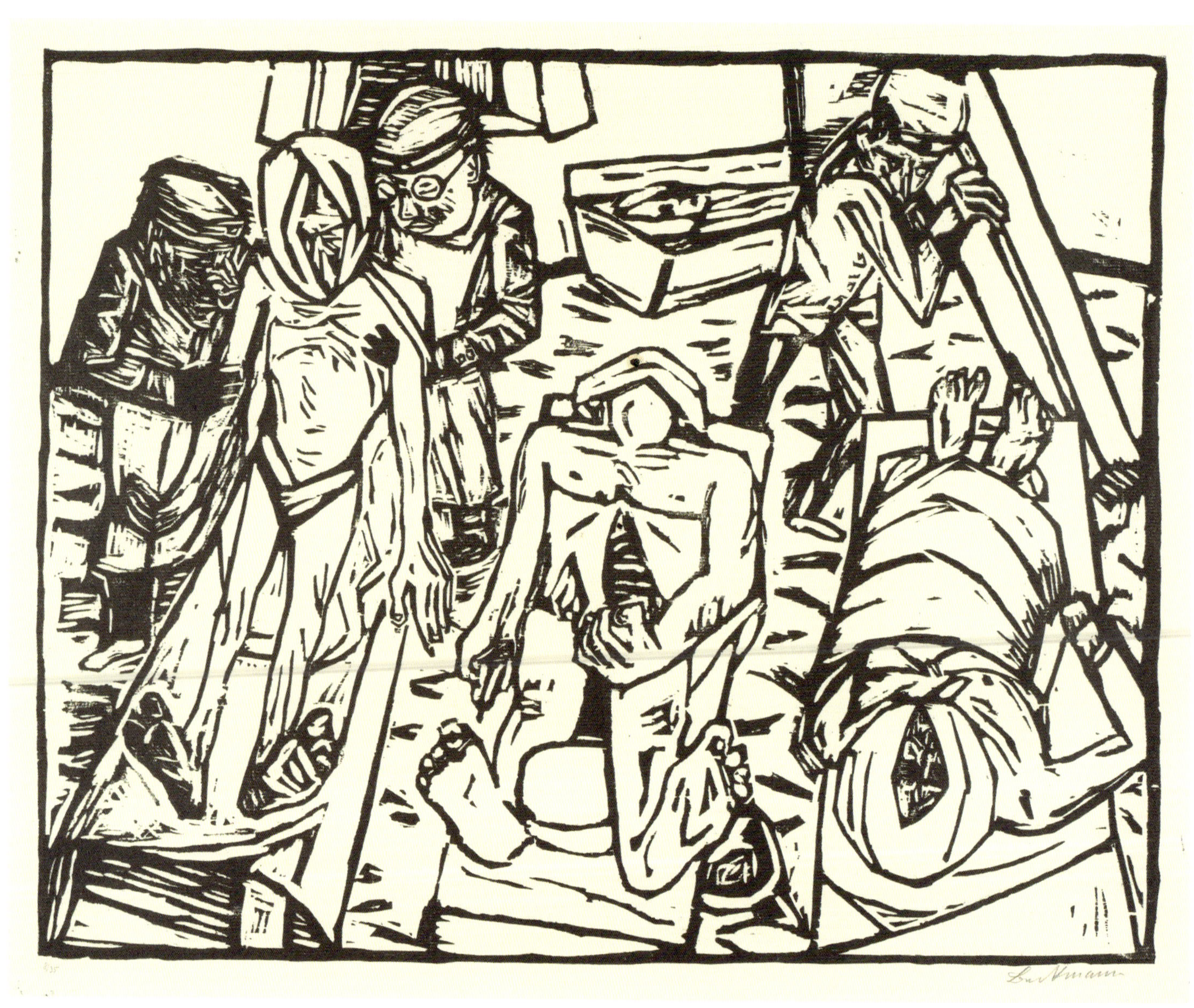

8. MORGUE, PRINTED 1922, PUBLISHED 1924

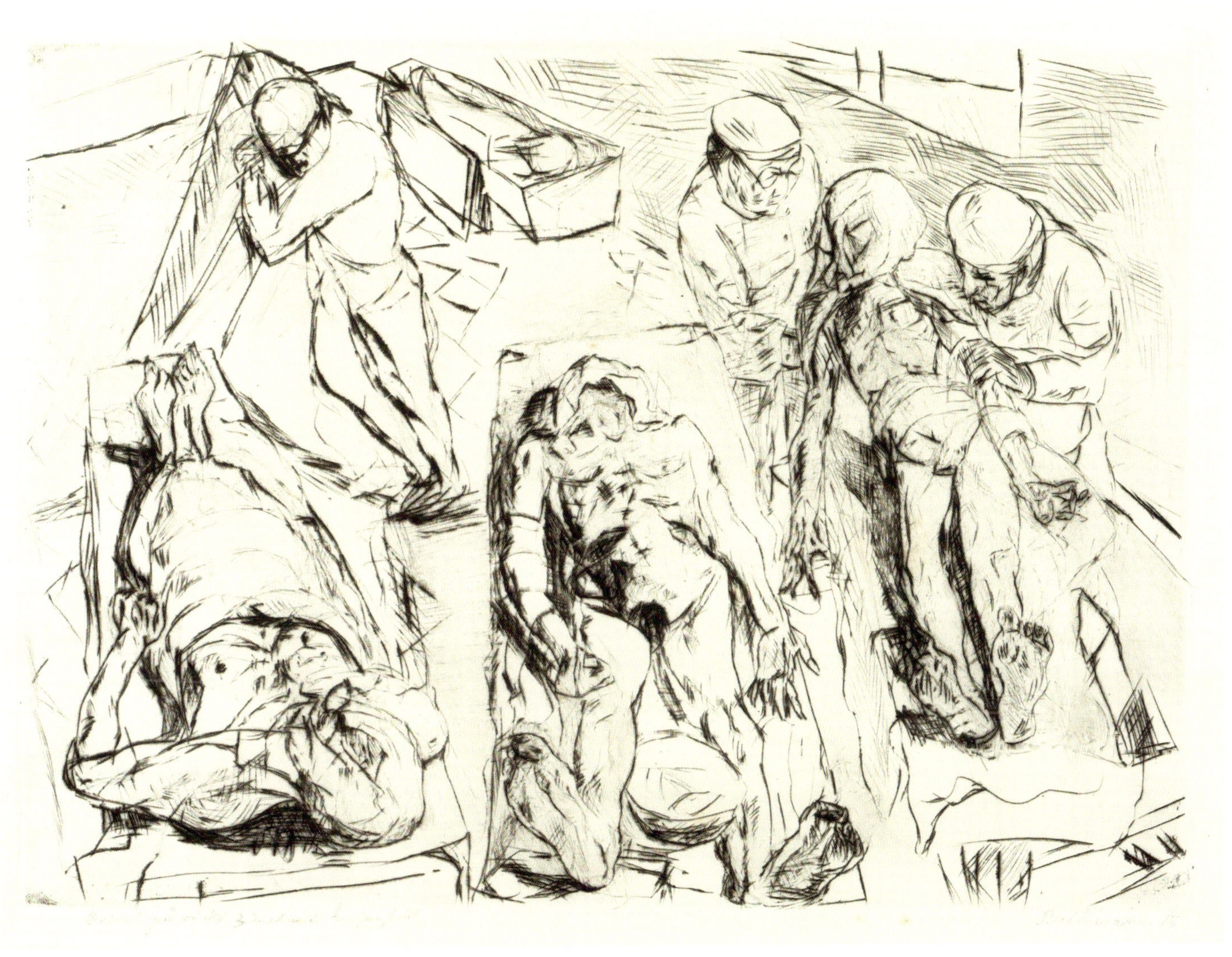

9. MORGUE, PRINTED 1915, PUBLISHED 1918

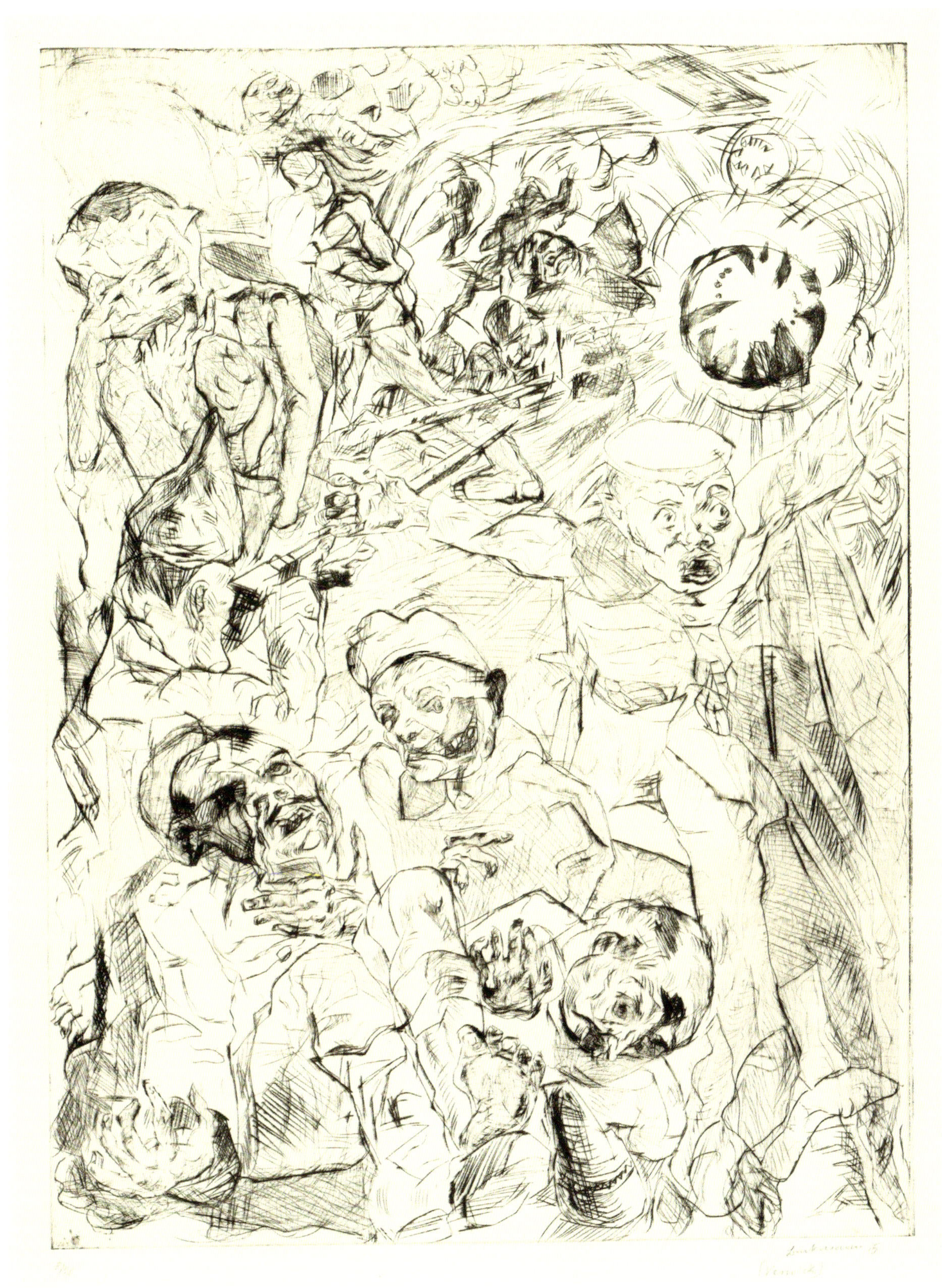

10. THE GRENADE, 1915, PUBLISHED 1918

The stylistic change in Max Beckmann's oeuvre that had been triggered in part by World War I is clearly evident in his drawings. His *Portrait des Oberstabsarztes Prof. Dr. Philaletes Kuhn* (Portrait of Senior Medical Officer Prof. Dr. Philaletes Kuhn) of 1915 revolves around the head, which Beckmann first outlined probingly and then rendered ever more precisely. The finely drawn bald skull has almost a landscape quality, expansive—and only then does Beckmann's harder stroke capture the eyebrows, nose, and left ear more precisely, and the physiognomy takes on concrete form. The entire head is positioned precisely within the image and is anchored by the powerfully drawn collar of the uniform, whereas the rest of the clothing and hence also Kuhn's corporeality is merely suggested and thus barely tangible. For Beckmann, the human being is primarily represented by a head or a face in his drawings. The artist will pursue this interest in physiognomy further and in 1919 title an extensive portfolio of prints *Gesichter* (Faces), playing with the double meaning of *Gesicht*, which has distinct plural forms depending on the sense: *Gesichter* (faces) and *Gesichte* (visions).

In the case of Kuhn, in addition to the physiognomy, Beckmann still placed great weight on the head leading to the chin, while two fingers, pointy and expressively elongated in the Gothic manner, help stabilize the head and lend it stability. These fingers have at once a decadent, overly refined quality and a precise, dissecting one, and under Beckmann's eye they are almost transformed into precision instruments. Medical analysis and a doctor's treatment, the instrumental and the animalistic, remain in balance, so that Kuhn's gaze is divided into two extreme ways of seeing without Beckmann being willing to give preference to either of them: we recognize a distanced observation in Kuhn but at the same time a horrified perception. These impulses determine each other, so that they can provide help.

Olaf Peters

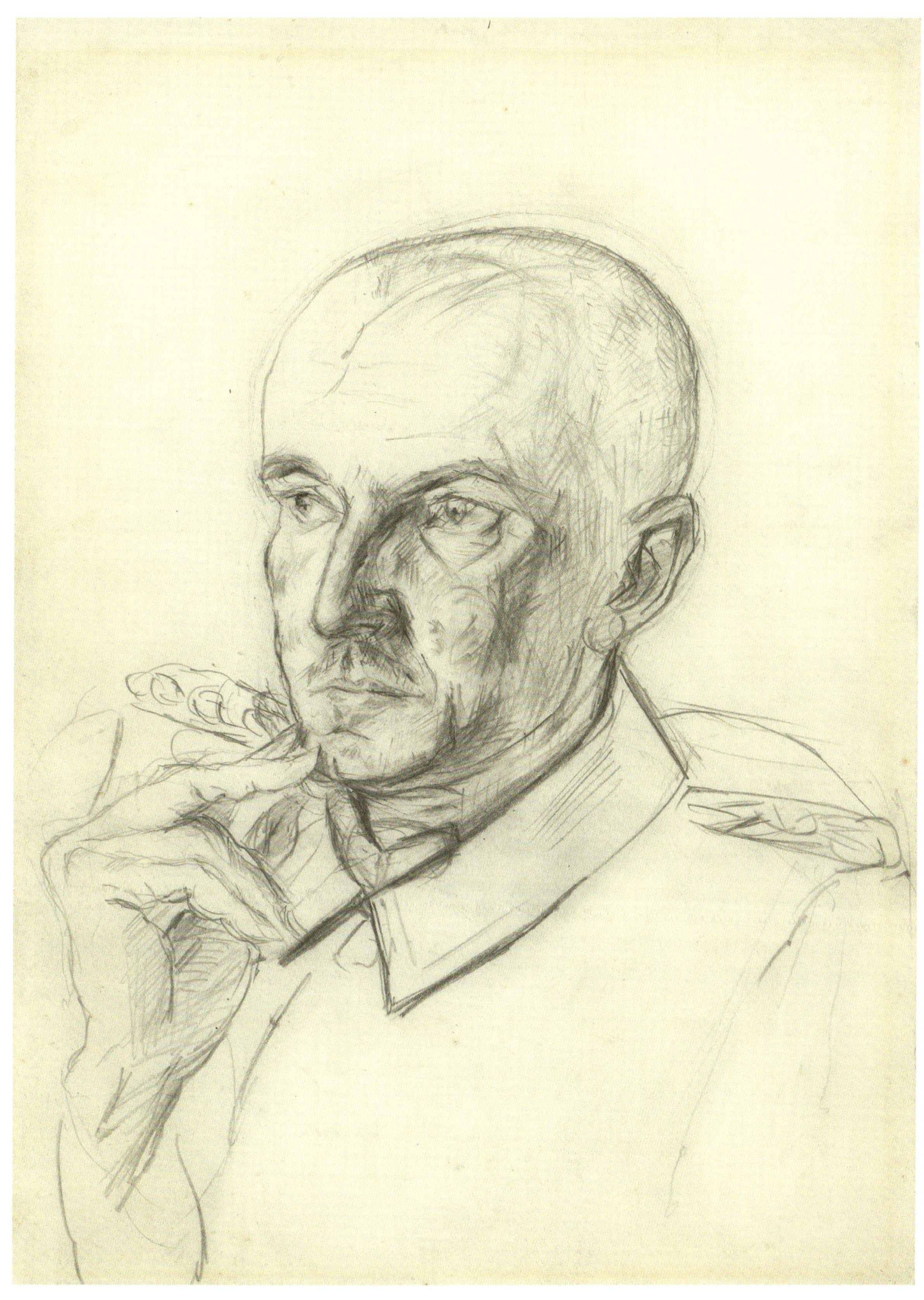

11. PORTRAIT OF SENIOR MEDICAL OFFICER PROF. DR. PHILALETES KUHN, 1915

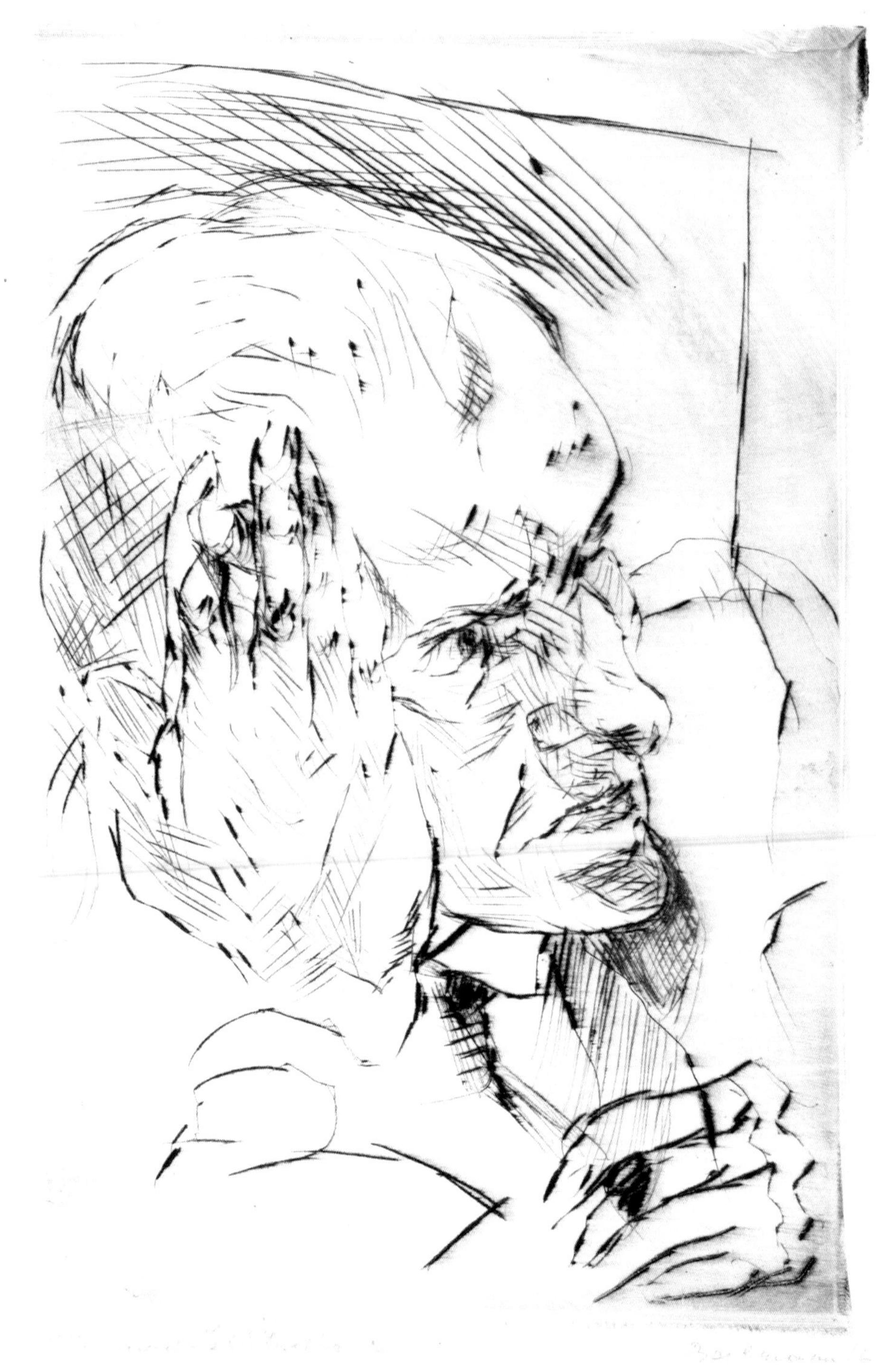

12. SELF-PORTRAIT, HAND TO CHEEK, 1916

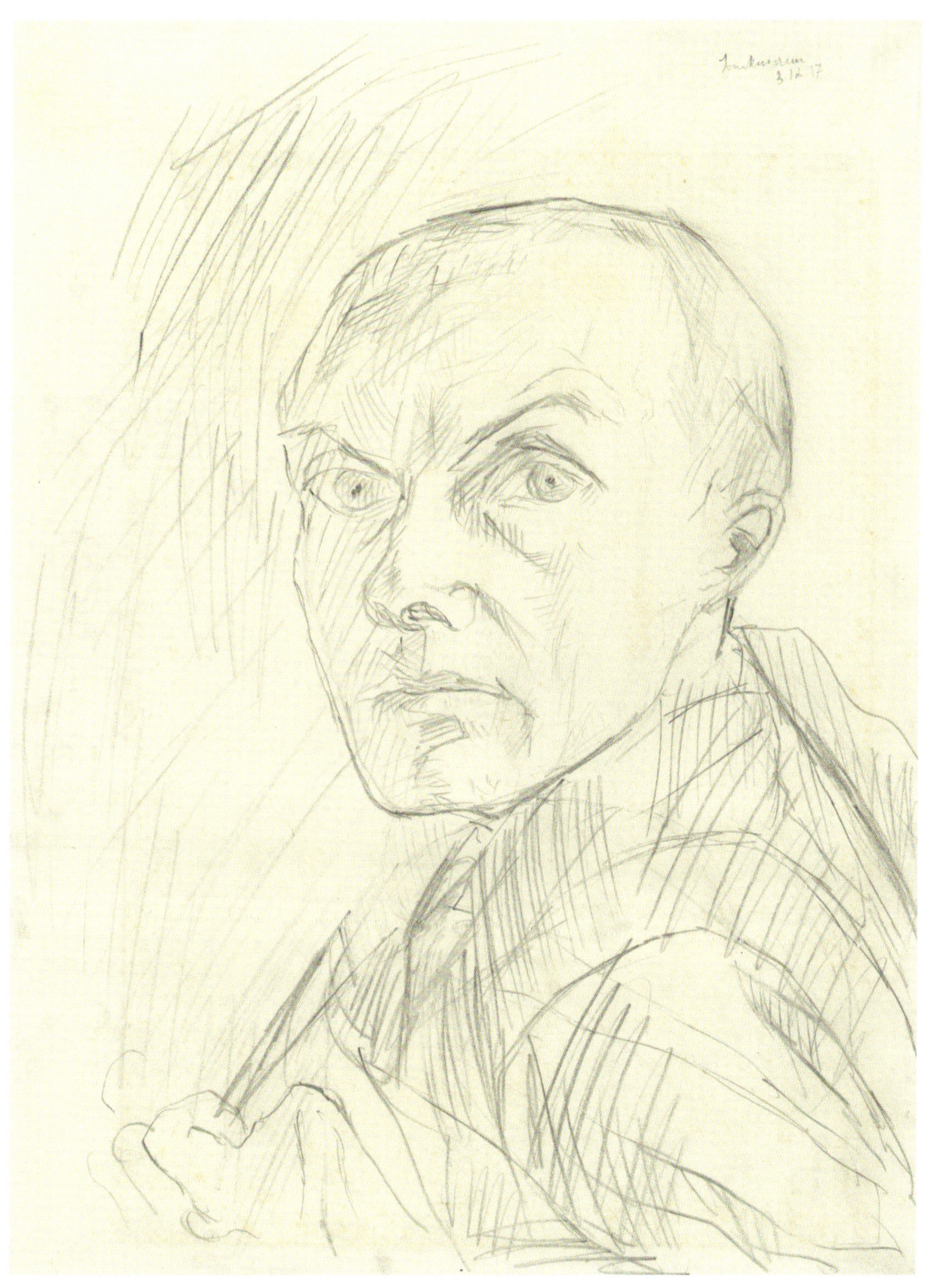

13. SELF-PORTRAIT IN HALF PROFILE TO THE LEFT, 1917

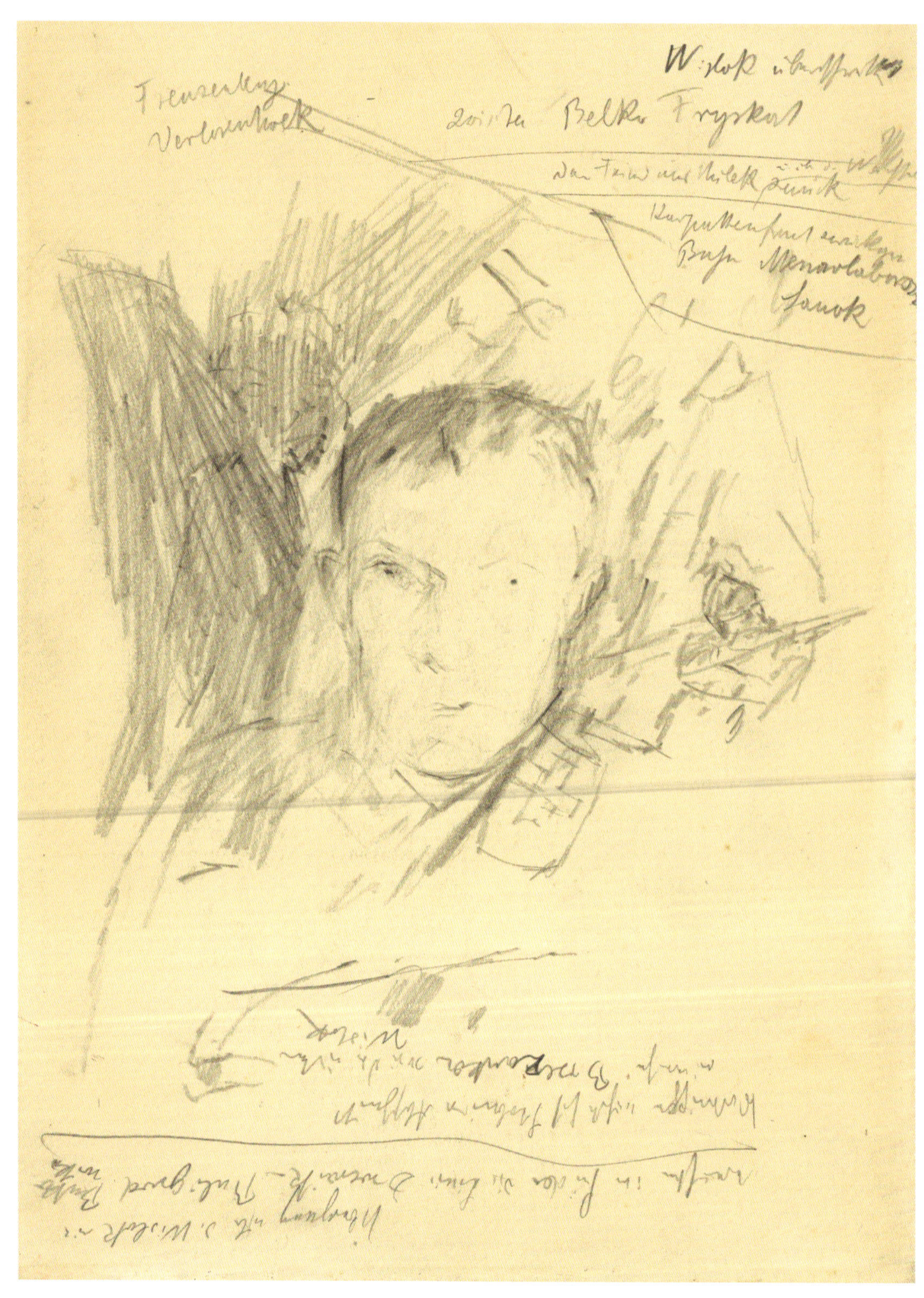

14. SELF-PORTRAIT AS MEDICAL ORDERLY, 1915

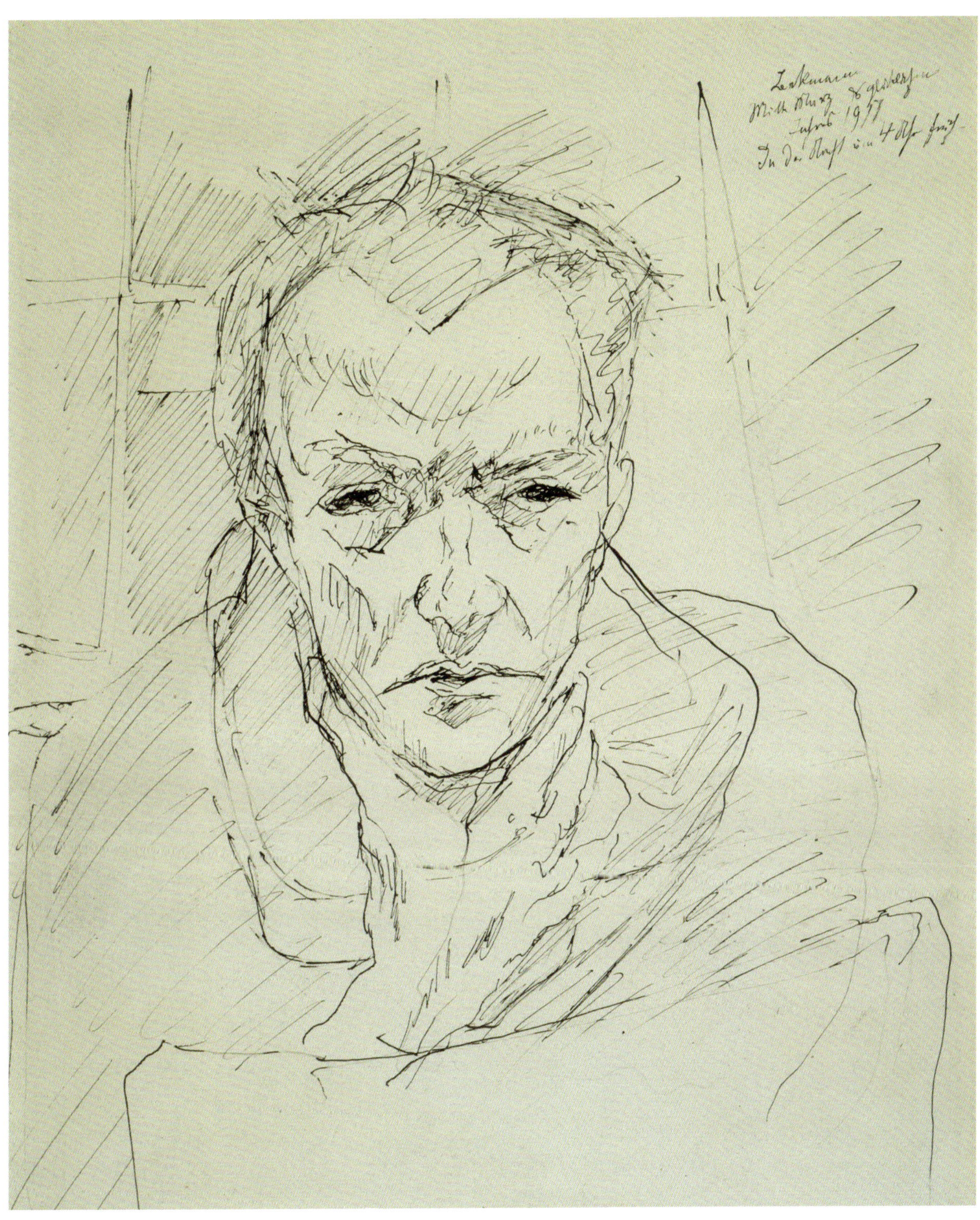

15. SELF-PORTRAIT, 1917

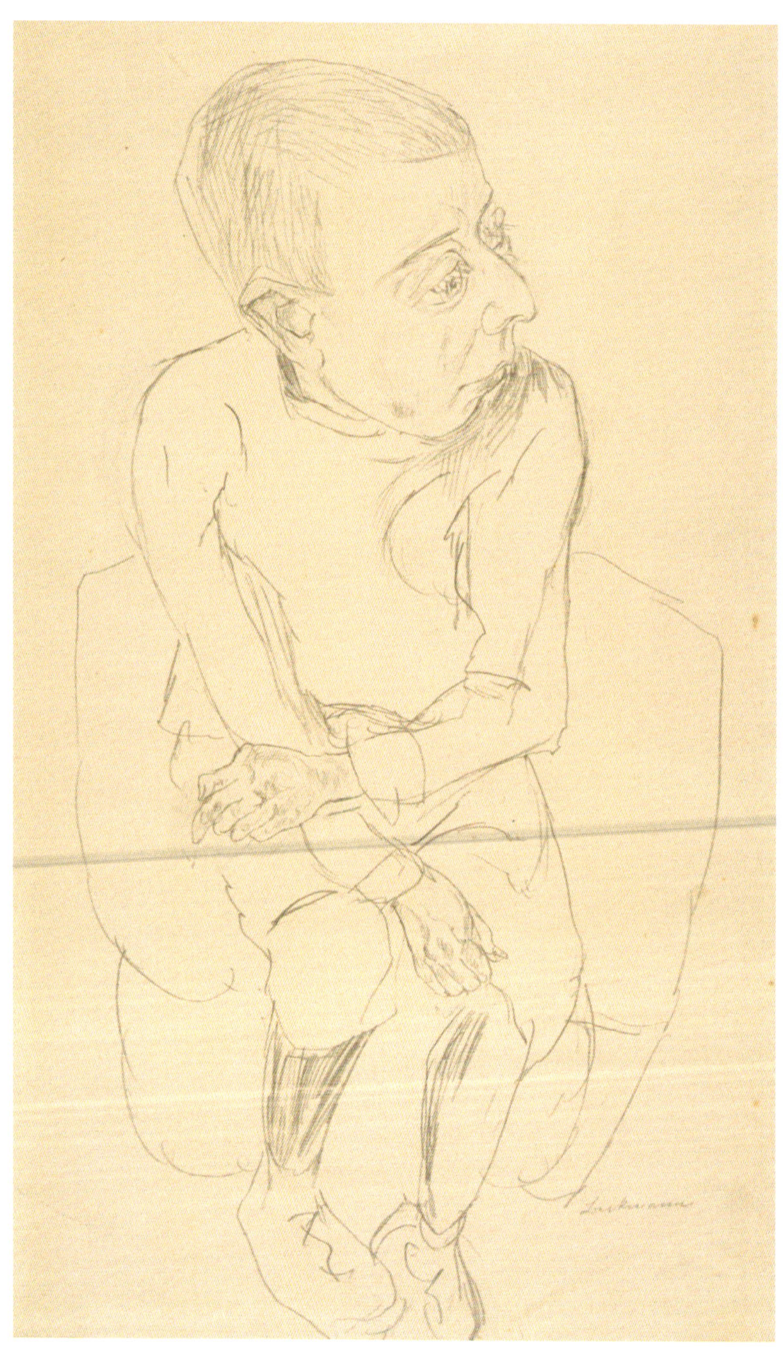

16. SEATED BOY, 1918

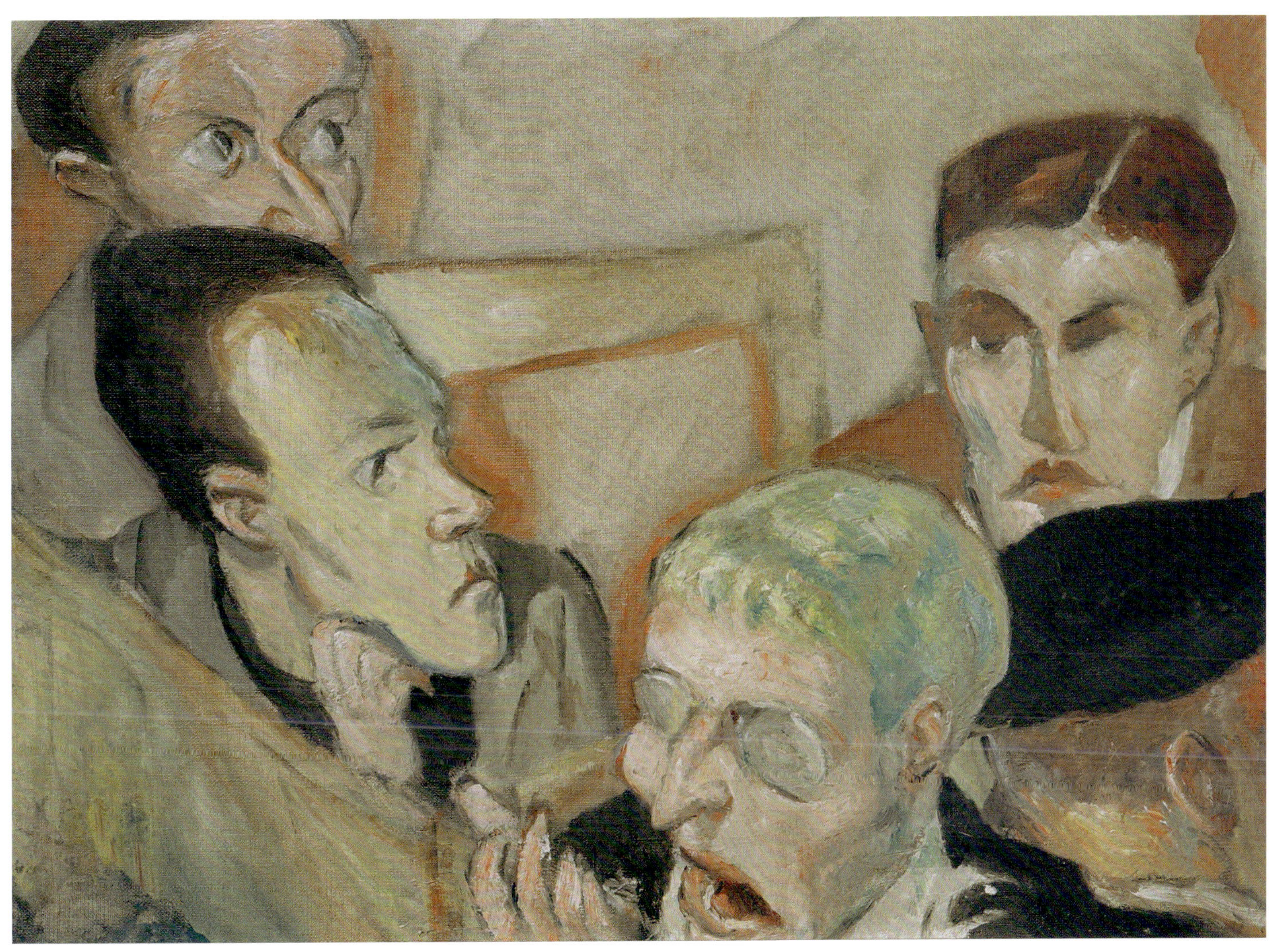

17. THE DEFENDANTS, 1916

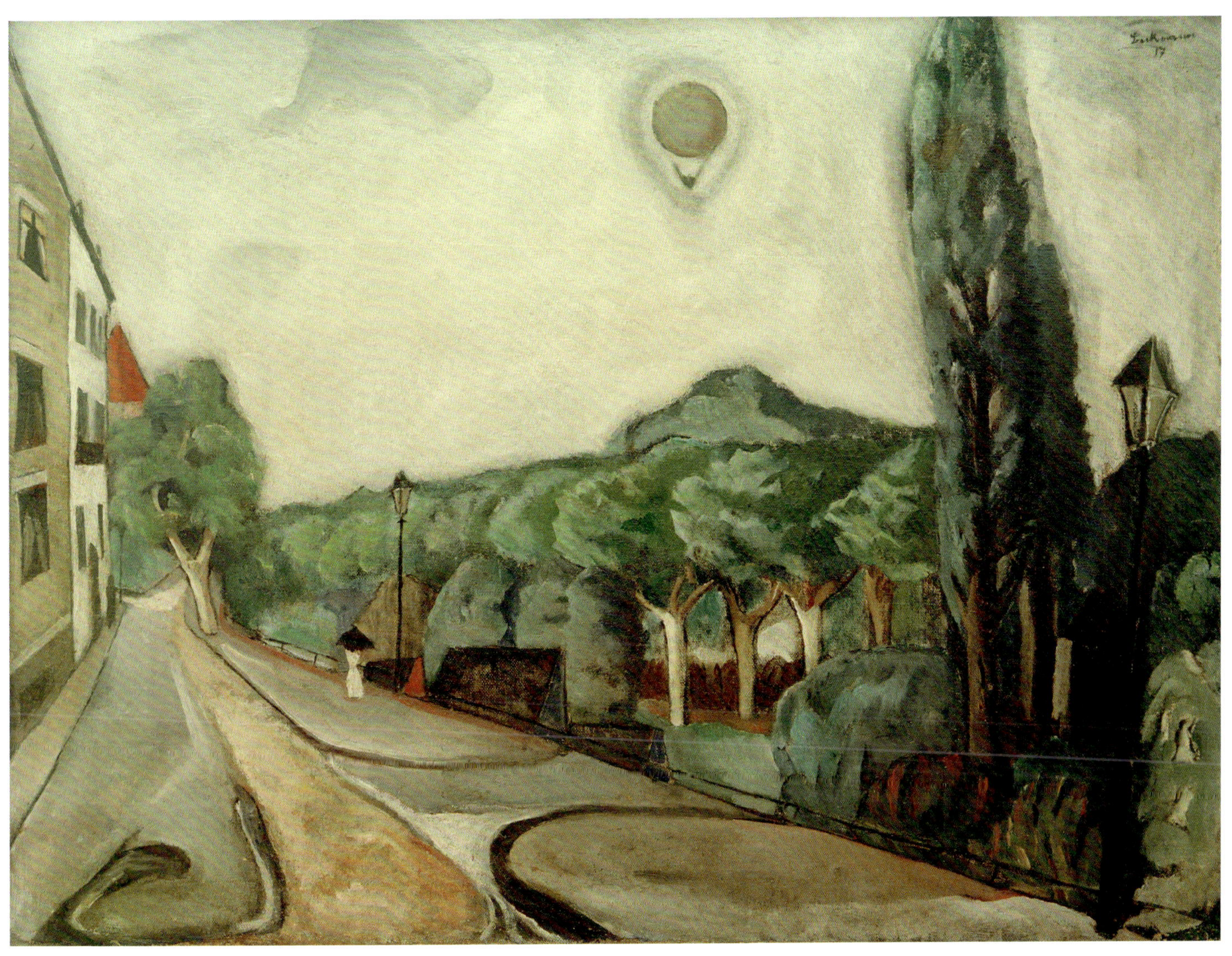

18. LANDSCAPE WITH BALLOON, 1917

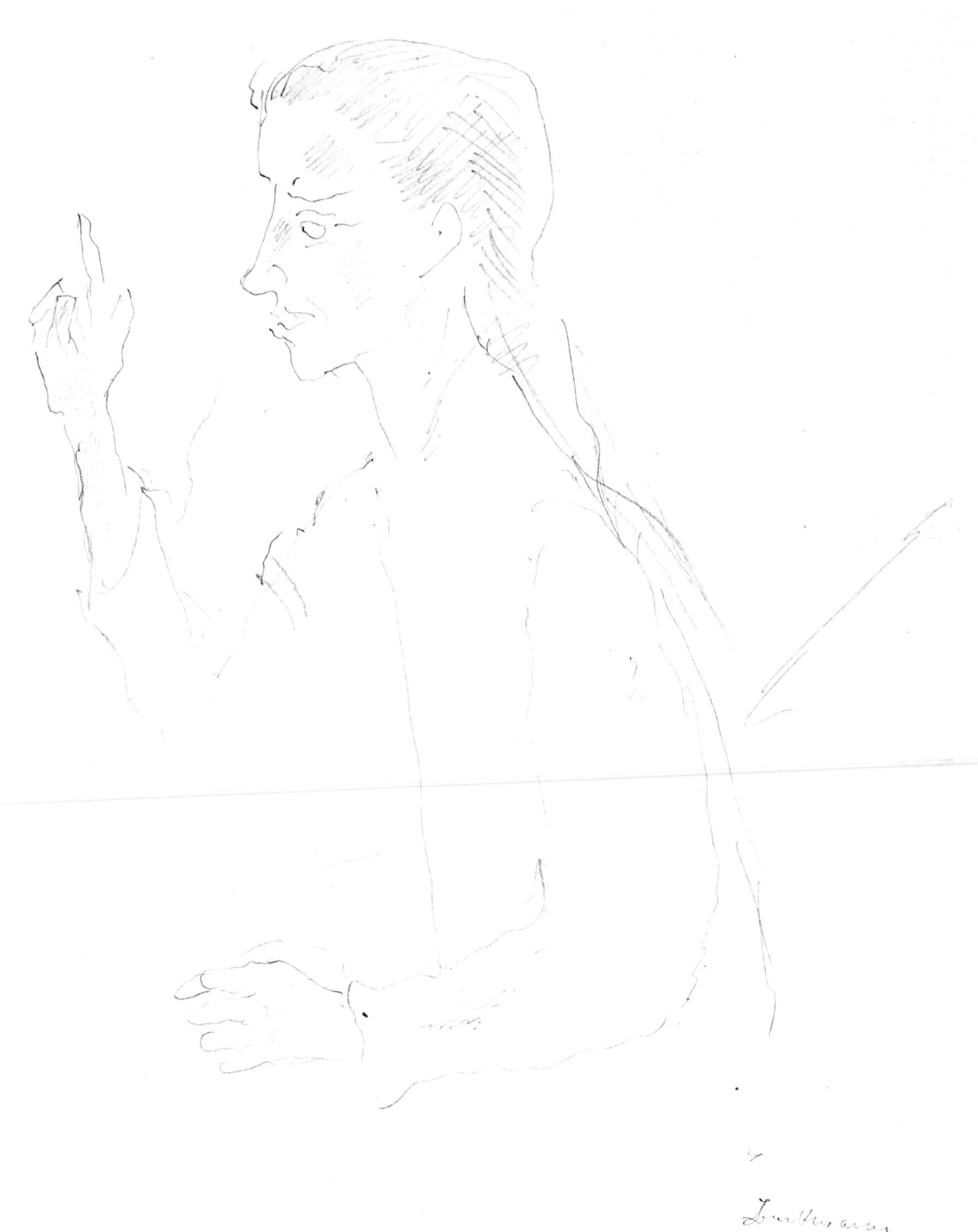

19. HALLUCINATION I, 1916

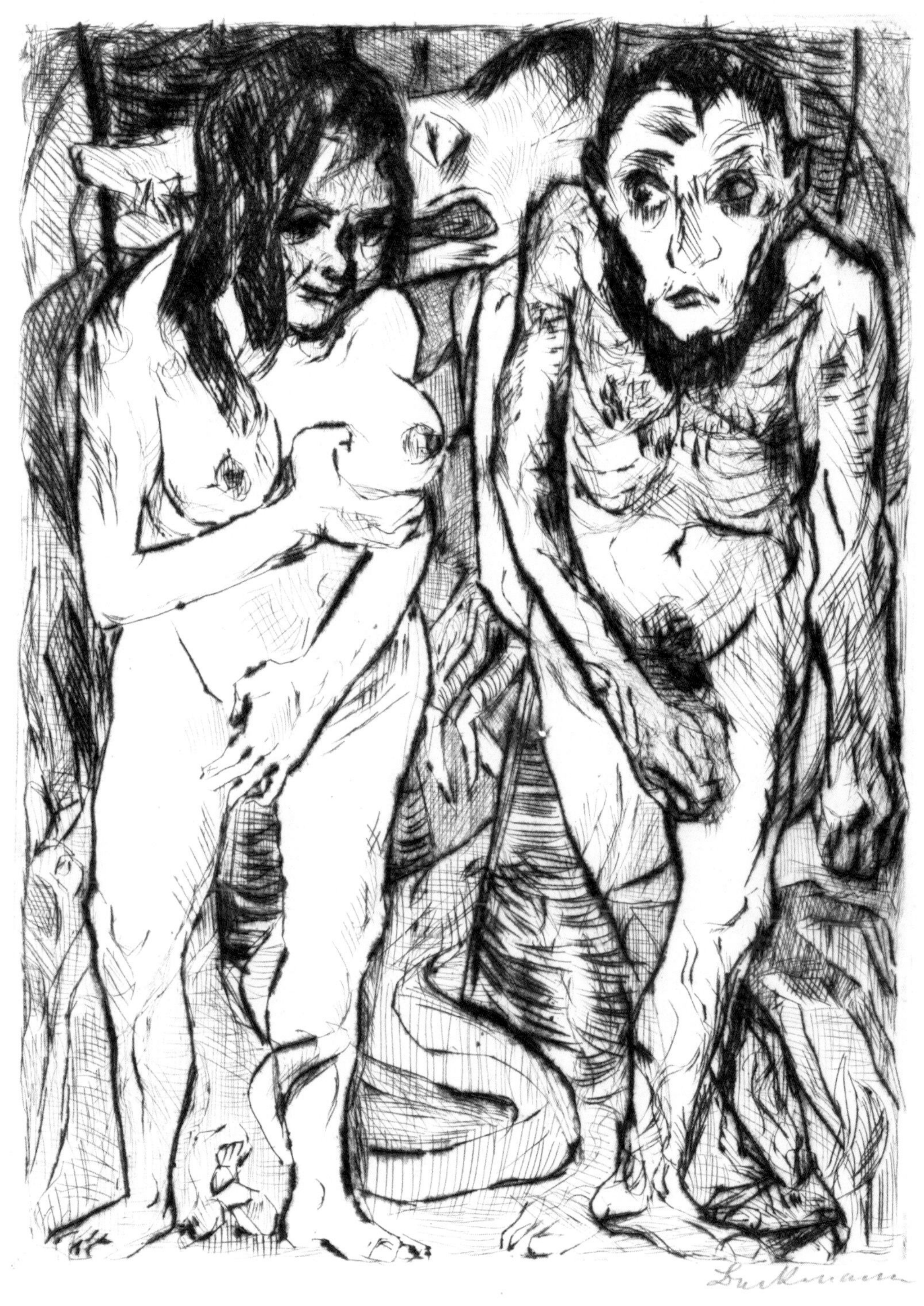

20. ADAM AND EVE, PRINTED 1917, PUBLISHED 1918

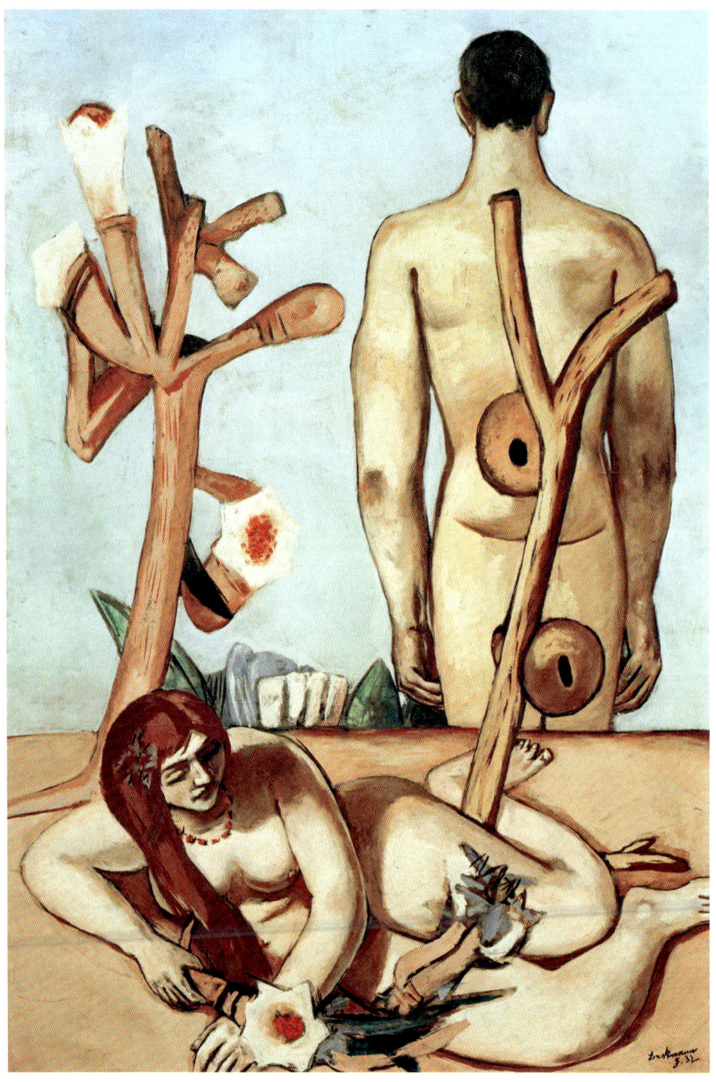

Max Beckmann, *Adam and Eve*, 1932, oil on canvas. Private Collection. Photo: akg-images

During the years from 1916 to 1918, Beckmann became a new artist: he left his early work behind, after having volunteered in the war as a medical orderly; his first marriage failed, and after a nervous breakdown he moved to Frankfurt am Main, withdrawing into the home of friends, the husband-and-wife painters Fridel and Ugi Battenberg. Alongside his alarming 1917 *Selbstbildnis mit rotem Schal* (Self-Portrait with Red Scarf) (Staatsgalerie Stuttgart), he now produced religious paintings whose formal language can be traced back above all to intense study of the northern European art of the late Middle Ages and early modern period. Their reduced coloration and a nested, splintered spatiality sometimes reveal the influences of Cubism.

Adam und Eva (Adam and Eve) depicts a human couple in a contemporary style, with the woman offering her breast rather than the apple. The same scene is depicted in an etching executed in parallel [Plate 20]. Beckmann adopts a gesture shown in Rembrandt van Rijn's *Adam and Eve* etching from 1638 while substituting the apple for the seductive breast. The man reacts defensively—toward both Eve and the grotesque snake in equal measure—raising one hand and stiffly stretching out the other away from his body. This gesture anticipates Christ's death on the cross, a theme that Beckmann took up that same year in *Kreuzabnahme* (Descent from the Cross) [Plate 23], as a later consequence of the Fall. It is striking for the hard contours of the figures and their emphatic plasticity in contrast to the flat parts of the painting. These are indications of Beckmann's stylistic change during the second half of the 1910s.

In 1932 the painter returned to this theme [see ill. on this page], once again when facing a reorientation of his art. Once again, he interpreted the relationship of the sexes as polar: the sensuous woman crouched on the floor and the man distancing himself by gazing afar. This painting was purchased in 1933 by Stefan Lackner, from a Beckmann exhibition in Erfurt that had already closed, and that became the basis for a lifelong friendship between the collector and the artist who was defamed by the National Socialists.

Olaf Peters

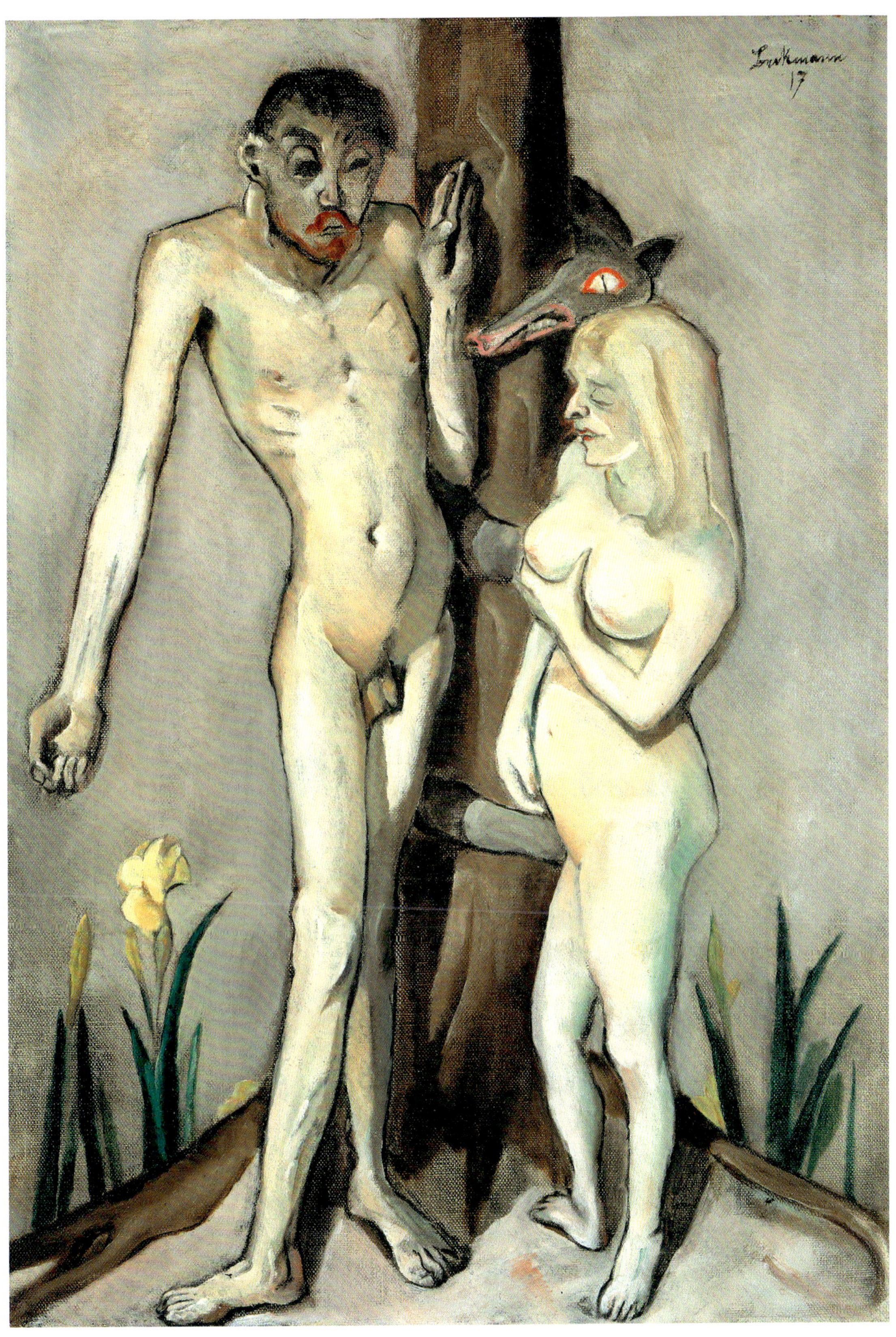

21. ADAM AND EVE, 1917

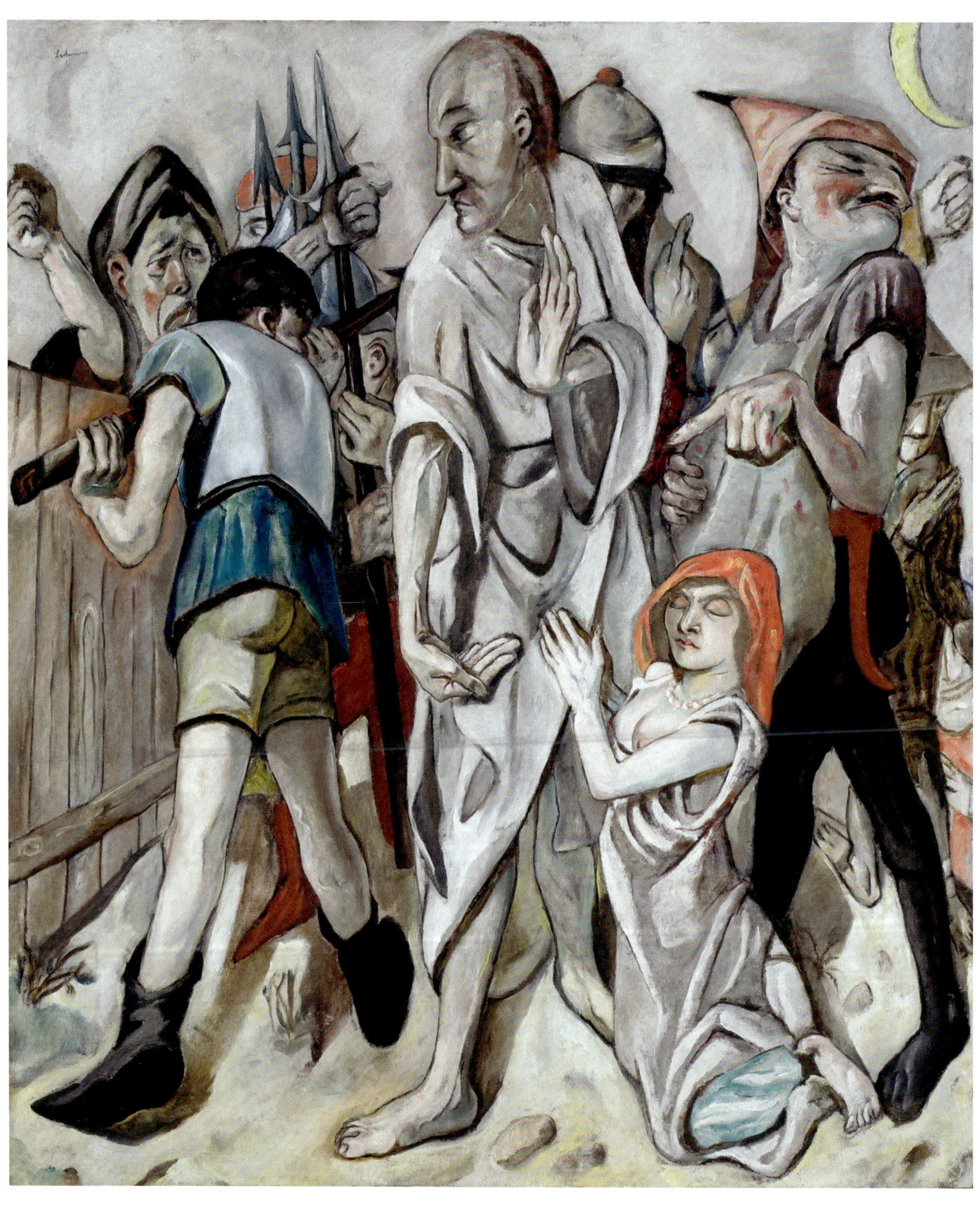

22. CHRIST AND THE SINNER, 1917

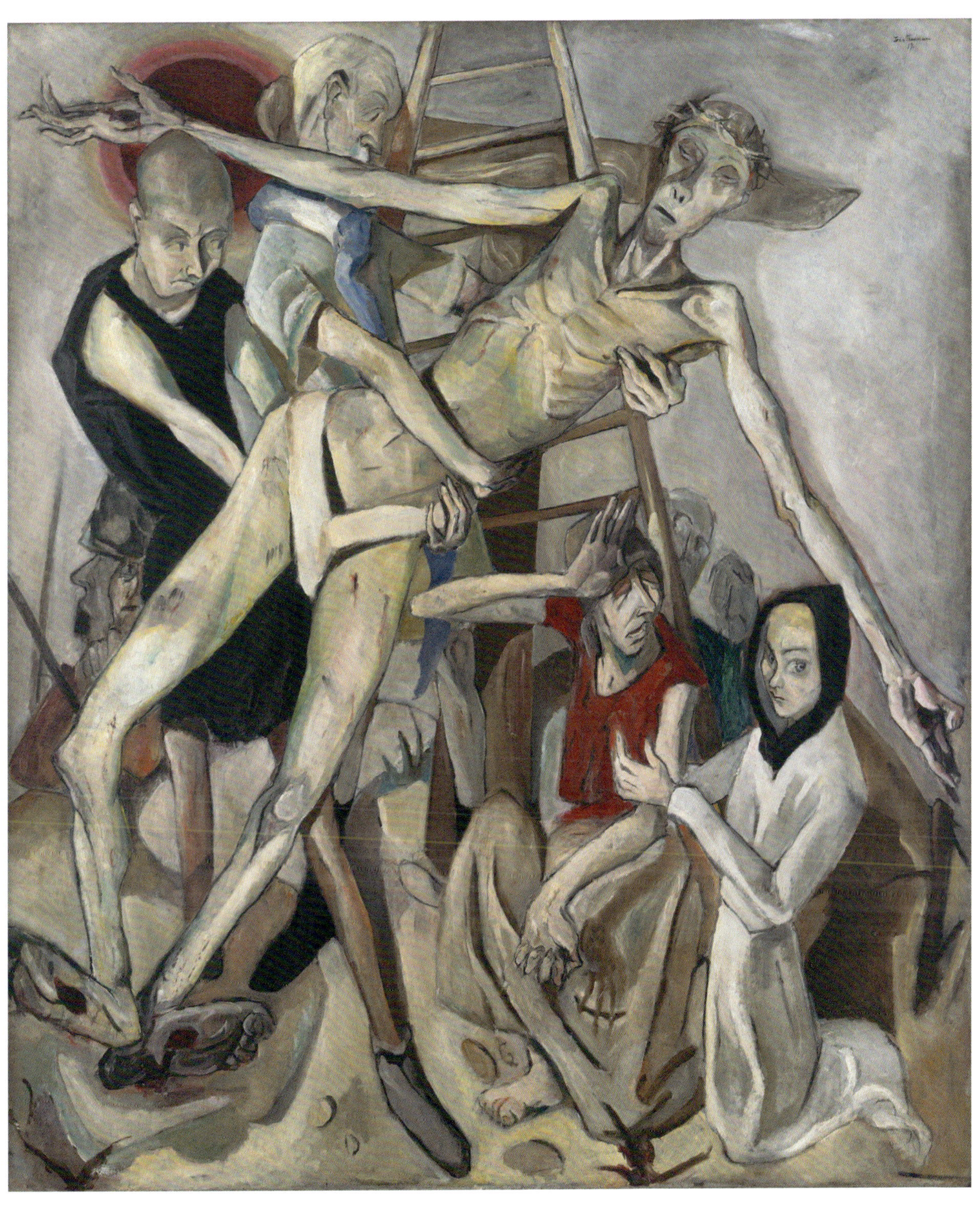

23. DESCENT FROM THE CROSS, 1917

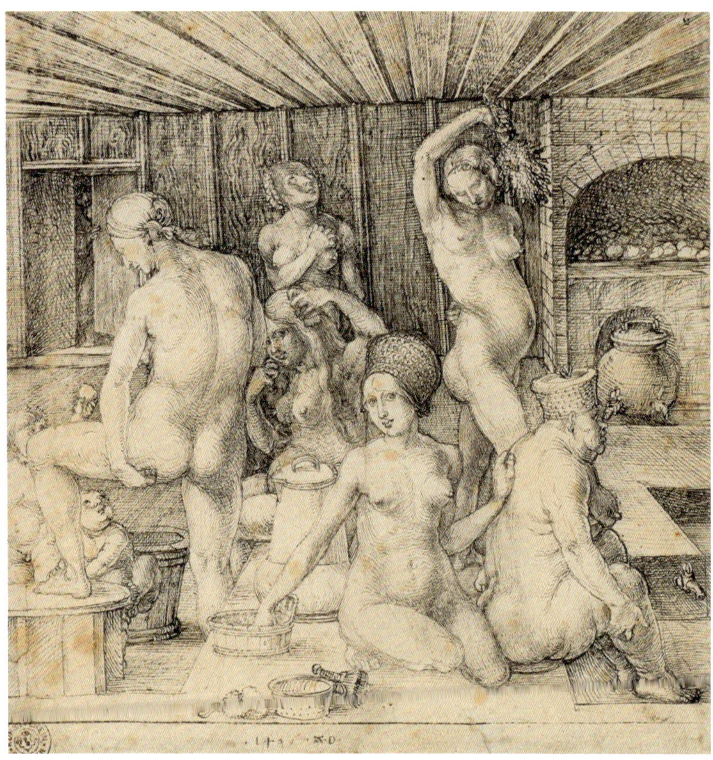

Albrecht Dürer, *Women's Bath*, 1496, pen and black ink on paper. Kunsthalle Bremen - Der Kunstverein in Bremen. Kupferstichkabinett. Photo: Kunsthalle Bremen - Die Kulturgutscanner - ARTOTHEK

This complexly nested image is almost overfilled with figures and shows children and women in a room built of wood. The central axis of the painting is defined above by a middle-aged woman on a swing and below by an old woman depicted as a seated nude seen from behind. According to Beckmann, the latter was intended to illustrate not only a certain ugliness but also the tragedy of aging. Additional figures are arranged in a circle around the two of them and engage the viewer's eye. Two infants crawling on the floor and moving away from each other form the starting point and can direct the gaze in different directions. Beckmann has found a composition here that he would vary again and again. The theme of the painting connects to older art—for example, Albrecht Dürer's eponymous drawing of 1496 in the Kunsthalle Bremen [see ill. on this page]—and in combination with the form illustrates that the artist's self-image was historically informed: "The most important thing to me is to get back to a clear and absolutely solid form: the roundness in the plane, the depth in the sensation of the plane, the architecture of the image. Locking in as great a sum of vitality as possible in crystal-clear lines and planes! [...] The painting [*Frauenbad*] should look like a Gothic stained-glass window." That was how the painter expressed himself to his Munich-based publisher Reinhard Piper in July 1919, and he aimed programmatically for a "metaphysics in representationalism."

Olaf Peters

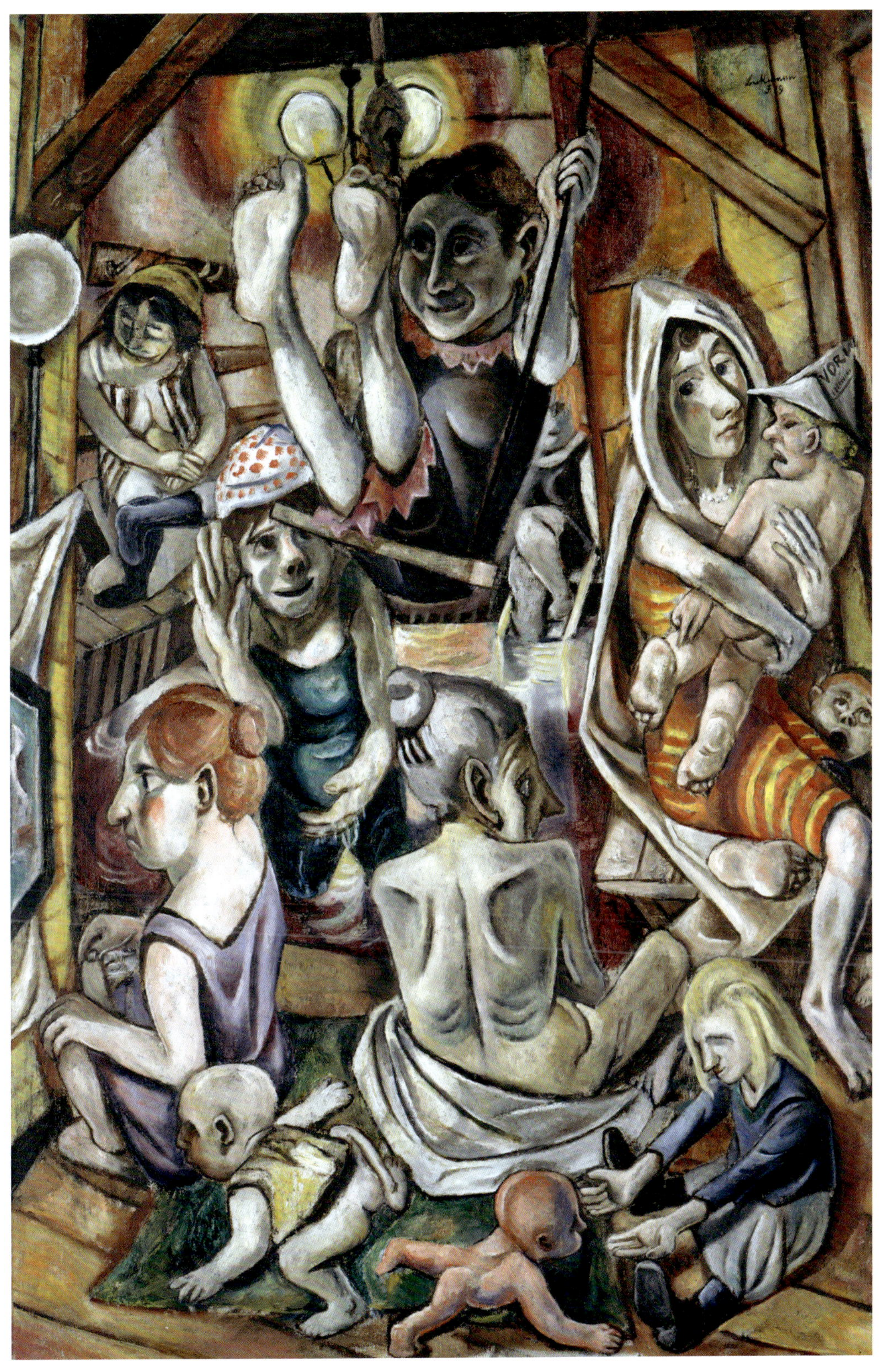

24. WOMEN'S BATH, 1919

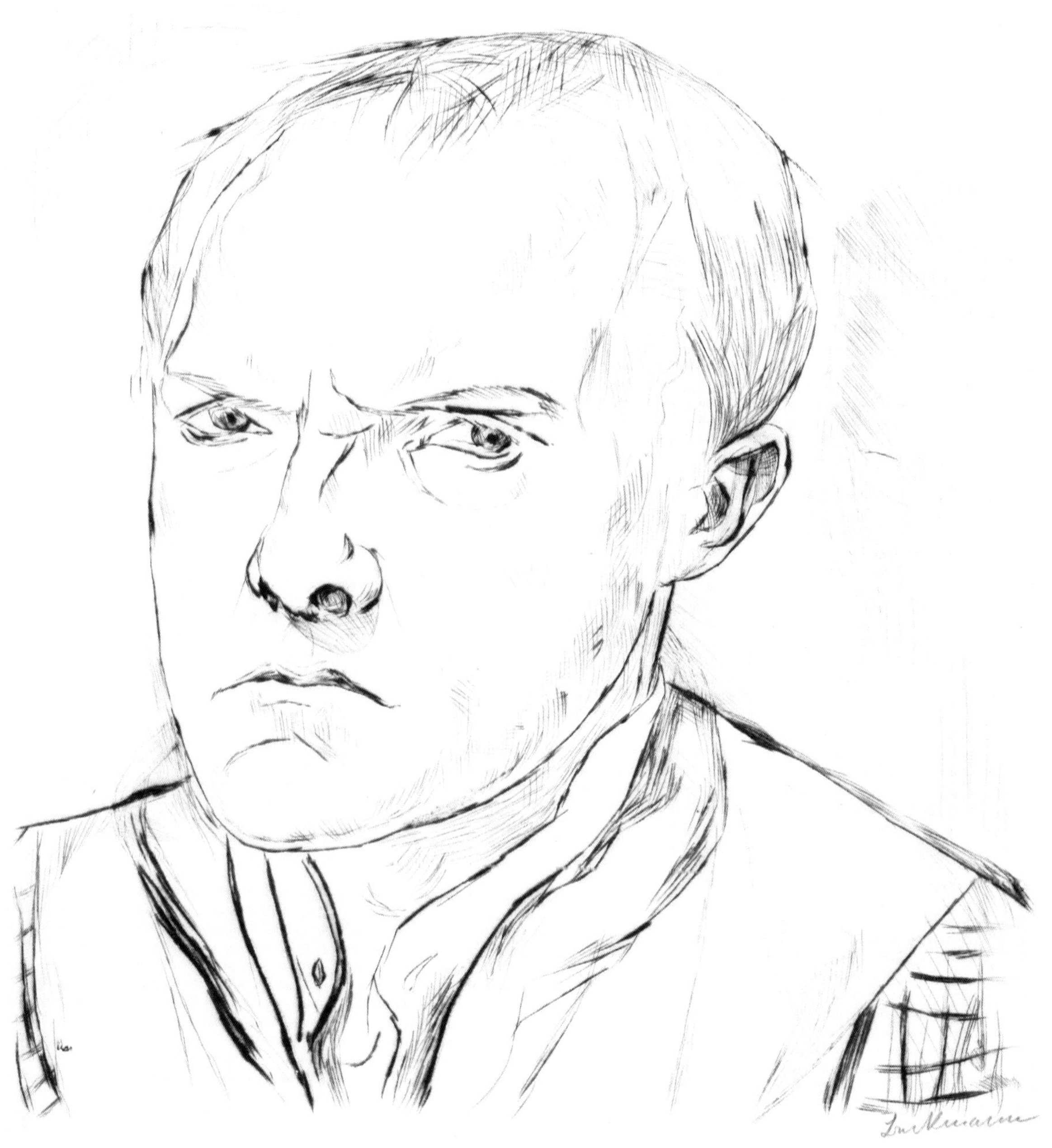

25. SELF-PORTRAIT, PLATE 1, FACES PORTFOLIO, PRINTED 1918, PUBLISHED 1919

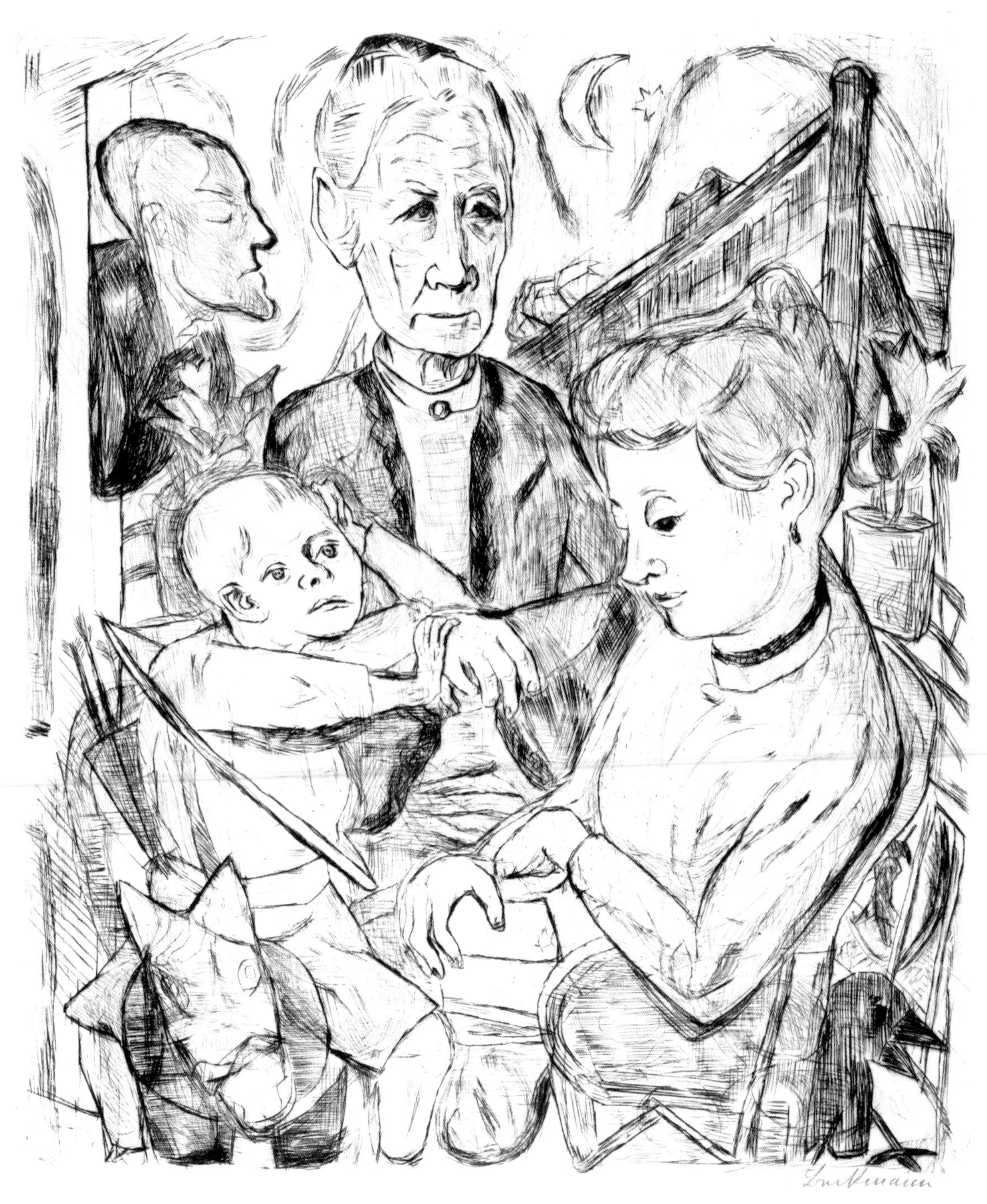

26. FAMILY SCENE (BECKMANN FAMILY), PLATE 2, FACES PORTFOLIO, PRINTED 1918, PUBLISHED 1919

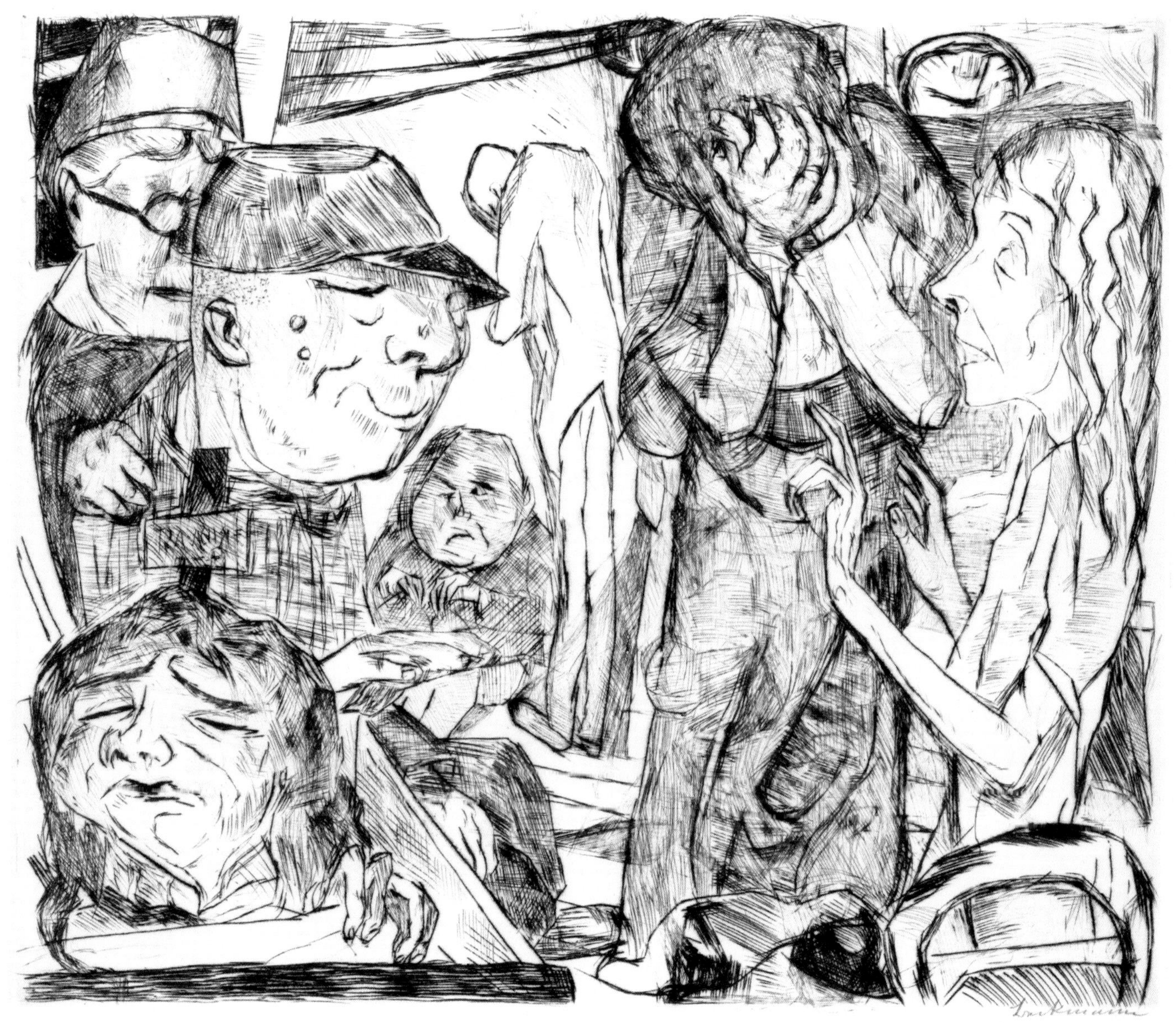

27. MADHOUSE, PLATE 3, FACES PORTFOLIO, PRINTED 1918, PUBLISHED 1919

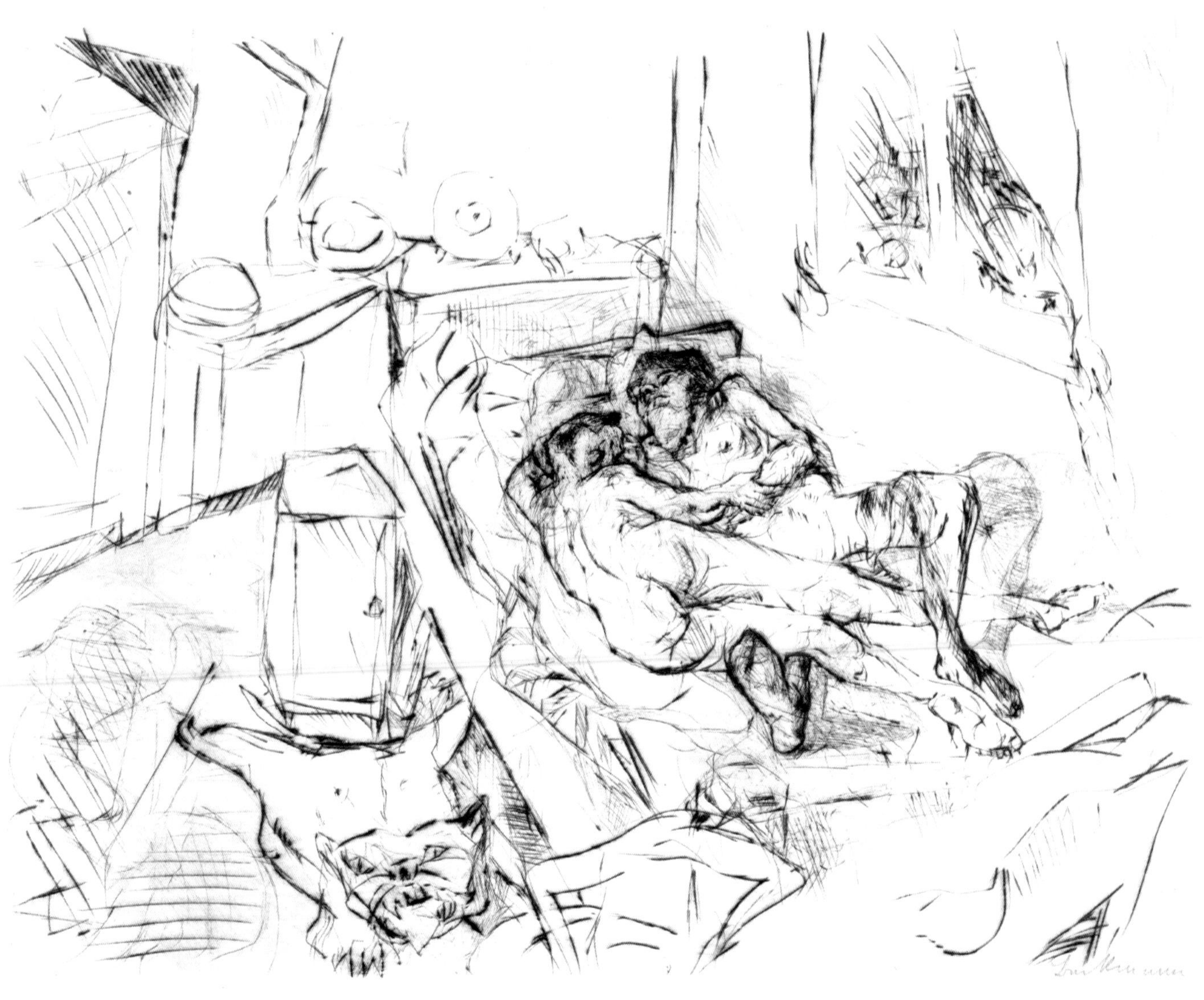

28. LOVERS I, PLATE 4, FACES PORTFOLIO, PRINTED 1916, PUBLISHED 1919

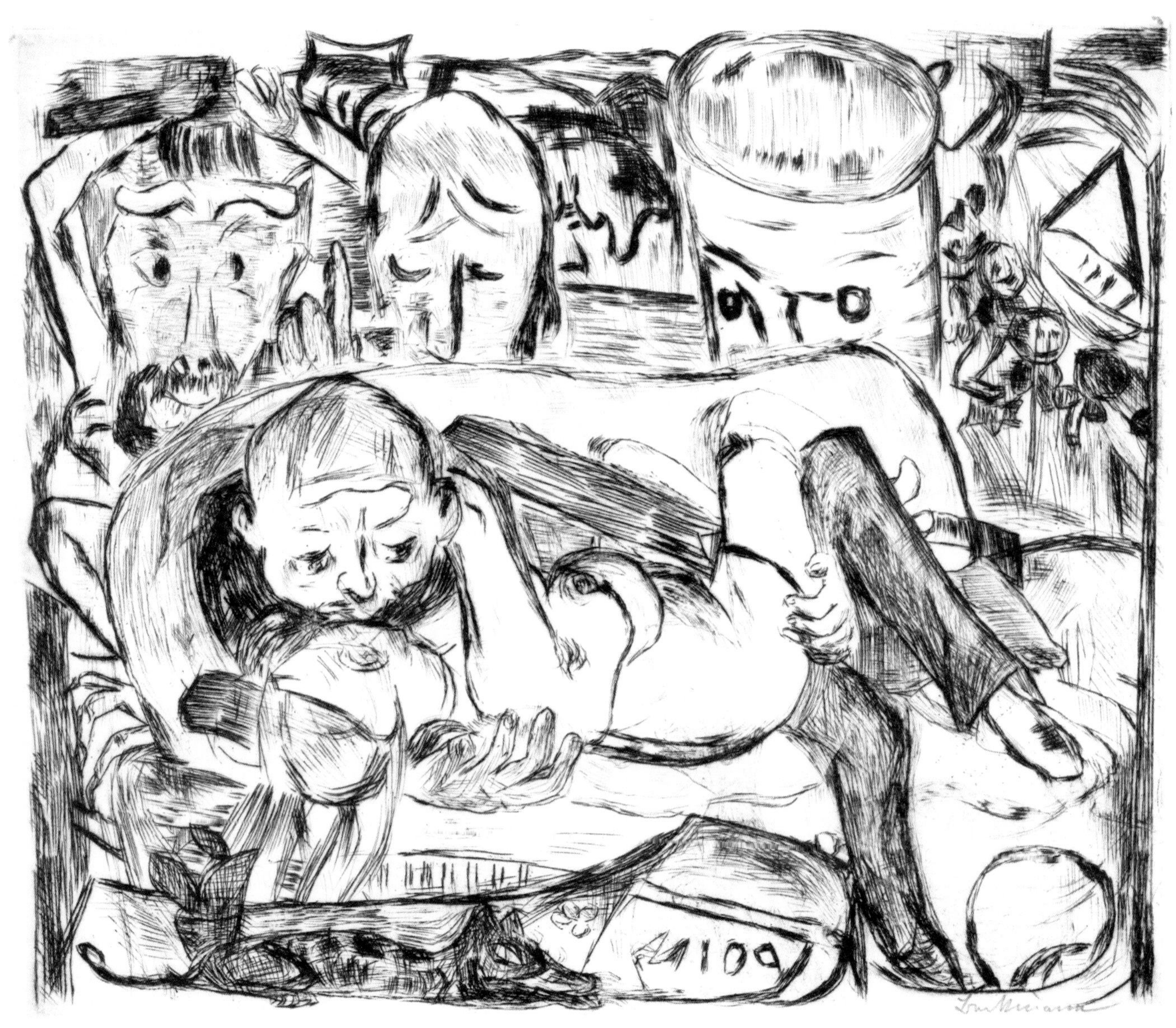

29. LOVERS II, PLATE 5, FACES PORTFOLIO, PRINTED 1918, PUBLISHED 1919

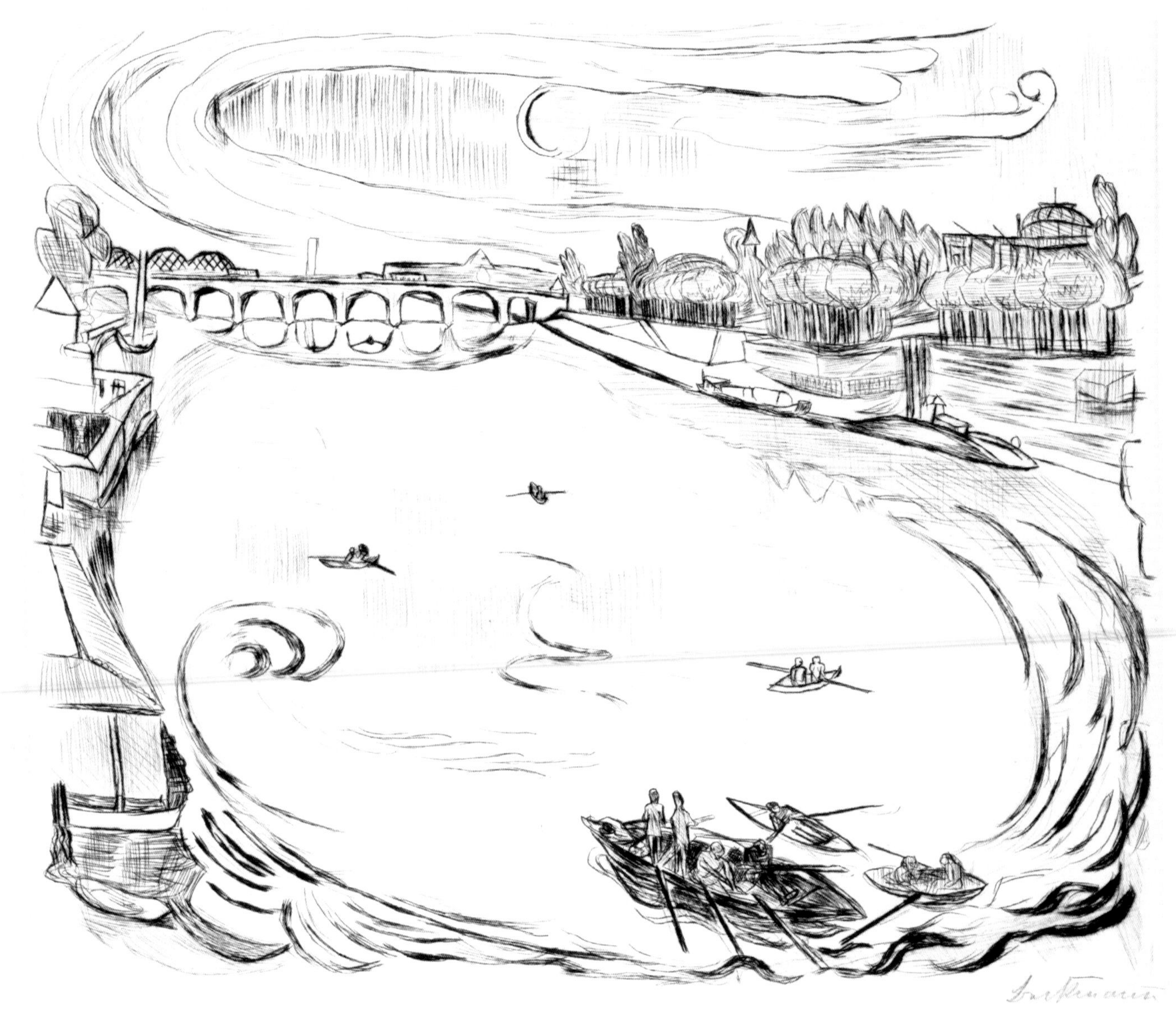

30. MAIN RIVER LANDSCAPE, PLATE 6, FACES PORTFOLIO, PRINTED 1918, PUBLISHED 1919

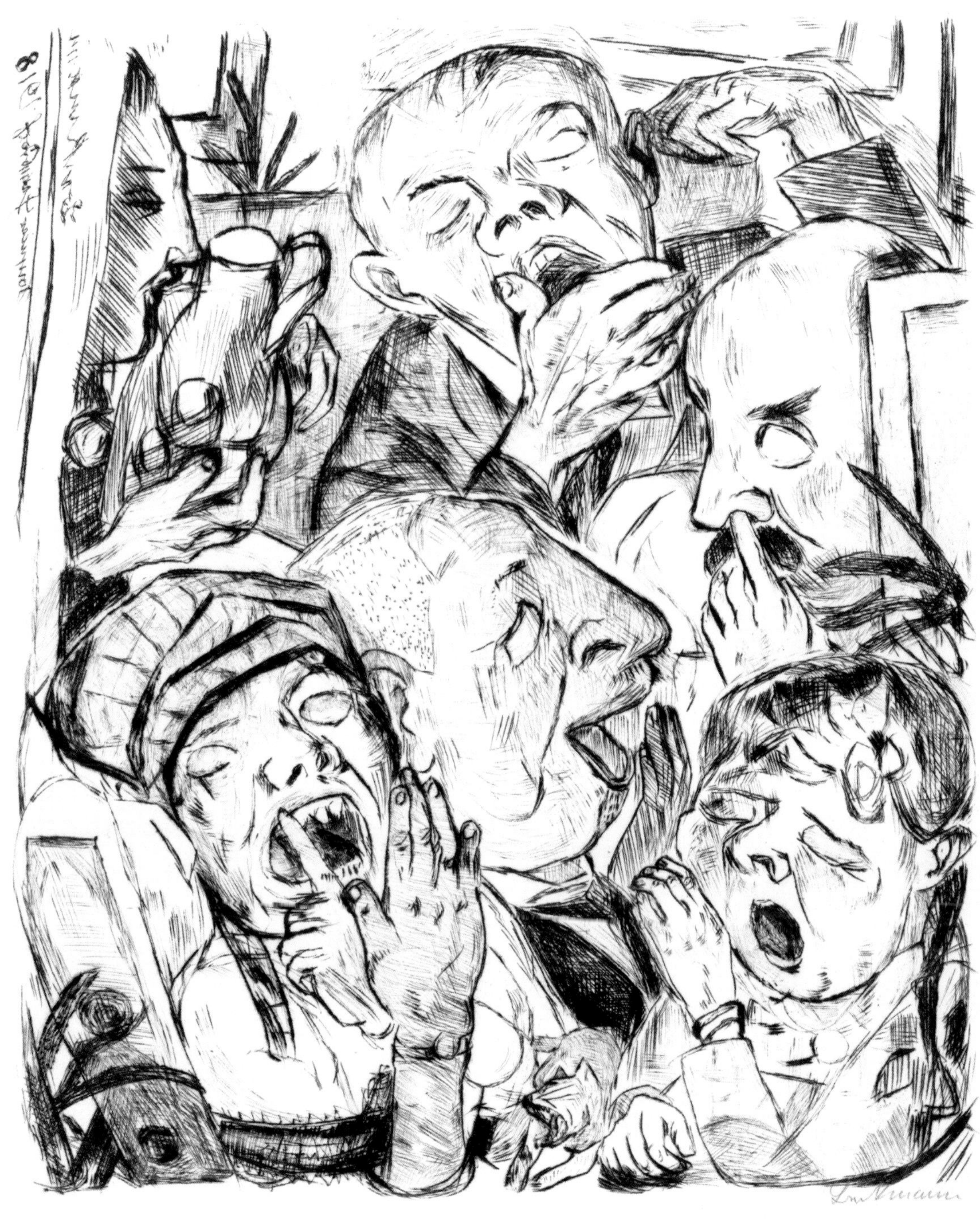

31. THE YAWNERS, PLATE 7, FACES PORTFOLIO, PRINTED 1918, PUBLISHED 1919

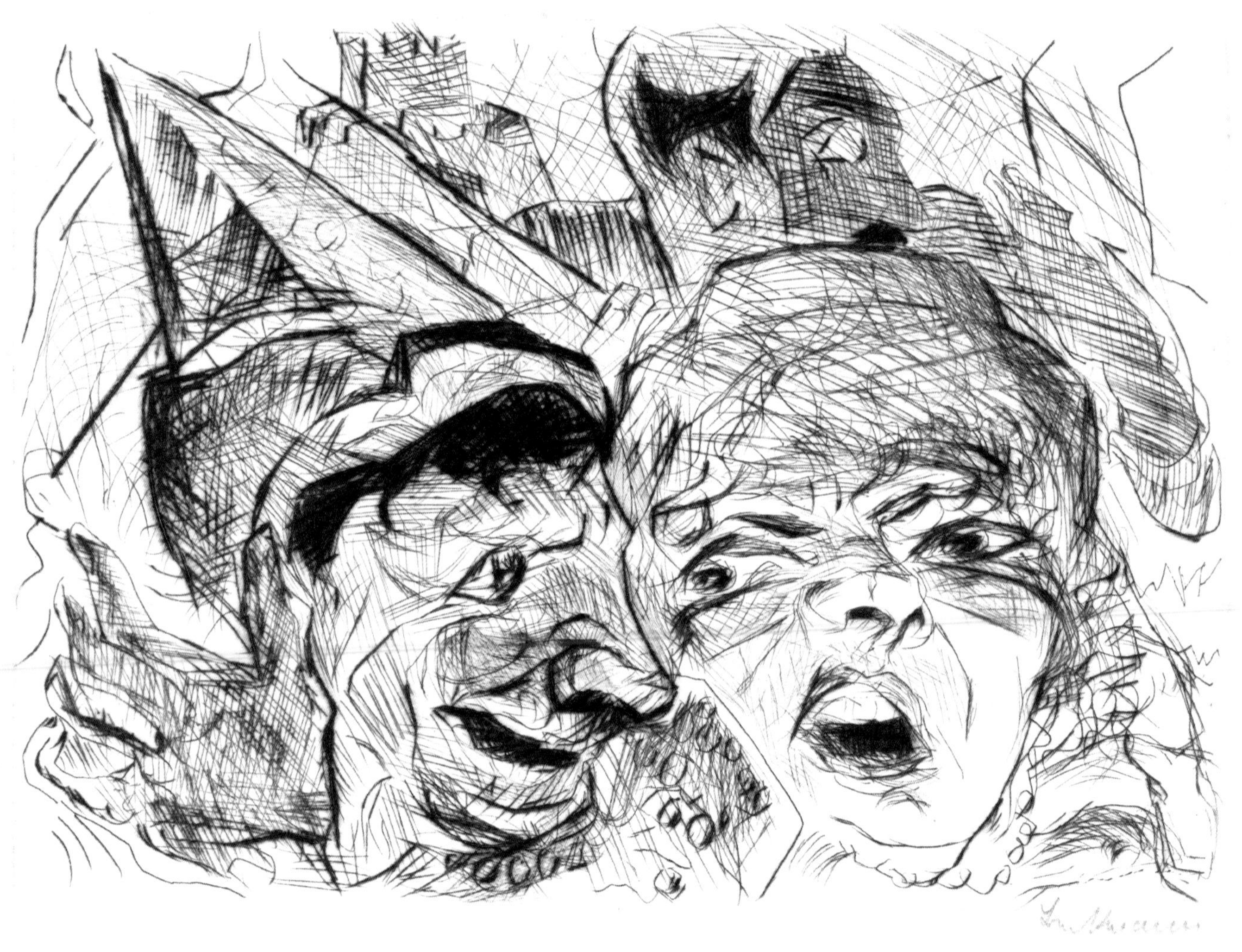

32. THEATER, PLATE 8, FACES PORTFOLIO, PRINTED 1917, PUBLISHED 1919

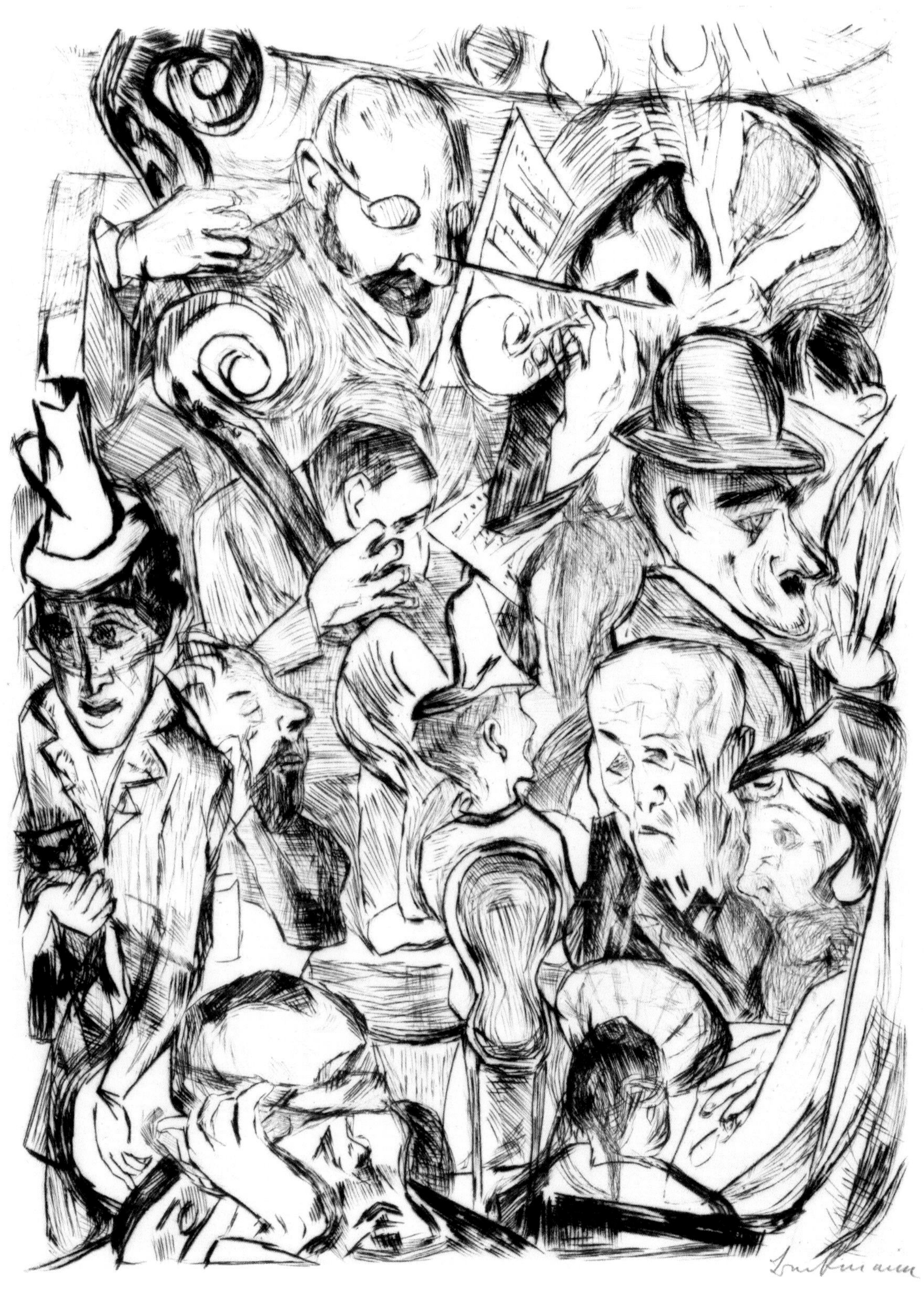

33. CAFÉ MUSIC, PLATE 9, FACES PORTFOLIO, PRINTED 1918, PUBLISHED 1919

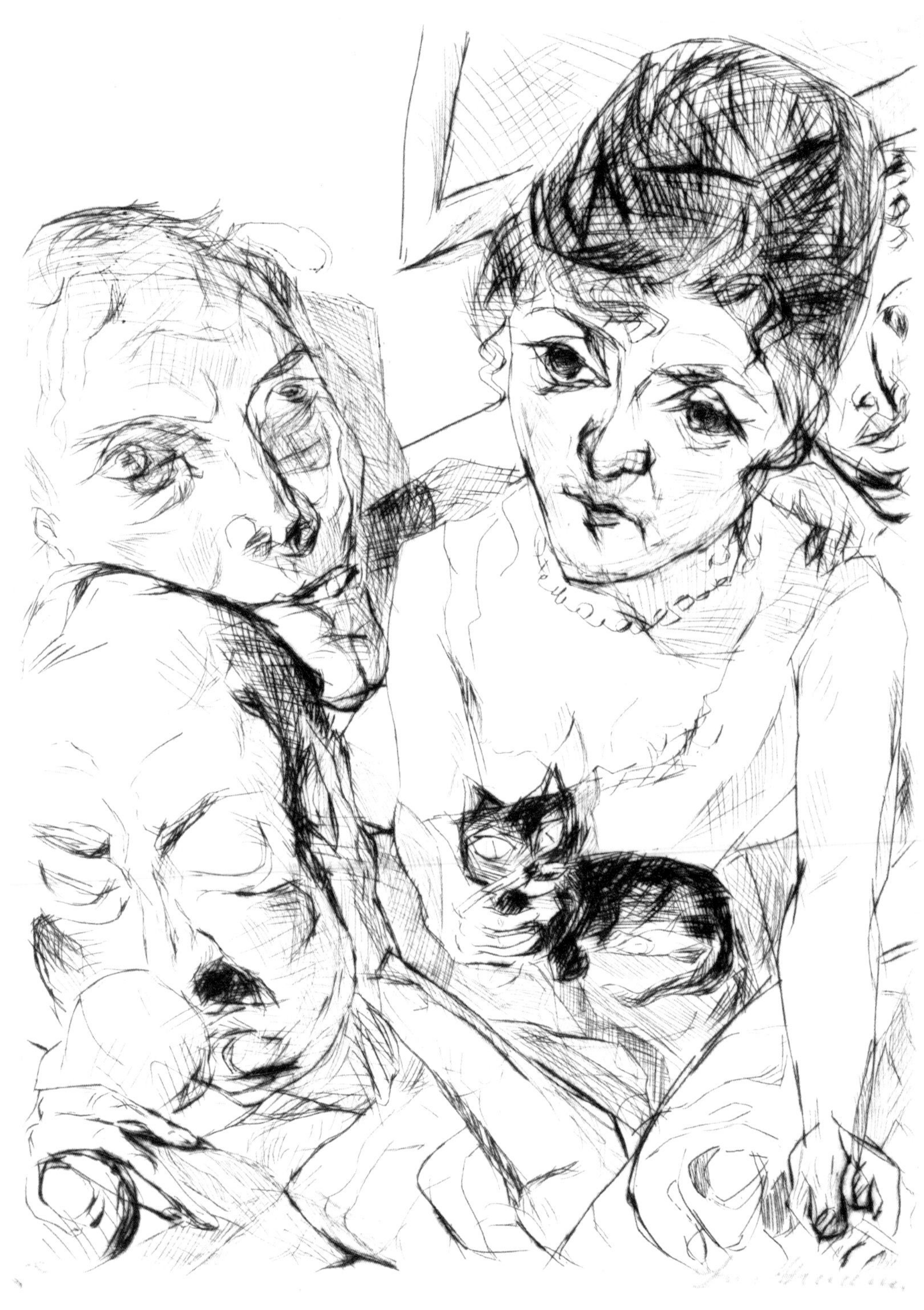

34. EVENING (SELF-PORTRAIT WITH THE BATTENBERGS), PLATE 10, FACES PORTFOLIO, PRINTED 1917, PUBLISHED 1919

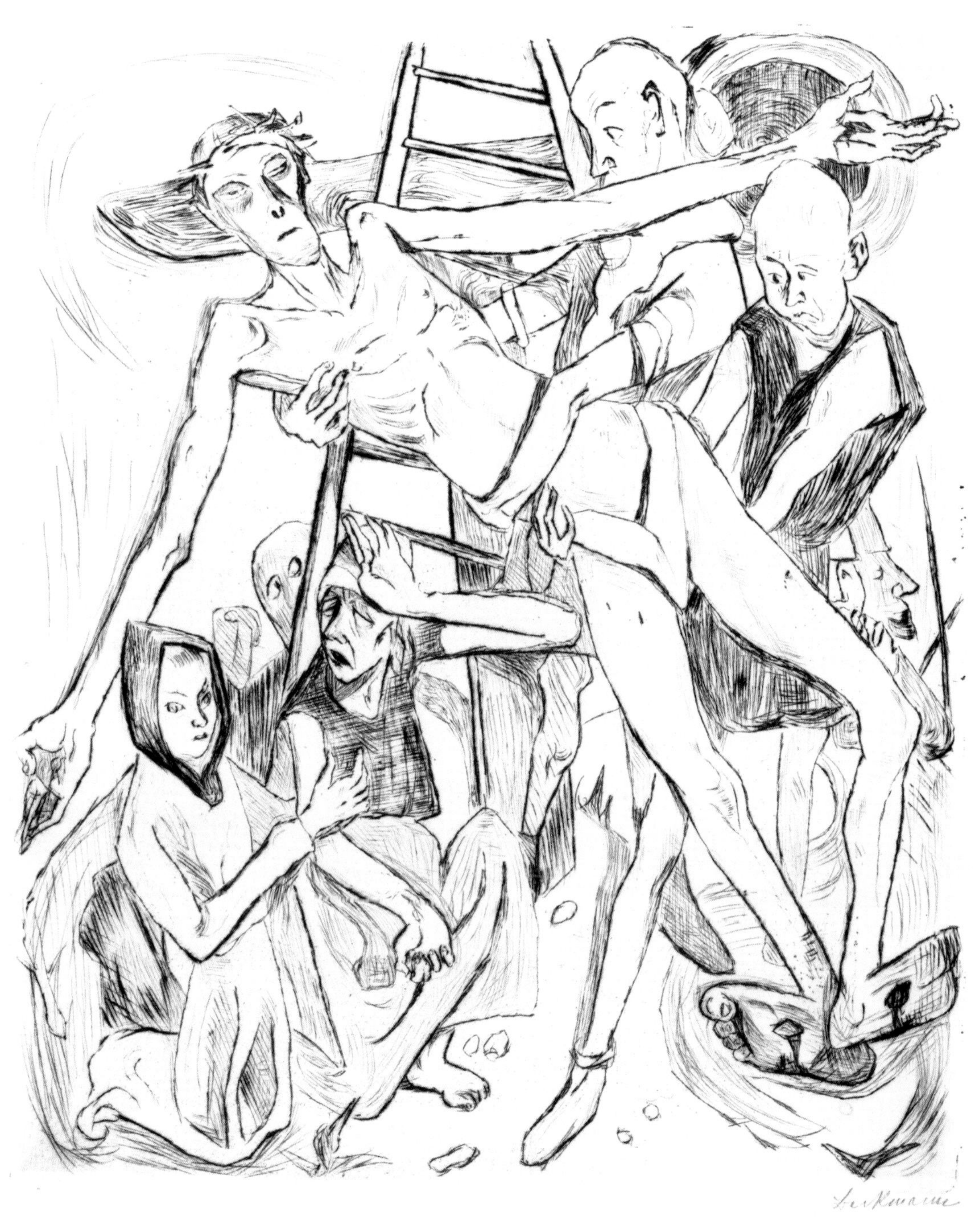

35. DESCENT FROM THE CROSS, PLATE 11, FACES PORTFOLIO, PRINTED 1918, PUBLISHED 1919

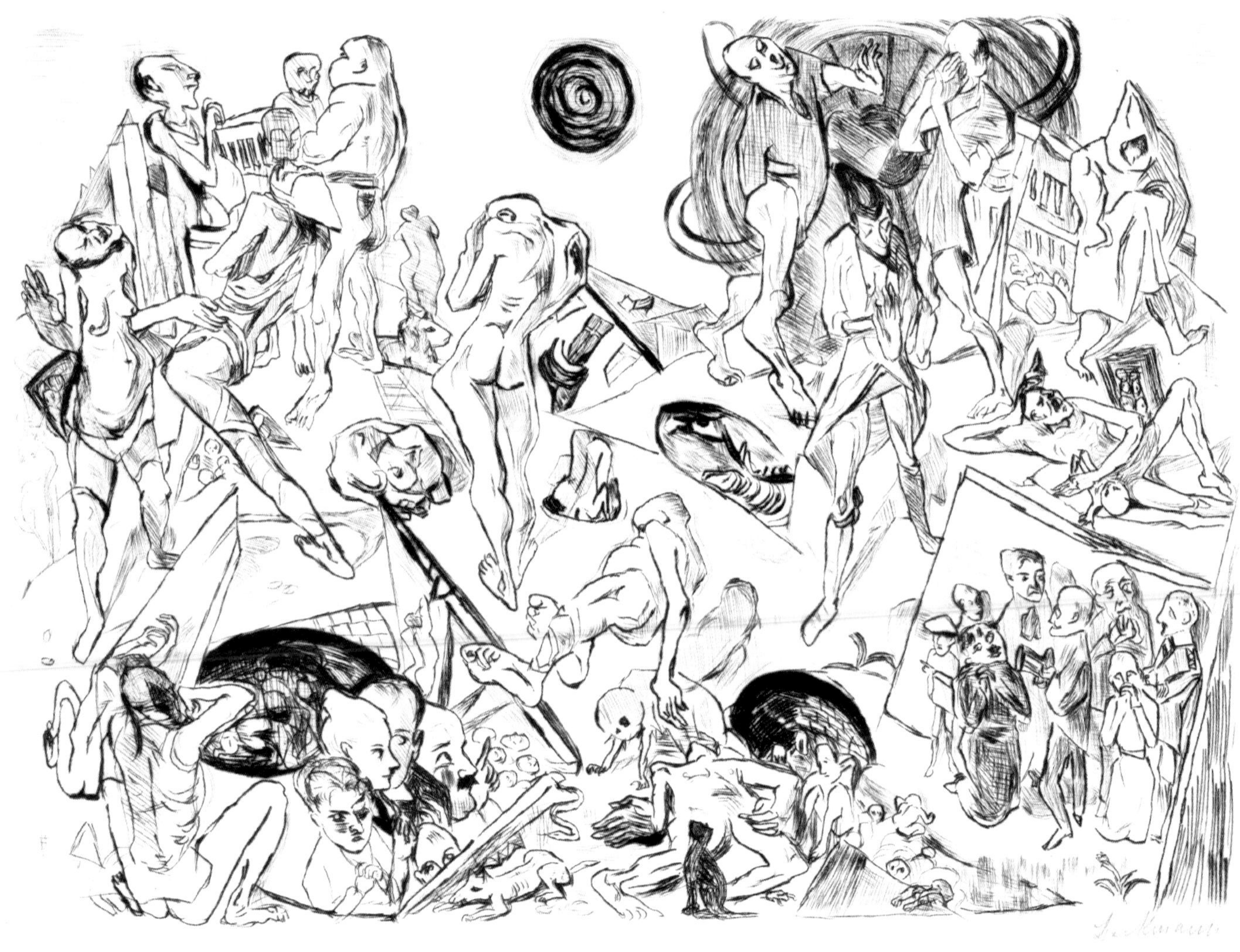

36. RESURRECTION, PLATE 12, FACES PORTFOLIO, PRINTED 1918, PUBLISHED 1919

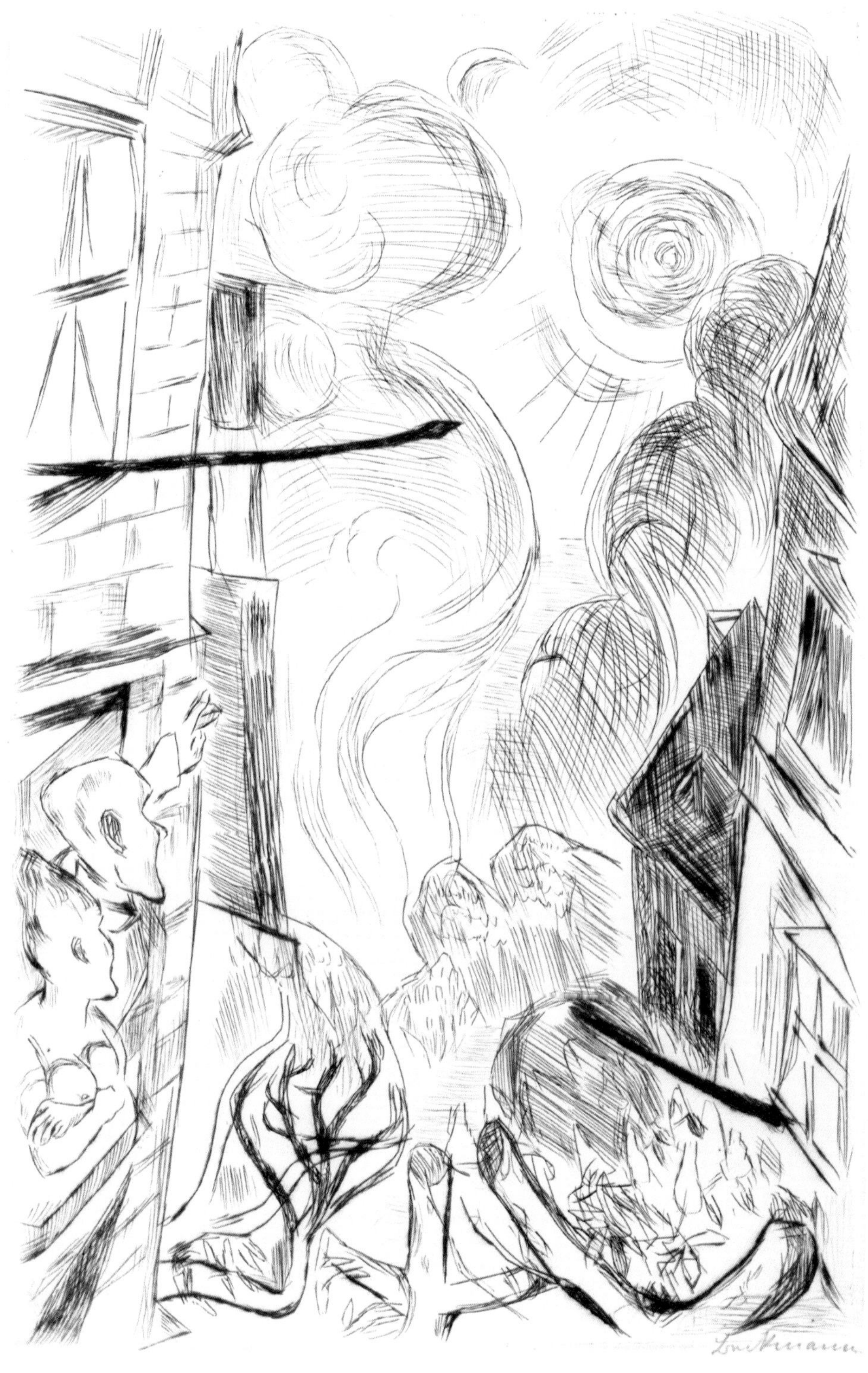

37. SPRING, PLATE 13, FACES PORTFOLIO, PRINTED 1917, PUBLISHED 1919

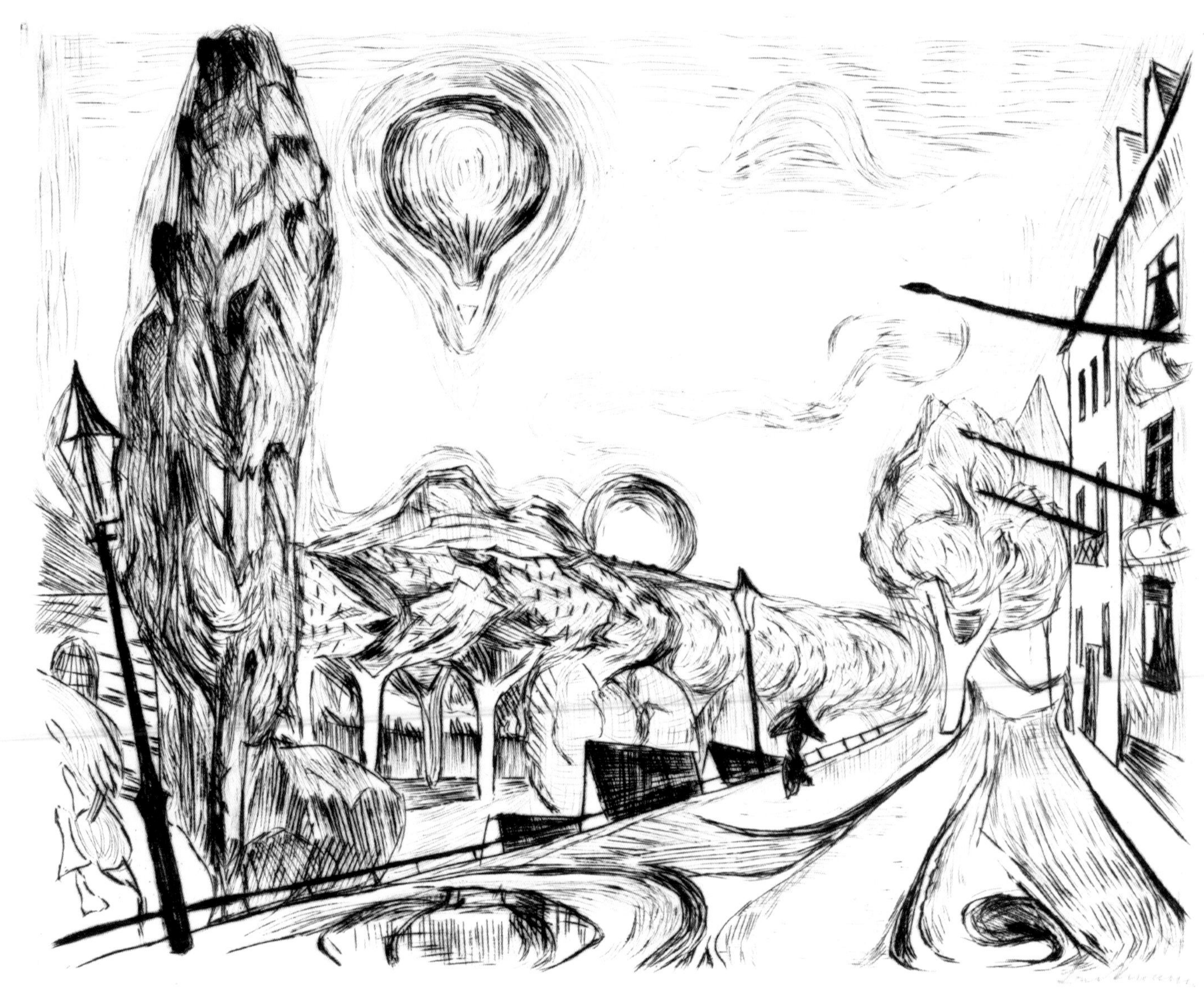

38. LANDSCAPE WITH BALLOON, PLATE 14, FACES PORTFOLIO, PRINTED 1918, PUBLISHED 1919

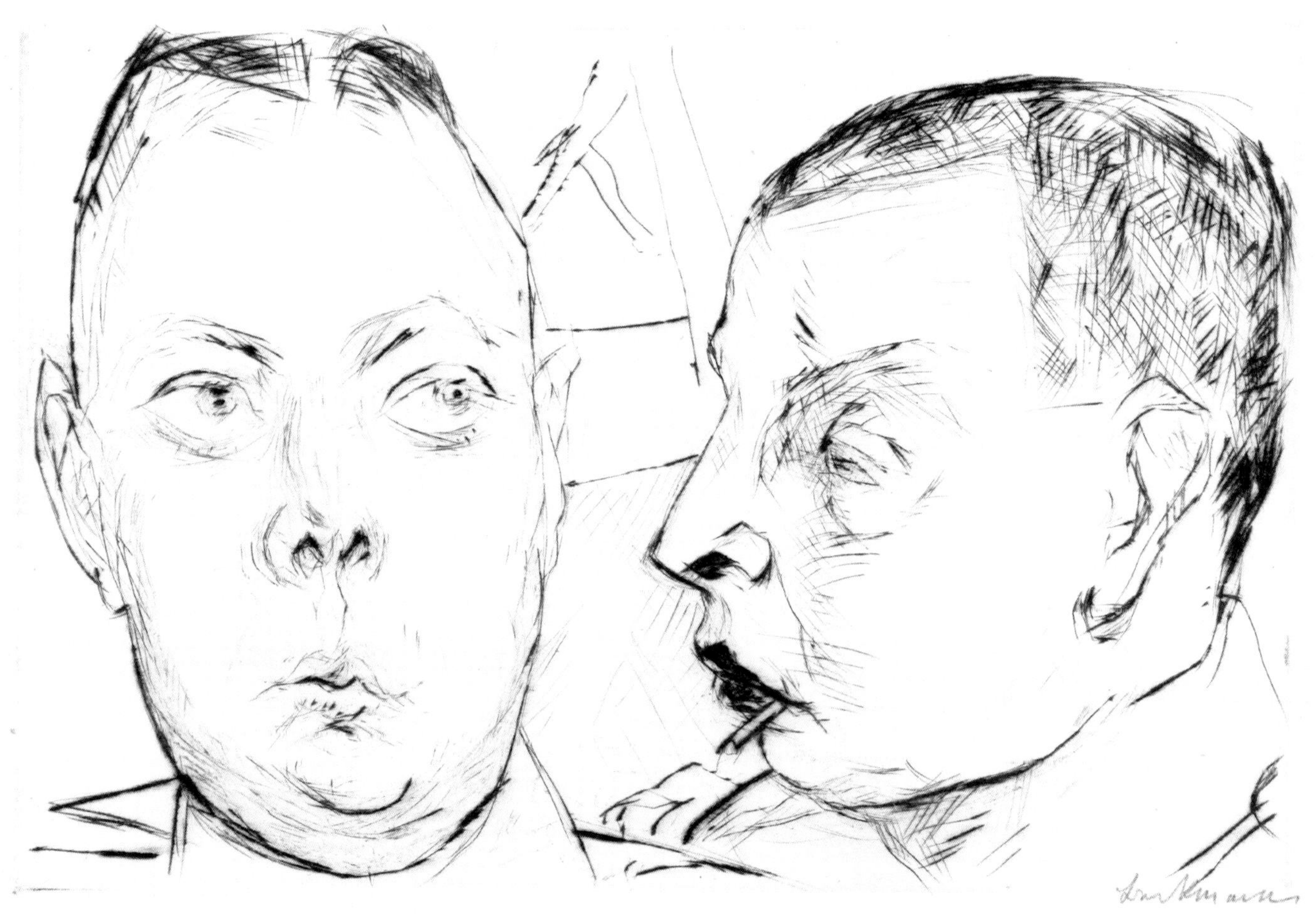

39. TWO AUTO OFFICERS, PLATE 15, FACES PORTFOLIO, PRINTED 1915, PUBLISHED 1919

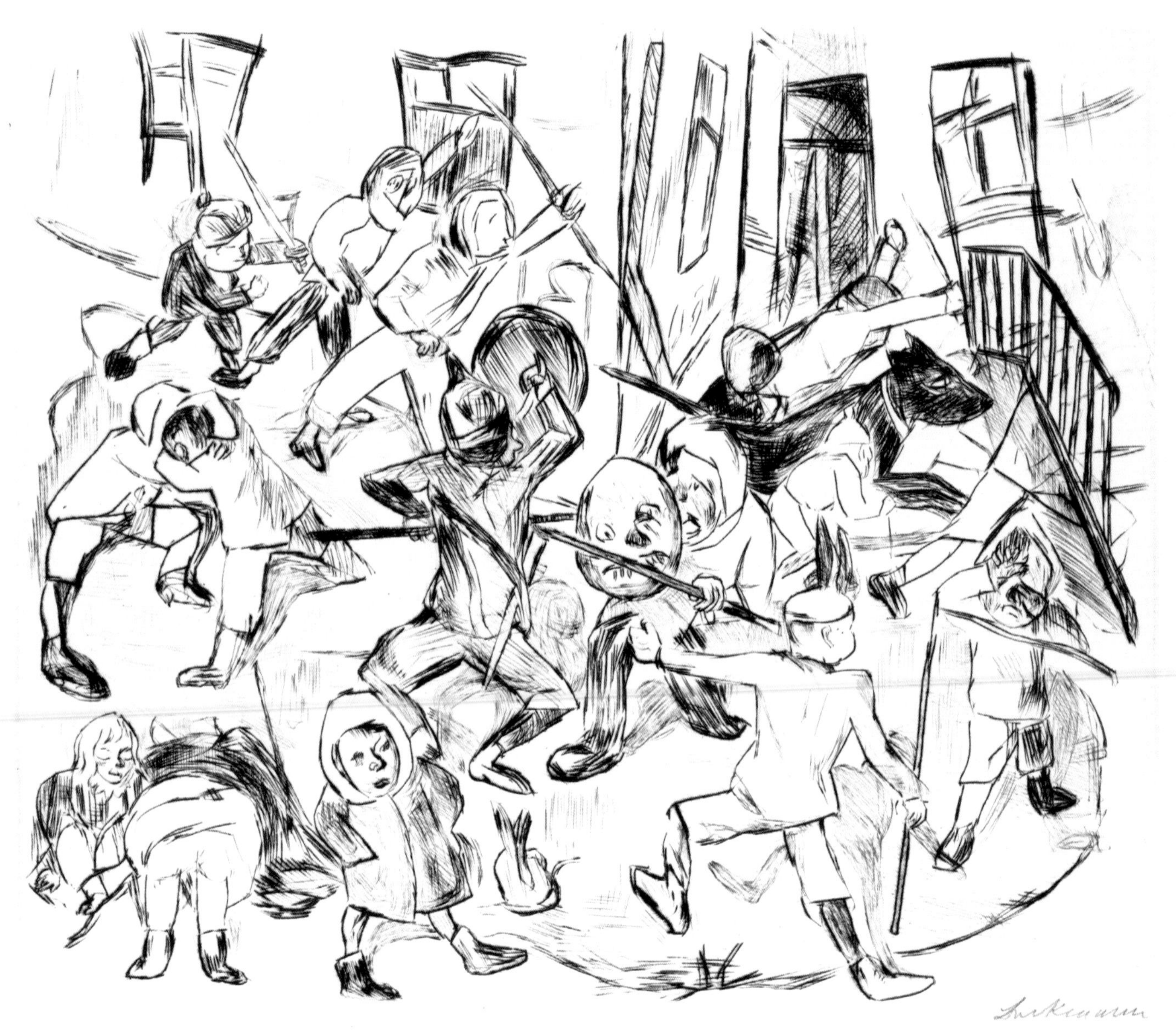

40. PLAYING CHILDREN, PLATE 16, FACES PORTFOLIO, PRINTED 1918, PUBLISHED 1919

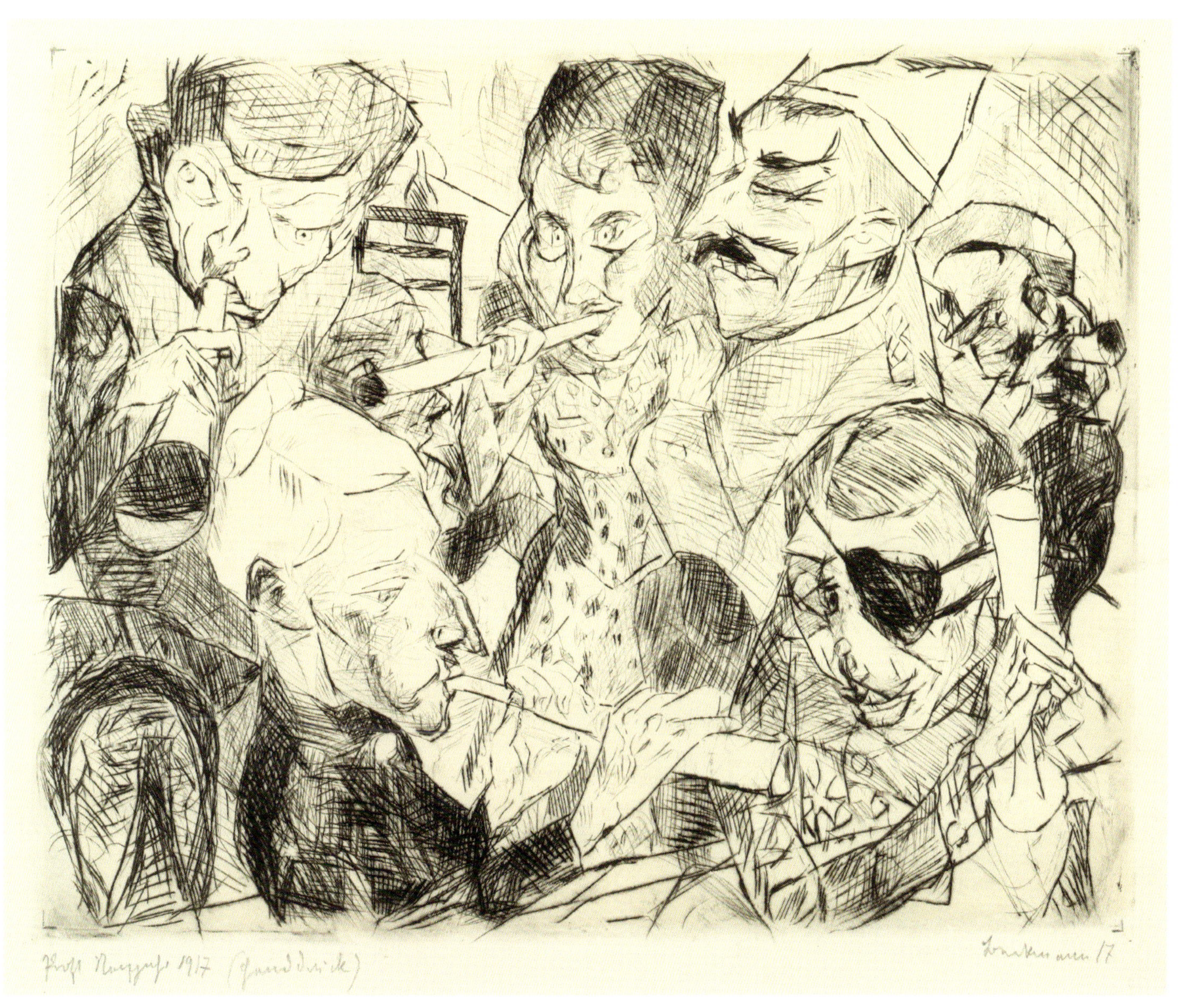

41. HAPPY NEW YEAR, PLATE 17, FACES PORTFOLIO, PRINTED 1917, PUBLISHED 1919

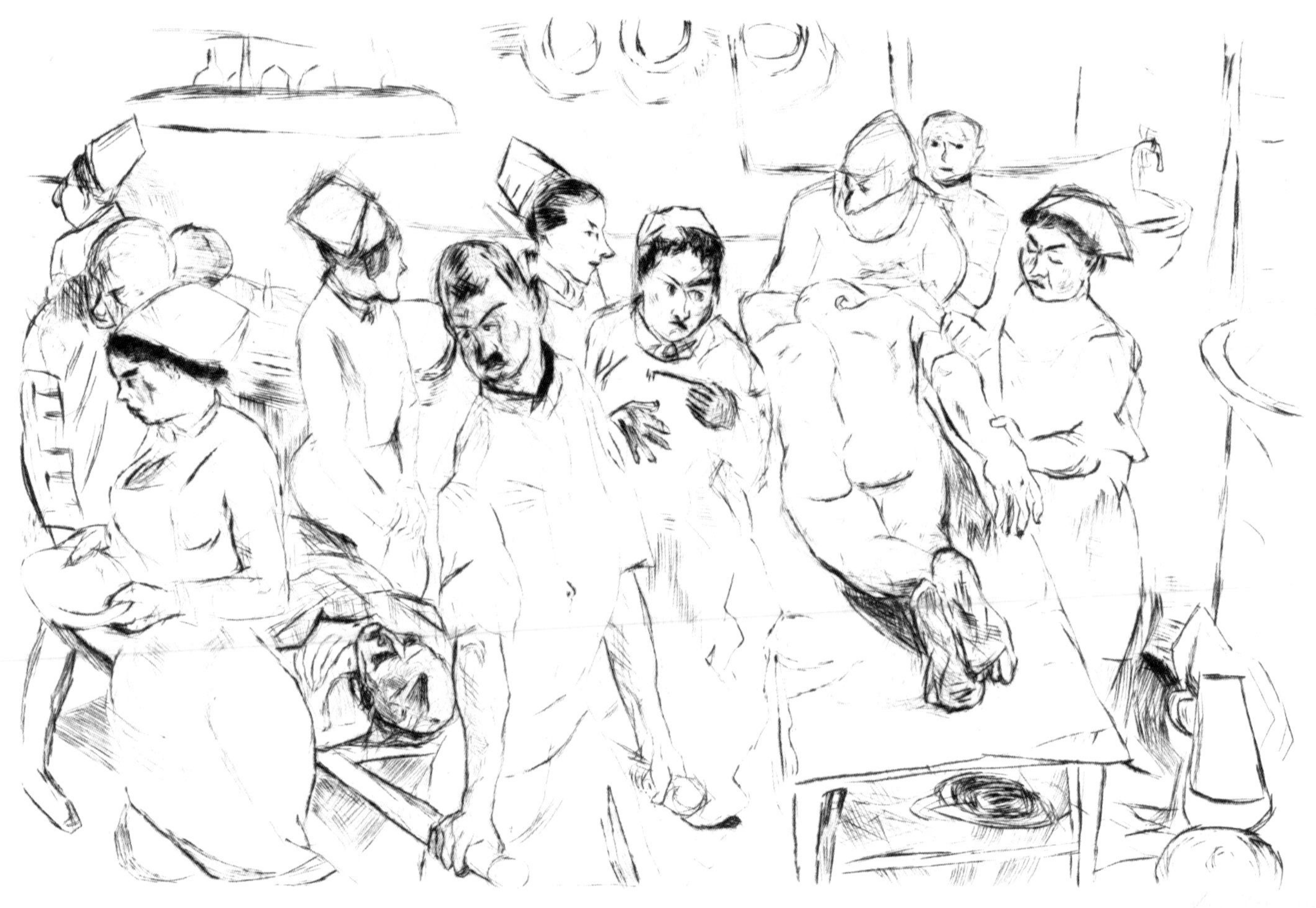

42. THE LARGE OPERATION, PLATE 18, FACES PORTFOLIO, PRINTED CA. 1914, PUBLISHED 1919

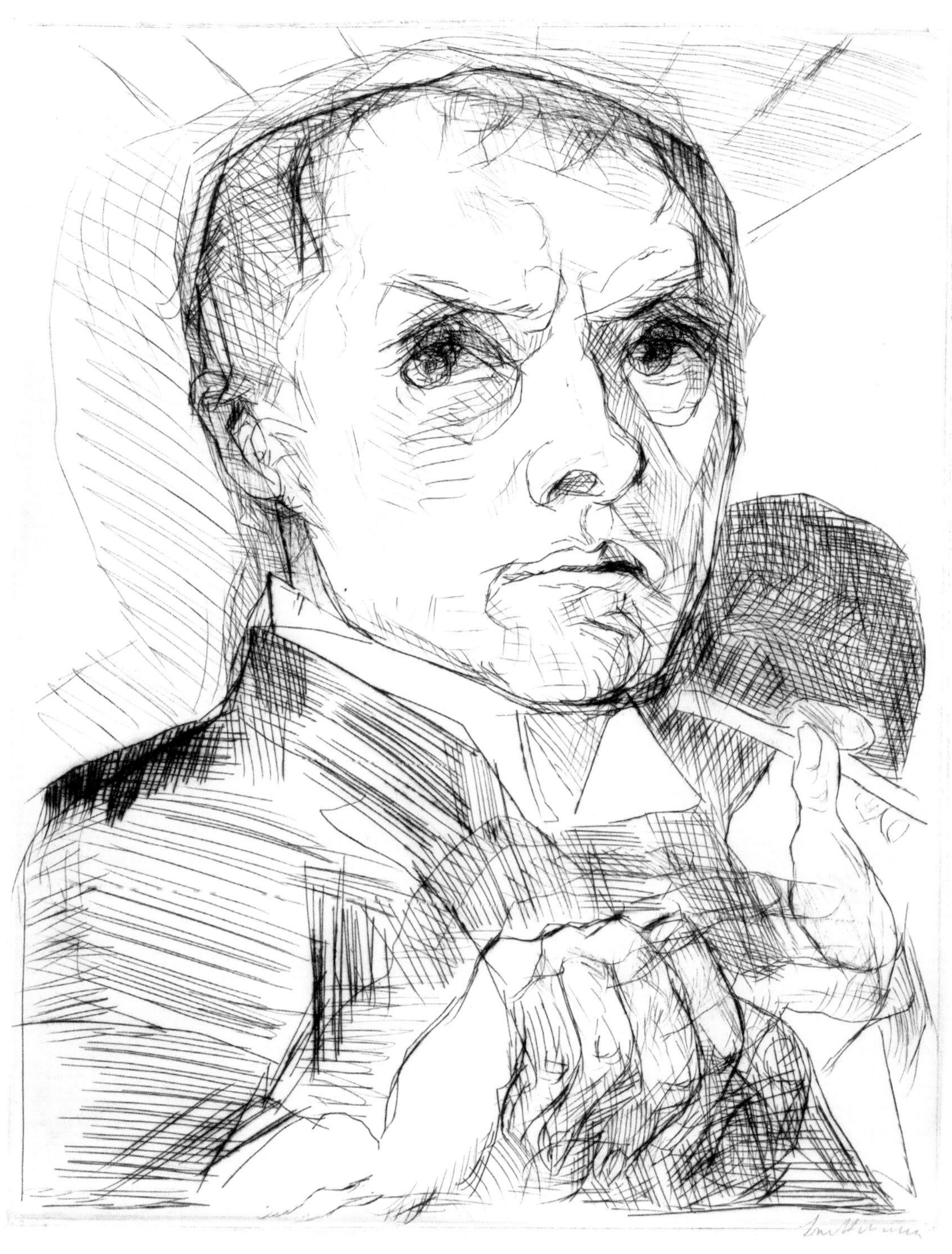

43. SELF-PORTRAIT WITH STYLUS, PLATE 19, FACES PORTFOLIO, PRINTED 1916–17, PUBLISHED 1919

FROM WAR TO STABILIZATION

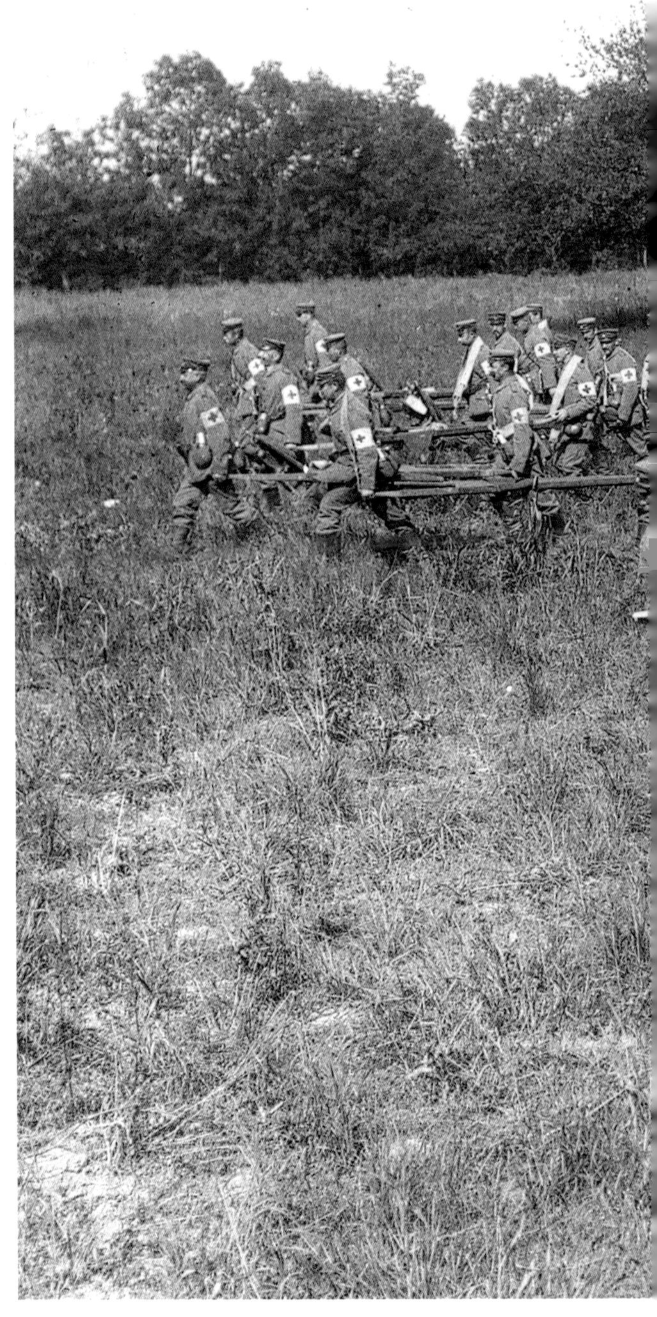

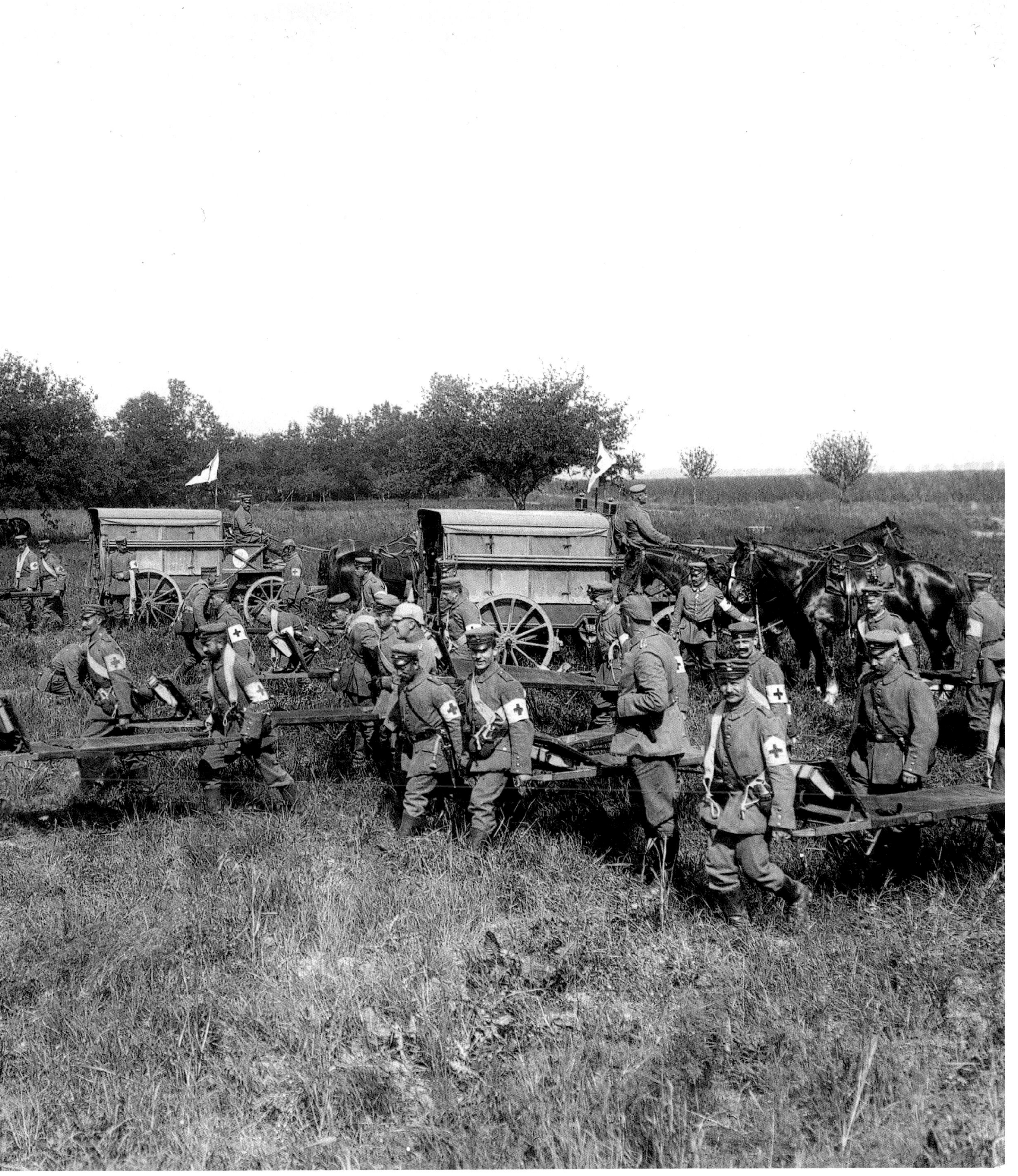

German army medics on the way to the combat area on the Western Front to rescue the wounded, 1914. Photo: Haeckel Collection / ullstein bild via Getty Images

THE WAR AS CONCLUSION AND NEW BEGINNING

Christiane Zeiller

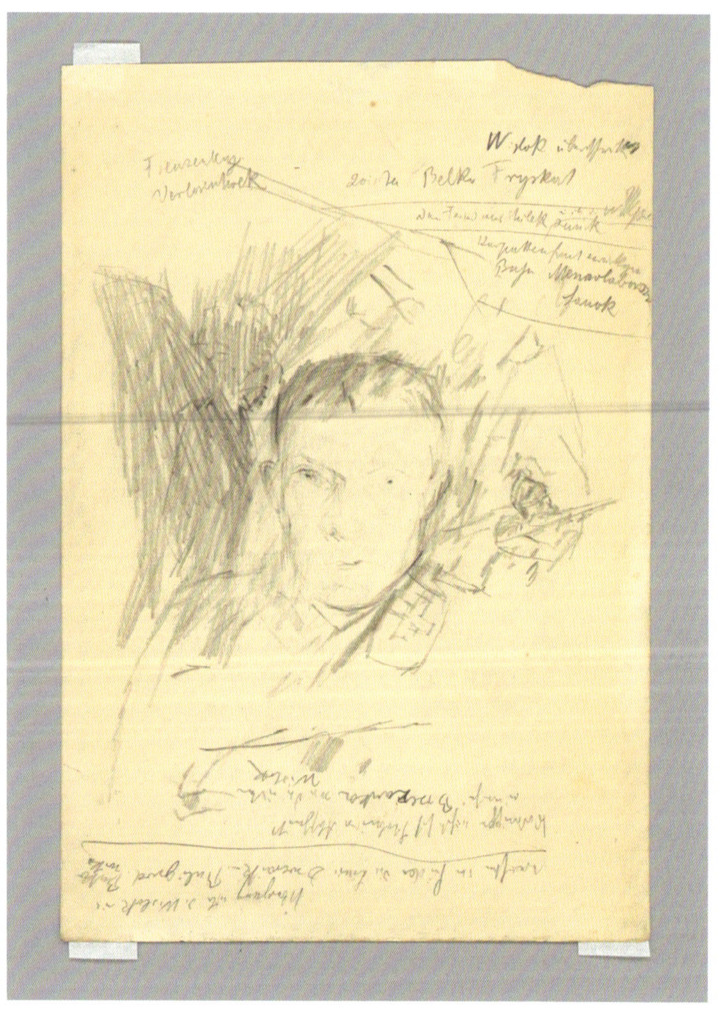

Max Beckmann's far-reaching personal and artistic crisis, triggered by his experiences of World War I, has been addressed many times. It is clearly evident in his work, but it also left behind traces in sources that have thus far been less well known. Beckmann's *Briefe im Kriege* (Wartime Letters) will be examined along with his wartime sketchbook and selected works with regard to what they reveal about the changes in the painter's style.

Beckmann's fifty-two letters to his wife, Minna Beckmann-Tube, have been lost and have been handed down only thanks to their early publication. She published this complex group of letters—which at times reads more like a diary than correspondence—with Bruno Cassirer in Berlin in 1916.[1] In January 1913, Beckmann noted in his diary, which ends in April 1913, that he did not want to read a great deal but instead write to his wife "diligently about everything, including the entirely tangential."[2] For the painter, the tangential should never be equated with the insignificant—quite the contrary.

Because the original source of the letters of the months from September 1914 to the summer of 1915 no longer exists—when and under what circumstances the letters were lost can no longer be determined—scholars have cited the edition published by Bruno Cassirer from the outset. They were incorporated word for word in the later edition of the letters.[3] One is struck when reading them by the characteristics of a correspondence having been reduced to a minimum, with no salutations or complimentary closes, for example. It is reasonable to assume that Minna excluded the all-too-personal from her edition with an eye to a public readership. The letters are merely dated and go straight into descriptions of the everyday. Because the original sources have been lost, it is no longer possible to determine the extent of interventions or abridgements.

An annotated proof copy has survived in Beckmann's papers, which the publisher had sent the painter so he could indicate the placement of illustrations.[4] The type area and line breaks are the same as the Bruno Cassirer edition; the page breaks have changed because of deletions and the insertion of illustrations. This document makes it possible to identify several interventions by Beckmann and his wife: for example, the first paragraph of his letter of June 7, 1915, ends in the proofs with the words "*und trinke um zwölf Uhr Kaffee*" (and drink coffee at twelve o'clock). The painter added in his hand: "As you know, I have to illustrate the military songbook for the A.O.K. [army higher command]." This addition, with its orthography corrected, was included in the print version. Its purpose was obvious: to inform readers as completely as possible about his artistic activities, in this case his drawings for the booklet *Kriegslieder des XV. Korps, 1914–1915: Von den Vogesen bis Ypern* (War Songs of the Fifteenth Corps, 1914–1915: From the Vosges to Ypres), published by Paul Cassirer in Berlin in 1915—one of the two important commissioned works that Beckmann produced during his wartime service.[5]

In addition, there are later editions apparently intended to emphasize their character as letters: "*Ich bin müde heute, werde wohl nicht viel schreiben können.*" (I am tired today, presumably won't be able to write much.) This sentence—it is unclear whether it was written by Minna or by Max—is found only in the printed version, not in the proofs. It is possible that Beckmann actually began his letter with these words but perhaps also as it is in the proofs: "*Es ist so viel bequemer für mich, zu zeichnen wie zu reden.*" (It is so much easier for me to draw than to speak.) In the proof copy, there are several such examples of smoothing out, deleting, and adjusting that scholars have yet to compare to the published edition.

The most extensive deletion and the most important one for this essay concerns the penultimate letter of the set, which Beckmann wrote to his wife from Flanders on June 8, 1915. The famous version of the letter ends with a description of a specific drawing, probably the portrait of the young Belgian woman Céline Durnez:[6] "Yesterday I sketched the girl once again with an immense exertion of strength. I think I succeeded in capturing her to an extent. I tried to express everything essential immediately, while also always keeping hold of the objective."[7]

This letter ends with this description of the portrait drawing—seemingly. In the proofs, however, it is followed by a passage entirely deleted by Beckmann. It is significant for the stylistic change that Beckmann had already announced prior to World War I but that was accelerated by it. The deleted continuation reads: "*Ich will die Person machen, aber mit dem Rhythmus, mit dem ich geboren bin. Das beides zu vereinigen ist wahnsinnig schwer, und man kommt dem Ziel manchmal näher, manchmal wieder ganz weit weg. Versinkt in Realismus oder in leere Stilvexerei.*

1. Max Beckmann, *Self-Portrait as Medical Orderly*, 1915, pencil. Private Collection

Die Verschmelzung ist nur mit aller höchster Konzentration und Energie zu erreichen und ist auch dann im letzten Moment noch 'Gnade.'" (I want to do the person but with the rhythm with which I was born. Uniting the two is insanely difficult, and sometimes one gets closer to the goal, sometimes one is far away again. Descended into realism or into empty stylistic vexation. The fusion can only be achieved with the utmost concentration and energy and even then there is still "grace" in the final moment.)

These three sentences reveal the artist as a seeker in the middle of a profound artistic crisis. The description of the struggle ("insanely difficult") and the reference to fate ("grace"), which helps determine success or failure ("grace") contradicted the image Beckmann wanted to convey of himself as a strong painter unerringly pursuing his goal. Nor did he see himself as free of the risk of unintentionally falling into realism or meaningless stylistic exercises—a development he had observed in the work of fellow artists and criticized not without mocking polemicism.[8] He pointed this out to Minna by clearly distancing himself from "arabesques" and "calligraphy" and antithetically contrasting them with "the vitally pulsating," "intensified roundness," and "fullness and plasticity."[9]

The deleted lines already articulate the traces that the war had left on Beckmann at the time of the letter—he had been volunteering for more than nine months. Around the same time, he produced his devastating *Selbstbildnis als Sanitäter* (Self-Portrait as Medical Orderly) [Fig. 1]. It exposes the painter as literally torn apart; his tense face appears to be illuminated by a stroboscopic flickering. His right eye looks blinded; his upper body seems to be dissolving, as are his features, which are almost snuffed out, not the determined or even grim features otherwise so characteristic of Beckmann's self-portraits. The artist's extraordinarily unstable head-and-shoulders portrait drawing is surrounded by figural sketches of fighting soldiers, some of which have been crossed out, as well as hasty, stenography-like notes of diverse occurrences at the front. Other self-portrait drawings produced shortly before this one also feature hurriedness in the strokes, tension, and—in the case of *Selbstportrait beim Zeichnen* (Self-Portrait While Drawing)[10] [see ill. on p. 116] and *Selbstportrait 1917* (Self-Portrait 1917) of two years later [Plate 15]—signs of premature aging. But that Beckmann seems to dissolve in the background in the self-portrait seen here is unique and truly symbolizes the erasing of the prewar Beckmann. The concentration and energy mentioned in the deleted passage as essential for his project of creating "vital" portraits have now left him.

Beckmann's state of increasing exhaustion and traumatization led to *Oberstabsarzt* (Senior Medical Officer) Dr. Philaletes Kuhn [Plate 11] arranging for his transfer in August 1915 to Strasbourg, far from the murderous daily routine of the war in Flanders. He was employed at the Kaiserliches Institut für Hygiene und Bakteriologie (Imperial Institute for Hygiene and Bacteriology) to draw cell cultures, but shortly thereafter the war caught up to him psychologically and he had a nervous breakdown.[11]

During his time volunteering as a medical orderly, Beckmann always had a sketchbook in hand, which he used in 1915 and 1916.[12] It contains two related groups of drawings, the first of which was probably made in Flanders, that is, in the middle of the action, but the second probably dates from his time in Strasbourg, depicting the horrors of war at the front retrospectively. This book also has numerous notes, from addresses and train schedules to a draft of a request to be discharged from military service. The sketches assimilate events Beckmann witnessed in East Prussia and Flanders. More than a dozen drawings, several of which are titled, were not used for works, even though they testify to a specific pictorial idea. Why that is the case will be discussed below.

One especially drastic case is a drawing from the first of the two groups mentioned—the sketches made in Flanders—that Beckmann initially planned to use for an etching. It is labeled: "*Kopf auf d. Lanze und Leute mit durchschnittenen Kehlen*" (Head on lance and people with cut throats) [Fig. 2, top]. In the sketch in question, a human head on a pike and other figures can be seen in the background; the linework appears rushed and agitated; the frame is only partially drawn. Seeing beheaded people and other images of the everyday horrors of the war such as the dead, wounded, and ill continued to have a psychological effect on him for years. His statement in a conversation with the young poet Lili von Braunbehrens, in which he described his mental state, should be interpreted accordingly: "I have drawn nearly all of them, these dead men. Perhaps they held it against me; after all, they visited me."[13]

The specificity of the scene in the sketch suggests Beckmann experienced it in Flanders. During the same period, he encountered wounded men in surgery, and for a time he was bunked above a morgue. He must have been immersed in the murderous war with all his senses. His letters to Minna also testify to this, describing the stench of decay, the sound of thundering cannons, the color of the blood of the wounded, the music of the "wild insanity of this gargantuan murder,"[14] and the "bottomless chasm" into which he felt himself being pulled.[15]

The morgue and the military hospital became places of the quotidian and of horror in equal measure and made their way into his prints [Plates 8, 9 and 42].[16] Beckmann had planned from the outset to turn several of his pictorial ideas into prints rather than paintings. The pointy, splintered character of drypoint etching seemed suited to a world lying in rubble, and Beckmann began to make etchings from them while still in Strasbourg.

The second sketch on the same sheet (fol. 9 verso) [Fig. 2, bottom] was presumably the point of departure for the drypoint etching *Kleine Operation* (Small Operation),[17] but it has the almost trivial title *Der Verbandsraum* (The Surgical Dressing Room). Several figures are schematically visible, accompanied by notes that are difficult or impossible to read. A patient is lying on an operating table parallel to the picture plane. The cursory sketch is like a stenograph of a scene he observed in the military hospital; in the etching, it is condensed and dramatized: a badly wounded man appears in the center, with a deep, gaping head wound and mangled leg. He has Beckmann's features, which is another indication that the artist was by this point anything but an objective observer of the scene—the horror of a reality that was at the same time banal had caught up with him too much for that.

The sketchbook also has drawings that were not turned into prints directly but may have provided impetus for works on related subjects. The sketched titled *Vergewaltigung* (Rape) [Fig. 3, bottom] has an arrangement of figures that resembles an operation scene. The figure lying defenseless on the left in the middle is flanked by two figures; two more figures can be made out in the background, but it is impossible to say whether they are facing the action or away from it. The rape Beckmann witnessed may have later influenced his mas-

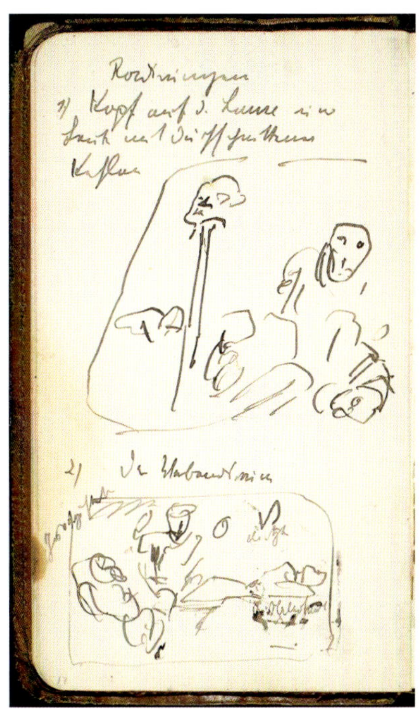

2. Max Beckmann, *Two Sketches for Etchings*, 1915, pen and black ink. *Sketchbook 9*, folio 9 verso. National Gallery of Art, Washington, D.C.

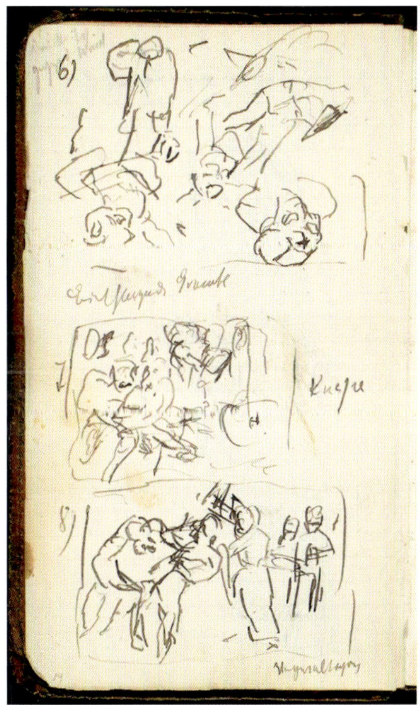

3. Max Beckmann, *Three Sketches*, bottom: *Rape*, 1915, pen and black ink. *Sketchbook 9*, folio 10 verso. National Gallery of Art, Washington, D.C.

terpiece *Die Nacht* (The Night) of 1918–19[18] [see ill. on p. 17], which moves the tortured and violated figure of the woman to the center. Unlike the graphic versions of the etchings, there are no longer compositional parallels here; in terms of its subject matter, however, a painting such as *The Night* cannot be understood without the horrifying experiences of his wartime service, during which he wrote to his wife: "I would drag myself through all the sewers of the world, through every conceivable humiliation and abuse in order to paint. That I have to do."[19]

The pathos of several works from before he was deployed in the war sometimes seem almost forced. The painter's search for relevant themes for humanity repeatedly brought him to Christian mythology,[20] which along with antiquity remained an inexhaustible source of inspiration and engagement until the end of his life. Now his oeuvre was enriched with works such as *The Night* that explored the depths of human action without mythological or historical garb. Beckmann was welcoming this in retrospect when he observed: "The war dragged me violently out of a milieu that was beginning to become dangerous for me."[21] The famous quotation "My art can gorge itself here"[22] also documents a cathartic role he subjectively perceived as necessary that the war played for him and many other artists of his generation.

The sequence of sketches and their titles in that first part of *Sketchbook 9* reads like a recording of the horrors he experienced: *Die Beschiessung* (The Bombardment), *Der Blendschuss* (The Flare), *Typhus* [*Lazarett*] (Typhoid Military Hospital) (all three: folio 11 verso); *Die Flucht im Schützengraben* (Refuge in the Trench), *Die Granate* (The Grenade)[23] (both folio 12 recto); *In den Drahtverhauen* (In the Barbed Wire), followed absurdly by *Tanz* (Dance) (both folio 14 recto). These sketches directly document his experiences and make a work such as *Die Schlacht* (The Battle) of 1907 seem by contrast almost academic and theatrical, despite the high quality of its technique.[24] It lacks the scale of human tragedy, the immediate experience of the real battle, the massacre seen by the painter and described in the letters to Minna. This is also true of contemporaneous dramas drawn from his reading of daily newspapers, such as *Szene aus dem Untergang von Messina* (Scene from the Destruction of Messina)[25] and *Untergang der Titanic* (Sinking of the Titanic).[26] One senses in both works a distance that aligns those current dramas with the ancient tragedies.

His subject matter and how it was related changed after his wartime service, based on his immediate experiences in the field and the trenches. Thanks to an intense revival of the print, especially the drypoint etching, Beckmann now found a new language that continued its effect in his painting. In the early years after returning from the war, the latter had a hardness and brittleness compared to the ecstatic and almost baroque works of the prewar period that are physically related to the burrs engraved into the metal plate and sometimes conveys an impression of shattering glass just like these documents of his printmaking. Not until the early 1920s did his forms become rounder and smoother again, filling with life, so to speak.

The "second" part of *Sketchbook 9*, with drawings such as *Hitze* (Heat) (folio 45 verso) and *Der Schützengraben* (The Trench) (folio 46 verso) and *Lazarett* (Military Sick Bay) (folio 47 verso), was presumably first used by Beckmann in Strasbourg. This is suggested by the position of these sketches within the book. But an increased degree of execution also leads one to suspect it. It can be explained by greater distances from the events: the sketches immediately after the experience are clearly more cursory. In the sketchbook, they are followed almost exclusively by notes.

The only self-portrait in the sketchbook represents an exception; it was very probably drawn in Strasbourg. In the face of his traumatizing experiences, the subjects of the other sketches, and compared to *Self-Portrait as Medical Orderly*, it seems surprisingly youthful at first. At the same time, however, the drawing is alarmingly uncontoured, clumsy, and shaky, and it is certainly related to the ill-defined, hesitant line of *Self-Portrait as Medical Orderly*. The softer graphite here favors a vaguer line compared to that of the more precise pen used for the sketches in this book. The unfinished self-portrait appears as if Beckmann had given up, resigned, during the drawing process. But the fact that he did not tear out the page or reject and cross out the self-portrait may indicate that he felt that this moment of obvious lack of orientation was also worthy of preservation.

The ratio of sketches in *Sketchbook 9* that were implemented to those that were not is revealing and is connected to the profound changes to Beckmann's style, choice of themes, and techniques as a result of the war. It has been shown that themes like that of the sketch *Rape* continued to influence his painting even years later. Other themes, by contrast, were dealt with by the sketch and not translated in any other work, whether print or painting.[27] This is because a sketch such as *Head on Lance and People with Cut Throats* was no longer suited to the new "program" he had formulated in February 1914. In it he described concisely his desire to "produce something living."[28] Drastic depictions of the mangled dead or seriously injured are no longer found in his paintings after the war.

The second *Auferstehung* (Resurrection),[29] which Beckmann began while in Strasbourg, and which translates his lived experience into the context of Christian mythology, no longer seemed a suitable way to convey what he had experienced. This monumental work attempts to translate the events of the war into a vision of an apocalyptic catastrophe without the promise of salvation that is central to Christian accounts of the Resurrection. Beckmann criticized the flight into religious subject matter as painted absolution: "Complete withdrawal in order to achieve that famous purity people talk about as well as the loss of self in God, right now all that is too bloodless and also loveless for me."[30]

Its gigantic format—*Resurrection* was by far his largest format by that point, even though the prewar period did not lack large formats—presumably also played a role in Beckmann abandoning the undertaking as a failure, writing on the canvas in pencil a memo to himself: "*zur Sache!*" (get to the point!). "Objectivity of the inner vision"[31] became his credo. Not until *Selbstbildnis mit Griffel* (Self-Portrait with Stylus) of 1916–17[32] did Beckmann once again present himself with his usual determination, as a visionary who persuades by means of his art, in the service of human beings. He now saw his place among them, in the city. He reclaimed for himself as painter the task of giving them "a picture of their fate" and confessed that it could be done "only if we love humanity."[33]

He was following his conviction that the human being is god, expressed in 1927 in his text "Der Künstler im Staat" (The Artist in the State).[34] Beckmann's contribution has an editor's note that somewhat distances itself from his remarks, which could be superficially misunderstood by some readers as blasphemy: "We are proud to publish the great artist's

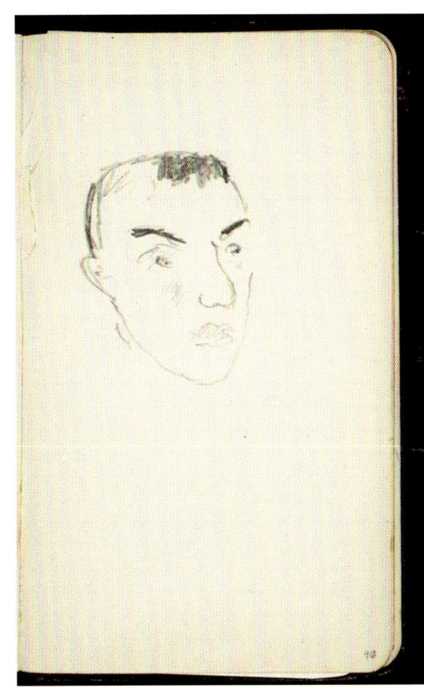

4. Max Beckmann, *Self-Portrait*, 1915, pencil. *Sketchbook 9*, folio 61 recto. National Gallery of Art, Washington, D.C.

moving confession, although we do not want in any way to associate ourselves with certain extreme metaphysical conclusions detached from their deeply human meaning."[35] Wilhelm Hausenstein had shown himself to be clearly more tolerant of Beckmann's remarks in 1924, writing that a "blasphemy of an energetic positivist is preferable" to its opposite: "the metaphysical blurriness of all-too-many Expressionists, who do not know what they believe and in whom stirs not the dear Lord but a literary ersatz demon. Beckmann's blasphemy is a correlate of his sense of clarity, closeness, density, and radicalness in the painting."[36]

Despite his objections cited above, Beckmann took up religious subjects in three of his seven paintings from 1917 [Plates 21–23]. Much as in *The Night* of the following year, his experiences in the war form the matrix for all three works, which draw on them. The design and colors of Adam and the dead Christ are inspired by the many dead soldiers the painter saw on a daily basis. Here, too, it is striking how much these works differed from those before the war on the same subjects in terms of the figures, style, and atmosphere.[37]

The breakdown that Beckmann suffered in Strasbourg in the summer of 1915 resulted first in leave and ultimately in his being discharged from military service. The painter sought refuge in Frankfurt am Main with a friend from student days, Ugi Battenberg, and his wife, Fridel. He found his way back to oil painting only slowly. According to his list of paintings, when Beckmann went to war in September 1914, he had completed five paintings since the beginning of the year.[38] In the year of his breakdown, 1915, there were just two oil paintings; the following year, the number was the same, but one remained unfinished—the second *Resurrection*, which he had begun in Strasbourg. The year 1917 was the strongest since returning from the war in terms of the number of paintings finished. His self-confidence was also back to the prewar level when he outlined to Reinhard Piper his plan to have chapels built—interestingly, for gigantic formats, which he was still thinking of painting at this time—despite the failure of the second *Resurrection* and despite his general reorientation. He perceptively described himself as "rather megalomaniacal."[39]

The war and the psychological crisis it caused forced Beckmann to take a break from painting. In Wervik he had still longed for painting, for color, "an instrument that one can't do without for long. All I have to do is just think of gray, green, and white, or of black-yellow, sulfur yellow, and violet, and a shudder of pleasure runs through me. Then I wish the war were over and I could paint."[40]

Translated from the German by Steven Lindberg

1 Max Beckmann, *Briefe im Kriege* (Berlin: Bruno Cassirer, 1916).

2 Diary entry of January 7, 1913. The Max Beckmann Archiv is currently producing a complete digital edition of Max Beckmann's diary; the project, directed by Oliver Kase and compiled by Nina Peter and the present author, is planned for release in early 2024. Beckmann's diary entries are cited in this essay from the original manuscripts.

3 Max Beckmann, *Briefe*, ed. Klaus Gallwitz et al., 3 vols. (Munich: Piper, 1993–96), 1:91ff.

4 Unpublished proofs with handwritten annotations, 44 pages (proofs cut out and pasted to blank sheets of paper), Bayerische Staatsgemäldesammlungen, Max Beckmann Archiv, Max Beckmann Nachlässe.

5 The other commission was a mural in Wervik: a fresco for the swimming pool of field hospital no. 9 of the fifteenth corps (destroyed). See *Max Beckmann: Die Gemälde*, ed. Barbara and Erhard Göpel with Anja Tiedemann, 3 vols. (Ahlen: Franz Dieter und Michaela Kaldewei Kulturstiftung, 2021), cat. no. 186. (Cited hereafter as Göpel/Tiedemann followed by catalog number.)

6 *Porträt einer jungen Belgierin* (Portrait of a Young Belgian Woman) is illustrated on page 61 of *Briefe im Kriege* (see note 1), where it appears under the letter of May 20, 1915, but it may belong to the immediate

context of the letter cited here. See also the note in Stephan von Wiese, *Max Beckmanns zeichnerisches Werk, 1903–1925* (Düsseldorf: Droste, 1978), cat. no. 302. (Cited hereafter as Wiese followed by catalogue number.)

7 Max Beckmann to Minna Beckmann-Tube, June 8, 1915, in Beckmann, *Self-Portrait in Words: Collected Writings and Statements, 1903–1950*, ed. Barbara Copeland Buenger, trans. Barbara Copeland Buenger and Reinhold Heller with David Britt (Chicago, IL: University of Chicago Press, 1997), 175–76.

8 Max Beckmann, "Thoughts on Timely and Untimely Art," in Beckmann, *Self-Portrait in Words* (see note 7), 113–17.

9 Max Beckmann to Minna Beckmann-Tube, March 16, 1915, in Beckmann, *Self-Portrait in Words* (see note 7), 149.

10 *Selbstportrait beim Zeichnen*, 1915 (Wiese 280).

11 See my essay on Beckmann's stay in Strasbourg: Christiane Zeiller, "'Es ist sehr eigentümlich hier man kann sich sehr auf sich selbst concentrieren': Max Beckmann in Strassburg," in *Max Beckmann: Beiträge, 2004–2005*, Hefte des Max Beckmann Archivs 8 (2006), 95–107.

12 Christiane Zeiller, *Max Beckmann: Die Skizzenbücher / The Sketchbooks*, ed. Max Beckmann Gesellschaft and the Bayerische Staatsgemäldesammlungen, 2 vols. (Ostfildern: Hatje Cantz, 2010), no. 9.

13 Max Beckmann, "Gespräch mit Lili von Braunbehrens über das Gemälde 'Auferstehung II'" (presumably 1916), in Beckmann, *Die Realität der Träume in den Bildern: Schriften und Gespräche, 1911 bis 1950*, ed. Rudolf Pillep (Munich: Piper, 1990), 19.

14 Max Beckmann to Minna Beckmann-Tube, March 28, 1915, in Beckmann, *Self-Portrait in Words* (see note 7), 154–55, esp. 154.

15 Max Beckmann to Minna Beckmann-Tube, September 5, 1915, in Beckmann, *Briefe* (see note 3), 144 (no. 139).

16 *Grosse Operation* (Large Operation), presumably 1914. See James Hofmaier, *Max Beckmann: Catalogue Raisonné of His Prints*, 2 vols. (Bern: Galerie Kornfeld, 1990), cat. no. 81. (Cited hereafter as Hofmaier followed by catalog number.)

17 Hofmaier 82.

18 Göpel/Tiedemann 200.

19 Max Beckmann to Minna Beckmann-Tube, April 26, 1915, in Beckmann, *Self-Portrait in Words* (see note 7), 161.

20 Cf. *Sintflut* (The Flood), 1908 (Göpel/Tiedemann 97), *Auferstehung* (Resurrection), 1909 (Göpel/Tiedemann 104); *David und Bathseba* (David and Bathsheba), 1910 (Göpel/Tiedemann 128); *Kreuztragung* (Bearing of the Cross), 1911 (Göpel/Tiedemann 139).

21 Reinhard Piper, *Mein Leben als Verleger: Vormittag, Nachmittag* (Munich: Piper, 1964), 328.

22 Max Beckmann to Minna Beckmann-Tube, April 18, 1915, in Beckmann, *Self-Portrait in Words* (see note 7), 159.

23 Realized as the drypoint *Die Granate* (The Grenade), 1915 (Hofmaier 80 / Plate 10).

24 Göpel/Tiedemann 85.

25 Göpel/Tiedemann 106. The very word "scene" points to a stage-like context.

26 Göpel/Tiedemann 159.

27 Of the seventeen sketches of the first block in *Sketchbook 9*, only three were definitely implemented; the implementation of two more is at least probable. Only sketches with frames and titles are counted here.

28 Max Beckmann, "Statement for Exhibition at Hamburg Kunstverein, *Max Beckmann (Gemälde), Walter Geffcken (Gemälde), Jules Pasquin (Zeichnungen)*," in Beckmann, *Self-Portrait in Words* (see note 7), 129.

29 Göpel/Tiedemann 190.

30 Max Beckmann, "Creative Credo," in Beckmann, *Self-Portrait in Words* (see note 7), 181–85, esp. 185.

31 Max Beckmann, "Catalogue Foreword for Exhibition at J. B. Neumann Graphisches Kabinett, Berlin, *Max Beckmann Graphik*," in Beckmann, *Self-Portrait in Words* (see note 7), 178–80, esp. 180.

32 Hofmaier 105.

33 Beckmann, "Creative Credo" (see note 30), 184.

34 Max Beckmann, "Der Künstler im Staat," *Europäische Revue* 3, no. 4 (July 1927): 288–91, esp. 289; Max Beckmann, "The Artist in the State," in Beckmann, *Self-Portrait in Words* (see note 7), 284–90, esp. 286.

35 Beckmann, "The Artist in the State" (see note 34), 287.

36 Wilhelm Hausenstein, "Max Beckmann," in Curt Glaser et. al., *Max Beckmann* (Munich: Piper, 1924), 50–72, esp. 64.

37 See *Adam und Eva* (Adam and Eve) of 1907 (Göpel/Tiedemann 67), *Kreuzigung* (Crucifixion) of 1909 (Göpel/Tiedemann 119), and *Kreuztragung* (Christ Carrying the Cross) of 1911 (Göpel/Tiedemann 139).

38 Max Beckmann kept records of his paintings, their date of origin, and buyers. These three notebooks are Book 1 (1904–34), Book 2 (1934–49), and Book 3 (1949–50). Books 1 and 2: Bayerische Staatsgemäldesammlungen, Max Beckmann Archiv, Max Beckmann Nachlässe. Book 3: Columbia University New York, Rare Book and Manuscript Library.

39 Piper, *Mein Leben als Verleger* (see note 21), 320.

40 Max Beckmann to Minna Beckmann-Tube, June 8, 1915, in Beckmann, *Self-Portrait in Words* (see note 7), 176.

SELF-PORTRAITS AS DRAFTSMAN

BECKMANN WITH THE SKETCHBOOK

Dietrich Schubert

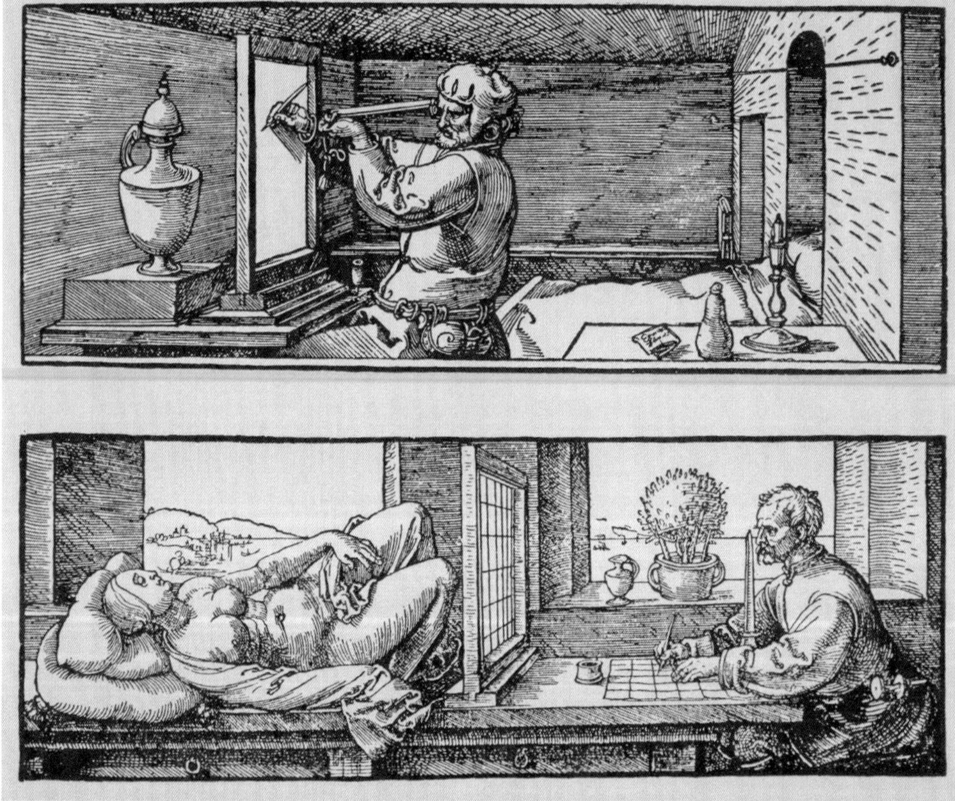

1. Albrecht Dürer, *Draftsman Making a Perspective Drawing of a Reclining Woman*, from *The Treatise on Measurement*, 1525, woodcut

DRAWING ONESELF: THE HISTORY OF THE SELF-PORTRAIT

Max Beckmann was one of those passionate egocentrics who repeatedly reveal themselves in self-portraits. Before we address his work in this genre as a draftsman, a brief introduction will suffice by examining a few pertinent prototypes. As early as 1525,

Albrecht Dürer produced a view of an artist measuring and recording a female nude in perspectival foreshortening [Fig. 1]. It was a study for Dürer's *Underweysung der Messung* (Treatise on Measurement) and it remains influential.[1] Depicting oneself as an artist in front of a mirror in the studio became an important subject of modern art history derived from the Renaissance, especially because Leonardo da Vinci had reflected on the interdependencies of seeing, rendering the visible, and perceiving the world in his treatise on painting.

Such self-depictions entailed not only technical problems but also psychological ones; looking at oneself and at the viewer provided information about the mental state of the artist in his or her social context.[2] A drawing by Matthias Grünewald, dated 1529 [Fig. 2], the original of which has not survived, conveys with exemplary expressivity a visionary appearance with his eyes raised toward heaven and his brush or pencil in front of his shoulder. Beckmann doubtless knew this depiction of the artist as a seer of invisible realms, as a quasi-prophet.[3]

Depictions of artist-friends posed working in the studio also belong to the group under discussion here: in 1641, in a small etching 4 inches tall, Rembrandt van Rijn depicts a studio scene. The draftsman is posed in front of a sheet of paper and illuminated by candlelight with a pen in his right hand, and an inkpot in his left. He is studying a sculptural bust of a girl. This testifies to a realistic stance in opposition to the fashion of numerous personifications and series of allegories in which naked female or male figures represent an idea or thing; for example, in 1612 Hendrik Goltzius presented Drawing as a winged female genius sketching a figure of Diligence, who is also nude (Harvard Art Museums / Fogg Museum). Rembrandt radically distinguished himself by adopting a different approach.

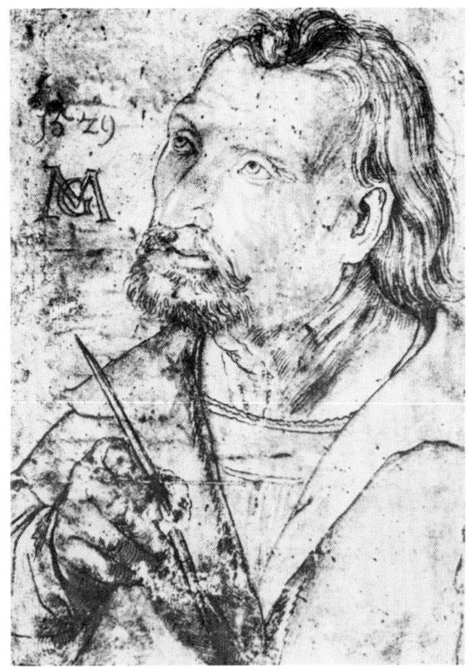

2. Matthias Grünewald, so-called *Self-Portrait*, 1529, chalk or charcoal on paper. Universitätsbibliothek, Erlangen. Photo: W. Hütt

Rembrandt depicted himself as a painter before an easel with a canvas in a major work in 1660 (Louvre, Paris); this painting was widely influential—including on Paul Cézanne and Vincent van Gogh—in part because it was accessible to the public in the Louvre. An unfinished etching offers a view into a studio where a nude female model is posed, slightly shifted from the central axis with her back turned, while a seated draftsman on the left is working with sketching paper. The *non finito* of this print radiates a particular modernity. By contrast, in an ink drawing Rembrandt appears as a half-length figure seated at a table wearing a smock posed in his studio [Fig. 3]. He gazes directly at the mirror, while his right hand appears in the foreground of the sheet—actually his left hand mirror-reversed in the image.[4] There is a more elaborate etching from 1648 that is intimately related to this one: at just over 6 inches (sixteen centimeters) tall, Rembrandt presents himself as right-handed, drawing at a bright window with a view onto a landscape [Fig. 4].[5] The drawing and the

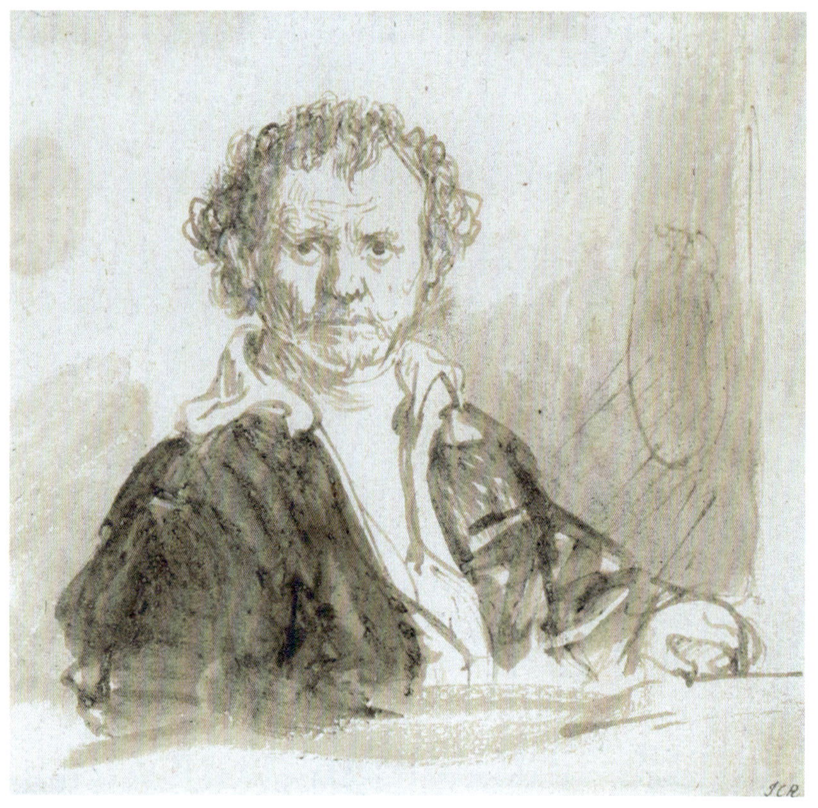

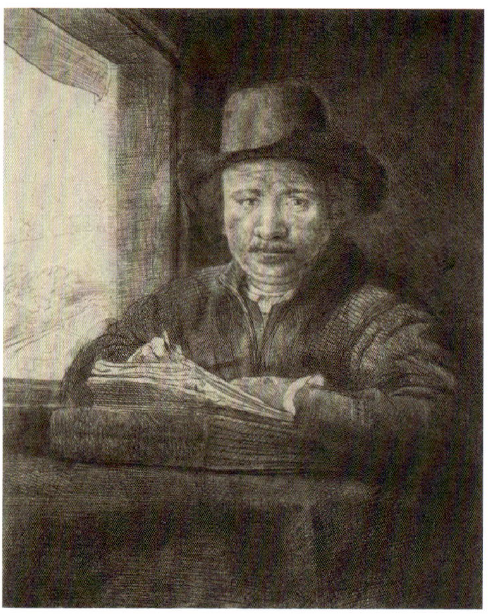

3. Rembrandt (Rembrandt van Rijn), *Self-Portrait at the Drawing Table*, ca. 1648, ink on paper. Kupferstichkabinett, Staatliche Museen zu Berlin. Photo: bpk / Kupferstichkabinett, SMB / Jörg P. Anders / Art Resource, NY

4. Rembrandt (Rembrandt van Rijn), *Self-Portrait Drawing at the Window*, 1648, etching. The National Gallery of Art, Washington, D.C. Rosenwald Collection

etching had different intended audiences; the drawing was for singular contemplation by an individual whereas the etching aimed to reach the broader art market.

In a painting probably dating from several years later, Rembrandt depicted himself in an oblique view to the right, his illuminated right hand on an open sketchbook held in his left hand. The original canvas from around 1653, once in the collection of the painter Joshua Reynolds, appears to be lost. Specialists have identified copies that appear to convey successfully what the painting was, since a print was also circulated.[6] The latter accentuates the distribution of the light in front of the dark, neutral ground just as the painting did: it is not a natural, logical light from an empirical perspective; rather, Rembrandt illuminated the parts that are important for the composition, that is to say, he exercised artistic freedom to create a dramatic effect akin to stage lighting in a theater.

A budding artist in the eighteenth century was expected to learn from the drawings of masters and to study and copy engravings of paintings to which they had no access. The young Francisco de Goya y Lucientes studied for four years with José Luzán, who had him copy prints. In 1778, Goya published his etchings after paintings by Diego Velázquez. Later, at the height of his enormous powers, Goya portrayed artists such as Francisco Bayeu (Museo del Prado, 1795),[7] who was also one of his teachers. One outstanding example of Goya's portraits is that of Everisto Pérez de Castro, who pursued a diplomatic career until 1838. In the latter's portrait, Goya emulated Rembrandt by painting in a free manner with chiaroscuro accents, placing the head in front of a dark ground, illuminating his white shirt in a suggestive way and creating a transition to the hand at the lower left, in which Pérez holds a pen above sheets with drawings.

In 1799 Goya published the cycle *Los caprichos* (The Caprices), which opens with a self-portrait in a black top hat. The preliminary drawing for folio 43 of 1797 shows an artist bent intently over a table with an etching plate [Fig. 5]. A cloud representing his imagination, in which we recognize Goya's face, rises above his head. Bats flap their wings in the gloomy space behind his back. In the etching that followed, these details are more precise, the depressive artist is more brightly lit; two drawing implements lie on the table; and, on the side of the table facing forward, we read the insight: "*Il sueño de la razón produce monstruos*" (The sleep of reason produces monsters).[8]

Since the epoch of Romanticism after 1800, the artist has frequently been depicted drawing or working at the easel—from Caspar David Friedrich to Max Klinger and Lovis Corinth. In 1891, Klinger published an illuminating essay on the difference between painting and drawing, and its impact was still felt by Beckmann and Käthe Kollwitz. In a letter Klinger sent from Paris on February 24, 1885, he calls drawing "the true organ of the imagination in fine art."[9]

With an eye to Beckmann, however, we turn to the realist Adolph Menzel: drawings for his cycle *Künstlers Erdenwallen* (Artist's Earthly Pilgrimage) of 1834.[10] On the sheet *Schule* (School), the student is instructed by the elderly master to draw antique works; we recognize the head of *Laocoön* on the left. After attending a course in plaster casting at the Berlin academy, however, Menzel drew what he saw in life, and did so standing up (which is also documented in photographs). In a pencil sketch on a small sheet from around 1845 [Fig. 6], he captured himself in a view from below, pausing a turn of his body, with his palette in his right hand even though he was left-handed. Although the sheet looks unfinished, its open style of drawing is progressive and points ahead to modernism after 1900. This free drawing style with thin and thick strokes eschews isolated contours and seeks to fill the significant strokes with life just as its figure conveys inner and outer movement in the transitory moment.

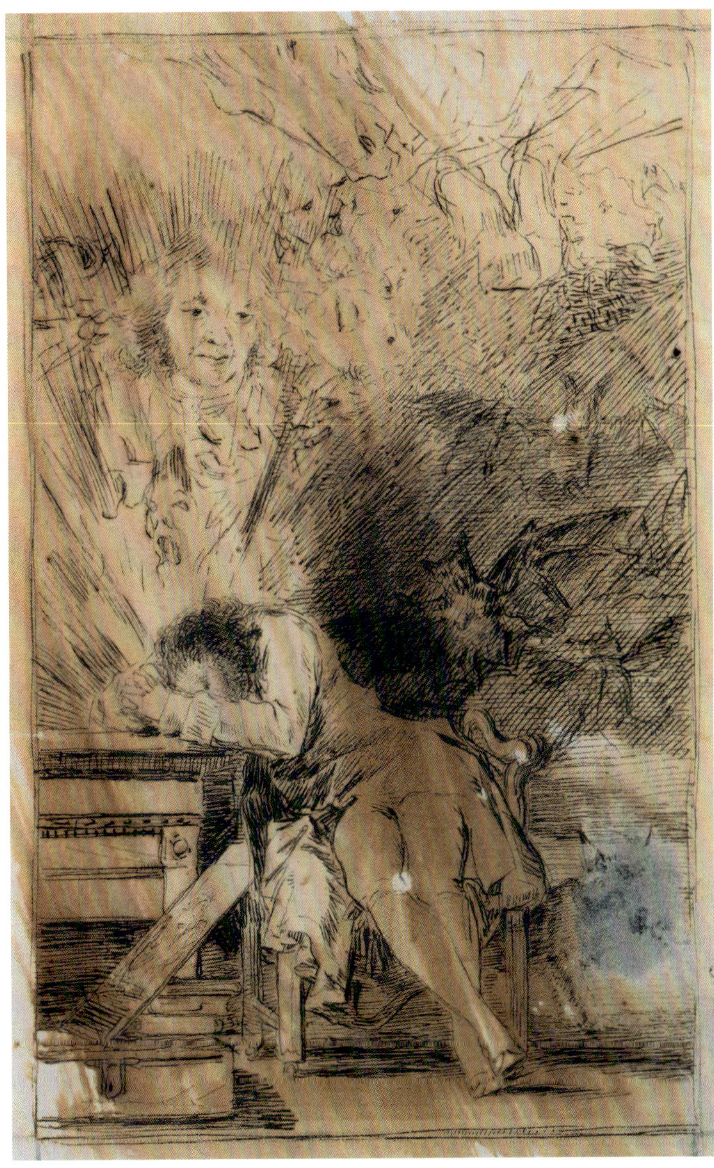

5. Francisco de Goya y Lucientes, *The Sleep of Reason Produces Monsters*, 1796-97, feather sepia on paper. Museo del Prado, Madrid. Photo: Album / Art Resource, NY

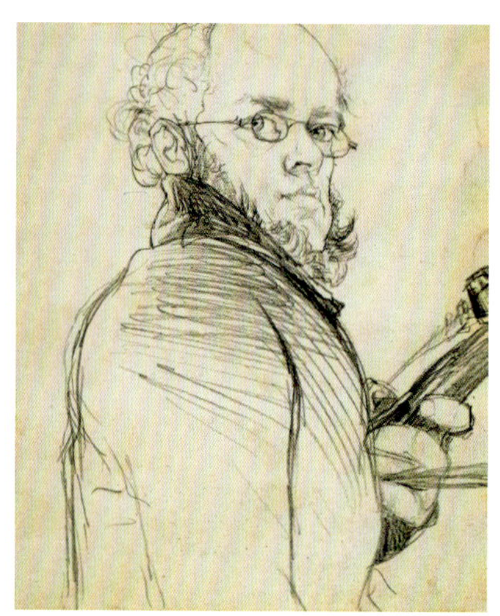

6. Adolph Menzel, *Self-Portrait with Palette*, ca. 1845, pencil on paper. Private Collection. Photo: Pels-Leusden, Zürich

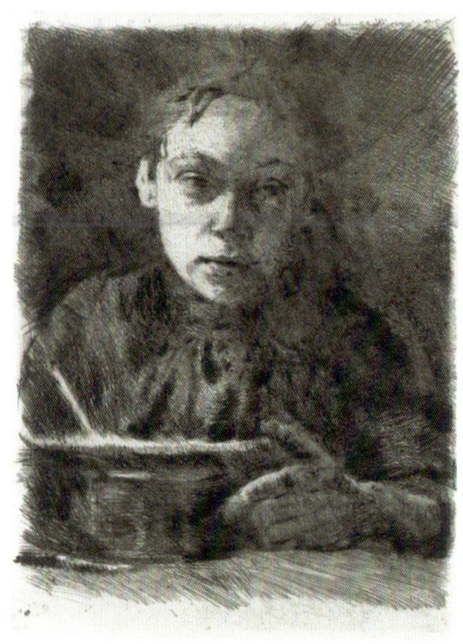

7. Käthe Kollwitz, *Self-Portrait at the Drawing Board*, 1893, etching and drypoint on paper. Kupferstich-Kabinett, Staatliche Kunstsammlungen Dresden, Photo: Herbert Boswank

The tradition of learning from plaster casts of antique statues had already been rejected by Rembrandt. His studio produced the significant sheet (Hessisches Landesmuseum Darmstadt) showing a group of art students drawing a naked female model in a studio. The paradigm shift is from the model of ancient art to the model of nature, of social reality, of visible reality.[11] That became the credo not only of Menzel but also of the realist Gustave Courbet, who portrayed himself repeatedly, for example, in 1845 drawing at a table on which lies the piece of chalk with which he was working (Louvre, Paris) and of his experience as a political prisoner in 1873 after the Paris Commune uprising.

Kollwitz began her career with drawings and prints in the tradition of these realists, such as in *Self-Portrait at the Drawing Board* [Fig. 7] and repeatedly challenged herself artistically. Corinth was another indefatigable draftsman and etcher until the beginning of World War I.[12] He produced numerous self-portraits before and around 1900, for example, in a mirror behind a nude model in an etching from 1913 or in seven studies of his face—à la Rembrandt—on one sheet in [Fig. 8]. Corinth often portrayed himself in ironic roles in the *theatrum mundi*, or "theater of the world." Until 1925, he used a mirror to portray himself as a draftsman again and again to document the effects of aging. Corinth and Beckmann knew each other from their years in the Berlin Secession. In August 1914, the older artist did not have to go to war, while the younger one volunteered to serve as a medical orderly. Beckmann was therefore not fighting on the front lines, like Otto Dix, Franz Marc, Waldemar Rösler, Albert Weisgerber, and other artists.

DRAWING IN THE WAR: 1915

Seeking balance like a circus acrobat, like a kind of tightrope walker, between dark and

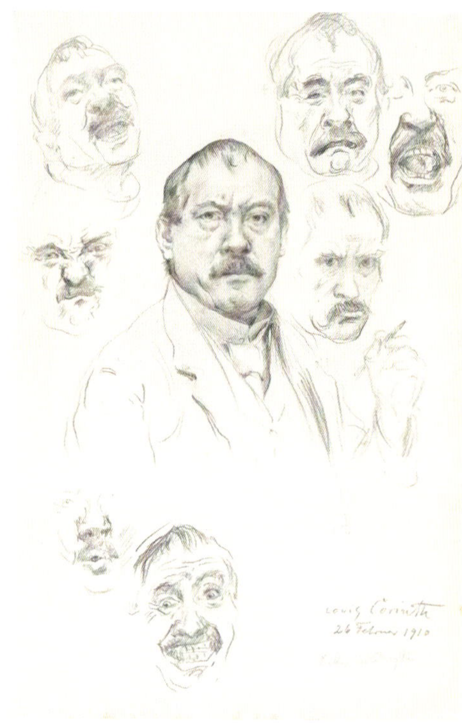

8. Lovis Corinth, *Studies for a Self-Portrait*, February 1910, pencil on paper. Kunsthalle Bremen - Die Kulturgutscanner - ARTOTHEK. Photo: Kunsthalle Bremen - ARTOTHEK

light, between nonbeing and being, between black and white (the elements of drawing), and the beautiful and the ugly, became Beckmann's central concern. In a lecture on his painting in London on July 21, 1938, he asserted God as the unity between the corporeal and the creative, creating again and again "a great and eternally changing terrestrial drama."[13] In the 1921 etching *Seiltänzer* (Tightrope Walkers), with two people on a rope high above a set—a proof of it is captioned "our self-portrait"— he proffered the figurative symbol of this, which is also a parable for the tensions between the sexes, in this instance himself and his wife, Minna. Their relationship had lost its harmony in real life. In the painting *Das Trapez* (The Trapeze) from two years later

[Plate 73], several men and women with blank expressions contort themselves and cannot come together; they appear paralyzed as if by magic[14]—whereas prior to 1914 the painter had found the vitality of the figurative works of Théodore Géricault and Eugène Delacroix exemplary. In those years before the war, he was painting, much like Corinth, with freer, looser brushwork and no lines. Around 1910 he drew chiaroscuro masses without isolated contour lines, of which many sheets of seashore scenes and the unfinished self-portrait of 1912 are exemplary. They can best be understood and defined as painterly drawings.

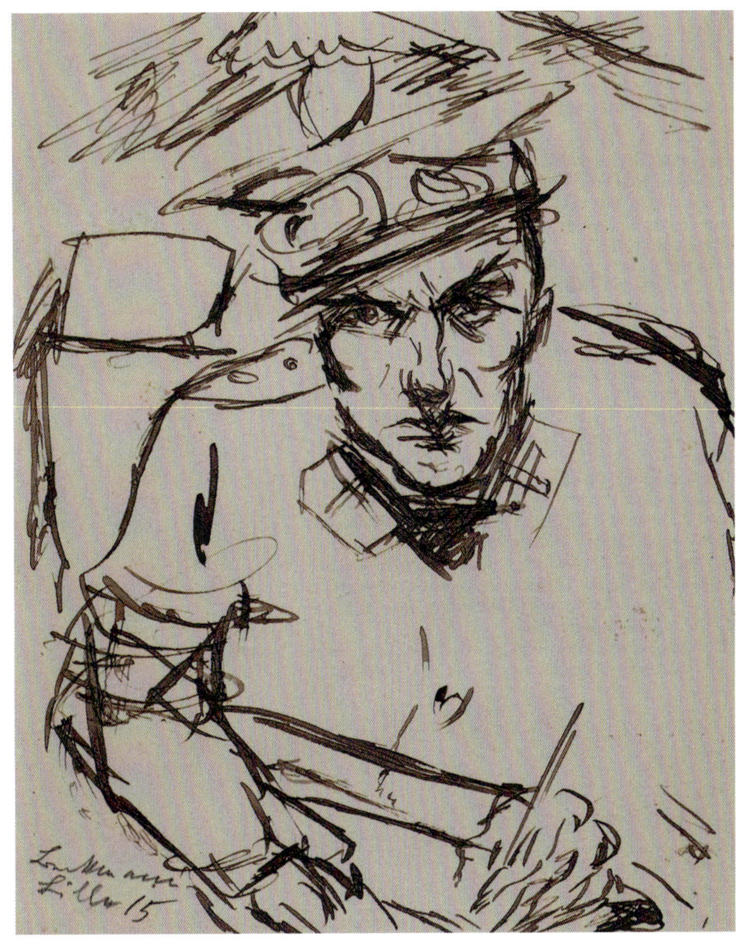

9. Max Beckmann, *Lille 1915*, ink on paper. Private Collection. Photo: Dietrich Schubert, Heidelberg

While on the Western Front near Ypres and Wervik in 1915, Beckmann produced an ink sketch showing himself with the driver's glasses he had worn on a trip to Lille (April 3, 1915) pushed back over his head. He was documenting himself not simply as an observer but as someone who was trying to render what he had seen, including dangerous things, signed at bottom left "Beckmann Lille 15" [Fig. 9].[15] The artist was a voluntary orderly in Feld-Lazarett 9 in the XV. Armeekorps. His early motto was: "I made drawings. That protects a person from death and danger."[16] This sentence, first expressed in a letter October 3, 1914, to Minna, was psychological self-deception, for although drawing may offer a certain "power" over things—in the spirit of Friedrich Nietzsche—it by no means provides security against death in war, as we know well from the fate of the artists killed.[17] Because Beckmann did not to participate in combat, and was not part of a munitions column or in an entrenchment battalion, like his friend the painter Lieutenant Waldemar Rösler near Messines, he was able to draw and write many letters; they are a valuable source. In a letter composed in Roeselaere on March 16, 1915, Beckmann wrote: "Yesterday I was off duty. Instead of going on some short trip or another, I plunged like a wild man into drawing and made self-portraits for seven hours. I hope ultimately to become ever more simplified, ever more concentrated in expression, but I will never—this much I know—give up fullness, roundness, the vitally pulsating. Quite the contrary, I want to intensify it more all the time—you know what I mean by intensified roundness: no arabesques, no calligraphy, but rather fullness and plasticity."[18] These sentences should be understood as a program and be considered for the present essay.

On April 24, 1915, while looking through his new drawings he saw that there were "more than seventy. Seen as a whole, they please

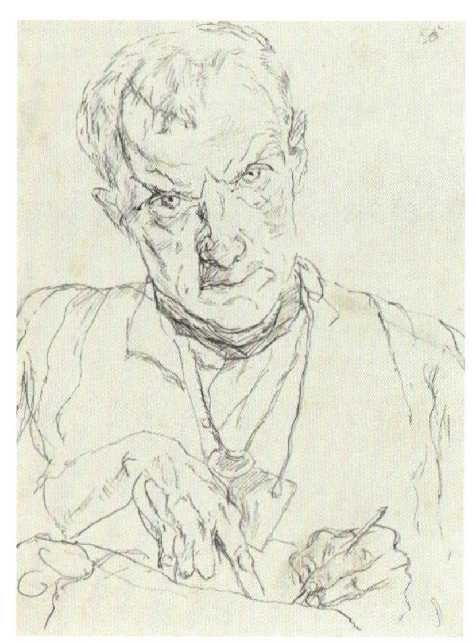

10. Max Beckmann, *Self-Portrait while Drawing*, May 10, 1915, ink on paper. Staatsgalerie Stuttgart, Graphische Sammlung. Photo: © Staatsgalerie Stuttgart

11. Max Beckmann, *The Flemish Woman Seline in the Café Rubens*, April–May 1915, pencil on paper. Private Collection. Photo: von Wiese

me more than individually. It's then possible to see the will they share, which I'm not aware of in the individual drawing, since I only feel and do not think when I draw."[19] At the end of the month Beckmann reported that he had even experienced sulfur nearby: "I really wasn't very scared. A strange, fatalistic feeling of safety surrounded me, so that I was able to draw calmly while not too far from me sulfur grenades hit and the poisonous yellow and green clouds slowly wafted by."[20]

An ink drawing made using a mirror while in the sick ward in Wervik is dated "10.5.15 Verwik" [Fig. 10]. With rapid strokes and trembling hand, Beckmann seems older than he was. His desire to be a witness in this international historical event of the great European war is evident from his intense gaze into the mirror.[21] Although Beckmann did not have to fight in the trenches at the front, while walking through the trenches he experienced terrible things such as the death of a corporal in front of the dugout. On the other hand, looking at the fabulous hips of the women gave him "immense erotic fantasies" (May 23)! Anxiety and gloomy thoughts grew more frequent, as on May 24, 1915: "I had a wonderful apocalyptic dream again. Now probably just about my twentieth."[22] But in the west he also enjoyed the sunsets over the English trench and was very satisfied. In the Café Rubens in early June, he drew a Flemish woman who fascinated him, Seline [Fig. 11], as well as a family; he also sketched portraits of soldiers: Ernst Pflanz, twice, and a Bavarian with a cigar dated "Verwik 17.4.15."

The large, solid form he managed to capture in sketches reveals connections to the portraits that Van Gogh drew in Nuenen in 1885 and painted in Arles in 1888. In 1919, Beckman said to the publisher Reinhard Piper: "Van Gogh is always wonderful. I have much more from him than from Cézanne. Especially as a draftsman, he cannot be placed highly enough! Van Gogh and Dostoevsky are the two reincarnations of Christ."[23] It is not known whether Beckmann was aware that many of Van Gogh's drawings were copies of oil paintings (which still had to dry) and had such a sure stroke for that reason.[24] Beckmann did not, however, succeed with a "large drawing of a young girl" and tore it up. Later he wanted to escape it all, writing on June 7: "Life is a wild, chaotic torture—I wish I were sitting on Mars reading Titan and asleep."[25]

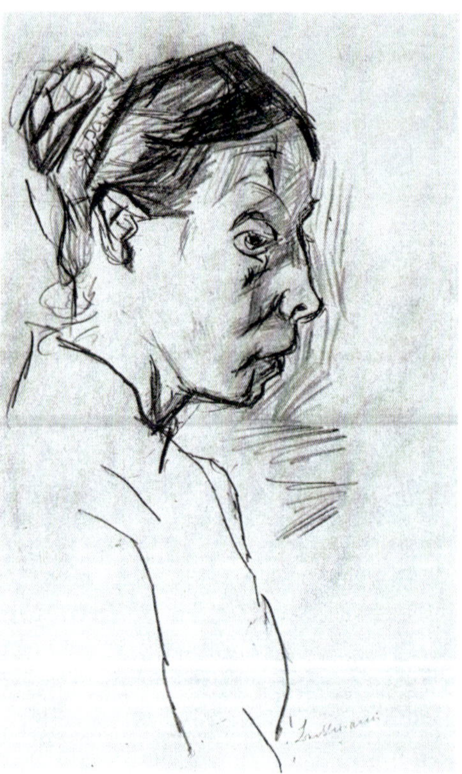

It was long claimed that Beckmann suffered a psychosomatic breakdown near Ypres. But news from Rösler, a lieutenant and company leader in an entrenchment unit near Messines, who met Beckmann in August 1915 while on leave in Brussels—"Beckmann was here on Sunday; he draws undisturbed"—disproves

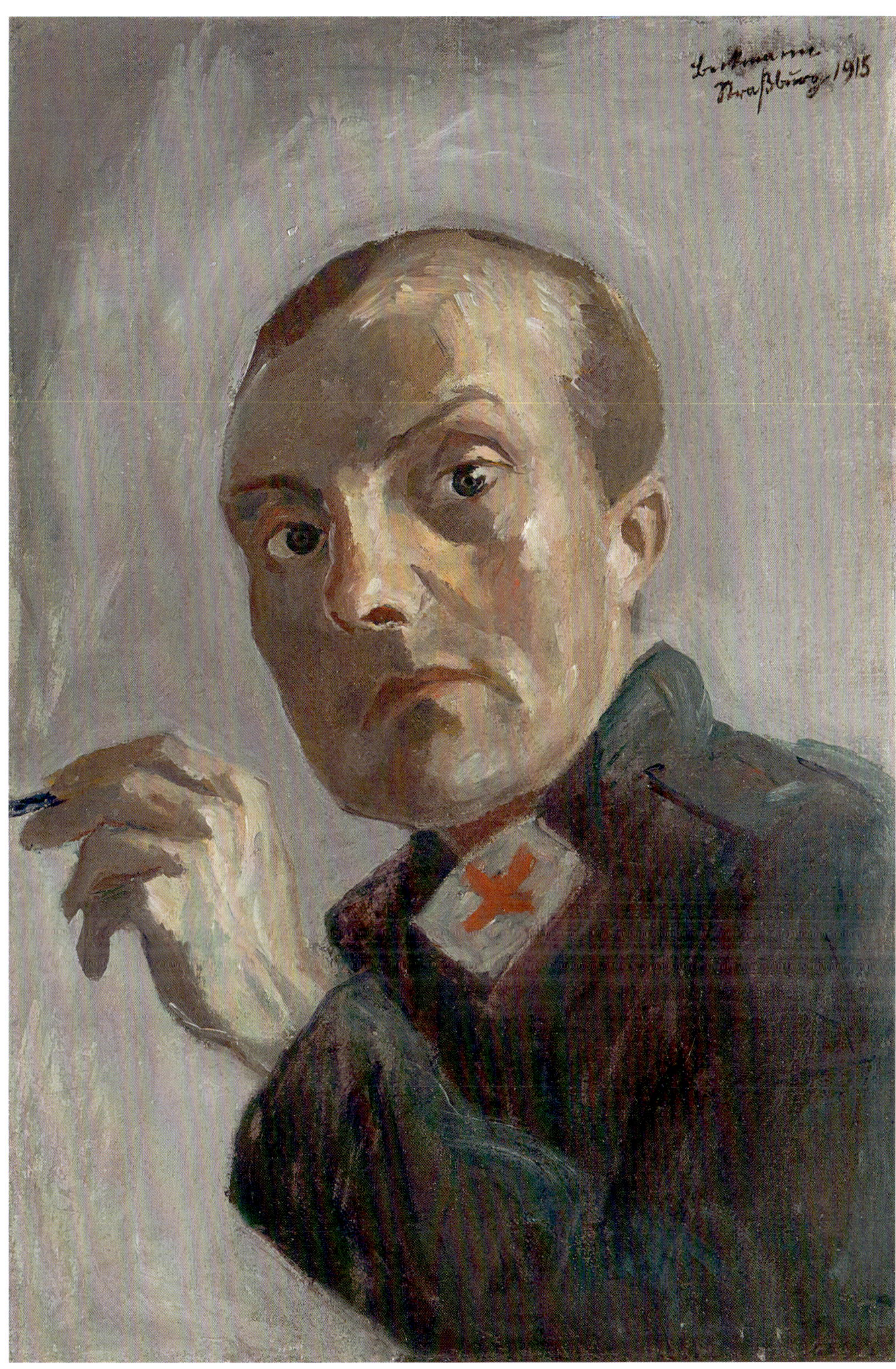

12. Max Beckmann, *Self-Portrait as Medical Orderly*, 1915, oil on canvas. Kunst- und Museumsverein im Von der Heydt-Museum Wuppertal. Photo: Antje Zeis-Loi, Medienzentrum Wuppertal

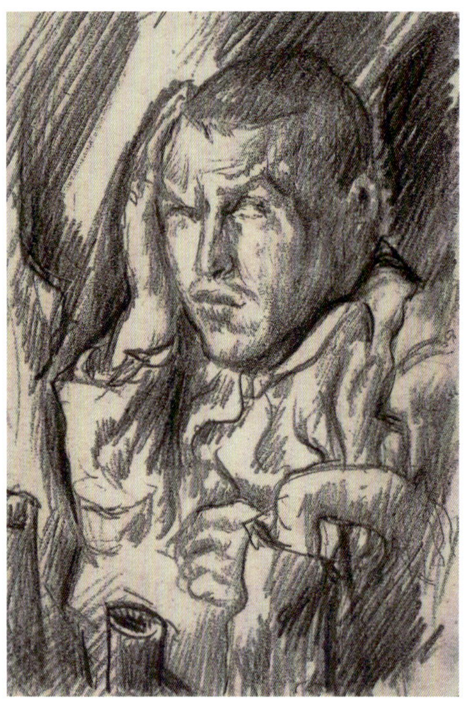

13. Otto Dix, *Self-Portrait at Night in the Dugout before Reims*, postcard from the front, March 20, 1916, Kunstsammlung Gera. Photo: Holger P. Saupe

that assumption.[26] He was then posted to a hygiene institute in Strasbourg, where he made a cursory self-portrait, wearing a green uniform jacket with the Red Cross symbol and looking into the mirror, his hand raised to draw or paint, labeled "Strassburg '15" at top right [Fig. 12]. Beckmann had easy duty there, writing:[27] "You can concentrate on yourself very well." He also offered an illuminating remark in a letter of September 5, 1915: "Work always helps me past my various paranoia attacks."

Around that time, in late September, after lengthy training, Otto Dix was ordered with MG-Trupp 390 (Machine Gun Troop 390) into the bloody fights of the Second Battle of Champagne, south of Rethel. The postcards from the front that Dix sent to his family in Gera and to his girlfriend in Dresden provide a foundation from which to judge his experiences in the hell of modern war, with its machine guns and grenades. Like Dürer in a self-portrait drawing from around 1492, of which Dix had a reproduction, he drew himself in a dugout at night on March 20, 1916 [Fig. 13], drawing or writing a letter, with a worried expression and a dark sense that peace would not come.[28] The postcard from the front is significant; there is no indication of place, but it was probably sent from around Aubérive, and just as important was a card from June 1916 from a machine gun position outside Reims, expressing a desire for peace. From there Dix was sent to the devastating battle on the Somme, near Péronne, which he survived.[29]

At the end of 1915, Beckmann did not return to Berlin but went instead to his friends Fridel and Ugi Battenberg in Frankfurt am Main. He depicted himself with them in a great, expressive etching in 1916, which he titled *Der Abend* (Evening). In 1917, he produced a self-portrait drawing with pen and black ink now in the Sprengel-Museum in Hannover that depicts him drawing, seen in a mirror from the front [Fig. 14]. It might have been a composition study for an oil painting that he produced in 1917 showing him in the corner of an open veranda, wearing a red neckerchief. The thin linework in that drawing is jittery, lifeless, bodiless, spaceless, even provisional and he has rendered himself using a mirror. Beckmann holds the pen out of sight in his left hand and places his right hand (holding a cigarette) on his chest in a confessional attitude.[30] A stylistically similar self-portrait from March 1917 was sketched with trembling strokes, "at night, at four in the morning," from the front with his hand at his neck like a sick man [see Plate 15].[31] The angular form in the foreground is presumably the drawing board. Beckmann did not seek a cerebral art of form but sought instead an art of existence that remained indebted to visible reality—that is to say, an art of reality, like that also postulated by the poet Eduard von Keyserling in the face of the Great War in 1916.[32]

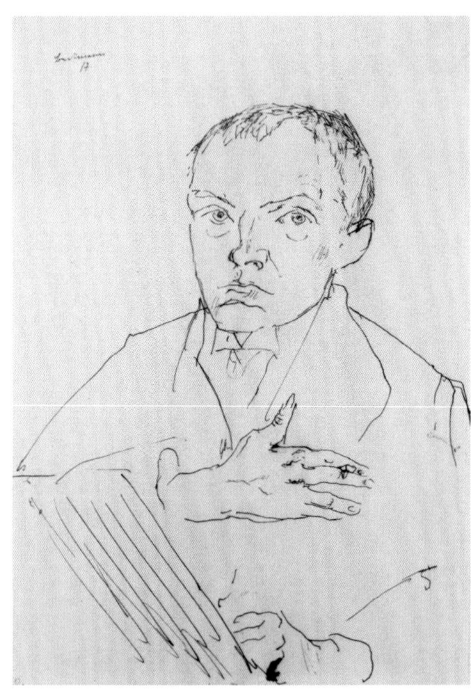

14. Max Beckmann, *Self-Portrait*, 1917, pen and ink on paper. Sprengel-Museum Hannover. Photo: Döring and Lenz

Forcing the terrible monster of the flinching realities of life into "crystal-clear, razor-sharp lines and planes"—as Beckmann described his will to design, in the spirit of Nietzsche's philosophy of vitalism, as part of a will to power[33]—is documented by the great etching *Selbstporträt mit Griffel* (Self-Portrait with Stylus) of 1917 [Fig. 15]: a pathos-laden image of Beckmann portraying himself with the use of a mirror with his eyes darkened and radial lines above his head that perhaps indicate thoughts. He pushes the raised fist of his left hand up to the front edge of the image, revealing the drawing stylus in his right hand, which appears in the reverse due to the mirror. Beckmann submitted this sheet to an exhibition of graphic arts at J. B. Neumann in Berlin in 1917. He wanted to keep his graphic works on his war experience together in time (letter to R. Piper, April 16, 1918) and published them only after the war, but that did not happen. He published this self-portrait as folio 19 with eighteen others in the portfolio *Gesichter* (Faces), edited and with a text by Julius Meier-Graefe and published by Reinhard Piper in 1919. The two self-portraits, folios 1 and 19, document Beckmann's self-centered egocentrism getting out of hand.[34] The visionary depiction of *Self-Portrait with Stylus* goes beyond the simple reproduction of looking at nature, and also beyond simple methods of photography (as do his engravings of war scenes):[35] that is to say, the artist mentally tackles the things that have affected him as an individual and that he still wants to address in his art. Beckmann was able to orient himself around the preface to

15. Max Beckmann, *Self-Portrait with Stylus*, Plate 19, *Faces* portfolio, printed 1916–17, etching on paper. Published 1919. Publisher: Marées-Gesellschaft, R. Piper & Co., Munich. Printer: Franz Hanfstaengl, Munich. The Museum of Modern Art, New York. Gift of Edgar J. Kaufmann, Jr. Photo: © The Museum of Modern Art/ Licensed by SCALA / Art Resource, NY

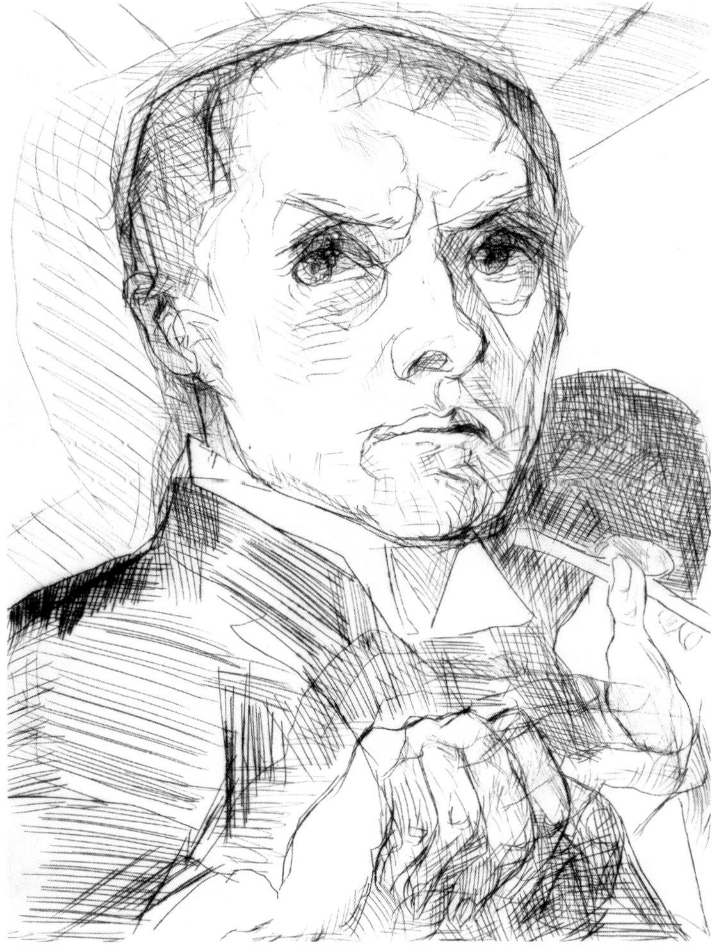

the novel *Pierre et Jean* by Guy de Maupassant (1888), which sets forth the thesis that the work of a realistic artist must go beyond the banal photograph of life and create a kind of vision that is more complex than reality itself. In his text "*Bekenntnis*" (Confession) of 1918, Beckmann postulated that he wanted to depict empathetically the fate of humanity, which is possible only "if we love humanity."[36] His verbal love is, however, very much relativized when he writes to Neumann on November 7, 1920, arrogantly, even haughtily: "There are so few complete people. Most are just pygmies."[37] This hypertrophic judgment of humankind (whom he supposedly loved) was consciously or unconsciously influenced by Nietzsche's *Zarathustra*, second part, "On Redemption," in which the philosopher addresses the blind and the cripples: "Verily, my friends, I walk among men as among the fragments and limbs of men. [...] And how could I bear to be a man if man were not also a creator and guesser of riddles and the redeemer of accidents? [...] Will—that is the name of the liberator and joy-bringer [...]. But now learn this too: the will itself is still a prisoner."[38] In his first years in Frankfurt, up to 1916, Beckmann was working on a large painting on canvas, an important work: his second *Auferstehung* (Resurrection) (now in Stuttgart), which he also called *Die Erscheinung der Toten* (The Manifestation of the Dead). This giant, unfinished painting that assimilates the experiences of the way in a visionary heightening of the earth breaking open, in part in Cubist forms with oversized figures that recall Grünewald was a project for an apocalyptic scene like a *Last Judgment* that he had been planning during the war. However, the scene becomes a kind of nihilistic theater, because instead of Christ the Judge in the sky Beckmann depicts the darkened sun like a black sack.[39] We do not see primarily a vision of resurrection toward the light above, as before, but rather a pessimistic vision of the end of the world essentially inspired by Jean Paul's "*Rede des toten Christus vom Weltgebäude herab, dass kein Gott sei*" (Declaration of the Dead Christ from the Edifice of the World That There Is No God). The work remained unfinished because it could not be finished. In a trench (shelter) at front right, we see the painter with his wife, Minna; his son, Peter; and the two Battenbergs witnessing the event [Fig. 16].

CLOSENESS TO AND DISTANCE FROM *NEUE SACHLICHKEIT*

Kurt Pfister's book *Deutsche Graphiker der Gegenwart*, published in 1920, included Beckmann's etched self-portrait with his eyes turned to the side, holding a stylus—the observer of the *theatrum mundi*, as he liked to call the world of society.[40] The arts of the early 1920s were marked by conflicts of values and artistic styles and by enormous contrasts in themes. In his essay on Dix in 1923, the writer and art critic Carl Einstein observed: "The poles of contemporary art are stretched apart to the breaking point. Constructors, abstractionists established the dictatorship of form; others, like Grosz, Dix, and [Rudolf] Schlichter, demolish the real with pithy objectivity, unmask this era, and force it into self-irony. Painting, a medium of cool execution; observation an instrument of relentless attack."[41]

There were the artists who took a position on the bloody war, its events, its victims, and its consequences for society, such as Käthe Kollwitz, Otto Dix, George Grosz, Otto Griebel, and Rudolf Schlichter, that is, the critical realists (verists); and there were those who tended to an idyllic world view (neo-Biedermeier), such as Georg Schrimpf, Alexander Kanoldt, the fashion painter Christian Schad, Carlo Mense, and Kay Nebel. They caused the war and its social consequences to be forgotten. In the exhibition "*Die Neue Sachlichkeit: Deutsche Malerei seit dem Expressionismus*"

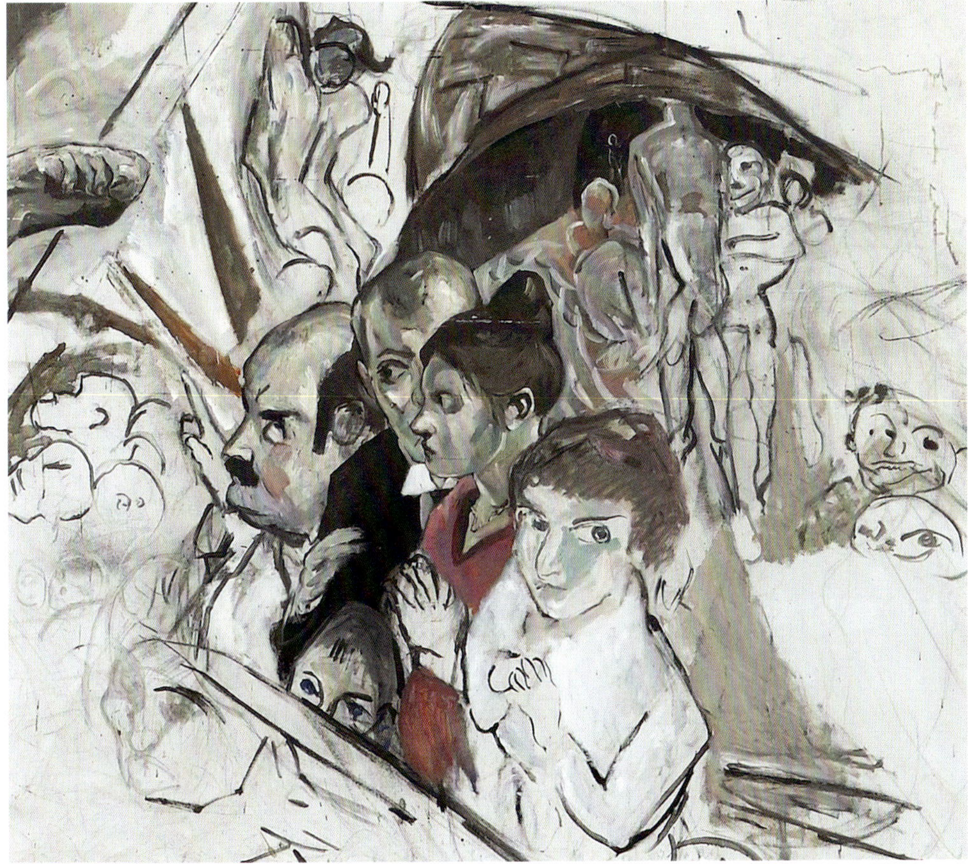

16. Max Beckmann, *Self-Portrait in the Shelter*, detail of *The Resurrection*, 1916–18, oil and charcoal on canvas. Staatsgalerie Stuttgart. Photo: © Staatsgalerie Stuttgart

in 1924–25, the curator Gustav F. Hartlaub in Mannheim gave most of the space—that is, the most paintings—to the latter.[42] The twelve works by Georg Schrimpf embodied pure idyll, Kay Nebel was merely modern kitsch, which Hartlaub apparently did not see; the realist Willy Jaeckel was missing entirely. The painter and graphic artist Ludwig Meidner moved between these fronts, portraying himself several times as a draftsman or etching in an individual late Expressionist style.[43] Hartlaub timidly did not include in his show Dix's radical war painting *Schützengraben* (Trench) of 1922–23, which Meier-Graefe had reviled in a reactionary way in July 1924, although it had an explosive effect and would have separated the fashionable proponents of the *Neue Sachlichkeit* from the critical verists, which Hartlaub was already trying to do with his division into two wings.[44] Beckmann in particular advocated representationalism "in a new art form," paired with objectivity and the effort to cause the invisible to shine through the visible. Although he was represented in Hartlaub's construct by five works (some of them still Expressionist)—nine more paintings were added after the exhibition opened[45]—he increasingly distanced himself from the so-called *Neue Sachlichkeit*: "that is becoming a fashion now, and I have to do everything to escape the bustle that will now grow more and more," he wrote on July 21, 1925, to his young (second) wife, Mathilde. The occasion was a review of the *Neue Sachlichkeit* show in the *Frankfurter Zeitung* on July 20, in which that newspaper called Beckmann the "definitive

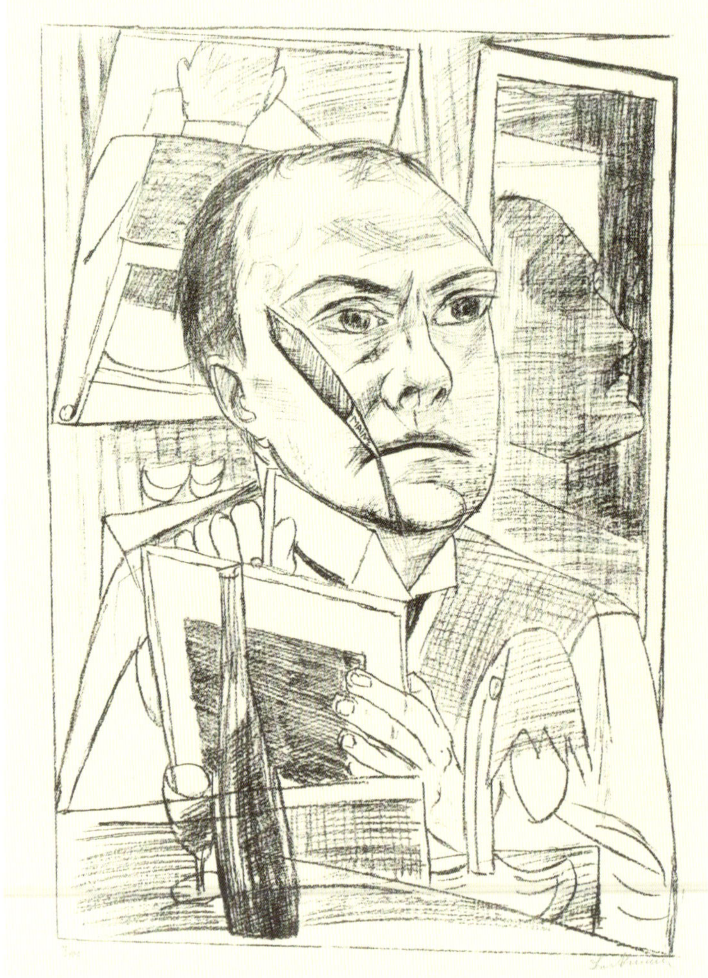

17. Max Beckmann, *Self-Portrait in the Hotel*, Plate 1, *Trip to Berlin* portfolio, 1922, lithograph. Publisher: J. B. Neumann, Berlin. Printer: C. Naumann's Druckerei, Frankfurt am Main, Germany. The Museum of Modern Art, New York. Photo: © The Museum of Modern Art/ Licensed by SCALA / Art Resource, NY

leader"—which is not accurate and did not please him because he had found an individual path forward.[46]

Like other artists in the Weimar Republic, Beckmann worked on cycles of prints for the public, but he never produced a cycle on the war and its consequences; he wanted to be the arranger of current events: that led to a semipolitical cycle on contemporary events in 1919: *Die Hölle* (Hell) with a self-portrait on the cover. In part inspired by German late Gothic and Parisian Cubism, these prints represented an effort to synthesize figures and tight spaces on the picture plane, but in several of them (e.g., *Die Strasse* [The Street]) the composition is so overfilled that they look like failures.[47] In the year of his exhibition at the Kunstverein Frankfurt, Beckmann published the cycle of lithographs *Jahrmarkt* (Annual Fair) in April 1921. In his review of that exhibition in the *Frankfurter Zeitung* of April 23, 1921, Wilhelm Hausenstein called the artist a "*Malerzeichner*" (painter-draftsman), which was also said of Max Liebermann.[48]

This was followed in 1922 by the ten prints of the cycle *Berliner Reise* (Trip to Berlin). Its cover shows the artist standing with a suitcase in front of an advertising column that announces the titles of the prints inside. The first folio is a self-portrait in a bar or hotel with a sketchbook and pen in his right hand [Fig. 17], a bottle of wine before him, a cigar in his mouth, in front of mirrors in which his profile is reflected in the shadow.[49] In keeping with his theory of art, Beckmann was clearly transforming the round into the plane and building up the composition in an almost tectonic way. Now, as in his paintings, he found his new style of larger forms and of a synthesis of space and plane, which meant a certain abstraction from reality. The inspiration he had found in the paintings of the naive painter Henri Rousseau, nicknamed "le Dounaier" (customs officer), in Paris faded.[50] Nevertheless, Beckmann was well informed about earlier artists. On December 27, 1925, he wrote to Reinhard Piper to thank him for Charles de Tolnay's book on Pieter Bruegel the Elder as draftsman: "another especially great one."

Because Beckmann admired Eugène Delacroix, it is reasonable to assume that he was familiar with his theory of drawing, namely, not employing the isolated line. As Delacroix had emphasized, the single, isolated line and the contour do not exist in nature but are rather abstractions by the human imagination and hand. It was necessary to draw out of the centers of the motifs with parallel hatching—"*par les milieux*" (by means of the inner masses)—and not by means of contours as the followers of Jean-Auguste Dominique Ingres had done.[51] This dispensing of the isolated line was rigorous and established the French colorism from which the draftsman Vincent van Gogh also worked out a clear concept in 1885, with an eye to Rembrandt and Frans Hals; in the autumn of 1887, Van Gogh wrote to the painter Horace M. Levens that true drawing means modeling with color.[52]

PROSPECT

As the democracy of the Weimar Republic was gradually destroyed by the Nazis step by step, many artists, especially the sociocritical verists, had to fear for their existence. Otto Dix in Dresden, who was not a member of any political party, portrayed himself in 1933, the first year of the National Socialist dictatorship, as a draftsman with a drawing pad and in 1934 as a soldier in a steel helmet in the (Old Master–style) painting *Triumph des Todes* (The Triumph of Death).[53] During these early years of the National Socialist dictatorship, several artists, especially the critical realists, portrayed themselves in a way that attempted to communicate the spiritual and physical threat to their existence as part of the message.[54] Although Beckmann had already been dismissed from the Städel-Schule in Frankfurt on April 15, 1933, just as Dix was from the Kunstakademie in Dresden in April as well, he as in less danger than Dix, who

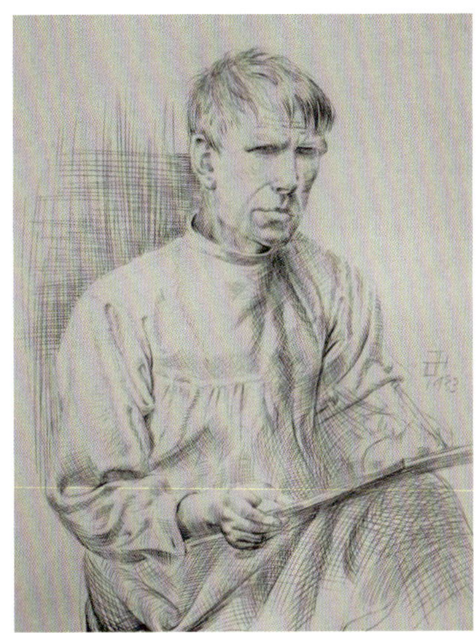

18. Otto Dix, *Self-Portrait* 1933, silverpoint on paper. Photo: Fritz Löffler

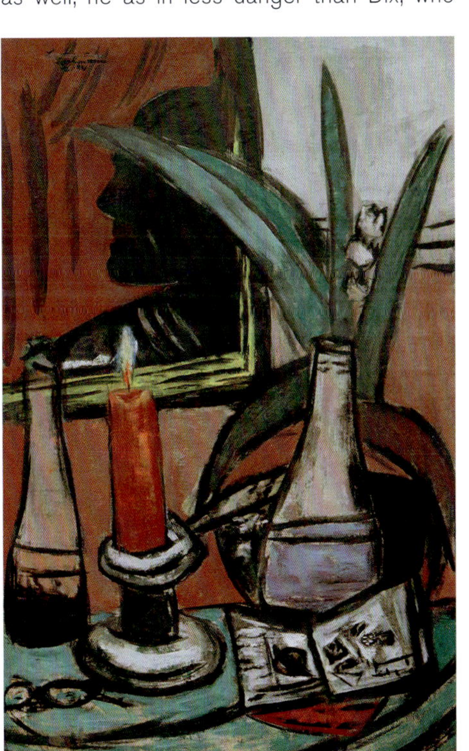

19. Max Beckmann, *Self-Portrait in a Large Mirror with Candle*, 1933, oil on canvas. Private Collection, Southern Germany. Photo: akg-images

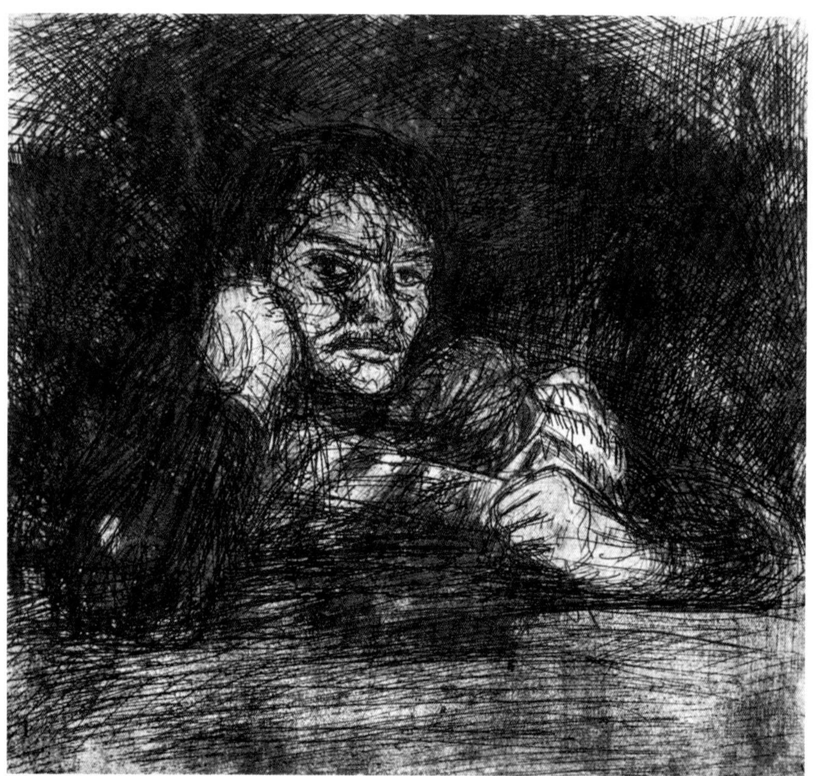

20. Alfred Hrdlicka, *Self-Portrait as Draftsman at Night*, 1959–61, etching. Private Collection. Photo: Dietrich Schubert, Heidelberg

was being persecuted for the fifty etchings of *Der Krieg* (War) of 1924, which were reviled as a "sabotage of the military" owing to their verist character. And, famously, Beckmann's paintings remained on view for a time in the Nationalgalerie in Berlin, to which he had moved in January.[55] At this time, Dix adopted a drawing technique that the Old Masters had practiced in the fifteenth century: the silverpoint. In his self-portrait of 1933 [Fig. 18], he is wearing the white smock he had worn as a professor at the academy. He gazes piercingly at his own face to confirm his own existence and to show the outside world that he is close to the famous early German artists of the late Gothic: Grünewald, Baldung Grien, Lucas Cranach, and Albrecht Dürer.[56] Was he now trying to protect himself from defamation by Nazi functionaries? We know of no self-portraits as draftsman by Beckman from these early years of the dictatorship. But in *Selbstbildnis im großen Spiegel mit Kerze* (Still-Portrait in a Large Mirror with Candle), with a burning candle, he added a profile of his head in black in 1933, which has been interpreted as a reference to a possible, coming threat [Fig. 19].[57] But the burning candle precisely in the axis of his profile is an optimistic symbol of life. In the open book in the foreground, we recognize Saturn, Beckmann's astrological sign; he believed that he was influenced by that planet god, and viewed himself as a child of Saturn.

A continuity can be found tracing from Rembrandt to Beckmann to the Viennese sculptor and graphic artist Alfred Hrdlicka. Hrdlicka admired the bleakness of Rembrandt's etchings as exemplary, and in a similar way depicted himself as a draftsman in his early work of 1959–61 [Fig. 20].[58] The darkness of night surrounds the sculptor, who portrays himself in a melancholic state, almost depressed. At that time, the so-called "Art Informel," was dominant in Vienna. Hrdlicka had to face the phalanx of abstract, nonobjective painters and sculptors, such as Josef Mikl and Karl Prantl, and assert himself. For the tricentennial of Rembrandt's death in 1969, Hrdlicka wrote the essay "Mein Rembrandt" (My Rembrandt), thereby reclaiming the Old Master for himself. The year before Hrdlicka had produced an etching as a variation on Rembrandt's *Night Watch* in eight steps.[59] Hrdlicka's artistic credo was: "In the human effort to grasp the world, clarity clearly ranks above abstraction."

In the century-old battle of realism versus abstraction, which continues to smolder and to feed the discourse on the arts, Hrdlicka joined Oskar Kokoschka on the side of the critics and opponents of nonobjective art, and he expressed his conviction in several texts; Kokoschka had also done so in his text on Edvard Munch and in his 1954 essay

"Gegenstandslose Kunst?" (Nonobjective Art?),[60] describing the abstract as a "flight from the world." Nietzsche would have labeled abstraction as a "slander of the world." Hrdlicka once said: "All realists have always had to be capable of being the best at abstraction."

Translated from the German by Steven Lindberg

1 Svetlana Alpers, *The Art of Describing: Dutch Art in the Seventeenth Century* (Chicago: University of Chicago Press, 1983), 43; Ulrich Pfisterer and Valeska von Rosen, eds., *Der Künstler als Kunstwerk* (Stuttgart: Reclam, 2005).

2 See Kirk T. Varnedoe, ed., *Modern Portraits: The Self & Others*, exh. cat. Columbia University, New York (New York: Wildenstein, 1976); Anthony Bond and Joanna Woodall, *Self-Portrait: Renaissance to Contemporary* (London: National Portrait Gallery, 2005). See also Alfred Neumeyer, *Der Blick aus dem Bilde* (Berlin: Gebr. Mann, 1964); Renate Trnek, ed., *Selbstbild: Der Künstler und sein Bildnis*, exh. cat. Akademie der bildenden Künste, Vienna (Ostfildern: Hatje Cantz, 2004), and Jacques Derrida, *Memoirs of the Blind: The Self-Portrait and Other Ruins*, trans. Pascale-Anne Brault and Michael Naas (Chicago: University of Chicago Press, 1993); Tobias G. Natter, ed., *The Self-Portrait from Schiele to Beckmann*, exh. cat. Neue Galerie, New York (Munich et al.: Prestel, 2019).

3 *Grünewald in der Moderne: Die Rezeption Matthias Grünewalds im 20. Jahrhundert*, ed. Brigitte Schad and Thomas Ratzka, exh. cat. Galerie der Stadt Aschaffenburg (Cologne: Wienand, 2002), 29; Werner Frick and Günter Schnitzler, eds., *Der Isenheimer Altar: Werk und Wirkung* (Froiburg: Rombach, 2010), 48 (in the text by Anna Schreurs-Morét).

4 Wilhelm Pinder, *Rembrandts Selbstbildnisse* (Königstein: Langewiesche, 1956), 75; Richard Hamann, *Rembrandt* (Berlin: Safari, 1948), 23–24; Christopher White and Quentin Buvelot, *Rembrandt by Himself* (London: National Gallery Publications, 1999; The Hague: Royal Cabinet of Paintings Mauritshuis, 1999), no. 47; Holm Bevers, *Rembrandt Drawings from the Berlin Kupferstichkabinett*, exh. cat. Rembrandt House Museum, Amsterdam (Ostfildern: Hatje Cantz, 2007), cat. no. 17, 98; Volker Manuth, *Rembrandt: Die Selbstbildnisse* (Cologne: Taschen, 2019), 94; also important here, Otto Pächt, *Rembrandt* (Munich: Prestel, 1991), 65–78.

5 White and Buvelot, *Rembrandt by Himself* (see note 4), cat. no. 62. On Rembrandt's diverse portraiture, see the impressive interpretations by the philosopher Georg Simmel: Georg Simmel, *Rembrandt: An Essay in the Philosophy of Art*, ed. and trans. Alan Scott and Helmut Staubmann with K. Peter Etzkorn (New York: Routledge, 2005; orig. pub. in German in 1916), 61–66 and 66–68.

6 White and Buvelot, *Rembrandt by Himself* (see note 4), cat. no. 70. The Gemäldegalerie in Dresden has a good copy in oil: Harald Marx and Gregor J. M. Weber, *The Old Masters Picture Gallery in Dresden*, trans. Dorothy Ann Schade-Maurice (Munich: Deutscher Kunstverlag, 1993), 315.

7 Pascal Bonafoux, *Portraits of the Artist: The Self-Portrait in Painting* (New York: Skira/Rizzoli, 1985); Robert Hughes, *Goya* (New York: Alfred A. Knopf, 2003), 44–45.

8 Margret Stuffmann, *Goya Zeichnungen und Druckgraphik*, exh. cat. Städelsches Kunstinstitut, Frankfurt am Main (Stuttgart: Cantz'sche Druckerei, 1981); Werner Hofmann, Edith Helman, and Martin Warnke, *Goya: "Alle werden fallen"* (Frankfurt am Main: Europäische Verlagsanstalt, 1981), 24, 31.

9 Max Klinger, *Malerei und Zeichnung, Tagebuchaufzeichnungen und Briefe*, ed. Anne Hübscher (Leipzig: Reclam, 1985), 113; on this, see Dieter Gleisberg, "'Ich muss mir stets ein kleines Monument errichten' : Max Klinger in seinen Selbstdarstellungen," in *Max Klinger*, ed. Dieter Gleisberg, exh. cat. Städelsches Kunstinstitut, Frankfurt am Main (Leipzig: Edition Leipzig, 1992), 13–25; Friedrich Gross, "Klingers graphische Modernität," in *Max Klinger Zeichnungen Zustandsdrucke Zyklen*, exh. cat. Villa Stuck, Munich (Munich: Prestel, 1996), 68–77.

10 On Menzel, see Siegmar Holsten, *Das Bild des Künstlers: Selbstdarsstellungen* (Hamburg: Christians, 1978), 65; Werner Hofmann, ed., *Menzel der Beobachter* (Munich: Prestel, 1982), 35–36; Jost Hermand, *Adolf Menzel* (Reinbek bei Hamburg: Rowohlt, 1986), 15.

11 Claus Grimm, *Rembrandt selbst: Eine Neubewertung seiner Porträtkunst* (Stuttgart: Belser, 1991), 8, fig. 2. On Rembrandt's principle of chiaroscuro, see Christoph Wagner, "Umbra et potentia: Visuelle Metaphern," in Werner Busch et al., eds., Ähnlichkeit und Entstellung: Entgrenzungstendenzen des Porträts (Berlin: Deutscher Kunstverlag, 2010), 47ff.

12 Klaus Gallwitz, *Lovis Corinth: Das Portrait*, KV Karlsruhe 1967; on Corinth, in addition to the monographs, see Oliver Jehle, "Durch alle Finsternis: Corinths späte Selbstbildnisse," in Busch et al., Ähnlichkeit und Entstellung (see note 11), 135–36.

13 Max Beckmann, *Self-Portrait in Words: Collected Writings and Statements, 1903–1950*, ed. Barbara Copeland Buenger, trans. Barbara Copeland Buenger and Reinhold Heller with David Britt (Chicago, IL: University of Chicago Press, 1997), 298–307, esp. 303. Beckmann may also have been recalling the speeches in Nietzsche's *Zarathustra*, although the tightrope walker (in the preface) falls! In 1948, Beckmann wrote: "We are all tightrope walkers"; Max Beckmann, "Letters to a Woman Painter," in Beckmann, *Self-Portrait in Words* (see note 13), 312–17, esp. 317.; see Olaf Peters, *Vom schwarzen Seiltänzer: Max Beckmann zwischen Weimarer Republik und Exil* (Berlin: Reimer, 2005).

14 Klaus Gallwitz, *Beckmann in Frankfurt* (Frankfurt am Main: Insel, 1985), 56; Holger Jacob-Friesen, *Max Beckmann: Druckgraphik*, Staatliche Kunsthalle, Karlsruhe (Heidelberg: Kehrer, 2005), 113. The significance of these more profound contexts is discussed in Thomas Noll, "Spiegelungen des Selbst: Beckmann in seinen Bildern," in *Signatur und Selbstbild*, ed. Sebastian Karnatz and Nico Kirchberger (Berlin: Reimer, 2019), 90–111, esp. 90 and 98.

15 In blue ink that has oxidized to brown; see Reinhard Piper, *Mein Leben als Verleger* (Munich: Piper, 1964), 319; Stephan von Wiese, *Max Beckmanns zeichnerisches Werk, 1903–1925* (Düsseldorf: Droste, 1978), cat. no. 258; Thomas Döhring and Christian Lenz, *Max Beckmann: Selbstbildnisse; Zeichnungen, Druckgraphik*, exh. cat. Neue Pinakothek, Munich (Braunschweig: Braus, 2000), no. 23 (auctioned by Hauswedell & Nolte in Hamburg in 2004). On this, see Dietrich Schubert, *Max Beckmann: Vom Vietzker-Strand zur Departure* (Petersberg: Michael Imhof, 2021), 68 and fig. 47; see also Christian Lenz, *Max Beckmann* (Münster: Rhema, 2022), 55–56.

16 Max Beckmann to Minna Beckmann-Tube, October 3, 1914, in Beckmann, *Self-Portrait in Words* (see note 13), 140–41, esp. 140; see Erhard Göpel, *Beckmann der Zeichner*, 2nd. ed. (Munich: Piper, 1958); Andreas Stolzenburg, "'Meine Kunst kriegt hier zu fressen': Beckmann im Ersten Weltkrieg, 1914/15," in *Max Beckmann: Zeichnungen aus dem Nachlass Mathilde Q. Beckmann*, exh. cat. (Leipzig: Museum der Bildenden Künste,1998), 16–39; *Max Beckmann: Der Zeichner*, exh. cat. Galerie Albstadt, Städtische Kunstsammlungen (Albstadt: Galerie Albstadt, 2001), esp. Christian Lenz, "Beckmann als Zeichner," 7–25, and Claudia Schönjahn on the war sketches, 51–56.

17 See Dietrich Schubert, *Künstler im Trommelfeuer des Krieges, 1914–1918* (Heidelberg: Wunderhorn, 2014).

18 Max Beckmann to Minna Beckmann-Tube, March 16, 1915, in Beckmann, *Self-Portrait in Words* (see note 13), 149.

19 Max Beckmann to Minna Beckmann-Tube, April 24, 1915, in Beckmann, *Self-Portrait in Words* (see note 13), 169.

20 Max Beckmann to Minna Beckmann-Tube, Verwick (he always spelled the town either that way or as Verwik), April 28, 1915, 163–64, esp. 163. It should be noted that the German military was the first to employ poison gas, near Ypres, even though it was banned and prohibited—making it a war crime. See Olivier Lepick, *La Grande Guerre chimique, 1914–1918* (Paris: Presses universitaires de France, 1998).

21 Von Wiese, *Max Beckmanns zeichnerisches Werk* (see note 15), cat. no. 280; Dietrich Schubert, *Max Beckmann, Auferstehung und Erscheinung der Toten* (Worms: Werner, 1985), 75; Wolfgang J. Mommsen, ed., *Kultur und Krieg: Die Rolle der Intellektuellen, Künstler und Schriftsteller im Ersten Weltkrieg* (Munich: Oldenbourg, 1996); Corinna Höper, *Kollwitz, Beckmann, Dix, Grosz: Kriegszeit*, ed. Sean Rainbird, exh. cat. Staatsgalerie Stuttgart (Tübingen: Wasmuth, 2011), 95–96; Uwe M. Schneede, *ICH! Selbstbildnisse in der Moderne* (Munich: C. H. Beck, 2022).

22 Max Beckmann to Minna Beckmann-Tube, May 24, 1915, in Beckmann, *Self-Portrait in Words* (see note 13), 172–73, esp. 173.

23 Quoted in von Wiese, *Max Beckmanns zeichnerisches Werk* (see note 15), 64–65 and n. 187; described as the "derivation" method in Christian Lenz, "Max Beckmann und Van Gogh," *Hefte des Max Beckmann- Archivs*, no. 3 (2000): 31. The hypertrophic view of Van Gogh as a kind of Christ may have been inspired by Meier-Graefe's talks around 1919, when he was writing his *Vincent van Gogh*, published in a large format by Piper in 1921.

24 See especially the outstanding catalogue by Colta Ives et al., *Vincent van Gogh: The Drawings* (New York: Metropolitan Museum of Art; Amsterdam: Van Gogh Museum; New Haven, CT: Yale University Press, 2005).

25 Max Beckmann to Minna Beckmann-Tube, June 7, 1915, in Beckmann, *Self-Portrait in Words* (see note 13), 175. The drawings are in Uwe M. Schneede, ed., *Der Zeichner und Grafiker Beckmann*, exh. cat. (Hamburg: Kunstverein, 1979), 25 and 26; von Wiese, *Max Beckmanns zeichnerisches Werk* (see note 15), p. 61; "Titan" was Beckmann's favorite book by Jean Paul, as is clear from Reinhard Piper's memoirs (see note 15).

26 In the letters and postcards that Rösler sent to his family, Kurt Badt, and Richard Engelmann, I found this sentence in a letter to the sculptor Engelmann in Weimar on August 5, 1915; see Dietrich Schubert, "Lovis Corinths Text 'Krieg und Kunst' vom Dezember 1915 und Waldemar Röslers Reaktion im Schützengraben," *Jahrbuch der Berliner Museen*, n.s. 56 (2014): 139–50, and Schubert, *Max Beckmann* (see note 15), 78 and 86; see also Stolzenburg, "'Meine Kunst kriegt hier zu fressen'" (see note 16). As late as 2011, Corinna

Höper was still writing about a "total psychological breakdown"—a legend that should be retired; Höper, *Kollwitz, Beckmann, Dix, Grosz* (see note 14), 99.

27 Uwe M. Schneede, ed., *Max Beckmann: Selbstbildnisse*, exh. cat. Hamburger Kunsthalle (Stuttgart: Hatje, 1993), cat. no. 8; see my review in *Kritische Berichte* 21, no. 3 (1993): 91–97. On his duty in Strasbourg, see Christiane Zeiller, "'Es ist sehr eigentümlich hier, man kann sich sehr auf sich selbst concentrieren': Max Beckmann in Strassburg," *Beckmann-Beiträge, 2004–2005*, Hefte des Max-Beckmann-Archivs 8, ed. Christian Lenz (2006): 95–107; Uwe M. Schneede, ed., *1914: Die Avantgarden im Kampf*, exh. cat. Kunst- und Ausstellungshalle der Bundesrepublik Deutschland, Bonn (Cologne: Snoeck, 2014); Schubert, *Max Beckmann* (see note 15), 84–85; Lenz, *Max Beckmann* (see note 15), 60–61, 296 n. 5.

28 See Dietrich Schubert, *Otto Dix mit Selbstzeugnissen*, 9th ed. (Reinbek bei Hamburg: Rowohlt, 2019), 21–25; Bertrand Lorquin, ed., *Allemagne: Les années noires*, exh. cat. Musée Maillol, Paris (Paris: Gallimard, 2007), 73–89, and frontispiece. Dix, a noncommissioned officer, had to keep fighting the following years up to the autumn of 1918 in France, Russia, and Flanders. See Ulrike Lorenz, *Otto Dix: Grüsse aus dem Krieg; die Feldpostkarten der Otto-Dix-Sammlung in der Kunstgalerie Gera* (Gera: Kunstgalerie Gera, 1991), 21–22; Dietrich Schubert, *Künstler im Trommelfeuer, 1914–1918* (Heidelberg: Wunderhorm, 2014), 222–24; Olaf Peters, *Otto Dix: Der unerschrockene Blick: Eine Biographie* (Stuttgart: Reclam, 2013), 41–42.

29 On the large-scale attack of the British and French in July 1916 on the Somme and Otto Dix, see Gerd Krumeich, Gerhard Hirschfeld, and Irina Renz, *Die Deutschen an der Somme, 1914–1918: Krieg, Besatzung, Verbrannte Erde*, 2nd ed. (Essen: Klartext, 2016), 191–211.

30 See *Max Beckmann in Frankfurt*, exh. cat. (Frankfurt am Main: Städel-Museum, 1983), cat. no. 108; Christian Lenz in Döhring and Lenz, *Max Beckmann* (see note 15), 160.

31 Not in Döhring and Lenz, *Max Beckmann* (see note 15); it was exhibited at the Centre Georges Pompidou in Paris and Tate Modern in London in 2002–3, see Sean Rainbird, ed., *Max Beckmann*, exh. cat. (London: Tate Publishing, 2002), cat. no. 17, 47.

32 Eduard von Keyserling, *Die kommende Kunst*, quoted in Käthe Kollwitz, *Die Tagebücher* (Berlin: Akademie, 1989), 226 (February 21, 1916).

33 Beckmann famously expressed himself in this way when he wrote his "*Bekenntnis*" in 1918 and published it in 1920 in *Schöpferische Konfession*, ed. Kasimir Edschmid. Especially before the war began in 1914, he read the writings of Friedrich Nietzsche, and during the war read *Zarathustra* near Wervik, for example, on March 28, 1915. On the "will to power," see Hans Barth, *Wahrheit und Ideologie* (Frankfurt am Main: Suhrkamp, 1974), 215–21.

34 The portfolio was initially going to be titled *Welttheater* (Theater of the World), but Meier-Graefe proposed *Gesichter* (Faces), which Beckmann adopted. Ursula Harter and Stephan von Wiese, *Max Beckmann und J. B. Neumann: Der Künstler und sein Händler in Briefen und Dokumenten, 1917–1950* (Cologne: Walther König, 2011), 38–39; Alexander Dückers, ed., *Gesichter der Zeit: Ein Panorama aus Physiognomien in Zeichnung und Graphik*, exh. cat. Kupferstichkabinett, Berlin (Berlin: Nikolai, 1999), 72–73; Döhring and Christian Lenz, *Max Beckmann* (see note 15), esp. Lenz, "Sachlichkeit den inneren Gesichten," 9–42; Schubert, *Max Beckmann* (see note 15), chap. 3, 91–92, and fig. 75. See also the half-length figure holding a pencil and turning over his left shoulder, in two versions dated December 3, 1917, from the estate of Barbara Göpel (Kupferstichkabinett, Berlin); see Göpel, *Beckmann der Zeichner* (see note 16), cat. no. 13; Andreas Schalhorn, *Das Vermächtnis Barbara Göpel* (Berlin: Staatliche Museen zu Berlin, 2018).

35 James Hofmaier treated the various war engravings as a loose group of works in James Hofmaier, "Max Beckmann als Graphiker," *Max Beckmann*, ed. Siegfried Gohr, exh. cat. (Cologne: Josef-Haubrich-Kunsthalle, 1984), 153–54.

36 Max Beckmann, "Creative Credo" (September 1918) in Beckmann, *Self-Portrait in Words* (see note 13), 181–85, esp. 184.

37 Harter and von Wiese, *Max Beckmann und J. B. Neumann* (see note 34), 49; Thomas Noll in Karnatz and Kirchberger, *Signatur und Selbstbild* (see note 14), 108 n. 59. Christian Lenz also comments on this problem of Beckmann's inclination/disinclination vis-à-vis people and uses the opportunity to sweepingly dismiss the works of Dix and George Grosz once again; see Lenz, *Max Beckmann* (see note 15), 94.

38 Friedrich Nietzsche, *Thus Spoke Zarathustra*, in *The Portable Nietzsche*, ed. and trans. Walter Kaufmann (New York: Penguin, 1976), 250–53. The ambivalence between wanting—that is to say, the will bound in the *Lebensstrom* (Georg Simmel) as "thing-in-itself" ("lack of freedom of the will," diary, July 4, 1946)—and the free will in the drive to create (*Zarathustra*, second part, "On Redemption": "The will is a creator"), on the one hand, and being caught up in the drives of the body, on the other hand, was Beckmann's crux into the 1940s. (On this, see the passage in the fourth act of his drama *Das Hotel*.) As late as July 4, 1946, he commented in his diary on cursed "vegetative corporeality," that is, the sexuality that dominated Beckmann—from which he hoped work on his art could provide the final salvation. *Gestaltung ist Erlösung* (Creation is salvation) was the faith and

the motto that he proclaimed in 1948 in his fictive letters to a woman painter. But salvation from what?!" the reader asks, and refers to Nietzsche's profound text no. 853 in the (posthumous) book *Der Wille zur Macht* (The Will to Power). Art is the salvation of the one who perceives, who perceives tragically; art is the salvation of the sufferer. In the later paintings of the 1940s, Beckmann was still confronting the young, erotically charged woman with the sculptural torso of a man whom she can no longer reach (*Atelier*, 1946). Cf. the letters to a woman painter: "the will to form carries in itself one part of the salvation you are seeking." Max Beckmann, "Letters to a Woman Painter," in Beckmann, *Self-Portrait in Words* (see note 13), 312–17, esp. 317. On this, see Dieter Gleisberg, "Gestaltung ist Erlösung" in *Max Beckmann*, exh. cat. (Leipzig 1984), 2–8.

39 Concerning Grünewald's topicality at the time, it is important to recall that his great altarpiece in Colmar was brought to Munich at the end of the war in 1918 to be restored and exhibited and was admired by many artists. In 1919, Reinhard Piper published a large-format volume of plates with a text by Oskar Hagen: *Grünewalds Isenheimer Altar*; cf. the review by Eckart von Sydow in *Feuer*, no. 2 (1920): 715–16. On the *Auferstehung* paintings of 1908 and 1916–18, see Schubert, *Max Beckmann* (see note 19); brief information in Amy K. Hamlin, "Figuring Redemption: Christianity and Modernity in Beckmann's *Resurrection*," in *ReVisioning: Critical Methods of Seeing Christianity in the History of Art*, ed. James Romaine and Linda Stratford (Eugene, OR: Cascade, 2014), 294–309; Hubertus Kohle, "Transzendieren ohne Transzendenz?," *Das MÜNSTER* 51, no. 2 (1998): 135–45; most recently, Lenz, *Max Beckmann* (see note 15), 66–71, with assessment of the older literature.

40 Kurt Pfister, *Deutsche Graphiker der Gegenwart* (Leipzig: Klinkhardt & Biermann, 1920); see *Max Beckmann: Zwanzig Selbstbildnisse—eine Privatsammlung*, auct. cat. (Berlin: Villa Grisebach, 2007), no. 60.

41 Carl Einstein, "Otto Dix," trans. Dan Raneau, in *The Weimar Republic Sourcebook*, ed. Anton Kaes, Martin Jay, and Edward Dimendberg (Berkeley: University of California, 1994), 190–91, esp. 490; orig. pub. as "Otto Dix," *Das Kunstblatt* 7, no. 3 (1923): 97–102, esp. 97; Paul F. Schmidt, "Die deutschen Veristen,": *Das Kunstblatt* 8 (1924): 367–72.

42 Gustav F. Hartlaub, ed., *Neue Sachlichkeit: Deutsche Malerei seit dem Expressionismus, 14. Juni–13. Sept. 1925*, exh. cat. (Mannheim: Städtische Kunsthalle, 1925). In his preface Hartlaub remarked that "an extensive collection" of Beckmann's works was added "at the height of summer." For another perspective, see Franz Roh, *Nach-Expressionismus: Magischer Realismus; Probleme der neuesten europäischen Malerei* (Leipzig: Klinkhardt & Biermann, 1925); Franz Roh, "Otto Dix und die heutige Malerei Deutschlands," *Neue Zürcher Zeitung*, March 7, 1929. More recently, see *Realismus und Sachlichkeit: Aspekte deutscher Kunst, 1919–1933*, ed. Roland März and Gottfried Riemann, exh. cat. Nationalgalerie, East Berlin (Berlin: Staatliche Museen, 1974); see also Dieter Gleisberg, *Conrad Felixmüller: Leben und Werk* (Dresden: Verlag der Kunst, 1982), 55; Gleisberg distinguished between critical verism and the anemic Biedermeier of the so-called *Neue Sachlichkeit*; on the exhibition in Mannheim in 1925, see Karoline Hille, *Spuren der Moderne: Die Mannheimer Kunsthalle von 1918–1933* (Berlin: Akademie, 1994), 84–85; Olaf Peters, *Neue Sachlichkeit und Nationalsozialismus: Affirmation und Kritik, 1931–1947* (Berlin: Reimer, 1998).

43 See *Kunst im Aufbruch: Dresden, 1918–1933*, ed. Joachim Uhlitzsch (Dresden: Staatliche Kunstsammlungen Dresden, 1980), cat. no. 391 (etching from 1922).

44 On this, see Dietrich Schubert, "Ein Schützengraben von 1916–18: Julius Meier-Graefe und Otto Dix," *Marburger Jahrbuch für Kunstwissenschaft* 45 (2018): 275–304; see, in particular, Werner Spiess, "L'imperatif iconographique: La Nouvelle Objectivité et ses implications politiques dans l'Allemagne," *Cahiers du Musée National d'Art Moderne Paris*, nos. 7–8 (1981): 209–32, and Jean Clair, "'Nouvelle Objectivité' et art national socialiste: L'inversion des signes," in *L'art face à la crise, 1929–1939* (Saint-Étienne: CIEREC, 1980), 43–61.

45 See Hille, *Spuren der Moderne* (see note 42), 142.

46 Max Beckmann to Mathilde Kaulbach, July 21, 1925, in Beckmann, *Briefe*, ed. Uwe M. Schneede, vol. 1 (1899–1925) (Munich: Piper, 1993), 343; Schubert, *Max Beckmann* (see note 15), 155–68. The painter preferred to speak of "representationalism in a new art form," as he wrote to Wilhelm Hausenstein on March 12, 1926. Cf. Franz Roh, "Gegenständlichkeit: Grundsätzliches zur Wendung neuester Malerei," *Der Cicerone* 17 (1925): 1113–18. In 1930, the writer Joseph Roth published "Schluss mit der 'Neuen Sachlichkeit,'" *Die Literarische Welt*, January 17 and 24, 1930. Equally informative about Beckmann's attitude to the so-called *Neue Sachlichkeit*, are his letters to J. B. Neumann: Harter and von Wiese, *Max Beckmann und J. B. Neumann* (see note 34), such as the one on January 25, 1926, in which he complains to Neumann that Nierendorf prefers his competitor Otto Dix. Nierendorf did indeed mount a large Dix exhibition from February 1926 onward, in which *Schützengraben* and the fifty etchings of *Der Krieg* were presented (see note 40).

47 See Paul F. Schmidt, "Max Beckmanns '*Hölle*,'" *Der Cicerone* 12 (1920): 841–47; for a comprehensive treatment, see Alexander Dückers, *Max Beckmann: Die Hölle, 1919*, exh. cat. Kupferstichkabinett, Berlin

(Berlin: Frölich und Kaufmann, 1983); Günter Aust, "Max Beckmann und die Spätgotik," in *Ikonographia: Anleitung zum Lesen von Bildern*, ed. Bazon Brock (Munich: Klinkhardt & Biermann, 1990), 249–80; cf. Harter and von Wiese, *Max Beckmann und J. B. Neumann* (see note 34), 40.

48 Julius Elias, *Max Liebermann*, Graphiker der Gegenwart 8 (Berlin: Neue Kunsthandlung, 1921), 7: "He had to draw, just as he had to paint."

49 *J. B. Neumanns Bilderhefte: Max Beckmann* (Berlin: Neumann, 1922), 57; Paul F. Schmidt, "Neue Graphik von Max Beckmann," *Der Cicerone* 15 (1923): 180–84. See also Schneede, *Der Zeichner und Grafiker Beckmann* (see note 22), cat. no. 100; Höper, *Kollwitz, Beckmann, Dix, Grosz* (see note 19), 102–3; Harter and von Wiese, *Max Beckmann und J. B. Neumann* (see note 34), 74; Thomas Noll, "Spiegelungen des Selbst: Max Beckmann in seinen Bildern," in *Signatur und Selbstbild: Festschrift für Albert Dietl zum 60. Geburtstag* (Berlin: Reimer, 2019), 90–111.

50 Schneede, *Der Zeichner und Grafiker Beckmann* (see note 22), 96; see also Döhring and Lenz, *Max Beckmann* (see note 15), cat. no. 69. On the issues of form, see Christoph Wagner, "Max Beckmann im interkulturellen Dialog mit Henri Rousseau," in *Kulturelles Gedächtnis und interkulturelle Rezeption im europäischen Kontext*, ed. Eva Dewes and Sandra Duhem (Berlin: Akademie, 2008), 567–93.

51 Eugène Delacroix, entry for January 11, 1857, in *The Journal of Eugène Delacroix*, trans. Walter Pach (New York: Covici, Friede, 1937), 530–34, esp. 531; *Journal, 1822–1863*, ed. André Joubin (Paris: Plon, 1982), 607; see Kurt Badt, *Eugène Delacroix: Werke und Ideale; drei Abhandlungen* (Cologne: DuMont Schauberg, 1965), 33–34. In Bertall's 1849 caricature of a duel between them, Ingres is "*le Thiers de la ligne*" and Delacroix "*le Proudhon de la couleur*"; each bears his motto: "*La couleur est une utopie—Vive la ligne!*" (Color is a utopia—Long live the line!) and "*La ligne n'est qu'une couleur*" (The line is nothing but a color); see Dietrich Schubert, *Vincent van Gogh: "Sternennächte"* (Regensburg: Schnell + Steiner, 2022), 30–31.

52 See *Liebermann und Van Gogh*, ed. Martin Faas, comp. Julia Klarmann, exh. cat. Villa Liebermann, Berlin (Cologne: Wienand, 2015), 35–47.

53 Diether Schmidt, *Otto Dix im Selbstbildnis*, 2nd ed. (Berlin: Henschel, 1981); Schubert, *Otto Dix* (see note 28), 112; Andreas Strobl, *Otto Dix: Eine Malerkarriere* (Berlin: Reimer, 1996), 127–28; Rainer Rochlitz, "Otto Dix entre vérisme et allégorie," in *Otto Dix: Dessins d'une guerre á l'autre*, exh. cat. Centre Pompidou, Paris (Paris: Gallimard, 2003), 29–45, and Ulrike Lorenz, "Dix dessinateur," ibid., 47–65; Olaf Peters, ed., *Otto Dix*, exh. cat. Neue Galerie New York (Munich: Prestel, 2010). For numerous references, see Peters, *Neue Sachlichkeit und Nationalsozialismus* (see note 42), 71–79.

54 März and Riemann, *Realismus und Sachlichkeit* (see note 42); Kristina Hoge, "Selbstbildnisse im Angesicht der Bedrohung durch den Nationalsozialismus," PhD. diss, Universität Heidelberg, 2004, pp. 28–29, 107; Lorquin, *Allemagne* (see note 28).

55 On the context, see Klaus Gallwitz, *Beckmann in Frankfurt* (Frankfurt am Main: Insel, 1984), 15.

56 Aust, "Max Beckmann und die Spätgotik" (see note 47). In the winter of 2016–17, the Kunstsammlung Gera showed an exhibition of silverpoints by Dix. See also Sylvie Lecoq-Ramond, *Un maitre ancien du XXe* siècle*: Otto Dix et l'art de Grünewald*, exh. cat. (Colmar: Musée d'Unterlinden, 1996); *Dix: Katalog der Gemälde, Zeichungen und Druckgrafik aus dem Bestand der Kunstsammlung Gera*, ed. Holger P. Saupe and Claudia Schönjahn (Bonn: VG Bild-Kunst, 2022), esp. Elvira Mienert on the silverpoints, 74–79.

57 Karin von Maur, ed., *Munch, Nolde, Beckmann ... : Private Kunstschätze aus Süddeutschland*, exh. cat. Staatsgalerie Stuttgart (Heidelberg: Braus, 2004), 84; Knut Soiné, "Der Weg im Dunklen: Max Beckmann in Berlin, 1933–1937," *Niederdeutsche Beiträge zur Kunstgeschichte* 43–44 (2004–5): 315–44. In April 1933, the first National Socialist exhibition of "degenerate art" was held at the Kunsthalle Mannheim, which included paintings by Beckmann. In 1935, however, he was represented by *Selbstportrait im Spiegel mit Kerze* in the Munich exhibition "Berliner Kunst in München."

58 M. Lewin, *Alfred Hrdlicka Druckgraphik* (Berlin: Europa, 1989), cat. no. 75. Hrdlicka's relationship to Rembrandt is a case of "propagating connection from art to art," that is, of art historical context, as is shown in Kurt Badt, *Kunsttheoretische Versuche*, ed. Lorenz Dittmann (Cologne: DuMont-Schauberg, 1968), 141–75. When I sent Gary Schwarz's book of Rembrandt etchings in original size to Hrdlicka in Vienna, he immediately took it to his graphic studio—as his wife, Barbara told me—in order to draw on copperplates. His Rembrandt text appears in Alfred Hrdlicka, *Schaustellungen: Bekenntnisse in Wort und Bild* (Munich: Deutscher Taschenbuch-Verlag, 1984), 92–94.

59 Dietrich Schubert, "Funktionen und Formen der Handzeichnung im Werk Hrdlickas," in *Alfred Hrdlicka: Der Tod und das Mädchen; Werke, 1944–1997*, exh. cat. Kunstmuseum, Kloster Unser Lieben Frau, Magdeburg (Magdeburg: Magdeburger Museen, 2000), reprinted in Schubert, *Alfred Hrdlicka: Beiträge zu seinem Werk* (Worms: Werner, 2007), 83–105; Christian Walda, *Der gekreuzigte Mensch im Werk von Alfred Hrdlicka* (Vienna: Böhlau, 2007).

60 Oskar Kokoschka, "Gegenstandslose Kunst?," *Universitas* 9, no. 12 (1954): 1297–98.

SMASHED GLASS

MAX BECKMANN'S PRINT PORTFOLIO *HELL*

Elisa Tamaschke

PROLOGUE

Among Max Beckmann's surviving letters from World War I are accounts from the military hospital and the front that are in keeping with our informed idea of the horrors there: convulsive bodies, disfiguring wounds, screams, amputations, overfilled tent camps, the odor of decay, and rain. We are prepared visually for these factual descriptions because they have often been translated into drawings, prints, paintings, literature, and film. War is the form of hell that we can imagine.

In Beckmann's intense descriptions, war is also filled with strangely inconsequential, atmospheric details. For example, he repeatedly describes sounds and noises. In September 1914, when he was still in the East, he wrote to his wife, Minna, with reference to nature: "Outside the wind is howling in the old pines, and up in the castle the poor, shot-up men are listening to its song. Presumably they can't sleep much, and thousands of flies torment them, so that pine branches had to be placed over their faces."[1] Rushing wind, the buzzing of flies, but also a strange stillness, silent as the grave, come together eerily here, putting the inexorable and brutal course of life before our eyes. In May 1915, he observed how bullets in a forest that threatened his life struck "the pines [...] with a loud bang."[2] The songs of the soldiers, their music,[3] and of course the gunfire of machine guns and infantry were also part of this horizon of noises. Beckmann learned to distinguish German and French cannons.[4]

He also repeatedly communicated observations about color: quite Romantically, for example, "rosy evening air";[5] elsewhere he wrote—and as a reader it is easy to imagine here a painted vision by Matthias Grünewald, whom the artist admired: "This morning I was at the dusty, white-gray front and saw wonderful, enchanted, and glowing things. Burning black, like golden gray-violet to destroyed loam yellow, and pale, dusty sky, and partially and entirely nude men with weapons and bandages. [...] Magnificent pink and ashen limbs with the dirty white of the bandages and the gloomy, heavy expression of suffering."[6] These descriptions by Beckmann emphasize that he was an artist who was involved in the war.[7] He reacts to events with all his senses, recording them in letters but also drawing them, until he broke down around the middle of 1915 and was no longer fit for action—fortunately, in the end, since he was still alive.

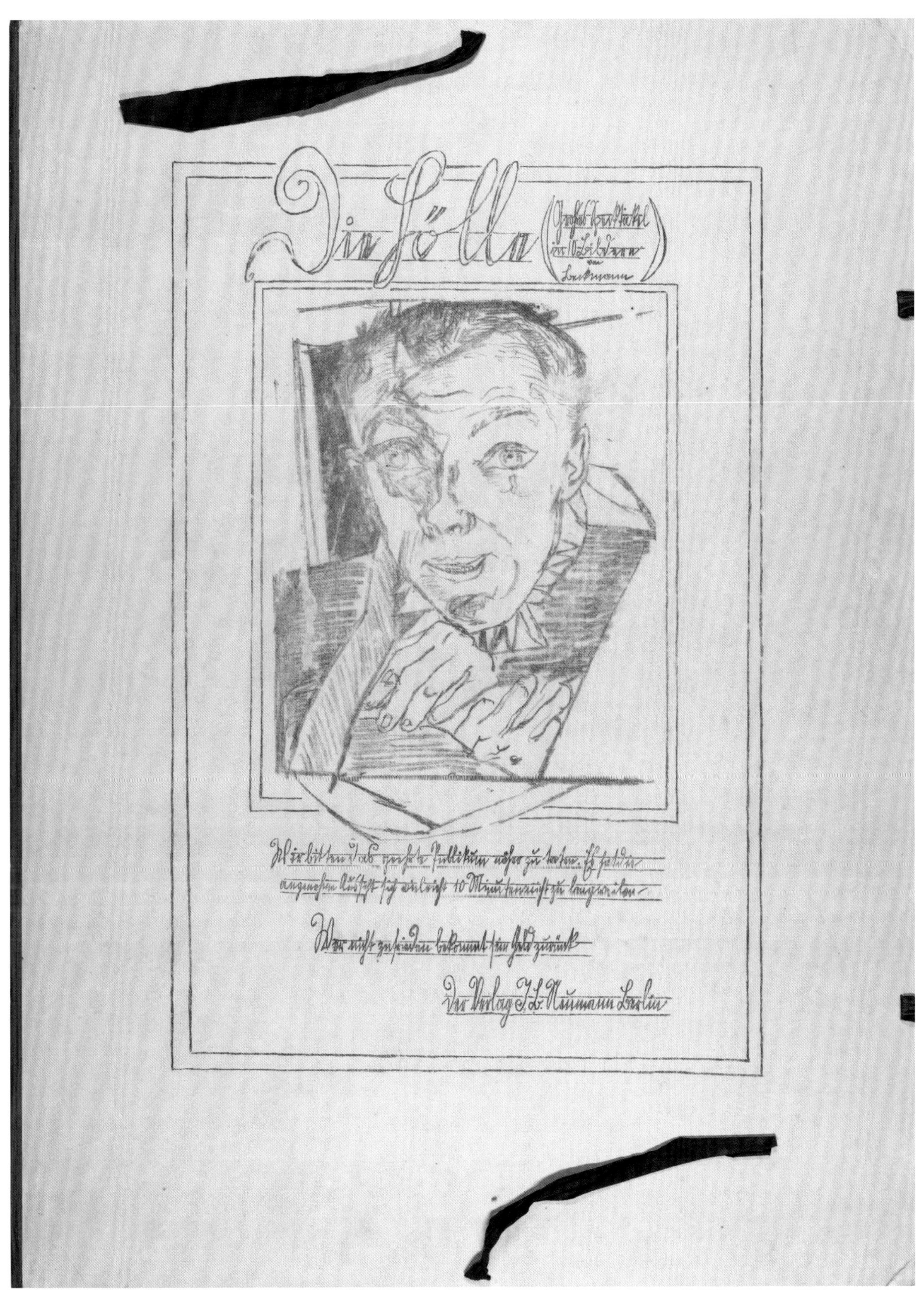

44. SELF-PORTRAIT, FRONT COVER, HELL PORTFOLIO, 1919

Soon after his breakdown, Beckmann moved to Frankfurt am Main. He repeatedly visited his former home, Berlin—in March 1919, for example—and experienced first-hand the violence of the street battles raging there, whose relentlessness represented a kind of continuing of the war. Paul Ferdinand Schmidt pointed out in the journal *Cicerone* as early as 1920 that the visit must have had a formative influence on the making of Beckmann's print portfolio *Die Hölle* (Hell), the subject of the present text, because numerous motifs from the specific circumstances of the postwar era appear in it.[8] J. B. Neumann Verlag published the portfolio in an edition of seventy-five signed copies and paid Beckmann two installments totaling 7,000 marks for it—the annual salary of a skilled worker, though inflation caused its value to plunge.[9] In addition to the deluxe collector's edition, a thousand "*Hell* booklets" were published: a smaller photolithographic reproduction with a red cover that cost two marks.[10] According to Neumann, it did not help attract the desired broad audience. In his memoirs Neumann wrote of the failure of the booklet and also of the portfolio: he had "in mind a popular edition of this series, so that this extraordinary work would also be affordable to the general public who could not afford the original lithographs. [...] But it [the books] met with no great response. I was thus forced to give way most of the copies of the edition of a thousand to people who wanted to have the booklet. The original prints were that much more shocking in their enormous format, and many patrons of the arts regarded my sales offer as an insult. Not a single copy was sold."[11] It goes without saying that its failure to sell at the time contrasts strongly with the production of texts about the portfolio by art historians. Important interpretations—indeed, the first decoding of motifs—were made by Christian Lenz[12] and Alexander Dückers,[13] but Jörn Pabst,[14] Holger Jacob-Friesen,[15] and Rose-Carol Washton Long[16] also made pioneering observations, alongside experts on Beckmann's prints and drawings, such as James Hofmaier[17] and Stephan von Wiese.[18]

On its surface, *Hell* is not about war. The scenes depicted are of a postwar city: they show violent acts, obscenities, indifference and ignorance, desperation and hunger. Now we will dedicate ourselves to these "terrible horrors,"[19] reflecting on which is the greater hell: war, or having survived it, perverted by it.

HELL

Beckmann invites us into hell. On the cover print of the portfolio [Plate 44], we encounter a self-portrait by the artist. He looks directly at the viewer with eyes that are certainly not unfriendly.[20] His face appears worn out; his hair is short and stubbly; his bony hands are folded before his chest, without the gesture seeming fully explicable. Dückers noted that the double frame drawn around the portrait makes it look like Beckmann's head is seen through a window hatch, perhaps of a ticket booth.[21] The clown-like jagged collar around the artist's neck also suggests that the venue of this scene is a variety theater. Could the paper banderole winding about his neck and out of the edge of the image be a roll of admission tickets? The title of the portfolio appears in beautiful cursive writing above his head. The ruled lines recall those of school notebooks to help draw letters of equal height. Explaining the title, *Hell* is an addition in brackets hawking its wares: "Great spectacle in ten pictures by Beckmann."

Underneath the first picture frame, again added on ruled lines, not by Beckmann himself but by the Verlag J.B. Neumann, is the following message: "We ask the esteemed public to step up. It has the pleasant prospect of not being bored for perhaps ten minutes. Anyone who

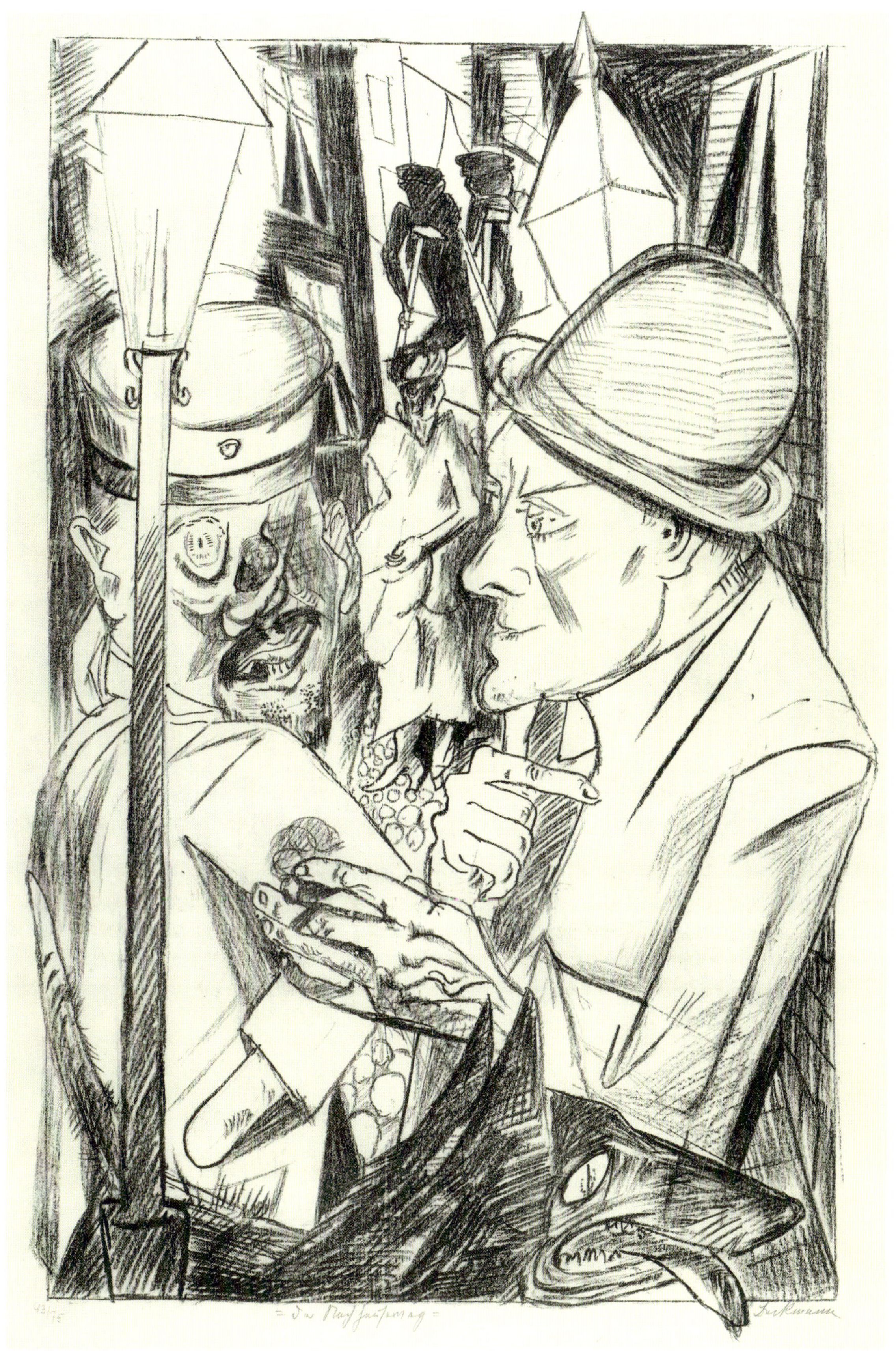

45. THE WAY HOME, PLATE 2, HELL PORTFOLIO, 1919

is not satisfied will have his money returned. The J. B. Neumann publishing house in Berlin." A number of things should be emphasized here: the cursive script, the announcement of a great spectacle in pictures, and the call to step up. The use of cursive parodies the word "hell." It negates the dread that will unfold on the pages that follow. Like a Pied Piper, this cover page and the artist himself seduce, still in a harmless manner, albeit with a taste of sensationalism, the viewers to step up and participate in a spectacle. It has been pointed out that Beckmann originally used the formulation "*einzutreten*" (come in) in a draft sketch for the text, rather than the "*näher zu treten*" (step up) used later.[22] This subtle correction of the wording emphasizes the visual character of the sheets, which are not entered in the manner of the fairground—the *hineintreten*, or "step right in," of the classical barker's cry—but rather approached (and entered only in a metaphorical sense). Dückers previously drew attention to the strong description of the picture as picture by referring to the various solutions for a frame around the motifs—and to the motifs overstepping these framing lines.[23] The unusual size of the pages, 34 x 23 7/8 in., permits the association that the prints are being presented to the viewers on a wall, since their size makes them more appropriate for that form of presentation rather than easily leafing through the pages, in turn suggesting that the viewers are stepping up to a window through which they observe the kaleidoscopic spectacle unfold.[24]

The second sheet, *Der Nachhauseweg* (The Way Home) [Plate 45], establishes the narrative setting for the scenes that follow. In a narrow street at night, Beckmann, who has again integrated a self-portrait, encounters a soldier injured in the war. A gas streetlamp illuminates the scene. Brazenly staring at the soldier's appearance, the artist reaches out with a sinewy hand, holding a cigarette, and touching the man's stump of a right arm. The soldier looks around and turns his disfigured face toward Beckmann and to the viewers. It remains unclear whether he is shocked about having been touched; after all, the wartime injury robbed him of the possibility to convey reactions or emotions through facial expressions. His right eye is torn wide open and drips black; he no longer has a left eye or nose.

Beckmann makes a pointing gesture with his right index finger. Is he gesticulating toward himself to suggest a connection to the solider? Beckmann stands here as someone uninjured in the war facing someone injured in the war. Does he want to say: "I too experienced the war. I share your impressions"? Is it a request that the soldier tell him his stories? Is he offering to walk with him part of the way home?

At this point, it is necessary to take a closer look at the formal dynamic of the print: the injured man is all but pulled into the image by the movement of the hand grasping his arm; part of his back is still outside the frame. Beckmann's pointing gesture and the fact that his shoulder juts out beyond right the edge of the image, by contrast, create a dynamic that goes back out of the painting to the right, though first it concentrates in the encounter of the two main figures. The dog with its tongue hanging out, which occupies the entire width of the foreground, is also moving in a direction that leads to the right edge and out of the image. If one imagines the presentation of the cycle on a wall, everything in the formal logic of the image can be understood as reference, a leading to the next image. The cover print with the invitation to the viewers to step up is thus reinforced, and here it is spoken directly to someone who participated in the war and was badly wounded, who has already suffered one hell and is now part of another one.

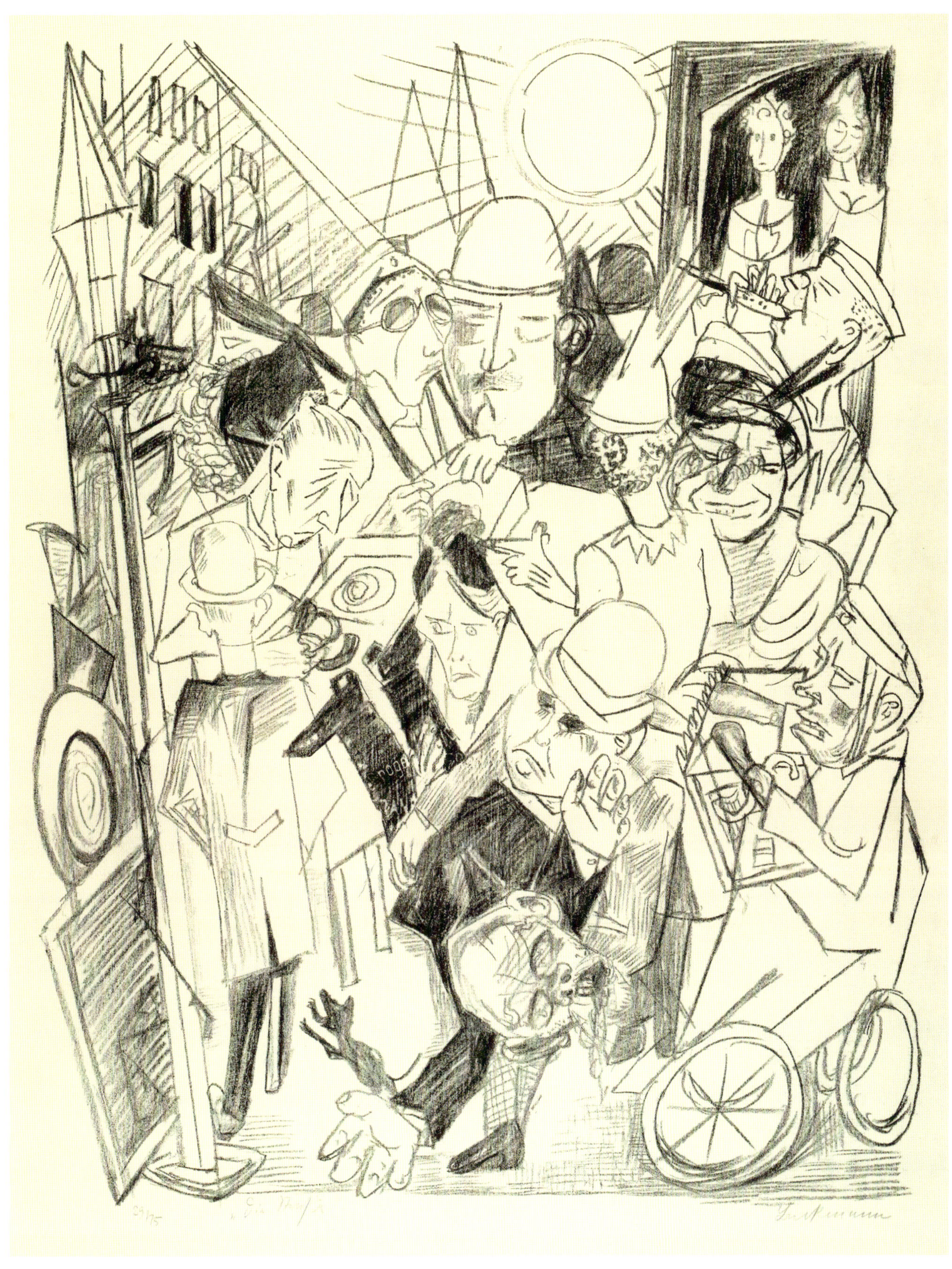

46. THE STREET, PLATE 3, HELL PORTFOLIO, 1919

The narrow lane in which the two meet is lined by apartment buildings. In the middle ground of the image stands a prostitute; her behind is exposed, shining through the fabric of her dress. In the shadows at the end of the lane, two more men with crutches, probably also injured in the war, appear and disappear, turning around a corner. The title—*The Way Home*—succinctly emphasizes its ordinariness. It can also cause one to reflect on the fact that the possession and good fortune of having a home could by no means be taken for granted in 1919, the year the cycle was made, especially in the case of those returning from the war, so that the way home took on at least two meanings.

On the third sheet, *Die Strasse* (The Street) [Plate 46], the way is broad, save for the narrowness of the street at night; numerous people are busily underway on it. Beckmann defines the teeming crowd of people primarily by their faces and, accordingly, by types; the motif is composed of the heads jumbled together. Very portly men with hats; wizened, presumably elderly women; a young lady with a chic hat and Pierrot collar; opposite her, a woman with rosy cheeks; and between them three men who have returned from the war: one wearing glasses that shield his eyes and a vendor's tray or collection bag; another is tootling on a flute; and in the right foreground a man missing limbs pushes his way into the picture frame with a mobility cart.

A scene is played out in the foreground that can seemingly be interpreted only metaphorically: one of the portly men is strenuously carrying or holding a rigid man as if he were a papier-mâché figure or a corpse. He is apparently assisted by an old woman behind him, who looks out from the center of the interlocked chaos of the crowd and holds one of the legs with her hand. The hands of the man being carried are extended far above him; his hands are bloated. He is dressed in a black suit, which distinguishes him from the crowd of people. But his face also causes him to stand out: with his giant, wide-open eyes, he looks like a skull; drool—or his last breath—is escaping from his gaping mouth. This person is closer to death than to life, perhaps death has been captured visually in his form, and he is being edged out of the picture with a decisive gesture.[25] None of the others are reacting to this macabre scene; rather, all of the people are introspective, concentrating on themselves: hardly anyone has eyes that appear to see and look around; even the button eyes of one of two doll-like women who are staring down at the crowd from an elevated position like a kind of opera loge, presumably do not see.[26] *The Street* shows the bustle of city life, which can probably only be generated by eyes closed to reality. The sun shines unrelentingly above it all, heralding the natural continuation of time.

The fourth sheet, *Das Martyrium* (The Martyrdom) [Plate 47], is one of the motifs of the cycle that have been already addressed in great detail in the literature. As Lenz showed as early as 1974, it concerns the theme of the assassination of the socialist Rosa Luxemburg.[27] On January 15, 1919, Luxemburg was in the hideout to which she had fled after being released from prison in 1918, where she was arrested by a militia and then put on trial in the Eden-Hotel by the headquarters of the Garde-Kavallerie-Schützen-Division. As she was transported from the hotel, the soldiers beat her. Unconscious, she was dragged into a car, where she was shot, and her corpse was thrown into the Landwehrkanal. Karl Liebknecht was also arrested, put on trial, and then murdered like her.[28] In contrast to *The Street*, where disillusionment and the mercilessness of the present are rendered

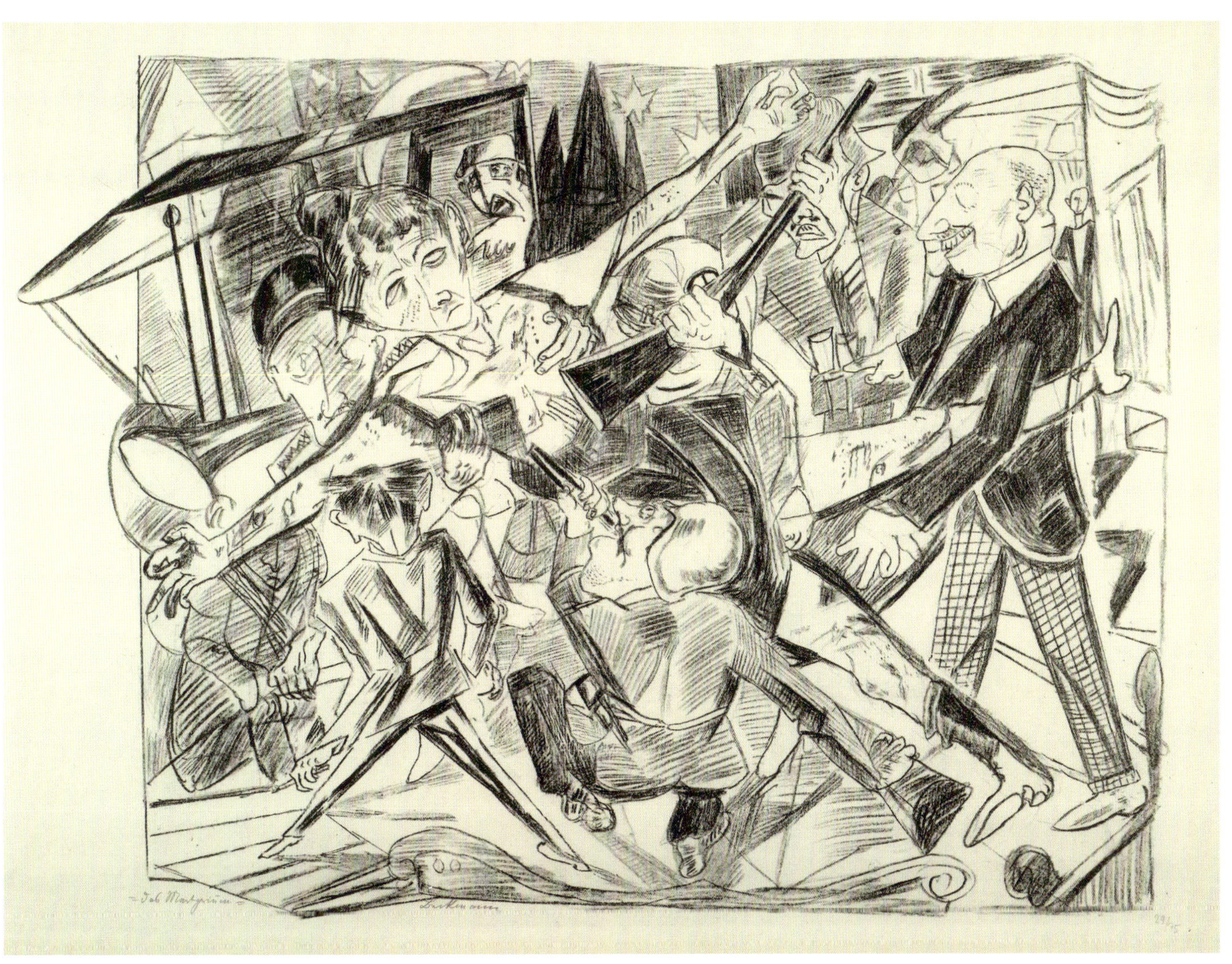

47. THE MARTYRDOM, PLATE 4, HELL PORTFOLIO, 1919

atmospherically and visually, this motif depicts a historical event that was nearly contemporaneous.

The Martyrdom is one of only two horizontal formats in the series. A brutal panorama unfurls on it: the abused, beaten body of a woman—namely, Luxemburg—extends across nearly the entire diagonal of the motif. Her arms are extended as if she were being crucified. She is surrounded by numerous men, some wearing helmets, who cruelly threaten her, beat her with rifle butts, grab and degrade her. Visually, her body sinks down between the men and their actions. Her slender face and above all her empty eyes,[29] serve as a warning of the dehumanizing degradation to which she is being subjected. She has become a shell; her spirit no longer occupies her body over which the men have seized control. And her hands? Her index fingers are bent down into palms, as if broken. She points to herself with arms outstretched in a gesture of crucifixion.[30] In the *Isenheim Altarpiece* by Grünewald, an artist whom Beckmann revered, John the Baptist makes his famous gesture of pointing at the crucified Christ. In addition to the possibly self-referential gesture of the woman, there is also a male "pointer" in Beckmann's work: to the right of the woman's head are the head and hand of another helmeted man. He points to the woman with his index finger; his face conveys horror.

Dückers and Schubert have described the scroll form in the foreground of this scene as creating the impression of a country fair or theater stage.[31] There is also a curved form in the lower right corner: the pit between a stage and the audience is suggested here. Schubert asks whether Beckmann wanted to reduce the "bloody reality to a kind of theatrical scene," as if he had relativized the spectacle.[32] These stage scrolls are not found on the other sheets of this portfolio, but they are only logical in the context of the spectacle of *Hell*: the viewers are voyeurs looking at a crime whose progress they can no longer influence. The form and motifs reflect the reality of the murder of Luxemburg and the historically documented people on the streets of Berlin who did not help her. One such figure is a man standing in the background on the right, watching with his arms interlocked behind his back. Another is the figure of the man at front left with legs spread and hair standing on end, electrified.[33] The brutality does not just lie in the violent act of beating but also in casually observing it.

The man pointing angrily at Luxemburg serves as a transition to the next sheet of *Hell*: *Der Hunger* (Hunger) [Plate 48]. It was noted above that in the context of Beckmann's admiration for Grünewald, his gesture might refer to the latter's John the Baptist. In *Hunger*, as Dückers was the first to demonstrate,[34] a figure of John the Baptist appears quite literally. In the background of the table scene that fills the image, a sculpture of John stands on a pedestal, which is surely most likely what we are seeing. His arms are outstretched as if to make a proclamation. Yet one could almost imagine that he is a master of ceremonies presenting the scene in the foreground to a public hungry for spectacles. At his feet lies the Lamb of God with his attribute, the cross. In the center of this once again stage-like scene, including a large curtain, is a round table positioned under the glaring light of a ceiling lamp. Sitting around the table, absorbed in prayer, are, according to Dückers, Beckmann's mother-in-law, Ida Tube-Römpler; his son, Peter; possibly Beckmann himself, seen from behind; and a female friend of the family.[35] Their empty plates are very small; not a lot of food would fit on them; and the serving bowl, also small, contains too little to suffice for those gathered. The most striking figure in this work

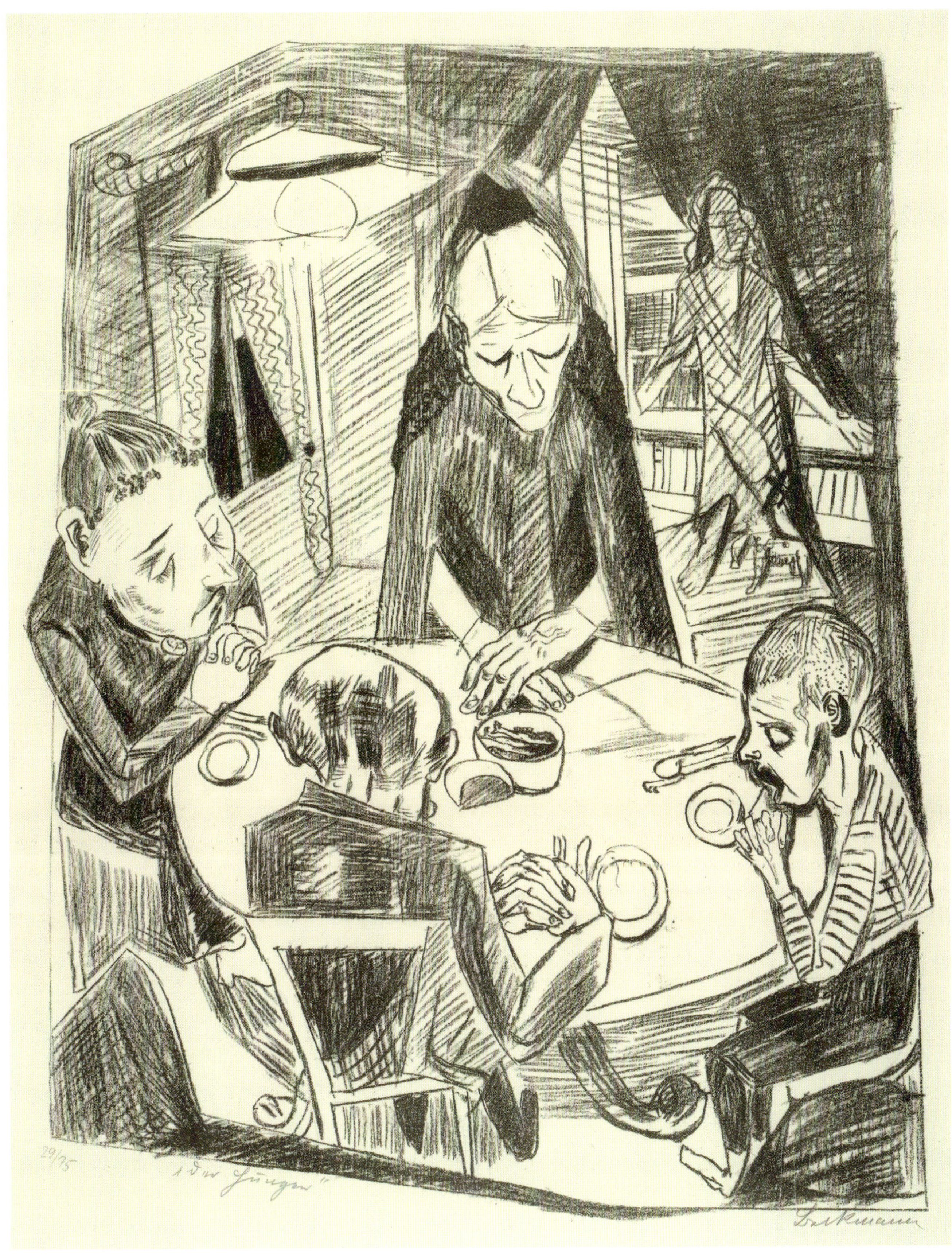

48. HUNGER, PLATE 5, HELL PORTFOLIO, 1919

is Beckmann's mother-in-law. John the Baptist is posed behind her to one side at the same height perspectivally. His open gesture with his arm, and above all the symbolically associated Christian confession or pronouncement is adopted by Tube-Römpler in that she places her hands—completing the circle of John's gesture—one above the other in prayer. In contrast to her, the others interlace their hands. This emphasizes her praying gesture. Tube-Römpler's cape emphasizes her upright, monolithic presence in the space and recalls the Virgin of Mercy's protective cloak. The two women keep their eyes closed meditatively; by contrast, Peter, who is bent over in exhaustion, looks desperately at the sparse meal with hungry eyes outlined in black. For the Christian interpretation, Dückers cited the penitential sermon of John the Baptist, Mt. 3.2: "Repent ye."[36] But it seems worthwhile here to repeat Mt. 3.2 in full: "And saying, Repent ye: for the kingdom of heaven is at hand." Could this hungry evening prayer truly have offered hope for the kingdom of heaven, or could that have been the only hope that remained?

The silence of the scene of evening prayer contrasts with the truly visible volume of the following sheet, *Die Ideologen* (The Ideologues) [Plate 49].[37] The figures in *Hunger* silently seek an inner dialogue; in *The Ideologues*, we believe we hear them overpowering one another. The crowded space filled with people provides a strong contrast with the almost hall-like expanse of the room in *Hunger*. The figures in *The Ideologues* have gathered; in their center stands a man at a lectern, or is he seated at the head of a table? He gesticulates and speaks, a preacher in a new era.[38] Are the ideologues present following a common ideology? The chaos of chair backs, heads, and hands makes one thing clear above all: no intellectual order can result from this spatial muddle. Scholars have made various attempts to connect those depicted with real people. That cannot be ruled out on principle; after all, Luxemburg is also part of this great series of prints, but Pabst's view should be underscored: he emphasizes in the context of interpreting these people that Beckmann was not primarily concerned about the portrait character of his motifs but rather about their universally valid truth.[39]

In the medley of *Hell*, *The Martyrdom* has a kindred work in *Die Nacht* (Night) [Plate 50]. Both motifs are horizontal formats—the only ones in the cycle—and certainly have been extensively interpreted by scholars. Their formal dynamics burst out of the picture frame; their motivic components shatter splinter-like: these motifs signify explosions. Beckmann had executed an early version of *Night* in oil in 1918–19 and now took it up again. A family in an attic is being tortured by three men who clearly intend to kill them. Two of them are hanging the father from a rafter using a sheet; his head and limbs are contorted in death throes. His left arm is being broken. His wife's wrists are bound; her bodice split; her bottom exposed; her stockings and undergarments torn from her body. With her legs spread wide, she appears to have slipped on the floor, debased. Her child is being grabbed by the third attacker. He is starting to open the window as if he intends to throw him out of it. The brutal extermination of a family is the theme. The men torturing the husband have bandaged heads. Are they wounded men who have returned from the war or rebellious street fighters? *Night* is a pendant not only to *The Martyrdom* but also to *Hunger*. The family in *Night* was also eating dinner. On the table at which they had been seated, and onto which the father is now being heaved, lie a displaced tablecloth and a plate. This table and this space, an attic, are even shabbier than the already quite paltry room in *Hunger*. The kingdom of heaven for

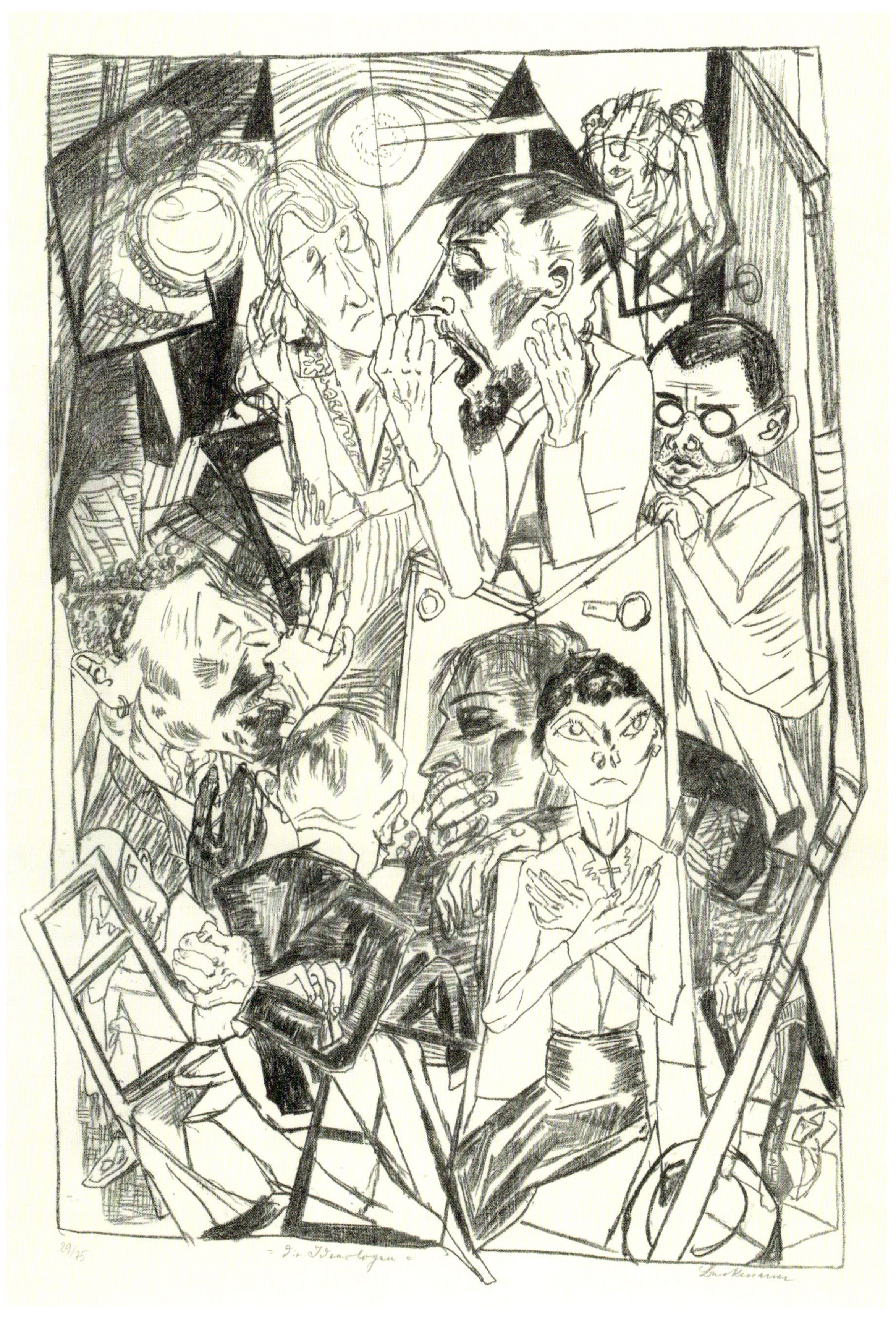

49. THE IDEOLOGUES, PLATE 6, HELL PORTFOLIO, 1919

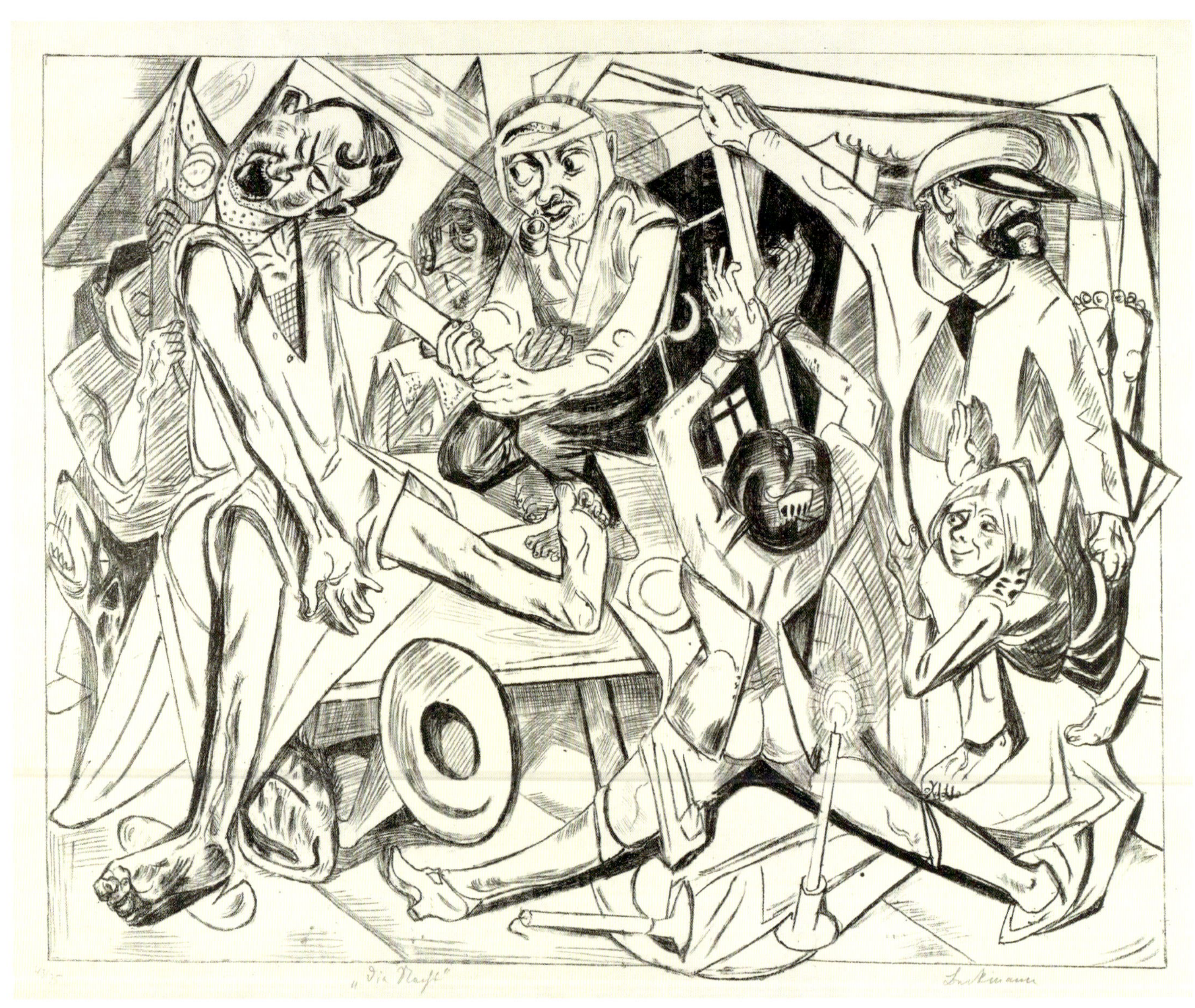

50. NIGHT, PLATE 7, HELL PORTFOLIO, 1919

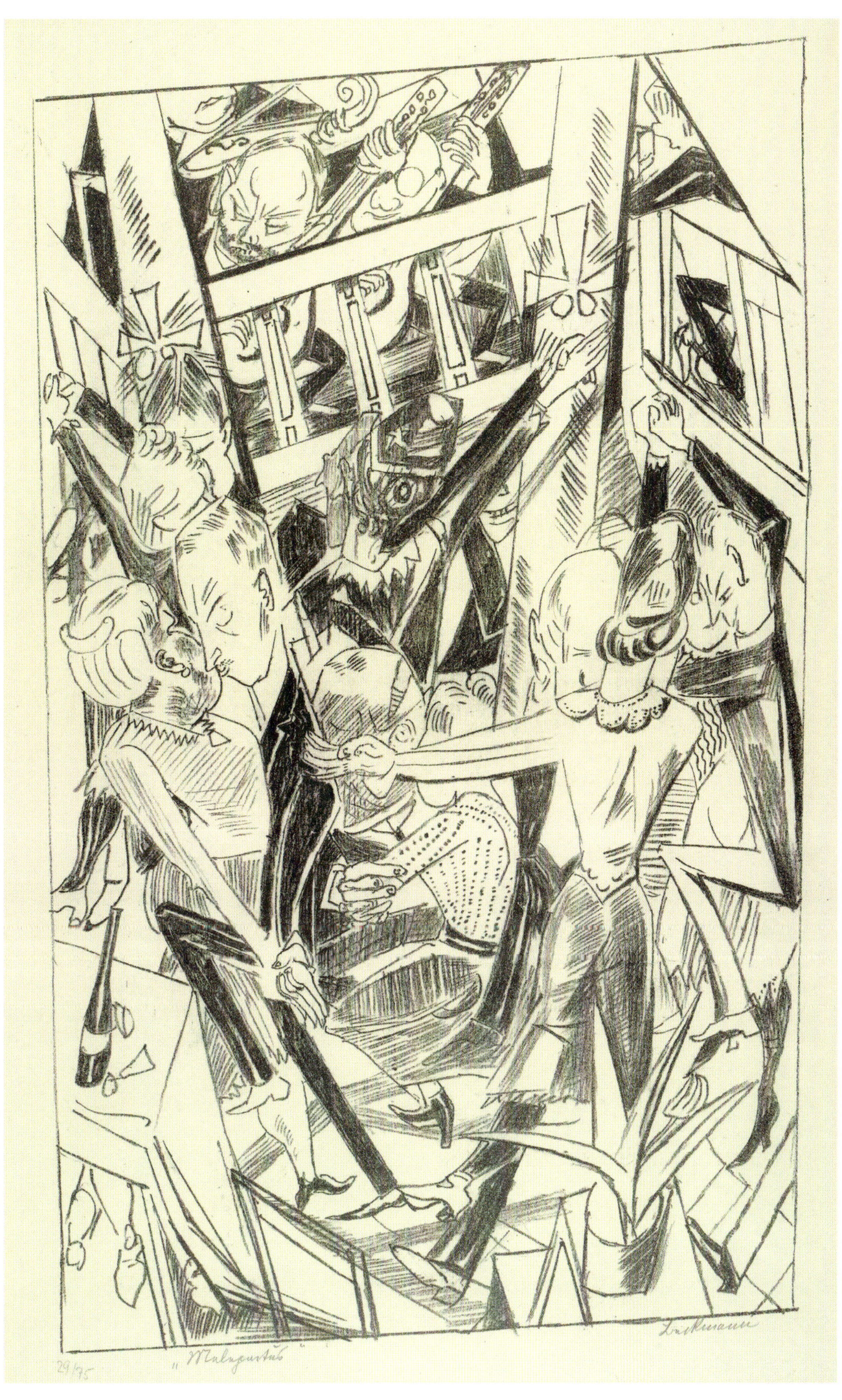

51. MALEPARTUS, PLATE 8, HELL PORTFOLIO, 1919

which they pray in the latter, which John the Baptist announced in his sermon on repentance, is blasted into the air in *Night*. Violence is victorious.[40] A woman with a Pierrot collar sits at a table in the background watching the happenings impassively. Who is she? A dog howls in the left corner.

The next two sheets become musical. In *Malepartus* [Plate 51],[41] six couples dance ecstatically in a tiny space that opens up funnel-like toward a gallery on which the musicians are playing no less ecstatically. The faces of the couple in the center are covered by the horizontally extended arms of another couple, but the war wounds to the man's face are still visible—a skull with teeth and the top of his head are exposed. His left eye is the only open one in this print and it peers directly at the viewers. This gruesome eye that bears witness to death in the middle of the supposed vivacity of the dancing is the true center of the image.

The musical encounter in *Das patriotische Lied* (The Patriotic Song) [Plate 52] is more intimate. The passages in Beckman's letters during World War I in which he reports on the patriotic songs of the soldiers have often been cited, including in the present prologue.[42] In *Hell*, the active war is over and, moreover, lost, but the songs continue to be performed by a man playing the violin and another playing the accordion. A group of men are gathered around a table; two of them are presumably soldiers; the third, in the foreground on the left, has a beard, is older, and is singing along ardently. The soldier on the left next to him rests his head on the table in despair. The other soldier occupies the foreground; he has opened his mouth, presumably to sing; his right hand is raised as if he is trying to bolster his song. Cups bearing the eagle symbolizing the Prussian-German empire stand on the table. The men appear caught in a state of bewilderment and attempt to hold on to something irretrievably lost; the atmosphere evokes Erich Kästner's "Sachliche Romanze" (Real Romance) of 1928. It says of the lovers: "When for eight years they had known each other / (And they did know each other, no doubt about that), / They suddenly found their love was missing, / As others will lose a stick or a hat. // They were sad, but kept up appearances gaily, / Sought kisses, as if with nothing to fear, / And looked at each other and knew no further, / At last she was weeping; and he stood near. // From the window far out one could wave to the shipping, / He said it must now be a quarter-past-four / And time to look round for a place to drink coffee, / Someone was practicing scales next door. // They went in the smallest cafe, and stirred / The cups which they had been handed. / When evening came they were still sitting there. / They sat alone, and they said no word / And simply could not understand it."[43] In contrast to that couple, the ones gathered around the table in Beckmann's work cling to the fateful love of the fatherland, a vanished political system, but it is quite clear: a sinister past is more real than the present reality. The men seem to have no future. A woman also sits at the table; her facial features, especially her mouth, recall Beckmann's mother-in-law, Tube-Römpler. Her son Martin had died in battle in Russia in 1914. The patriotism feebly upheld here took her child.

On the ninth sheet of *Hell, Die Letzten* (The Last Ones), the briskly dancing bodies of *Malepartus* become rifles and machine guns aimed from an apartment or hut on a barricade at a mad crowd on the street—the "last ones" of the title—and the wall of the building across the street [Plate 53]. Whereas in *Malepartus* the dynamic was directed funnel-like inward, now it moves outward through the large window like a vortex or undertow. Brutally

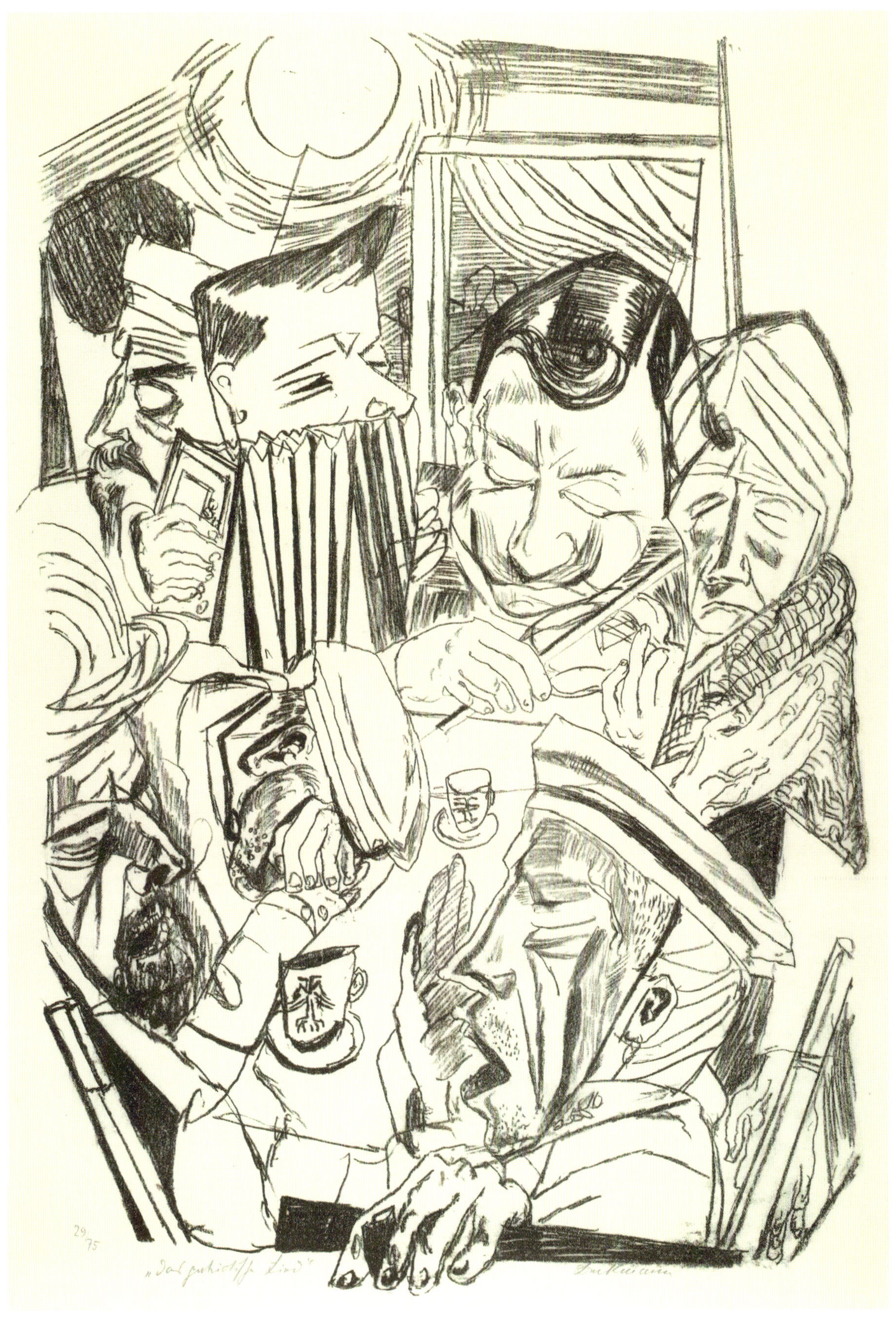

52. THE PATRIOTIC SONG, PLATE 9, HELL PORTFOLIO, 1919

injured figures shoot at those who have gone crazy. A dead man lies in the foreground, his bloody intestines gushing out of his belly. No one takes notice of him. Dückers related this sheet to the historical context of the street battles of the "German revolution" and the Spartakusbund (Spartacus League) and probably rightly proposes that Beckmann drew inspiration for this print in photographs accompanying newspaper reports.[44] In an alternative drawing of the same motif cited by Dückers, Beckmann had integrated the words and sentence "VERBRÜD(ERUNG) / WIR SIND TOT" (FRAT[ERNIZATION] / WE ARE DEAD).[45] Indeed, it seems to be truly a wish for death, and not a desire to change a social situation that drives these men and shows them to be the "last ones," because they are the only ones who still want to fight.

Die Familie (The Family) [Plate 54] concludes *Hell*. Beckmann once again portrays himself; his mother-in-law, Tube-Römpler; and his son, Peter: In his written memories of his father, Peter Beckmann recorded an event from his childhood with reference to the print in *Hell*: "in which he [Beckmann] and Buschchen [Ida Tube-Römpler] point beyond the evil in a calm pose while the dumb Peter drags home from a playground in Berlin a steel helmet and tin cans he had found among the belongings left behind by soldiers who had disarmed there. The latter were in fact hand grenades."[46] Tube-Römpler's gesture has been interpreted as a defense against the strict artist-father and as taking sides with the innocently playing son,[47] but Peter's account seems very understandable. Beckmann and Tube-Römpler reject the young boy's game. Beckmann with his experience as a medic in the war and the mother who had been robbed of a son who died in combat are expelling the war objects, and hence the war itself, from their home. As a child from the next generation, Peter does not understand the scope of the conflict. He echoes the innocence with which the young men set off for the battlefields in 1914, believing it would be easy.

EPILOGUE

The two horizontal-format works—*The Martyrdom* and *Night*—have traditionally been viewed as the major prints of the portfolio. That seems evident. The murder of Luxemburg, addressed in *The Martyrdom*, was a key event in German history after the war, and it remains so today. This depiction of it in art so soon afterward is outstanding. Beckmann's presentation of it alludes in its forms to the crucifixion of Christ but nevertheless he does not exaggerate the terrible reality of the circumstances of her assassination. Indeed, despite their oppressive radicalness, none of the motifs in this portfolio appear to have exaggerated its subject matter. The hell that Beckmann sketches here is rendered in an expressive but realistic form. The motif of *Night* occupies a special place in the artist's oeuvre: after all, it has a precursor in oil that is largely identical; second, the title is echoed in various ways later, for example, in the portfolio *Stadtnacht* (City Night), which is also, already on its title page, about a scene of an attack at night in a domestic environment.

Like Beckmann's print portfolio *Gesichter* (Faces), *Hell* begins and ends with self-portraits by the artist. Compared to the other faces rendered in the portfolio under discussion, they are delicately drawn; Tube-Römpler, too, is clearly portrayed rather than stereotyped. These two figures and the men with wartime injuries in *The Way Home* are the central ones of the portfolio. Hence the first and last prints are the most important for the portfolio's message. Beckmann, Tube-Römpler, and the men injured in the war are also depicted at the same eye level in their respective prints; they appear as unities. Their

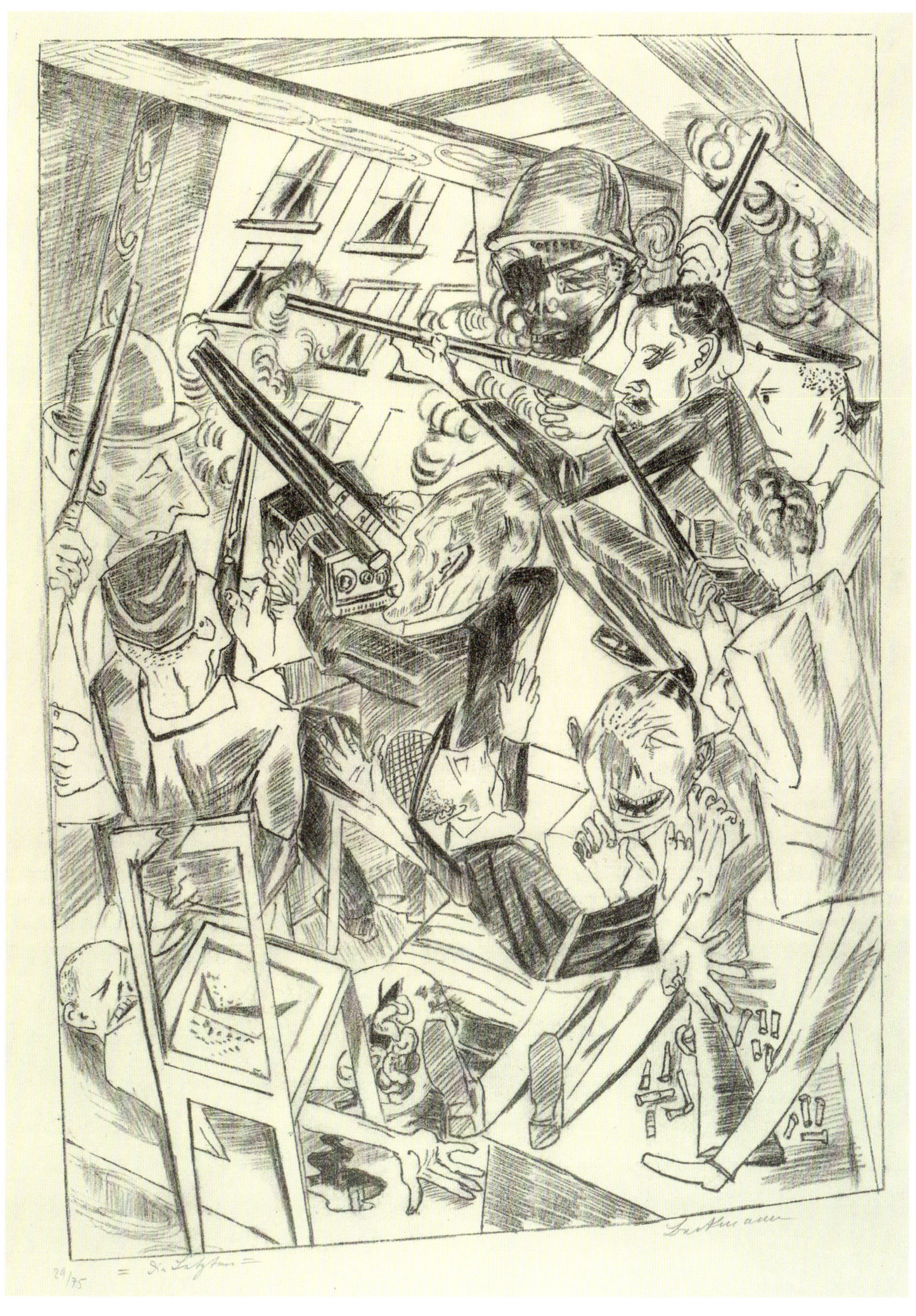

53. THE LAST ONES, PLATE 10, HELL PORTFOLIO, 1919

individual faces belong in the context of motivic tales of the contemporaneous experience of a hell based on the experience of a different kind of hell. They are admonishers. The encounter between Beckmann and the man injured in the war in *Night* illustrates the war and its consequences and also marks the narrative precondition for the circumstances of the sheets that follow.

Despite the many people depicted in the portfolio, there are hardly any friendly interactions. Even in the more intimate scenes, such as *Hunger* and *The Patriotic Song*, they are next to one another—albeit immersed in an inner dialogue—rather than with one another. There is neither consolation nor hope, for hell is not a place of hope. This contrasts with the biblical story of the prodigal son, which Beckmann, interestingly, related in five gouaches in 1918,[48] only four of which survive [see ill. on pp. 150–151]: in the parable, the father's joy over the return of the son who was thought dead is central, and he admonishes his other son, who had dutifully remained home, to share it. The motif that Beckmann chose for the final illustration of the parable is the happy togetherness of the family in their home; outside a cow stands in the field, and the moon shines calmly above it.

When the young Peter plays with hand grenades in *The Family*, a seed may already have been sown in him that may bring new disaster. The order "Out!" from Beckmann and the defensive gesture of Tube-Römpler are the reactions of those who have experienced and suffered. But who listens to the admonishers? Beckmann casts the viewers out of the portfolio just as he lured them in in the first place. Throwing them out is not associated with any mollifying of the torments of hell but surely is a manifesto against the war, against the idea that war should be understood as a game. In *Hell*, Beckmann shatters his motifs like windowpanes. In formal terms, they splinter into "crystal-clear, razor-sharp lines and planes."[49] If it was observed at the beginning of this essay that the viewers approach the images like windows, it turns out that they have broken glass.

Translated from the German by Steven Lindberg

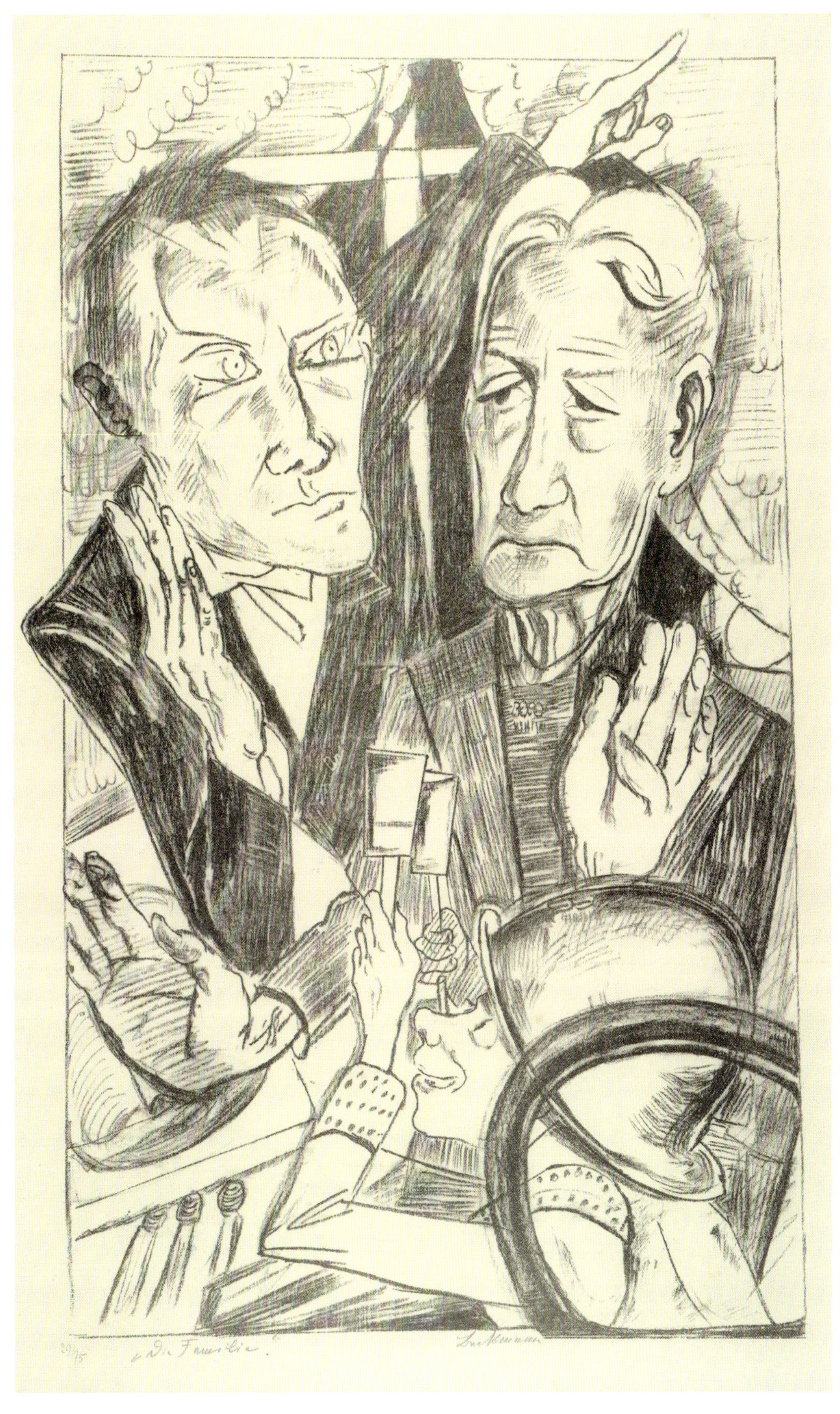

54. THE FAMILY, PLATE 11, HELL PORTFOLIO, 1919

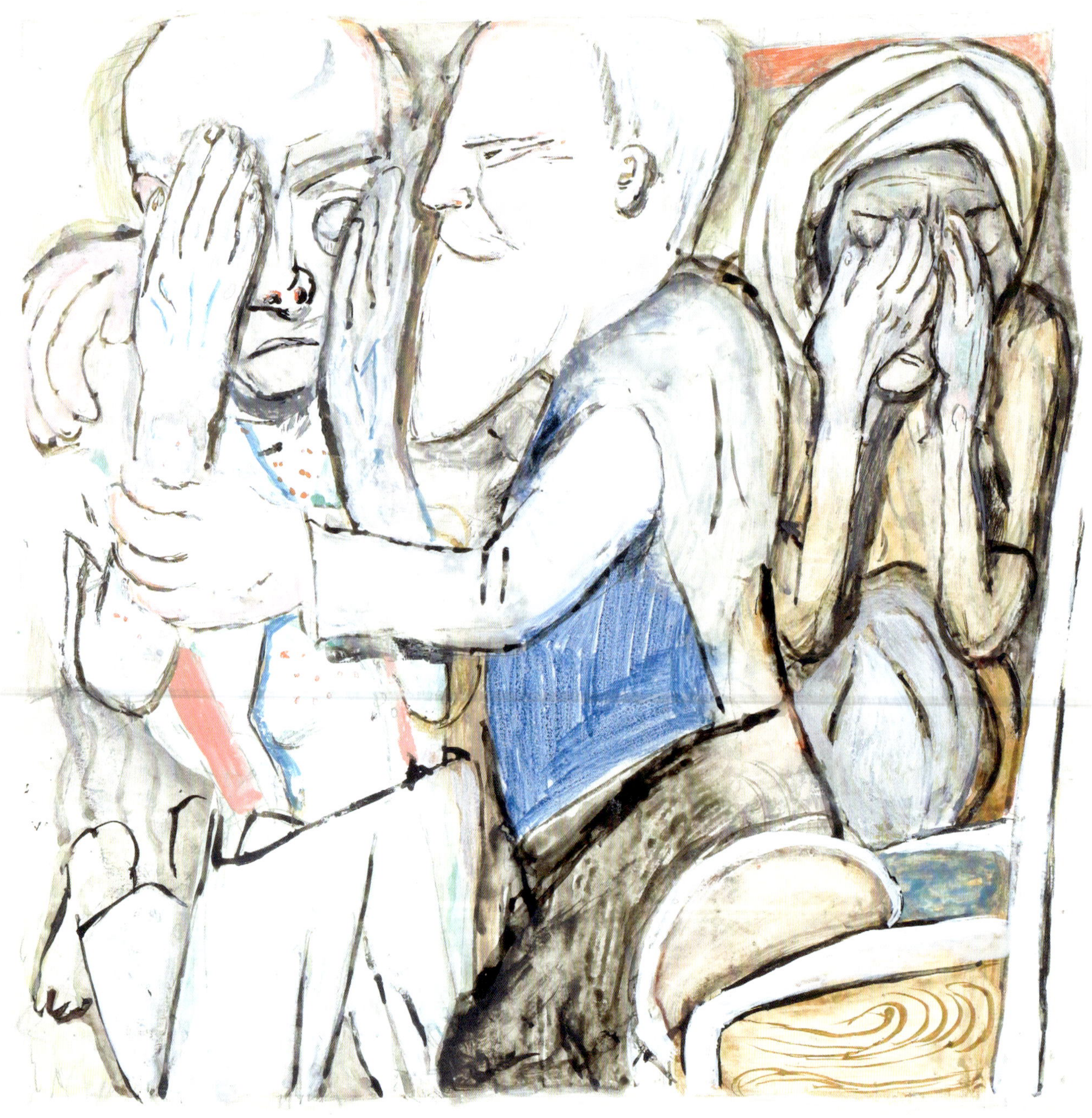

Max Beckmann, *The Return of the Prodigal Son,* ca. 1918, gouache and watercolor over ink and pencil drawing on parchment. The Museum of Modern Art, New York. Purchase. Photo: © The Museum of Modern Art/Licensed by SCALA / Art Resource, NY

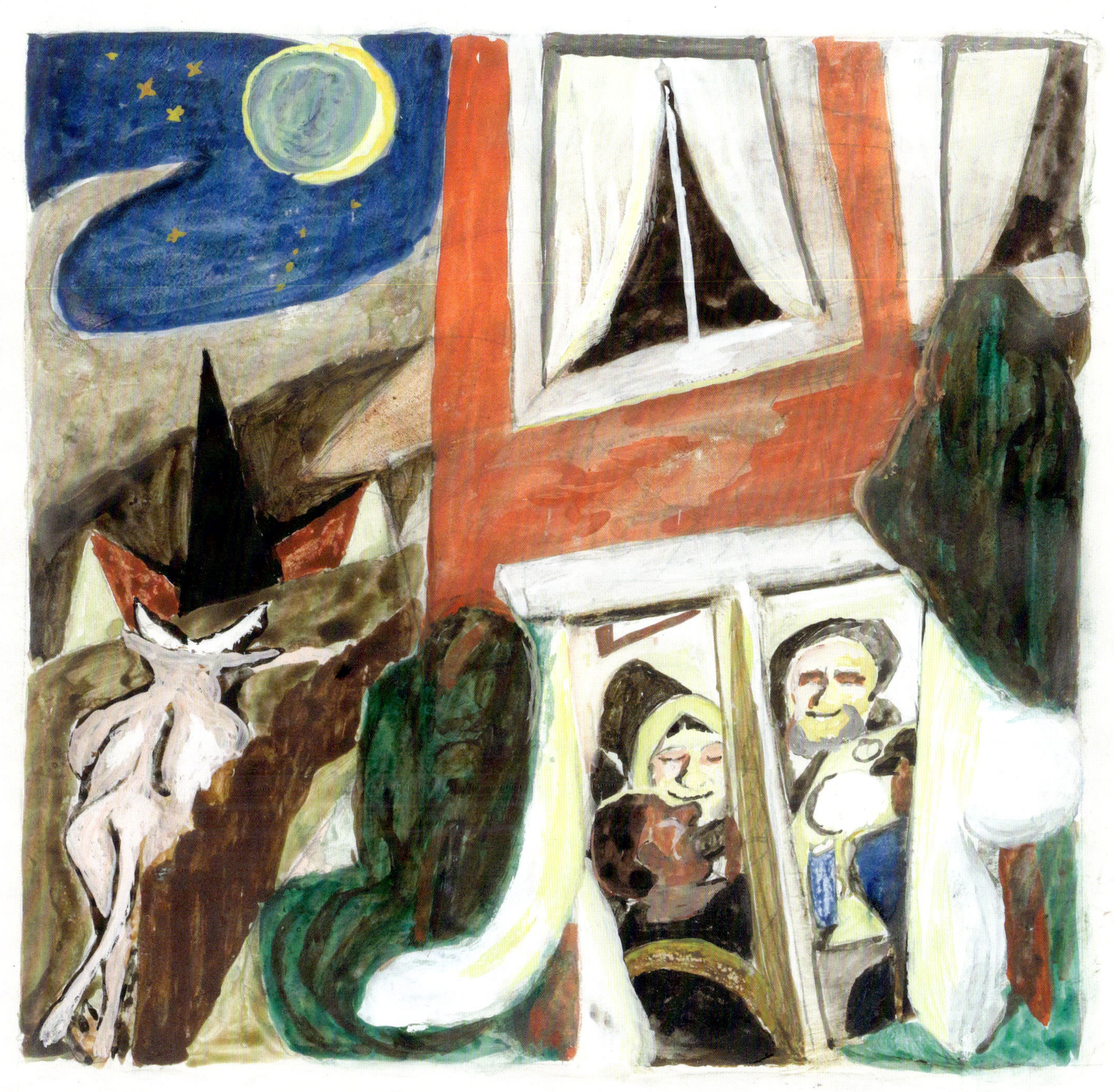

Max Beckmann, *The Feast of the Prodigal Son,* ca. 1918, gouache and watercolor over ink and pencil drawing on parchment. The Museum of Modern Art, New York. Purchase. Photo: © The Museum of Modern Art/Licensed by SCALA / Art Resource, NY

1 Max Beckmann to Minna Beckmann-Tube, September 28, 1914, in Max Beckmann, *Briefe*, ed. Klaus Gallwitz, Uwe M. Schneede, and Stephan von Wiese with Barbara Golz, vol. 1 (1899–1925) (Munich: Piper, 1993), 97.

2 Max Beckmann to Minna Beckmann-Tube, May 21, 1915, in Beckmann, *Briefe* (see note 1), 135.

3 Max Beckmann to Minna Beckmann-Tube, March 28, 1915, in Beckmann, *Briefe* (see note 1), 112.

4 Max Beckmann to Minna Beckmann-Tube, March 27, 1915, in Beckmann, *Briefe* (see note 1), 110.

5 Max Beckmann to Minna Beckmann-Tube, March 28, 1915, in Beckmann, *Briefe* (see note 1), 112.

6 Max Beckmann to Minna Beckmann-Tube, June 7, 1915, in Beckmann, *Briefe* (see note 1), 140.

7 Dietrich Schubert has also pointed to Beckmann's aesthetic, artistic perspective in his wartime letters; see Dietrich Schubert, *Künstler im Trommelfeuer des Krieges, 1914–18* (Heidelberg: Wunderhorn, 2013), 295–96, and Dietrich Schubert, *Max Beckmann vom Vietzker-Strand zur Departure: Die Kristallisation seiner Werturteile und seine bildnerische Praxis, 1904–1939* (Petersberg: Michael Imhof, 2021), 72.

8 P. F. Schmidt, "Max Beckmanns 'Die Hölle,'" *Der Cicerone* 12 (1920): 841–47, esp. 841; see also Alexander Dückers, *Max Beckmann: "Die Hölle," 1919*, exh. cat. (Berlin: Kupferstichkabinett—Staatliche Museen Preussischer Kulturbesitz, 1983), 9.

9 Dückers, *Max Beckmann* (see note 8), 25.

10 Ursula Hart and Stephan von Wiese, eds., *Max Beckmann und J. B. Neumann: Der Künstler und sein Händler in Briefen und Dokumenten, 1917–1950* (Cologne: Walther König, 2011), 40.

11 J. B. Neumann, "Sorrow and Champagne," in Hart and Wiese, *Max Beckmann und J. B. Neumann* (see note 10), 285–323, esp. 291. On the lack of sales, see Holger Jacob-Friesen, "Die Hölle," in *Max Beckmann: Druckgrafik, 1914–1924*, exh. cat. (Karlsruhe: , 2005, 57.

12 Christian Lenz, "Max Beckmann: 'Das Martyrium,'" *Jahrbuch der Berliner Museen* 16 (1974): 185–210. See also *Max Beckmann: Selbstbildnisse Zeichnung und Druckgraphik*, ed. Thomas Döring and Christian Lenz, exh. cat. Neue Pinakothek, Munich, Herzog-Anton-Ulrich-Museum, Braunschweig (Heidelberg: Braus, 2000), 180–88.

13 Dückers, *Max Beckmann* (see note 8).

14 Jörn Pabst, "Anmerkungen zur Genese der Mappe *Die Hölle* von Max Beckmann," *Hefte des Max-Beckmann-Archivs*, no. 6 (2002): 9–19.

15 Jacob-Friesen, "Die Hölle" (see note 11), 56–59.

16 Rose-Carol Washton Long, "Ambivalence: Personal and Political," in *Of "Truths Impossible to Put in Words": Max Beckmann Contextualized*, ed. Rose-Carol Washton Long and Maria Makela (Bern: Peter Lang, 2008), 103–34.

17 James Hofmaier, *Max Beckmann: Catalogue Raisonné of His Prints*, vol. 1 (nos. 1–179) (Bern: Galerie Kornfeld, 1990), 379–400.

18 Stephan von Wiese, *Max Beckmanns zeichnerisches Werk, 1903–1925* (Düsseldorf: Droste, 1974).

19 Schmidt, "Max Beckmanns 'Die Hölle'" (see note 8), 841.

20 J. B. Neumann sardonically called them Mephistophelian; see Neumann, "Sorrow and Champagne (see note 11), 289.

21 Dückers, *Max Beckmann* (see note 8), 74.

22 Max Beckmann, *Die Skizzenbücher / The Sketchbooks*, ed. Max Beckmann Gesellschaft, Munich, and Bayerische Staatsgemäldesammlungen, Munich, trans. Allison Gallup and Steven Lindberg, 2 vols., vol. 2, Sketchbook 21, fol. 5r (1919) (Ostfildern: Hatje Cantz, 2010), 504.

23 Dückers, *Max Beckmann* (see note 8), 79; on overstepping the line of the frame, see also, for example, Jacob-Friesen, "Die Hölle" (see note 11), 57.

24 The size of the prints and the painting-like character has been noted continuously in the literature; see, for example, Lenz, "Max Beckmann: 'Das Martyrium'" (see note 12), 185, and Dückers, *Max Beckmann* (see note 8), 56.

25 Various authors have tried to identify the dead man as a real person: Lenz considers whether Gustav Landauer may have been intended in Lenz, "Max Beckmann: 'Das Martyrium'" (see note 12), 198; Dückers argues for Kurt Eisner in Dückers, *Max Beckmann* (see note 8), 84.

26 Dückers, *Max Beckmann* (see note 8), 84.

27 Lenz, "Max Beckmann: 'Das Martyrium'" (see note 12).

28 Lenz gives a detailed account of the historical circumstances and also refers to a lost painting by Beckmann on the theme of Liebknecht's assassination; see Lenz, "Max Beckmann: 'Das Martyrium'" (see note 12), 195, siehe auch Dückers, *Max Beckmann* (see note 8), 86f.

29 Lenz reads them as closed: Lenz, "Max Beckmann: 'Das Martyrium'" (see note 12), 186, Dückers refers to her "blank gaze"; Dückers, *Max Beckmann* (see note 8), 86

30 Dückers refers to her "fingers cramped in pain"; Dückers, *Max Beckmann* (see note 8), 88.

31 Dückers, *Max Beckmann* (see note 8), 88; Schubert, *Max Beckmann* (see note 7), 112.

32 Schubert, *Max Beckmann* (see note 7), 112.

33 See also Lenz, "Max Beckmann: 'Das Martyrium'" (see note 12), 186: Lenz emphasizes Beckmann's view "that the events could not be blamed solely on a wild band of undisciplined soldiers but that civil circles, representatives of the bourgeoisie, were also directly involved." One can only agree with that statement. Lenz interprets the figure in the foreground seen from behind as a young man; Dückers, more plausibly, as a journalist; Dückers, *Max Beckmann* (see note 8), 86.

34 Dückers, *Max Beckmann* (see note 8), 90. Dückers included Grünewald's John as a comparative illustration in his discussion of the print.

35 Dückers, *Max Beckmann* (see note 8), 90.

36 Dückers, *Max Beckmann* (see note 8), 92.

37 Lenz, "Max Beckmann: 'Das Martyrium'" (see note 12), 198.

38 See also Dückers, *Max Beckmann* (see note 8), 94.

39 Pabst, "Anmerkungen zur Genese" (see note 16), 17.

40 In "Sorrow and Champagne," J. B. Neumann wrote analogously of *Hell*: "Whereas in the Middle Ages one could still avoid hell by being virtuous, there was no escaping the hell that had swallowed all of us"; Neumann, "Sorrow and Champagne (see note 11), 290.

41 Malepartus was the name of a nightclub in Frankfurt, where Beckmann was living at the time; see Lenz, "Max Beckmann: 'Das Martyrium'" (see note 12), 201, and Dückers, *Max Beckmann* (see note 8), 102. Dückers also points to the eponymous foxhole in the *Reynard the Fox* fable. In Goethe's version of the fable, the first canto states: "His castle, Malepartus, he has shut, / And in the desert built a Hermit's hut. / So lean and pale and haggard he hath grown / By his best Friend he scarcely would be known." Johann Wolfgang von Goethe, *Reynard the Fox*, trans. Thomas James Arnold (London: Nattali and Bond, 1855), 15. It is not certain whether Beckmann included this in his choice of a title, but the quotation fits seamlessly into discussions of the situation of people in the period after the war and Beckmann's depictions of them.

42 Dückers refers to the proof copy of this sheet in the Städelsches Kunstinstitut in Frankfurt am Main, on which Beckmann wrote in his own hand, clarifying the title: "Wartesaal (Deutschland, Deutschland über alles)" (Waiting Room [Germany, Germany, above All]); see Dückers, *Max Beckmann* (see note 8), 104.

43 Erich Kästner, "Real Romance," in Kästner, *Let's Face It: Poems*, trans. Patrick Bridgwater (London: Jonathan Cape, 1963), 41.

44 Dückers, *Max Beckmann* (see note 8), 108.

45 Dückers, *Max Beckmann* (see note 8), 109.

46 Peter Beckmann, (Belser: *Max Beckmann. Leben und Werk*, Stuttgart and Zürich 1982), 44; for more detail, see also Peter Beckmann, "Beckmann's Path to His Freedom," trans. Barton Byg, in *Max Beckmann: Retrospective*, ed. Carla Schulz-Hoffmann and Judith C. Weiss, exh. cat. Saint Louis Art Museum et. al. (Munich: Prestel; New York: W. W. Norton, 1984), 11–13, esp. 13; see also Dückers, *Max Beckmann* (see note 8), 109.

47 Lenz, "Max Beckmann: 'Das Martyrium'" (see note 12), 203.

48 On this, see Christian Lenz, "'Sachlichkeit den inneren Gesichten': Max Beckmanns Selbstbildnisse der Jahre 1900 bis 1924," in *Max Beckmann: Selbstbildnisse* (see note 12), 9–42, esp. 25–29.

49 "The stronger my determination grows to grasp the unutterable things of the world, the deeper and more powerful the emotion burning inside me about our existence, the tighter I keep my mouth shut and the harder I try to capture the terrible, thrilling monster of life's vitality and to confine it, to beat it down and to strangle it with crystal-clear, razor-sharp lines and planes." Max Beckmann, "Creative Credo," in Beckmann, *Self-Portrait in Words: Collected Writings and Statements, 1903–1950*, ed. Barbara Copeland Buenger, trans. Barbara Copeland Buenger and Reinhold Heller with David Britt (Chicago, IL: University of Chicago Press, 1997), 181–85, esp. 183–84.

THE ARTIST IN THE STATE, 1927

Max Beckmann

The artist in the contemporary sense is the conscious shaper of the transcendent idea. He is at one and the same time the shaper and the vessel. His activity is of vital significance to the state, since it is he who establishes the boundaries of a new culture. Without a universal new transcendent idea the very notion of a new state is incomplete. The concept of a state must first be derived from this transcendent idea, and the contemporary artist is the true creator of a world that did not exist before he gave shape to it. Self-reliance is the new idea that the artist, and with him, humanity, must grasp and shape. Autonomy in the face of eternity. The goal must be the resolution of the mystic riddle of balance, the final deification of man.

Should this goal be achieved in a work of art, then the work itself becomes a symbol and an energy-engendering medium for the development of the partially still-slumbering forces in the responsible man. Appraisal of the finished product is an aesthetic question to be measured according to the highest degree of the collective vitality of the engendered balance. In this sense, artist and statesman are both components of the overall process, since like the artist, the statesman seeks the realization of the transcendent idea in the concrete expressive product of the effected balance, that is, in the organization of the state.

Law on the one hand and the complete achievement of balance on the other are the essence of humanity's goal. Should this goal ever be achieved, the cosmic game in which we are now engaged will come to an end and a new one will begin, in the face of which deified humanity will once again disguise its true role.

Humanity's first revolutionaries perceived their primary purpose as a struggle against God. They adopted more or less the role of Prometheans or other delinquent angels. We fought against God, we swore at him, we hated him, or we ridiculed him—depending on our inclination or talent. Let us realize at last that we were always fighting only against ourselves. We no longer have anything to expect from without, only still from within. For we are God—by Jove, perhaps an altogether inadequate and pathetic God, but God all the same.

The collective intellectual products of humanity constitute God. This is and always has been the case. God is the collective consciousness of the world conceived in eternal evolution—or as I would rather put it, in its eternal unraveling. Its thermometer, the gauge of its achieved

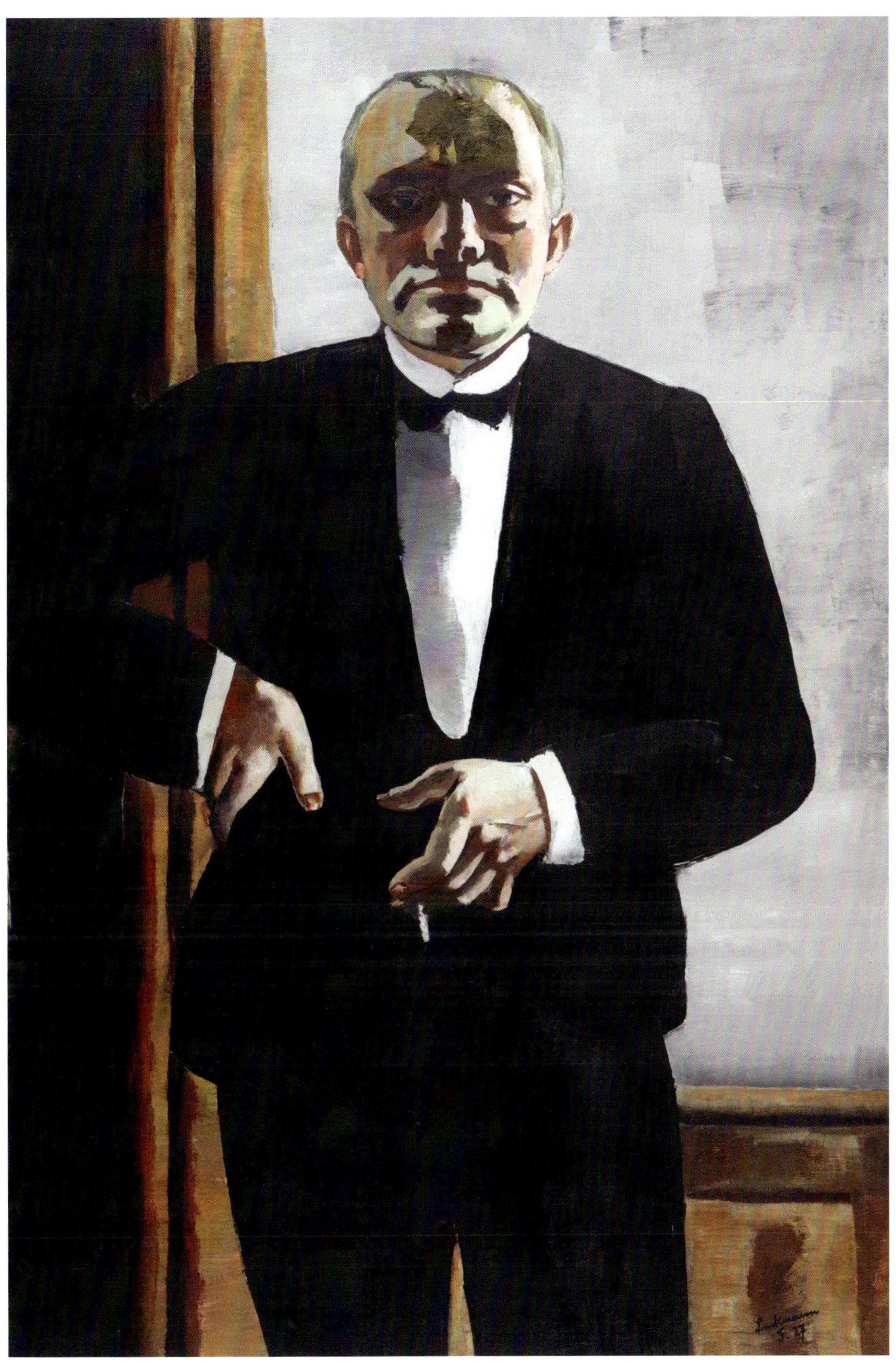

Max Beckmann, *Self-Portrait in Tuxedo*, 1927, oil on canvas. Harvard Art Museums/ Busch-Reisinger Museum, Association Fund

balance or its accomplishment, is embodied in art, and thereafter in all the other products of the human brain.

What we have here is a picture of ourselves. Art is the mirror of God embodied by man. The fact cannot be denied that this mirror has in the past been greater and more rousing than it is today. Yet we know that even childhood in its innocent fashion sometimes engenders things that are often more beautiful than all the works of grown-ups. I view the period of humanity in which we live today as the transitional age from humanity's youth to its manhood. We are just beginning to be grown-up, and in the process permit some beautiful dreams of our youth to fall by the wayside. But no one can deny the fact that even the adult has it in his power to apply his consciousness to the creation of things that may yet surpass the shimmer of the muffled magnificence of our childhood achievements (in India, China, Egypt, and Europe's Middle Ages). We have arrived at this transitional juncture. The old gods lie in smithereens at our feet, and the old churches in their twilight perpetuate a dark, unreal, deceptive sham existence.

Chastened and devoid of all faith, matured into its adulthood, humanity stares into the empty void, not yet aware of its strength.

What we're missing is a new cultural center, a new center of faith. We need new buildings where we can practice this new faith and this new cult of man's balance, buildings in which to collect and present all that has become whole as a consequence of our newly acquired balance. What we are after is an elegant mastery of the metaphysical, so as to live a stalwart, clear, disciplined romanticism of our own profoundly unreal existence. The new priests of this new cultural center must be dressed in dark suits or on state occasions appear in tuxedo, unless we succeed in developing a more precise and elegant piece of manly attire. Workers, moreover, should likewise appear in tuxedo or tails. Which is to say: We seek a kind of aristocratic Bolshevism. A social equalization, the fundamental principle of which, however, is not the satisfaction of pure materialism, but rather the conscious and organized drive to become God ourselves. The external sign of success in this state system would no longer or only secondarily consist in money; the collective approbation would go to the individual who had achieved the greatest sum of balance and who would merit the greatest degree of power and influence. Power and influence are to be assigned on the basis of self-reliance. I am well aware that all this is a utopian vision. But someone has to make the first step, if only in the realm of ideas.

If we are not willing to adopt the faith that one day in the course of human development we ourselves will become God, that we will be free, that we will finally and clearly recognize or see through that incomprehensible, weak, and impossible charade that we still call life, see it in all its hidden expediency—then the entire flux of humanity will from the very beginning have been nothing but a foolish farce. To focus this transcendent wish, we must join together. To strengthen this faith and transform it into reality, we must create the new art form, the new state from. This shared hope, this common faith will be the new core of what in olden times was filled by the longing for redemption through God's intercession. What we want today is to believe in ourselves. To be God, each one of us must share responsibility for the development of the whole. We can no longer depend on anything other than ourselves.

Children must already learn in school that they themselves are God. The purpose of such instruction is to free every creature from its metaphysical dependence and to make it reliant upon itself. Only in this way can the essential and new strengths of humanity be unleashed, the strengths that will bring the eternally fluctuating generations of man, which we embody, to a final standstill, allowing for a free state of being.

If the practically impossible were possible again, if we could build a new center of faith, then surely it would be this one. And it is imperative that we establish that new center, lest humanity sink into the foulest morass it has ever known. In accordance with this new faith, it is essential that the aesthetic education of humanity be far more strenuously pursued in childhood. The recognition of the law of balance in art, whether in painting, poetry, music, or sculpture, is an essential complement to the moral lesson of self-reliance and self-deification. Here is the basis for the transcendent positive potential perceived through the balance achieved in the work of art. This is a replacement for prayer. Our purpose is the last and final focus of the new and ultimate religion of mankind. Oh, our goal is still far off—how well I know it!—but let us harbor the thought, even if the center of which we speak is today still a utopia. We ourselves are the future generations and all those to come. We will reencounter this resolve in the next life, and it will help us—indeed, it will continue to help us emerge from this pathetic slave's existence we now call life. Locked up like children in a dark room, we sit, beholden to God, waiting for the door to be opened, waiting to be led off to our execution, our death. Only when the faith becomes firmly established that we ourselves have a say in the outcome of our lives, only then will our self-reliance grow stronger. Only by combating the weak, the egoistic, and so-called evil in ourselves for the sake of universal love will we succeed together as one humanity in achieving those great and decisive works; only then will we find the strength in ourselves to become God—that is, to be free, to decide for ourselves whether to live or to die. Only then will we become the conscious masters of eternity—free from time and space.

This is humanity's goal. Humanity's new faith, new hope, new religion. Bolshevism took the first steps toward the fulfillment of this vision by the state. Yet what Bolshevism lacks is art and a new faith. It lacks centralization—the dogmatic centralization of this faith, as well as a centralization of art in this faith.

Max Beckmann

Self-Portrait in Words: Collected Writings and Statements, 1903–1950, ed. Barbara Copeland Buenger, trans. Barbara Copeland Buenger and Reinhold Heller with David Britt (Chicago, IL: University of Chicago Press, 1997), 287–90.

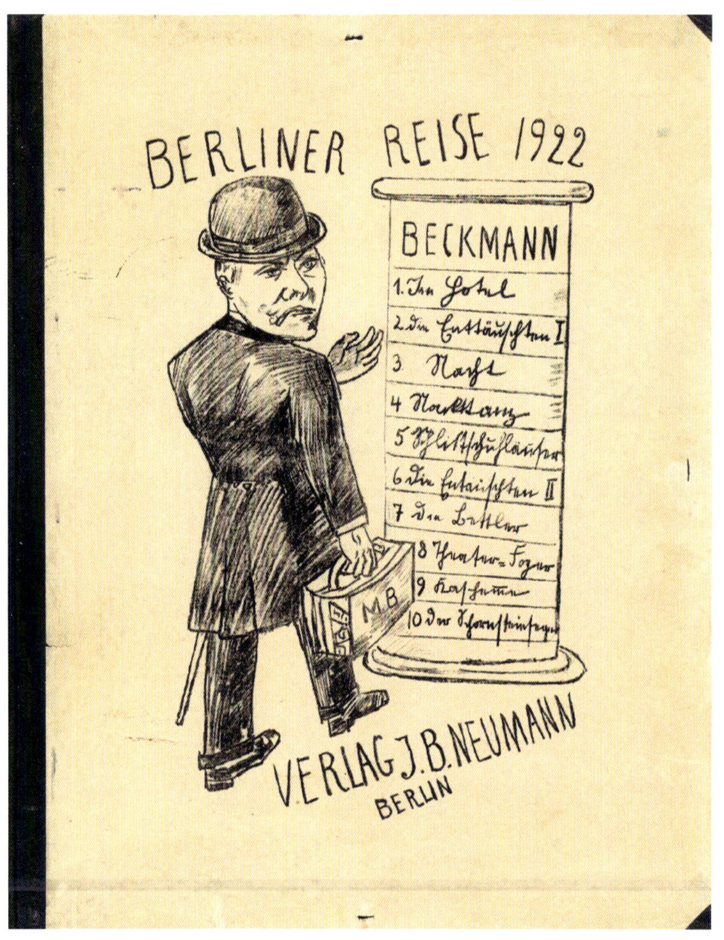

Max Beckmann, Cover, *Trip to Berlin* portfolio, 1922, lithograph. Private Collection

The medium of the print was crucially important to Beckmann's artistic development from the mid-1910s onward. He used it to explore radical formal innovations and at times to realize and record visual ideas that could not be turned into paintings because of the circumstances of the time (see the portfolio *Die Hölle* [Hell]). The seven lithographs that comprise *Stadtnacht* (City Night) were used to illustrate twenty poems by the writer Lili von Braunbehrens that were published under that title by Reinhard Piper in 1921. They were intended to represent evening strolls and tours through Frankfurt am Main, but Beckmann also explores intimate public and private spaces. The portfolio is introduced by the murder of a woman in an apartment by a hooded man, during which her husband screams through a broken window but does not come to her aid.

Licentious activities are shown in the prints *Trinklied* (Drinking Song) and *Stadtnacht*, with boozing and debauchery. By contrast, *Möbliert* (Furnished) depicts a family scene; a child winds a gramophone whose horn occupies the midpoint of the composition and pushes the parents to the edge. This bourgeois household contrasts with the spartanly decorated garret occupied by two resigned war veterans in *Vorstadtmorgen* (Suburban Morning). The figure in *Der Kranke* (The Sick One), in turn, looks ready to be extinguished at any moment, like the wobbly candle next to him; he has stretched out his arms in front of himself as if already dead, and his face radiates unreally, almost crazily into the beyond. Beckmann titled a self-portrait *Verbitterung* (Bitterness), turning himself into a distanced and somewhat cynical observer of the postwar situation in the young Weimar Republic. The sharply angled and reduced forms and social description of the prints elevate them into an urgent testimony of critical verism, a movement with which Beckmann was associated at the time. The 1919 series *Die Hölle* and *Berliner Reise* (Trip to Berlin) of 1922 belong in this same context and address such issues further in a narrative way; by contrast, *Jahrmarkt* (Annual Fair) is striking for its terrifying succinctness.

Olaf Peters

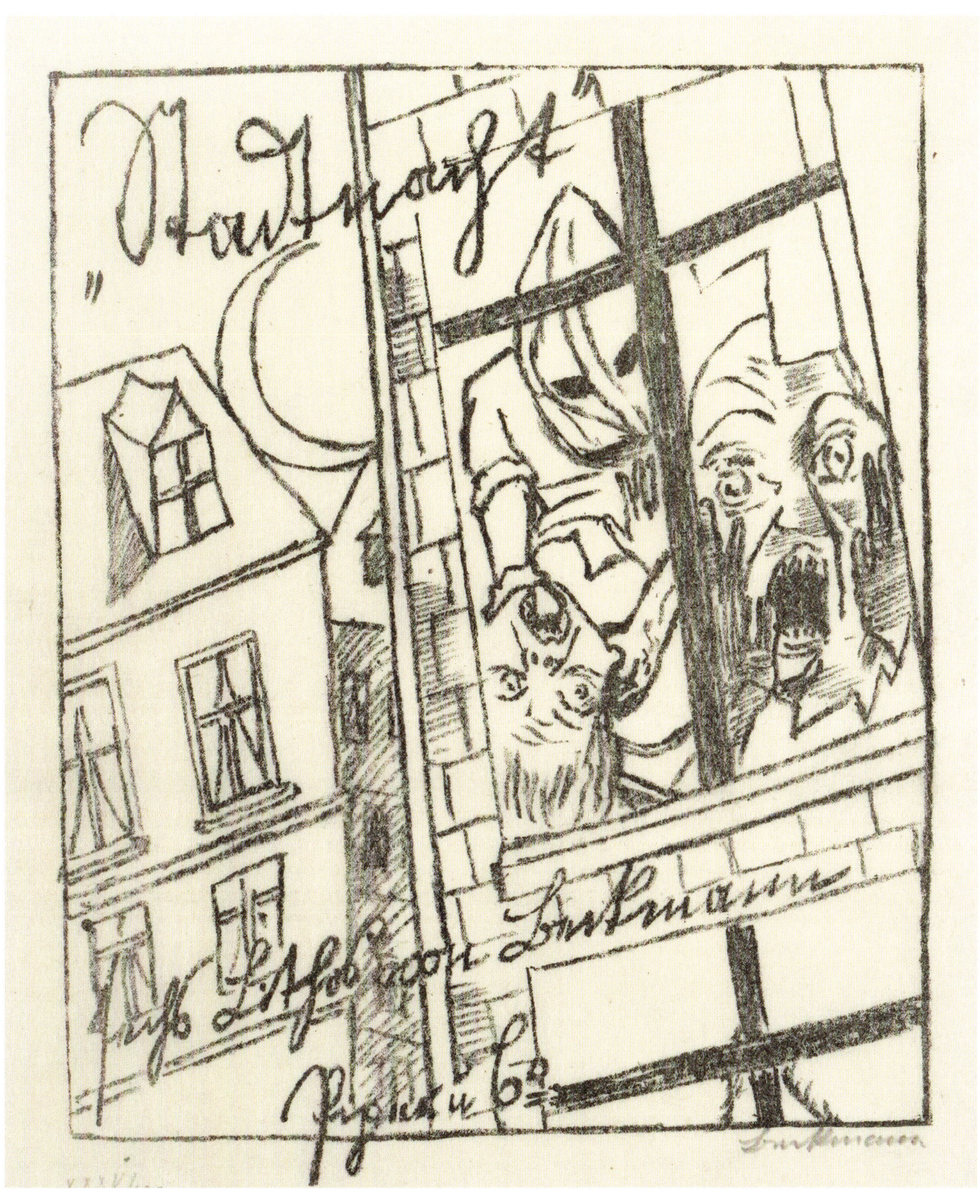

55. TITLE PAGE, CITY NIGHT PORTFOLIO, 1920

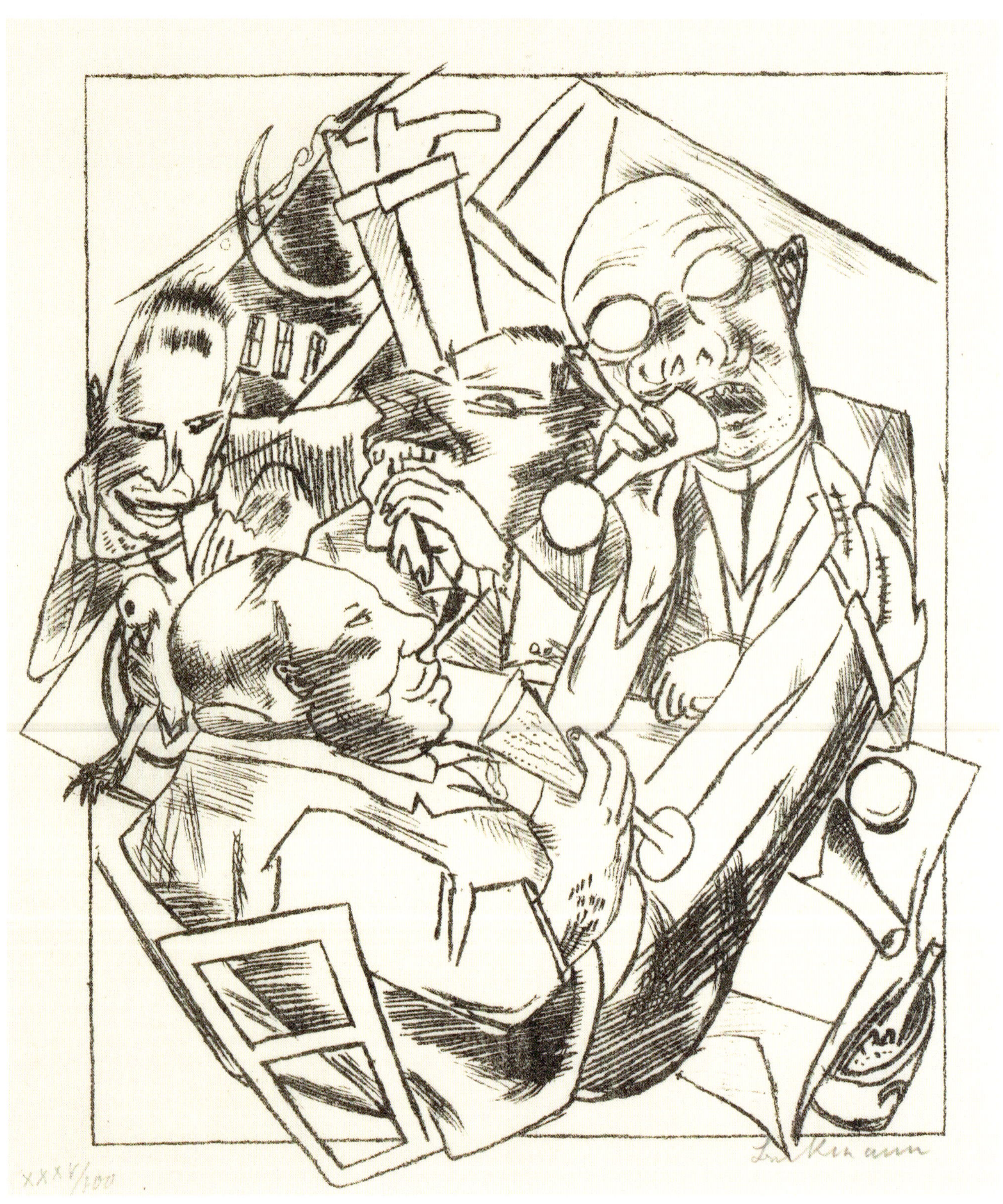

56. DRINKING SONG, PLATE 1, CITY NIGHT PORTFOLIO, 1920

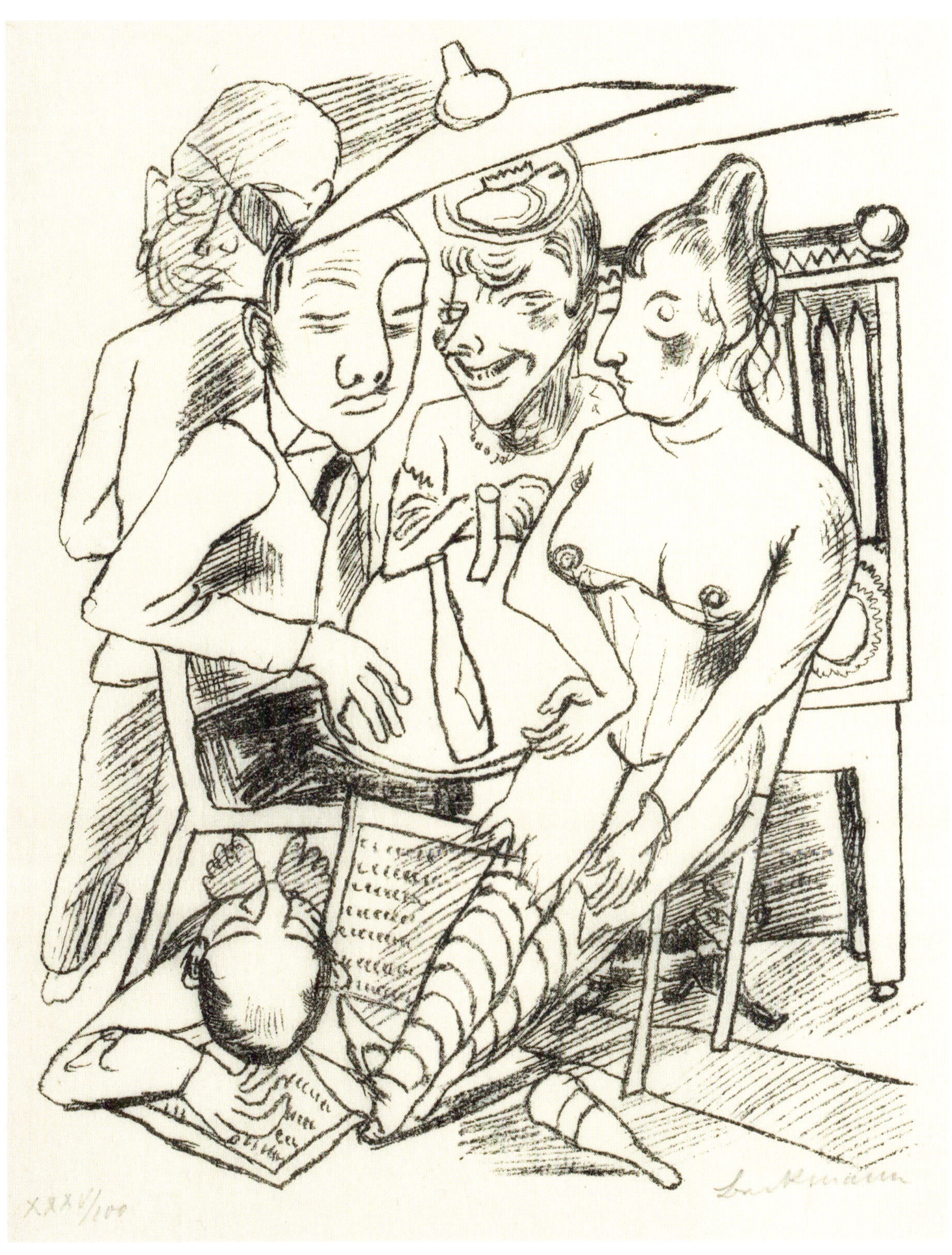

57. CITY NIGHT, PLATE 2, CITY NIGHT PORTFOLIO, 1920

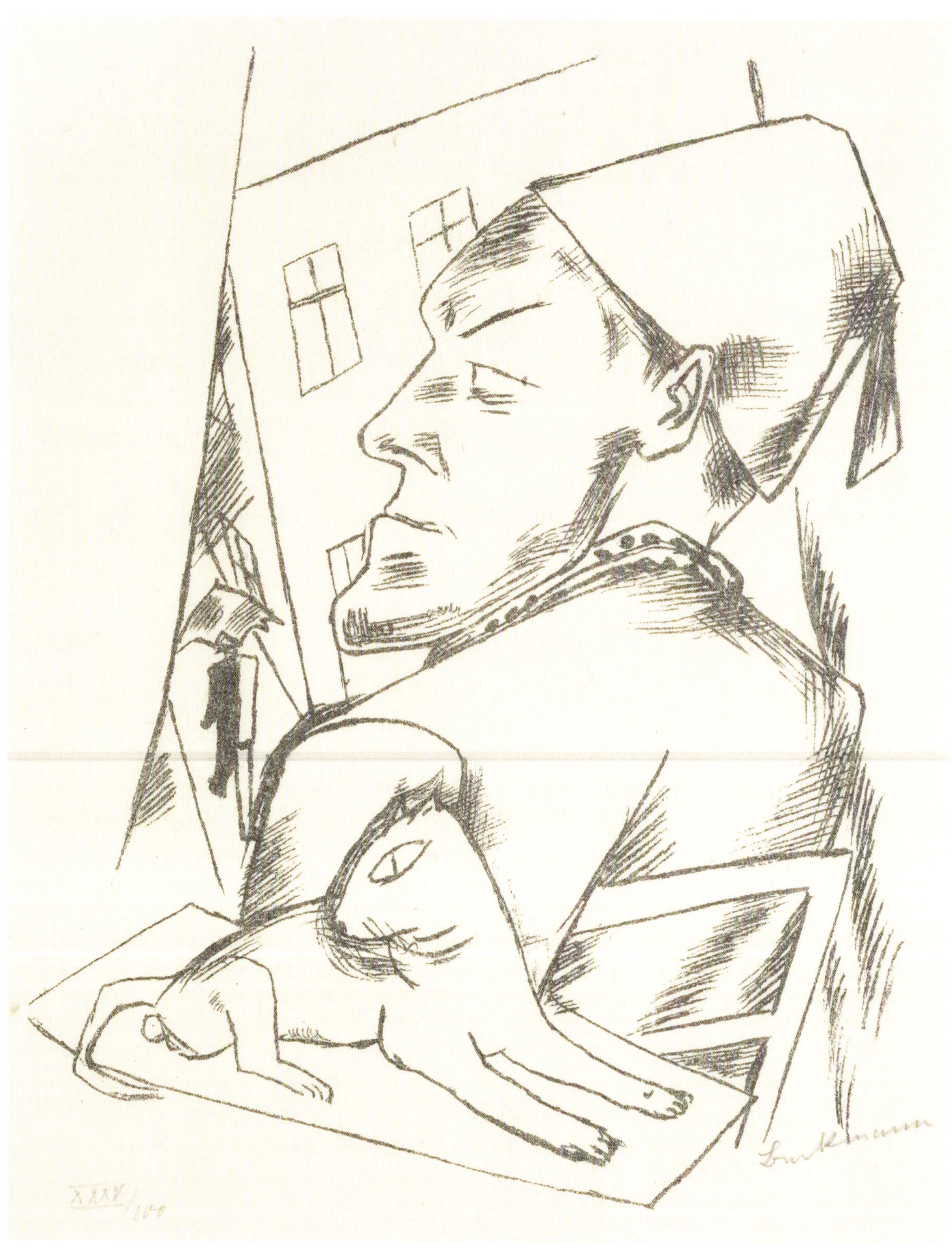

58. BITTERNESS, PLATE 3, CITY NIGHT PORTFOLIO, 1920

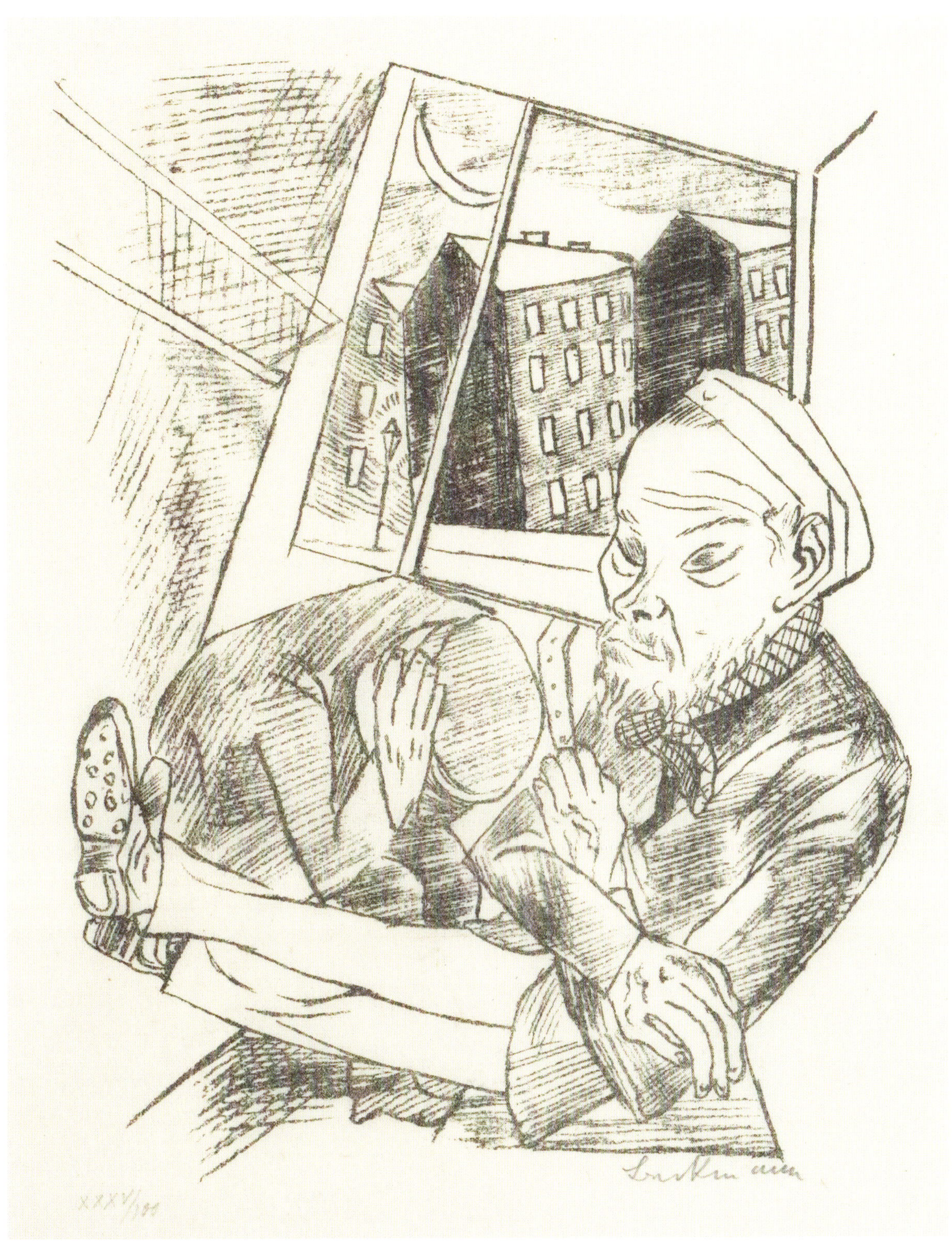

59. SUBURBAN MORNING, PLATE 4, CITY NIGHT PORTFOLIO, 1920

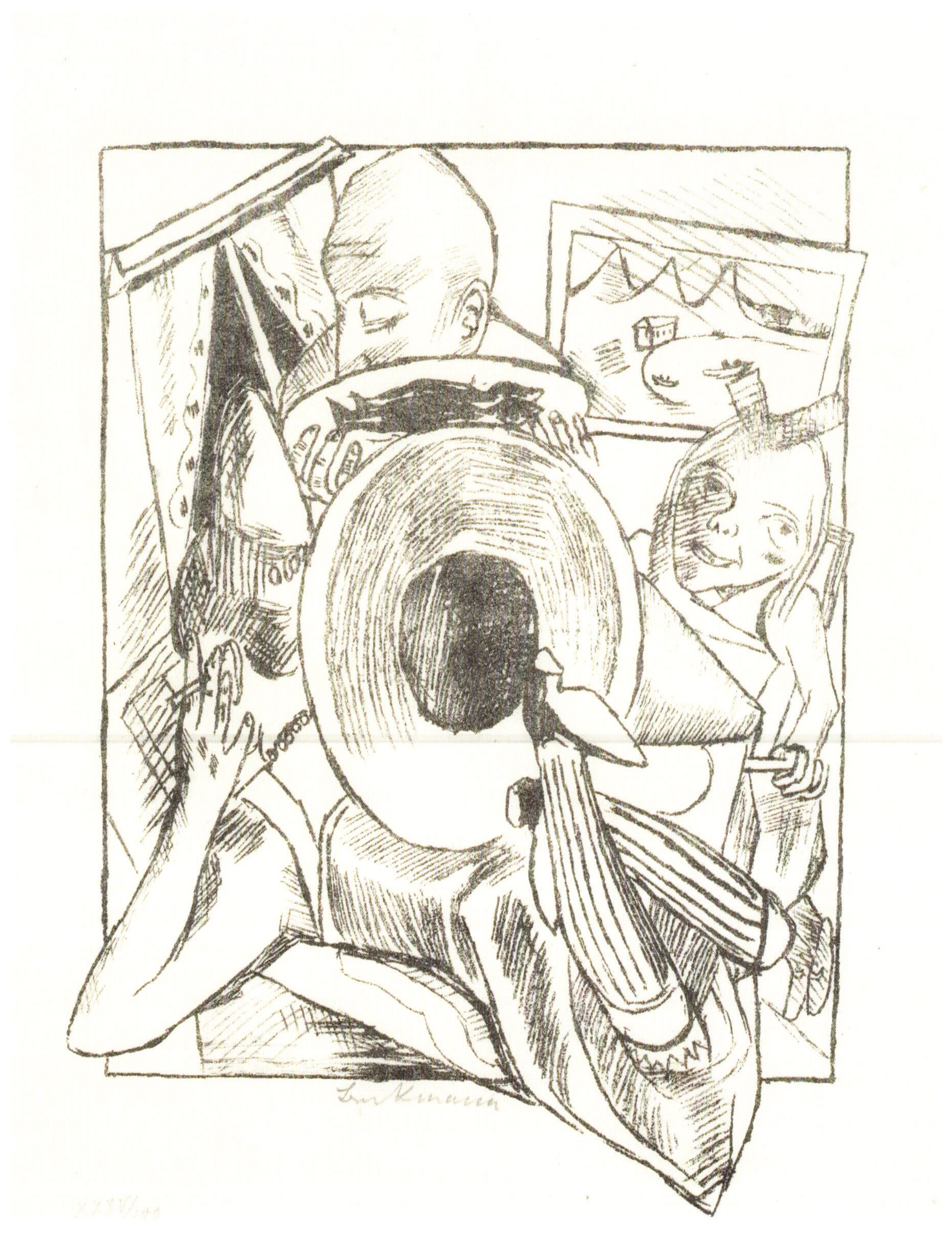

60. FURNISHED ROOM, PLATE 5, CITY NIGHT PORTFOLIO, 1920

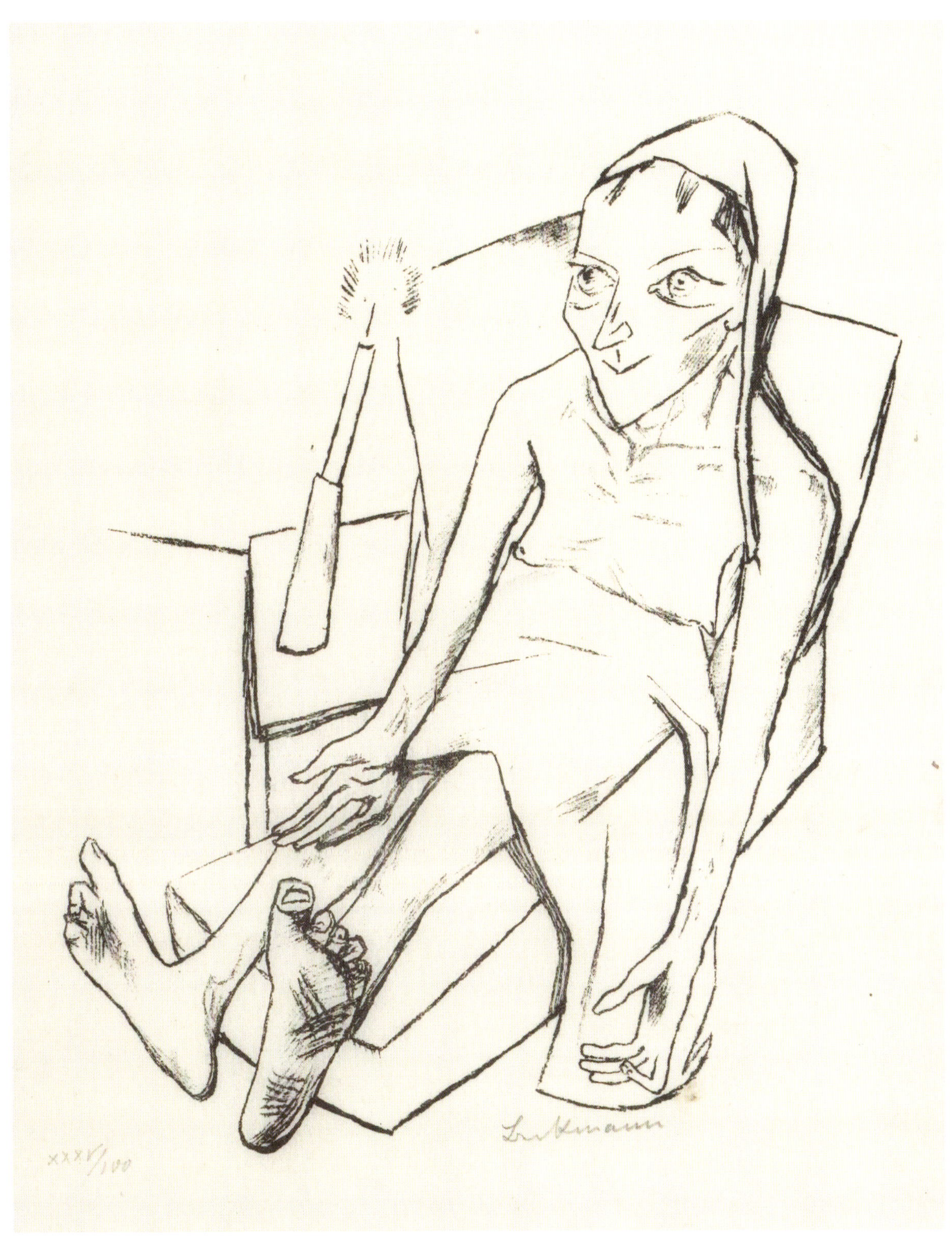

61. THE SICK ONE, PLATE 6, CITY NIGHT PORTFOLIO, 1920

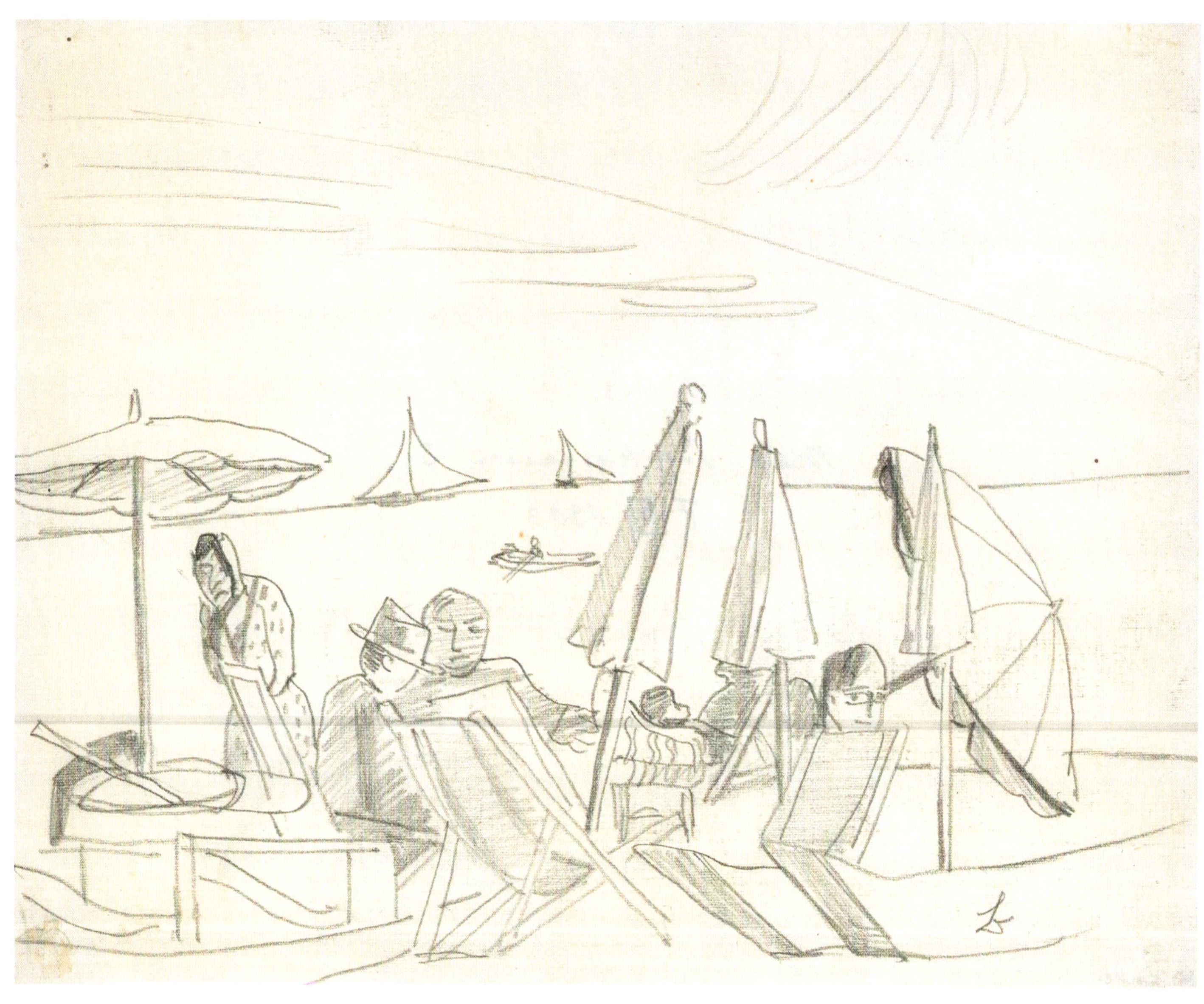

62. BEACH SCENE, CA. 1924

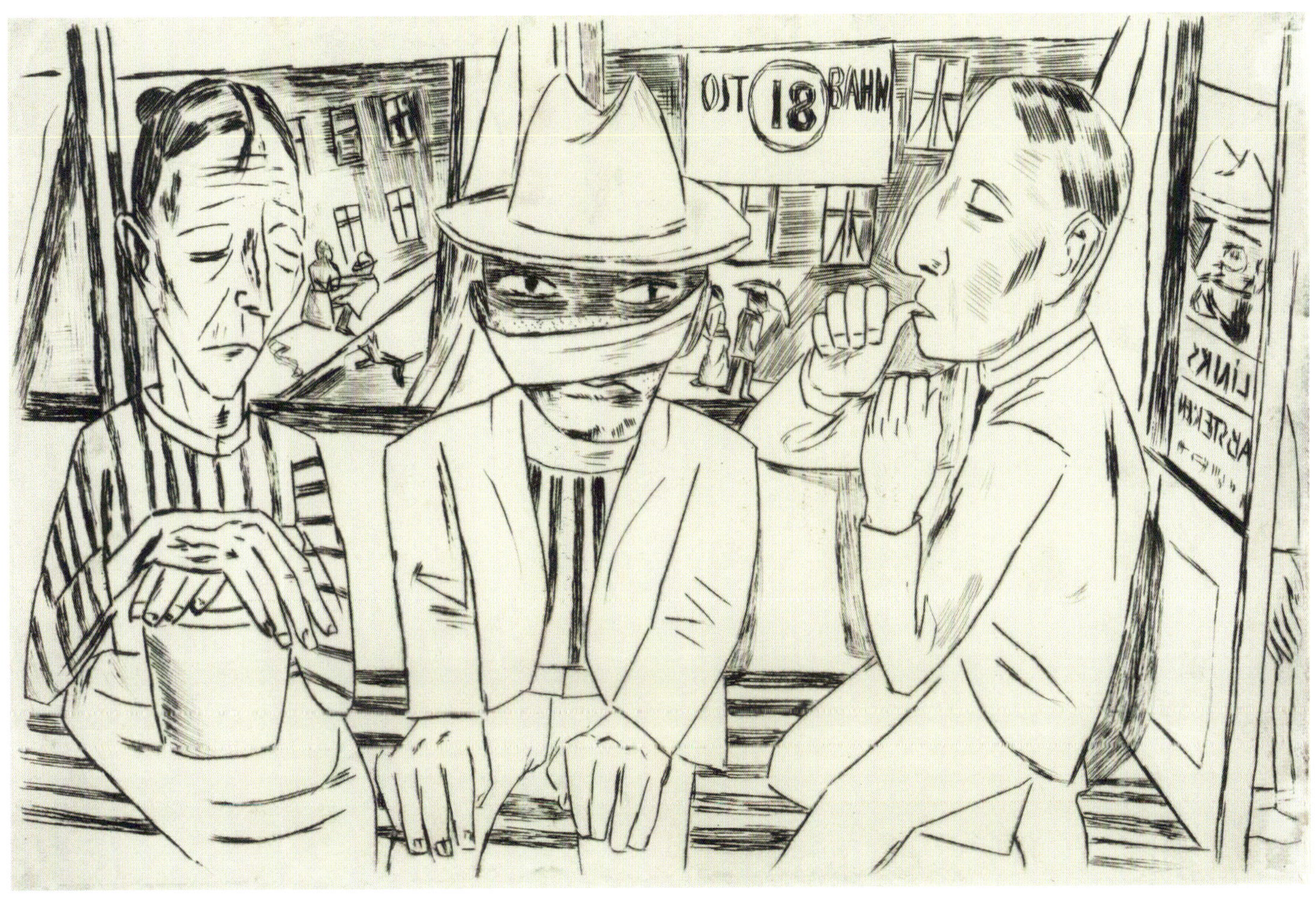

63. IN THE TRAM, 1922

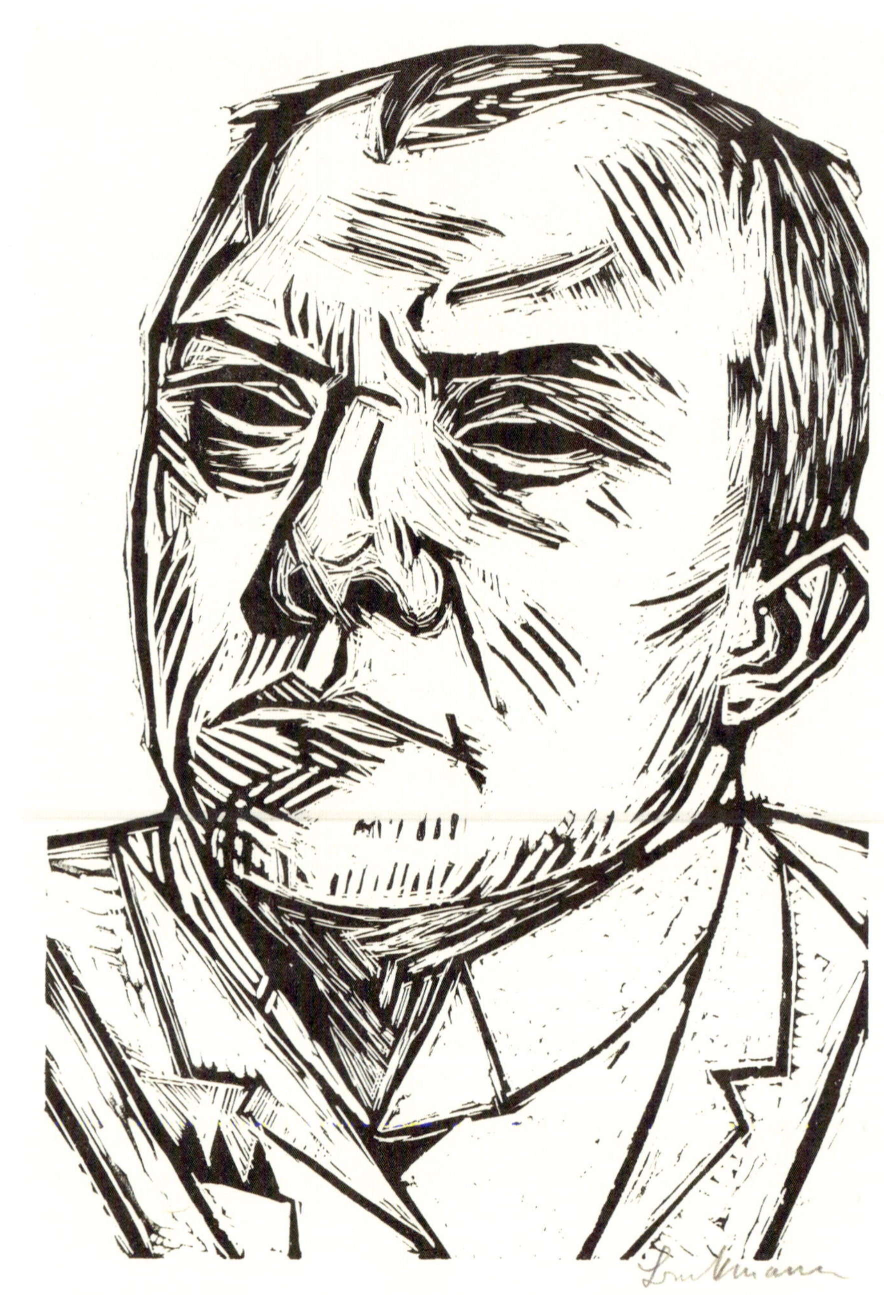

64. SELF-PORTRAIT, 1922

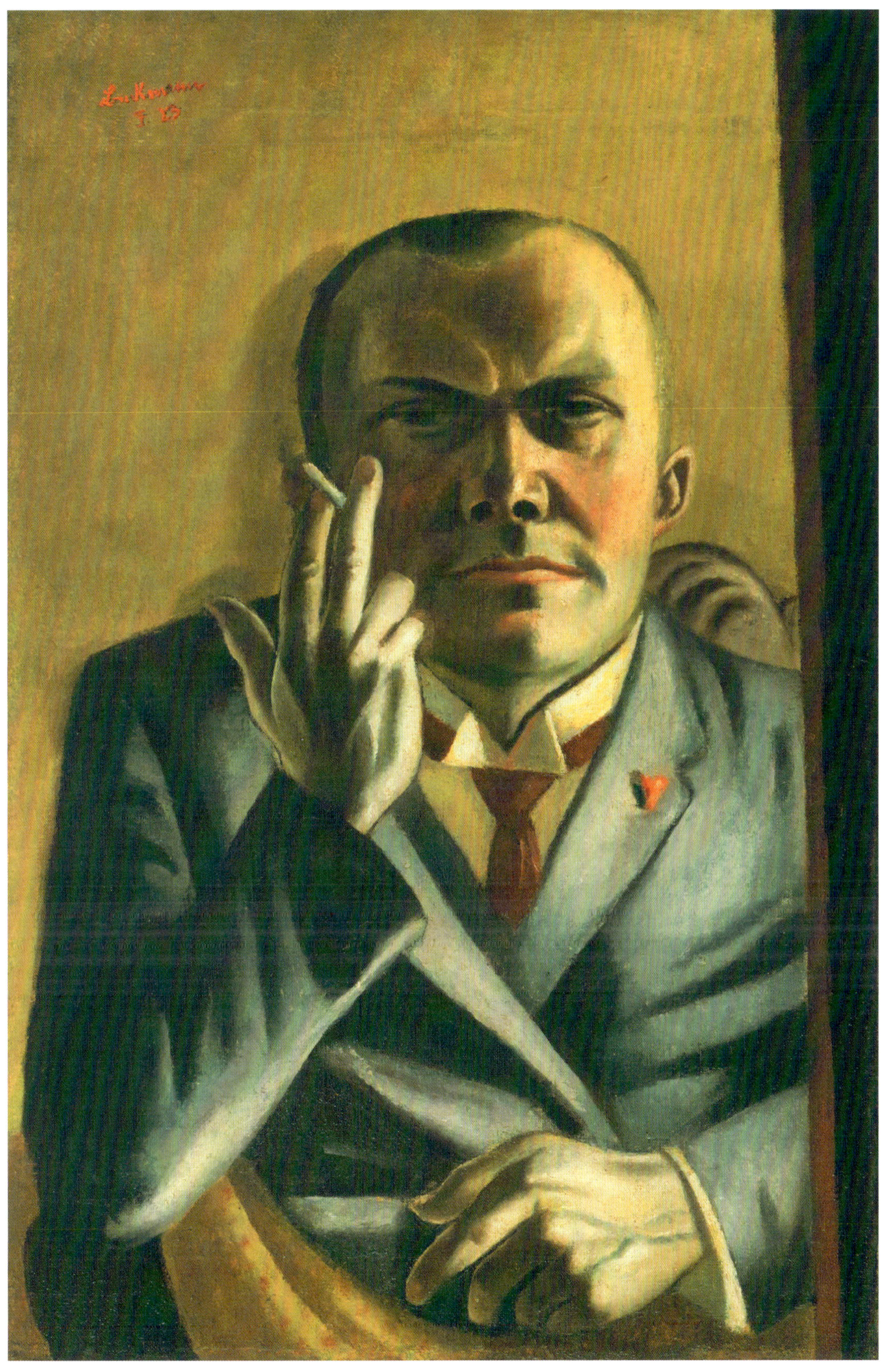

65. SELF-PORTRAIT ON YELLOW GROUND WITH CIGARETTE, 1923

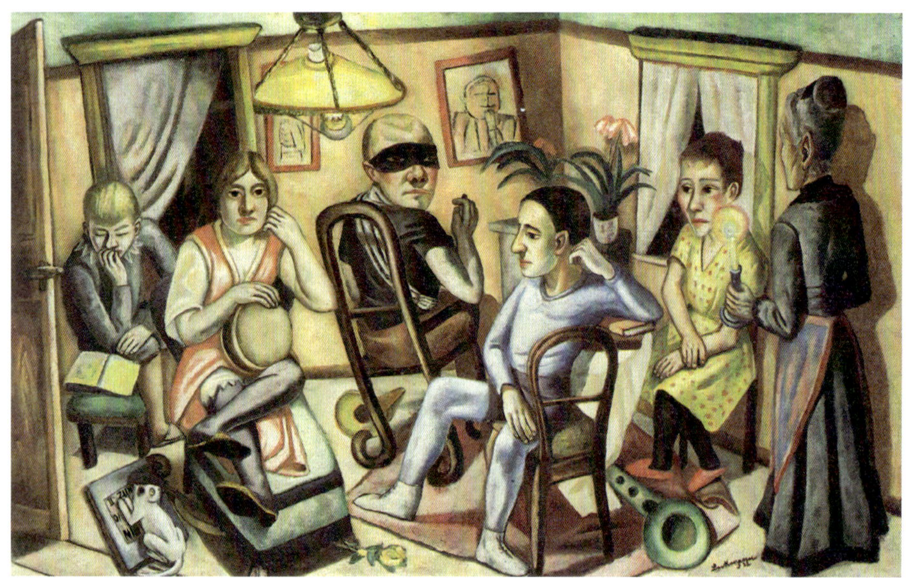

Max Beckmann, *Before the Masquerade*. 1922, oil on canvas. Pinakothek der Moderne, Bayerische Staatsgemäldesammlungen. Photo: bpk Bildagentur / Pinakothek der Moderne, Bayerische Staatsgemäldesammlungen / Art Resource, NY

Beckmann compresses his family into a low horizontal format, conveying a picture of bewilderment and speechlessness. Beckmann himself is located on the left with a bandaged head and glassy stare, lying on a recliner, holding a horn in his hand, with a cigarette stub jammed between his narrow lips. His then-wife, Minna (the divorce followed in 1925 but they were already living apart from each other), is standing in her underclothes with her back to the viewer and doing her hair; her dark eyes peer out of the oval mirror toward the viewer. Beckmann's mother-in-law, Ida Concordia Minna Tube, is sitting with her second daughter, Annemarie, at a round table and has raised her hand in front of her face. She is no longer looking at the open book in front of her, as she is the first to process the horror of what she has read. Annemarie is also gazing into the void and has propped her head melancholically. This group of figures is rounded out by a person sitting on a chair and reading a newspaper (the *Berliner Lokal-Anzeiger*), who has yet to be identified. Beckmann's son, Peter, is lying, like a frog, on the floor under the table at his feet, reading a book.

In this small format—as opposed to the large paintings *Die Nacht* (The Night), *Fastnacht* (Carnival) and *Der Traum* (The Dream) that he produced between 1918–19 and 1921—Beckmann dedicates himself to his own state of mind and that of others. He latently connects it to current events, which are introduced into the painting by the woman reading the newspaper. We do not, however, see any connectedness in reaction to the circumstances of the time but instead an almost arbitrary-looking present in the same place at the same time. The room has a stage-like character and numerous props surround the figures: candles, lamps, a flowerpot, gramophone, kite, cats, and a sculpture of a crowned saint crammed between the corner of the room and an opened grand piano. The theater metaphor will now repeatedly be connected to Beckmann's pictorial inventions but here it is rather an imaginary group portrait that captures the decline of a family into solipsistic activity or immobility. Two years later, the 1922 painting *Vor dem Maskenball* (Before the Masquerade) [see ill. on this page] is a variation on the theme, with the important difference that Beckmann places himself in the center in a black mask and from this point on increasingly paints himself in a state of subjection.

Olaf Peters

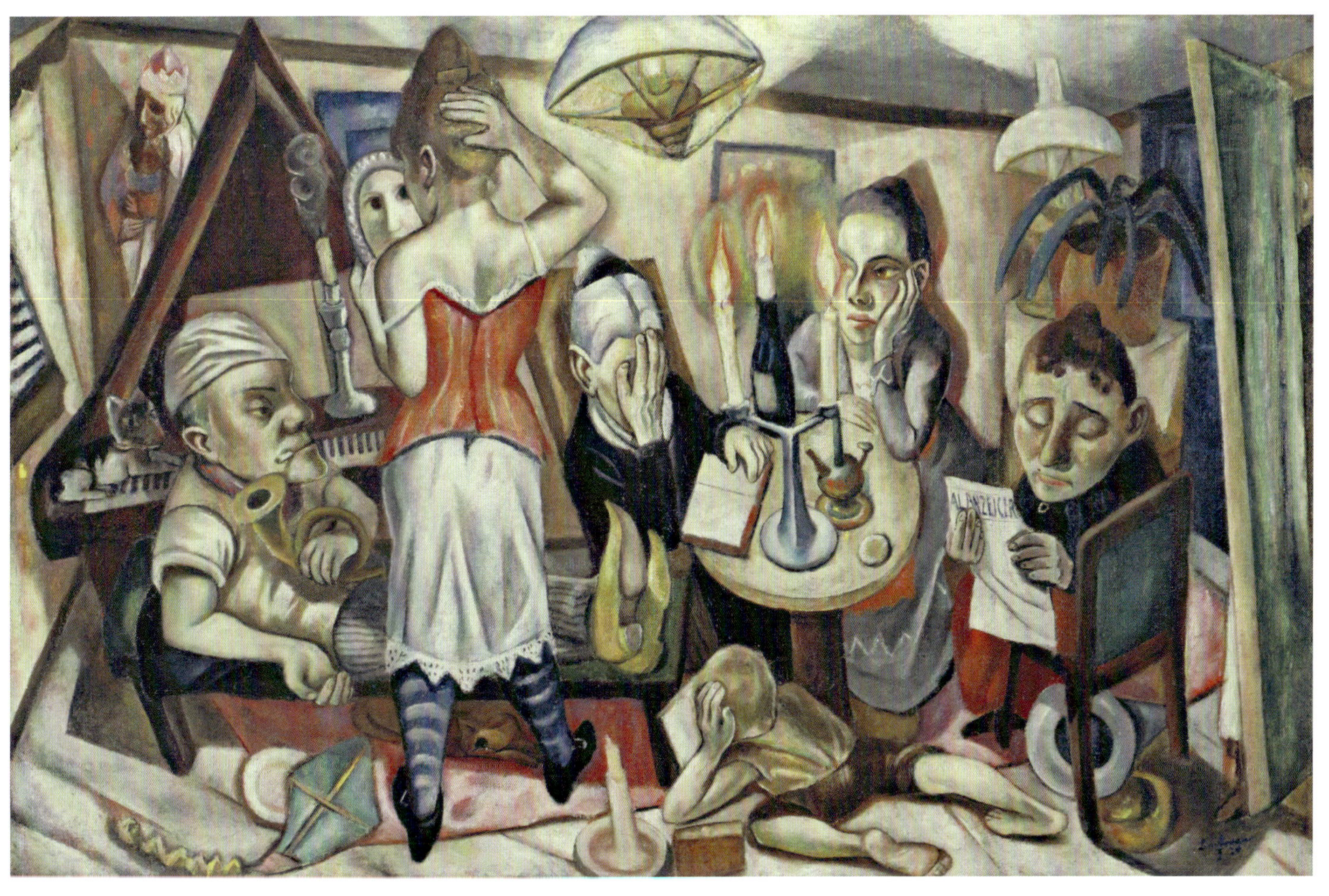

66. FAMILY PICTURE, 1920

This relatively narrow painting is a very personal image for Max Beckmann and marks the beginning of the sometimes-eccentric vertical formats of the 1920s. The painter continued to develop them, by way of *Der Traum* (The Dream [Plate 72] of 1921 and the 1925 *Galleria Umberto* [Plate 101]. From 1932–33, he will make them the point of departure for his triptychs. In *Fastnacht* (Carnival), Beckmann depicts two close friends: Fridel Battenberg and Jsrael Ber Neumann. Beckmann had been living with fellow artists Fridel and her husband, Ugi, in Frankfurt am Main since the mid-1910s, following his separation from his wife, Minna, and their son, Peter. Beckmann did not depict Fridel's husband next to her but rather his Berlin-based art dealer. Neumann made an effort to support the latest art; he began exhibiting work by Beckmann already in 1917, and in 1919 presented the first Dada exhibition in Berlin—the famous "Erste Internationale Dada-Messe" (First International Dada Fair) did not take place until the following year at Otto Burchard's gallery in Berlin. Beckmann—the figure lying bent on the floor, wearing a grotesque animal mask—suddenly found himself at the center of the avant-garde art scene, though he maintained a skeptical distance from it and strove to create his own position. *Carnival* represented a crucial step in that direction.

The scene as a whole plays out in a crowded room overflowing with objects and living creatures. A comparison to medieval carved altarpieces is suggested by the packed, closed-off, and filled up composition. Beckmann was thus ostentatiously putting himself in the tradition of Northern European, even specifically German art. At the same time, he was exploring the relatively recent avant-garde movement of Cubism, whose splinters and facets can also be observed in his contemporaneous prints (see the portfolio *Die Hölle* [Hell], Plates 44–54). Proponents of both Cubism and the Dadaism, who were represented by Neumann, had developed a radical avant-garde approach to collage that in turn exploded the organic, physical body of the traditional easel painting. Beckmann's approach was to reflect on that development but also to fight it almost compulsively. This synthesis of older and very recent art was his effort to find an individual response and is also seen in *Carnival*.

Olaf Peters

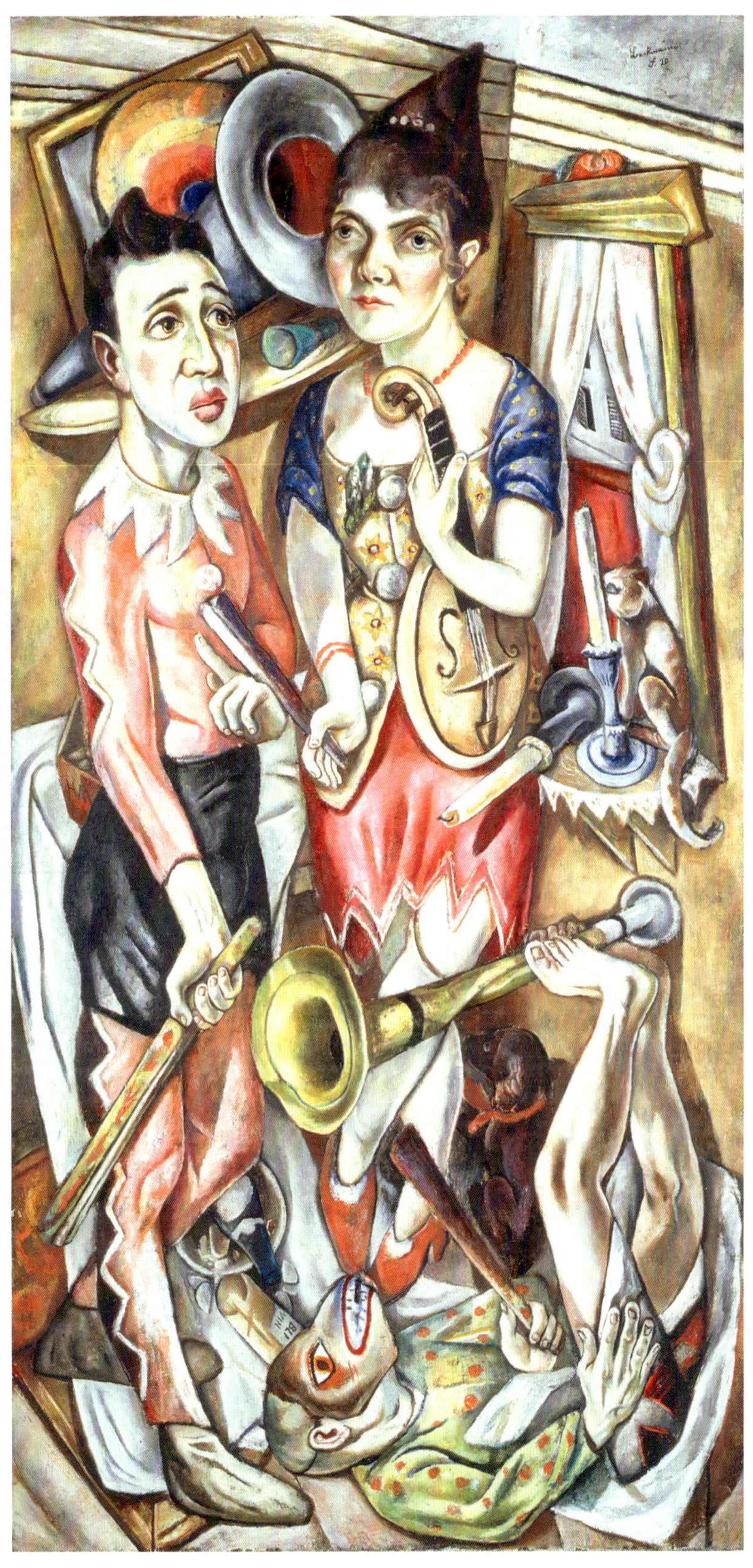

67. CARNIVAL, 1920

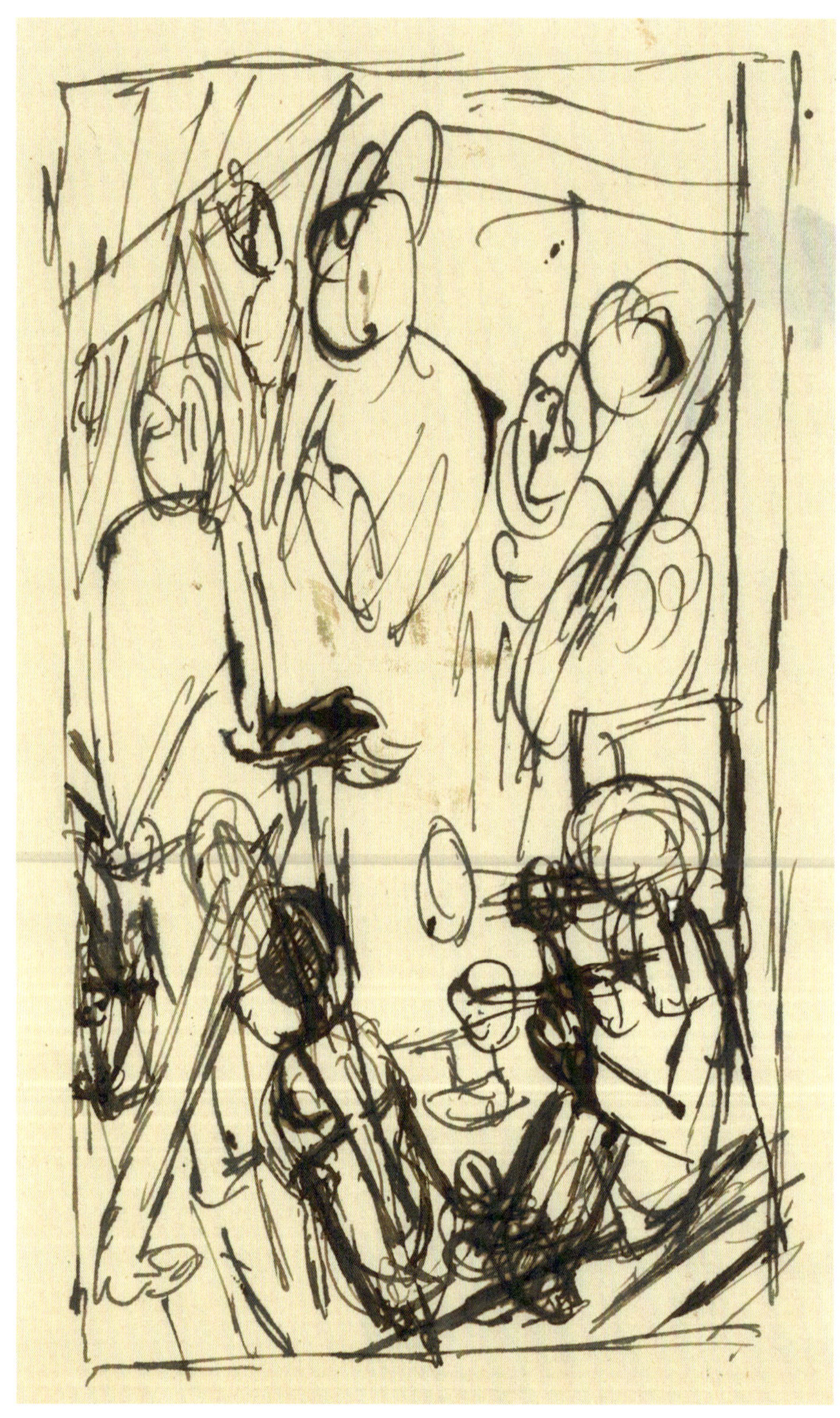

68. CARNIVAL (DESIGN FOR PAINTING), 1920

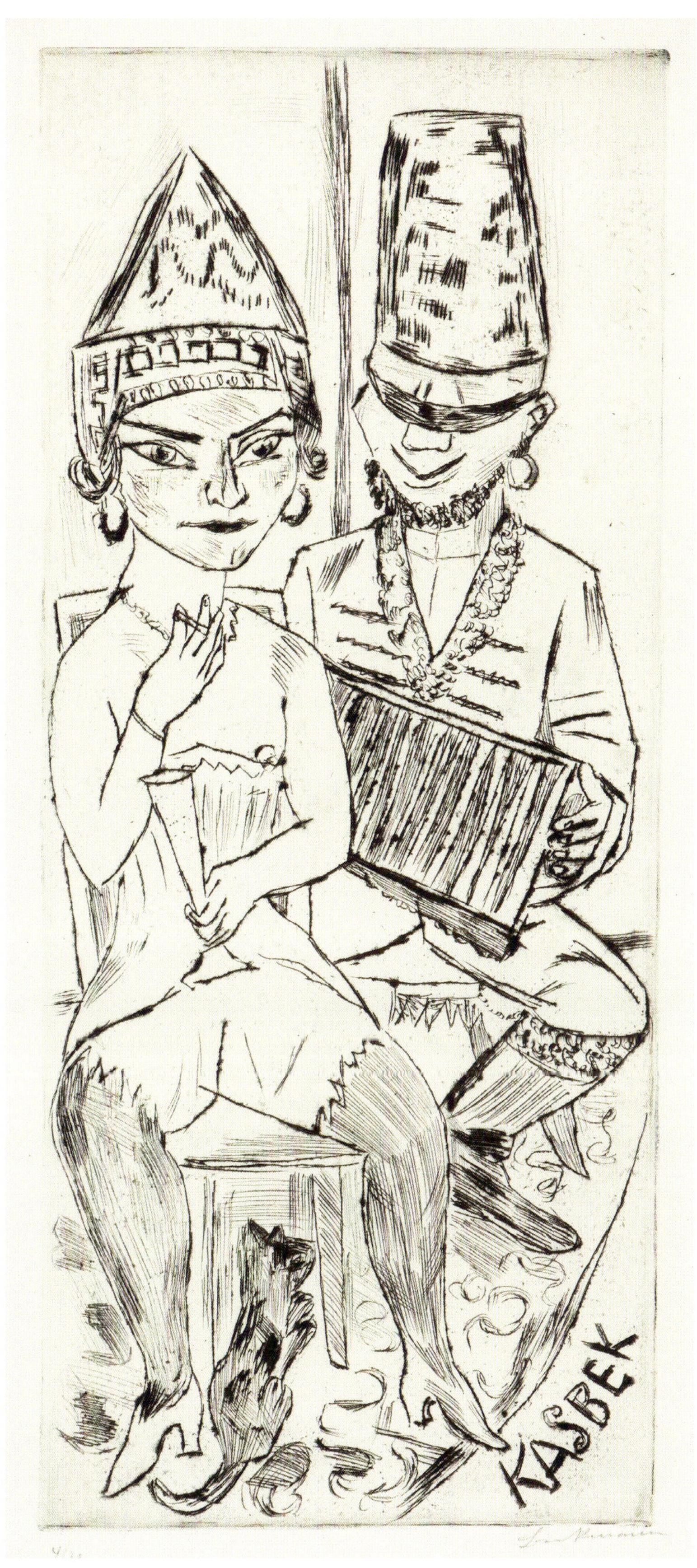

69. KASBEK, 1923

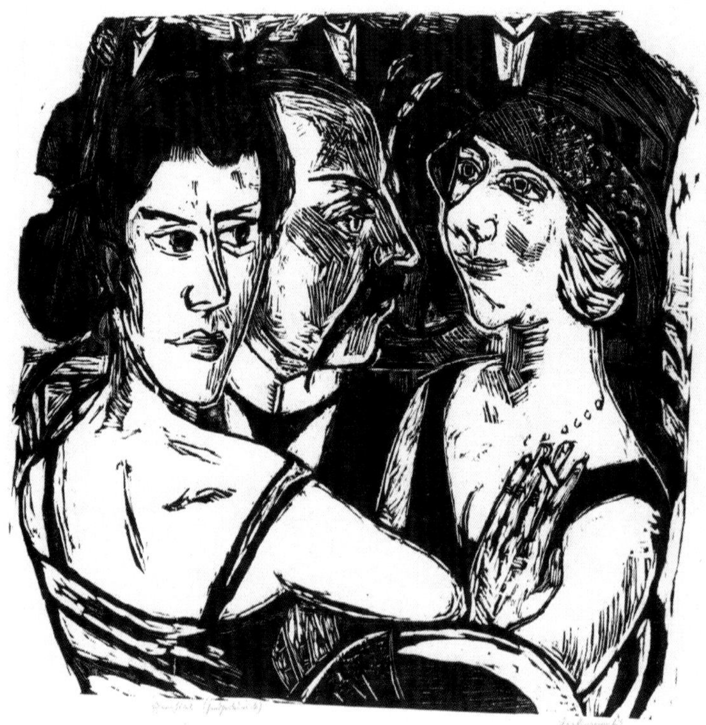

Max Beckmann, *Group Portrait, Eden Bar*, 1923, woodcut (proof). Private Collection

After intensely experimenting with various printing techniques and publishing several print portfolios, some of which were quite extensive, in 1923 Beckmann seized the study of forms of expression temporarily. The results were extremely succinct and would serve as models in later years. Among the woodcuts, *Gruppenbildnis, Eden-Bar* (Group Portrait, Eden Bar) should be emphasized; it presents a close-up view of two women and a man in the bar of the eponymous hotel [see ill. on this page]. This large print confronts us with a technique associated with Expressionism but viewed through an objective gaze. By contrast, *Tamerlan* of that same year is scratched into the printing plate with a drypoint needle. The title refers to a nightclub. Rather than a dramatic close-up, the gaze becomes lost in this narrow vertical format in a maze of stairs and crowds of figures that seem to bring Giovanni Battista Piranesi's *Carceri d'invenzione* (Imaginary Prisons) of 1760 into the young Weimar Republic.

The left half of the image is defined by the stairways, on which waiters rush past with champagne glasses as industriously as ants as they scurry outside the frame. On the right, by contrast, there is a circus scene in which a magician is sitting on a horned animal, which is in turn balanced atop a large ball. The lowest quarter of the sheet shows guests, who oblivious to the activities going on around them—neither the waiters nor the artistes. Beckmann himself appears among them, with his mysterious great love of the time, Naila (Hildegard Schmidt-Melms), an economist from Krefeld who received her doctorate in 1922 and was presumably Beckmann's lover briefly in 1923 but later separated from him. Her clearly recognizable face corresponds to that of the male artiste in the upper right half of the image. Beckmann, by contrast, remains a masklike schema and somewhat helplessly immobile. Leaving these biographical speculations aside, however, *Tamerlan* must be recognized as one of Beckmann's most radical pictorial inventions, one that he would take up again in abbreviated form in his 1937 *Selbstbildnis im Frack* (Self-Portrait in Tails) and his triptychs from the 1930s (see the right wing of *Departure*, and the left one of *Acrobats*).

Olaf Peters

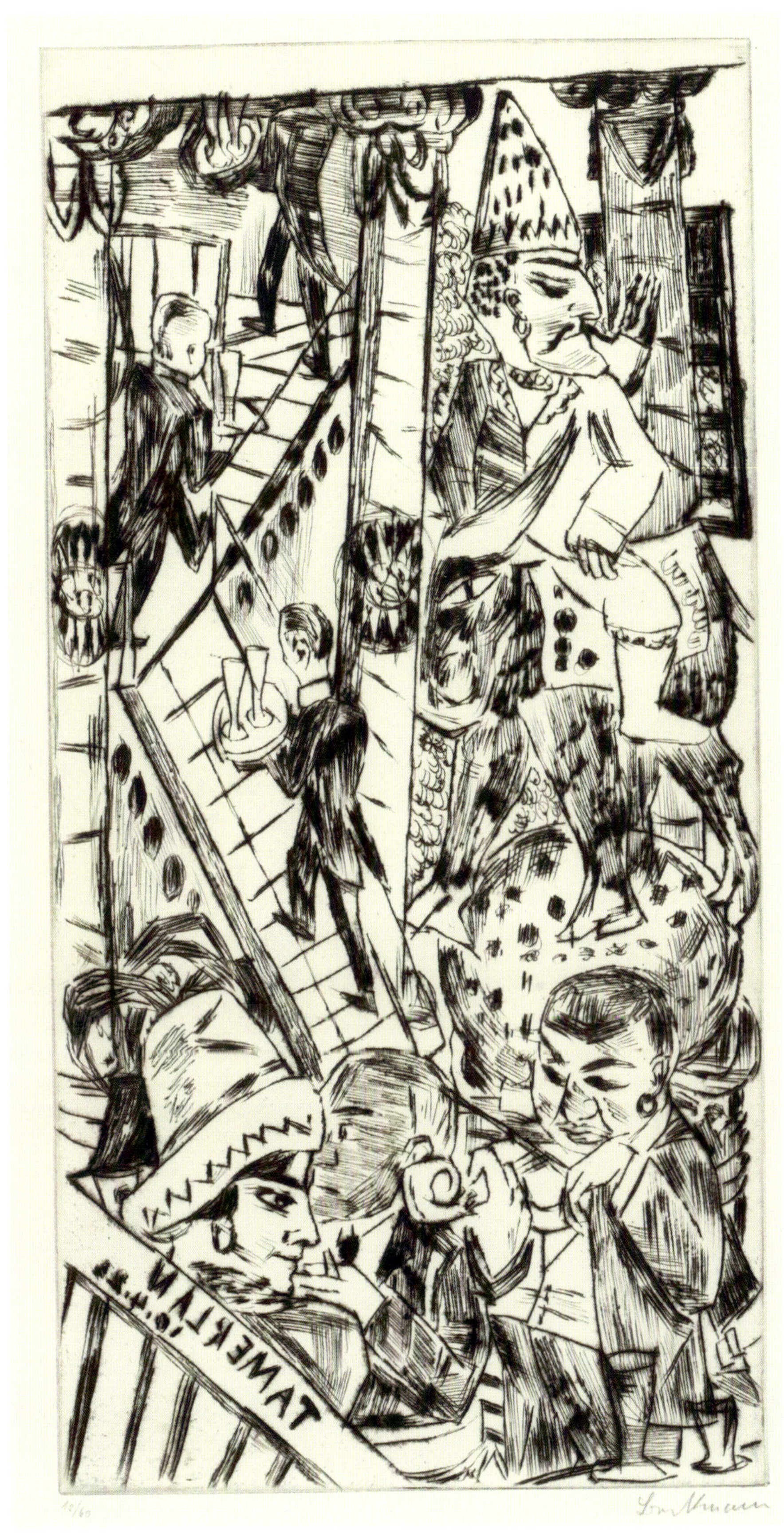

70. TAMERLAN, PRINTED 1923, PUBLISHED 1924

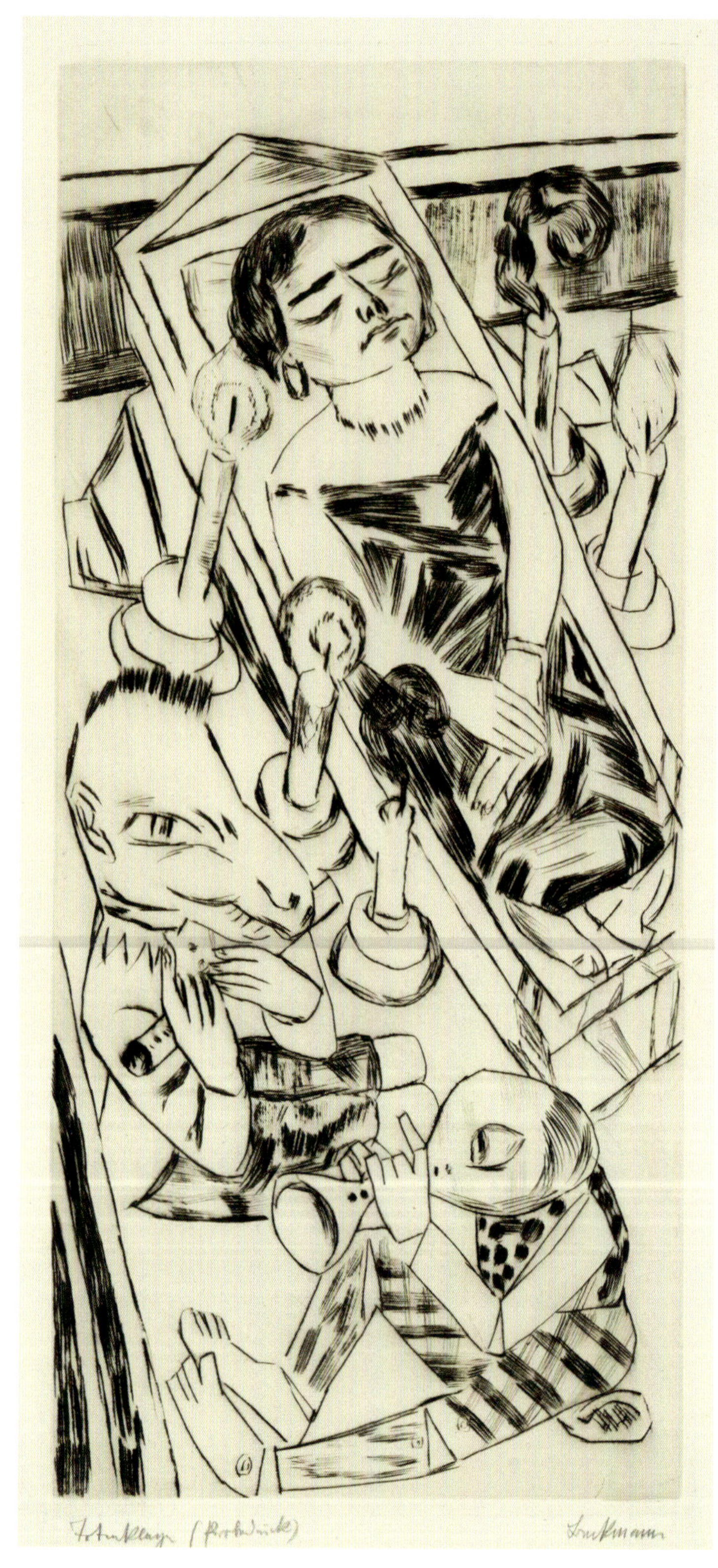

71. DREAM I (FUNERAL DIRGE), 1924

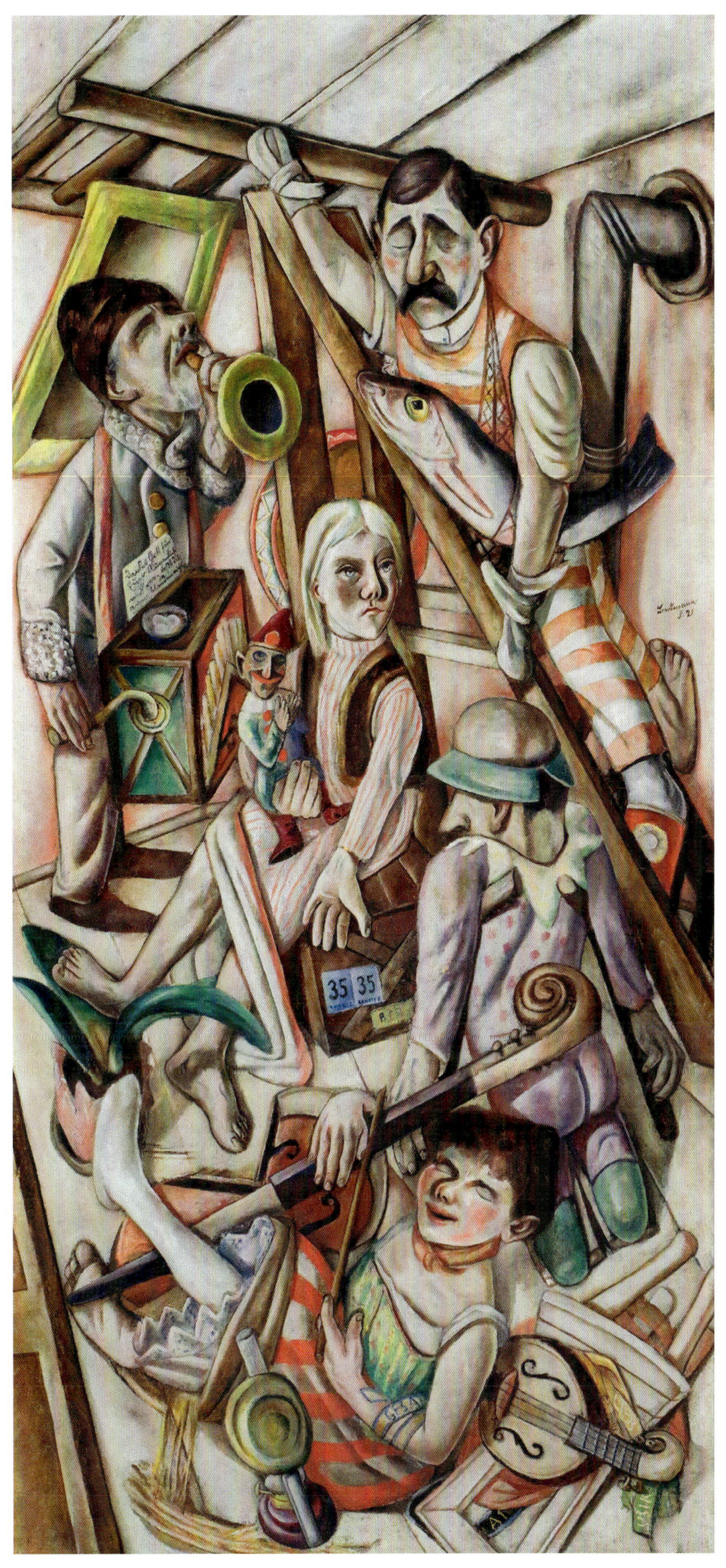

72. THE DREAM, 1921

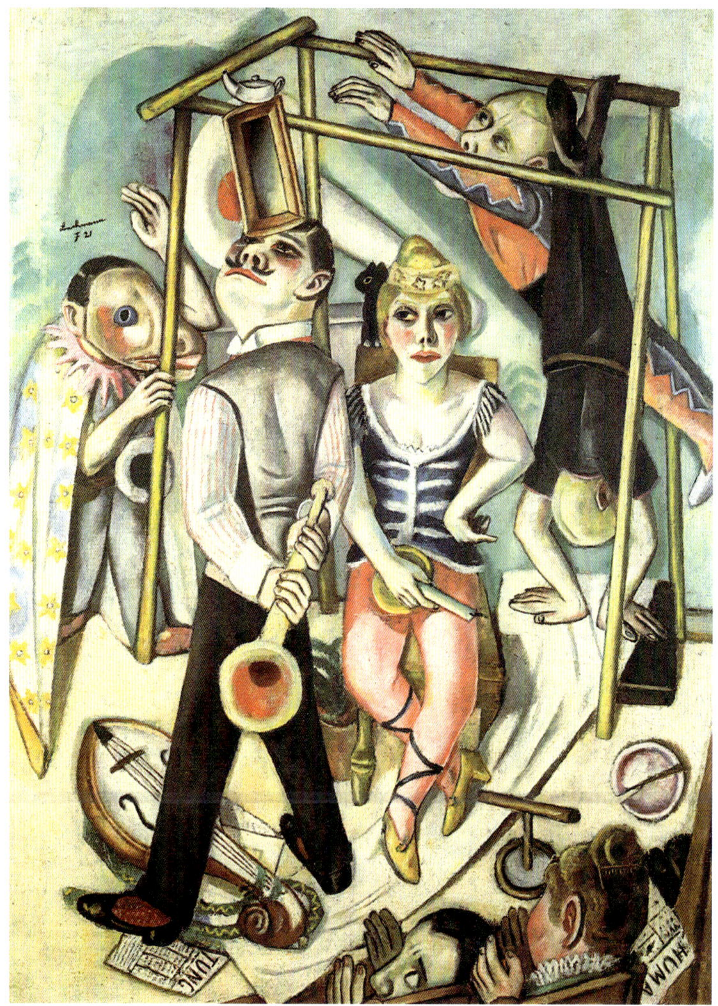

Max Beckmann, *Variety Show*, 1921, oil on canvas. Private Collection

The iconography of carnies and the circus is one of the central themes of Max Beckmann's art, along with the places and motifs of the café, dancehalls, and variety theaters. He took them up often in his paintings and prints of the early 1920s. *Das Trapez* (The Trapeze) shows seven artistes compressed into a cramped space within a vertical, rectangular image. They interlock, sometimes touching each other, and yet act independently of one another in a strangely detached way. In addition to and almost in contradiction with the solipsism that characterizes these figures, despite their connections, is a violence that Beckmann inscribes in the image: the artiste on the floor looks almost trampled down; the woman on the left side combines eroticism with compulsion. The man in a white leotard stuck under the ceiling is holding an iron chain in his mouth—another painful motif for the viewer—and responds to the figure pressed to the floor.

Several formal aspects of this painting already illustrate Beckmann's future development: these include its hard, black contours; its transformed palette, in which Beckmann replaces the primary colors previously used frequently as signals with a beguiling chord of lemony green, reddish pink, and indigo; the use of figurative motifs that subdivide, tense up, and construct the pictorial space. The fact that Beckmann returned to its composition for the left wing of his 1939 triptych *Akrobaten* (Acrobats) [see p. 266] shows the significance of this painting. There the painter quoted and varied *The Trapeze* in order to transition from an almost surreal, dream- or nightmare-like sequence to images with allusions to defamation and the dangers of war that were most certainly critical of their era.

Olaf Peters

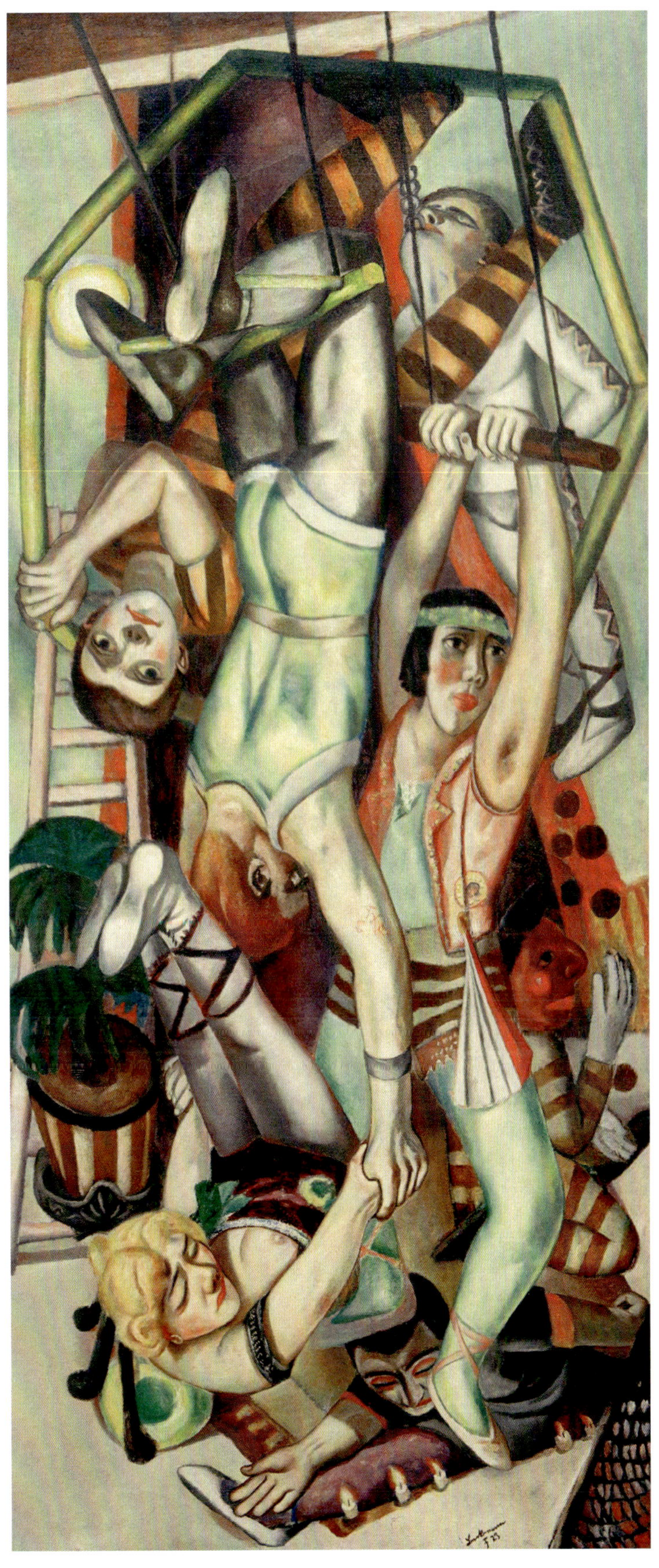

73. THE TRAPEZE, 1923

Max Beckmann, *New Construction*, 1928, oil on canvas. Private Collection. Photo: Christie's Images Ltd - ARTOTHEK

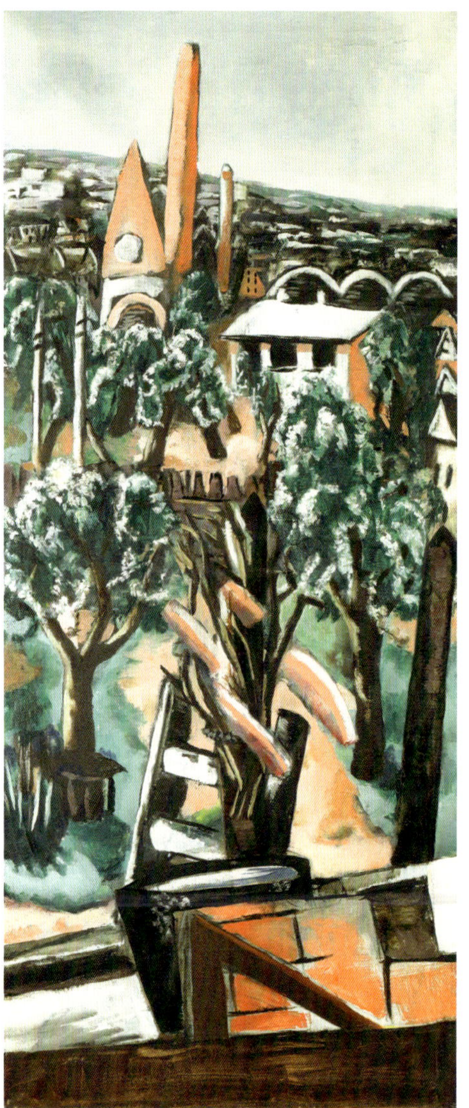

From the early 1920s onward, Max Beckmann increasingly returned to the subject of the landscape. He favored scenes depicting locales worked by humans, especially the landscape on the periphery of the city of Frankfurt am Main. Beckmann had moved there during World War I and remained until 1933. Beneath a hard, nearly white sky, interrupted by narrow, sharply cutting clouds, a miniature-like urban landscape stretches out across the horizontal format, marked by apartment buildings, allotment gardens, and several smaller factories with chimneys. Beckmann tips and nests the elements of the painting into one another, producing an almost mosaic-like restlessness. The representationalism of the *Neue Sachlichkeit* and the Cubist concept of space achieve a synthesis here that translates this excerpt from reality into a visual autonomy with a logic of its own. Beckmann thus was receptive to a contemporaneous avant-garde that was determined by Constructivism without abandoning his goal to study reality and to master it artistically.

Two subsequent paintings show Beckmann's stylistic development: the 1926 *Landschaft mit rauchendem Schornstein* (Landscape with Smoking Chimney) radically reduces the scenery, offering a vertical format with stripes, some of which are executed in monochrome, that pen nature in behind a fence. A smoking chimney towers above the scene, releasing a dark, dirty cloud of smoke in front of white clouds that trail to the right. *Neubau* (New Construction) of 1928 better differentiates the suburban landscape with its white-and-green blossoming trees and red buildings [see ill. on this page]. Construction is clearly ongoing here; a metropolis is growing, which was already being called the Neues Frankfurt at this time, in the sense of *Neues Bauen* (New Building). Beckmann is merely suggesting that transformation, which was implemented in Frankfurt from 1925 onward under municipal architect and planner Ernst May, which today is associated with the Weimar Republic. Beckmann was no illustrator of historic, socioeconomic change but instead favored a sometimes probing, sometimes gripping architecture of a pictorial structure that never ossifies but always remains alive.

Olaf Peters

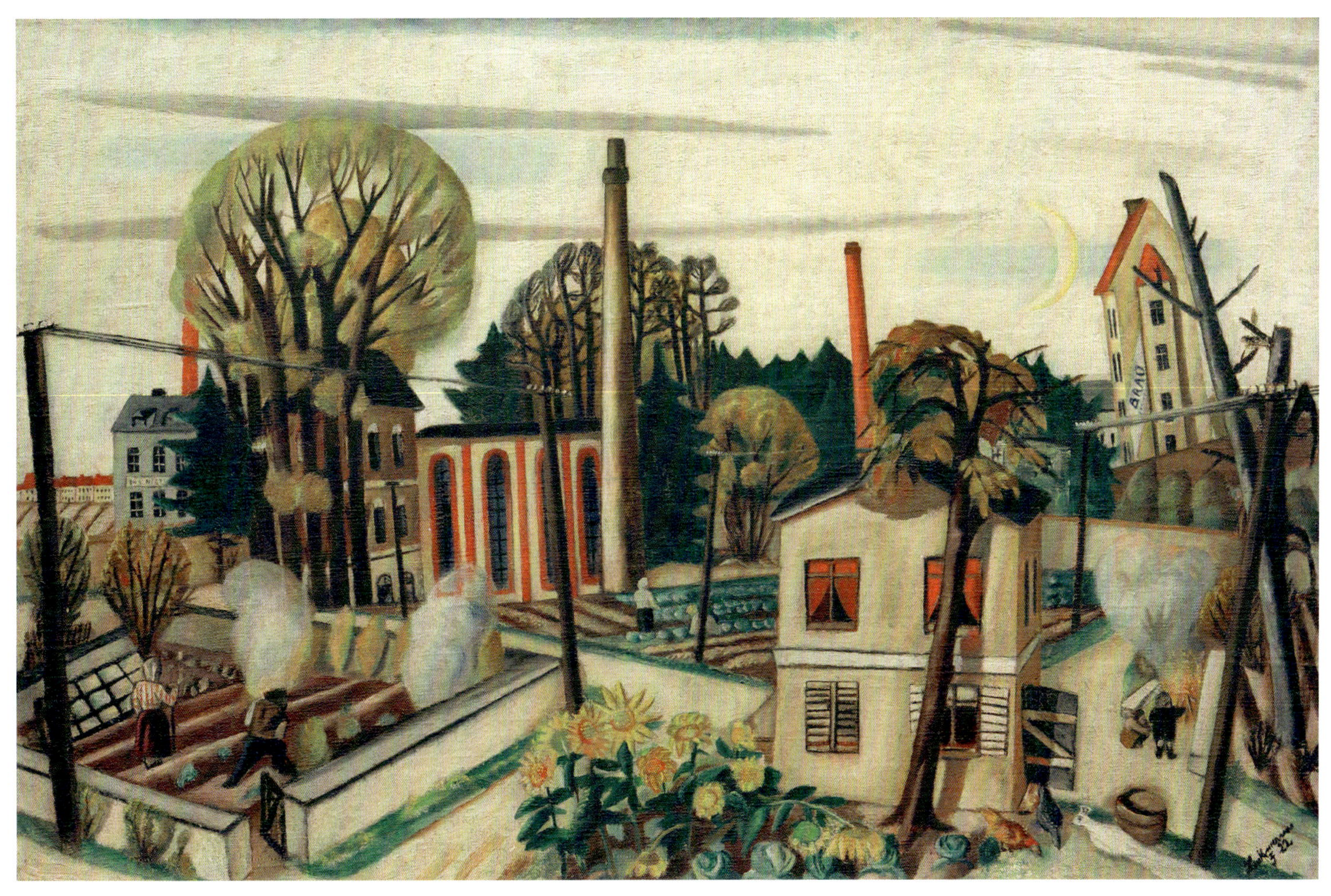

74. LANDSCAPE NEAR FRANKFURT (WITH FACTORY), 1922

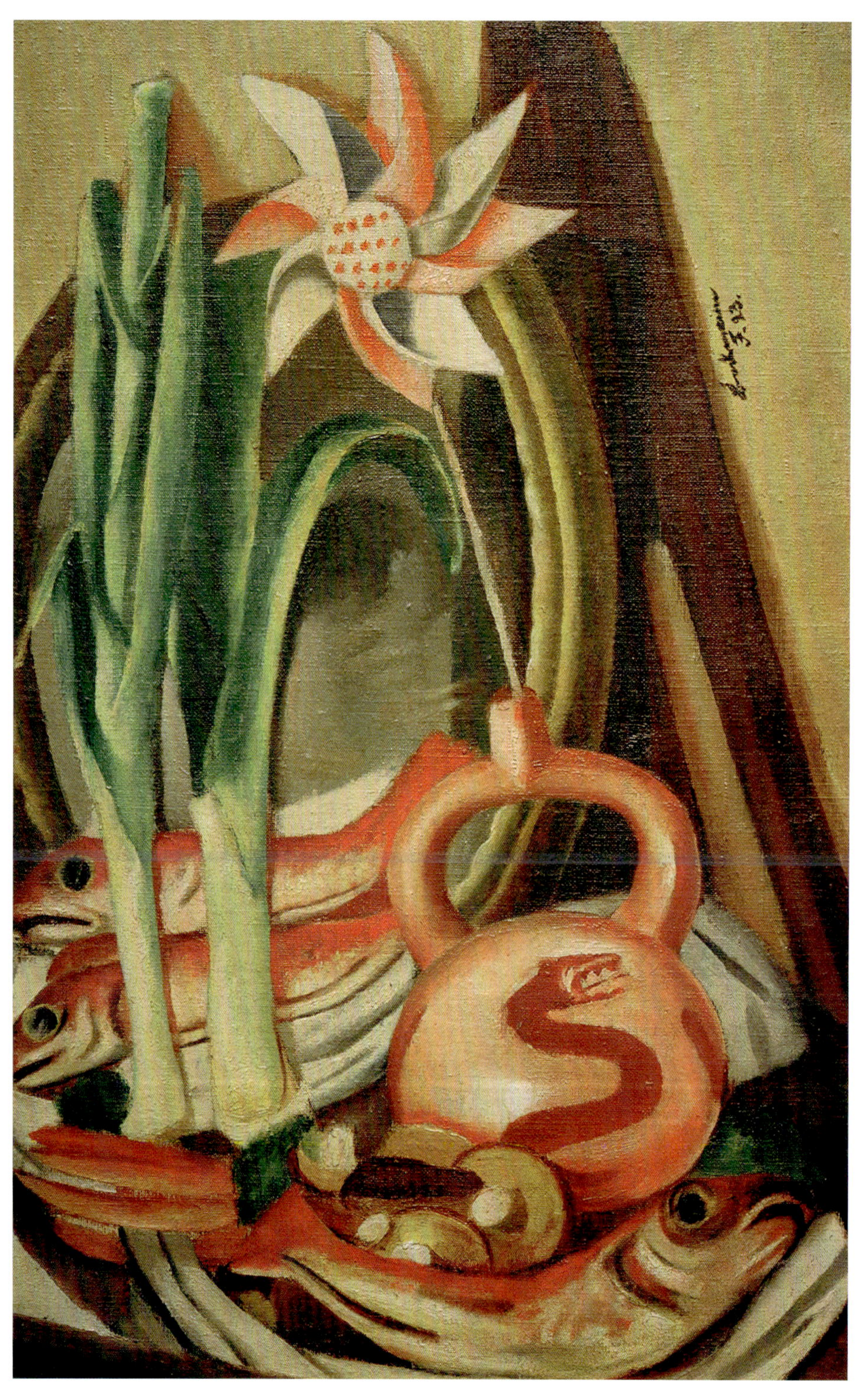

75. STILL-LIFE WITH FISH AND PINWHEEL, 1923

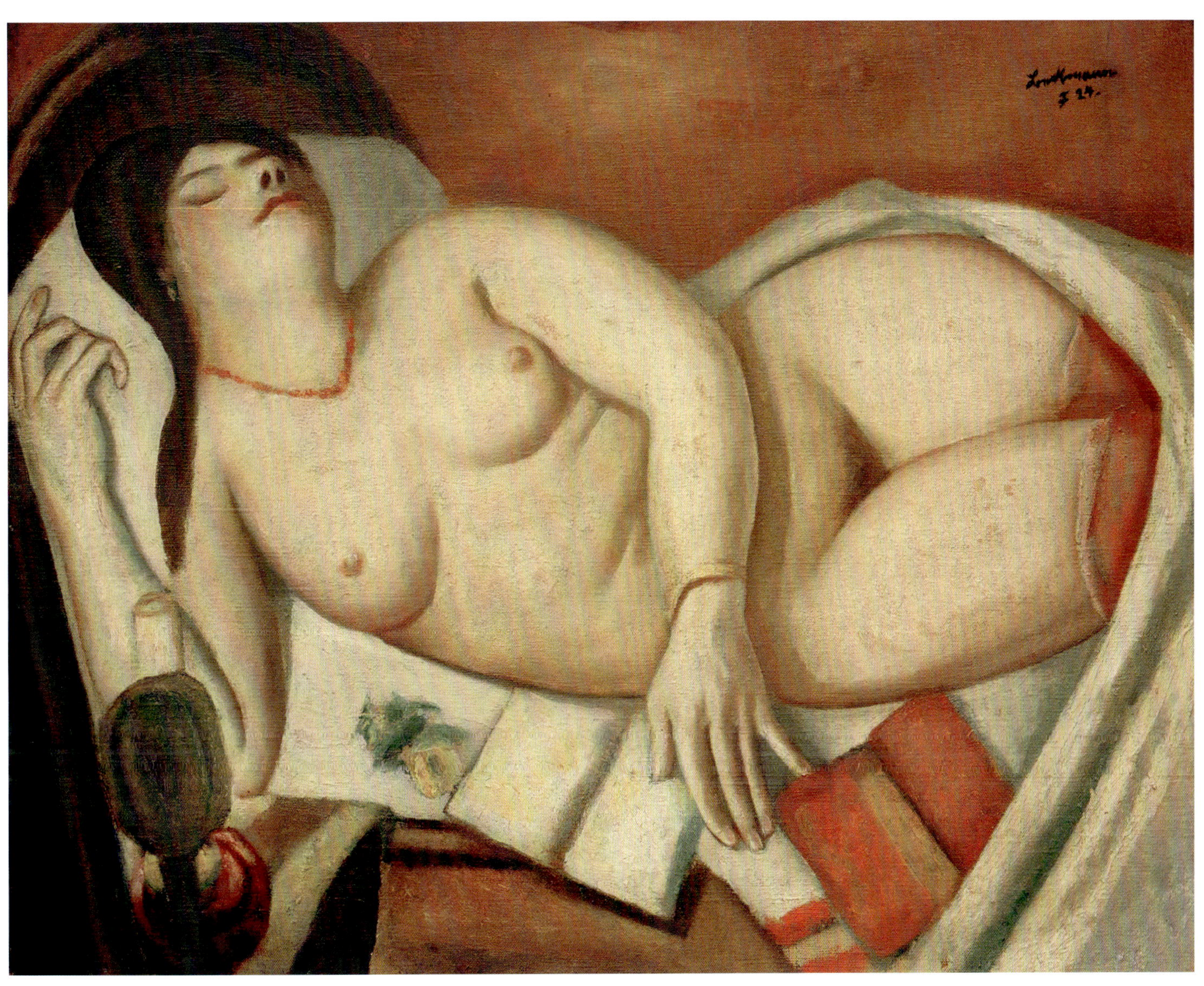

76. SLEEPING WOMAN, 1924

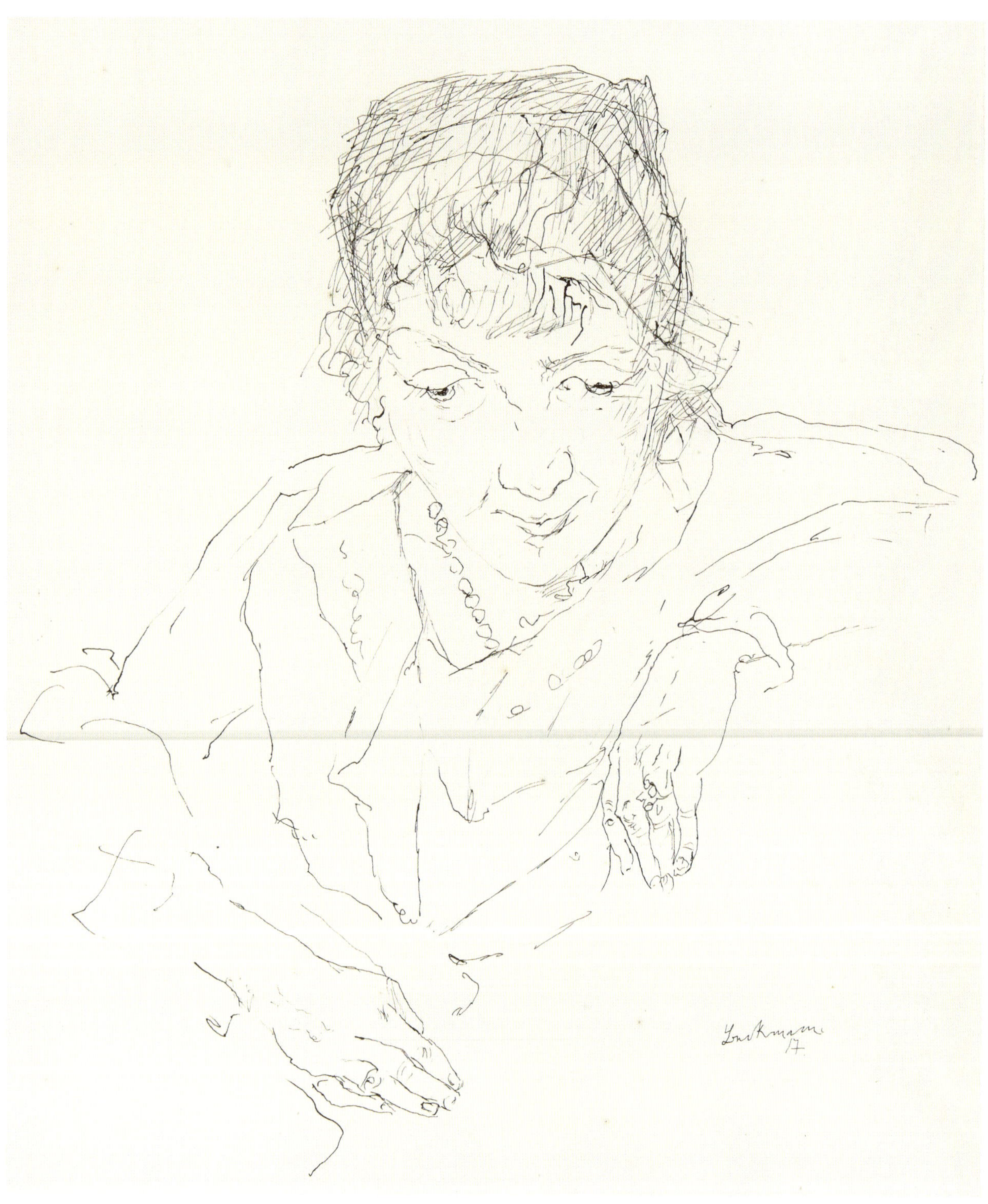

77. FRIDEL BATTENBERG, 1917

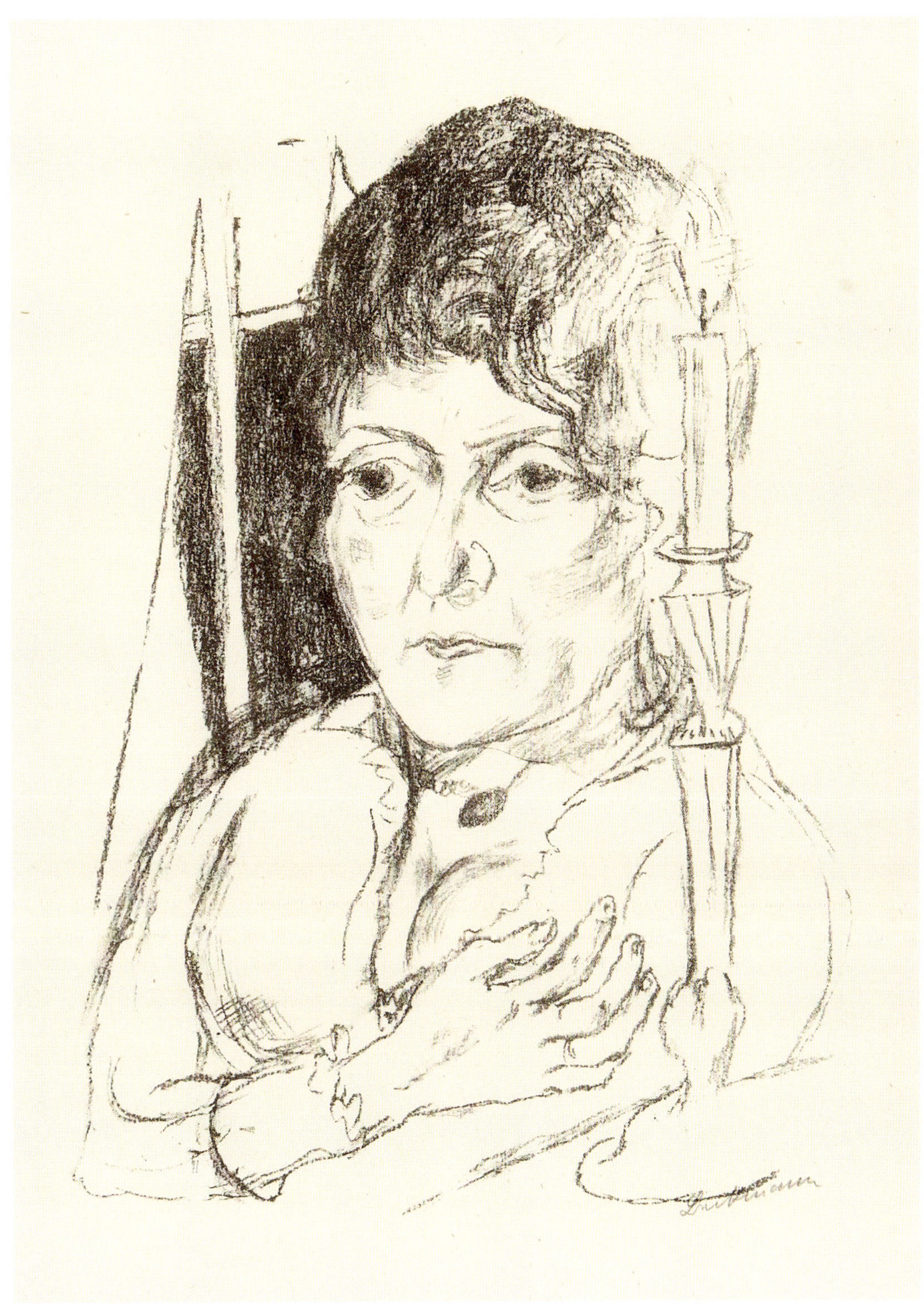

78. PORTRAIT OF FRIDEL BATTENBERG, 1917

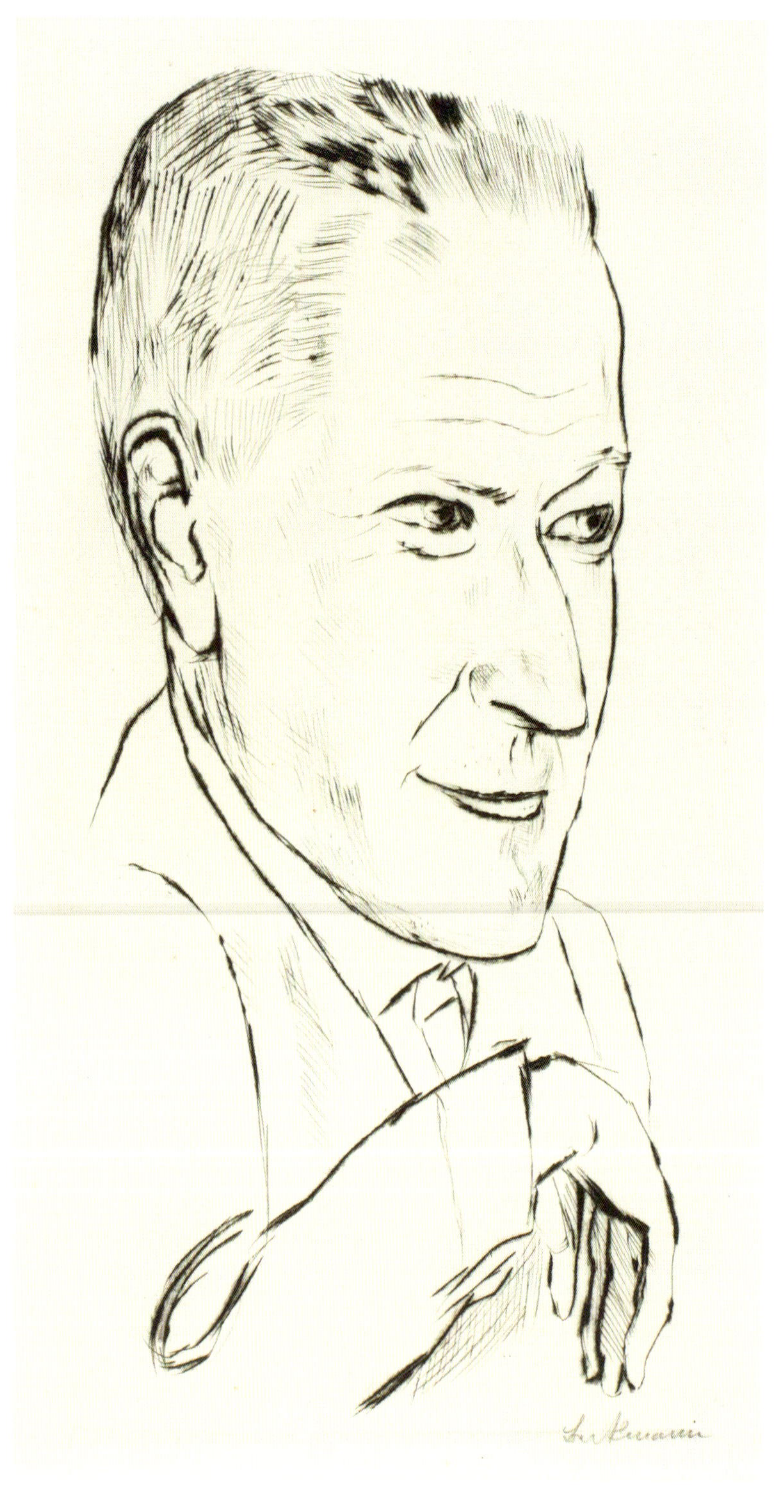

79. PORTRAIT OF REINHARD PIPER, 1920

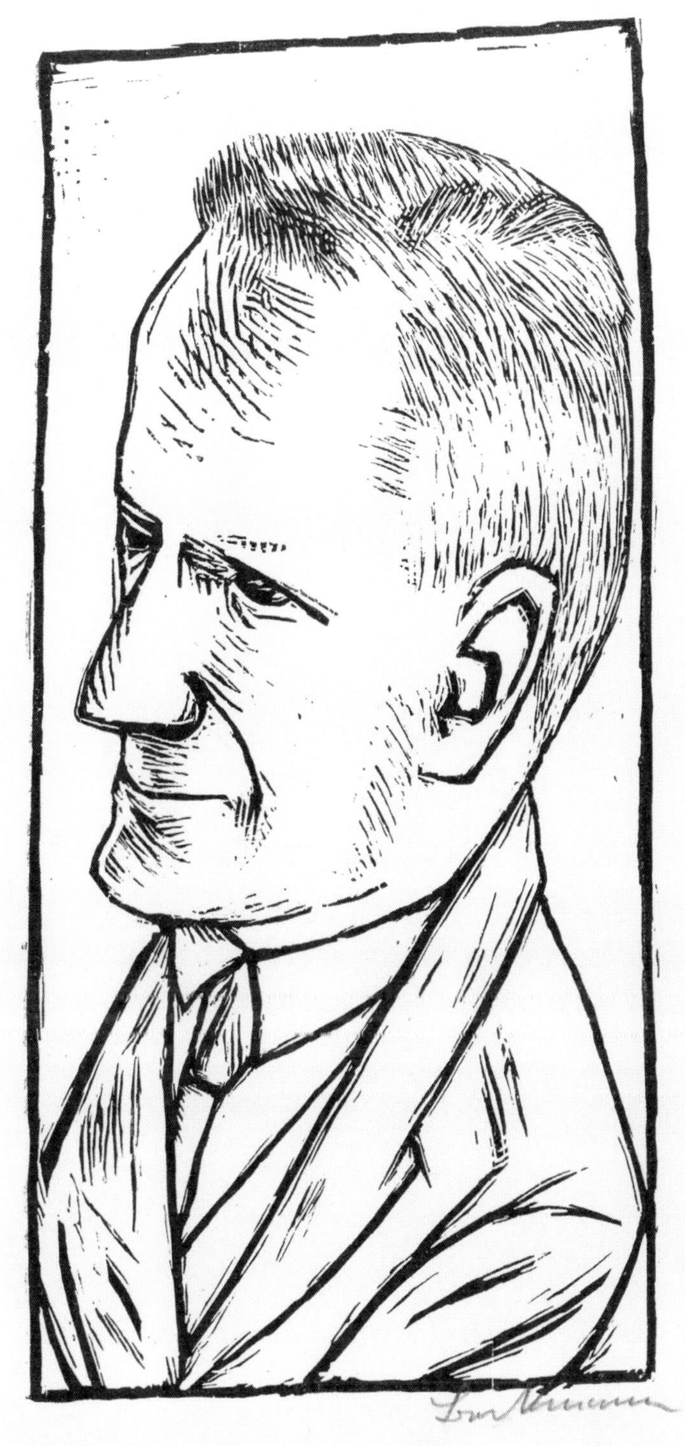

80. PORTRAIT OF REINHARD PIPER, 1922

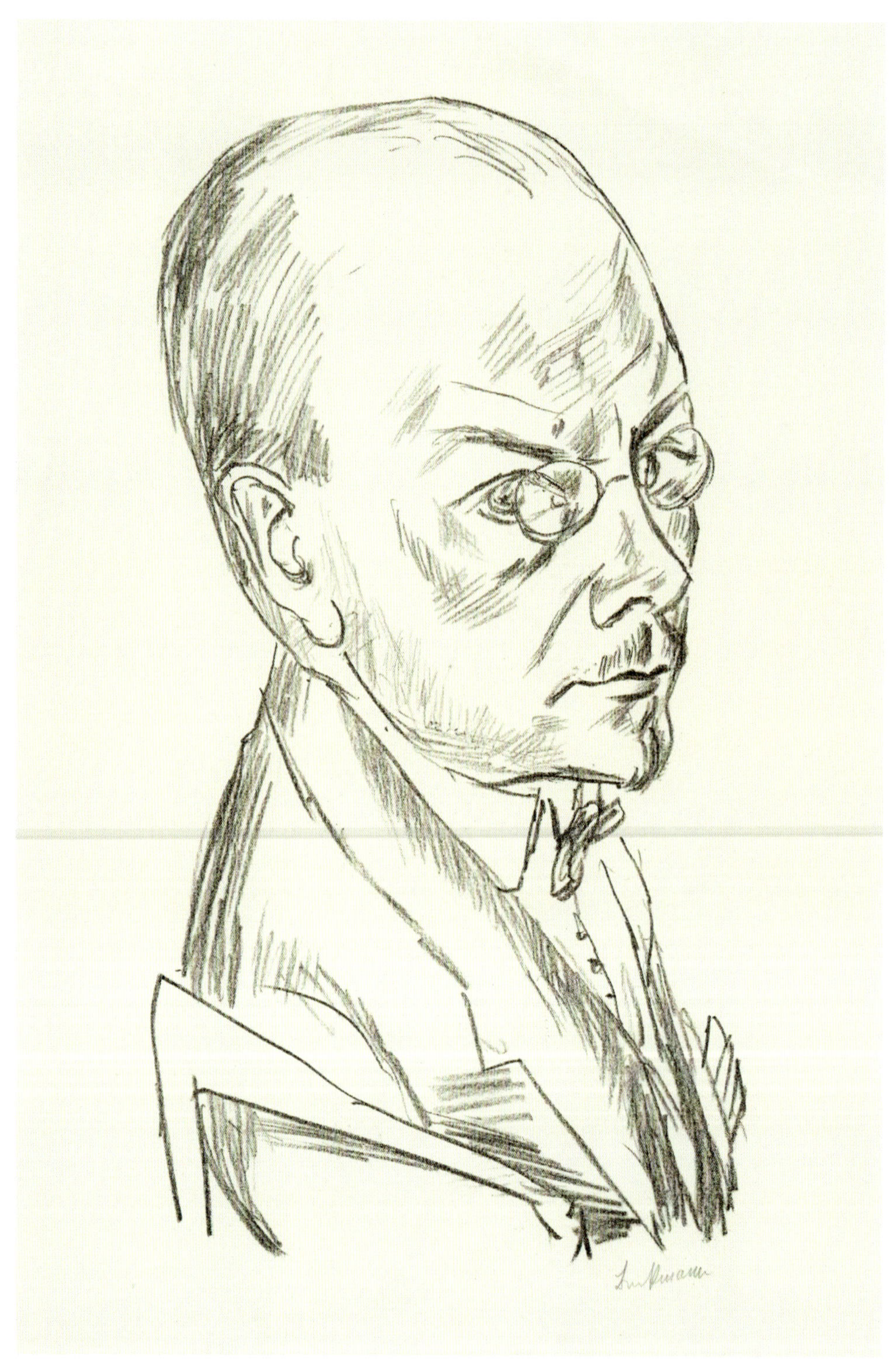

81. GEORG SWARZENSKI, CA. 1921

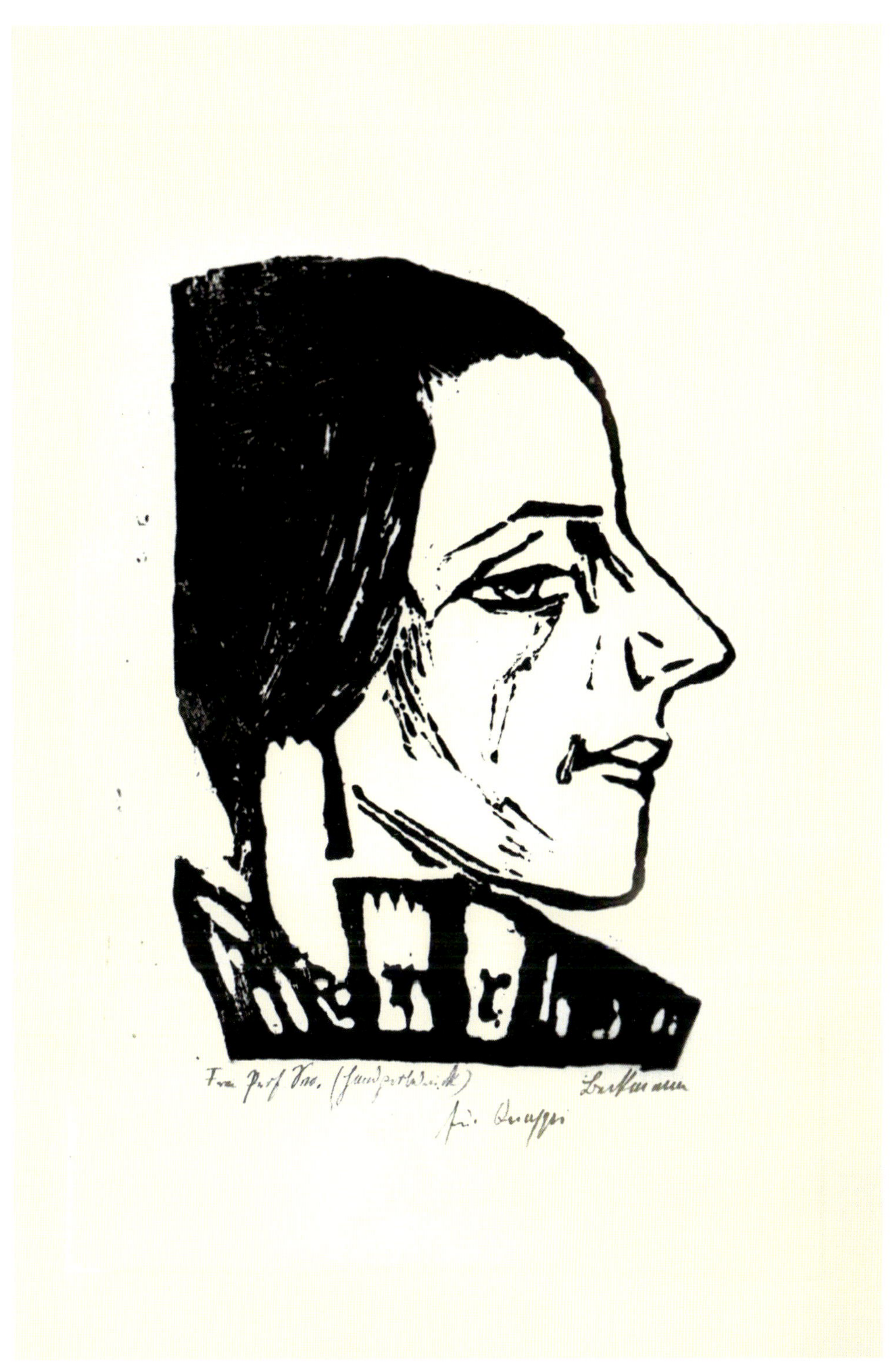

82. PORTRAIT OF MRS. MARIE SWARZENSKI, 1925

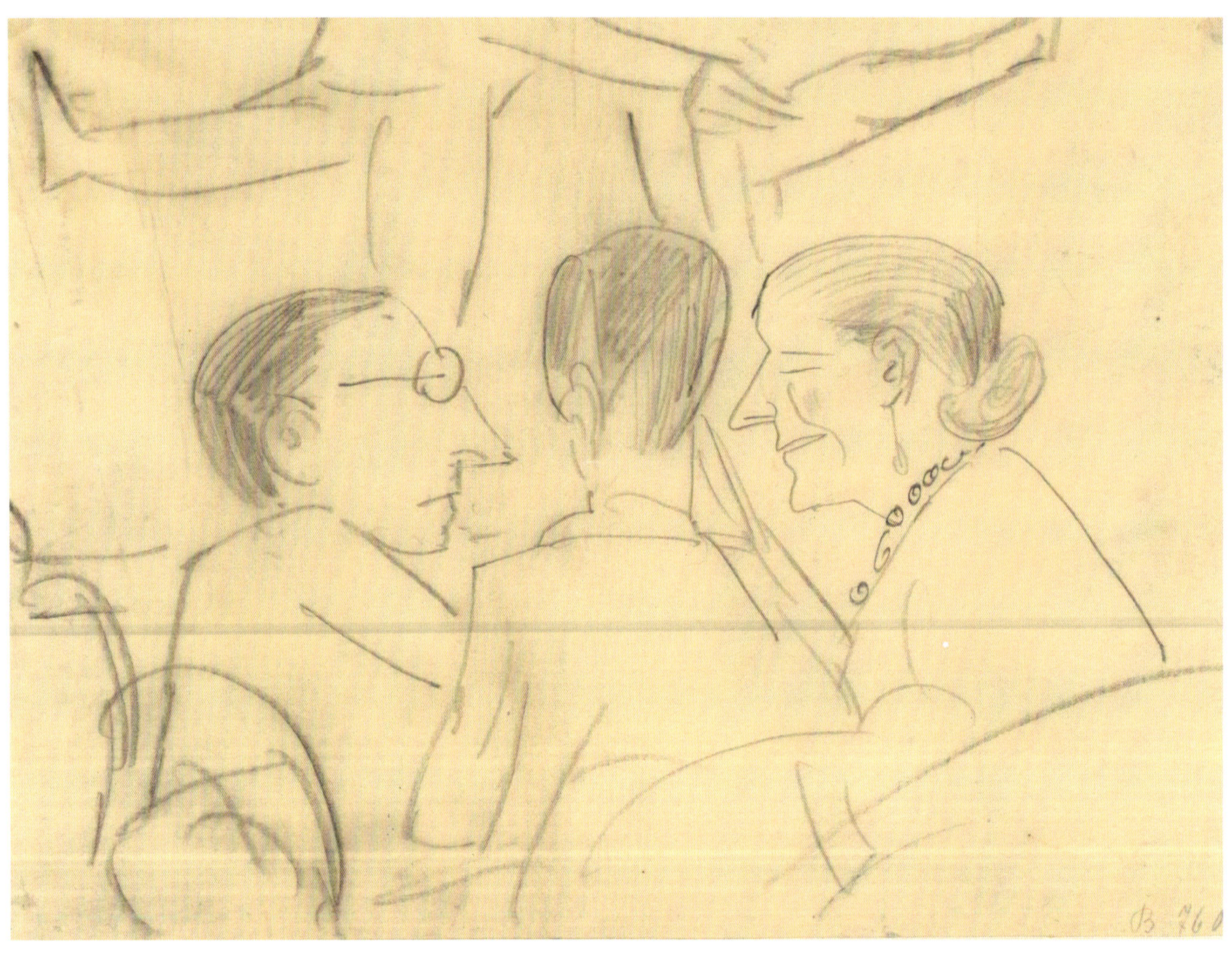

83. ENTERTAINMENT, CA. 1922

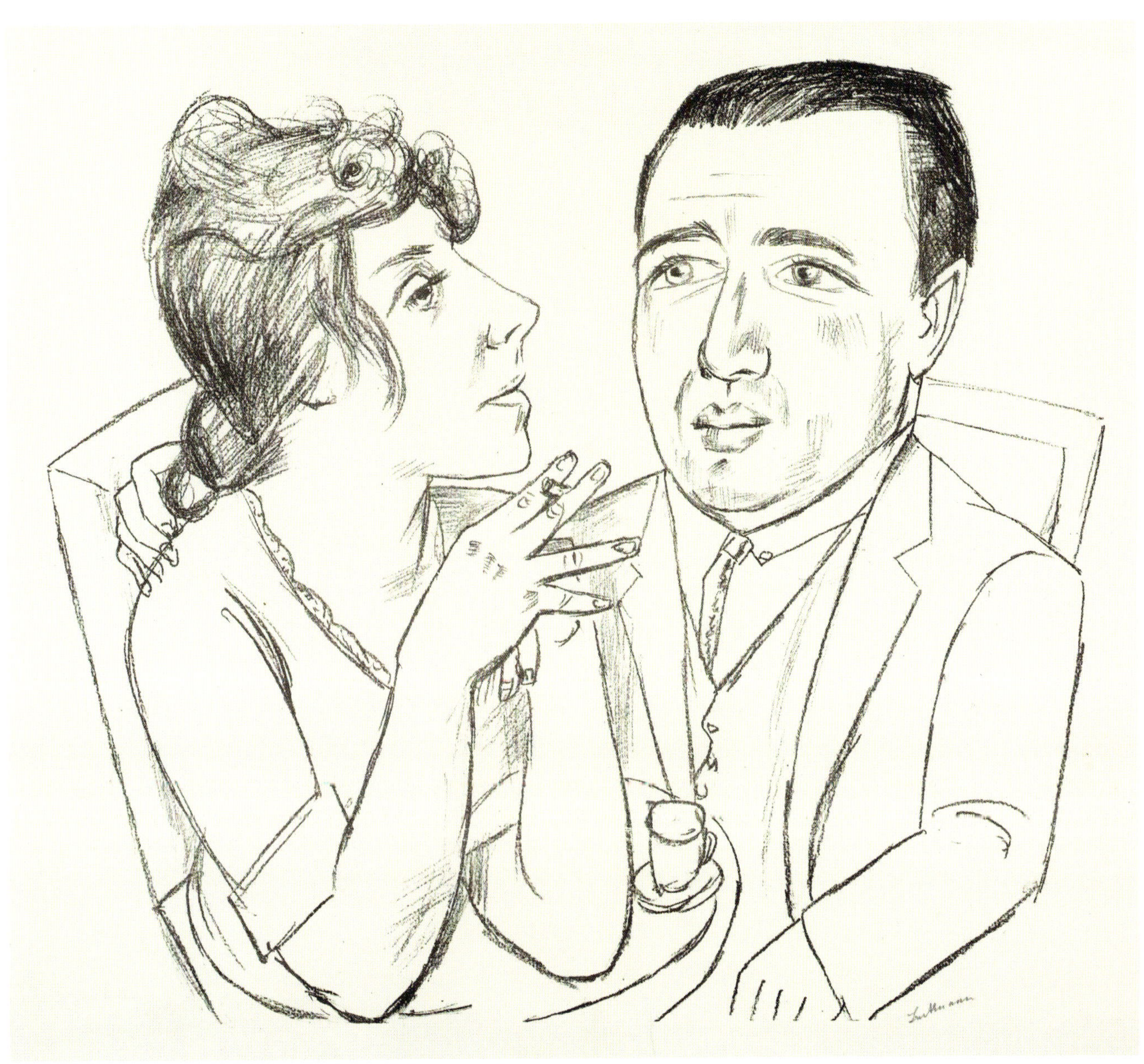

84. J.B. NEUMANN AND MARTHA STERN, 1922

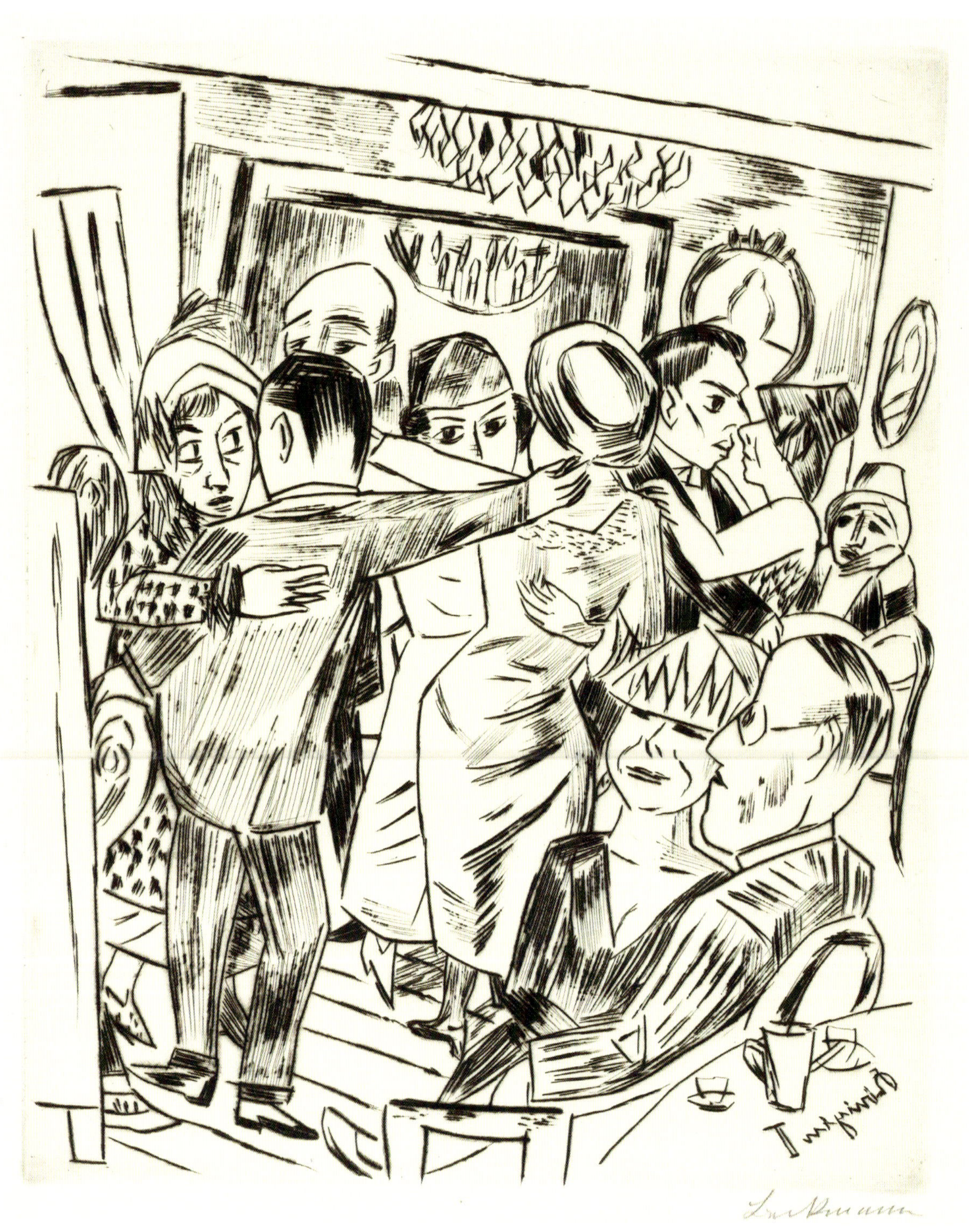

85. KÖNIGIN BAR II, 1923

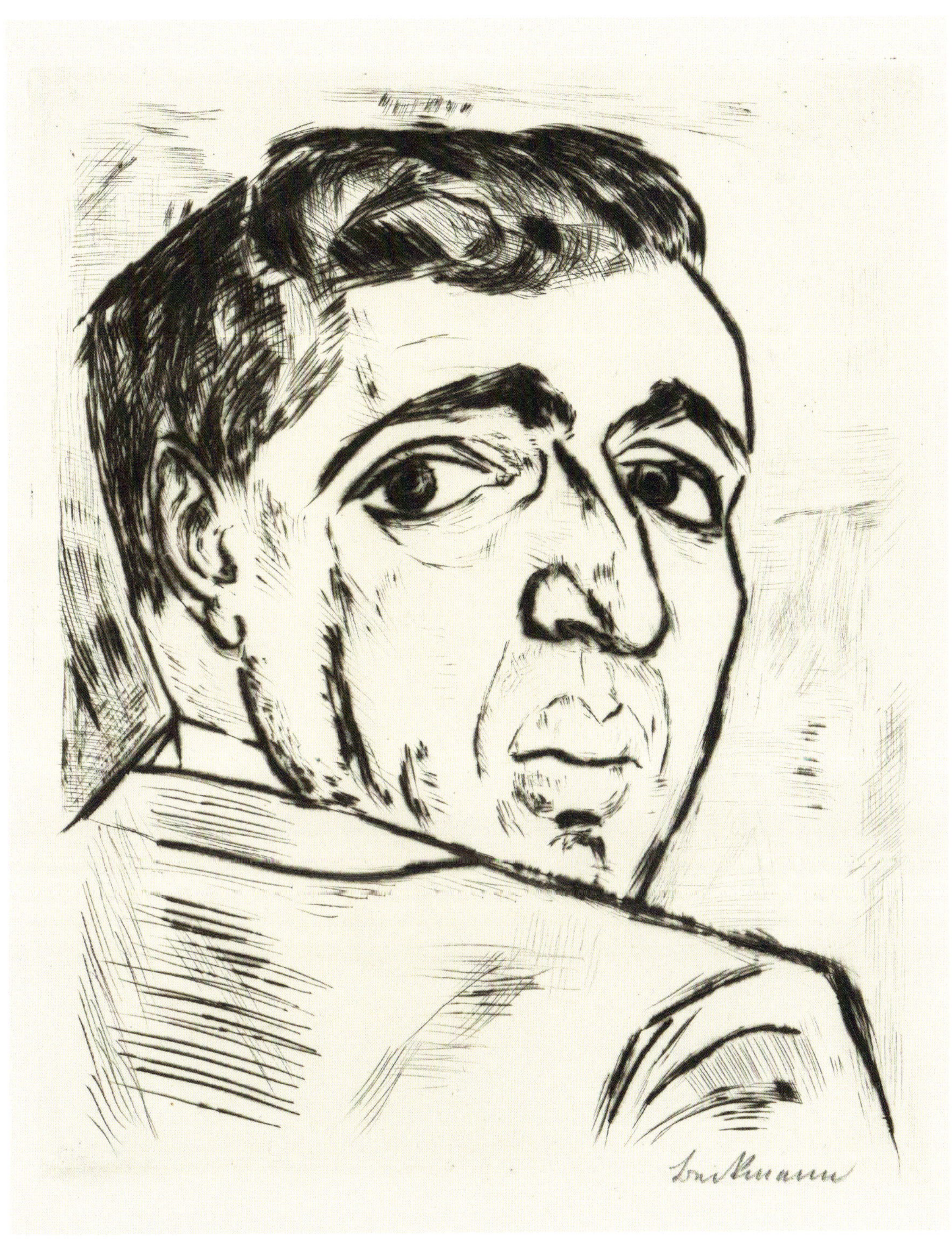

86. PORTRAIT OF J.B. NEUMANN, 1919

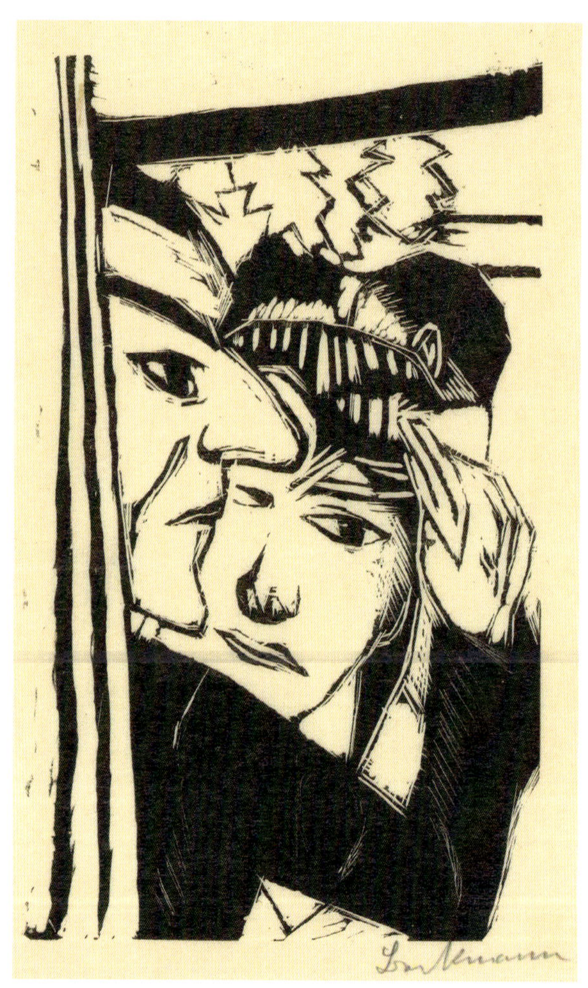

87. DANCING COUPLE, 1922

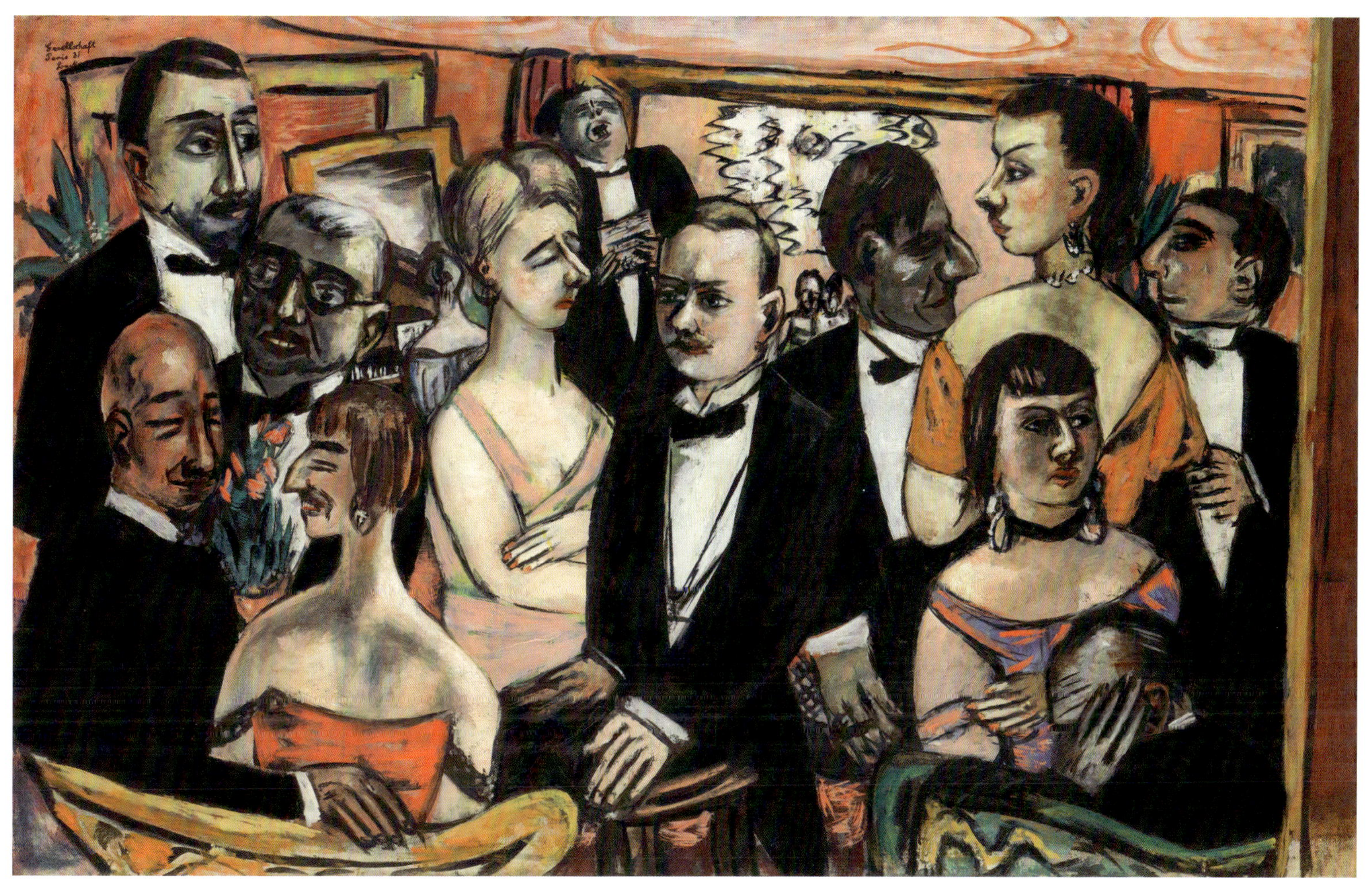

88. PARIS SOCIETY, 1925/1931/1947

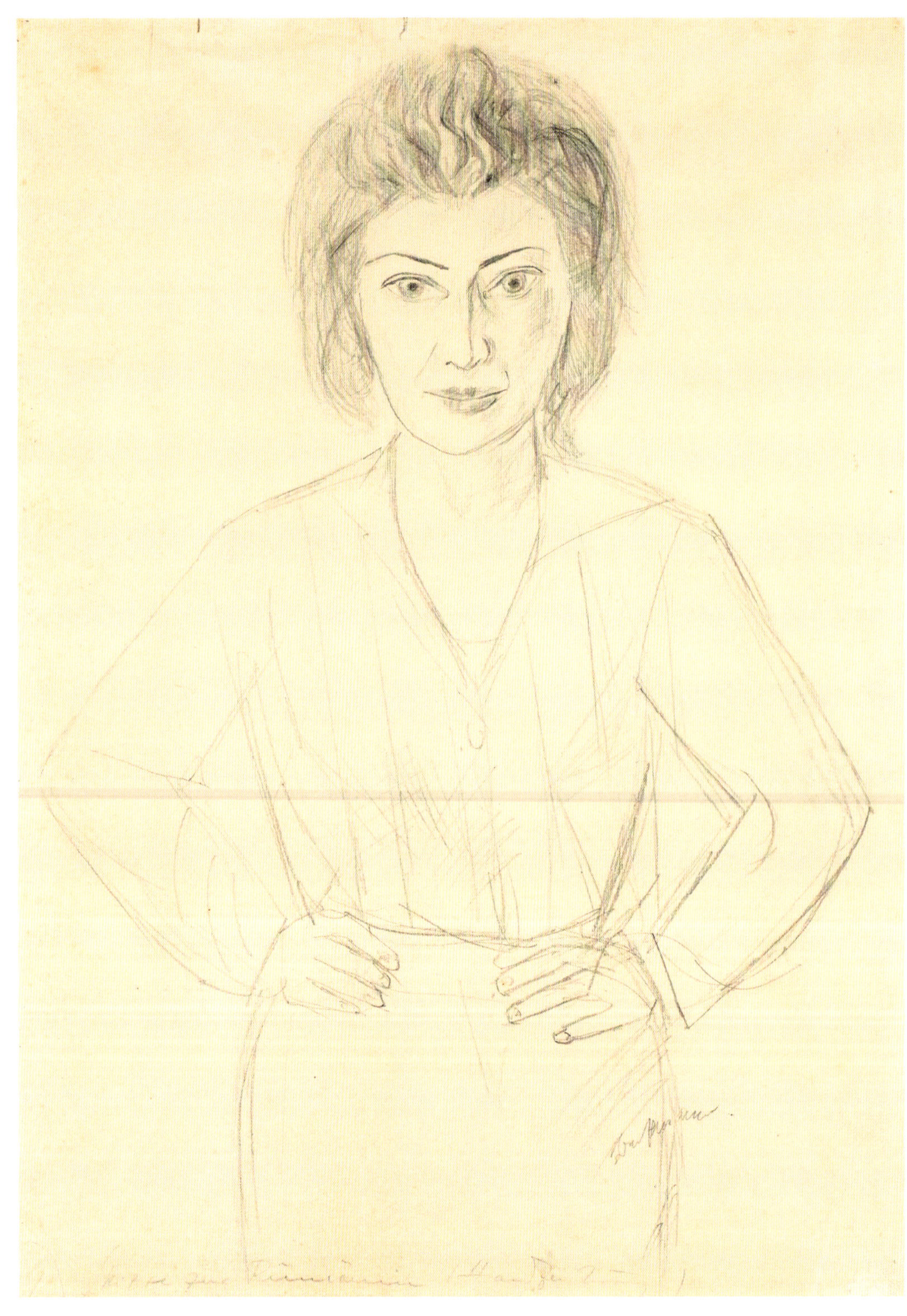

89. ROMANIAN WOMAN (SKETCH FOR THE PORTRAIT OF MRS. HEIDEN), 1922

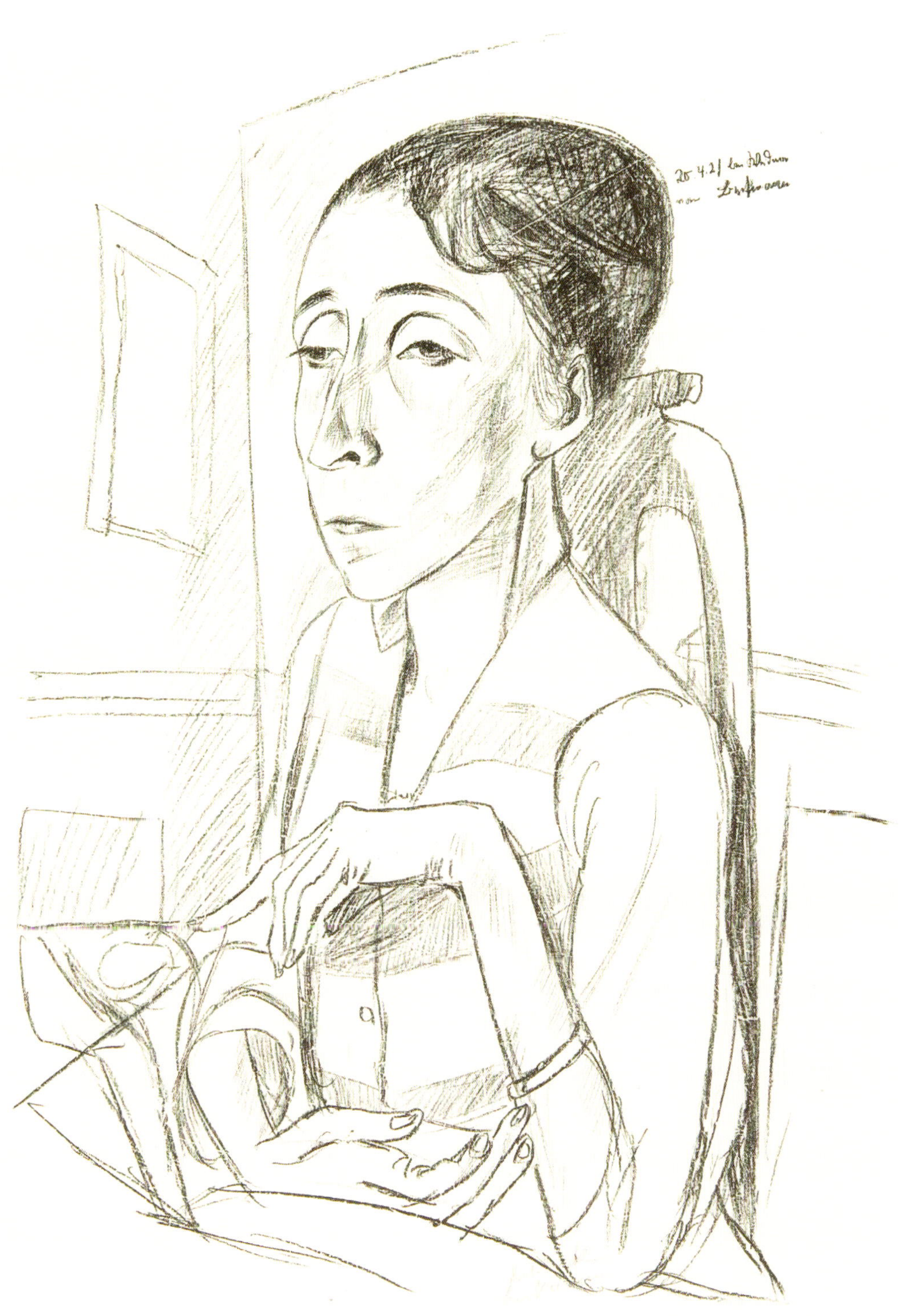

90. PORTRAIT OF THE DANCER SENT M'AHESA, 1921

Max Beckmann, *Self-Portrait with Saxophone*, 1930, oil on canvas. Kunsthalle Bremen - Der Kunstverein in Bremen. Photo: Kunsthalle Bremen - Lars Lohrisch - ARTOTHEK

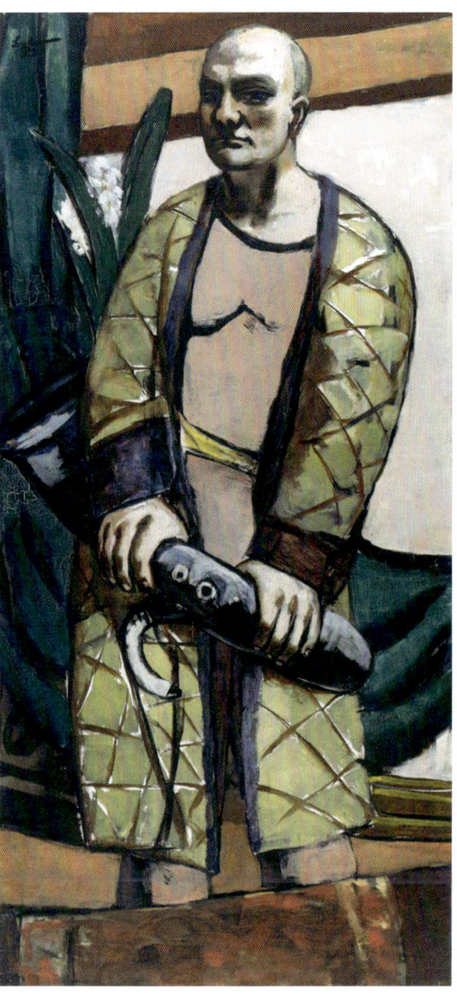

Max Beckmann associated his own existence with the ambition to become a self, an I. This was a lifelong task for him, marked by self-doubts and self-stylizations and expressed in countless self-portraits. They are all reflections on his own life; they articulate states of mind and intentions, fears and desires, social rank and ongoing efforts to be recognized. His *Selbstbildnis vor rotem Vorhang* (Self-Portrait in front of Red Curtain) of 1923 establishes a form that Beckmann will revisit again and again in major works of this genre: the partially frontal three-quarter-length portrait. Whether the 1926 *Selbstbildnis mit weißer Mütze* (Self-Portrait with White Cap) [Plate 103], *Selbstbildnis im Smoking* (Self-Portrait in Tuxedo) of 1927, *Selbstbildnis mit Saxophon* (Self-Portrait with Saxophone) of 1930 [see ill. on this page], or, at the end of his life, *Selbstbildnis mit blauer Jacke* (Self-Portrait in Blue Jacket) from 1950, they are all central efforts to adopt a stance or take stock of his own life.

The year 1923 was one of intense crisis in the Weimar Republic, marked by continued political unrest but above all by the difficult economic situation of hyperinflation. Beckmann appears unaffected by it, since he presents himself in elegant evening dress with a bowler and a cigar. His appearance was clearly connected with a visit to the theater, since the red curtain, cord, frames, and ornaments point to a public space. The painter was thus demonstrating his social ambition and at the same time revealing a degree of uncertainty, since he is presented as someone waiting in a lobby or foyer. The yellow-polka-dotted scarf lies around his neck and extends menacingly to the noose-like cord upward. The expression of stately self-assertion is undercut by latent awareness of his precarious instability, which is reflected in the almost incendiary-looking color of the curtain and in the nails of his right hand placed against his body. The portrayal has a forced personal character that had resonance with a familiar conversation partner from this period: Beckmann's publisher in Munich, Reinhard Piper, was, from 1924 at the latest, the first owner of this masterly yet open self-portrayal.

Olaf Peters

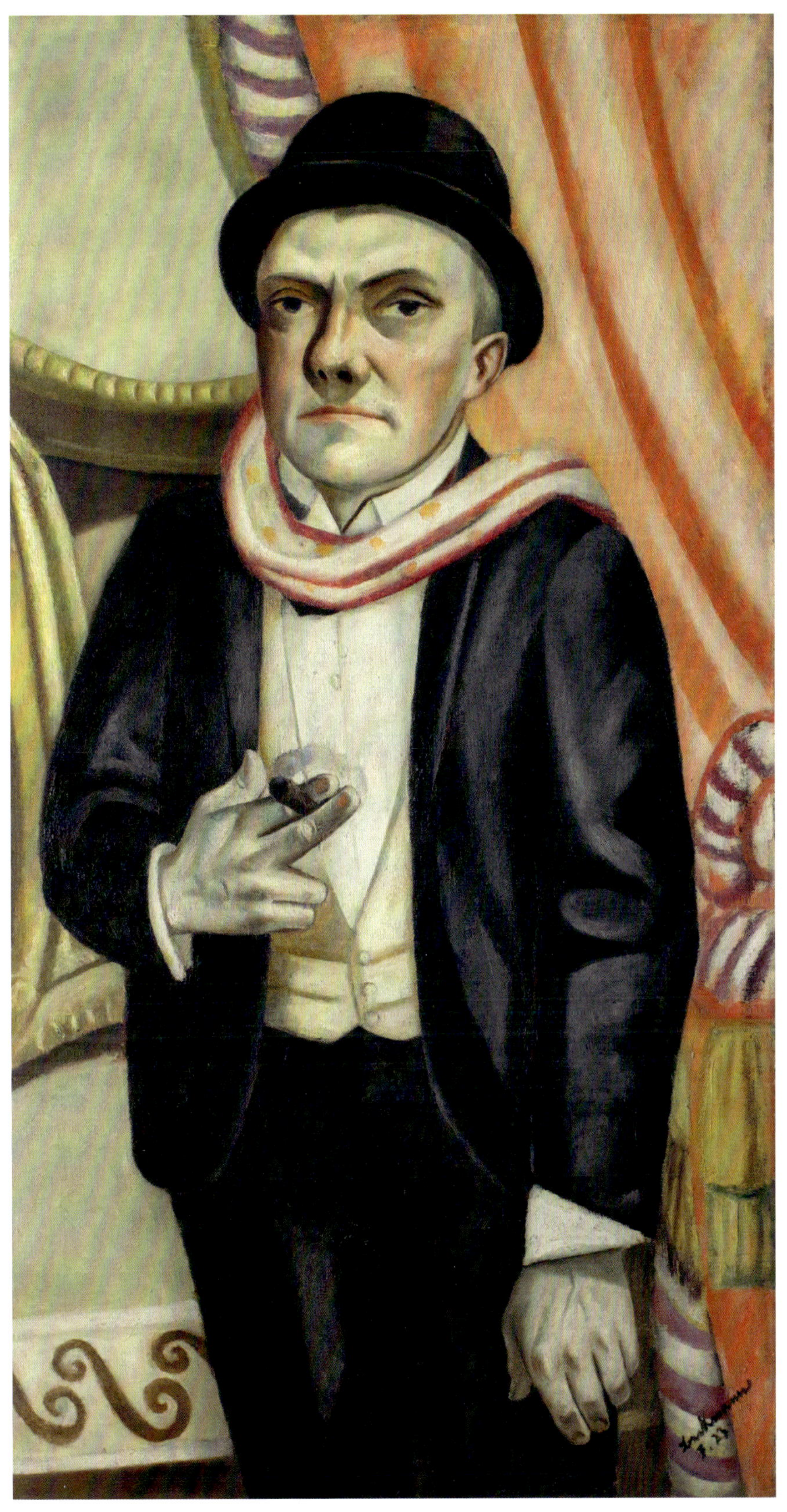

91. SELF-PORTRAIT IN FRONT OF RED CURTAIN, 1923

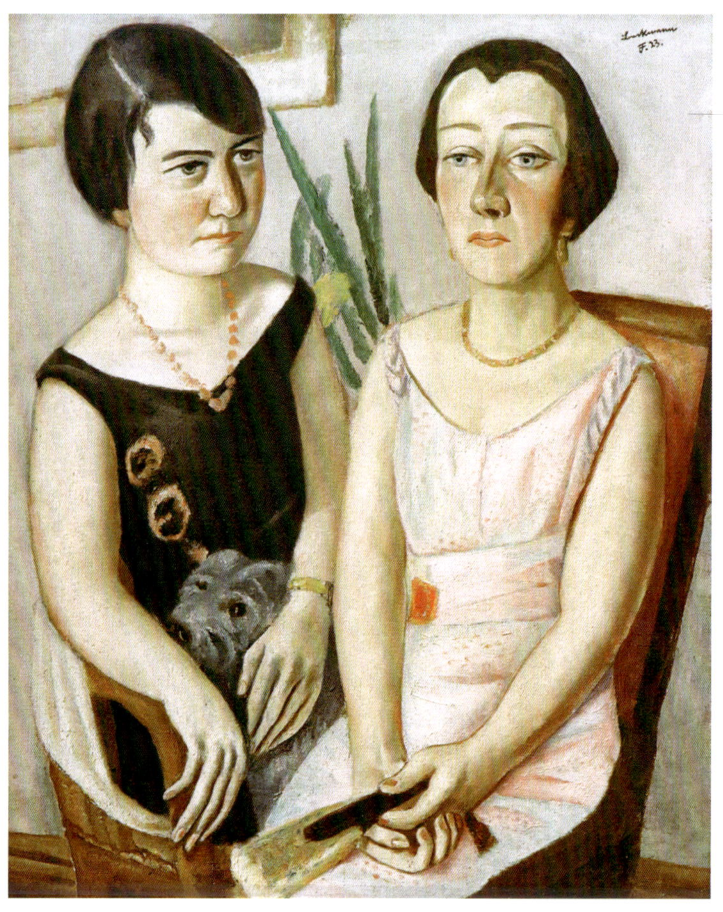

Max Beckmann, *Portrait of Carola Netter and Marie Swarzenski*, 1924, oil on canvas. Private Collection

In the mid-1920s, Max Beckmann produced a series of outstanding portraits that clearly move close to the *Neue Sachlichkeit* (New Objectivity) art movement. As a rule, however, Beckmann avoided depicting a type intended to represent a specific profession or different social strata, which would call into question the individuality of the sitter. For the painter, it was always about the personality, about the individual. This painting shows the banker's daughter Elsbet Götz, who was from a respectable bourgeois family in Hamburg with an appreciation for art. Her brother studied art history and worked as an assistant to Georg Swarzenski at the Städel-Museum in Frankfurt am Main. The museum director Swarzenski [see Plate 81] and the painter Beckmann were close friends.

Elsbet Götz took a path different from her brother and became a kindergarten teacher. She founded a private kindergarten, but because of her Jewish origin could no longer continue it after 1933. Jews were prohibited from caring for or educating non-Jewish, German children. Despite worsening circumstances, Elsbet Götz passed up an opportunity to emigrate from Germany in order to care for her mother. In 1942 she was deported to Theresienstadt where she met a lawyer from Cologne who had also been deported, whom she married in 1943. In October 1944, Elsbet Götz was brought to Auschwitz on one of the final transports and was murdered.

Twenty years before these tragic circumstances, Elsbet visited her brother, who was living in Frankfurt am Main, and on March 7, 1924, met Beckmann, who completed this portrait of her in October. Her brother did not purchase the painting, however, because it seemed to him unlike her. Her large eyes look vaguely into the distance; her arms form a trapezoid down to her calmly folded hands. Beckmann artistically arranges the folds of her green dress and shows a slender strip above her beautiful head that terminates at a vertical angle. Her dark hair and the direction of her gaze balance the composition. Overall, the figure situated in a warm red backdrop radiates a statuesque calm that testifies to her self-confidence and self-determination exhibited many years before her refusal to emigrate and thus giving the National Socialists the opportunity to murder Elsbet Götz.

Olaf Peters

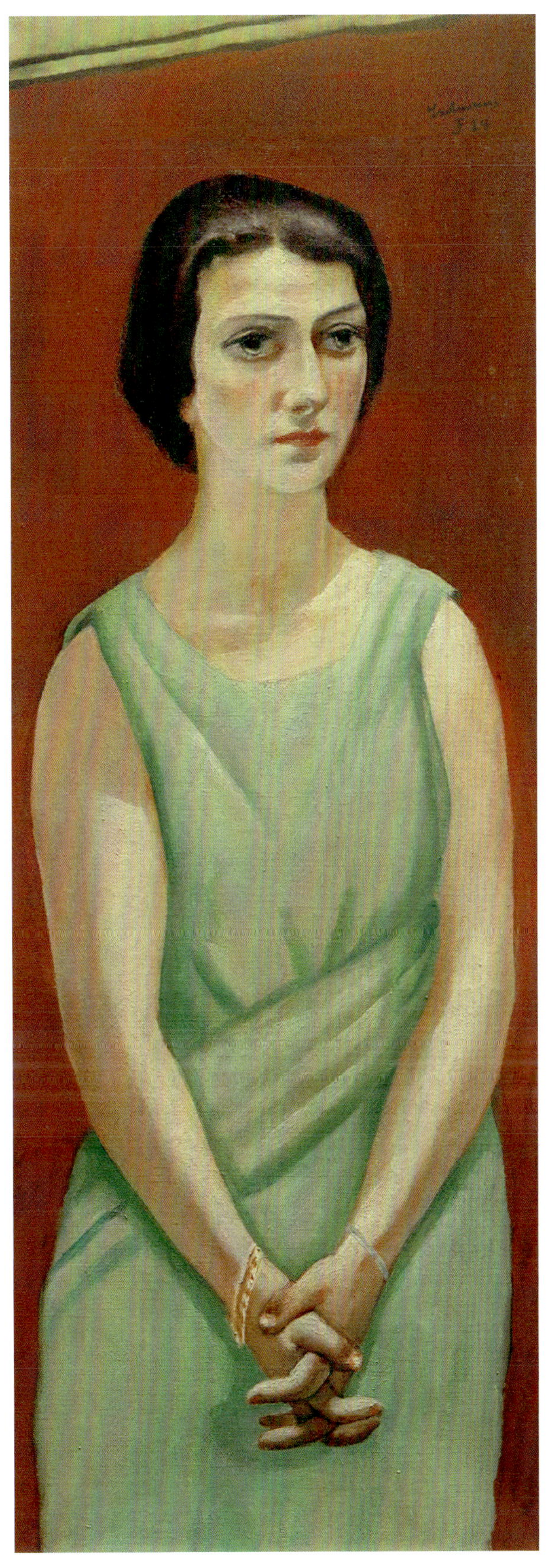

92. PORTRAIT OF ELSBET GÖTZ, 1924

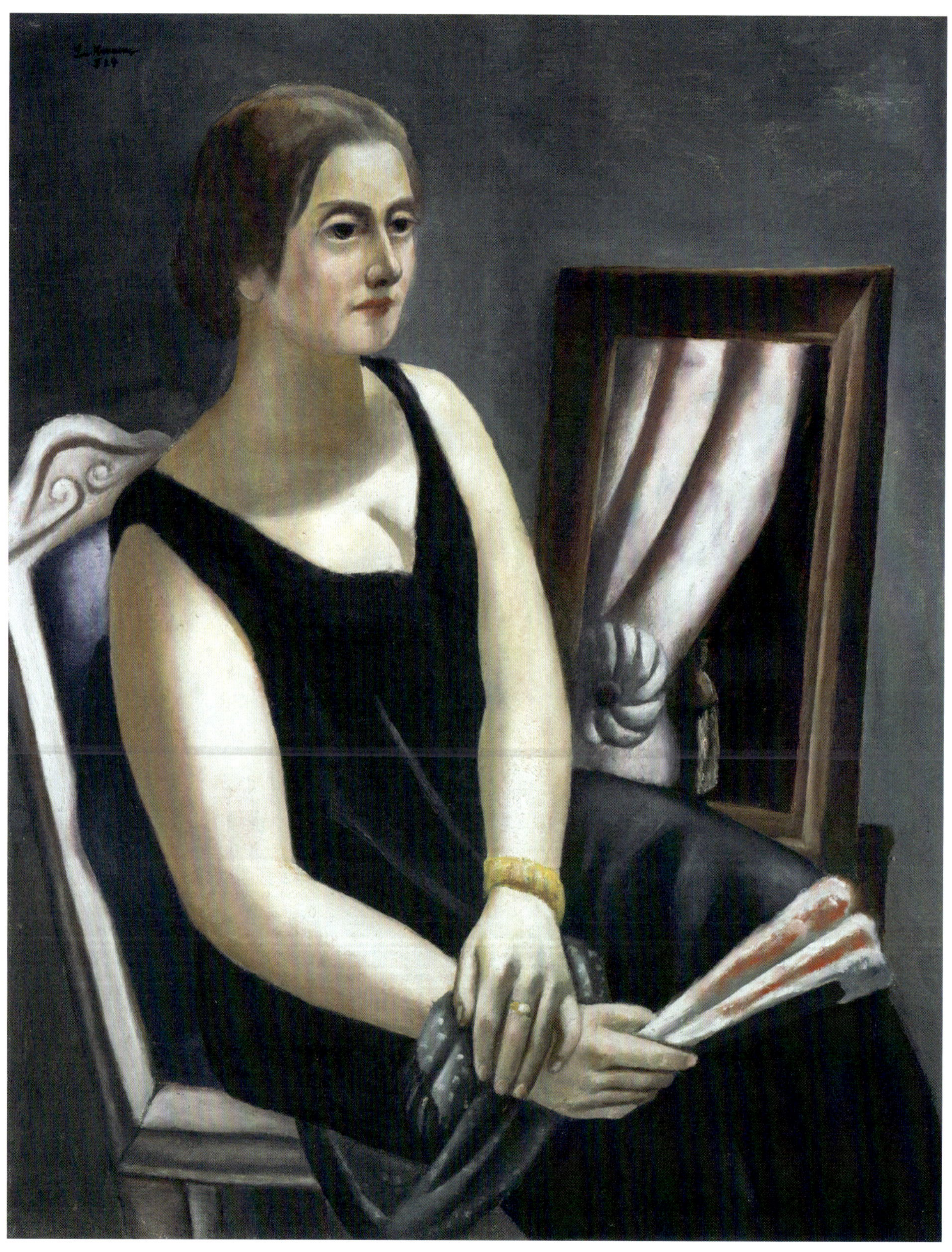

93. PORTRAIT OF MINNA BECKMANN-TUBE, 1924

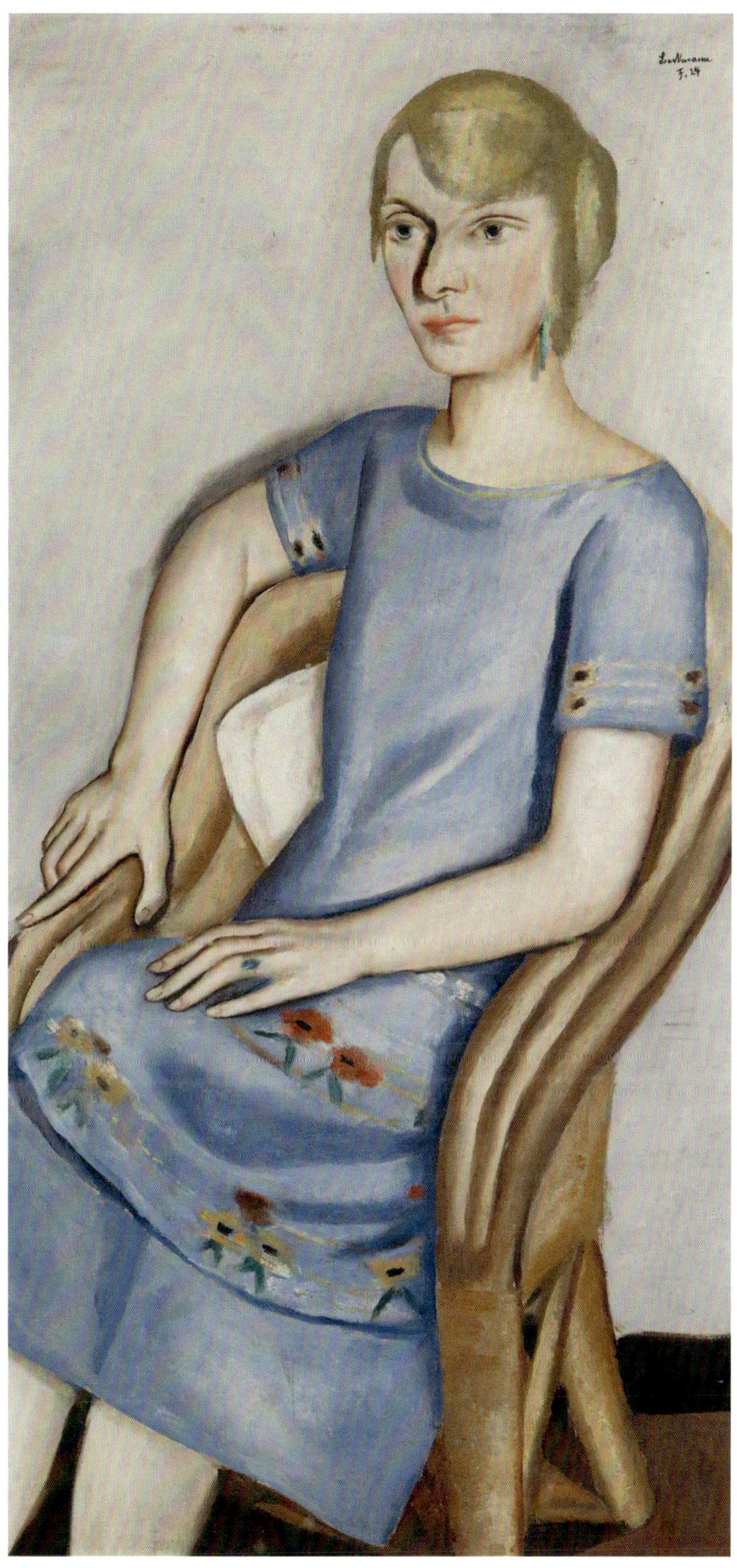

94. PORTRAIT OF IRMA SIMON, 1924

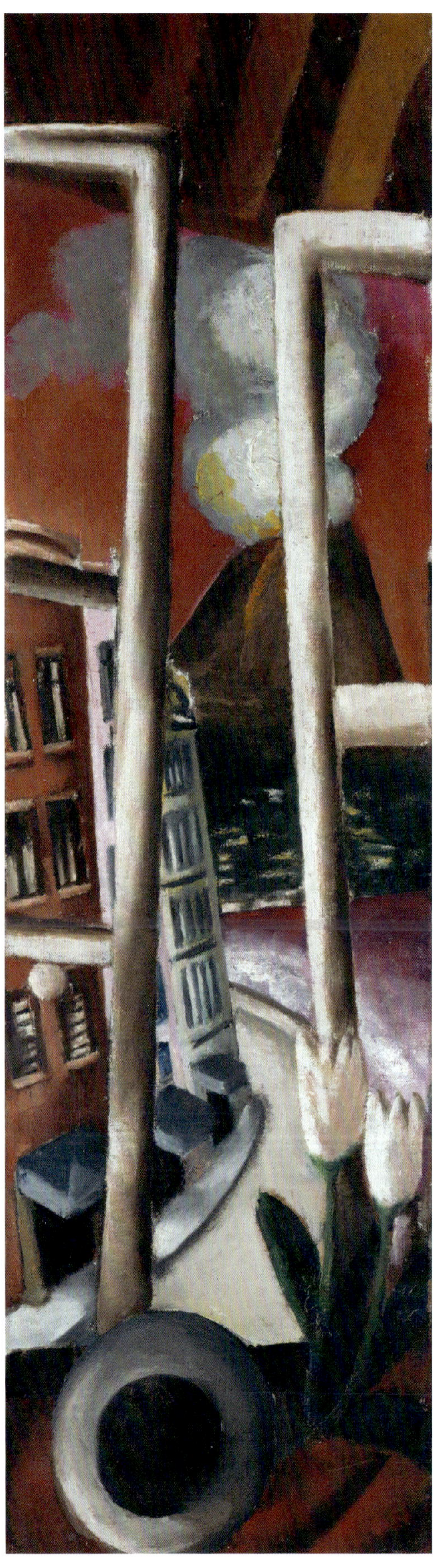

95. LANDSCAPE WITH VESUVIUS, 1926

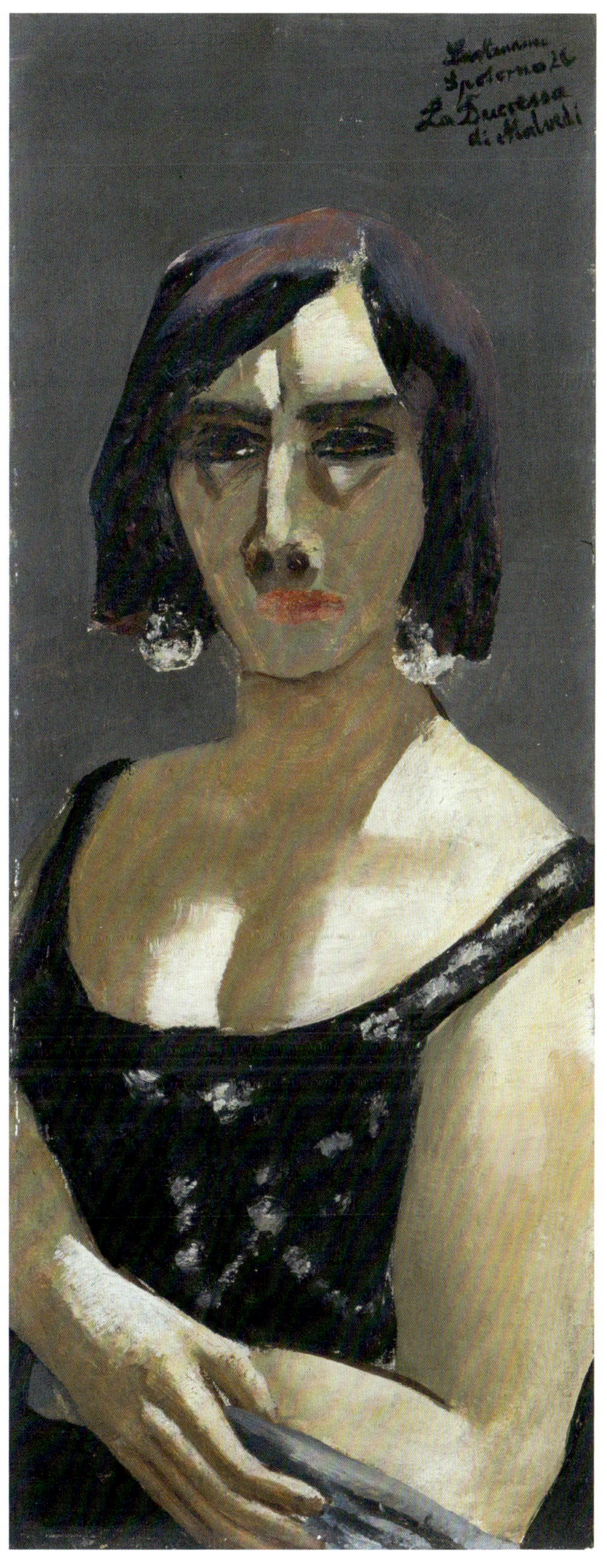

96. PORTRAIT OF LA DUCHESSA "DI MALVEDI," 1926

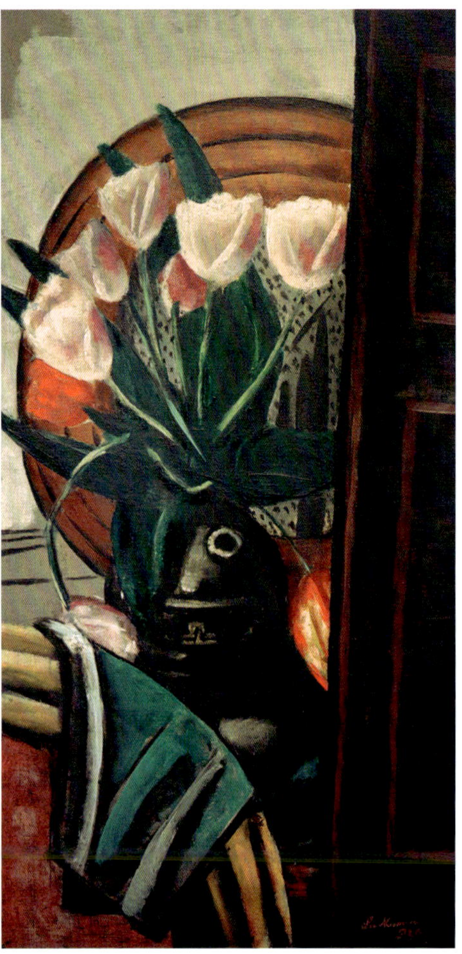

Max Beckmann, *Still-Life with Tulips*, 1928, oil on canvas. Private Collection. Photo: akg-images

Only from the mid-1920s onward did Max Beckmann again dedicate himself to the genre of the still-life with growing intensity. This shift was signaled by an enigmatic still-life from 1924 that seems to imbue its seemingly simple subject with great significance. From this point on, Beckmann expressed his general worldview symbolically in a condensed form, and still-lifes become a regular element in his highly complex, multifigure and multipart paintings. *Still-Life with Gramophone and Irises* stacks up various elements into an unstable construction that looks as if it could begin to slide away. But the painting retains its constructive tension, both in spite of and because of its compositional elements. This dichotomy offers proof of Beckmann's superior compositional abilities. He tested the quality of his paintings by looking at them in mirrors. It seems crucial to underscore that Beckmann appeared to bring inanimate objects to life, and this animation counters our perception of things that no longer seem passive. The surface on which the vase is standing echoes the numerous round forms in the painting, and the mirror—in which a masked woman is reflected—corresponds to the gramophone box. The gramophone horn is linked to the mask on the chair, whose leg becomes a paw.

In terms of its painting style, this work stands precisely on the threshold between transcendental objectivity—in 1918–19, the gramophone had played an important role in the major work *Die Nacht* (The Night) [see Fig. on p. 17]—and the freer, sometimes loose and fluid and sometimes impasto painting on canvas with a colored ground. The latter is demonstrated exemplarily by the flowers. The symbolism of the gramophone continues to be centrally important, because here it reveals a "chasm," in that Beckmann "brings out the negative of the form and emphasizes it physiognomically. This gives the void, the whole, an emblematic figure." And it proves Friedhelm W. Fischer's fundamental thesis: "Beckmann's work has a mysterious character. … The artist himself wanted the mystery and tried to preserve it." That applies as well to the material world, which seems to conceal something.

Olaf Peters

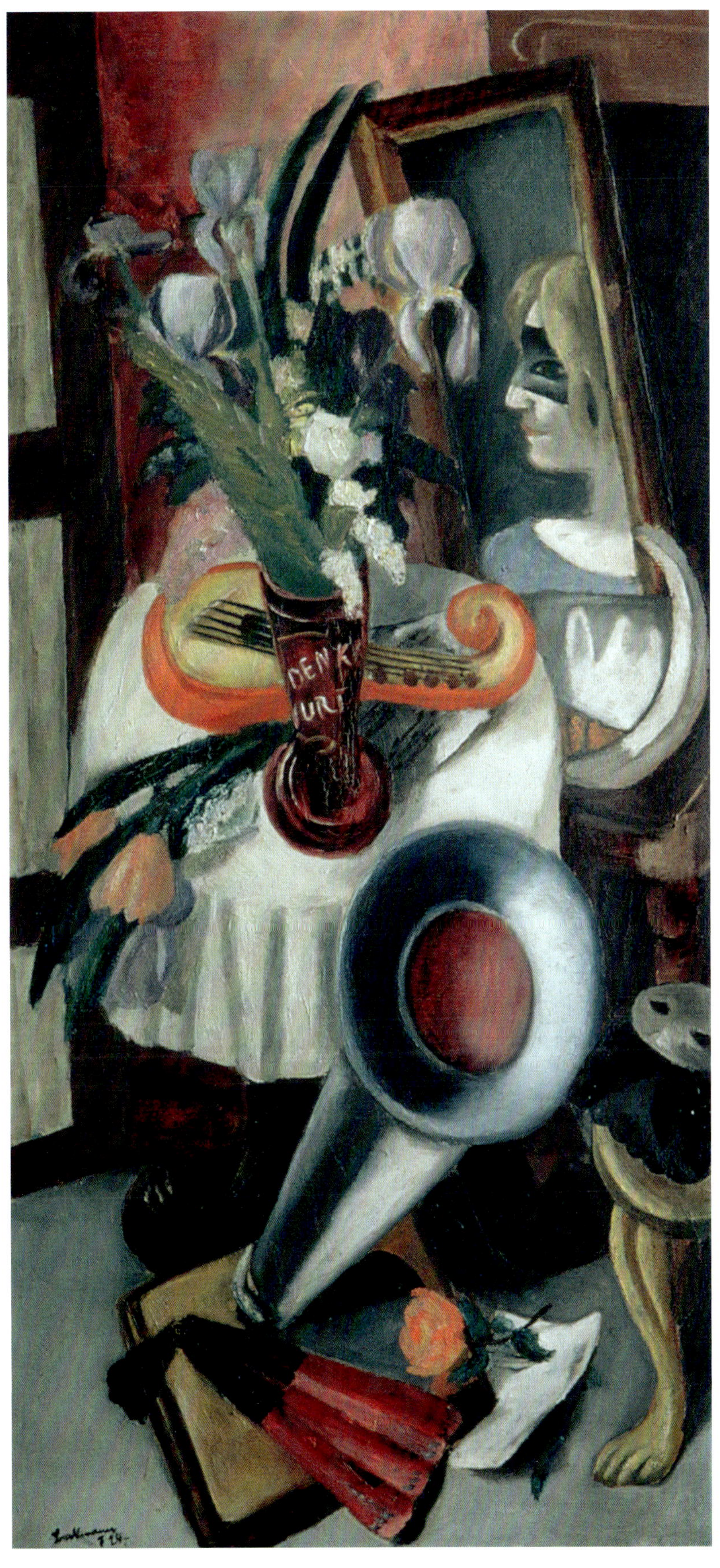

97. STILL-LIFE WITH GRAMOPHONE AND IRISES, 1924

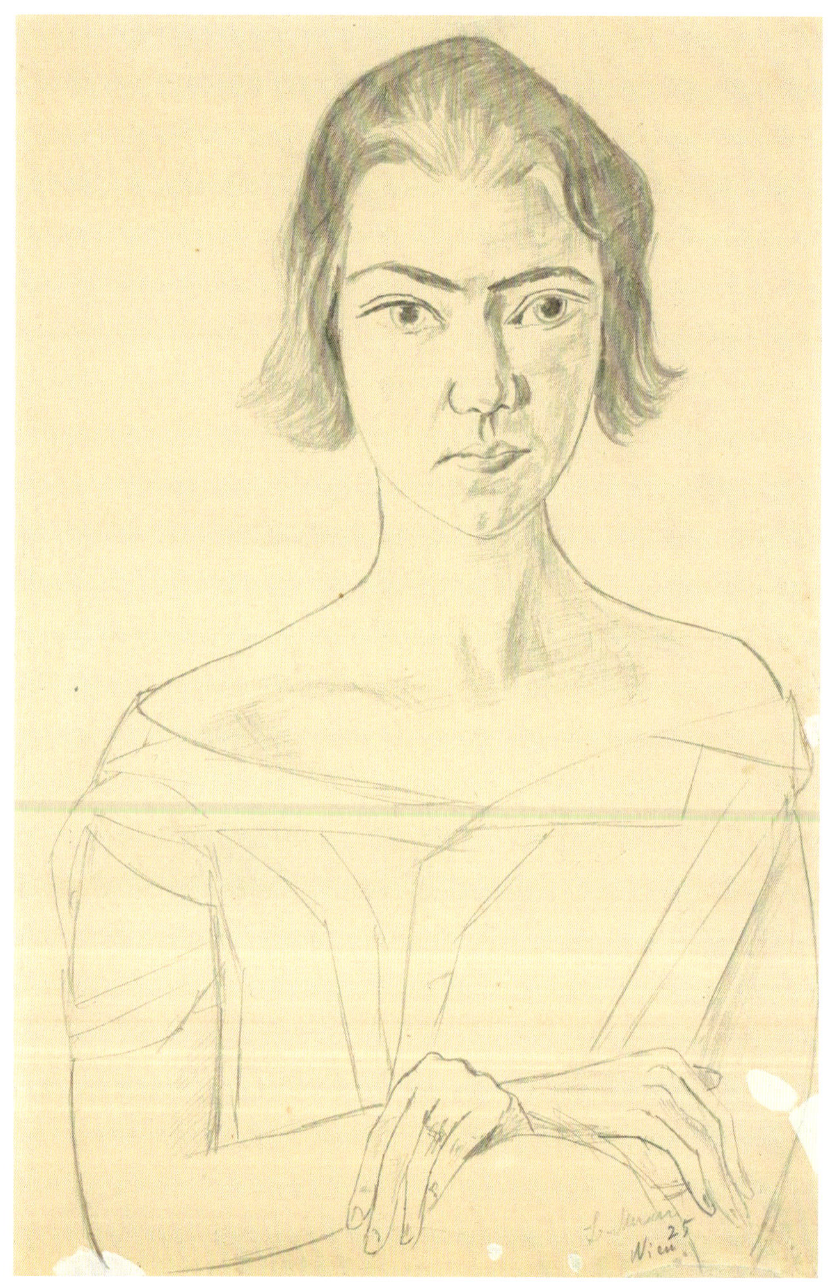

98. PORTRAIT OF QUAPPI, 1925

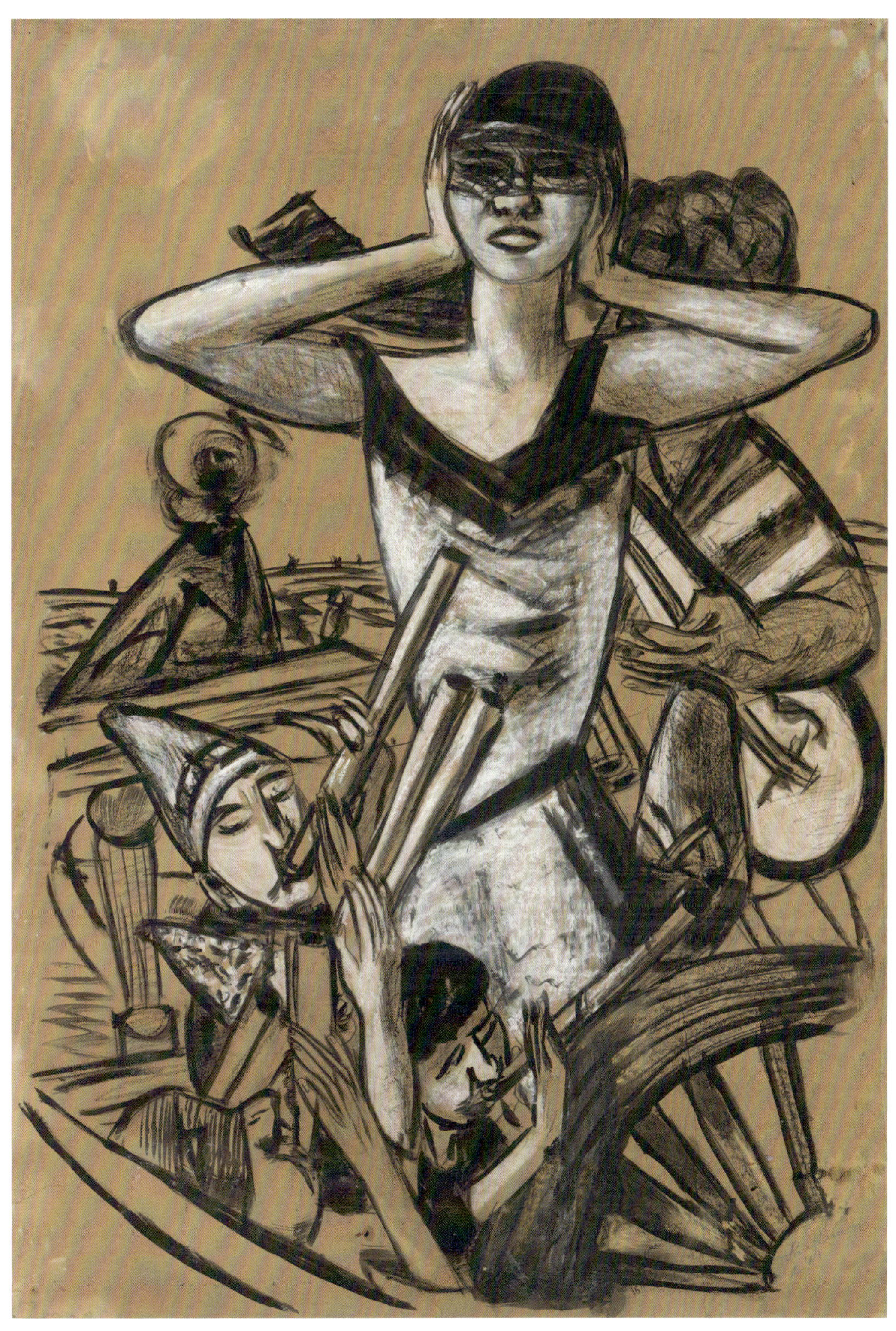

99. CARNIVAL IN NAPLES, 1925

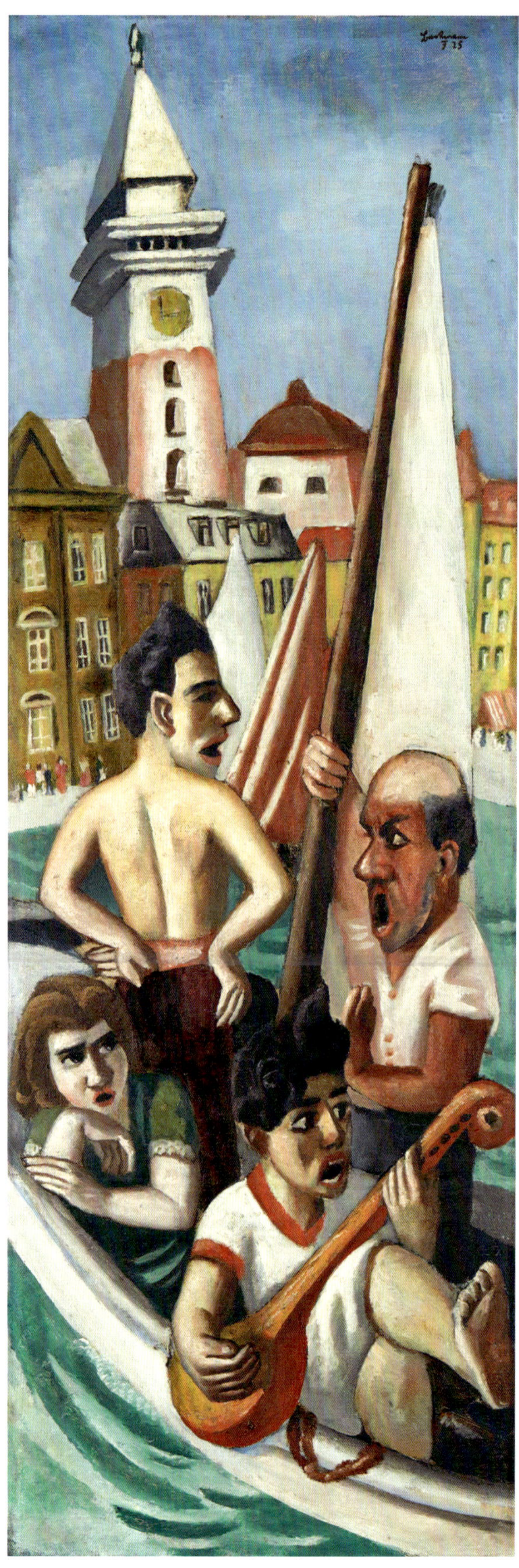

100. ITALIAN FANTASY, 1925

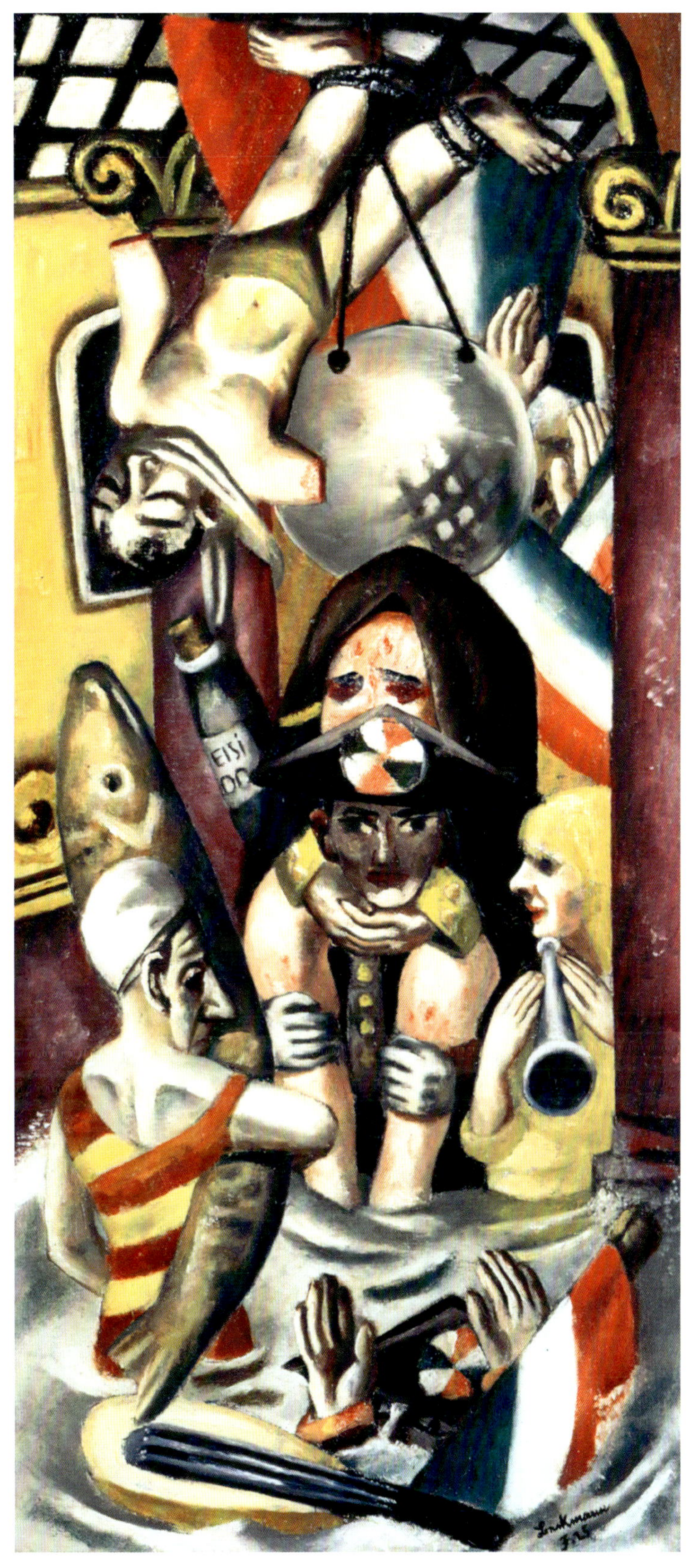

101. GALLERIA UMBERTO, 1925

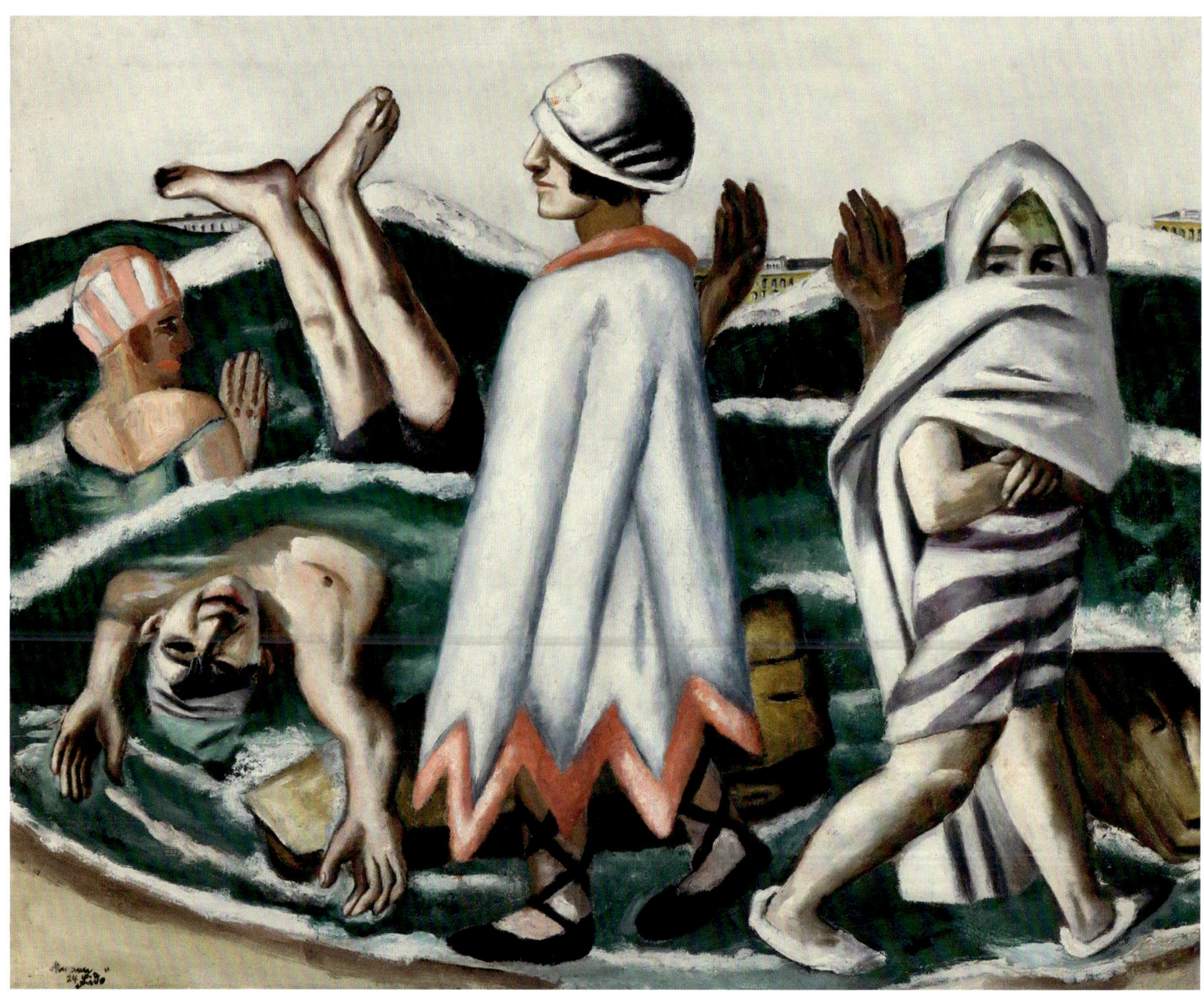

102. LIDO, 1924

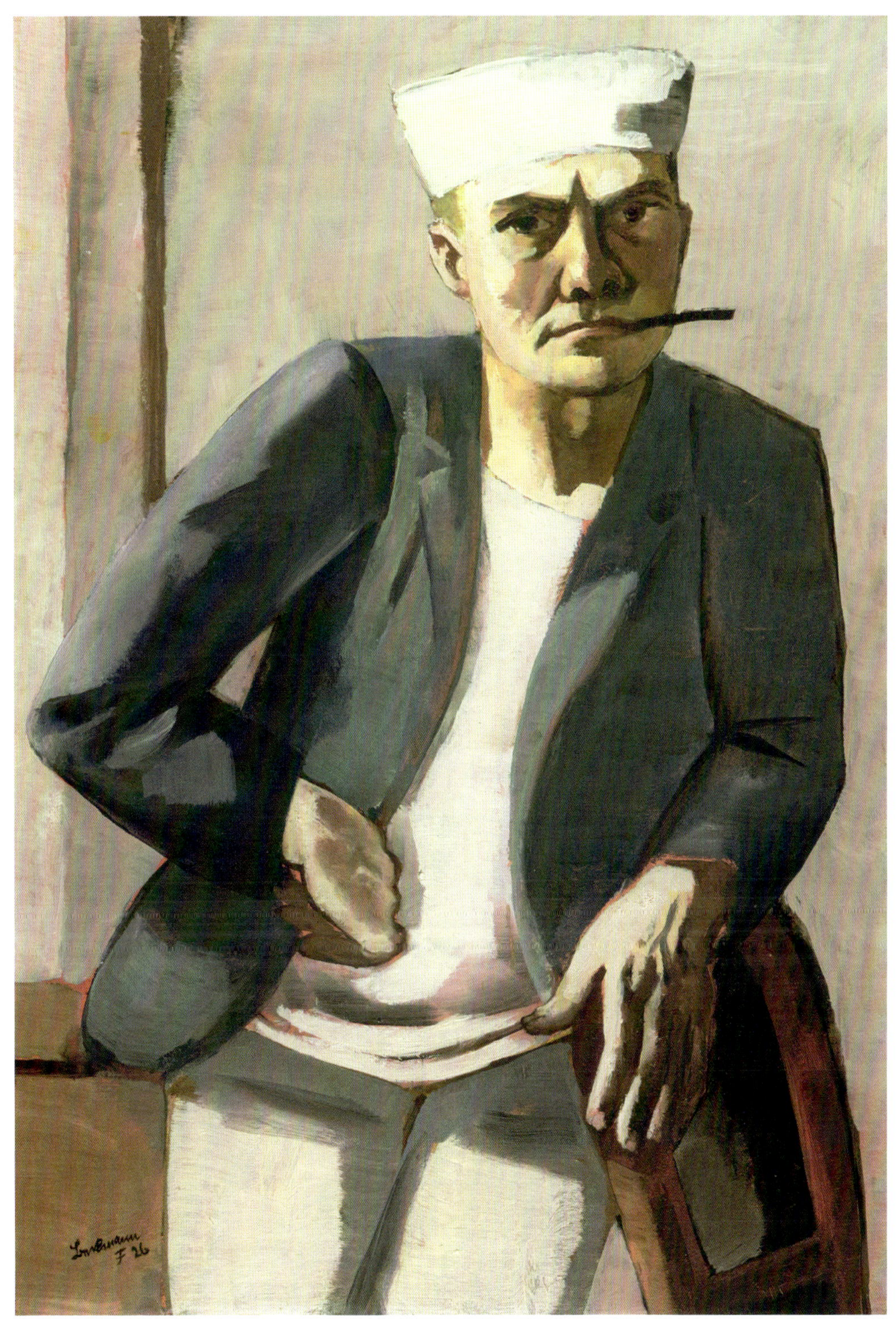

103. SELF-PORTRAIT WITH WHITE CAP, 1926

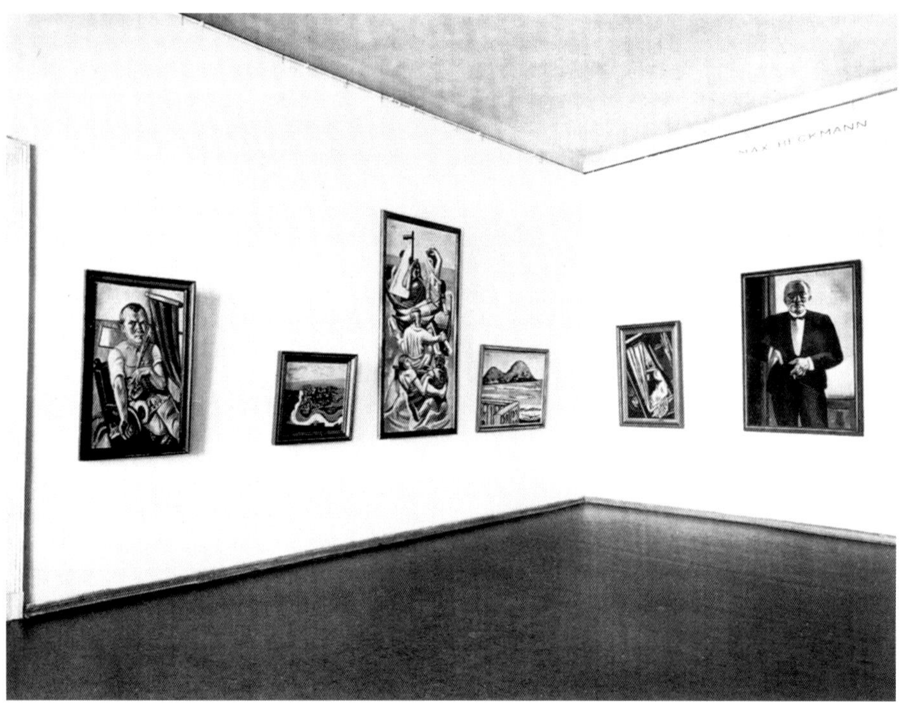

Beckmann room at the Kronprinzenpalais, Nationalgalerie, Berlin 1933

In the mid-1920s, Max Beckmann was recognized as a major figure of the *Neue Sachlichkeit* (New Objectivity). He was represented by a total of fourteen paintings in the exhibition in Mannheim in 1925 that lent the movement its name. That development increasingly disturbed the painter, who was always concerned about his autonomy because it assimilated and subordinated his artistic individuality to a general current. In late 1924, he was already beginning to turn to Italian themes, which can be traced back to several beach vacations in Italy. *Galleria Umberto* [Plate 101] is a first radical and almost surreal-looking attempt to explode previous ideas of the image using the example of the eponymous arcade in Milan. *Italienische Fantasie* (Italian Fantasy) [Plate 100] of 1925 continues this and at the same time brings it back into reality. *Die Barke* (The Bark) of 1926 represents a temporary end to this group of works. In its vertical format, we see a tower of figures oscillating between playful swimming and existential plight. Overlapping and obstructions of the view prevent a completely coherent grasp of the spatial arrangement. These paintings respond to the Fascism in Italy in a general way without referring to it directly. *Bad im August* (Swimming in August) of 1937 takes up this mood and motif once again during his exile in Amsterdam under the auspices of persecution.

For Beckmann, *The Bark* was "once again a magnum opus," as he wrote to his art dealer Jsrael Ber Neumann on June 26, 1926. On June 25, 1928, he informed Neumann that it was already in the possession of the Nationalgalerie in Berlin, along with the 1927 *Selbstbildnis im Smoking* (Self-Portrait in Tuxedo), and other works would follow. His success in the capital of the Reich was exceptionally important to the artist; ultimately, an entire room in the Kronprinzenpalais—the modern department of the Nationalgalerie—was dedicated to him, which the painter negotiated with the curator Ludwig Thormaehlen in September 1932. It was installed in 1933 [see ill. on this page], but it quickly fell victim to the destructive art policy of the National Socialists. In 1935, Beckmann himself traded *The Bark*, among other works, for the 1933 painting *Ochsen im Stall* (Oxen in the Stable), which may have seemed less controversial. But the oxen painting was not spared either and was confiscated in July 1937 as part of the action "Entartete Kunst" (degenerate art). *The Bark* remained in Beckmann's possession until 1946, when it was sent to the United States to Beckmann's close friend and supporter Stephan Lackner, who sold it in 1960 to the Beckmann enthusiast Richard Feigen.

Olaf Peters

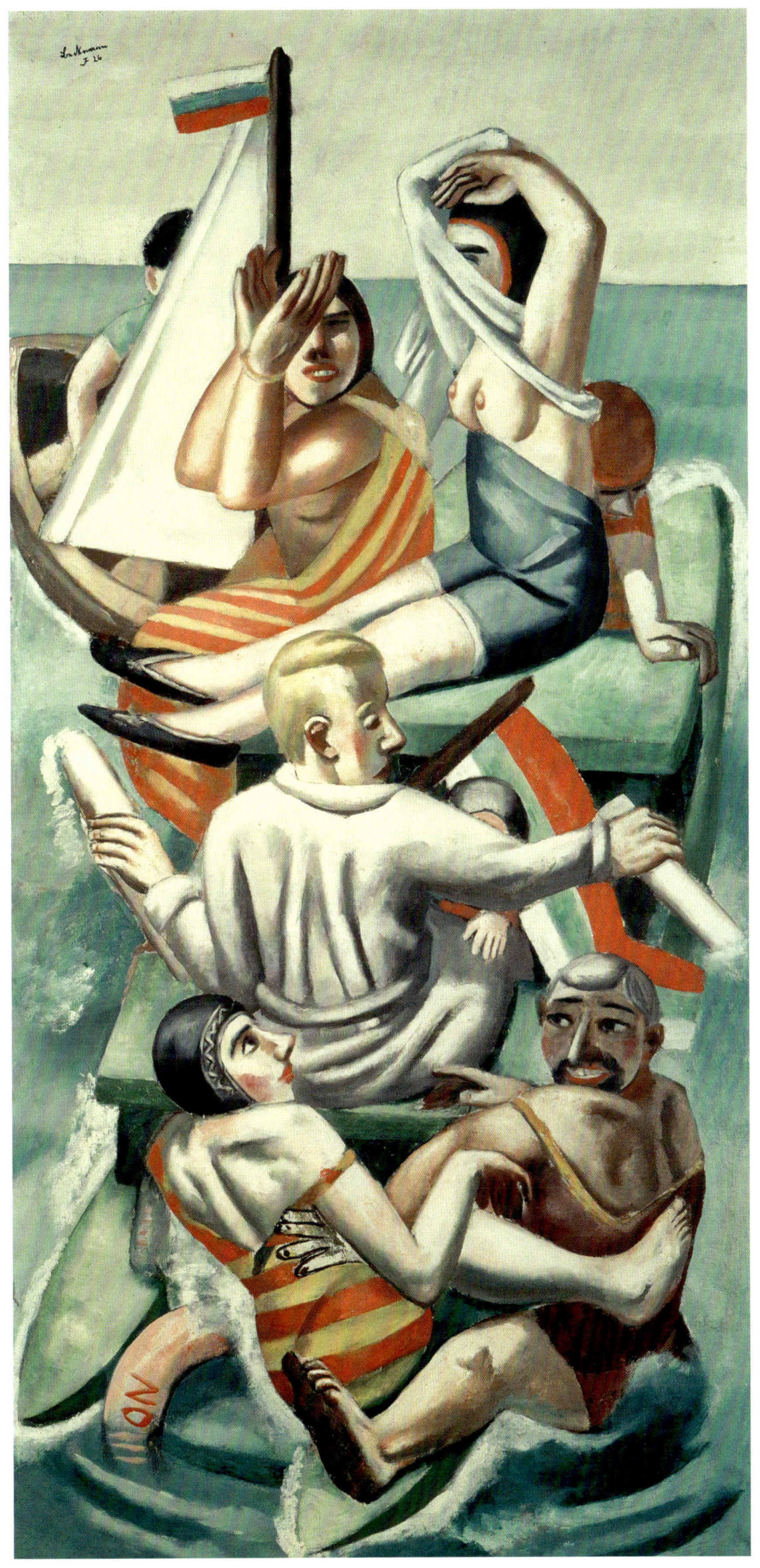

104. THE BARK, 1926

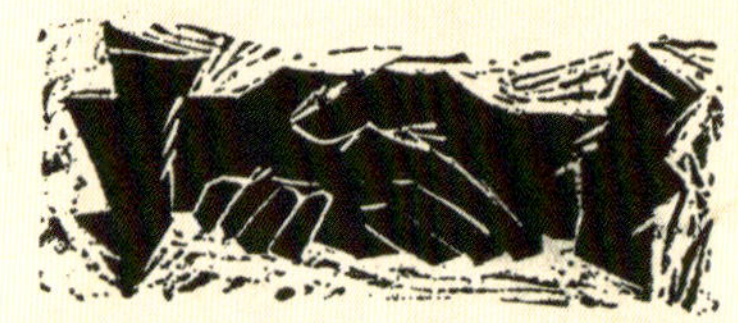

THE DIRECTOR OF THE NEW ART CIRCLE SPEAKS:

Ladies and Gentlemen:

It is now three years since I have been in your midst. When I first arrived in New York, I intended to exhibit the work of the man whom I am just now presenting to you.

After having shown this season Georges Rouault, the Frenchman, and Max Weber, the American, two of the most outstanding of contemporary artists, I am introducing this German artist, Max Beckmann, whose work I have had exclusively since 1913, except for a short intermission when Paul Cassirer, who was his first dealer, handled it.

The publications I made of Beckmann had no text; so again, in this case, his work may speak for itself. Furthermore, there are two books on Beckmann; one by Hans Kaiser, published by Paul Cassirer, Berlin, 1913, and one by Meier-Graefe, Glaser, Hausenstein and Fraenger, published by Piper, Munich, 1923.

My wish is that the response to this exhibition may be great enough to encourage the Neue Kunstgemeinschaft in its aim, which is to establish a friendly exchange of art between America and Germany. Next season I hope to show here works by Dix, Feininger, Gross, Heckel, Kirchner, Kokoschka, Nolde, and others of Germany, and to exhibit such Americans as Weber, Karfiol, Kuhn, Burlin, Scheeler, Becker, Levinson, Hondius, Howland, Burkhard and others, in Germany.

"MAX BECKMANN: ARTLOVER," J.B. NEUMANNS BILDERHEFTE. PUBLISHER: NEW ART CIRCLE, NEW YORK, 1927

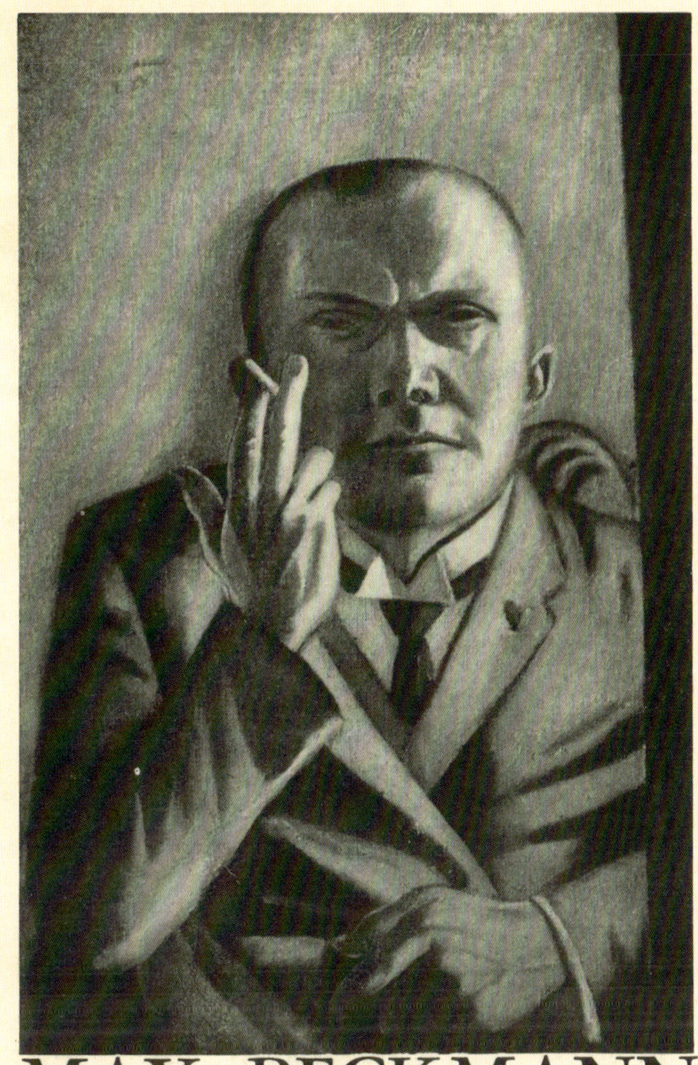

MAX BECKMANN

ARTLOVER
J. B. NEUMANNS BILDERHEFTE

NEW ART CIRCLE
NEUE KUNSTGEMEINSCHAFT
NEW YORK/BERLIN/MUNICH

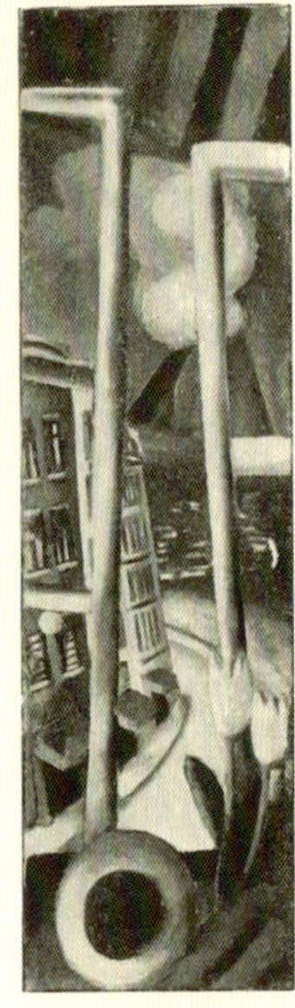

MAX BECKMANN
EXHIBITION 1927
NEW ART CIRCLE
J. B. NEUMANN/DIRECTOR
NEW YORK

2

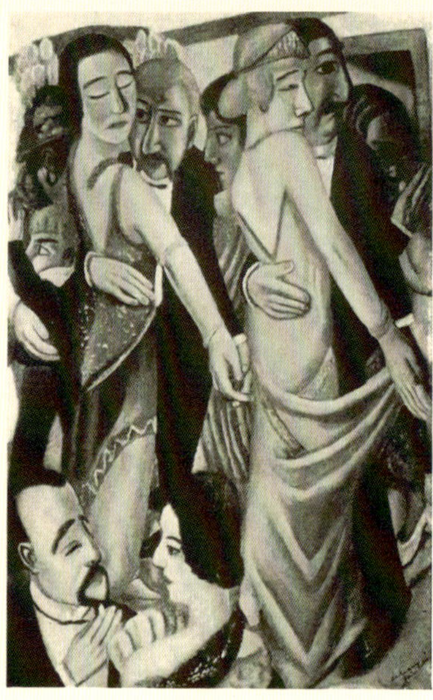

MAX BECKMANN EXHIBITION 1927
NEW ART CIRCLE/J. B. NEUMANN/DIRECTOR/NEW YORK

3

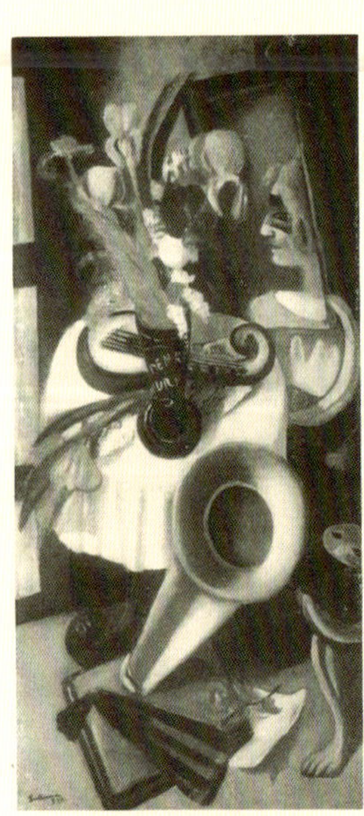

MAX BECKMANN EXHIBITION 1927
NEW ART CIRCLE/J. B. NEUMANN/DIRECTOR
NEW YORK

4

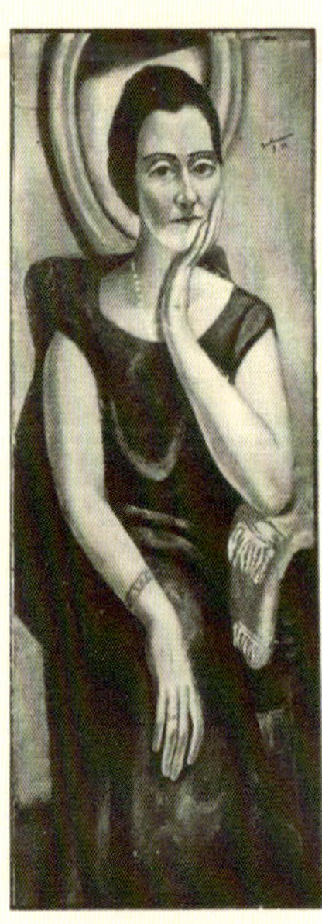

MAX BECKMANN
EXHIBITION 1927
J. B. NEUMANN/DIRECTOR
NEW YORK

5

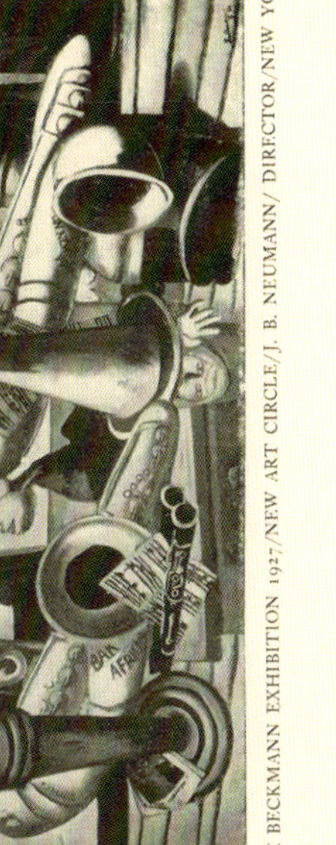

MAX BECKMANN EXHIBITION 1927/NEW ART CIRCLE/J. B. NEUMANN/ DIRECTOR/NEW YORK

6

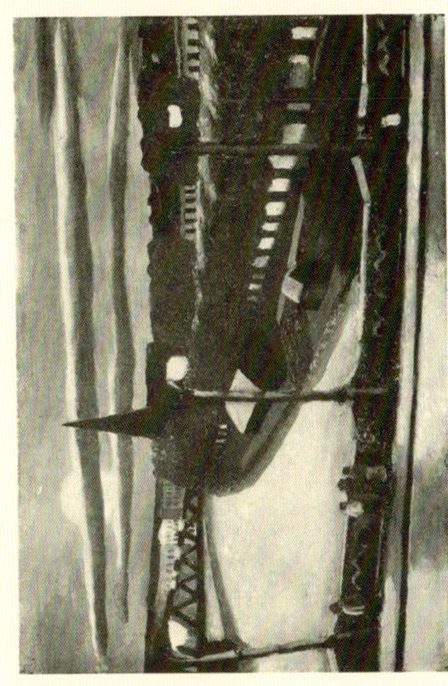

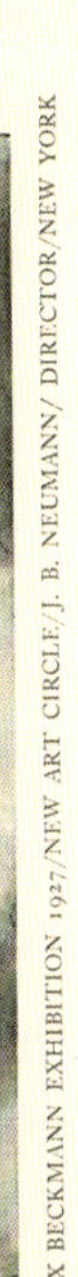

MAX BECKMANN EXHIBITION 1927/NEW ART CIRCLE/J. B. NEUMANN/ DIRECTOR/NEW YORK

7

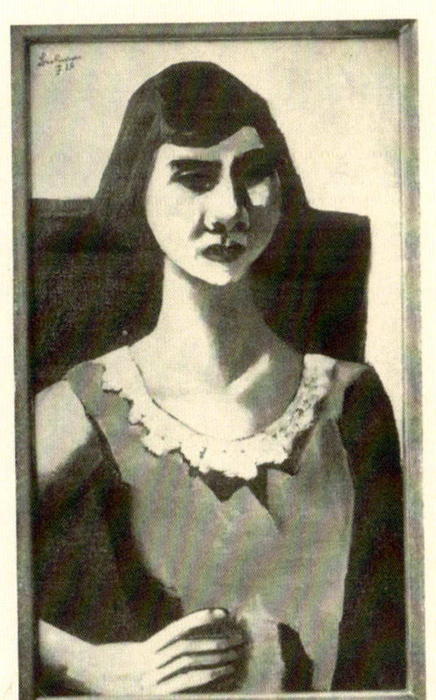

MAX BECKMANN EXHIBITION 1927
NEW ART CIRCLE/J. B. NEUMANN/DIRECTOR/NEW YORK

8

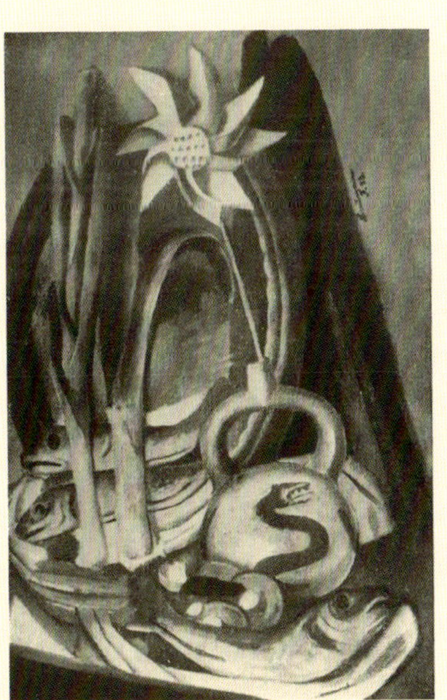

MAX BECKMANN EXHIBITION 1927
NEW ART CIRCLE/J. B. NEUMANN/DIRECTOR/NEW YORK

9

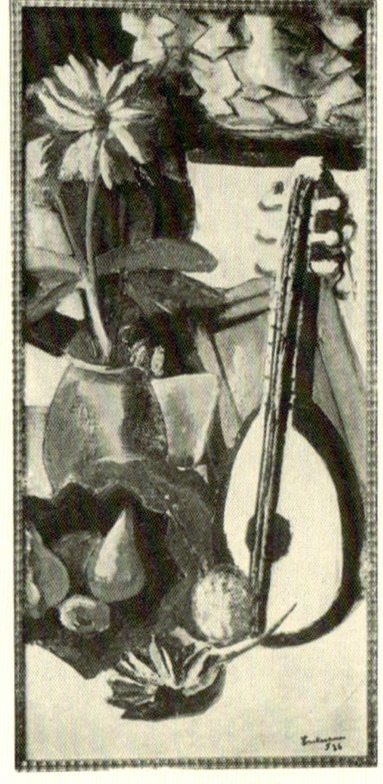

MAX BECKMANN EXHIBITION 1927
NEW ART CIRCLE/J. B. NEUMANN/DIRECTOR/NEW YORK

10

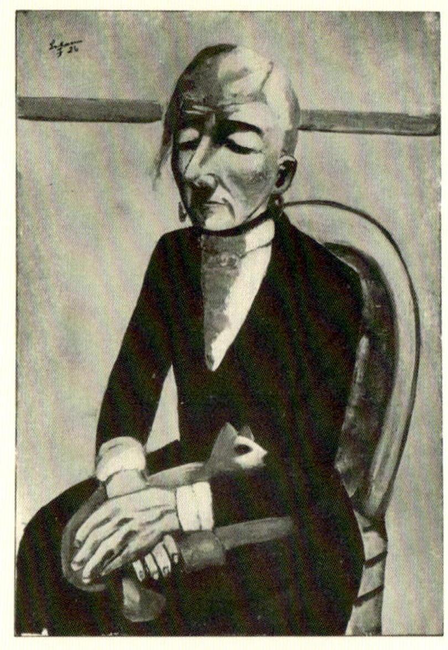

MAX BECKMANN EXHIBITION 1927/NEW ART CIRCLE
J. B. NEUMANN/DIRECTOR/NEW YORK

11

12

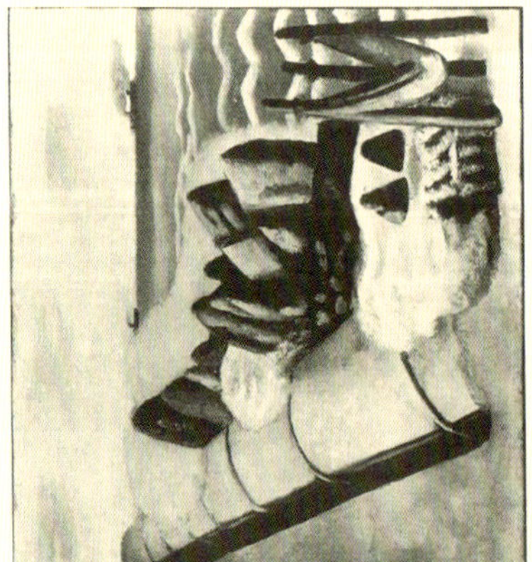

MAX BECKMANN EXHIBITION 1927/NEW ART CIRCLE
J. B. NEUMANN/DIRECTOR/NEW YORK

13

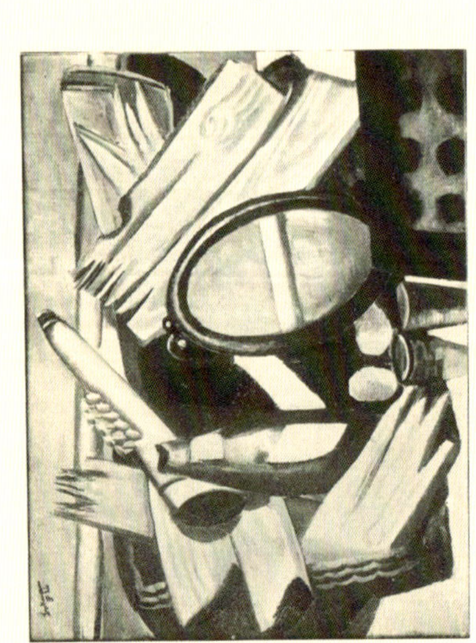

MAX BECKMANN EXHIBITION 1927/NEW ART CIRCLE
J. B. NEUMANN/DIRECTOR/NEW YORK

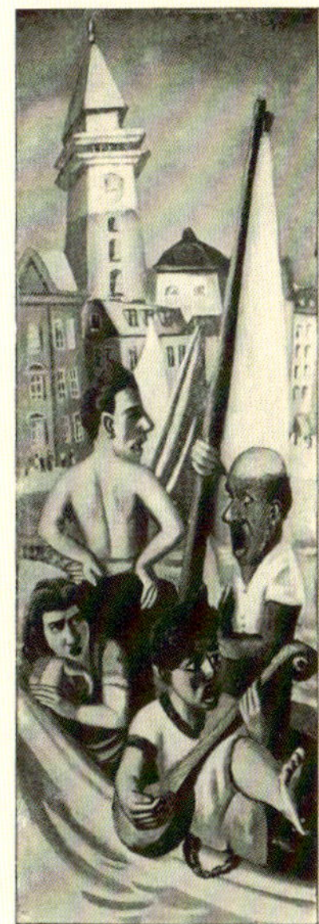

MAX BECKMANN
EXHIBITION 1927
NEW ART CIRCLE
J. B. NEUMANN/DIRECTOR
NEW YORK

14

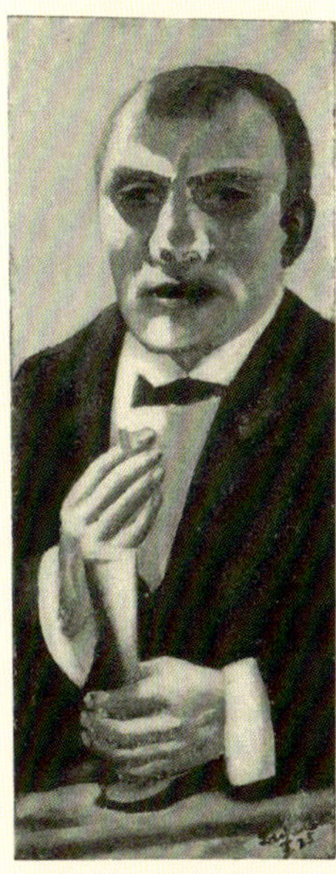

MAX BECKMANN
EXHIBITION 1927
NEW ART CIRCLE
J. B. NEUMANN/DIRECTOR
NEW YORK

15

MAX BECKMANN

Heinrich Simon

Real experts no longer dispute that it is an important phenomenon. A few who were until recently still resisting have since converted. Their emphatic enthusiasm is perhaps unconsciously intended to cover up their former critical stance.

The so-called public is, as always when on new artistic terrain, uncertain, divided into camps: crying hosanna, calling to crucify him. That should not be cause for reproach. "Ça dure vingt ans," Vollard used to say. Vision and hearing are by nature conservative in normal individuals—that is to say, those who are not gifted in these specific senses. The way we generally see and hear today is the result of yesterday's art. With music, this happens, on the one hand, more quickly, because a rather high percentage of truly musical people listen to serious music, and they naturally find it easier to keep up. With the broad public, which especially in "official" music events is thoroughly permeated by creatures who are not especially talented musically, on the other hand, it goes even more slowly than in the other arts. The average such listener has probably arrived at Haydn, Mozart, and the early Beethoven. His reverence for the Beethoven of the later quartets would not pass a test that truly probes the soul. With painting, it is precisely the reverse. Because everyone, even those not decidedly gifted visually, believes to have a relationship with the image, above all thanks to the ability to grasp objects, thanks to the concept of taste, thanks to our innate sense of pleasure with colors, the circle of the "interested" is filled with the visual laity; consequently, even so-called collectors, regular visitors and lovers of galleries, and the art historically oriented include large numbers who are completely alienated by its latest manifestations, so alienated that even today they stop *before* the French Impressionists and essentially feel comfortable only in a "classical" atmosphere. It is, however, precisely in a so-called broad public that one finds one or the other uneducated person who does not feel too limited to the visual idiom (perspective, familiar ABC of color, traditional format, clarity of outline) of the past era but gladly turns to the more recent and the latest manifestations and almost understands them.

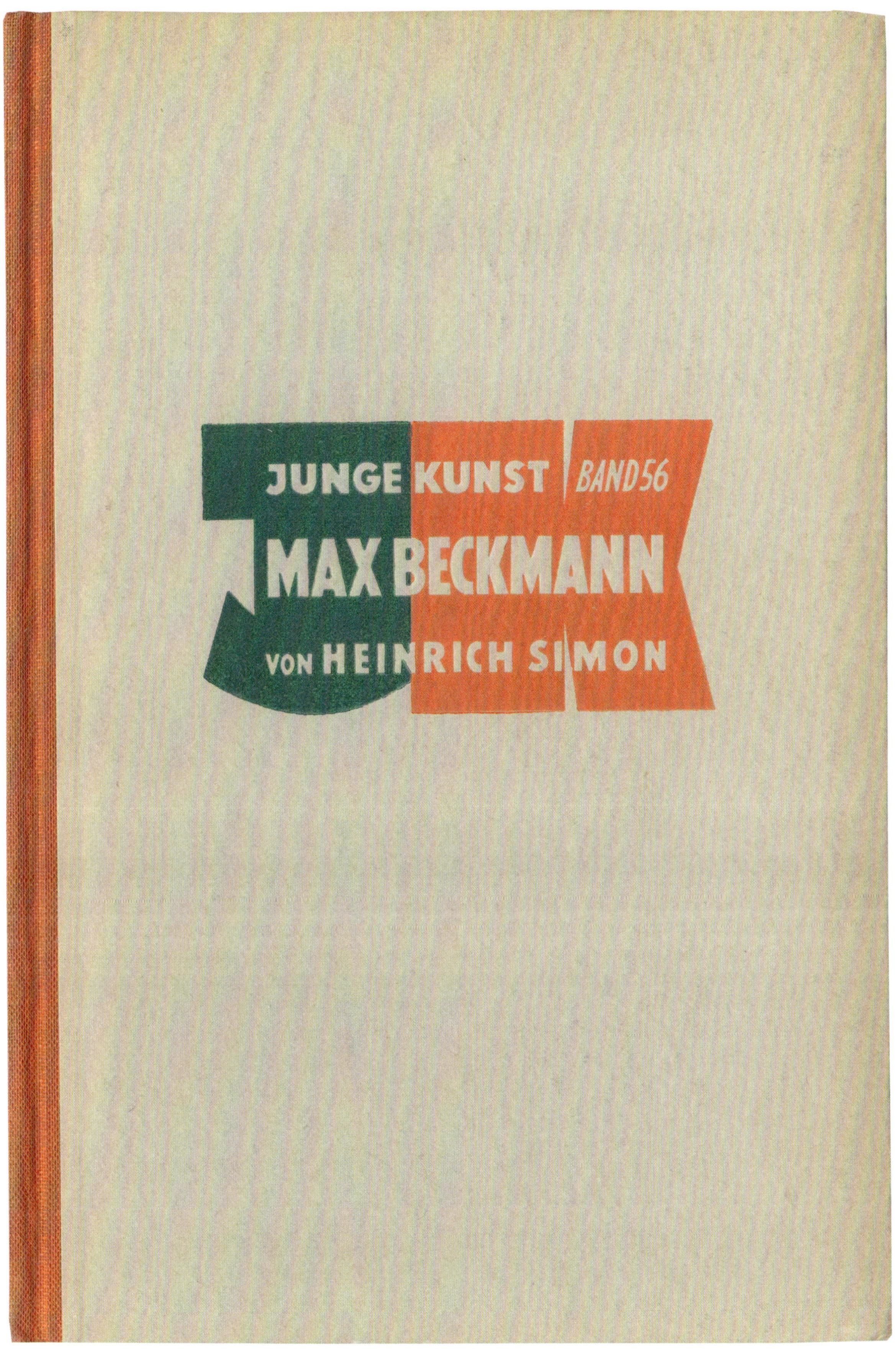

"MAX BECKMANN," HEINRICH SIMON. PUBLISHER: VERLAG VON KLINKHARDT, BERLIN & LEIPZIG, 1930

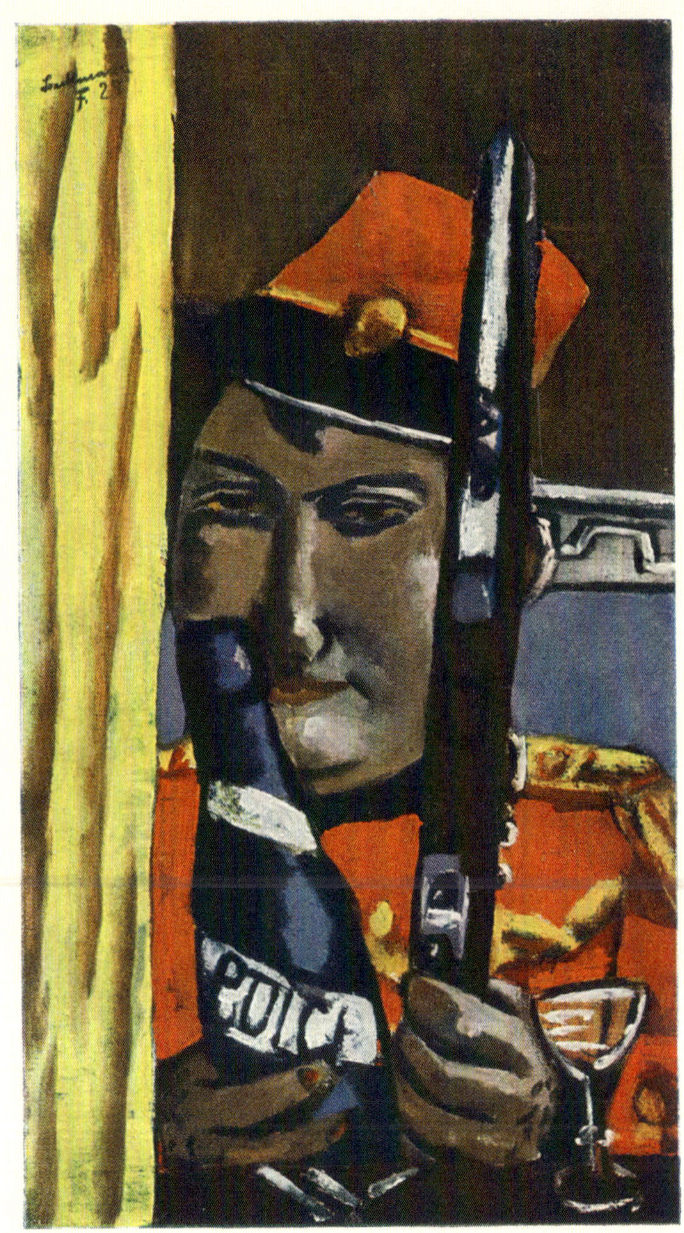

Der peruanische Soldat trinkt 1929
Stuttgart, Slg. Hugo Borst

JUNGE KUNST
BAND 56

MAX BECKMANN

VON

HEINRICH SIMON

MIT 32 TAFELN UND EINEM FARBIGEN TITELBILD

BERLIN UND LEIPZIG, 1930
VERLAG VON KLINKHARDT & BIERMANN

Consequently, precisely in the guild of collectors, there are many, also in Beckmann's case, who reject him as well as everything that does not fit into their Cinquecento schema, and whose backwardness is less obvious only because they no longer have the courage to speak frankly about more recent art commodities that have received the stamp of approval, such as Van Gogh or Corinth. On the other hand, one not infrequently encounters naive visual souls, especially in the younger generation, who recognize and admire this painter as unusual and important for his time without stumbling over the novelty of his formal idiom.

And the market? A complicated matter! In some cases, it is the true standard for the value of the rarity of great art that is gaining acceptance, which is, however, especially in relation to past values, subject to changes in current taste, and as a result sometimes walks blindly past great values and sometimes outlasts revisions and expulsions that have occurred. In some cases, it is a stock-market game played by a few skilled jugglers; it is deliberately staged inflation of prices by intelligent art dealers who are sufficiently enlightened about the obedience of the interested parties. In our day it is influenced by a penchant for the bizarre, for the marginal, by the pleasure the bourgeoisie derives from *épater le bourgeois voisin*. In short, it is the faithful mirror of the merry carnival of our time, which, because it lacks real thrones, while the urge to show reverence is only growing, now selects a chosen few and rewards their work at a thousand pounds each but is already throwing it away tomorrow. Collectors anxiously seek to sell, even at a loss, the pieces they have acquired to those who haven't yet seen the latest stock quotes. The benchmark for the true situation of the market is therefore less the fluctuating and only slowly stabilizing figure of the art trade but rather the fact that there is hardly a single important public art collection in Germany that does not feel obliged to own one important painting by Beckmann. Just as one can be skeptical about the reliability of judgment of our age in general, one can be skeptical about the judgment of museum directors—after all, they are not investing their own money but public funds, and the majority of them know perfectly well that they were given an office and are thus also obliged to have an opinion that is supposed to survive the future as well.

It has therefore become unnecessary, as it was just a few years ago, to wave the Banner of the Upright Seven, to fight for a new, important manifestation. The task today is: trying to understand even better an acclaimed figure of our time, finding his proper place in the ranks of the masters of our century, and discovering his exemplary quality that will influence coming generations.

It is—to introduce a few biographical facts here—no coincidence that Max Beckmann, who is forty-five, decided to begin teaching as head of a master class at the art school in Frankfurt just two years ago—even though his ability in his craft, his talent, already thrilled art lovers twenty years ago and made possible a career that was in every way based on this ability in the traditional sense. The paintings from that time make that understandable. One can sense role models in them, as one can in all healthy and mature art, but the technique, the taste, the individual style of the drawing and painting of that time are mastered in such a way that it must have required an enormous amount of energy not to have society braid the laurels that he had earned almost effortlessly into a wreath that would have been completely sufficient for a respectable and lucrative career as an artist.

Literatur

Karl Scheffler: Max Beckmann. Berlin. Bruno Cassirer 1913 (Kunst und Künstler XI).

Hans Kaiser: Max Beckmann. Berlin. Paul Cassirer 1913.

Heinrich Simon: Max Beckmann. Potsdam. G. Kiepenheuer 1919 (Kunstblatt III).

Paul F. Schmidt: Max Beckmann. Leipzig. Klinkhardt u. Biermann 1919 (Cicerone XI).

Benno Reifenberg: Max Beckmann. München. Piper 1921 (Ganymed III).

J. B. Neumann: Bilderhefte I/II 1920/1921.

Curt Glaser / Julius Meier-Graefe / Wilhelm Hausenstein / Wilhelm Fraenger: Max Beckmann. Piper & Co. München 1923.

Carl Einstein: Max Beckmann. Berlin. Propyläen-Verlag 1926 (in „Die Kunst des 20. Jahrhunderts").

Julius Meier-Graefe: Max Beckmann. München. Piper 1926 (in „Entwicklungsgeschichte der modernen Kunst").

Georg Swarzenski: Um Max Beckmann. Frankfurt/M. 1927 („Das neue Frankfurt", Heft 4).

Adolph Glassgold: Max Beckmann. New York 1927 (The Arts).

G. F. Hartlaub: Max Beckmann. Mannheim 1928.

Lilly v. Schnitzler: Max Beckmann. Querschnitt April 1928.

Fritz Wichert: Max Beckmann. Die Form 1928.

Wilhelm Hausenstein: Max Beckmann. München 1928 (Vorrede zum Katalog des Graph. Kabinetts).

20

1

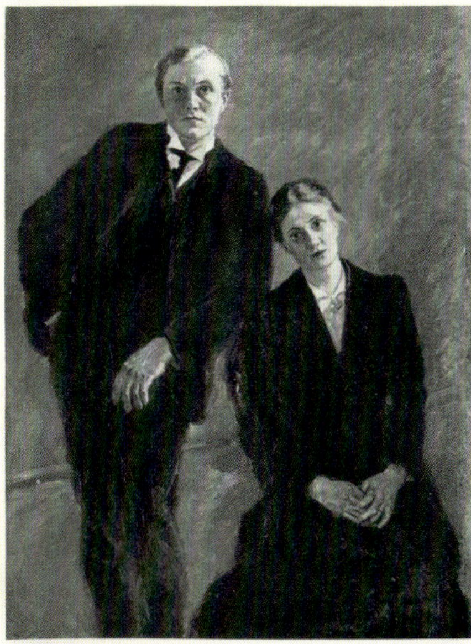

Doppelbildnis 1909
Halle, Museum

2

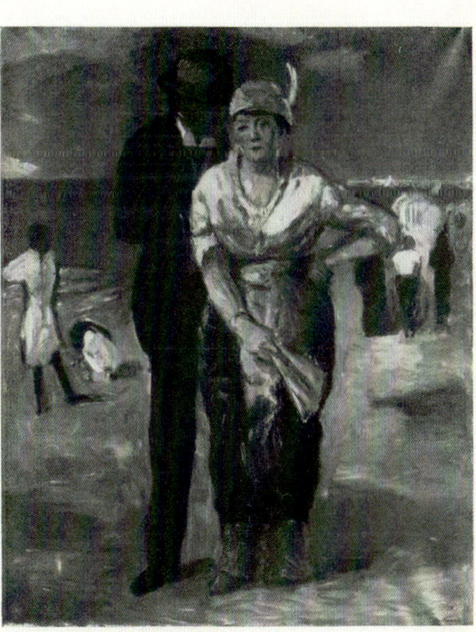

Paar am Strand 1913
Hamburg, Slg. Frau H. B. Simms

3

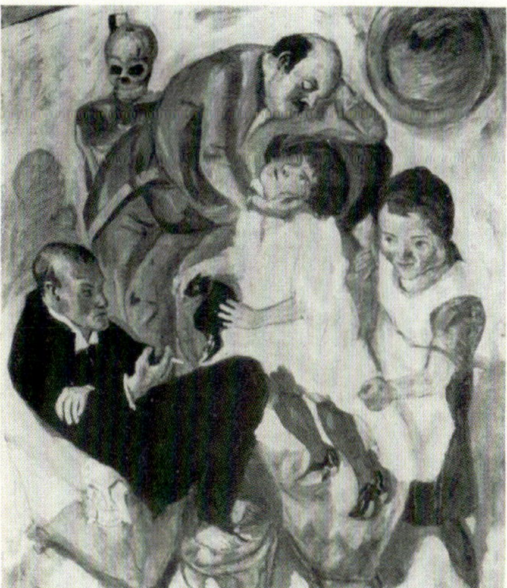

Gesellschaft 1915
Frankfurt, Slg. Ugi Battenberg

There are some who are unable to perceive any connection at all between these paintings and the later ones, who base their lack of faith in Beckmann on that alleged irreconcilability. There are others who declare the war to have been the guilty party and speak of a wartime psychosis that was only gradually overcome, who stand transfixed before his current still-lifes, which they say are finally, thank God, once again paintings by a recuperated Beckmann.

It is difficult to say which group should be awarded the palm for the greater error. To the former, who do not see that a transformation in design follows from the early paintings in a completely logical sequence, a breaking away from the traditional structure of the painting, and that the war—and herein lies a grain of truth of group two—influenced the tempo of this development, slowing it by interrupting the existence focused professionally solely on painting, driven by the compulsion that it exercised on every more profound observer: to think and act radically, that is, without the ballast of accepted ideas. And, at the same time, that exposes the error of the second group. The war was, of course, crucial for Beckman as a human being, and because he is certainly not by nature purely contemplative or solely artistic but rather a painter who feels a most profound connection to the political and moral events of his homeland and of the world, the war necessarily became visible in some fashion in his works as well. But anyone who declares his present paintings, which strike gentler and more peaceful tones here and there, to be the only real ones, that is, those once again in contact with the earlier Beckmann, completely overlooks the fact that what stands between the paintings of then and now—and herein lies a grain of truth of group one—is much less the war than a development from the traditional idea of the image to a completely different one, so that seen retrospectively these early paintings may belong to Beckmann but to a phase that had been finished off once and for all—and by Beckman himself.

That is the inner reason—whether conscious or unconscious, a difference that plays hardly any role in the life of a genius—why Beckmann decided so late, despite his great ability, not just to paint but also to teach others: his artistic drive forced him not to stick with the traditional idea of the image, which he felt was no longer current and no longer appropriate, but rather to develop a new, meaningful, and objective idea. For the conscious artist, that demanded time. Lots of time. Years of the most concentrated work not on theory—which would have resulted in something artificial—but on the practice of painting. Painting and painting again. And, in general, eliminating everything from his life that distracted his concentration, everything superficial, everything that took him prematurely, too prematurely along externally determined paths: clique, position, relationships. What mattered was not painting pretty pictures that were successful and brought in commissions. What mattered was not joining a group or asserting himself against criticism and public opinion. What mattered was constant experiments, like a chemist locked up in a laboratory, that would finally bring him, painting by painting, to a new valid idea. To a meaningful and objective one. And in that he differs quite fundamentally from other contemporary experimenters.

He was not the only one who sensed that the traditional idea of the image was dubious. That it *had become* dubious. How? Answering that would require writing the history of the idea of the image from the Renaissance to the present. It would require going into matters of a purely optical nature, would have to start with a psychological analysis of perspective in

4

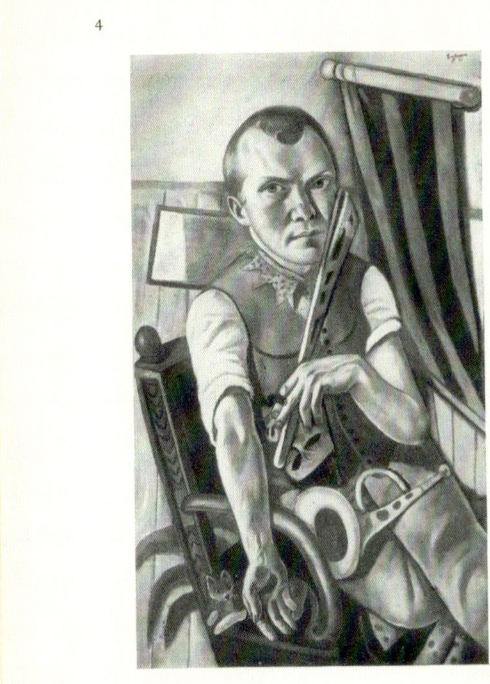

Selbstbildnis mit Pritsche 1921
Berlin, Slg. Alfred Flechtheim

5

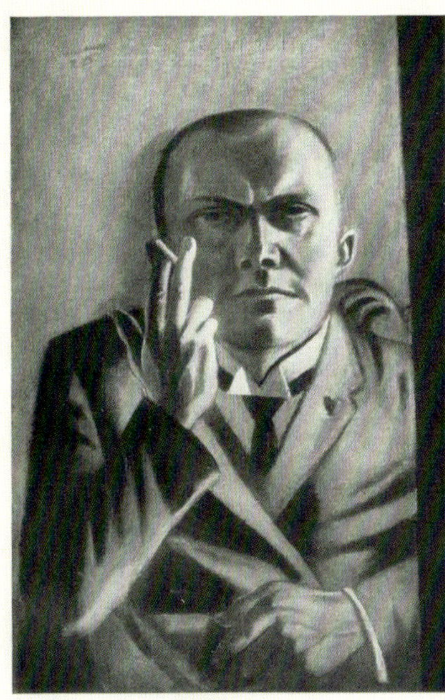

Selbstbildnis auf gelbem Grund 1923
Neuyork, Slg. Dr. F. H. Hirschland

6

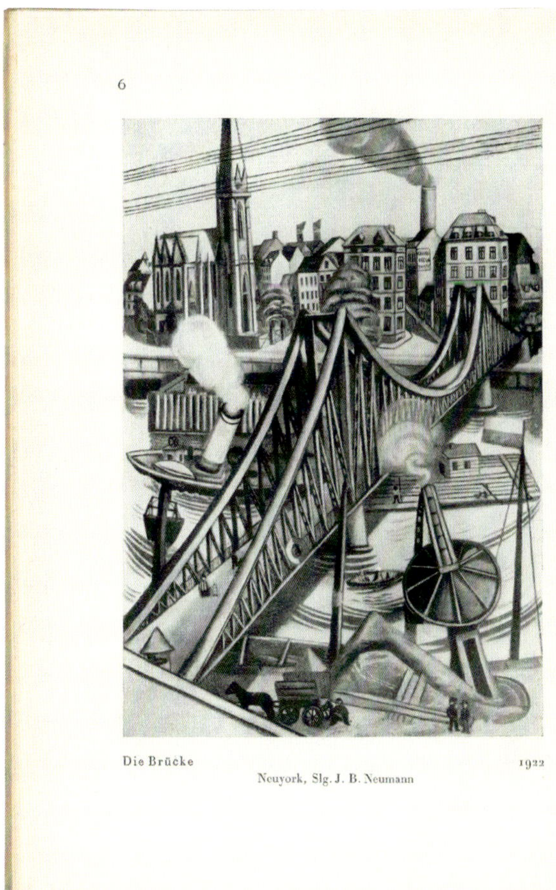

Die Brücke 1922
Neuyork, Slg. J. B. Neumann

7

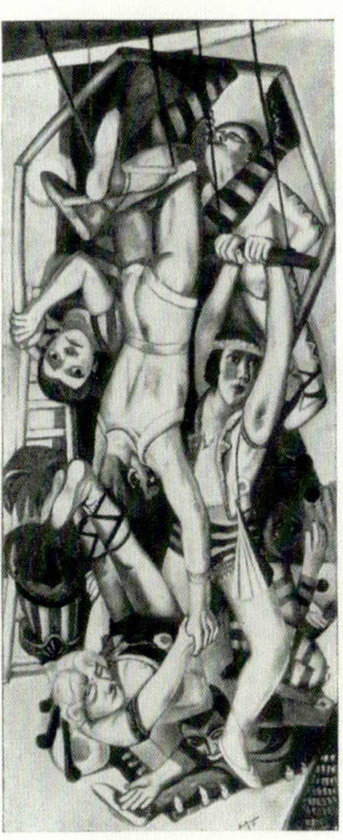

Das Trapez 1923
Berlin, Slg. Baron von Simolin

Dürer's work, would have to uncover how this way of seeing and depicting the seen is connected to the thinking of that time and its view of the world. It would have to follow the change of the visual image over the following centuries, and why, despite that change, the Renaissance construction—and sometimes variations on that deviated far from the original—was retained, seemingly as the ultimate solution, timeless like a natural law. How it then became looser, the first question marks appeared, whether it was at all possible to render nature other than in this peep box, in this comfortable vis-à-vis form, in which the viewpoint was fixed, like an old, tried-and-true household remedy, and now cheerfully and, once learned, effortlessly recreated a space, that looked like a beautifully, deceptively real space, an artificial space, so anyone could understand it. A space that—as its immortal contribution—taught us to take in, piece by piece, this chaotic nature that repeatedly escapes us because of its diversity, making it possible for us, thanks to a form adapted to human senses, to grasp and understand nature for the first time. No one has, to my knowledge, studied the role that photography played in the nineteenth century in *this* sense—by which I mean the extent to which it severely spoiled the enjoyment of a world so flawlessly and seemingly definitively reproduced by doing it in essence much better and even more effortlessly than the painters. There were, however, some—and supposedly they still exist today—who used photography's perfection in terms of the "correctness" of its visual image and, because they believe the traditional idea of the image to be the definitive one, quite legitimately worked with photography, sometimes officially, and sometimes holding the translation under the table, as we did in high school.

Surely, however, in addition to photography other factors of a more general nature contributed to skepticism breaching the sanctuary of the traditional idea of the image. But even the French Impressionists—as revolutionary as they saw themselves, and as they were indeed with regard to using nonlinear forms to produce space—generally clung to the rigidly constructed vis-à-vis image. The demonic pair of friends Van Gogh–Gauguin were the first to boldly venture out in this way, offering details that seemed violent and artificial compared to what had come before, sometimes seemingly seen from above, or with dimensions in some sections looking larger than in others in the same perspectival plane. In a word, they drew "incorrectly": Cézanne, although he was less conscious, less intellectual, had his way of reproducing nature that was more law, more principle. Perhaps precisely *because* he wrote fewer philosophical letters and instead dedicated himself more exclusively to painting! He must have tortured himself incredibly with these matters. It was new ground. He was stolid and essentially conservative. That is why he still wavered. Seen from the present, however, he was the one who broke most unaffectedly and most naturally from the vis-à-vis idea and introduced a dynamic bottom-to-top movement into the rigidity of the traditional idea.

It is, namely, the case that when we fix our eyes on a point, we see nothing at all but this point clearly, unless we stand so far back from the object to be taken in with the eye all at once that we also see it as a whole when we look at it. We poor mortals depend on the wandering of the eye to create an image of the world. That is laborious, and the way that the established Cinquecento image brought the world together was truly a brilliant idea. The human being tied to his clod of earth, for which the distant is per se already something foreign, uncanny, something that demands daring—because who knows who is hiding behind

8

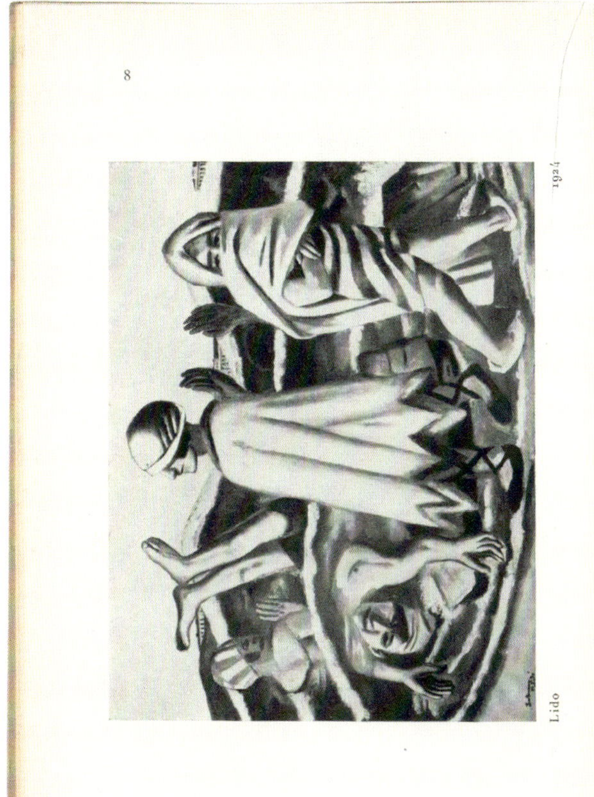

Lido 1924

9

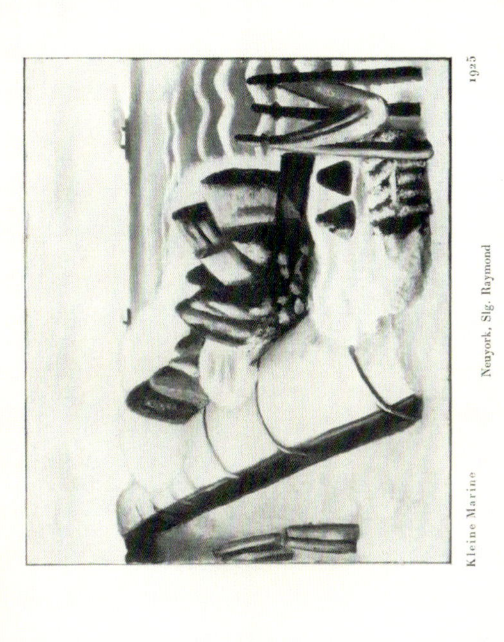

Kleine Marine 1925
Neuyork, Slg. Raymond

10

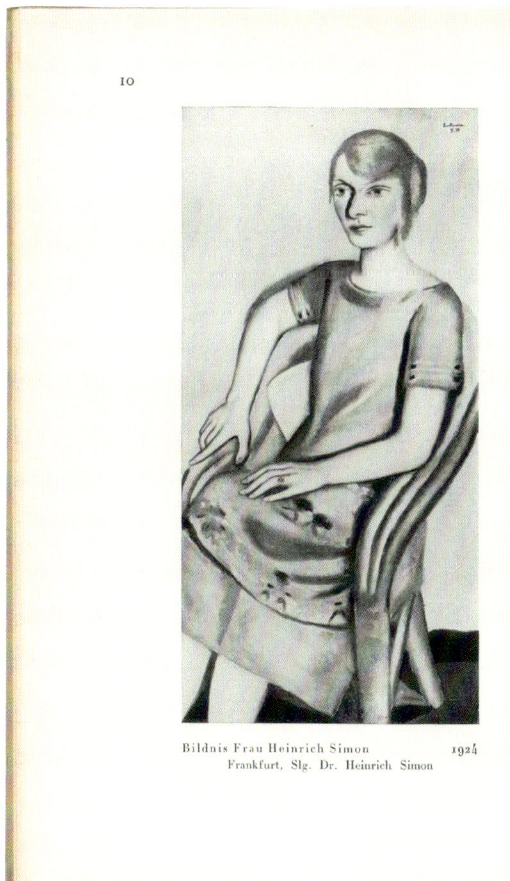

Bildnis Frau Heinrich Simon 1924
Frankfurt, Slg. Dr. Heinrich Simon

11

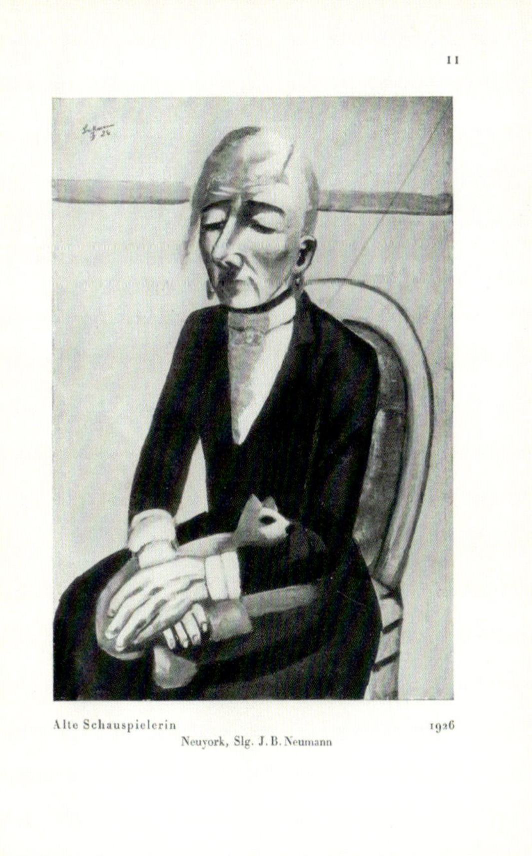

Alte Schauspielerin 1926
Neuyork, Slg. J. B. Neumann

12

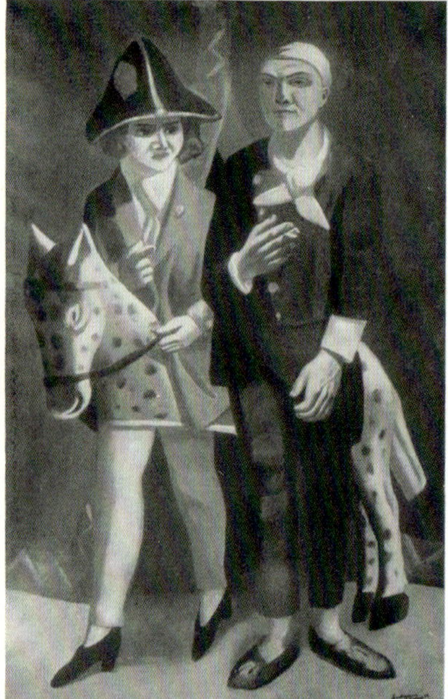

Karneval 1925
Frankfurt, Städel'sches Institut

13

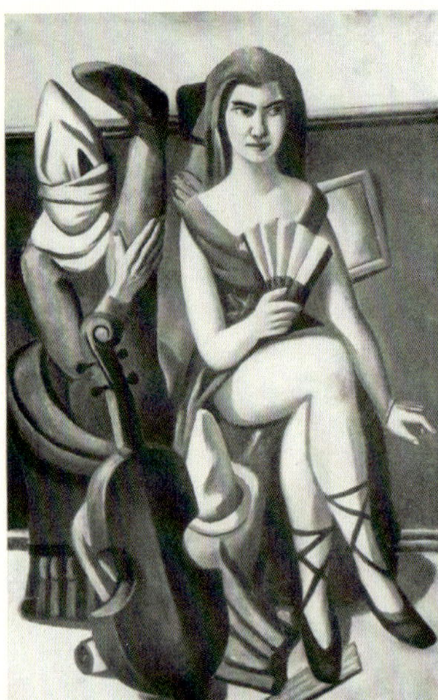

Pierette und Clown 1925
Mannheim, Kunsthalle

14

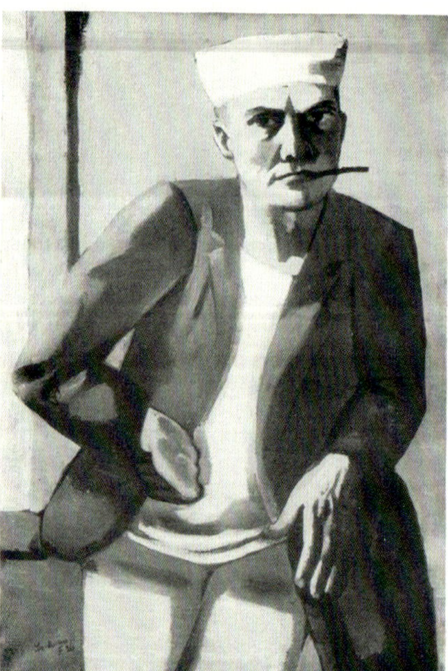

Selbstbildnis mit weißer Mütze 1926

15

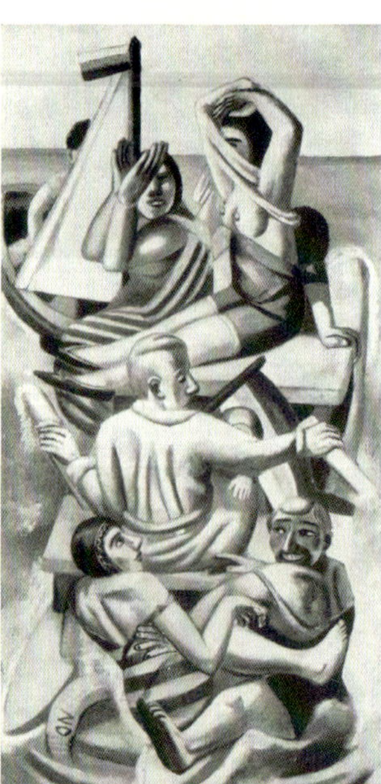

Die Barke 1926
Berlin, Nationalgalerie

the next tree—has everything beautifully and safely side by side in the image. Even his fellow man whose eyes deny what his mouth says, who appears disguised and in armor, menacing as a lord before whom eyes are cast downward in reverence, will perhaps, if in a good mood, offer a gracious gaze, like alms, lying in wait as a compeer for the bareness he is given—this other person has been precisely and faithfully rendered in the image, just as he is. A sensation that one saw something that was actually completely unreal, passing by so quickly, something so little exposed, something of which one has a vague notion but no clear idea, captured in the image. Imagine this life of earlier centuries: on the one hand, the isolation of the individual, no idea of the rest of the world except from stories, add to it the unrest of many wars, the rabble above and below, ambush and robbery, and then the beautiful, peaceful, revealing summary, the capturing of the world in the image. Like other sensations we seek today! We have ideas aplenty. About people: from extremely dressed up to completely naked, taken in from all sides, probed, analyzed, as if in the tailor's movable mirror, which permits every view, every nuance of a view. We know his visibility from all zones of the inhabited earth. And especially the landscape! We know it so well that it is difficult even for the person who can do anything—as far as the idea is concerned, namely the photographer—to find something striking that is not already on postcards. And if airplanes had not come to his aid, so that he could for a while—how much longer?—amuse his honored public with tricks: all from above, half from above, all from below, half from below, then presumably even he, the man with the camera that captures everything, would probably already be at the end of his glory. But what we do not have, what we want to read from the many ideas, are the essences of people and things. For example, not a factual assessment of what a person looks like but his special quality, such as his wisdom or strength of will or perfidy. In the past, that was displayed with naive openness: the person of the sixteenth or seventeenth century was truly more or less what he looked like. Then began the covering up, and not just with makeup and powder. And faces became masks. Now the painter begins to become something uncomfortable, namely: people begin to hide their perfidy from the outside; it is not immediately "visible." What gives the painter the right to drag it into the daylight, especially when the painting is paid for by its subject? But we are interested precisely in this exposure. Because you, Mr. Patient Sitter, don't really interest us, but how kindness, leadership, swindling, lust, break out of person—how it is possible to be dressed and still shamelessly naked, completely distinguished and yet as naive as a newborn child, terribly famous and yet so small, entirely nondescript and yet quite large—that interests us. We have plenty of ideas about people. Anyone who is not a herdsman in a remote pasture knows at least a hundred of that species in the most varied situations and costumes, from the swimming trunks in the public pool to the frock coat for the festive opening of the new slaughterhouse. And the glossy magazines print pictures of all the other swimming trunks, public pools, frock coats, openings, slaughterhouses. All of the regions, cities, summer and winter vacation homes, arctic and equatorial places are known and familiar to us. To have them depicted again by the painter is simply boring for us.

But just as a city is so devoted to a river that it seems to flow with it, just as trees when without leaves become anxious as if they were beginning to freeze, and when they bloom it is like a storm of love—that interests us. This living thing behind the ideas, which breaks out from them only for those who have eyes to see

16

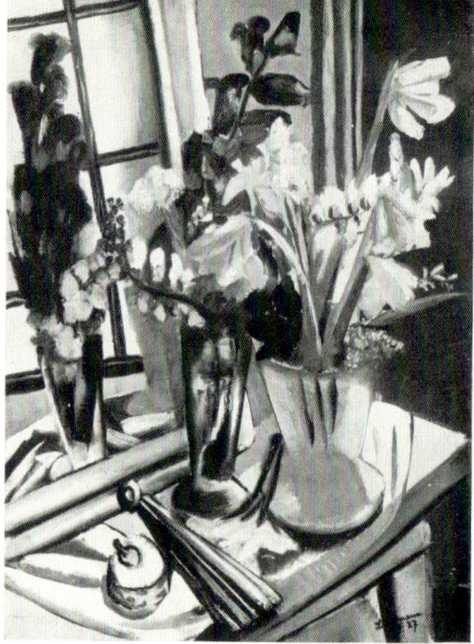

Blumen und Spiegel 1927
Frankfurt, Slg. Lily von Schnitzler

17

Damen am Fenster 1928
Frankfurt, Privatbesitz

18

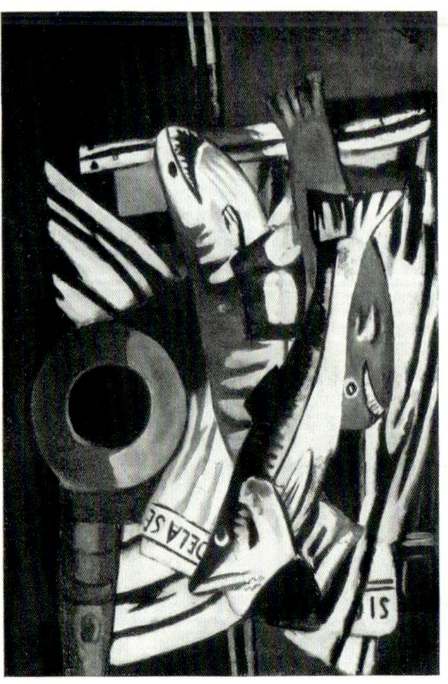

Fischstilleben 1927
Berlin, Slg. Baron von Simolin

19

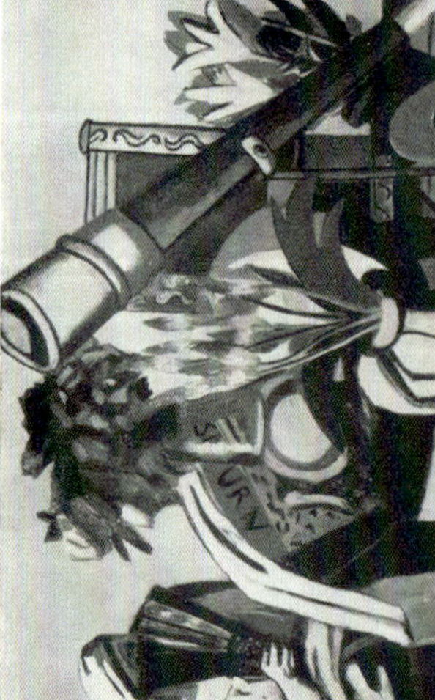

Interieur mit Fernrohr 1927
Berlin, Slg. Alfred Flechtheim

the connections that we do not see with "bare" eyes—that is what *our* painter should paint.

And that is what Beckmann paints.

But first something else about what he doesn't paint. The transformation of time cannot be explained and depicted from *one* thing. All formulas simplify too much. But one thing is certain: the remote is no longer foreign to us. The settled is the exception. The rule is movement. Sitting still makes one narrow. But it is not easy not remaining narrow even in movement, in that one only sees piecework, always only the individual. One has to still remember something seen yesterday and the day before yesterday; one has to see in motion that which one no longer sees. Perhaps, some argue, it is best to paint that which one does not see: the idea of movement, the idea of the human, the idea of landscape, the function, the mathematics, the music of things: *pure* concepts. A generation tortured itself with such attempts, and some of them are still torturing themselves.

There are surely clowns among them.

It is difficult to prove it. There is a profundity that is easily mistaken for shallowness. Anyone who wants to grasp the ungraspable is still vulnerable because he is performing a task that is in any event dubious. The mystic *and* the madman are close to God. Both babble. There are certainly true seekers of God among them: engineers convinced that they have found the element from which human beings are made and have discovered the curves that are the basis for all corporeal rhythm. But even assuming integrity and genuine gnosis: the mystic is understandable only to the mystic. This art is in any case a matter for a club. Even if all the members are gentlemen. The meaning of existence is, however, the real matter. The goal: to become every more real. To get ever-more spirit flowing into the material world. Not to reserve it, stored in bottles, solely for connoisseurs of opiate pleasures. Hundreds of people who merely sense the spirit are better than one who has it but is not in a position to convey it in a way that it can be understood with some effort. Being understandable means not moving so far from nature that magical signs are used to indicate the visible. Then concepts become formulas.

For we remain human. And with all our senses, with all creatural forms and colors, we want to transform ourselves into the godlike. *That* is not megalomania! Megalomania is the belief that we poor novices need only toss aside—like so many old items of clothing—materiality, corporeality, thingness, the how-we-are-made, and already we would find ourselves in the illustrious circles of the pure spirit. *This* path to "true" art was and is at best a noble megalomania, but in many cases surely nothing other than a comfortable way to avoid reforming and refining preexisting reality.

For the record: the gradual rejection of "mimetic painting" and the desire to get away from the boring, balanced, all-too-balanced image of the vis-à-vis was genuine, and was only natural given that the feeling for life had changed completely. But the pseudo-revolutionary gesture of dispensing entirely with reality, with any here and now, the construction into thin air of something one believes to be a law—that was a mistake. Not a rare mistake in an era tired of the past that lacks the patience to establish the foundation—which is hard enough if it is to be sufficiently solid for those born later to build on it—and impatiently wants to see the whole house standing finished—and begins with the roof.

It was Max Beckmann's first good deed not to remain content with his important talent—it would have lasted for a lifetime—and consume with leisure and dignity the interest on the result capital but rather to put his talent in the service of entirely new goals. And it was his second good deed that in an era that was only too willing to swallow any "experiment," even with the most inadequate means, he did not take that path but sought very painstakingly and conscientiously to make his painting adequate to a new, newly lived world.

He knew from the outset that he was not on the path of any arbitrariness, of any fixation on a boom, which says, like a hammy stage director: The old world no longer works, so presto! We'll make a new one. He knew that it was not enough simply to change the objects depicted, like the young girl who believes she is fashionable when she says the word "whore" in familiar company. He new the only path was via the form. By creating a pictorial space that was no longer the leisurely, respectably tempered, spoon-fed space of past centuries that effortlessly overcame all efforts of the roaming eye.

At the same time, however, in order to compete with the old masters, to be on the level of their former great overcoming of the material world, it could not be an arbitrarily constructed space, no playful exchange of up and down, to space born of the whims of eccentric contemporary taste, but had to have inherent laws. The painter had to go beyond himself to reach any valid possibility for a modern view of space.

Not his apparent eccentricities in the representational, not his brilliant combinations of colors, not the bitterness of his satire of his age, not his sensitivity in recording natural processes, but the creation of a spatial structure suited to the times, a new spatial style—that is the great achievement of Beckmann's art, and there above all lies its significance for the era.

The way he does it has something of the mystery of any well-crafted masterpiece. One can describe it approximately and yet not know whether one is forgetting the main point. It connects logically, even if probably not consciously, to the advances of the French, above all of Cézanne. The way he cuts the painting off at the bottom not where the visible vis-à-vis stops but instead, as it were, also paints the continuation that the eye makes until it reaches its essential object, its main accent, is sometimes found in Cézanne but also in Beckmann's early paintings, from a time when he presumably did not yet know Cézanne. But that was not enough. He did introduce a uniquely motoric aspect to the design by doing so. But it could easily result in a lack of balance, so that the remaining part of the painting in the back still clung to the old vis-à-vis technique. But allowing the entire picture to dissolve into such movement—composing in a suspended scale bowl, as it were—produced too much unrest and ran the risk of melting away. The space had to undergo a kind of articulation without the constructive rigidity that leads radially back to the point of sight. It had to be built in a way that one sensed something of its making, as it were. The eye should not travel *peu à peu*, as smoothly as a stagecoach, into the deeper parts of the painting but had to be dragged in, pushed in. Or the back parts had to be drawn out, chiseled out, so that they were there sooner than the good old eye anticipated. This was achieved by articulating the space as if cutting toward the back in layers, which were now placed closer to or farther from one another according to the painter's needs, or rather in keeping with the effect he desired. Like all comparisons of one art with another, this one is clumsy, but perhaps it clarifies Beckmann's new system if one recalls the way the music of our time strives less for a musical line that develops continuously from one beat to another but instead relates to the

20

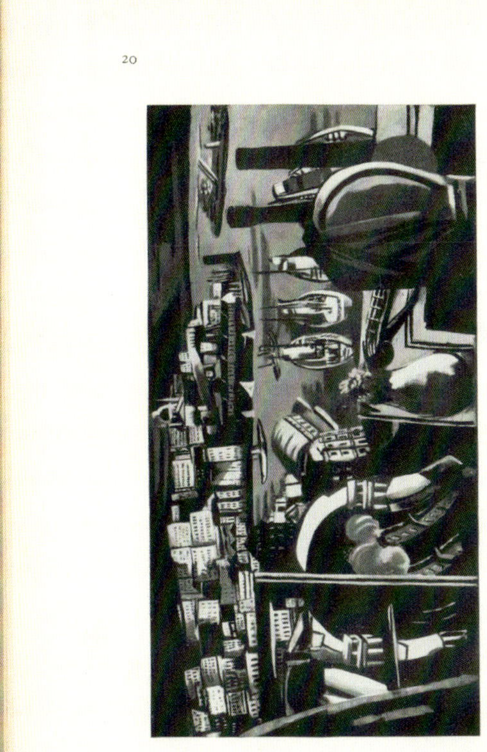

Genua 1926
Frankfurt, Slg. Frau von Rapaport.

21

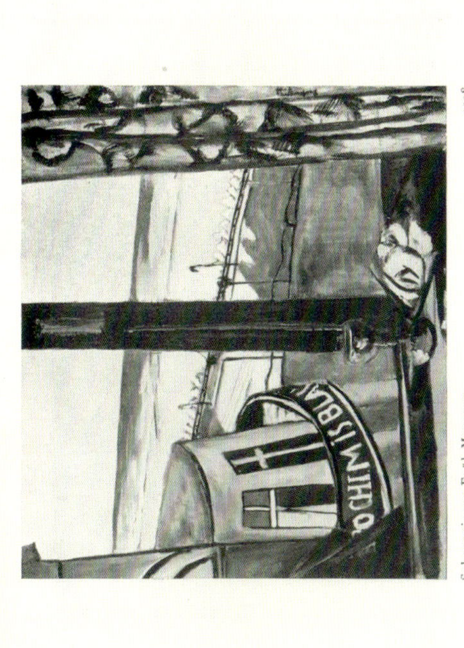

Scheveningen Früh Morgens 1928
Stettin, Museum

22

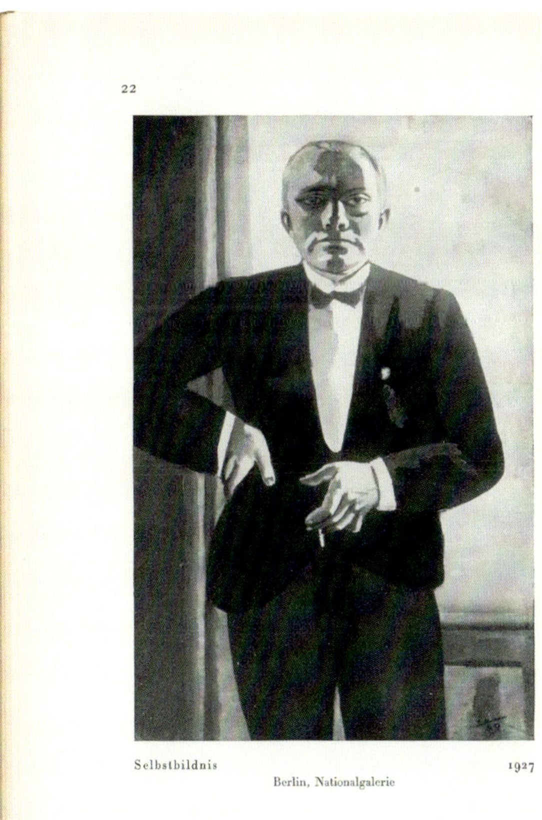

Selbstbildnis 1927
Berlin, Nationalgalerie

23

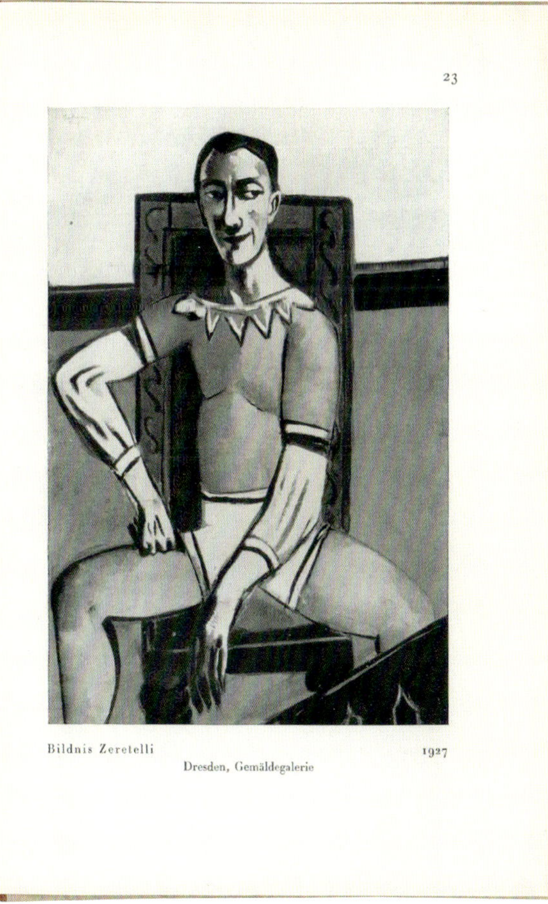

Bildnis Zeretelli 1927
Dresden, Gemäldegalerie

Bachian principle of setting groups—or blocks of beats—against other groups. It has nothing to do with a backdrop-like construction; there is nothing Beckmann's paintings resemble less than theater scenes. It is merely the definitive rejection of space established mathematically from the fixed point of sight forward; it is a space that still contains something of the original movement with which the eye creates the space by penetrating into the depths and then shooting back forward out of the depths. Because of the way it is divided up and put back together, however, the space does not convey an arbitrary, nervous impression but rather the effect of something built, something that follows laws.

This way of designing space is a discovery. Its special value derives from it being obtained not in an intellectual way but was found by painting, in essence by seeing. It therefore seems merely like a continuation of what was already starting. That seems to me to guarantee a suprapersonal significance. Where it is just a beginning is an idle question today. It is in any case a building block whose existence we can no longer deny.

There is a tendency today to mistake an original note for the originality of the creator. The particular is equated with the peculiar. It is therefore difficult to conclude that there are people in this distraught age for whom the special is not just a notion, a special case. The original is always so closely linked with the entirely personal, especially in the case of a phenomenon as trenchant and seemingly alien as Beckmann. When assessing him one is inclined to say that the loner Beckmann can best be understood and appreciated as a unique phenomenon. That this loner will perhaps be the only person in European painting, certainly in German painting, who will be the stylistic role model in the traditional, natural, eternal sense for the coming age, because he succeeded in finding, in inventing, the pictorial space suited to the time and working it out with the conscientiousness and martyrdom of all great art—that is one of the strange, recurring paradoxes of the evolution of the world.

Suited to the time. To speak of a spirit of the time is almost tasteless in an era like ours that is haunted by all times. But, of course, the essential, creative phenomena of any time are never completely isolated from one another. Sometimes the relationship is not a blood relationship. But all great men and discoveries of an age are at least cousins by marriage. Some are shocked that our entire solar system became "relative"; some are afraid that humanity is beginning to transform into one giant nomadic people. The break from the static object, the static life, the static law caused many to panic. Life in general is denied, making that very denial a substitute for religion. Painters ignore the subject; they are afraid to retain it lest they be judged outdated. They do not want to paint for others, even when they want to be purchased by others. They become ascetics; they destroy every memory of natural forms. Or they enter politics, painting pamphlets, manifestos, as socialists, communists, nationalists. They dispense with the effect of form and by switching out the objects without redesigning spatial style they are in essence, despite all their efforts to be contemporary, outdated.

Surely it is the only possibility: affirming the dissolution of the old forms. Surely it is the only creative option: taking up the struggle to create a new form. Beckmann's intellectual physiognomy, his knowledge about the matters of his time, about its elimination of old boundaries, its "relativizing" of old laws, its call for proud people to boldly storm the last bastions of traditional dogmas—this spiritual

24

Liegender Akt 1927
Stuttgart, Slg. Hugo Borst

25

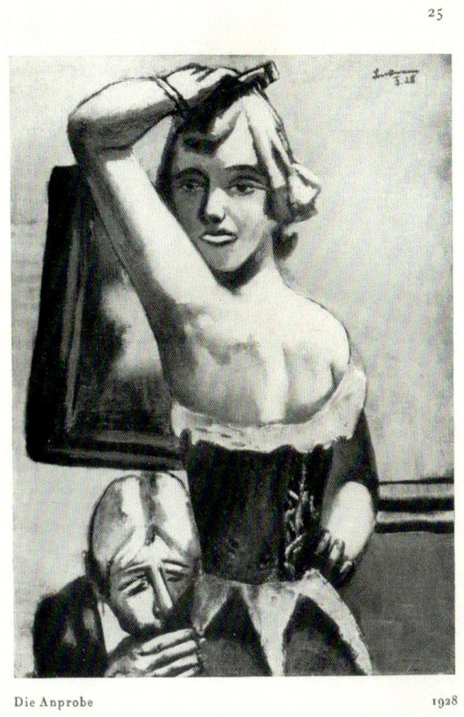

Die Anprobe 1928

26

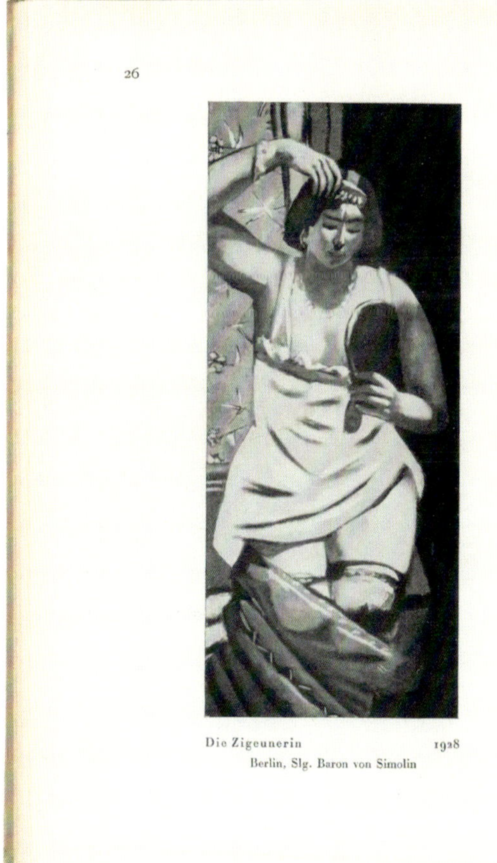

Die Zigeunerin 1928
Berlin, Slg. Baron von Simolin

27

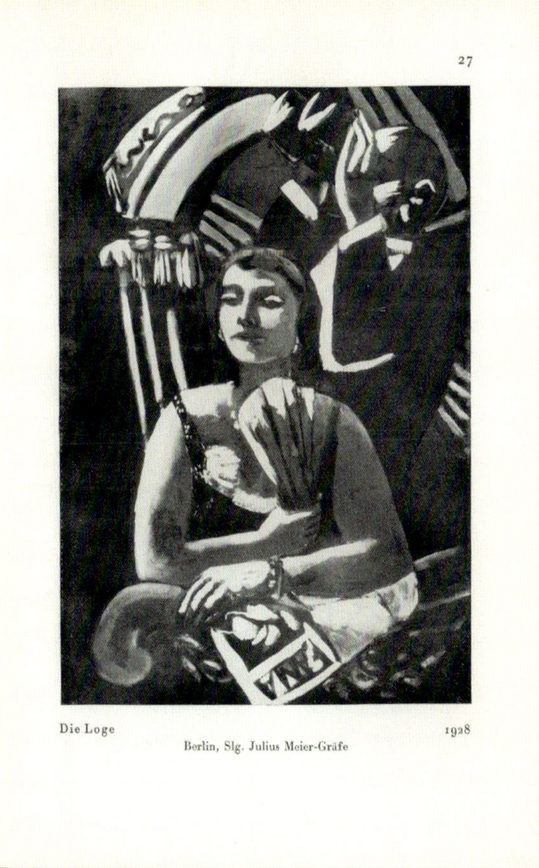

Die Loge 1928
Berlin, Slg. Julius Meier-Gräfe

cosmos of Beckmann the person is directly connected not primarily to *what* he paints but rather, very simply, very much in terms of his craft, with the space into which he places his people, his objects. From his new spatial world, one moves freely into the newly conceived space of the world. It is not, however, a flight into the void. With every single piece of the world that he paints, he wants to show: a new world is growing. He plays the wonderful game of the human spirit, which repeatedly builds from the same materials provided to it—with trees, fields, stars, flowers, seasons, people, hate, and love—a world, *its* world. But it is only truly new if that which holds it together is new: the space that surrounds it and the spirit that runs through it.

Translated from the German by Steven Lindberg

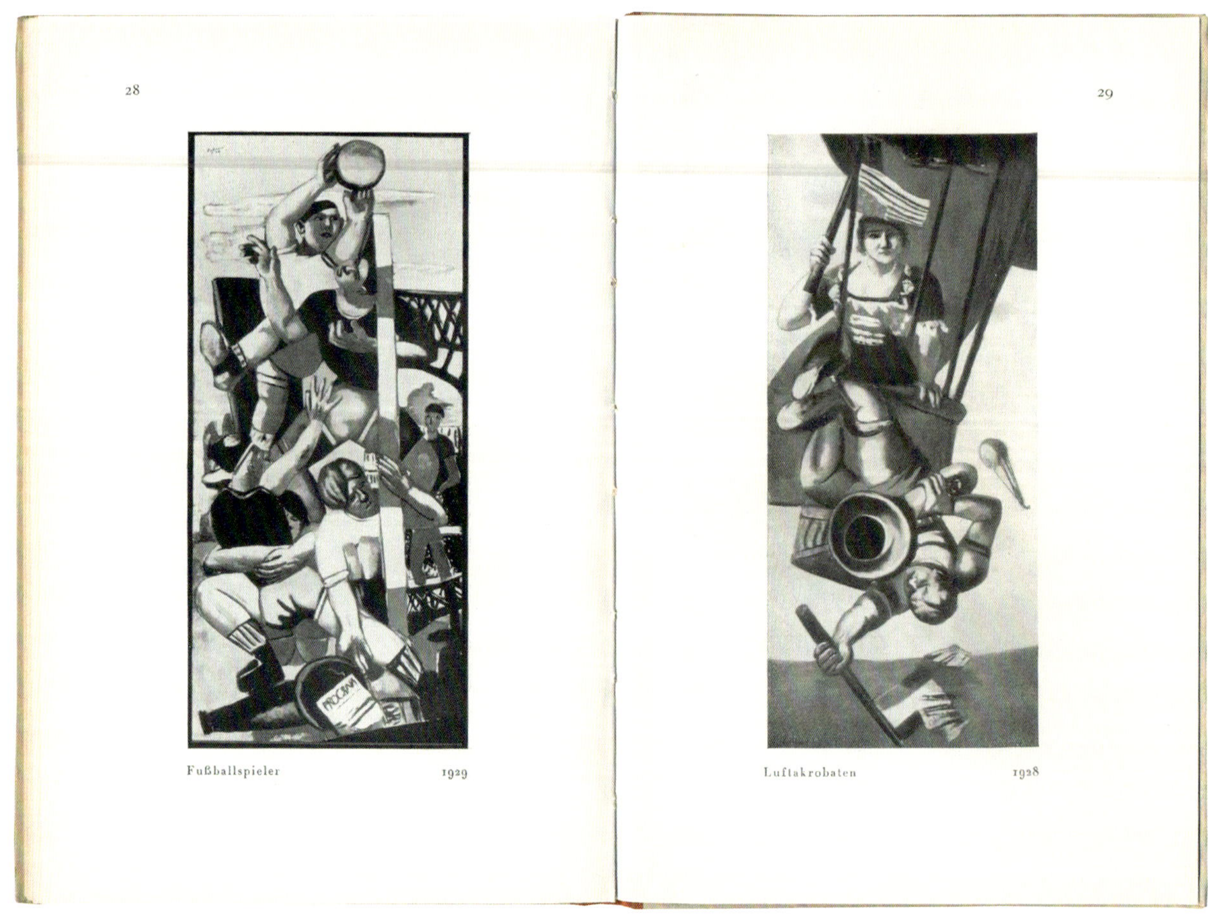
28

Fußballspieler 1929

29

Luftakrobaten 1928

30

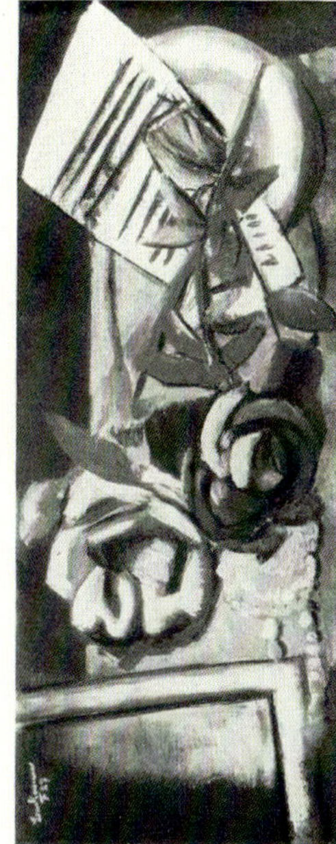

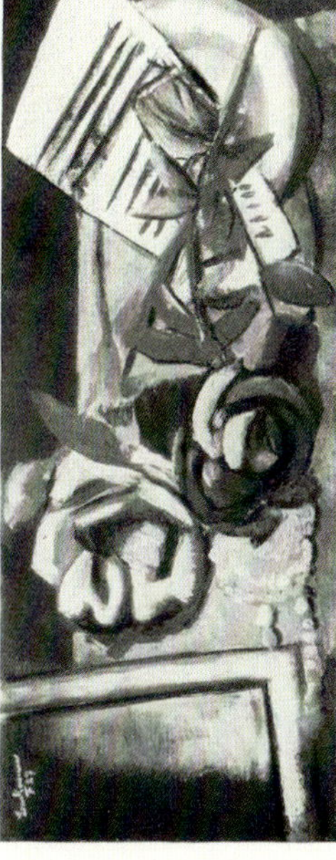

Rosenstilleben mit Spiegel — Berlin, Slg. Edith Rosenheim — 1927

31

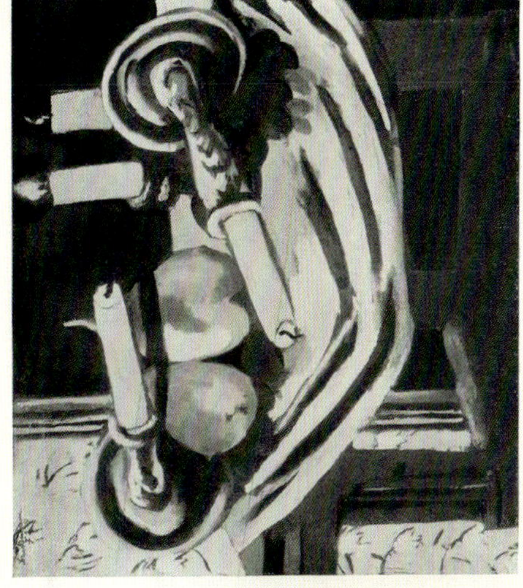

Stilleben mit Kerzen — Detroit (Mich.), Art Institute — 1929

32

Blick aufs blaue Meer (Scheveningen) 1928
Köln, Wallraf Richartz-Museum

Junge Kunst

Bd.
1. Biermann, Max Pechstein
2. Biermann, Paul Modersohn
3. Uphoff, Bernhard Hoetger
4. Ludwig Meidner, Autobiographische Plauderei
5. Däubler, César Klein
6. Kirchner, Franz Heckendorf
7. Hausenstein, Rudolf Großmann z. Zt. vergriffen
8. Schwarz, Hugo Krayn
9. Cohn-Wiener, Willi Jaeckel
10. Pfister, Edwin Scharff
11. Henry, Maurice de Vlaminck
12. Frieg, Wilhelm Morgner
13. v. Wedderkop, Paul Klee
14. Zahn, Josef Eberz
15. Henry, André Derain
16. Valentiner, K. Schmidt-Rotluff
17. Biermann, Heinrich Campendonk
18. Kuhn, Emy Roeder
19. Braune, Oskar Moll
20. Graf, Maria Uhden
21. Wolfradt, George Grosz
22. v. Wedderkop, Marie Laurencin
23. Hausenstein, Max Unold
24. Kirchner, Erich Waske
25/26 Hartlaub, Vincent van Gogh
27. Kolle, Henri Rousseau
28. Huebner, Lodewijk Schelfhout
29. Suermondt, Heinrich Nauen
30. v. Wedderkop, Paul Cézanne
31. Einstein, M. Kisling
32. Cohen, August Macke

Bd.
33. Biermann, Othon Coubine
34. Uphof, Christian Rohlfs
35. With, Marc Chagall
36. Wiese, Paul Gauguin
37. Graf, Georg Schrimpf
38. Huebner, Gustav de Smet
39. Bauer, Wilhelm Schmid
40. Wiese, Alexander Archipenko
41. Wolfradt, Otto Dix
42. Grohmann, W. Kandinsky
43. Raeber, A. H. Pellegrini
44. P. F. Schmidt, Alfred Kubin
45. Grohmann, F. Karl Gotsch
46. Basler, Henri Matisse
47. Wolfradt, Lyonel Feininger
48. Reifenberg, Karl Hofer
49/50. Schürer, Picasso
51. Osborn, Irma Stern
52. Biermann, Oskar Kokoschka
53. Schmidt, Emil Nolde
54. Osborn, Georg A. Mathéy
55. Henry, Juan Gris
56. Simon, Max Beckmann
57. Crevel, Renée Sintenis

1931 neu:
58. Thormaehlen, Erich Heckel
59. Colin, James Ensor
60. Justi, Georg Kolbe

In Vorbereitung:
61/62. Wilhelm Lehmbruck
63. L. Moholy-Nagy
64. Jean Lurçat

Jeder einfache Band
mit einer farbigen und 32 einfarbigen Tafeln kostet M. 2.50
Doppelband 25/26 in Halbleinen M. 4.50, Geschenkausgabe auf englisch Alfa, die Kunstdrucktafeln einseitig auf schwerem Kunstdruckpapier, in Leinen M. 6.50
Doppelband 49/50 in Halbleinen M. 3.50, in Leinen M. 4.–

KLINKHARDT & BIERMANN / BERLIN

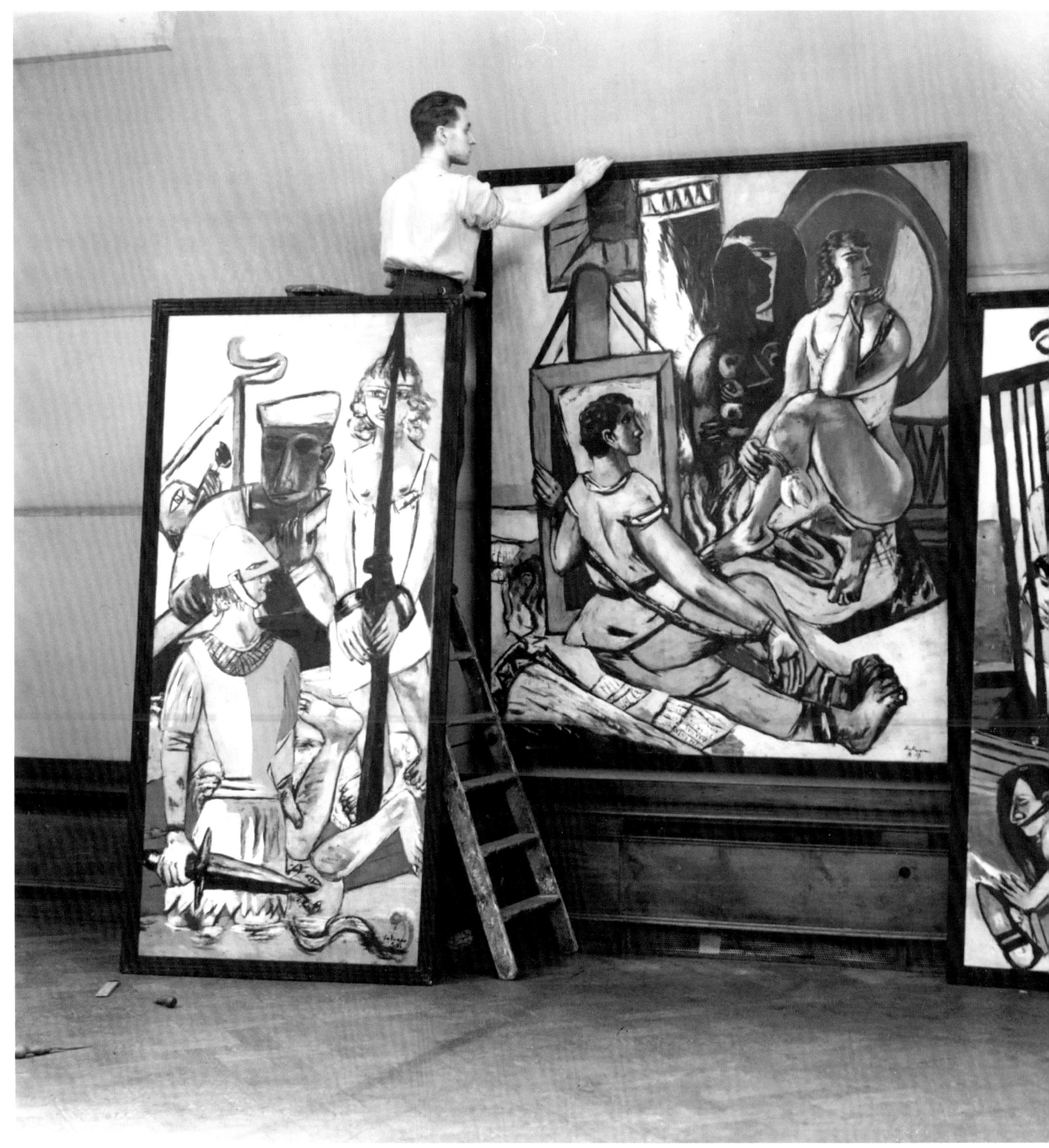

Two men prepare to hang Max Beckmann's triptych *Temptation* at the "Twentieth Century German Art" exhibition, New Burlington Galleries, London, 1938. The exhibition included work by German artists pilloried by Adolf Hitler in the "Degenerate Art" exhibition, Munich, 1937. Photo: Topical Press Agency / Stringer via Getty Images

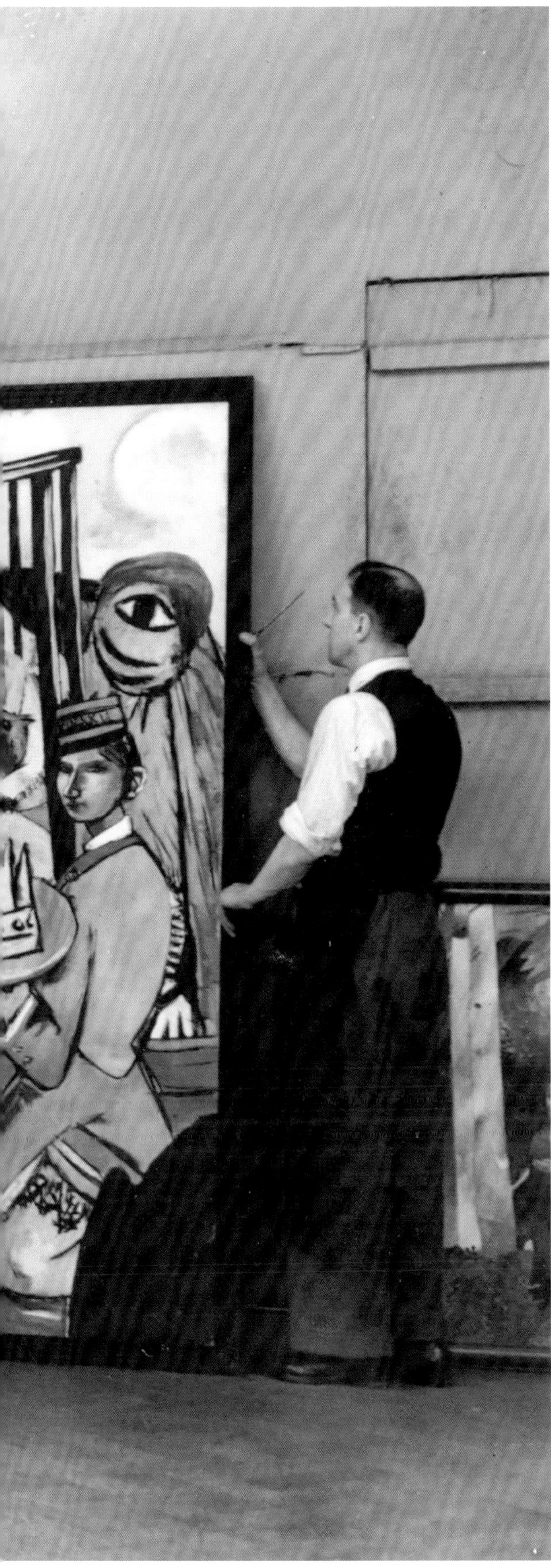

BEFORE AND AFTER

- "A WILD, CRUEL, SPLENDID LIFE"
- REFLECTED MODERNITY

"A WILD, CRUEL, SPLENDID LIFE"

THE YOUNG MAX BECKMANN, FRIEDRICH NIETZSCHE, AND THE PROBLEM OF A GERMAN MODERNITY

Jürgen Müller

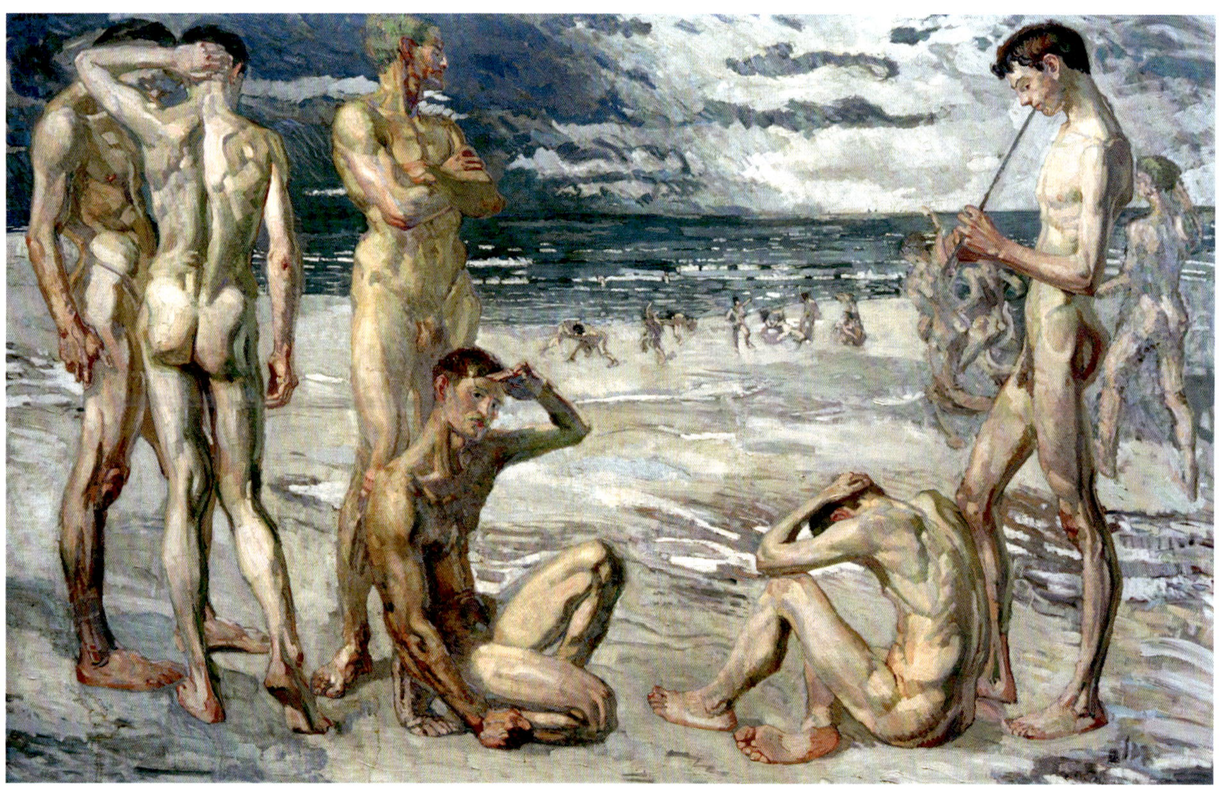

Modernity is an elusive and seductive concept because it holds out a promise. In the sense of contemporaneity, "modernity" represents a correspondence between a work and the present that goes hand in hand with it. In an emphatic sense, it can even symbolize taking the step into a future that is still unimaginable. Whatever one takes "modernity" to equal, it visualizes history as a sequence of the past, present, and future. "Modernity" means transition and marks the present as the place of mediation of the past and future. It is not a phenomenon with a single definition but rather exists in numerous varieties since it must take change into account. Modernity can therefore be understood as a technical, media event, as an abstraction and liberation into pure form, but also as a collective style and an attempt to renew life thoroughly. That necessarily raises the question of what should continue to exist in the course of an inevitable process of historical transformation and what turns out to be outdated.[1]

The counterpart to the concept of modernity is tradition. The word derives from the Latin verb *tradere*, or "to hand over." In the German, one speaks of *Überlieferung* (handing down, transmission) in this context. In contrast to modernity, tradition is a concept of conservation. It recognizes the past as valid. The conflict between the two concepts is irresolvable. Whereas the traditionalist makes the past the standard for the present, the modernist feels legitimized by the future. If the traditionalist feels justified by the rule of unalterable laws, the modernist experiences reality as mutable. And if the modernist can decide in favor of change, the traditionalist is tied to what is handed down. Philosophically speaking, freedom and necessity stand opposed. Can the present be understood on its own, or is the detour from the past necessary?

Max Beckmann's art is vital due to the conflict it embodies between modernity and tradition. The diary entries he wrote during his first stay in Paris express doubts about his vocation as an artist and concerns about the expectations of others. Modernity needs justification, even legitimation, and so a detour via tradition is imperative. It needs precursors one recognizes as related and declares oneself their successor. Throughout his career, the painter positioned himself like this, not always in ways that make sense. Nevertheless, such judgments of task provide artistic orientation. They help distinguish one from competitors and not infrequently take the form of a declaration that is supposedly irrevocable and tolerates no contradiction. Christian Lenz aptly writes in his study *Max Beckmann und die Alten Meister* (Max Beckmann and the Old Masters) that Beckmann's reflection of the present and recognition of the past sharpened his own profile.[2] Although never explicitly stated, it is bound up with a model of legacy and an assertion of legitimate succession. Beckmann's statements to this effect cannot be trusted absolutely, that would be to overlook how much he was indebted to the discourse on art of the Wilhelmine era at the beginning of his career.[3] Christoph Engels and Lenz underscore important key texts on art theory that influenced Beckmann's view of art. Wilhelm Worringer's book *Abstraktion und Einfühlung* (Abstraction and Empathy) of 1908 enjoyed immense success among artists.[4] In chapter 5 of that book Worringer states that the Northern people can be characterized by their ornament. It is an "abstract artistic volition" that characterizes their essence. The author fantasizes an essence of the Northern people with which an allegedly Northern, Gothic sense of form went hand in hand with centuries and epochs. Worringer historicizes in order to dehistoricize. With reference to Worringer, artists could be both simultaneously reassured of their Northern sense of form and their own modernity.

It is also a mistake to try to understand the young Beckmann from the perspective of his second phase of work and to try to reconstruct a linear development. His reading of Friedrich Nietzsche's writings is revealing about the early period. The philosopher is a constant reference in these brief notes and is mentioned no fewer than eleven times in his diary of the years 1903 and 1904. Even the purchase of

1. Max Beckmann, *Young Men by the Sea,* 1905, oil on canvas. Klassik Stiftung Weimar. Photo: akg-images

a paperback edition of Nietzsche's *Jenseits von Gut und Böse* (Beyond Good and Evil) for fifty pfennig is noted by Beckmann, who had just turned nineteen, and on the same page he observes: "I sometimes think that I have no feelings at all, that I am only acting the part of an artist, and that my contempt for everything else, for all that seems petty and stupid to me, is just something I need as a prompt so that I can play the part."[5] The inner conflict expressed here continues a little later when he writes: "It is raining outside, and I am so empty. A playactor in life, who would like to hear others tell him that he isn't one: Nietzsche said something to that effect, and it probably applies to me. Even now I still believe in the histrionic pleasure of self-abasement."[6]

The young Beckmann yearns for everything and at the same time calls it into question. He describes the appearance of his fiancée, Minna Tube, with words full of poetry, only to ultimately decide that he had to tear pages out of his diary because he had written "foolish and stupid things" about his dearest.[7] The diary entries are anything but profound. Rather, they sound engagingly precocious. They tell of a young man's search, of love, desire, and the task, expectations even he sees confronting him. He comments with self-irony on his *amour fou* for the overpowering philosopher: "Nietzsche. Well, *c'est la femme pour tous*. [...] Ideal for those who conduct their love affairs in quotations."[8]

It is hardly surprising that the painter uses the metaphor of the actor in an existential sense. Actors are exemplary human beings. They adopt roles and transform fiction into reality by making their own identity invisible. The metaphor of the actor is a kind of reversible figure.[9] It combines play and authenticity in a contradictory way. Is there an Archimedean point of our existence, or are there always only other masks of the self? Nietzsche's philosophy offers an orientation in that respect. It points to the fact that human beings are no longer in harmony with themselves. He thematizes the unassailability of the self, favors the role and the mask, and gives an exemplary account of the fate of the modern human being. The backdrop of Nietzsche's critique of civilization enables us to understand Beckmann's disgust with a second-hand life. After a passionate declaration of love for Minna, he writes: "Yes, perhaps—no, patently, undoubtedly—I am playing out an eternal, poor imitation."[10] The philosopher is mentioned in the diaries not only as a critic of the modern world but also in positive contexts and becomes the guarantor of a utopian promise of happiness: "Let me have people about me who are like music across the water at evening, when the day has long since become a dream. (Nietzsche) Yes, sure, but where are they."[11]

In Nietzsche's *Die Geburt der Tragödie aus dem Geist der Musik* (Birth of Tragedy from the Spirit of Music) of 1872, the philosopher considers it the task of culture to contribute to Germany's intellectual search for itself. Indeed, even more than that, art should help create a new morality. Polyvocal French modernism is rejected and the united force of a new German art evoked. This position is echoed in Beckmann's diary notes during his first stay in France. He is unable to take real pleasure in it and comments snootily on this fact in a diary entry about a café in Chalon-sur-Saône: "It's demeaning, I know, to read Nietzsche in this place. *Mais—*"[12]

But how could he become a painter of Nietzsche's philosophy, and how could his art fulfill the hope for a German modernity? Although the painter's commitment to Nietzsche is well noted, it has yet to be shown convincingly how it is expressed concretely in paintings and leads to an intelligible conception. In what follows I present several early works by Beckmann as examples and study their relationship to tradition. It is not enough to identify similarities. A genuine close reading of the paintings is necessary to judge how the qualities employed by others are transformed by him. Beckmann's early work in particular is by no means uniform. Numerous influences from Max Liebermann by way of Edvard Munch to Rembrandt van Rijn and other artists can be observed. Beckmann invents himself—an actor in search of a role suited to him.

A NEW DAWN

After returning to Germany from France, the young Beckmann intended to paint a programmatic work. His 1905 painting *Junge Männer am Meer* (Young Men by the Sea) [Fig. 1] is a *clavis* that makes it possible to reflect in an exemplary way on Nietzsche, imitation, and the connection of his early work to tradition. The artist was just twenty in the year it was painted, and the work represents a first attempt to find himself.[13] Benno Reifenberg even goes so far as to describe it as the painter's "journeyman's piece."[14] The work was shown in the third exhibition of the Deutscher Künstlerbund (German Artists' Association) in 1906 and received the Villa-Romana-Preis, which included an extended stay in Florence and prize money. Just one year later, it was in the possession of the museum in Weimar, thanks to the involvement of Harry Graf Kessler.[15]

Beckmann's attendance at the Grossherzogliche Kunstschule (Grand Ducal Art School) in Weimar introduced the artist to the classical forms of artistic *imitatio*.[16] Imitation was a key educational concept of the time. The young artist became familiar with the human body through nude studies. Copying existing paintings and drawing plaster casts were other important methods of imitation. Whether *imitatio artis* or *imitatio naturae*, imitation was at the center of academic instruction. For trained artists, however, it obtains a different significance in that it provides a starting point from where they position themselves. Imitation links the past and the future and can offer prospectives on both in alternation.

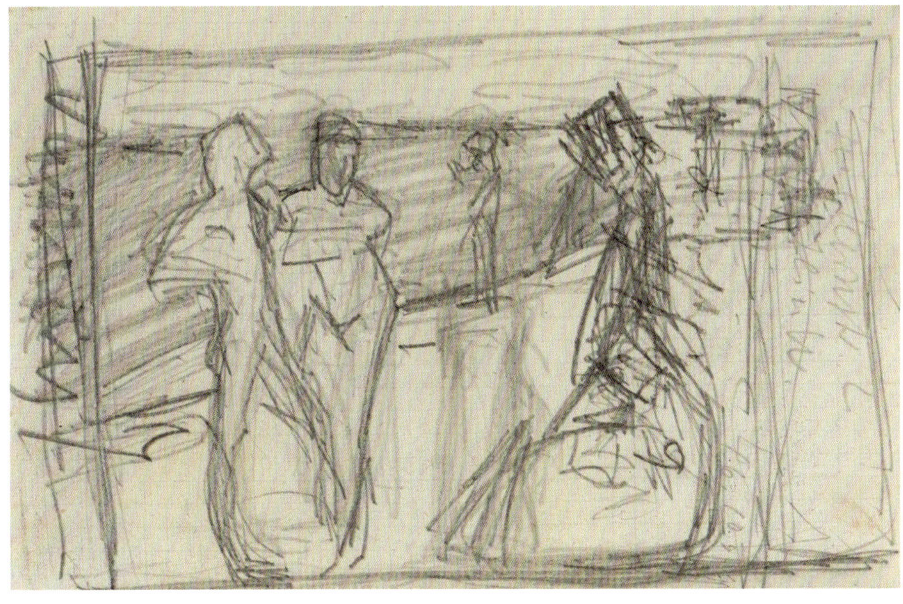

2. Max Beckmann, Preparatory sketch for *Young Men by the Sea*, 1903–04, pencil on paper. Max Beckmann, Diary, Vol. 3, 43 verso, Max Beckmann Archive, Bayerische Staatsgemäldesammlungen © Bayerische Staatsgemäldesammlungen, Sibylle Forster

Young Men by the Sea measures almost 5 by nearly 8 feet and thus has a pronounced horizontal format. The composition is determined by two diagonals, so that our gaze remains within the painting. Our eyes are led through the two groups of youths to the beach, to the playing and wrestling men, and then on to the horizon. Behind the flutist on the right, there is a third group, consisting of three people walking toward those playing on the beach. The work is distinguished by a lively, pastose application of paint and by a reduced palette of shades of gray, blue, green, yellow, and brown and by extreme lighting. Beckmann depicts the moment when the sky clears. The white clouds in the background move to the left and drive away the dark storm. The painter has made the colors of the figures and of the

3. Luca Signorelli, *The Education of Pan*, ca. 1490, oil on canvas. Formerly in the Gemäldegalerie, Staatliche Museen zu Berlin. Destroyed during World War II.

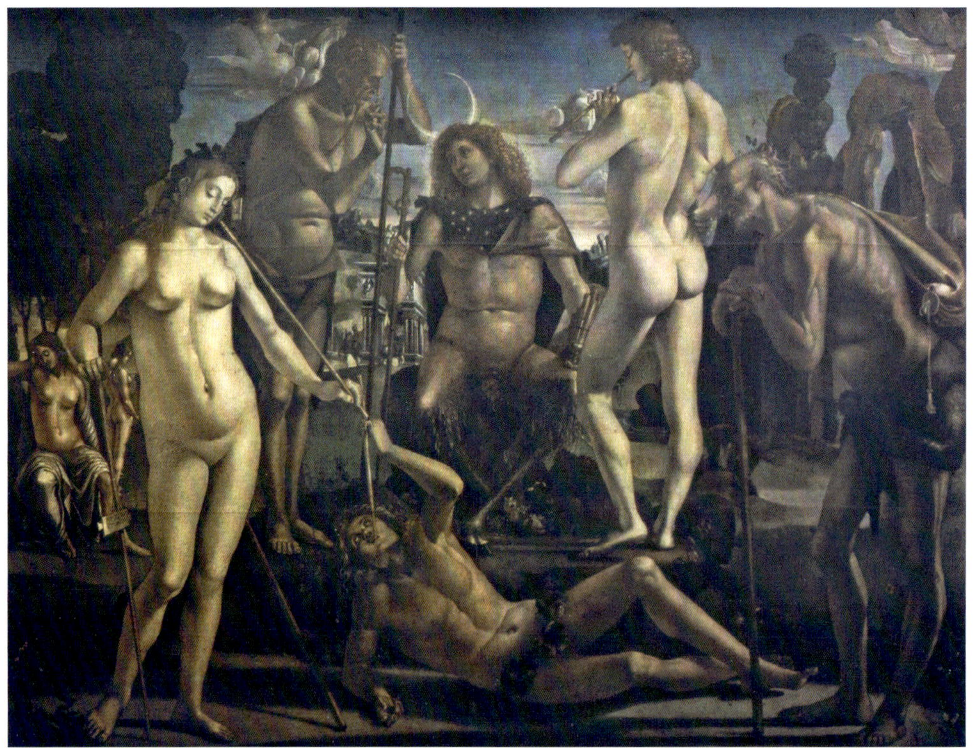

sand similar. The flutist and the youths continuing toward the right are brighter than the others. Indeed, the impression is of everything growing brighter. Blinding light determines the effect of the painting.

The people standing in the foreground correspond almost exactly to the height of the painting. All the figures are nude, and their bodies are elegantly elongated. Six young men stand or sit in characteristic poses, while the figure on the far right has placed one foot forward as if to concentrate on playing the flute. Numerous sketches for this painting are preserved in his diaries of the period [Fig. 2]. No single drawing corresponds to the final version of the painting. The painter initially designed a composition with three nude male figures but expanded it considerably for the completed work. Moreover, the scene cannot be assigned clearly to any genre. As a nude study, it is a history painting; as a depiction of the everyday pleasures of bathing, it is a genre painting. The painter was aware from the outset that the work was something special, and so he wrote his friend Caesar Kunwald on April 20, 1905: "I have painted a large work. Naked youths by the sea. Somewhat conventional, eh? But I don't think it looks very conventional. I am not exactly enthusiastic about it, but I learned a great deal in the process."[17]

In his first important figure painting, Beckmann attempts to part ways with the pleasant *peinture* of Impressionism. He uses an open painting style, plays with the effects of light and the colors of *plein air* painting; nevertheless, he employs a deliberate statue-like quality for his figures. It is not simply about the pleasures of bathing but also has an allegorical intention. Stylistically, the painting can be connected to Hans von Marée's art. It has also

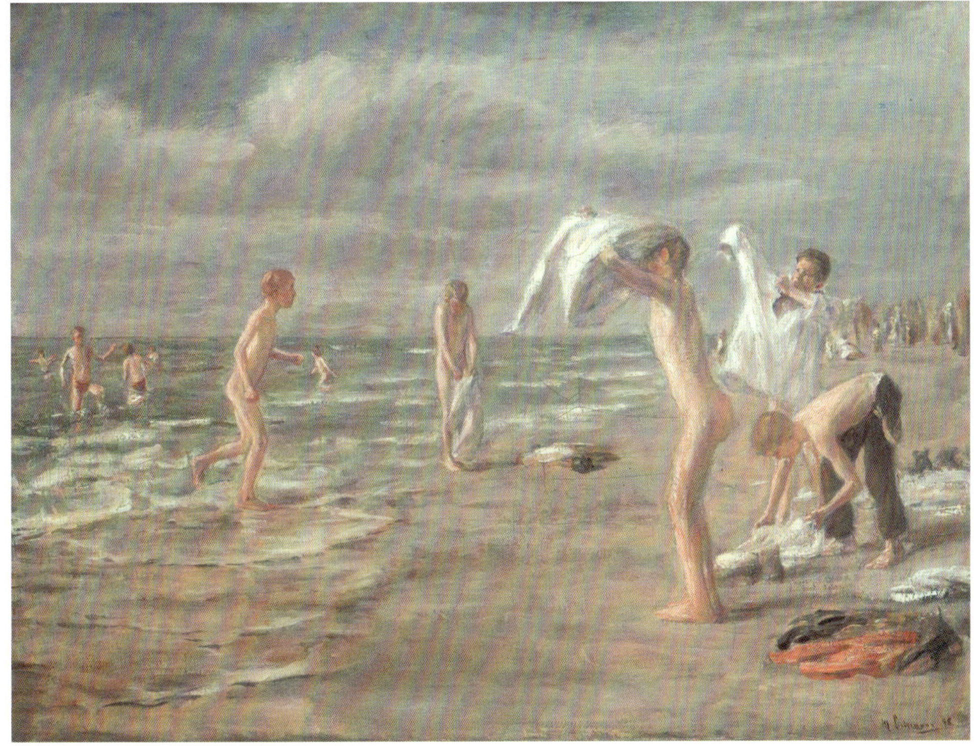

4. Max Liebermann, *Bathing Youths*, 1898, oil on canvas. Pinakothek de Moderne, Bayerische Staatsgemälde-sammlungen. Photo: bpk Bildagentur / Pinakothek der Moderne, Bayerische Staatsgemäldesammlungen / Art Resource, NY

been compared to Luca Signorelli's painting *L'educazione di Pan* (The Education of Pan) [Fig. 3] of ca. 1490.[18] Apart from the fact that both paintings have a youth playing a flute, however, there are no correspondences. The poses of the two figures do not correspond. It seems more plausible to think of Ferdinand Hodler's figurative ideal. But this reference also remains vague and associative since no concrete model or reason for such engagement can be identified. With regard to its theme, reference has been made to Max Liebermann's painting *Badende Jungen* (Bathing Youths) [Fig. 4], but it is a Rembrandt etching that is first known to address the theme of bathing youths. Although the works of these last two artists are close to Beckmann in subject, the artist nevertheless had recourse to other models.

It was suspected early on that the painter created this work under the influence of Nietzsche's philosophy of life and his documented reading of the poems of Richard Dehmel.[19] Nietzsche's philosophy emphasizes self-empowerment. His texts glorify deeds and taking action. Reading Nietzsche's texts can be a euphoric experience and may encourage taking risks. The philosopher identified a tendency in German culture to conform and called for the "unity of artistic style that manifests itself throughout all the vital self-expressions of a people." Instead, "the German" lives in the "chaotic hodgepodge of all styles" and does without an "original German culture."[20] But the thinker also tells of the possibility of entering a lost Paradise through the backdoor of a Dionysian life.[21]

Likewise, Beckmann holds out prospect for that hope. He evokes the emergence of a golden age, of a new "dawn" for which Nietzsche yearned.[22] In his painting he celebrates a new

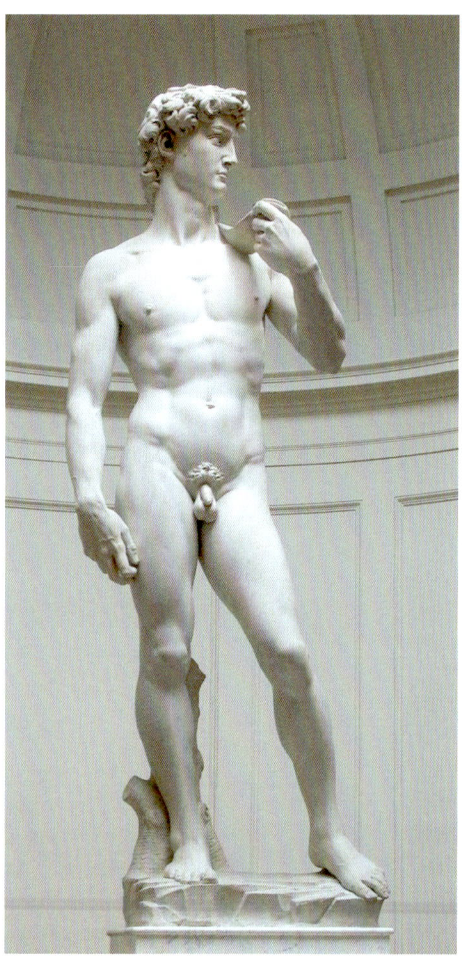

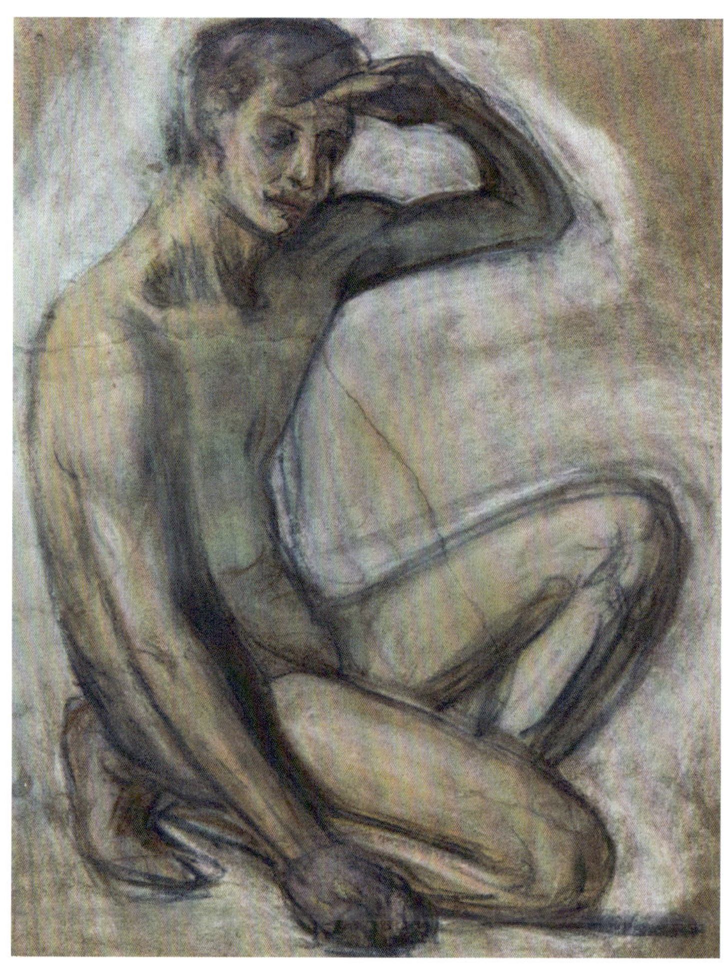

5. Michelangelo Buonarroti, *David*, 1501–04, marble. Galleria dell'Accademia, Florence

6. Max Beckmann, *Crouching Nude of a Youth*, ca. 1904, charcoal and pastel on paper. Private Collection

sensuality. It is hence appropriate that the flute is a Dionysian instrument and that the profile figure of the flute player is a motif that derives from Greek vase painting and that alludes to the context of a symposium. Most of the youths appear to be awakening from a deep slumber. One kneeling youth is keeping watch—possibly looking toward the future. The model for the nude seen from behind on the left half of the canvas is based on Michelangelo Buonarroti's *David* [Fig. 5]. The hand of the young man on the left next to him is also taken from that famous Renaissance sculpture. The kneeling youth who shields his eyes from the sun with his left hand mirrors an ancient posture passed down in both the *Crouching Venus* or the so-called *Arrotino*. The artist even made a separate study for this figure [Fig. 6]. The crouching figure is outlined with strokes of white chalk. The transition from the right to the left half of his body is especially successful and corresponds to a change from an illuminated side to a shaded one. It also underscores the dynamics of the contour line. Although he is crouching, the young man appears ready to take flight at any moment.

The seated figure to the right has a hand placed on the back of his head as does the standing one on the left. This posture recalls one of Michelangelo's *Slaves* in the Museo dell'Accademia in Florence, which were originally conceived for the Tomb of Julius II. The youth seated on the right, with his bent right leg shoved under his left, makes use of the motif of a seated figure in Ferdinand Hodler's painting *Der Frühling* (Spring) [Fig. 7] of 1901, which is now in the Museum Folkwang. But Hodler was not the author of that motif either; for his youth he had recourse to Agnolo Bronzino's *John the Baptist* [Fig. 8]. This adoption was certainly deliberate because of the subject, since both Hodler's youth and John are heralds of a Messianic age. To the extent that he uses the motifs he cites them only in part and metonymically, as it were, it is not simply to identify them at all. Moreover, when the painter cites Michelangelo's sculpture *David* in mirror reverse, it makes it more difficult to recognize. His handling of models is dissimulated.

This underscores that Beckmann did not assemble motifs indiscriminately but rather employed these Renaissance quotations mentioned to have a rebirth, to reawaken a sensuality that was thought to be lost. By evoking the senses—listening to the flute, looking into the distance, and hands touching behind heads—Beckmann expresses hope for a new physicality in human interactions, for a new "dawn." This interpretation is confirmed by the clever temporal structure that Beckmann employs as the scene suggests a sequence of events. Those crouching or sitting will rise alongside those standing and the group in the foreground will join those playing on the beach in the distance. The young man standing with arms crossed and watching the runners functions like a pivot point in this context. When the group in the foreground has broken up entirely, the dark sky will have cleared completely as well.

There is a study for *Young Men by the Sea* in a private collection that shows a group of

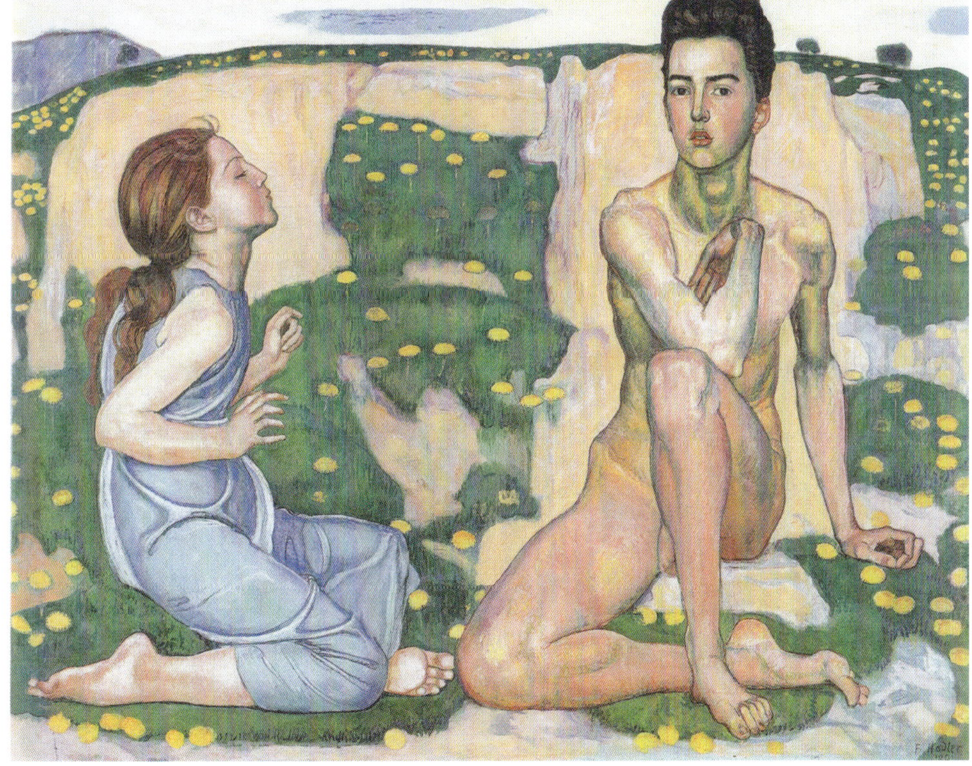

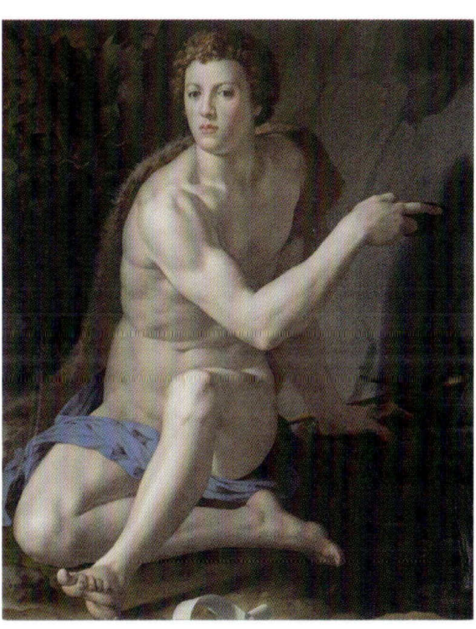

7. Ferdinand Hodler, *Spring*, 1901, oil on canvas. Museum Folkwang, Essen

8. Agnolo Bronzino, *John the Baptist*, 1550–55, oil on canvas. Galleria Borghese, Rome

ecstatically dancing young men [Fig. 9].[23] The drawing is impressive for its successful conception, since the four dancers become a single body in different phases of movement. It is not just the steps leading forward but also the vibrating linework, which sets everything in motion and even puts it into a trance. The flutist standing on the right is calm and graceful. With his instrument he sets the rhythm to which they all dance. The drawing makes it clear how much Beckmann is circling his theme of a new era being heralded by dance. Once again it is Nietzsche who provides the basic idea. In *Zarathustra*, dance is a leitmotif mentioned in numerous chapters.[24] The step from walking to dancing is a leap from the "spirit of gravity" into the lightness of a new existence. The philosopher says that life should be danced. The new human being will be a dancer. Dance is complemented by laughing: "And we should consider every day lost on which we have not danced at least once. And we should call every truth false which was not accompanied by at least one laugh." It is revealing that the painter ultimately rejected the concept of his original drawing. At the time, ecstatic dance would have been recognized as too obvious an adaptation of Nietzsche and the assertion of play and lightness would have seemed artificial. Beckmann decided on a more complex solution for the painting. It moves the temporal change into the future and represents a turning point that also holds out the prospect of changing from rest to movement. Nietzsche's idea of the dance of existence cannot be depicted and is reserved for the future and for the people to come.

Young Men by the Sea was intended to be a programmatic painting. It represents a conscious rejection of French Impressionism, promises a German Renaissance, and yet expresses the political demands of culture at the time. The age of imitating French art, Ferdinand Avenarius argued in a lead article in *Kunstwart*, must finally end.[25] Beckmann was under the spell of Nietzsche and turned against Parisian modernism. Only a few years later, however, his painting dissatisfied him. He found it impersonal and missed an "individualized feeling of life."[26] Looking again at its synthesis of Michelangelesque motifs, the painting certainly has the character of an academic stylistic exercise. The young painter also transformed Hodler's painting *Spring*, which already promised a new era.[27] In any case, it is no coincidence that Beckmann declared the Swiss painter, who was celebrated in Germany and especially in Weimar at the time, to be his favorite.

When Beckmann's stay in Paris ended in the spring of 1904, he planned to travel to Italy via France and Switzerland, but broke off his trip in Geneva. His mother's illness forced him to return prematurely to Germany, where he painted *Young Men by the Sea*. Just before returning from Switzerland, he wrote a letter to Caesar Kunwald: "As far as my painting style is concerned, I found here in Geneva, in Hodler's work, nearly everything that I had, in rather difficult struggles, developed myself as my future language."[28] Later, he would say nothing about Hodler as a role model. Subsequently it was Paul Cézanne who was repeatedly mentioned and said to have been the only one who impressed the young painter. For example, Beckmann wrote to Julius Meier-Graefe in a letter of September 10, 1919: "My great love, already in 1903, was Cézanne and has probably also remained so, when I think of the French masters."[29] Beckmann no longer recalled how much Hodler's painting had impressed him at this time, or that he wanted to see himself as like-minded, and even that his first important painting had been inspired by him. The episode described serves

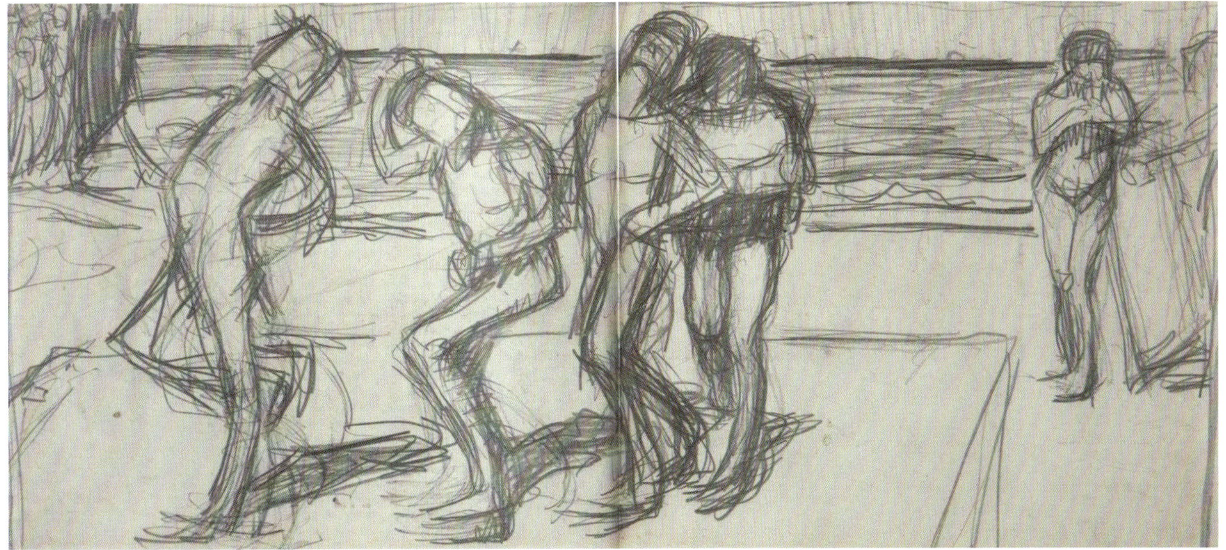

9. Max Beckmann, Preparatory sketch for *Young Men by the Sea*, 1903–04, pencil on paper. Private Collection

as an example. Beckmann mentions neither the adoption of specific motifs, nor is Hodler named as a source of inspiration. Yet it was not just the Renaissance that fascinated the young painter, but also Hodler's approach to tradition. As with the Swiss artist, one can distinguish between an internal and an external form when Beckmann adopts motifs. The Renaissance quotations of both artists are integrated into the overall design and then stylistically reformed. They function both as emblematic references to the motifs on which they are based and as part of the new context. It is not so much the aspect of repetition as the generative power of the painting and its dialogical character that should be emphasized here. In Michelangelo's *David*, the active human being is glorified. His hand becomes the symbol of action. Undaunted, he confronts his enemy. It requires no reflection. Thinking and acting are one.

Lenz and, most recently, Andreas Uhr show in their studies just how intense the painter's dialogue with his role models was. Despite the discovery of numerous examples, however, they do not offer a structural reflection on the phenomenon.[30] Their studies seem to address only the form of imitation that could be called influence or inspiration. But influence and inspiration remain diffuse quantities if the role models are not recognized as an opportunity for self-stylization. They illustrate not only a where from but also a where to. By contrast, my interpretation has surely made it clear that when I speak of imitation, I mean above all a practice quotation whose recourse to existing works always entails a certain calculation in order to enrich one's work both formally and semantically. The quotations identified function as a generative force. They permit the virtual copresence of another work that can in turn create associations with entire complexes of meaning. That makes the quotation aesthetically effective and heightens the complexity of the reuse. Recognizing a quotation requires an interplay of imagination and reason. In that sense, it necessarily transcends the purely sensory presence of the work to reach something that is not present that it nevertheless brings to bear. Quotations, one could say, are based on an aesthetic of the similar that requires the viewer's ability to make associations.

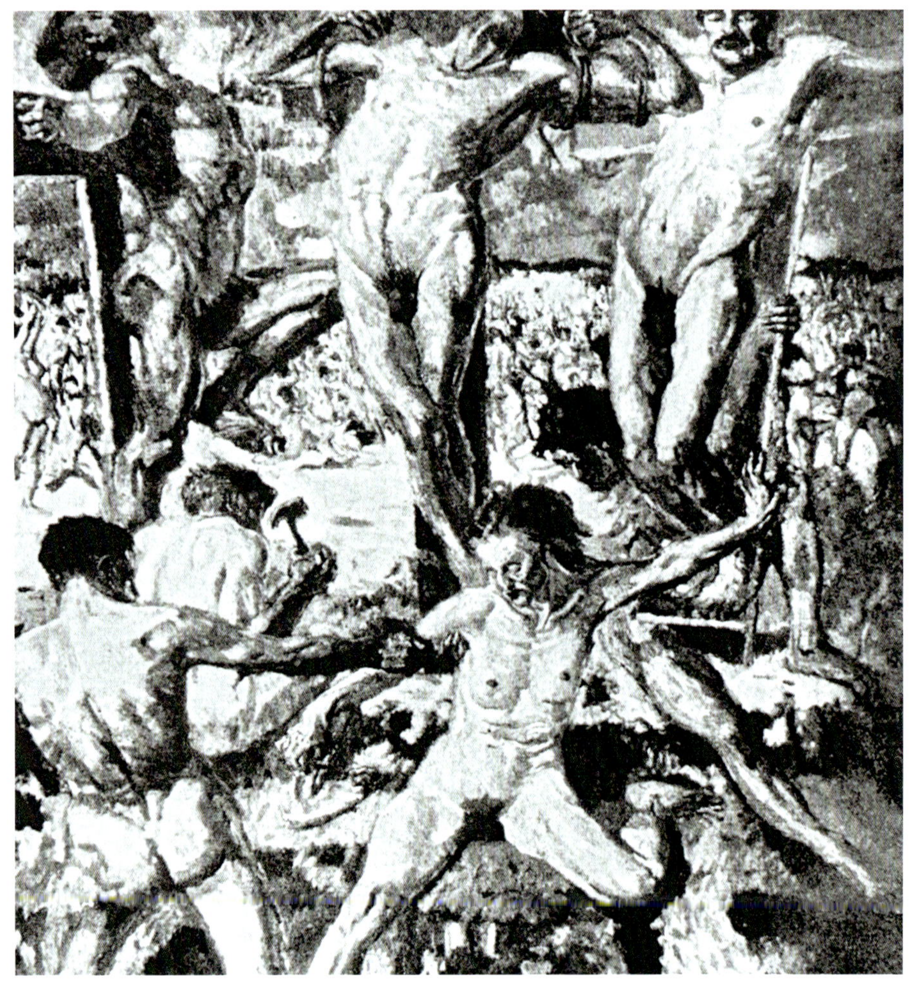

10. Max Beckmann, *Drama*, 1906, oil on canvas. Destroyed.

DIONYSIAN ART AS PATHOS FORMULA

Young Men by the Sea represents an important stage in Beckmann's search for an artistic position. At the time, his role models and experiments varied. His death scenes employed the stylistic idiom of Edvard Munch, as has been repeatedly noted, but Hodler remains a presence in the landscapes—think of *Kiefern, Grunewald* (Pines, Grunewald) and others. Yet Beckmann's study of the Italian Renaissance and motifs from Michelangelo soon continued in an unexpected way. The painter wished to present himself as a history painter and obtain large commissions. Nietzsche's philosophy again plays an important role. In *The Birth of Tragedy*, he called for a specifically German modernity that set out from Richard Wagner's ecstatic music and his idea of art as a *Gesamtkunstwerk* (total work of art).[31] The philosopher diagnosed the danger of a shattering of culture that went hand in hand with French modernism. He recommended that German artists engage with the origins of their own national identity. Luther's translation of the Bible and *Das Nibelungenlied* (The Song of the Nibelungs) seemed to him to promise an orientation in that regard.[32] However, he countered shattering modernity with a conception that aims at the overcoming of the individual in order to regard Dionysian ecstasy as the most noble task of contemporary art. The German philosopher writes that the heightening of Dionysian emotions could lead to the "complete self-forgetfulness" of the "subjective."[33] Beckmann flirted with the concept of being a Dionysian painter. Although he had already achieved success in the genres of landscape and portraiture, he was now interested in the *maniera grande*, in *terribilità* and large-format paintings. Nietzsche was the force behind it. Pathos and monumentality appear to be fitting opportunities to translate the Dionysian quality

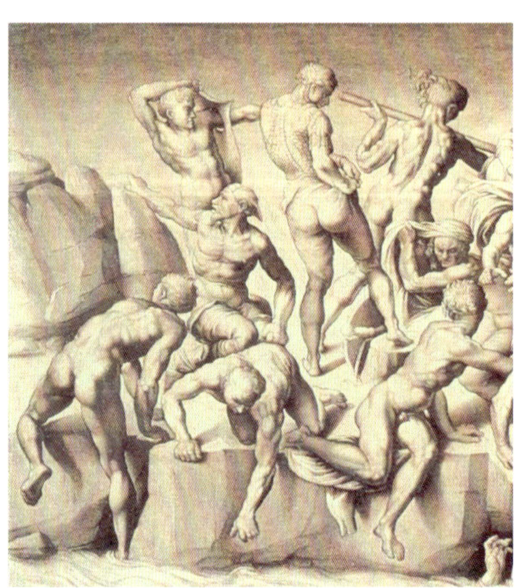

11. Bastiano da Sangallo, copy after Michelangelo Buonarroti, *Battle of Cascina* (detail), 1542, oil on panel. Holkham Hall, Norfolk

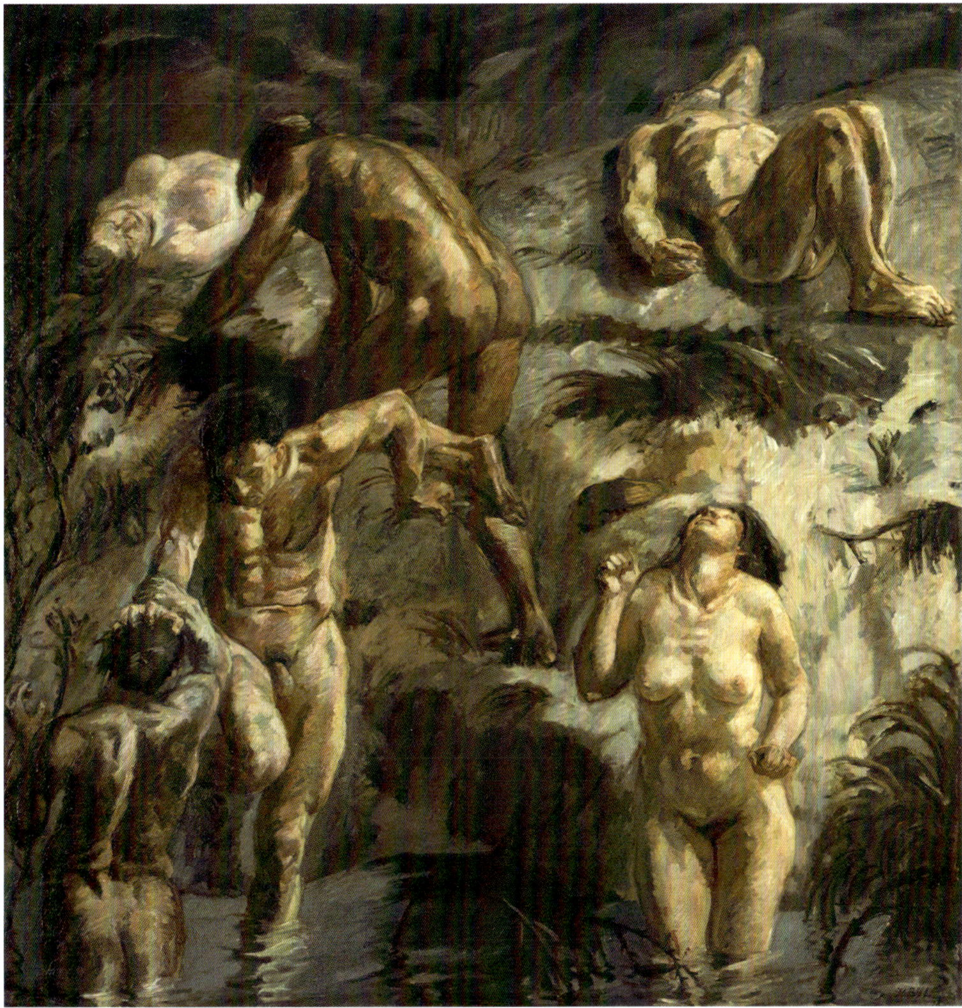

12. Max Beckmann, *The Flood*, 1908, oil on canvas. Hamburger Kunsthalle, Private Collection. Photo: bpk / Hamburger Kunsthalle, Privatsammlung / Elke Walford/ / Art Resource, NY

into the medium of painting. The goal is to overpower the viewer *à tout prix*. It demands an experience of breathless ecstasy and the elimination of an aesthetic distance.

This development begins with the painting *Drama* of 1906 [Fig. 10], which was destroyed in the war and survives only in a black-and-white photograph. It depicts a Crucifixion surrounded by an unusual scene. Beckmann employs an expressive gesturing figure for the first time here. History paintings demand that the painter be able to express extreme feelings and convey these emotions not only on the face but through stance and gesture. To communicate the theme of unbearable pain and make it possible to experience it viscerally, Beckmann placed a man and woman interacting immediately in front of the crosses. The man attempts to tear the woman away, pulling with all his strength on her right upper arm. Summoning up all of her available strength, she leans backward to remain in place. She turns her upper body away from the man, and her left arm is extended well to the right, as if it could grasp hold there and resist being torn away. Her left hand points upward in an expressive gesture of uncontrollable pain. The woman's body becomes a way of illustrating sorrow. The young painter

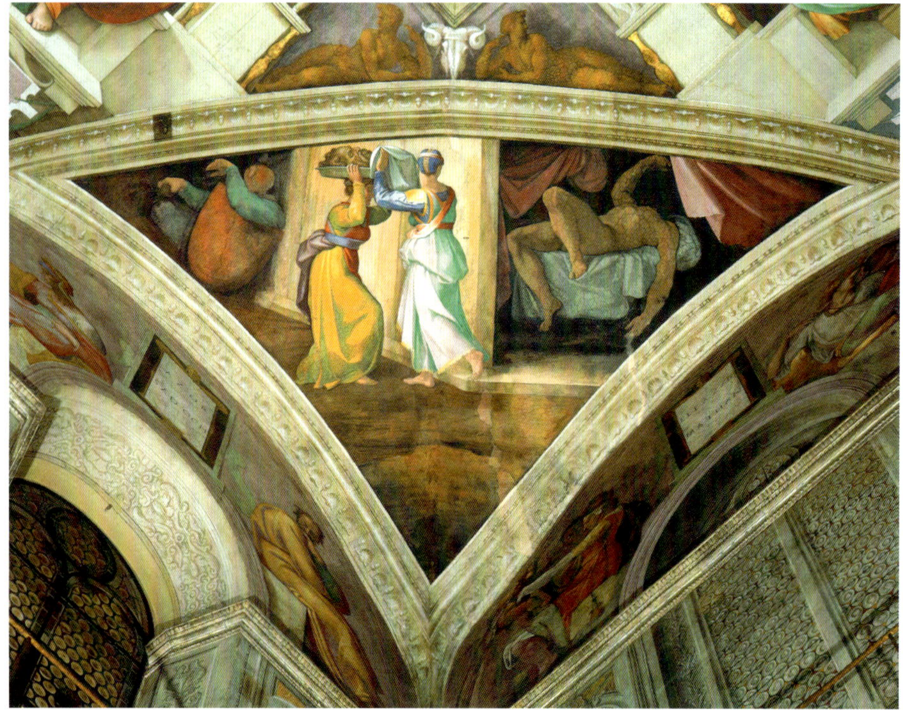

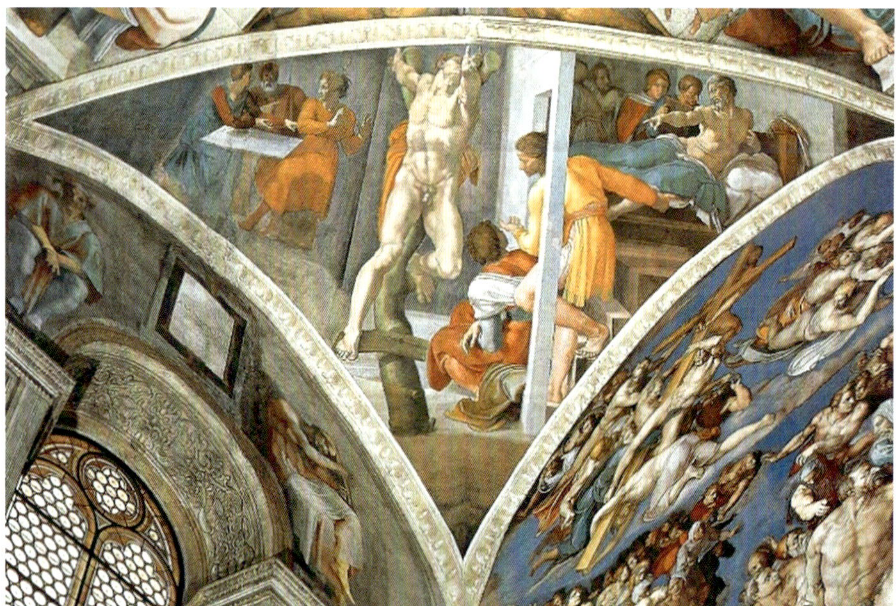

found orientation in Michelangelo's figurative ideal in *The Last Judgment*, imitating nothing less than Michelangelesque *terribilità*.[34] The art historical tradition has reserved that term for the overpowering intensity of emotional expression of the Pope's artist, contrasting it with Raphael's grace. The experience of such visual terror takes language to its limits and leaves the viewer in a state of silent horror. It is unusual to combine a Crucifixion with a scene of fighting as Beckmann has done, but surely it is scarcely possible to better express the pain suffered inside.

Lenz referred *en passant* to Beckmann's debt to Michelangelo and discovered a quotation from the *Battle of Cascina* in his painting *Die Sintflut* (The Flood) [Fig. 11]. But this is by no means sufficient to understand Beckmann's relationship to the Italian artist. It must be said that Michelangelo does not play a role in or get mentioned at all in the early diaries or in letters from this period. Beckmann did become familiar with his great role model early on by reading Wilhelm Henke's *Die Menschen des Michelangelo im Vergleich mit der Antike* (The Figures of Michelangelo in Comparison with the Antique) of 1871, as Andreas Uhr has written recently.[35] To illustrate the influence of the Renaissance artist, we must follow the hint Lenz provided and closely examine *The Flood* [Fig. 12]. The work was painted in 1908 and has a nearly square format of about 7 by 7 feet. Its title already provides an aid to reading it. For his dramatic depiction, Beckmann employed a steeply rising pictorial space to arrange six figures, one above the other. The people attempt to save themselves, leaving the water, climbing up, or sunk down in exhaustion. In the lower left corner, one man is pushing back another who is trying to reach dry land. All of these scenes express malevolence, impotence, and desperation. The female figure in the foreground on the right is intended to evoke sympathy in the viewer. She has closed her eyes and turned her head upward, but no help is to be expected from there. Humanity is beyond saving.

The painter depicts a threshold situation: the moment before the world goes under, when desperate people have turned away from God. The frenzy of their sinking is tied to hope for a new covenant and a new dawn. The painting's conception of the end of times corresponds to the artist dispensing with bright color. Shades of brown, green, and beige form a cool, uncanny accord. The figures are portrayed with the same palette as the background and do not appear grounded in the picture plane. Spatial orientation is neglected in favor of the physical presence of heavy bodies. It is as if they were slipping forward out of the painting and sinking into the water. The viewer's gaze futilely supports them.

The painter again employed figures by Michelangelo in his design. Contrary to what Lenz has written, however, it is not simply the climbing man at top left who is based on a motif from the *Battle of Cascina*: we are dealing with a real pasticcio here.[36] The highly foreshortened reclining male body on the upper right also recalls Renaissance models, which in turn originated in the central figure of the Laocoön group.[37] But Beckmann takes as his model Michelangelo's depiction of Holofernes in one of the pendentives of the Sistine Chapel [Fig. 13]. Finally, some of the figures in the group at front left can be connected to Michelangelo's famous fresco. The man bent forward with arms outstretched forward and backward recalls another of Michelangelo's pendentives with the motif of Haman [Fig. 14]. In Beckmann's painting, he is turned into a person with no pity who is pushing the man opposite him back into the water.[38] All of Michelangelo's motifs are modified insofar as the painter changes the angle of view and the viewer's standpoint. He rotates his figures forty-five or ninety degrees and has us look up or down upon them. These modifications suggest that the artist used a mannequin that enabled him to alter his model to create the desired impression.

Beckmann's *The Flood* is a figure study with a suitably bold composition. The artist spans an arc from the opposite corners so that we look from bottom left to top right and top left to bottom right. This results in a strong dynamic that corresponds to the dramatic motifs and has a breathtaking effect. In formal terms as well, Beckmann based his composition on Michelangelo's design for *The Last Judgment* in that he neglects depth and arranges the figures one above the other. But he shows the events from up close, and the picture breaks down into succinct single motifs: the man who is about to save himself, striving upward; the man who has run away from the waves and is lying exhausted in the upper right corner; the desperate woman who is aware of the helplessness of her situation. Beckmann sought to produce an overpowering impression. The painting may represent an ambitious attempt to seek out public commissions. The artist does not shy from pathos but knows how to combine it with a modern painting style. The message is of elemental force: something must perish so that something new can be born. At the same time, the theme of the flood offers the prospect of a new covenant in Nietzsche's sense.

Beckmann's interest in nudes in the tradition of the Italian Renaissance was clearly pronounced during this period and is also found in a female nude from 1908 [Fig. 15]. It was a study for the large-format *Auferstehung* (Resurrection) he was beginning at the time. The woman's body, painted in heavy impasto, is standing on a pedestal and is conceived as a gesturing figure. Whereas her upper body and raised left arm are turned into the painting, her right leg moves in the opposite direction. The background is rendered in

13. Michelangelo Buonarroti, *Judith and Holofernes*, 1509, fresco. Sistine Chapel, Vatican City, Rome

14. Michelangelo Buonarroti, *The Punishment of Haman*, 1511, fresco. Sistine Chapel, Vatican City, Rome

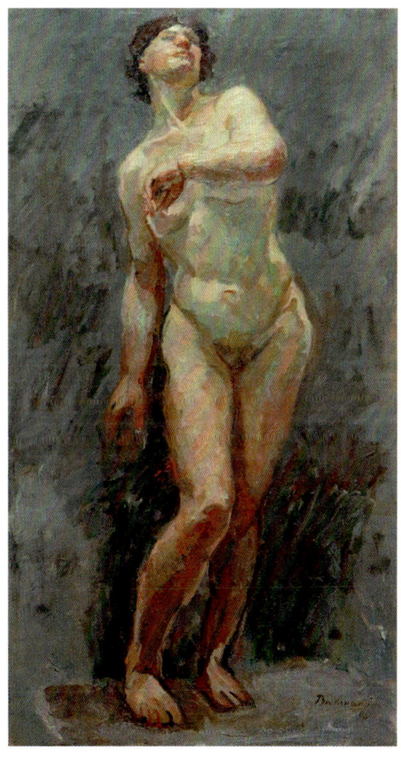

15. Max Beckmann, *Female Nude*, 1908, oil on canvas. Buchheim Museum. Photo: akg-images

the heavens provides her movement with a goal and produces extreme pathos.

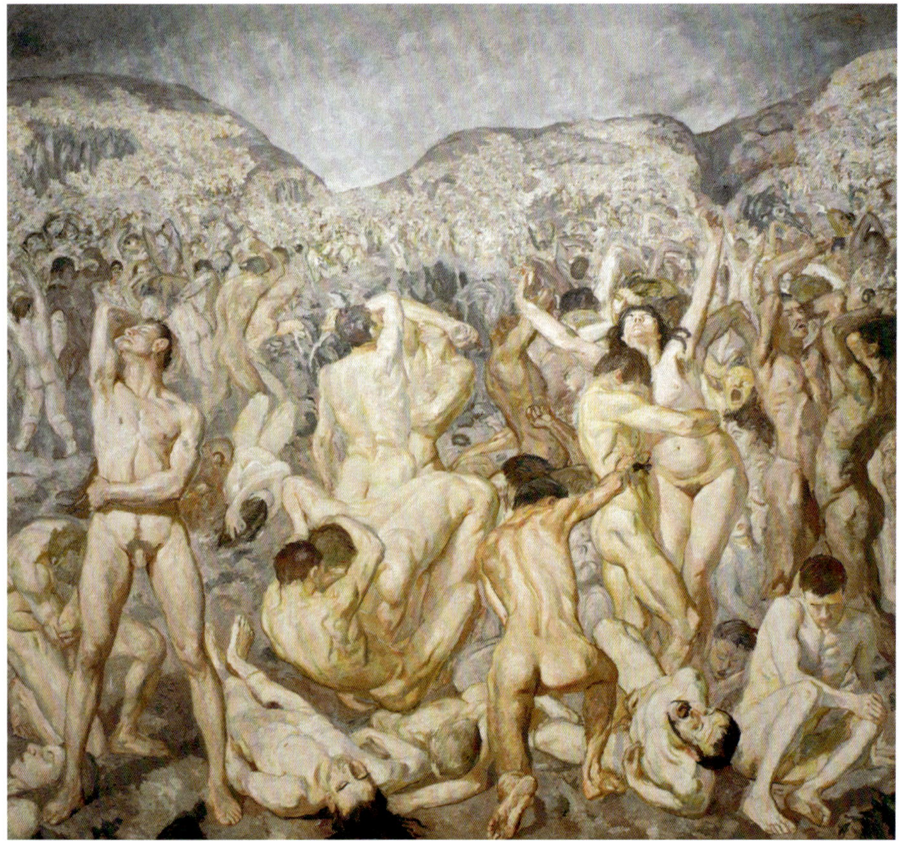

16. Max Beckmann, *The Battle*, 1907, oil on canvas. Museum Ludwig, on loan since 1992 Photo: © Rheinisches Bildarchiv Cologne

dark spots of impasto and causes the figure to stand out sculpturally. The artist chose a dramatic moment. Her gaze directed at the sky goes hand in hand with a turn toward the light. Whereas her legs and part of her stomach are still in shadow, her shoulders and upper body are already caught by highlights. The painter chose an interesting perspective for his female nude that enables us to view her simultaneously from her feet upward and from her head downward. The figurative ideal expressed here once again recalls the prophets and Sybils that Michelangelo developed in the Sistine Chapel but also in other works. The aesthetic achievement of Beckmann's study is its expressive dynamic. The woman's body seems aesthetic and energetic. It is the resurrection of the flesh, here reinterpreted as color with impasto skin tones. Her gaze into

Die Schlacht (The Battle), painted just a year earlier in 1907, once again shows the artist's masterly approach to tradition [Fig. 16]. The work measures about 9 ½ by nearly 11 feet. It features a rising pictorial space filled with fighting, desperate people. Numerous soldiers lie on the ground, dead or wounded. Beckmann created a panoramic scene of human bodies extending to the horizon. The artist again employed clever lighting. Whereas the figures in the foreground appear in bright highlights, the brightness fades toward the background. There is an early diary entry of January 1909 that one is tempted to relate to this painting: "Something rustling, sumptuous, like leafing through much silk, and wild, cruel, splendid Life."[39] In early scholarship, this painting was seen as a warning against the coming war, but that is not very plausible. Hans Belting unconvincingly recalled Michelangelo's *Battle of Cascina*, the reconstruction of which the artist could have seen in Florence.[40] But neither the spatial construction of the painting nor the fact that it depicts women makes the Italian model plausible. Lenz, by contrast, sees it as an attempt to come to terms with Michelangelo's relief *The Battle of Centaurs*.[41] The picture is also reminiscent of the powerfully Mannerist paintings of Cornelis van Haarlem [Fig. 17]. In terms of format, the construction of spatial depth, and the constant changing between front, back, and side views, Beckmann followed his Dutch role model. Van Haarlem was already trying to translate Michelangelo's aesthetic of large-format frescoes to the medium of easel painting. Van Haarlem made use of extreme horizontal formats that exceed our visual field, bringing the viewers inside the painting in order to overwhelm them. Beckmann had long been familiar with the art of the Mannerists, and the museum in Braunschweig has a work by Van Haarlem that may have inspired him to engage with it.

One might initially associate *The Battle* with the Massacre of the Innocents but its true theme is the battle of all against all. The painting is a symbol meant to evoke not the war but rather the Bronze Age. One sees neither blood nor knives nor swords. There are two men fighting, armed with stones and a bone, reminiscent of Cain and Abel. The right half of the scene shows a man and a woman who are clearly modeled on a Raptus group and hence a recollection of his stay in Florence. The young woman has raised both arms in horror, as she is embraced by a man with all his might. This couple joined by utmost violence creates a powerful dynamic. The woman is helplessly subjugated to the man, who presses himself against her forcefully. The figure in the lower right corner can also be connected to a model: one need only think of the antique sculpture *The Dying Gaul* [Fig. 18]. A photograph taken by Leopold Thieme when it was being painted show the preliminary drawing on the canvas with the figure of the suffering man already worked out on the left [Fig. 19]. Clearly, he was close to Beckmann's heart, because all of the desperation is focused here. The man has placed his lower arm next to his head, pointed upward, and closed his eyes. This figure is borrowed from a famous model: for his impressive gesture of despair, the artist employed Auguste Rodin's sculpture *L'âge d'airain* (The Age of Bronze) [Fig. 20]. The quotation becomes an intarsia of content, a known visual reference that lends its meaning to the picture.

Beckmann was playing with tradition and striving for a monumental impression. To summon up extreme pathos, the Italian Renaissance offered him a reservoir, an overflowing source with exemplary motifs. Michelangelo was the focus of his admiration, which could certainly be traced to his study and engagement with Rodin's sculptures. Beckmann was striving for nothing less than *terribilità* and addressing the challenge of a Dionysian art. Like Michelangelo in *The Last Judgment*, he neglected to convey a sense of spatial impression in favor of the figures. He brilliantly employed the art historical tradition for his own ends in order to present the ecstasy of extreme emotions. The heroically ecstatic is expressed in struggling bodies, in gestures, in

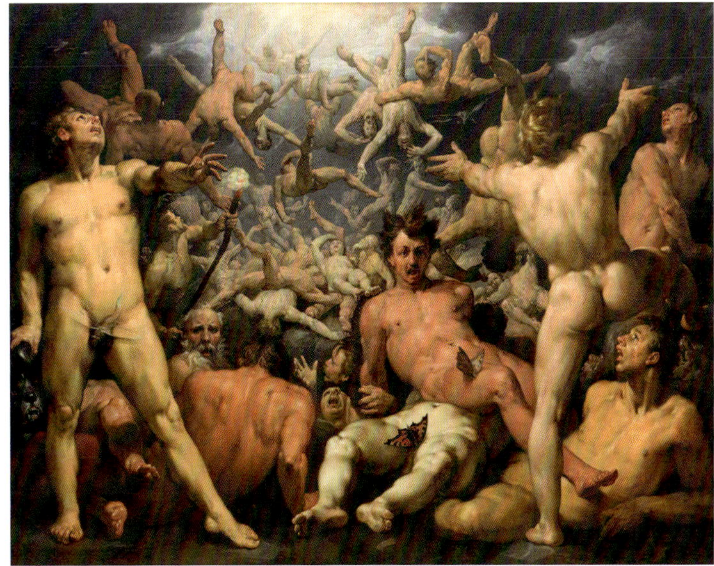

17. Cornelis van Haarlem, *The Fall of the Titans*, 1588-90, oil on canvas. Statens Museum for Kunst, Copenhagen

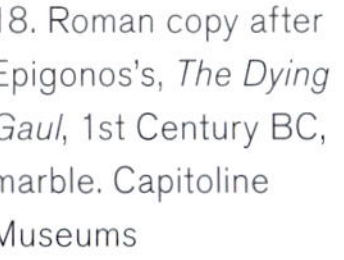

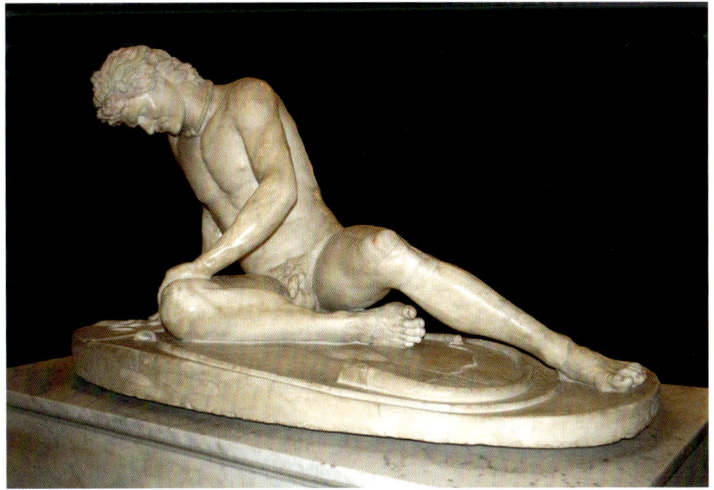

18. Roman copy after Epigonos's, *The Dying Gaul*, 1st Century BC, marble. Capitoline Museums

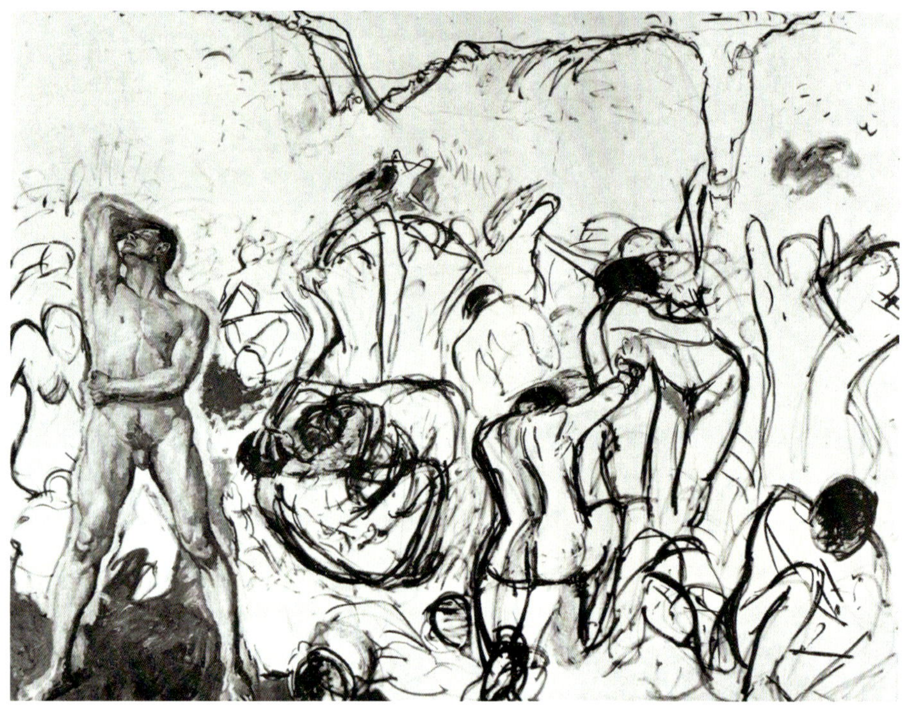

19. Max Beckmann, Sketch for *The Battle*, 1907, ink on canvas. Photo: Leopold Thieme

hopelessness and despair. Beckmann's gesturing figures in the tradition of Michelangelo represent the high point and his goal was to overwhelm the viewers. That concern put him in the tradition of Nietzsche's *Birth of Tragedy*. This painting expresses an extreme sense of a mission. His goal was the renewal of a national German art.

The reception of his painting was, however, negative. Beckmann did not reach the critics with his large-format history paintings. They were interpreted as the showy experiments of a young man, indeed even as academic gymnastics. Walter Cohen writes in *Kunstchronik*: "Max Beckmann submitted a giant parade of nudes, called *The Battle*, which no one knows what to do with: either this artist is very naive or a calculating bluffer."[42] In the journal *Kunst für alle*, Robert Schmidt even speaks a "ragout of nudes."[43] The painting's debt to tradition and Michelangelo was noticed, as is clear from a review by Ludwig Pietzsch in the *Vossische Zeitung*: "The artist is so eager to be considered and seem like a powerful artist, as Michelangesque. But neither his talent nor his artistic ability—drawing and painting—is sufficient for that. These paintings are supposed to appear grand but merely come across as repulsive and grotesque to the point of comedy."[44]

The artist's focus in his second creative phase is no longer on passionate depictions that overcome the viewers but rather on concentrated gestures as the expression of human corporeality. Beckmann's conception of art resists any conceivable connection of art, craft, and technology. How could it be otherwise, since if one is serious about bringing the modern world and industrial production in harmony, painting turns out to be a relic of an old world whose disappearance is almost the proof of a successful modernization process.

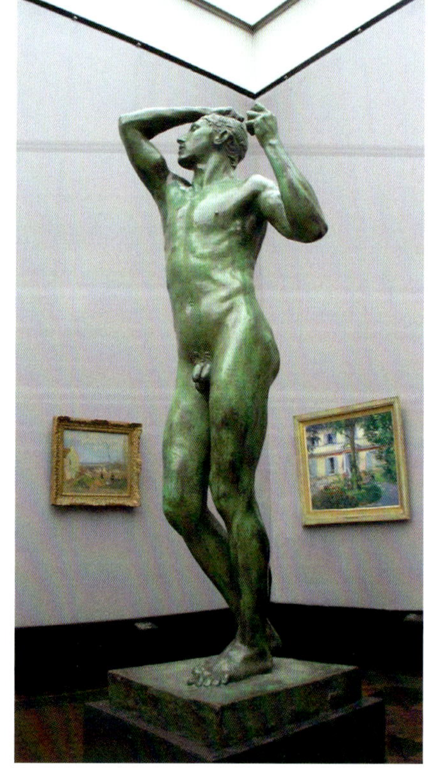

20. Auguste Rodin, *The Age of Bronze*, 1875-76, bronze. Alte Nationalgalerie, Berlin

All his life, he hated artists as engineers of progress. He remained oriented around the works and painters of the past, because it was the art of the past and its brilliant conception that endured for him and that he saw as lending its legitimacy to the present. He believed he could derive inspirations and stimuli from the art of Pieter Bruegel the Elder and from early German painting. As in Flemish paintings, the pictorial space is rendered without adhering to a sense of perspective. The artist embraces the ugly. We gaze into gaping maws and dark nostrils, discover the overly large feet of the protagonists, and get a sense of clumsy, uncouth corporeality. Now Beckmann's painting was distinguished by a concentration on a few figures, by extreme close-ups, a reduced number of attributes, and a minimal suggestion of space. The grotesque becomes the painter's real intention. But can one really still speak of the imitation of the Old Masters in the sense of a quotation?

In this essay, I have tried to connect Beckmann's paintings to the books in his library and his surviving letters and diary entries. The painter's reading of Nietzsche has served as the interpretative key to understanding his large figure paintings. No path circumvents the philosopher's writings. At the time, the painter was consulting his texts *en permanence*. Nietzsche had a firm hold on German culture of the time. The question can certainly be asked whether the artist truly followed the philosopher to the extreme and even whether that would be possible. Although he adopted numerous assessments, ideas, and metaphors, Beckmann could only pass over in silence the central idea of *Zarathustra* of the sublation of art in life.[45]

Beckmann's enthusiasm for Nietzsche was by no means an isolated case. If we consider the Bauhaus as the other end of modernity, the German philosopher appears again to be providing the cues. Lyonel Feininger's woodcut for the Bauhaus Manifesto of 1919 shows a cathedral as a metaphor for the reconciliation of art and life [Fig. 21]. The stars shine auspiciously above its spires and can be associated with Nietzsche's famous dictum from *Zarathustra* that one must still have chaos in oneself to be able to give birth to a dancing star.[46] In contrast to the idea expressed in the manifesto of a comprehensive reconciliation in the image of a cathedral to be built, Beckmann's concern was determined by the attempt to produce Dionysian paintings that he thought he could achieve by way of monumentality and pathos in the sense of Michelangelesque *terribilità*. To that end, the young artist presumably had far more recourse to models than I have been able to show and reconstruct here. Beckmann's painting was theater. It demanded playacting to produce images. Only selected gestures were adopted; nothing was said in the letters and texts about the borrowing of motifs. Role models could be added to construct ideal genealogies. On closer inspection, all authenticity turns out to be a masquerade. The world is a stage and is populated by actors. It cannot be otherwise. All art, to extend the thinking of a Nietzschean dictum, is an attempt and, if you will, a temptation.

Translated from the German by Steven Lindberg

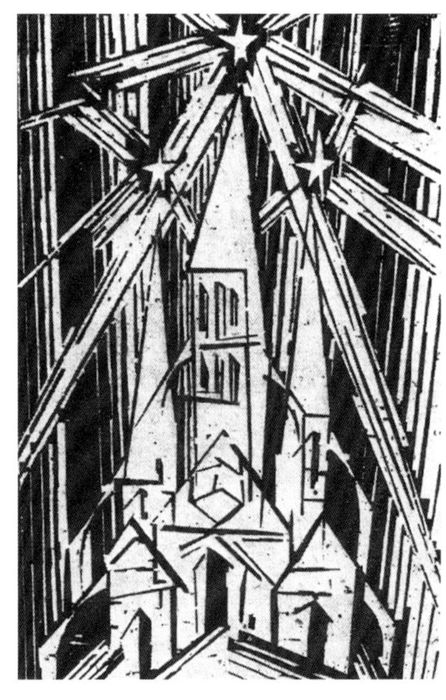

21. Lyonel Feininger, *Cathedral*, 1919, woodcut. Cover for the *Program of the State Bauhaus in Weimar.*

Acknowledgments

I wish to thank Sophie Kirsten and Martin Lottermoser for suggestions and corrections.

1 See Hans Robert Jauss, *Ästhetische Normen und geschichtliche Reflexion in der "Querelle des anciens et des modernes"* (Munich: Eidos, 1964).

2 See Christian Lenz, *Max Beckmann und die Alten Meister: "Eine ganz nette Reihe von Freunden* (Munich: Braus, 2000), 17.

3 On this, see the instructive study by Christoph Engels, *Auf der Suche nach einer "deutschen Kunst": Max Beckmann in der Wilhelminischen Kunstkritik* (Weimar: VDG, 1997), 189–98.

4 On February 8, 1918, the painter wrote to publisher Reinhard Piper about Worringer: "It is also very interesting that Worringer declared in a lecture here in Frankfurt, to the outrage of the assembled public, that Expressionism had reached a dead end and had no prospects." See Max Beckmann, *Briefe*, ed. Klaus Gallwitz, Uwe M. Schneede, and Stephan von Wiese with Barbara Golz, 3 vols., vol. 1 (1899–1925), comp. Uwe M. Schneede (Munich: Piper 1993), 164–65. See also Wilhelm Worringer, *Abstraction and Empathy: A Contribution to the Psychology of Style*, trans. Michael Bullock (London: Routledge & Paul, 1953).

5 Max Beckmann, diary entry of August 14, 1903, in Beckmann, *Self-Portrait in Words: Collected Writings and Statements, 1903–1950*, ed. Barbara Copeland Buenger, trans. Barbara Copeland Buenger and Reinhold Heller with David Britt (Chicago, IL: University of Chicago Press, 1997), 21–24, esp. 22.

6 Max Beckmann, diary entry of April 6, 1904, in Beckmann, *Self-Portrait in Words* (see note 5), 74.

7 Max Beckmann, diary entry of September 8, 1903, in Beckmann, *Self-Portrait in Words* (see note 5), 38, and Max Beckmann, diary entry of January 6 (or afterward), 1904, in Beckmann, *Self-Portrait in Words* (see note 5), 62–63, esp. 62.

8 Max Beckmann, diary entry of August 29, 1903, in Beckmann, *Self-Portrait in Words* (see note 5), 29–30, esp. 30.

9 See Ernst Robert Curtius, *Europäische Literatur und lateinisches Mittelalter* (Bern: Francke, 1948), 148–54.

10 Max Beckmann, diary entry of September 3, 1903, in Beckmann, *Self-Portrait in Words* (see note 5), 33–34, esp. 34.

11 Max Beckmann, diary entry of August 23, 1903, in Beckmann, *Self-Portrait in Words* (see note 5), 23–29, esp. 28.

12 Max Beckmann, diary entry of April 7, 1904, in Beckmann, *Self-Portrait in Words* (see note 5), 75–77, esp. 77. Reinhard Piper reports in his autobiography that Beckmann developed in Paris "a very strong aversion to the flood of Impressionist imitators." Reinhard Piper, *Mein Leben als Verleger: Vormittag, Nachmittag* (Munich: Piper, 1991; orig. pub. 1947–50), 328.

13 See, in general, Ernst-Erhard Güse, *Das Frühwerk Max Beckmanns: Zur Thematik seiner Bilder in den Jahren, 1904–1914* (Bern: Peter Land, 1977), 19–24; Barbara C. Buenger, *Max Beckmann's Artistic Sources: The Artist's Relation to Older and Modern Traditions* (Ann Arbor, MI: University Microfilms International, 1997) (PhD diss. Columbia University, 1979), 57–66; Christiane Zeiller, *Max Beckmann: Die frühen Jahre, 1899–1907* (Weimar: VDG, 2003), 145–98.

14 Benno Reifenberg and Wilhelm Hausenstein, *Max Beckmann* (Munich: Piper, 1949), 12.

15 Kessler mentions the work in his diary as a surprise and as the most interesting work in the exhibition. See Harry Graf Kessler, *Journey to the Abyss: The Diaries of Count Harry Kessler, 1880–1918* ed. and trans. Laird M. Easton (New York: Alfred A. Knopf, 2011), 369–70, esp. 370.

16 Talk of *imitatio artis* has traditionally always included competition with role models. Quintilian is fundamental to this idea, having observed in the tenth book of his *Institutio Oratoria* that imitation in the sense of merely repeating can never be satisfactory. It therefore goes without saying that *imitatio* does not mean the slavish imitation of models but also of creative appropriation that leads to artistic autonomy. *Imitatio artis* should by no means be understood to be creative stagnation. See Marcus Fabius Quintilian, *Institutes of Oratory; or, Education of an Orator*, trans. John Selby Watson, 2 vols. (London: Henry G. Bohn, 1856), 2:277–83 (10.2.1–27).

17 Max Beckmann to Caesar Kunwald on April 20, 1905, in Beckmann, *Briefe* (see note 4), 1:34 (no. 16).

18 See Lenz, *Max Beckmann und die Alten Meister* (see note 3), 19–20.

19 See Renate Hartleb, "Junge Männer am Meer, 1925," in *Max Beckmann: Gemälde, 1905–1950*, ed. Klaus Gallwitz, exh. cat. Museum der bildenden Künste, Leipzig, and Städelsches Kunstinstitut, Frankfurt am Main (Stuttgart: Hatje, 1990), 48.

20 Friedrich Nietzsche, *Unfashionable Observations*, trans. Richard T. Gray, Complete Works of Friedrich Nietzsche 2 (Stanford, CA: Stanford University Press, 1995), 9.

21 Friedrich Nietzsche, *Beyond Good and Evil*, in Nietzsche, *Beyond Good and Evil, On the Genealogy of Morality*, trans. Adrian Del Caro, Complete Works of Friedrich Nietzsche 8 (Stanford, CA: Stanford University Press, 2014), 1–203, esp. 41: "All that is profound loves a mask."

22 Friedrich Nietzsche, *Dawn: Thoughts on the Presumptions of Morality*, trans. Brittain Smith, Complete Works of Friedrich Nietzsche 5 (Stanford, CA: Stanford University Press, 2014).

23 Thomas Döring, Thomas Richter, and Andreas Uhr,

eds., *Max wird Beckmann: Es begann in Braunschweig*, exh. cat. Herzog Anton Ulrich Museum, Braunschweig (Munich: Hirmer, 2022), 164–65, cat. no. 63.

24 Friedrich Nietzsche, *Thus Spoke Zarathustra: A Book for All and None*, trans. Walter Kaufmann (New York: Penguin, 1978), 107–10, 112, 168–69, 195, 210, 217, 221, 224–28, 243–44, 293–96, 318, 320.

25 Quoted in Engels, *Auf der Suche nach einer "deutschen Kunst"* (see note 3), 14.

26 Max Beckmann, *Leben in Berlin: Tagebuch, 1908–1909*, ed. Hans Kinkel, 2nd ed. (Munich: Piper, 1985), entry of January 27, 1909.

27 In his comment on Beckmann's letter to Kunwald from Geneva, Uwe M. Schneede was the first to point out that Hodler was a model for Beckmann's *Junge Männer am Meer* and identified numerous aesthetic characteristics that the young painter adopted. See Beckmann, *Briefe* (see note 4), 1:398.

28 Ibid., 22 (no. 12).

29 Quoted in Engels, *Auf der Suche nach einer "deutschen Kunst"* (see note 3), 91.

30 Moreover, not all of the comparisons that Lenz proposed are convincing. Rembrandt's etching *The Fall* of 1638 has little to do with Beckmann's etching *Adam and Eve* of 1917. See Lenz, *Max Beckmann und die Alten Meister* (see note 3), 90. Justifying this comparison based on the motif of the dragon-like serpent is unsatisfactory, since numerous other examples of the same motif could be identified in the early modern period. More obvious comparisons for Beckmann's *Adam and Eve* would be Hans Baldung and Hans Sebald Beham.

31 Recall the famous passage on the necessity of the arts working together: "Every individual art can no longer invent anything new today, not just the fine arts but no less the art of the dance, instrumental music, and poetry. Now they have all developed their supreme ability in order to be able to invent themselves ever anew in the *Gesamtkunstwerk*, in the drama." Richard Wagner, "Das Künstlertum der Zukunft," in Wagner, *Frühe Prosa und Revolutionstraktate*, ed. Dieter Borchmeyer, Dichtungen und Schriften 5 (Frankfurt am Main: Insel, 1983), 261.

32 It is certainly reasonable to ask whether the presence of the *Nibelungenlied* and the Edda in Beckmann's library is connected to his reading of Nietzsche.

33 See Friedrich Nietzsche, *The Birth of Tragedy*, in *Basic Writings of Nietzsche*, ed. and trans. Walter Kaufmann (New York: Modern Library, 1968), 3–144, esp. 36.

34 David Summers, *Michelangelo and the Language of Art* (Princeton, NJ: Princeton University Press, 1981), 234-41.

35 We owe this discovery to Andreas Uhr, "Max Beckmann und die Alten Meister: Es begann in Braunschweig," in Döring, Richter, and Uhr, *Max wird Beckmann* (see note 23), 147–85, esp. 150.

36 See Lenz, *Max Beckmann und die Alten Meister* (see note 3), 28–29.

37 See Jürgen Müller, "'An exceeding marvel and altogether astonishing': Reflections on Michelangelo's Design of the Sistine Chapel," in *Capricci luterani? Michelangelo artista e poeta nel contesto del dibattito religioso del Cinquecento*, ed. Christine Ott et al. (Berlin: de Gruyter, 2023), 91–126.

38 Andreas Uhr sees this as the motif of Christ stepping down into the water from Veronese's *Baptism of Christ*, which is convincing as far as the motif of stepping is concerned but not for the position of the arm. See Uhr, "Max Beckmann und die Alten Meister" (see note 35), 150.

39 Beckmann, *Leben in Berlin: Tagebuch, 1908–1909*, ed. Hans Kinkel, 2nd ed. (Munich: Piper, 1985), entry of January 28, 1909, pp. 35–36.

40 In his study *Max Beckmann: Die Tradition als Problem in der Kunst der Moderne* (Munich: Deutscher Kunstverlag, 1984), Hans Belting pointed out that scholars had not been able to find a suitable interpretive frame for the painter. He has been described as a loner and existentialist whose reading of philosophy had guided him through his times. Belting rejects this and diagnoses a risk of biographism. Nevertheless, his study lacks precision. Too many names. Too many theses. Too little space is devoted to the attempt to explain the "whole Beckmann." One reads many fascinating things but sees nothing precisely. Translated as Max Belting, *Max Beckmann: Tradition as a Problem in Modern Art*, trans. Peter Wortsman (New York: Timken, 1989).

41 Lenz, *Max Beckmann und die Alten Meister* (see note 3), 28.

42 Quoted in Ursula Harter and Stephan von Wiese, eds., *Max Beckmann und J. B. Neumann: Der Künstler und sein Händler in Briefen und Dokumenten, 1917–1950* (Cologne: DuMont, 2011), 93.

43 Ibid., 22 and 26.

44 Quoted in Engels, *Auf der Suche nach einer "deutschen Kunst"* (see note 3), 123 (doc. no. 17).

45 The philosopher praises the dancer who has become an overman in words that are as seductive as they are passionate: "[Man] is no longer an artist, he has become a work of art: in these paroxysms of intoxication the artistic power of all nature reveals itself to the highest gratification of the primordial unity." Nietzsche, *The Birth of Tragedy* (see note 33), 37.

46 Nietzsche, *Thus Spoke Zarathustra* (see note 24), 17.

REFLECTED MODERNITY

MAX BECKMANN'S LATE WORK

Olaf Peters

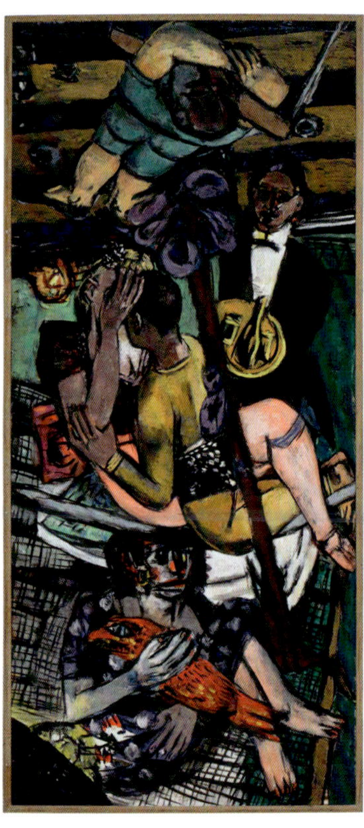

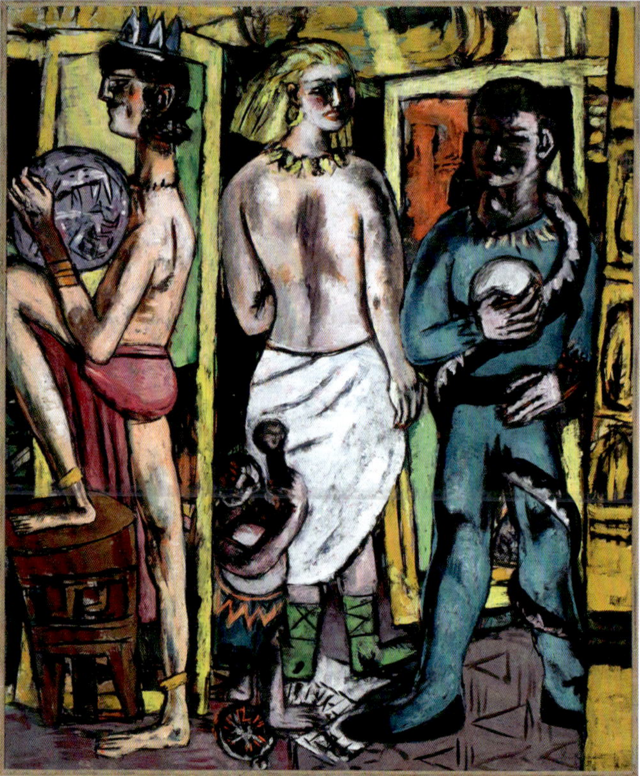

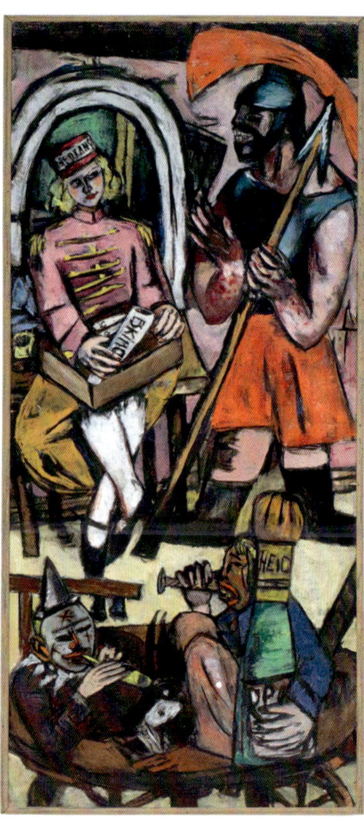

In Max Beckmann's view, the modern era required a new level of reflection. The painter did not submit to simple ideas of self-reflexive, progress-driven development. This essay will closely analyze two of Beckmann's triptychs that prove this.[1] They deserve attention because they support the thesis of this exhibition, which is that Beckmann repeatedly returned to the themes and forms explored during the period between 1915 and 1925 in the ensuing two decades between 1930 and 1950, the year of his death. This included recourses, self-quotations, variations, and repetitions. Together they reveal the continuity—despite all the caesuras—and the process of evolution in Beckmann's oeuvre.

THE WORLD OF THE WAR

Akrobaten (Acrobats) is Beckmann's third triptych [Fig. 1].[2] He produced it after fleeing National Socialist Germany for Amsterdam in November/December 1937. It was thus the first triptych of the ten years he spent in exile and it referred directly to the events of the time.[3] It is seemingly clear and simple in construction. In fact, however, closer inspection reveals a complex composition of varied, interlocking levels of form and content. The triptych presents a contemporary image of violence, exile, and the role of art in that period. The large central panel is dominated by three life-size figures. Standing on the left and looking out of the painting at the side panel is a crowned youth who has placed his bent leg on a stool. A large sphere rests on his knee, which he holds in one arm and presses to his chest. His face is turned away with a shifty grin. The almost scrawny figure, who is outlined by a tall frame behind him, confounds the viewer with his impossible stance and the Mannerist-looking, elongated rendering of his body and extremities. He is also distinguished by an enigmatic bearing that seems to conceal a secret.

To the right of the youth, almost back-to-back, stands a large, blonde, strong woman who wears nothing but a sheet wrapped around her hips. Her head is turned toward the viewer, her broad back, the white sheet, and her vivid boots emphasize this figure's centrality. She also occupies the panel's central axis and thus centers the overall composition. Beckmann repeats here a constellation already seen in the 1920 *Fastnacht* (Carnival) [Plate 67]. To the right of the woman, and in direct eye contract with her, stands an acrobat in a colorful leotard. He wears a dark cap and holds a bright glass or crystal ball, which he presses to his chest. A snake winds around his body, but rather than representing a mortal danger it seems to be his everyday companion. The viewer perceives the animal's head as a dark triangle next to the shaded but smiling features of the acrobat.

If one traces the gesture of the artiste's left hand diagonally through the painting, one spots a small drummer between the tall, rectangular frame in the background and the woman. He pushes his way out of the background to the front; extending his drumstick outward in a broadly sweeping gesture. His action suddenly dominates the panel. With the stature of a baby but with a man's face, the figure disrupts the balance of the figures who tower over him. But that initial impression is deceptive; the relationship between the figures is more complex. The drummer appears to spur on the youth with the implication that the youth derives his knowledge from him. In relation to the woman, the drummer seems like an ill-behaved child: loud, wild, unpredictable. The child seems ignorant, compared to the snake handler, because he is unaware of the acrobat's vaguely pointing gesture. Although the little one is calling the tune, he is oblivious to the scene behind his back. Even if he is able to disrupt the static structure of the main actors and their backdrops, he is unable to cause more disorder.

This view is rather different on the side panels. On the left, the viewer is confronted with a bold painterly composition that has a precursor in the magic realist *Das Trapez* (The Trapeze) of 1923 [Plate 73]. At least three layers can be distinguished here; they are united in the composition by repeatedly shifting the perspective. In a net spanned over a deep, sealike, green abyss, a woman in clownish makeup holds a large, yellowish-orange fish and has caught other smaller fish. Above her, two lovers are lying on a tightrope rather than balancing

1. Max Beckmann, *Acrobats*, 1937–39, oil on canvas. Saint Louis Art Museum, Bequest of Morton D. May

atop it. They appear to be bearing down on the woman holding the fish. The couple is inextricably intertwined in an ambiguous position—lying in each other's arms or wrestling each other, uniting or separating. Beckmann has created a highly ambiguous pair of figures here. A waiter attempts to approach them from the background to serve champagne but cannot reach them. The scene is closed off on top in a paradoxical way by an aerial acrobat who clings to the ceiling, more sleeping than swinging through the air on the trapeze. A tree, which has grown out of nowhere, is crowned by a large, violet blossom, and it holds the young man beneath the ceiling. Beckmann is taking up here two thematically identical paintings, *Varieté* (Variety Show) of 1921 [Fig. 2] and the 1923 *The Trapeze*, with similar constellations of figures. In *Variety Show*, an acrobat extends his hands outward toward a horizontal bar, and it is unclear whether he is trying to grab the bar in front of him or has released it after finishing his performance. The figure in front of him wearing a black leotard wedges him in place so that he seems hampered in flight and almost transfixed in space. In *The Trapeze*, there is a similar arresting of the figures, but here it seems to be part of the exercise; one figure hangs stiffly on a metal bar but without conveying any physical heaviness. The left panel of *Acrobats* presents a more complex scene of action compared to the two "precursor" paintings. The trapeze artist in *Acrobats* appears to cling under the ceiling while sleeping. If the painting were rotated 180 degrees, the figure would seem to be lying on floorboards. Because of the spatially unrealistic composition, an almost surreal mysteriousness reigns here that the earlier paintings did not demonstrate. Beckmann's recourse to the formulations of the early 1920s at first seems like a conscious strategy, but he manipulates it to intensify, complicate, and obscure.

By contrast, the right panel of the triptych is simpler to describe. Another pairing dominates two-thirds of the painting: a woman selling ice cream leans casually against a mirrored commode and listens with a smile to a powerful warrior with blood-smeared lower arms; he is waiting for his entrance and biding his time, or has not yet changed out of his costume after his performance. Directly under them, drunk clowns squat on a table. The figure on the left is at least trying to play the horn, but the other one blows her instrument mindlessly, almost biting it. In combination, they terminate the below with a cynical, sad cacophony and form a pendant to the women with the fish on the left panel.

With *Acrobats*, Beckmann conceived a triptych whose irregular spatial construction and dovetailing of different iconographies can scarcely be reconciled visually or mentally. Nevertheless, the palette and the iconography of the theater or circus interlock into a relatively harmonious whole. Disparity and coherence mediate visually into a contradictory unity that has to be perceived as such in its irresolvable tension and yet never breaks down into complete heterogeneity. One central element of this is the unifying effect of the format. It is of overriding importance that the two side panels together are approximately the format of the central panel, so that one can almost speak of a classical triptych.[4] It is important to establish this given the risk of the complete disparity of individual panels that are in fact autonomous, but it does not guarantee the internal coherence of the whole.

The common theme of the panels and an overarching harmony of color also bring them together: the trapeze artist, the snake handler, the right-hand clown, and the warrior all wear costumes of the same color. Equally important are the clown's faces, which can scarcely be called human, that appear at the bottom of each side panel. The irregular treatment of space for each side panel, at odds with any empirical experience of unity, emphasizes the irreality of the scene. It is also important to mention the divergent scales within the painting, which can both accentuate disparity yet also create visual coherence. The large and small figures in the central panel and medium-sized figures on the side panels are a deliberate design element in Beckmann's triptych. These do not reflect different spatial levels but rather represent a phenomenon of form and content that is related to medieval hierarchical proportion.

The figures depicted in the triptych can scarcely be satisfactorily identified. The diversity and polyvalence of several figures will be discussed here as examples because they may help the viewer to understand the enigmatic character of Beckmann's pictorial inventions and the resulting incoherencies they produce. A closer examination of the large, blonde central figure underscores that this pictorial invention is not enigmatic solely in terms of its iconography. Her legs are unnaturally positioned, as if she were performing in a ballet, and her feet are pointed 180 degrees apart—a stance that several figures in the painting share (see the snake handler and the warrior). Looking upward from the figure's feet, she is twisting and seems extremely deformed. Her lower back is already at a slight angle, and finally her head is turned backward almost violently. The main figure is turned awkwardly to look over her shoulder and almost face the viewer.

All of the other figures of the central panel relate to this female figure, who unites the iconographic traditions of the mother, Eve, the personification of Truth, and a Valkyrie. She is closest to the snake handler, so it is tempting to consider them as a couple. Their arms touch, and their eyes appear to meet. This proximity contrasts with the distance separating their feet: the small, green shoes of the woman are situated in the middle ground of the painting; her relatively small head is strangely close and far at once. The snake recalls the iconography of the modified Adam and Eve motif that Beckmann had employed as early as 1932 in the painting *Mann und Frau/Adam und Eva* (Man and Woman/Adam and Eve) [see ill. on p. 74] and that he revised in 1936 in a sculpture [Fig. 3]. The artiste's crystal ball and the motif of the bared chest of the woman, even though turned away, are associated with the

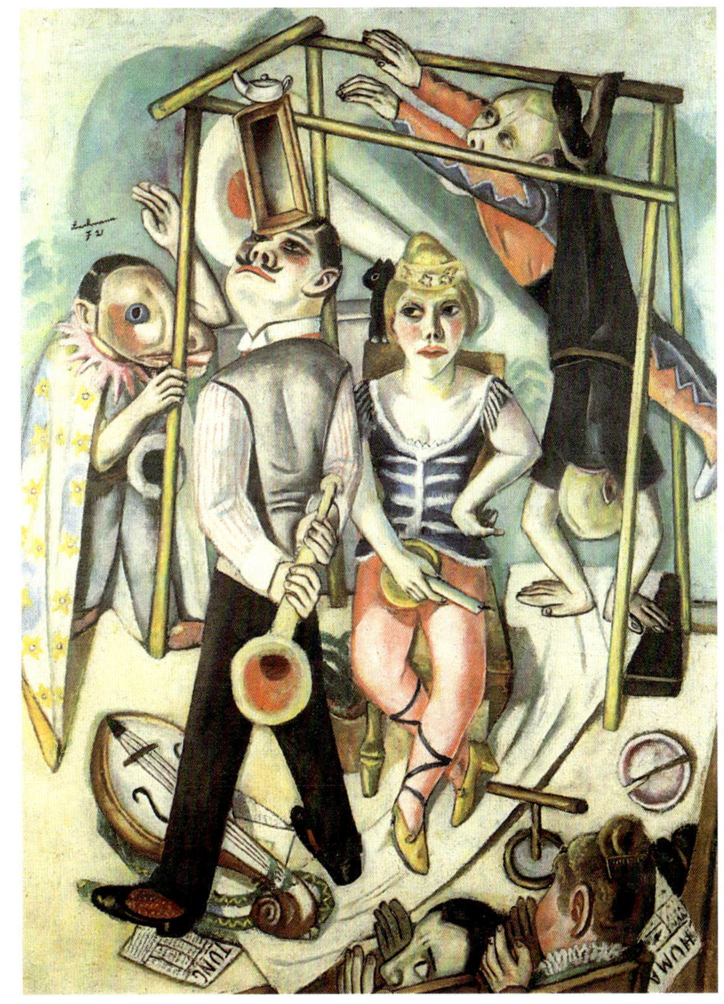

2. Max Beckmann, *Variety Show*, 1921, oil on canvas. Private Collection

iconography of Truth, bringing out the epistemological themes inherent in the panel.

Beckmann's intertwining of the motifs of temptation, knowledge, and truth results in an interesting relationship to the figure of the youth on the left. He is clearly separated from the two other protagonists of the central panel by the yellow frame. The motif of turning away is emphasized by being seen in profile while looking directly out of the painting. His sneering grin conveys a sense of cynical knowledge. This figure also has a sphere or ball but he is not casually or confidently holding it but instead clutching it possessively. The sphere is literally clamped between his bent thigh, cramped hand, and chest. At the same time, he is pressed against the edge of the painting and facing outward like the dwarf-like figure on the right edge of *The Trapeze*. A competition results between the two male figures in the painting: each has a sphere, and each is surrounded by a yellow frame that roughly corresponds to his statue and that draws the eye into the background like a stage set. The blonde woman representing "Truth" turns toward the figure on the right, who bears the burden of knowledge and can surely be read as the painter's barely concealed self-portrait.[5]

3. Max Beckmann, *Adam and Eve*, 1936, plaster. Hamburger Kunsthalle. Photo: bpk Bildagentur / Hamburger Kunsthalle / Elke Walford / Art Resource, NY

It is therefore no coincidence that this figure is the one making a significant if restrained gesture that points the viewer to the dwarf-life figure of the drummer. He too is operating behind the back of Truth, despite her turning around, and is another of Beckmann's strange pictorial inventions. His overly long arm is raised as if to strike and resembles a curve; the large drum is stretched in front of his body; and his unnaturally placed feet trample some type of clock. His befuddled, groggy face is puzzling—he even appears to be wearing an eye patch—his dark, straggly hair sticks to his forehead. This figure appears to be calling the tune, as Beckmann had said of the stoic drummer in his first triptych, *Abfahrt* (Departure) [Fig. 4] from 1932–35.[6] In 1937, the drummer had clear political connotations, and a viewer at the time could easily have associated him with the historical figure of Adolf Hitler because of his straggly hair and bewildered, fanatical expression.[7] It is thus no coincidence that the same face appears as a large portrait bust on the left wing of the 1942–43 *Carnival*—the triptych that most clearly represents an autobiographical reflection on exile. Its right panel—which takes up once again the iconography seen in the 1938 *Hölle der Vögel* (Hell of Birds) and the tale of Aeneas—is clearly the expulsion from Paradise, the forced move from Berlin to Amsterdam, and the left panel can be understood as a metaphorical illustration of the existence of the arts in an occupied country under threat from an armed, tyrannical power, since Beckmann again shows a figure playing the flute. Beckmann's triptychs are

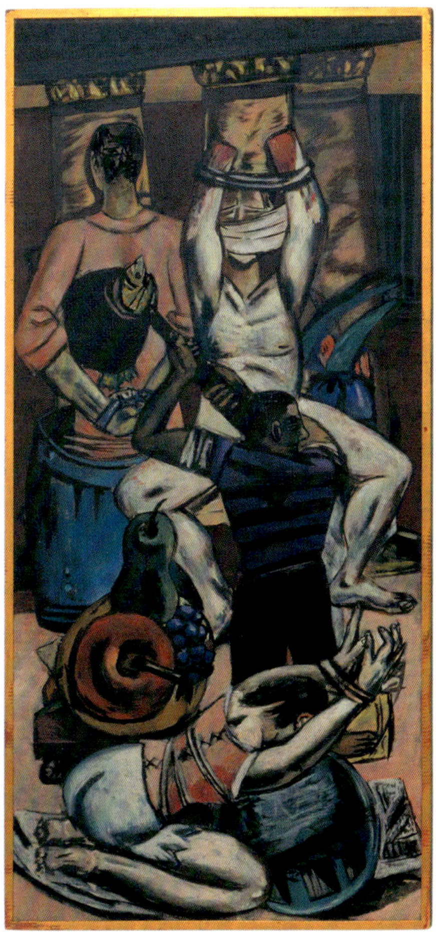
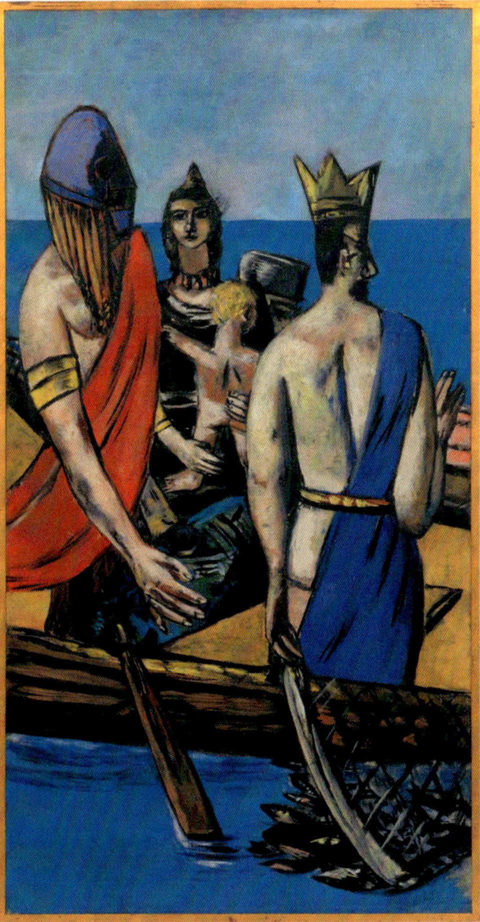
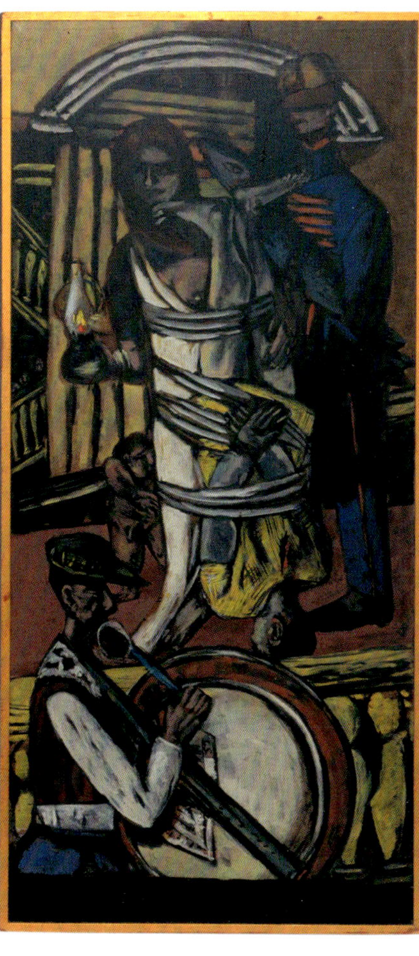

4. Max Beckmann, *Departure*, 1932–35, oil on canvas. The Museum of Modern Art, New York, Given anonymously (by exchange). Photo: © The Museum of Modern Art/Licensed by SCALA / Art Resource, NY

filled with allusions to contemporary history. *Acrobats*, however, is not simply a direct reference to history, but is part of it.[8]

Beckmann includes several figures that make the historical relevance of his panels clear. On the left panel, it is a circus milieu, which the figure of the waiter suddenly invades. He is, however, separated by a tree trunk from the couple he wants to serve, who take no notice of him and remain lost to the world and self-absorbed in their sexual existence. As emphasized above, the constellation of this couple is a multilayered, complex invention of the painter. The two are intertwined, the woman's left is crossed over the man's; the man grabs the woman's right arm, and she appears to be stroking his head. But their connection is less clear: the man's legs appear to be tied together. Fetters, interlocking, struggle, and passion intermingle. The man's knees are in an unnatural position, weighing on the stretched rope.[9]

The man grasps the woman's arm, but here too the significance of the action is unclear, above all due to the woman's gesture. She could either be delicately stroking her partner's head or self-defensively shielding her eyes from pain. Is she saying farewell, touching him gently, or is the fettered man subjecting her to violence despite his own powerlessness?

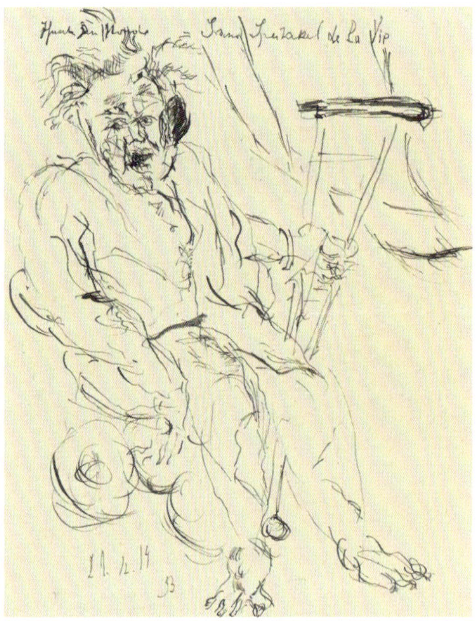

5. Max Beckmann, *Mann with Crutch in a Wheelchair,* 1914, ink on paper. Staatsgalerie Stuttgart, Graphisches Kabinett

All of these possibilities are interwoven in a referential pictorial invention whose meaning cannot be clearly determined based on the multiplicity of forms. The semantic levels of the painting are emphatically unclear or mysterious.

The significance of the trapeze acrobat in the upper part of the panel is ambiguous in this same way. He seems to be swinging, lying, sleeping, and clinging to the ceiling all at once, while being pressed upward by a large violet flower of a tree whose dark trunk runs diagonally through the painting, separating the waiter from the couple, and rooted in the safety net. A woman in a grotesque mask sits in a net with her legs drawn in and crossed. A large, orange fish is her victim, caught just as she is caught, and its eye is wide open and staring, surprised and aggressive at once, while baring its sharp teeth.

A similarly grotesque formation on the other side of the triptych corresponds to this scene. On the right, the viewer sees a sad figure, also with extremely bent legs, clutching a bottle of champagne and sullenly gnawing on a horn. Garishly made-up lips signal uninhibited desires, to which a cynical companion adds his song. The constellation above them is perhaps the easiest to read: a couple—a salesgirl and a warrior—are deep in conversation during intermission. Dressed in an alarming red, the warrior-like figure is another clear reference to contemporary history in 1938–39, during which time constant tension reigned in foreign policy. Spain was already engaged in a civil war, and World War II broke out when the Germans began a war of aggression against Poland just days after the painting was completed.[10] The figure is not just an actor and acrobat but also represents Ares/Mars himself. The god of war is attending a circus on which he will leave his bloody stamp. The worlds of the modern human beings and ancient gods meet, living together in an aesthetic phantasmagoria captured on canvases in a "tobacco storeroom" in Amsterdam.[11] The "swindle" of the world of the Greek gods that Beckmann criticized around 1920 has mutated into a grotesque *theatrum mundi*.[12]

The question of iconography is one of the most important issues concerning *Acrobats*. The iconographies of the theater, the circus, and the fair could certainly be called traditional themes of Expressionism as well as of Beckmann's paintings and prints of the early 1920s.[13] The painter also set his third triptych in this milieu, thus making it part of a "*Théâtre du Monde—Grand Spectacle de la Vie*" that he already associated with the war in 1914; the triptych naturally offers a broader perspective than the closeup of an individual's fate in the shocking drawing [Fig. 5]. The pictorial organization of this third triptych is fundamentally different from that of the two previous triptychs, *Departure* and *Versuchung* (Temptation). One can observe a successive process of bringing together pictorial inventions and concepts like those developed in *Filmstudio* of 1933 and the 1938 *Apachentanz* (Apache Dance). The iconography of the bar or café is associated with it. Then there was a series of themes, some of which had been addressed earlier, evoked by individual figures and their attributes: the Old Testament iconography of the Fall of Adam and Eve, the iconography of the war and that of Truth and the associated portrayal of the artist as *artifex vates*.[14] Beckmann's pictorial world is sometimes one of mystifying complexity. There are groups of motifs with historical connotations or political metaphors, for example, when Beckmann includes a drummer or the figure of a youth, whom his contemporaries would have recognized as references to two major works by the "degenerate" sculptor Wilhelm Lehmbruck. The latter's *Kniende* (Kneeling Woman) and *Emporsteigender Jüngling* (Rising Youth) are clearly cited,[15] and the entire scene is associated with a historical context that also refers to the defamation and confiscation of so-called "Entartete Kunst" (Degenerate Art), which began several months before these panels were conceived [Fig. 6].[16]

The triptych, which can be interpreted through many strands, details, and facets, is visually united by a macrostructure, but, unlike Pablo Picasso's nearly contemporaneous magnum opus *Guernica* (1937), it is not turned into a "metascenic unity of an event."[17] In Beckmann's case, there is a certain unity of content (iconography) and of form (color, symmetry), but it is shattered by the ostentations display of rifts within the work, so that one can indeed rightly speak of three autonomous panels that are brought together in the "pathos formula" of the triptych to create a coherent constellation that provides unity.[18]

The art historian Max Imdahl has demonstrated how Picasso's *Guernica* [Fig. 7] mediates history and myth with a genuinely

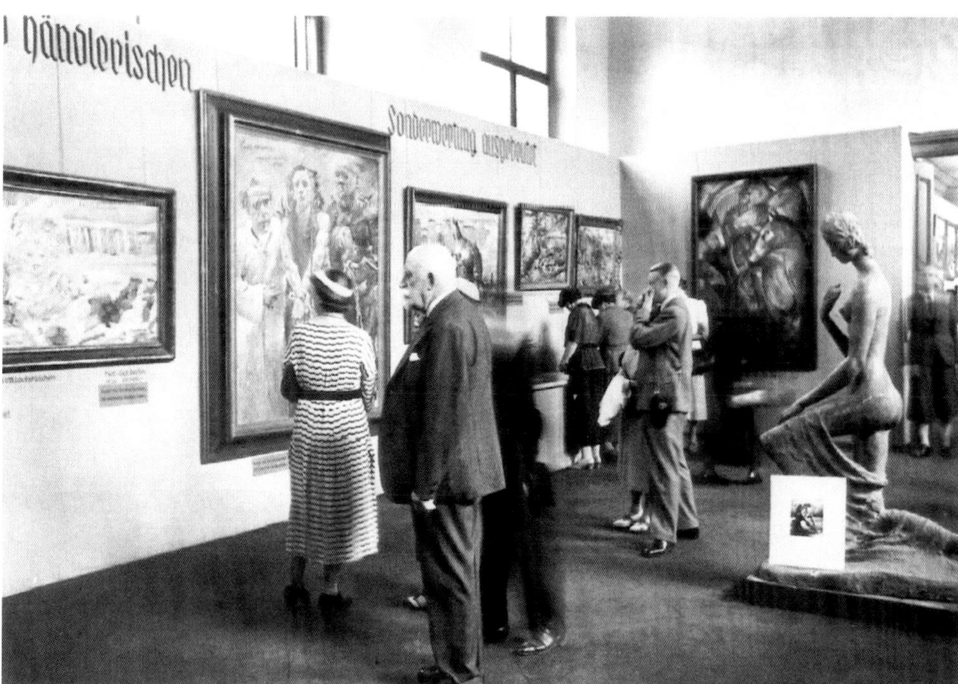

6. View of the "Degenerate Art" exhibition with Wilhelm Lehmbruck's *Kneeling Woman* (1911), Munich 1937

pictorial, clear coherence of the incoherent and the coherent that enabled him to come to terms with the senselessness of a historical event—in this case the bombing of the eponymous Basque city and religious center by the German Legion Condor.[19] By contrast, the theme of Beckmann's work is that such coming to terms is dubious and problematic. Although it is possible to grasp the world as a whole in the aesthetic concept of the theater of the world or in the pictorial concept of the triptych that is shattered but nevertheless makes connections, the painter did not understand the world as meaningful, as something that could be appropriated, or even as something one could come to terms with. There is no longer any meaning to be found in *Acrobats*; there may be flashes of it in certain respects, or it can be alluded to in fragments, but only to sink back into the dark enigma that the artist deliberately produces, which can sometimes "take on a powerful splendor," as Beckmann succinctly formulated it with reference to his first triptych, *Departure*, and applied to his work as a whole.[20]

THE PLAY OF THE GODS

Beckmann called the triptych *Blindekuh* (Blind Man's Buff) [Fig. 8] perhaps his "most extreme painting."[21] He worked on it from late June 1944 to September 1945 and retitled it frequently.[22] Nearly fifteen feet wide, with a central panel more than six and a half feet tall, it is Beckmann's largest triptych, produced during the final months of the German occupation of the Netherlands. The painter worked on it during the terrible agony of the Third Reich and ultimately finished it in an Amsterdam that had been liberated from its German occupiers.[23] Its central panel depicts a musical celebration by the gods,[24] which is connected to the contemporary social scenes on the wings by its bright colors and a seemingly homogeneous space.

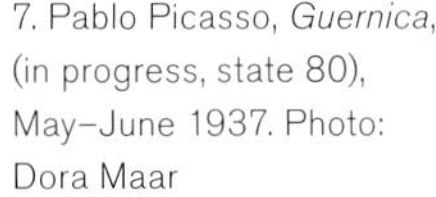

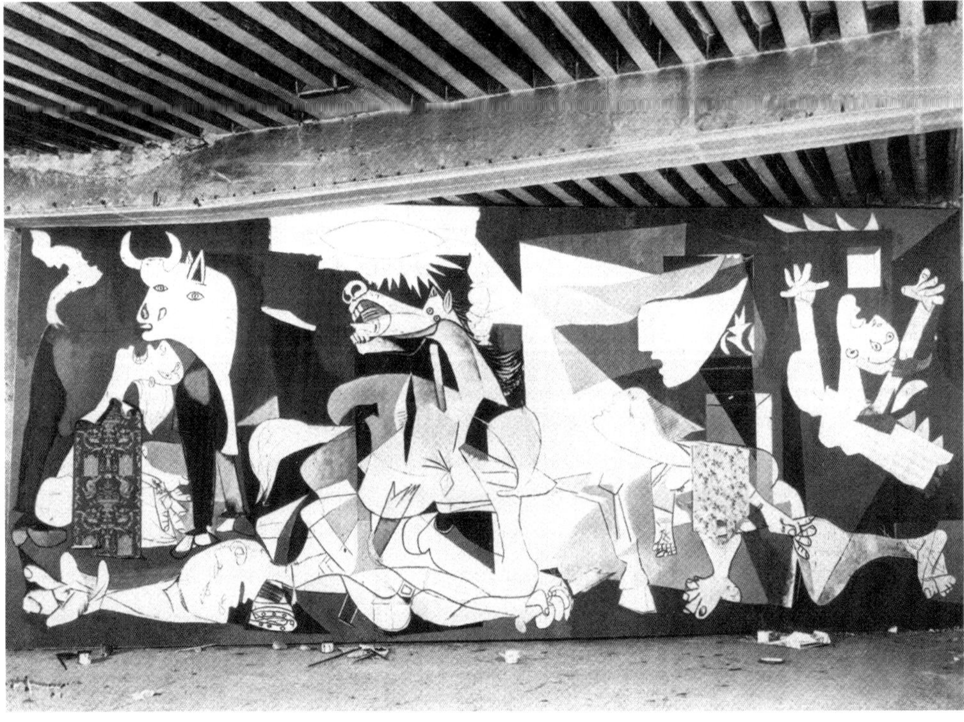

7. Pablo Picasso, *Guernica*, (in progress, state 80), May–June 1937. Photo: Dora Maar

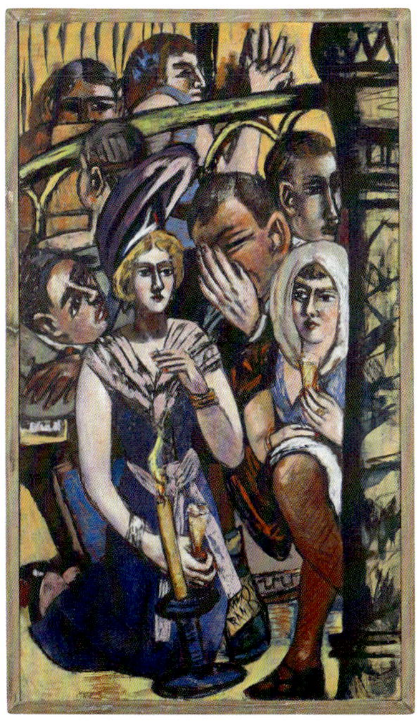
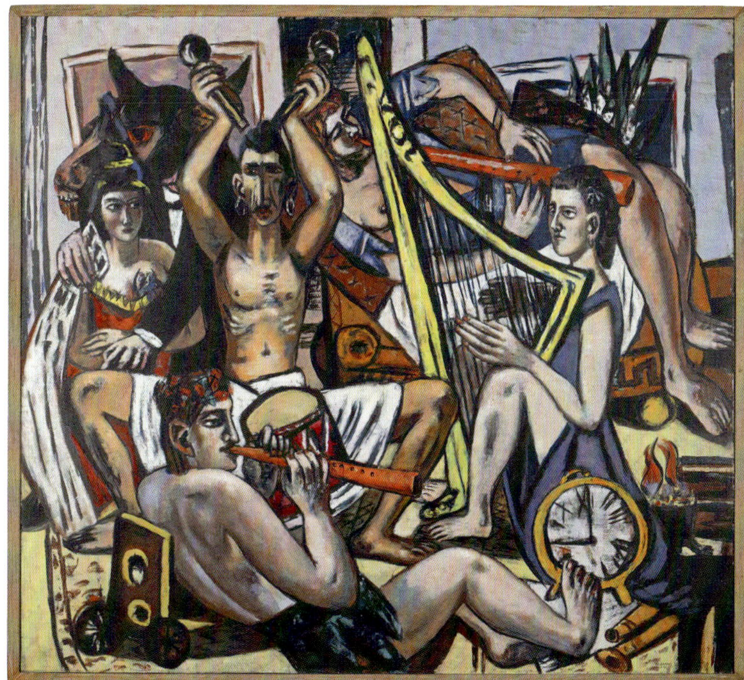
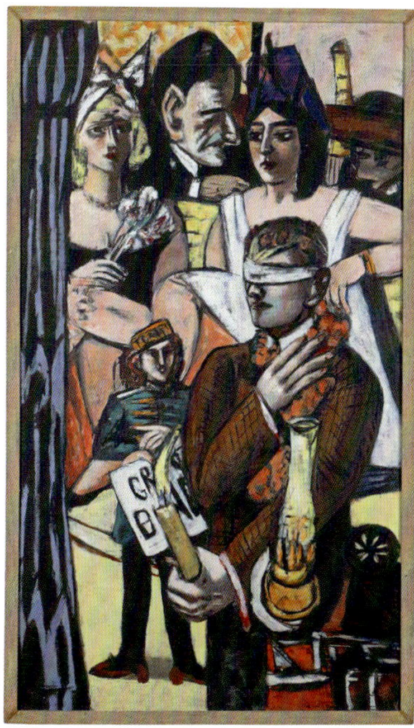

8. Max Beckmann, *Blind Man's Buff*, 1945, oil on canvas. Minneapolis Institute of Art, Gift of Mr. and Mrs. Donald Winston. Photo: Minneapolis Institute of Art

Blind Man's Buff is closely related to Beckmann's painting *Gesellschaft Paris* (Paris Society), which he began in 1925, continued to work on in 1931, and then completed in 1947. *Paris Society* [Plate 88] compresses in a compact space—in some respects as a caricature—a society in expensive evening wear that is alienated from itself. It is accompanied by a band that has been banished to the background and to which little attention is given. Its emptiness, world-weariness, despair, and vulgarity are exposed with dissecting sharpness. Beckmann sketches a picture of the ruling class of the grand bourgeoisie and nobility. At the same time, he addresses his own social and cultural ambitions, which he expressed in parallel, in an enigmatic and almost hybrid fashion, in the 1927 text "*Der Künstler im Staat*" (The Artist in the State) (see pp. 154–57).[25]

The triptych *Blind Man's Buff*, by contrast, seems to permit a quick glance behind the curtains of high society. It is as if *Paris Society* had been separated and pushed apart to serve as wings, so that the partially bored but also partially martial play of otherwise distant gods could be experienced from up close. Their activity and also inactivity are the reasons behind the depicted emotions of society's bustling and roaming.[26] Beckmann resumed work on the unfinished second *Auferstehung* (Resurrection) of 1916–18 [see Fig. 8 on p. 21], in which he and his family observe the salvation history as if at the theater, and shortly before conceiving *Blind Man's Buff*. *Blind Man's Buff* is essentially about the problematic relationship between contemporaneous society and a divine act: in 1918, an apocalyptic Last Judgment of the war being observed by contemporaries beneath a black, extinguished sun; in 1944, an epiphany of transcendent boredom and apathy, and perhaps also resistance in the face of the surrounding horrors of the war and the Holocaust. The historical context of the works in each case is the already foreseeable end of a murderous world war.

In 1944, one possibility to process contemporaneous events—in addition to current work in the studio and almost daily, albeit completely unsystematic reading—was a self-referential, fleeting turn to the past. That is why Beckmann began to work again on *Resurrection*, which had been left unfinished after working on it during the last two years of World War I, or at least to address the enormous work more seriously. He commented on this with the somewhat incomprehensible remark: "Everything repeats itself. Only reversed."[27] His repeated work on this early major work suggests that in 1944 he was again thinking about a programmatic, history-oriented work that would reflect on and interpret the immediate present, as he had proposed in his "*Bekenntnis*" (Confession, translated in English as "Creative Credo") (1918–20). In order to accomplish this task, he also went back to his own prints of the 1920s.[28]

Beckmann was often in a bad mood and nervous during these weeks and months. Like everyone else, he was waiting for the invasion of the Allied troops, whose progress he recorded constantly in his diaries from June 6, 1944, onward, along with the general progress of the war.[29] During the Allied advance, which did not lead to an invasion of Amsterdam, only the liberation of the southern part of the Netherlands, so that the Allied troops could continue advancing toward Germany, Beckmann had others read aloud to him. The reading material is revealing and points to a crisis of orientation and phase of reinvention: Beckmann had his wife, Mathilde "Quappi" Beckmann, read to him from the diaries of Harry Graf Kessler, who had been significantly responsible for the successful start of the painter's career in Weimar in 1905–06, and had the exiled writer Wolfgang Frommel read to him from Beckmann's own *Briefe im Kriege* (Letters in the War).[30] In this mood of existential uncertainty,[31] of a liberation that was finally coming, and hence of a foreseeable return to an existence as a free artist, which was mirrored in his reflection on the beginning of his own career nearly thirty years earlier, Beckmann began work on *Blind Man's Buff*.

The structure of the triptych is relatively simple, and the overpowering impression of the wall-sized painting results from the coherence of its color and composition, which lends the three panels an overall tone. The two side panels are composed with mirror symmetry and explicitly refer to each other; if placed together, they would convey an only slightly interpreted view of a continuous space with a large column standing in its center. As a partitioning element, the column separates the two "protagonists" of the outer panels, who apparently cannot find their way to each other. Only on closer inspection does the viewer realize that there are indeed two separate rooms. The one on the left has a woman kneeling in front of a candle, holding a champagne glass filled with ice cubes next to the candle and seemingly protecting its flame with her other hand. On the right panel, one sees a youth with eyes bound holding a candle—the painting's title comes from him—who moves through an apathetic gathering while receiving a message from a small female hotel messenger. The note may be telling him the way to his partner, at whom the messenger is pointing, if the side panels were not cut off and separated by the wide central panel.

The two young people are surrounded by a crowd of contrasting figures who are blended together like a montage and who, as in *Paris Society*, convey very different moods, oscillating between stoicism and horror. Their emotional reactions and their partially allegorical, personifying status—for example, on the left side of the right panel there is a Dutchwoman in traditional dress who stands for her nation—provide a dense backdrop of contrasts and context for the concentrated activity and waiting, respectively, of the two central figures. This is especially clear in the case of the woman, who is being addressed by a man rendered from a very confusing perspective and speaking from a depth in the painting that does not exist according to any spatial logic. She apathetically ignores both this address and the man crying behind her. The figure of the crying man cites an emotive formula from *Paris Society* and thus refers primarily to the catastrophe of World War II but also to the failures and letdowns of earlier political hopes and artistic ambitions.[32]

The painting *Paris Society* [see Plate 88] has an unambiguous political note and presents stylized portraits of Prince Anton von Rohan in the center and the desperate German ambassador in Paris, Leopold von Hoesch, in the front on the right, who appears to be crying and seeking reconciliation and confidence. In 1931, a secret plan for a German-Austrian customs union was revealed, causing a foreign policy uproar that did not help Beckmann's career plans in Paris, especially since Rohan and the Frankfurt banker Albert Hahn were involved. One also sees some of his acquaintances from Frankfurt (the music historian Paul Hirsch at front right and Hahn on the right edge) as well as Parisian celebrities (the man standing at the left edge is presumably the couturier Paul Poiret).[33]

The triptych, which at least when viewed against this backdrop offers a veiled denunciation of the passive apathy and blunted effect of himself and of others, is also a historical programmatic painting thanks to its conceptual reference to *Paris Society*. *Blind Man's Buff* updates *Paris Society* and interprets it with a pessimistic ideology, which makes the political directness of the earlier painting more universally applicable. A diary entry of March 24, 1945, indicates that closely associated exhausting work with the effort to repress the "most horrible things"—presumably reports of liberated concentration camps or horrors of the war.[34]

Like Picasso's *Guernica*, *Blind Mans' Buff* raises questions about how one can be partially responsible for something but at the same time helpless in the face of higher powers, whereas the Spanish artist captured in a modernist pathos formula the brutal consequences of the war in his native country. Beckmann's central panel is about helplessness because it presents the bizarre playing of the gods whose performance the painter is using to interpret the history of his day. At the same time, he is referring to transcendental ideas that are projected onto the present in order to "make the contemporary timeless and the timeless contemporary."[35] Reclining or squatting, the gods play their instruments listlessly, and in some cases with resignation. Their performance has presumably already gone on too long to judge from the clock—which appears to be missing the starting and ending numbers one and twelve—while a demonic minotaur in a tuxedo with bloodshot eyes grabs a woman in order to dance, but she shows no fear. She might even feel protected, observing with a detached gaze the archaic-looking Indian drummer, who prominently occupies the focus of the panel, which is shifted slightly to the left. It is unclear whether the drummer's sullenly rigid, idol-like face heralds the end of the game, a final drumbeat that breaks off the whole bustle. He is the monumental counterimage to the befuddled drummer of *Acrobats*.

The crucial thing about this strangely glowing and yet cold image is the impression of a basic atmosphere of passivity and resignation that does not express any interplay at all but rather a solipsistic lack of coherence. The playing is, on the one hand, devoted and arcadian and, on the other hand, sad and resigned, evoking an impression of the disrupted harmony of a seemingly "insane cosmos," as Beckmann expressed it in his diaries a little later.[36] Above all this, a poisonous, sulfur-yellow atmosphere spreads, immersing the agonizing wait and hesitant lingering of the figures at the end of the war in an uncanny, iridescent light. One is struck by the monumentality of the work, which bursts its format, producing discontent and a sense of discrepancy between the format and the depiction. The large painting is filled edge-to-edge with figures that Beckmann has placed one above the other in the style of the "Gothic verticalism" of his works from the early 1920s, making them seem even more crowded by crossing the edges of the painting.[37] Like an explosion of color and form captured in a moment, the overall impression created by means of a homogeneous palette and simple composition is dissociated again and again. It vanishes in the face of a particular searching vision that creates stability, which cannot organize the disorienting abundance into the fragments of reality that have been burned into the abstract canvas. This impression is also reinforced by the fact that, because of the nearly identical, planar, and unhierarchical structure of the side panels, Beckmann's dealer Curt Valentin had to ask which was the left and which the right panel of the triptych.[38] An astonishing occurrence. Dissolution, disconnectedness, and unrest are terms that could describe the vivid experience of *Blind Man's Buff*. Beckmann achieves a new quality: visually, the painting becomes a garish dance of colors and forms that spread as if in a kaleidoscope and take seeing to the edge of exhaustion.

In terms of its subject matter, *Blind Man's Buff* concludes the previous triptychs, some of which should be interpreted as very "historical": *Akrobaten* (1937–39) as a reflection on exile and "degeneration," as suggested above; *Perseus* (1940–41) as a reflection on the occupation and war of conquest; *Schauspieler* (Actors) (1941–42) as a reflection on the negation of state sovereignty; and *Karneval* (Carnival) (1942–43) as another reflection on expulsion, exile, and artistic production under occupation. All that can only be summarized here. The work is the polyvocal illustration of personal involvement, helplessness in the face of anonymous powers, and the impossibility of unambiguous knowledge. Located in the milieu of the grande bourgeoisie and the aristocracy, it sketches at the same time an almost nostalgic counterimage of the final stage of the war as he experienced it himself, which was certainly marked by hardship. Mathilde (Quappi) Beckmann in particular repeatedly recorded in her diaries the shortages of supplies and drastically increasing prices for food. Friends such as the art historian Erhard Göpel provided the couple with modest luxuries, such as coffee and so on now and again, and they never went hungry thanks to regular sales of paintings, auctions on the black market, and a comparatively privileged situation, even in the very hard winter of 1944–45, during which tens of thousands of people died. On the contrary, Quappi occasionally reported that they were even in a position to provide for starving children or strangers at their door.[39]

But *Blind Man's Buff* is just an interpretation of the present marked by fantasy. As a clear attempt to create a magnum opus, it compelled Beckmann in a metaphorical sense to continue as an artist, to attempt to create clarity about his own oeuvre not least by taking a position and openly expressing a return to his earlier work. For these reasons I am discussing this major work in such detail and addressing its fundamental issues. *Blind Man's*

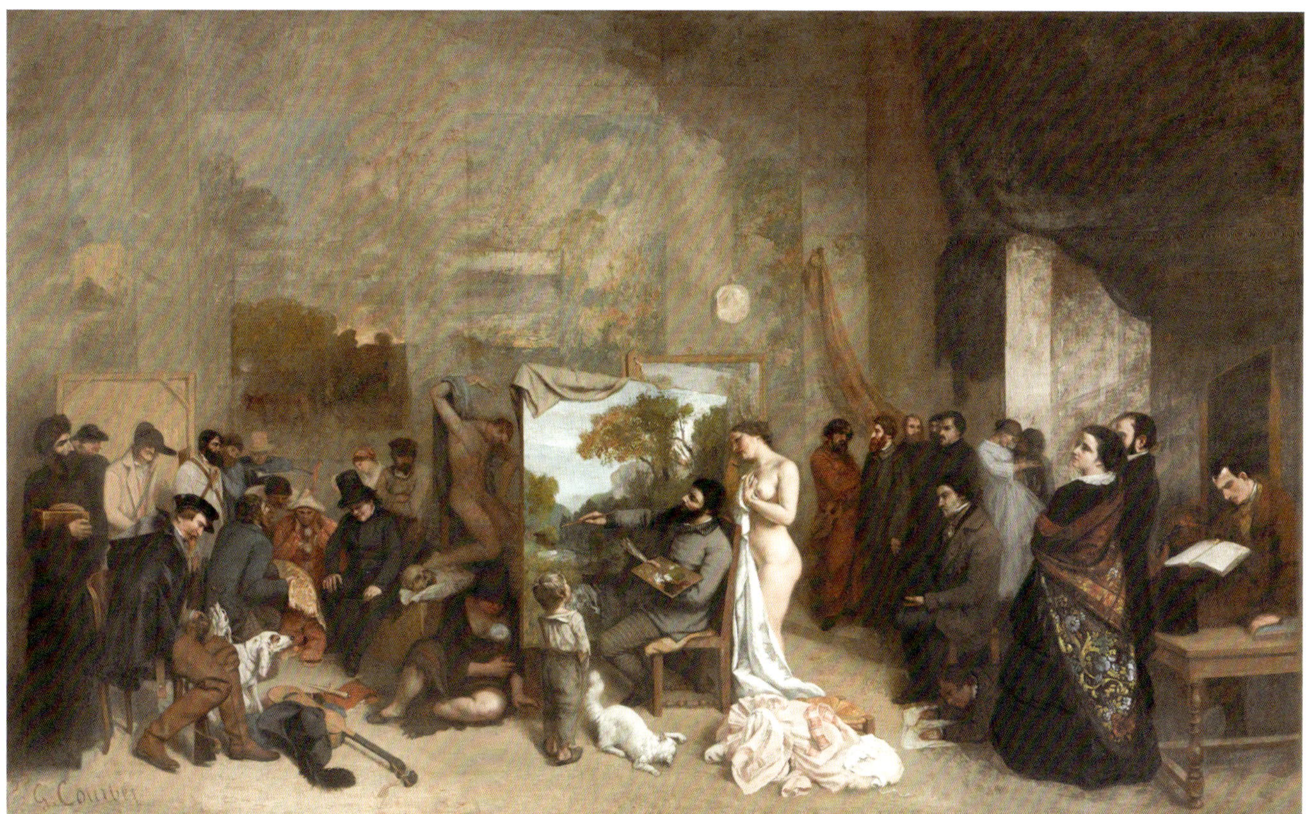

9. Gustave Courbet, *The Painter's Studio*, 1854–55, oil on canvas. Musée d'Orsay, Paris. Purchased with the support of the public and the Society of the Friends of the Louvre, 1920. Photo: Patrice Schmidt © RMN-Grand Palais / Art Resource, NY

Buff marks the beginning of Beckmann's late mythopoetic painting without representing a fundamental break in his oeuvre, which was in some respects established in self-reflexive retrospect with regard to his own works. This painting is the prelude to the late work in which Beckmann summed up his own painting and graphic art during the last five years of his life with a pessimism based on his experience of exile and war.

In the triptych *Blind Man's Buff*, Beckmann summed up his artistic ideas and realized a painting strikingly rich in allusions that could therefore function both as a summary of his life thus far and as a point of departure. In addition to the aforementioned role played by *Resurrection*, *Paris Society*, and the prints of the 1920s as foundations for a new image of society, Beckmann returned self-referentially to works such as the 1921 *Der Traum* (The Dream) [Plate 72], for the constellation of the central panel in general, and *Im Artistenwagen* (In the Artistes' Wagon) from 1940, for the figure of the observer on the left edge of the left panel. At the same time, the painter also returned to the influential role models for his early career, such as Luca Signorelli's *The School of Pan* from around 1488 [see Fig. 3 on p. 250] from the Kaiser-Friedrich-Museum in Berlin. That work, which burned during a bombing attack on the capital in the final days of the war, was an important influence on the prizewinning painting *Junge Männer am Meer* (Young Men by the Sea) from 1905 [see Fig. 1 on page 246], which established Beckmann's early career; he made a new version in 1943, around the same time that Beckmann was having Harry Graf Kessler's diary read aloud to him.

Beckmann also continued grappling with French modernism. First, he included a "self-portrait among the gods" in the form of a Minotaur wearing a tuxedo—a motif that alludes all too clearly to Surrealism and Picasso's work of the 1930s.[40] Second, the structure of the painting alludes to Gustave Courbet's monumental *L'atelier du peintre* (The Painter's Studio) [Fig. 9].[41] Courbet had referred to his giant painting a "real allegory," in a subtitle that called it the conclusion of a phase of his life lasting seven years.[42] Beckmann may have found resonance in this point of view and wanted to create an analogy for the conclusion of his own equivalent time in exile. In both works, the members of society are banished to the sides of the composition, while art reigns in the center. In Courbet's work, that took the form of the self-portrait of the painter working on a landscape and flanked by a model. She is at once his muse and an allegory of Truth. In Beckmann's work, it is the moody gods who determine the fate of humanity, who indifferently play their music in the face of the war's end and do not allow the lovers to unite. But it is also the painter himself, who wears evening dress in the self-portraits of 1923 and 1927 [see Plate 91 and p. 154] and in the role of the ox claims the position of his eternal rival Picasso and himself becomes God, something he had already called for in 1927 in his key text "*Der Künstler im Staat*" (The Artists in the State) but had not yet attempted in his art.

After the experience of a second world war, again lost and Germany now incriminated with terrible crimes,[43] he continued to work on an aesthetic solution to the essential problems of the early 1920s. After a critical diagnosis of the time as a decline of traditional values and of "cultural, aesthetic, and moral multiplicity,"[44] how can one create a unity to provide existential orientation? With his new paintings, of which there had been hints from the second half of the 1930s onward, but they only came together aesthetically as a result of the existential experiences of exile and war, he was able to overcome the moment of negation—in the sense of the inversion of traditional, Christian iconographies like those of *The Dream* of 1921.

Blind Man's Buff explicitly took up the ambition of the giant, long-abandoned *Resurrection* to "give people a picture of their fate." However, the painter no longer associated this with the programmatic, self-contradictory building of a "new church"[45] on the foundation of the old, smashed tablets and in an emphatically national stylistic idiom. With his new triptych, Beckmann was instead positioning himself equally in the art historical tradition and in French-influenced classical modernism. He was reflecting generally on the "intellectual products of humanity"[46] while at the same time referring to his own painting and graphic oeuvre, which he was now gradually updating and in part revising in his late works of the 1940s. In an artistic synthesis of a perspective so personal that it is sometimes impossible to understand, which results from the free aesthetic play with the aforementioned multiplicity of idioms derived from classical modernism, Beckmann's oeuvre reflects a crisis in painting of the early 1930s that is often not sufficiently recognized today, in addition to the existential challenge of National Socialism and ultimately the experience of exile.

Yet *Blind Man's Buff* is also undeniably evidence of the syncretic, metaphysical speculations in which Beckmann indulged all his life from the time of his early reading of Arthur Schopenhauer but especially after the National Socialists took power.[47] That does not make the matter simpler for us. *Blind Man's Buff* can, however, easily be interpreted as a reflection on a worldview influenced by Gnosticism that Beckmann had already developed around 1920. But that cannot be seen as its cause. Rather, the specific interpretative, instrumentalizing function of Gnosticism must be considered: it made it possible to interpret his experience of World War I, and he reflected on it as an interpretation that was linked to a specific time and hence was not universally valid.[48] In Beckmann's case, his processual, polysemantic pictorial invention constitutes an inherently fragile worldview than can scarcely be absorbed visually. The fundamental heterogeneity of his oeuvre cannot be derived from a preexisting worldview that determines the result, as it were. Each individual work doubtless has an interpretation of world events that offers a perspective, but it was very clear to the artist himself that, on the one hand, it was fictional at its core and, on the other hand, that it generated the painting:

> *I saw my paintings radiating on distant gods in the dark night—but—was that still me?—no—far from me, my poor self, they circled as autonomous creatures who looked down at me in scorn, "here we are" and "You n'éxiste plus"—oh ho—battle of the self-born gods against their inventor?—Now I too must bear—whether I want to or not—until beyond the great wall—then I will perhaps be myself and "dance the dance" of the gods—beyond my will and beyond my idea—and yet I myself. For all that should be clear to you is that I am fabricate such splendor from your unrestrained mystery. ("Oh—is it not us?!")*[49]

Transcendence and immanence are mediated and mirrored here in the metaphorical image—reflected on from an aesthetics of production—of a battle of "self-born gods" against "their inventor," so that in the end they can no longer be distinguished. He recognizes his own art as an illusory game and allows it to be valid as such. In the spirit of Nietzsche, who in his early text *Die Geburt der Tragödie aus dem Geiste der Musik* (The Birth of Tragedy from the Spirit of Music) had spoken of the necessary Apollonian illusion in the phase of the terrible Dionysian abyss,[50] this game is presumed to be at once necessary and fictional. I mention in passing that Beckmann was translating into painting precisely the two terms of Nietzsche's title: music and tragedy.

Beckmann's oeuvre reflects constant self-reflection and self-questioning. It could be said concisely that in his case it was about a kind of religiousness or, more precisely, a speculative "need for metaphysics" in Schopenhauer's sense, whose sources are sometimes free flowing and ubiquitous. The seventeenth chapter of the second volume of Schopenhauer's magnum opus *Die Welt als Wille und Vorstellung* (The World as Will and Representation) begins: "No beings, with the exception of man, feel surprised at their own existence [...]. It then marvels at its own works, and asks itself what it itself is. And its wonder is the more serious, as here for the first time it stands consciously face to face with death, and besides the finiteness of all existence, the vanity and fruitlessness of all effort force themselves on it more or less. Therefore, with this reflection and astonishment arises the *need for metaphysics* that is peculiar to man alone; accordingly, he is an *animal metaphysicum*."[51]

Beckmann's work should not be described as the implementation of preconceived pictorial ideas but rather as an never-ending artistic productivity borne from the will to continue and interpretate reality drawing on philosophy, literature, and religion because he wanted to believe but at the same time knew there was nothing more to believe in in the sense of a solid tradition that is passed down.[52] Painting had already lost any conviction in the validity of traditional faith during World War I, under the impression of Nietzsche's philosophy and his diagnosis of European nihilism and the discussion of the relativity of values, which had also affected the discourse of art critics at the time.[53] Beckmann's paintings offer an aesthetic solution to this no longer circumventable

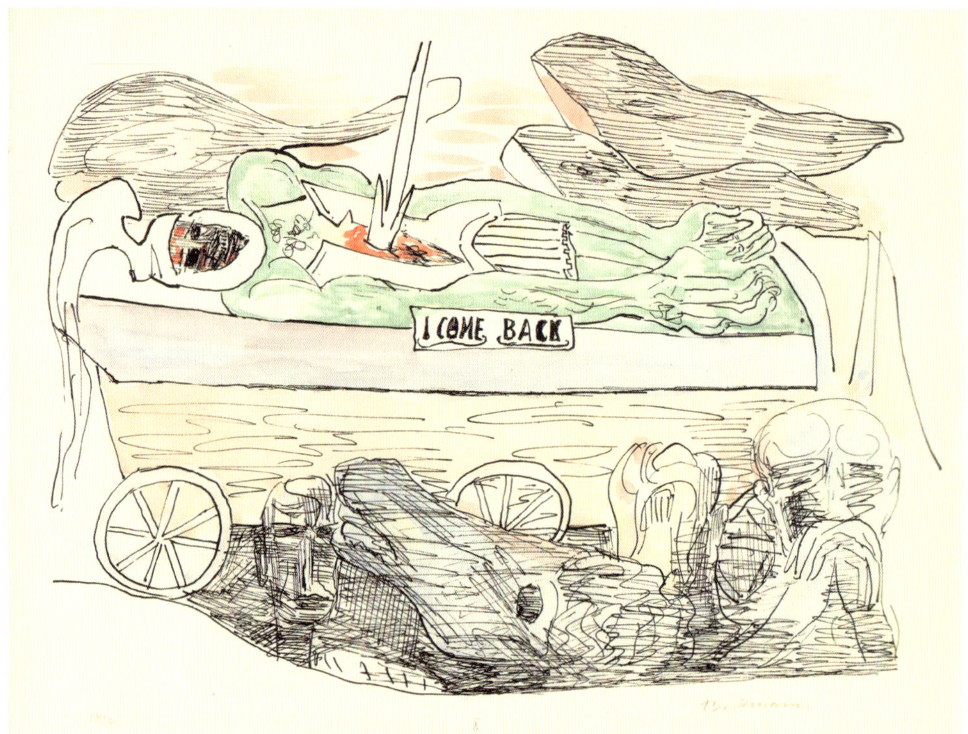

10. Max Beckmann, *The Dream of War*, Plate 10, *Day and Dream* portfolio, 1946. Private Collection

mental state of modernity because it calls into question but nevertheless holds out the prospect for recurring to traditional art, simulating new connections of meaning that have perhaps not yet been fathomed,[54] and faith. This resulted in the painter turning to the open play of an interpretive production of art that was well aware of its biographical and historical roots and particularity and thematized them in a self-reflexive way. Then one can once again say with Nietzsche, who understood "*myth* as a concentrated image of the world … as a condensation of phenomena": "But without myth every culture loses the healthy natural power of its creativity: only a horizon defined by myths completes and unifies a whole cultural movement."[55]

Beckmann could no longer recognize this unity. But as an individual he tried to realize such a unity in a solipsistic way, since painted myth at least graciously covered the black walls of the void surrounding humanity. With his artistic myth, he created a latent meaning, by no means one-dimensional but rather a multi-relational "fabric of ideas."[56] The artist wants to and must produce illusions to make existence bearable, even if, in the middle of the twentieth century, he no longer shares Nietzsche's optimism—then still tied to Richard Wagner's oeuvre—in a cultural movement that could produce unity. Nevertheless, Beckmann hoped to grant these fictions or illusions validity in a field of aesthetic options that is marked and determined by objective positions and his own subjective dispositions. More than any other work by the painter, *Blind Man's Buff* struggles with the claim to artistic recognition that he sought to guarantee by means of diverse allusions: allusions to the art of the Renaissance, to highly intellectual Symbolist art, to Courbet's realism of the nineteenth century, of the now historical achievements of the avant-garde, and its enduring will to painting that interprets the world. Beckmann was indeed wringing out a summa of modern art, and *Blind Man's Buff* is the prelude to his late work after the exile that was literally liberated, albeit pessimistically refracted owing to the circumstances of the time and the already emerging Cold War [Fig. 10].

Translated from the German by Steven Lindberg

1 On Beckmann's triptychs in general, see Charles S. Kessler, *Max Beckmann's Triptychs* (Cambridge, MA: Belknap Press of Harvard University Press, 1970); *Max Beckmann: Die Triptychen im Städel*, exh. cat. (Frankfurt am Main: Städtische Galerie im Städelschen Kunstinstitut, 1981); Peter J. Gärtner, *Der Traum von der Imagination des Raumes: Zu den Raumvorstellungen auf einigen ausgewählten Triptychen Max Beckmanns* (Weimar: VDG, 1996); Reinhard Spieler, *Max Beckmann: Bildwelt und Weltbild in den Triptychen* (Cologne: DuMont, 1998).

2 On this painting, see Kessler, *Max Beckmann's Triptychs* (see note 1), 37–42; Margot Ortwein Clark, *Max Beckmann: Sources of Imagery in the Hermetic Tradition* (Ann Arbor, MI: UMI Research Press, 1997), 268–85; *Max Beckmann: Die Triptychen im Städel* (see note 1); Spieler, *Max Beckmann* (see note 1), passim, and discussions based on it in Olaf Peters, *Vom schwarzen Seiltänzer: Max Beckmann zwischen Weimarer Republik und Exil* (Berlin: Reimer, 2005), 267–80.

3 This dating is based on a letter from Max Beckman to Jsrael Ber Neumann, in which he reported working on the triptych. Max Beckmann to Jsrael Ber Neumann, December 2, 1937, in *Max Beckmann und J. B: Neumann: Der Künstler und sein Händler in Briefen und Dokumenten, 1917–1950*, ed. Ursula Harter and Stephan von Wiese (Cologne: Walther König, 2011), 239.

4 See Wolfgang Pilz, *Das Triptychon als Kompositions- und Erzählform in der deutschen Tafelmalerei von den Anfängen bis zur Dürerzeit* (Munich: Wilhelm Fink, 1970), 17–21.

5 Cf. Max Erpel, *Max Beckmann: Leben im Werk; Die Selbstbildnisse* (East Berlin: Henschel, 1985), cat. no. 176.

6 See Max Beckmann, "Gespräch mit Lilly von Schnitzler über das Triptychon *Abfahrt*," in Beckmann, *Die Realität der Träume in den Bildern: Schriften und Gespräche, 1911 bis 1950*, ed. Rudolf Pillep (Munich: Piper, 1990), 46. On the relationship between Beckmann and the Schnitzlers, see *Erwerbungen, 2008–2010* (Munich: Max Beckmann Archiv, 2010).

7 On this, see Albrecht Tyrell, *Vom 'Trommler' zum 'Führer': Der Wandel von Hitlers Selbstverständnis zwischen 1919 und 1924 und die Entstehung der NSDAP* (Munich: Wilhelm Fink, 1975), and Ian Kershaw, *Hitler, 1889–1933: Hubris* (London: Allan Drury, 1998).

8 See also *Max Beckmann: Exile in Amsterdam*, exh. cat. Van Gogh Museum, Amsterdam, and Pinakothek der Moderne, Munich (Ostfildern: Hatje Cantz, 2007), esp. the discussion by Christian Lenz, 46–53.

9 For a detailed discussion of the iconography of bars and fetters, see Carla Schulz-Hoffmann, "Bars, Fetters, and Masks: The Problem of Constraint in the Work of Beckmann," trans. Barton Byg, in *Max Beckmann: Retrospective*, ed. Carla Schulz-Hoffmann and Judith C. Weiss, exh. cat. Saint Louis Art Museum et. al. (Munich: Prestel; New York: W. W. Norton, 1984), 15–52.

10 On this, see the standard work *Das Deutsche Reich und der Zweite Weltkrieg*, ed. Militärgeschichtliches Forschungsamt (Stuttgart: Deutsche Verlags-Anstalt, 1979–2008).

11 Max Beckmann, "On My Painting," in Beckmann, *Self-Portrait in Words: Collected Writings and Statements, 1903–1950*, ed. Barbara Copeland Buenger, trans. Barbara Copeland Buenger and Reinhold Heller with David Britt (Chicago, IL: University of Chicago Press, 1997), 298–307, esp. 303.

12 See Beckmann, *Die Realität der Träume* (see note 6), 28, and on the concept of the "theater of the world," see Stephan Lackner, "Das Welttheater des Malers Max Beckmann," in *Max Beckmann: Welt-Theater; Das graphische Werk, 1901–1946*, ed. Jo-Anne Birnie Danzker and Amélie Ziersch, exh. cat. Villa Stuck, Munich (Stuttgart: Hatje, 1993), 17–21, translated as Stephan Lackner, *Max Beckmann: Memories of a Friendship* (Coral Gables, FL: University of Miami Press, 1969); and Christian Lenz, "Das grosse dritte Auge Beckmanns: Die Welt ein Theater, das Leben ein Schauspiel, ein Traum," in *Max Beckmann: Beiträge, 2017* (Munich: Max Beckmann Archiv, 2017), 27–67. On the friendship between Max Beckmann and Stephan Lackner, see *Stephan Lackner, der Freund Max Beckmanns* (Munich: Max Beckmann Archiv, 2000).

13 See, in general, Donald E. Gordon, *Expressionism: Art and Idea* (New Haven, CT: Yale University Press, 1987).

14 On this, see Kurt Badt, "Artifex vates und Artifex rhetor," in Badt, *Kunsttheoretische Versuche: Ausgewählte Aufsätze*, ed. Lorenz Dittmann (Cologne: DuMont Schauberg, 1968), 39–83.

15 See Dietrich Schubert, *Wilhelm Lehmbruck: Catalogue raisonné der Skulpturen, 1898–1919* (Worms: Werner, 2001).

16 See *Degenerate Art: The Attack on Modern Art in Nazi Germany, 1937*, ed. Olaf Peters, exh. cat. Neue Galerie New York (Munich: Prestel, 2014), with bibliography.

17 For a detailed discussion, see Max Imdahl, *Picassos Guernica* (Frankfurt am Main: Insel, 1985), 67–96, esp. 90.

18 For an application of Aby Warburg's concept of the *Pathosformel* (pathos formula) to the modern triptych,

see the classic study by Klaus Lankheit, *Das Triptychon als Pathosformel* (Heidelberg: Winter, 1959).

19 See Max Imdahl, "Zu Picassos Bild 'Guernica': Inkohärenz und Kohärenz als Aspekte moderner Bildlichkeit" (1982), in Imdahl, *Gesammelte Schriften*, 3 vols. (Frankfurt am Main: Suhrkamp, 1996), 3:398–459, and Imdahl, *Picassos Guernica* (see note 17).

20 See Max Beckmann to Curt Valentin, February 11, 1938, in Max Beckmann, *Briefe*, ed. Klaus Gallwitz et al., 3 vols. (Munich: Piper, 1993–96), 3:29.

21 On this painting, see especially Kessler, *Max Beckmann's Triptychs* (see note 1), 69–76; Dagmar Walden-Awodu, *"Geburt" und "Tod": Max Beckmann im Amsterdamer Exil; Eine Untersuchung zur Entstehung seines Spätwerks* (Worms: Werner, 1995), 118–22; Spieler, *Max Beckmann* (see note 1), passim, and, based on that, Peters, *Vom schwarzen Seiltänzer* (see note 2), 382–400.

22 Christiane Zeiller has identified sketches from late June 1944 as the beginning of the artistic preparation for the triptych; the diary mentions work on a new triptych in September 1944. See Max Beckmann, *Die Skizzenbücher / The Sketchbooks*, ed. Max Beckmann Gesellschaft, Munich, and Bayerische Staatsgemäldesammlungen, Munich, trans. Allison Gallup and Steven Lindberg, 2 vols. (Ostfildern: Hatje Cantz, 2010), vol. 1: Sketchbook 1, 103, fols. 90v and 92r. The painting had been titled previously *Das Konzert* (The Concert), *Grosses Cafe* (Large Café), *Die grosse Bar* (The Large Bar), *Ochsenfest* (Ox Feast), and *Cabaret*. This illustrates the openness of Beckmann's approach to iconography. The definitive title was established before the painting was finished.

23 On the final phase of the war in the Netherlands, the northern parts of which remained under occupation and were largely spared the wartime actions, see Werner Warmbrunn, *The Dutch under German Occupation, 1940–1945* (Oxford: Oxford University Press, 1963), 13–17; Gerhard Hirschfeld, *Fremdherrschaft und Kollaboration: Die Niederlande unter deutscher Besatzung, 1940–1945* (Stuttgart: Deutsche Verlags-Anstalt, 1984), 33–38. On Beckmann in this period, see *Max Beckmann: Exile in Amsterdam* (see note 8), and Christian Lenz, *Max Beckmann* (Münster: Rhema, 2022), 171–232.

24 According to Quappi Beckmann, Beckmann himself identified the figures of the central panel as gods. See Kessler, *Max Beckmann's Triptychs* (see note 1), 70.

25 See Barbara C. Buenger, "Max Beckmann: 'Der Künstler im Staat,'" in *Überbrückt: Ästhetische Moderne und Nationalsozialismus; Kunsthistoriker und Künstler, 1925–1937*, ed. Eugen Blume and Dieter Scholz (Cologne: Walther König, 1999), 191–200.

26 On the effort to identify the people depicted, see Christian Fuhrmeister and Sabine Kienlechner, "Max Beckmann und der Widerstand in den Niederlanden: Überlegungen zu *Schauspieler* (1941/42), *Karneval* (1942/43), *Blindekuh* (1944/45) und *Argonauten* (1950)," in *Max Beckmann: Von Angesicht zu Angesicht*, exh. cat. Museum der bildenden Künste, Leipzig (Ostfildern: Hatje Cantz, 2011), 38–52, esp. 45–47.

27 Max Beckmann, diary entry on February 24, 1944, in Max Beckmann, *Tagebücher, 1940–1950*, 2nd ed. (Munich: Piper, 1987), 82.

28 See Max Beckmann, diary entry on March 28, 1944, in Beckmann, *Tagebücher* (see note 27), 86.

29 On the invasion in June 1944 and the westward advance of the Allies, see *Das Deutsche Reich* (see note 10), vol. 8, and Gerald Weinberg, *Eine Welt in Waffen: Die globale Geschichte des Zweiten Weltkriegs* (Stuttgart: Deutsche Verlags-Anstalt, 1995), 713–42.

30 See Beckmann's diary entries of September 18, 21, and 24, 1944, in Beckmann, *Tagebücher* (see note 27), 98–99. See also Mathilde Beckmann's diaries, which from early September 1944 repeatedly report on the nerve-racking waiting for the Allied invasion, which for tactical reasons did not occur until May 1945. Mathilde Beckmann Diaries, Archives of American Art (hereafter AAA), Washington, DC.

31 Because of the strained state of his health, Beckmann feared he would not survive until the end of the war. See his diary entry of March 28, 1945, in Beckmann, *Tagebücher* (see note 27), 114.

32 In this context, see Barbara and Erhard Göpel, *Max Beckmann: Katalog der Gemälde*, 2 vols. (Bern: Kornfeld, 1976), 1:244, and the discussions in Buenger, "Max Beckmann" (see note 25), 196–98.

33 On the artistic context of these ambitions, see *Max Beckmann and Paris: Matisse, Picasso, Braque, Léger, Rouault*, ed. Tobia Bezzola and Cornelia Homburg, exh. cat. Kunsthaus Zürich, and Saint Louis Art Museum (Cologne: Taschen, 1998), and Christian Lenz, "Max Beckmann und Paris," in *Max Beckmann: Beiträge, 2019* (Munich: Max Beckmann Archiv, 2019), 16–56.

34 See Beckmann, *Tagebücher* (see note 27), 114.

35 Beckmann's note from around 1950 in Beckmann, *Die Realität der Träume* (see note 6), 78.

36 See Beckmann's diary entry of July 17, 1950, in Beckmann, *Tagebücher* (see note 27), 396.

37 On the concept of "Gothic verticalism," see Sixten Ringbom, *From Icon to Narrative: The Rise of the Dramatic Close-up in Fifteenth-Century Devotional Painting*, 2nd ed. (Doornspijk: Davaco, 1983; orig. pub. 1965), 156–57.

38 See Curt Valentin to Max Beckmann, February 19, 1947; Curt Valentin Papers, Series III, Box 4; MoMA Archives, New York. Valentin, who was able to sell the work immediately—see his letter of March 17, 1947—received a sketch from Beckmann with the note that the smaller wing should be hung in relation to the middle of the central panel. See Max Beckmann to Curt Valentin, February 25, 1947, in Beckmann, *Briefe* (see note 20), 3:148–50, esp. 149.

39 See the diary entries of March 11 and 18, 1945 (Book 7) in Mathilde Beckmann Diaries, AAA, Washington, DC.

40 On the Surrealist journal *Minotaure*, which was published between 1933 and 1939, and on Picasso's variations on this mythological theme, see *Pablo Picasso: A Retrospective*, ed. William Rubin, exh. cat. (New York: Museum of Modern Art, 1980–81), 312–35.

41 On Courbet, see Michael Fried, *Courbet's Realism* (Chicago: University of Chicago Press, 1990), 148–88, and Werner Hofmann, *Das Atelier: Courbets Jahrhundertbild* (Munich: C. H. Beck, 2010).

42 See Klaus Herding, "Das Atelier des Malers: Treffpunkt der Welt und Ort der Versöhnung," in *Realismus als Widerspruch: Die Wirklichkeit in Courbets Malerei*, ed. Klaus Herding (Frankfurt am Main: Suhrkamp, 1978), 223–47, esp. 226.

43 See Beckmam's diary entries of May 9, 19, and 20, 1945, in Beckmann, *Tagebücher* (see note 27), 120–21, which reveal his shock over the horrors discovered and at the same time a certain critique of the judgement or "deformation" of the Germans. As late as November 30, 1945, after seeing a film on Stalingrad, Beckmann noted: "In the image of humanity, the disparagement and brutalization of the vanquished is always atrocious." Beckmann, *Tagebücher* (see note 27), 144.

44 See, with a wealth of evidence that helps to underscore the problems Beckmann was addressing at the time, Ulrich Schulz-Buschhaus, "Multiplizität der Kultur und Einheit des Lebens: Über ein Fin-de-siècle-Motiv in Robert Musils *Mann ohne Eigenschaften*," in *Fin de Siècle*, ed. Rainer Warning and Winfried Wehle (Munich: Wilhelm Fink, 2002), 321–73, esp. 322.

45 See Max Beckmann, "Creative Credo," in Beckmann, *Self-Portrait in Words* (see note 3), 181–85, esp. 185.

46 See Max Beckmann, "The Artist in the State," in Beckmann, *Self-Portrait in Words* (see note 3), 284–90, esp. 288.

47 The influence of Helena Blavatsky's *Secret Doctrine*, which he read several times, is only evident from around 1934 onward. See *Die Bibliothek Max Beckmanns: Unterstreichungen, Kommentare, Notizen, Skizzen in seinen Büchern*, ed. Peter Beckmann and Joachim Schaffer (Worms: Werner, 1992), and Thomas Noll, "Max Beckmann und die Geheimlehre der Helena P. Blavatsky," in *Max Beckmann: Beiträge, 2004–2005* (Munich: Max Beckmann Archiv, 2006), 45–74.

48 The wealth of motifs from Christianity and classical mythology in the painter's late work is an indication that there were competing interpretive models for Beckmann. Cf. *King Saul* (1947); *Christus in der Vorhölle* (Christ in Limbo) (1948); *Der verlorene Sohn* (The Prodigal Son) (1949); and *Perseus' (Herkules') letzte Aufgabe* (Perseus' [Hercules'] Last Duty) (1949).

49 Beckmann's diary entry of October 19, 1943, while working on his triptych *Karneval* (1942–43), in Beckmann, *Tagebücher* (see note 27), 72.

50 See Friedrich Nietzsche, *The Birth of Tragedy*, in *Basic Writings of Nietzsche*, ed. and trans. Walter Kaufmann (New York: Modern Library, 1968), 3–144, sections 2 to 4.

51 Arthur Schopenhauer, *The World as Will and Representation*, trans. E. F. J. Payne, 2 vols (New York: Dover, 1966), 2:160. Mathilde Beckmann urgently pointed to the crucial, almost "uncanny" significance of Schopenhauer for Beckmann in a diary entry of May 2, 1943 (Book 2). Mathilde Beckmann Diaries; AAA, Washington, DC.

52 On the loss of the Christian tradition and faith in the nineteenth century, see Walter Rehm, *Experimentum Medietatis: Studien zur Geistes- und Kulturgeschichte des 19. Jahrhunderts* (Munich: H. Rinn, 1947), 7–95. The author analyses the authors Jean Paul and Fyodor Dostoevsky, who were central for Beckmann.

53 For a comprehensive account of Beckmann's "worldview," see Christian Lenz, "Die Weltanschauung Max Beckmanns, nach schriftlichen Zeugnissen," in *Max Beckmann: Beiträge, 2016* (Munich: Max Beckmann Archiv, 2016), 47–88.

54 That is why Beckmann spoke of discovering backdrops and a visual theater (Bildtheater). See Beckmann, *Tagebücher* (see note 27), 338.

55 Nietzsche, *The Birth of Tragedy* (see note 50), section 23, 135 (emphasis original).

56 See Beckmann's diary entry from late July 1944, in Beckmann, *Tagebücher* (see note 27), 94.

CHECKLIST

1
Self-Portrait in Bowler Hat, 1921
Drypoint
53.7 x 41.9 cm (21 1/8 x 16 1/2 in.)
The Museum of Modern Art, New York. Gift of Edward M. M. Warburg

2
Society, 1915
Etching, drypoint
33.6 x 47.5 cm (13 1/4 x 18 3/4 in.)
Sprengel Museum Hannover

3
Declaration of War, Plate 3, Annual Fair portfolio, 1914
Drypoint etching
20 x 24.9 cm (7 7/8 x 9 3/4 in.)
Staatliche Museen zu Berlin, Kupferstichkabinett

4
Café (Two Old Women in Foreground), printed 1916, published 1918
Drypoint
36.2 x 44.3 cm (14 1/4 x 17 7/16 in.)
Publisher: J. B. Neumann, Berlin
The Museum of Modern Art, New York. Gift of Samuel A. Berger

5
Street II, 1916–17, dated 1917
Drypoint
Publisher: J. B. Neumann, Berlin
Printer: Max Beckmann, Frankfurt
The Museum of Modern Art, New York. Gift of Victor S. Riesenfeld

6
Open Latrine House (Villa Kratzfried), 1915
Ink on paper
23.5 x 32 cm (9 1/4 x 12 5/8 in.)
Kunsthalle Bremen

7
Hilly Landscape against the Sun, 1915
Ink on paper
24 x 31.8 cm (9 1/2 x 12 1/2 in.)
Kunsthalle Mannheim

8
Morgue, printed 1922, published 1924
Woodcut
52.8 x 75.5 cm (20 13/16 x 29 3/4 in.)
Publisher: Paul Cassirer, Berlin
The Museum of Modern Art, New York. Gift of Abby Aldrich Rockefeller (by exchange)

9
Morgue, printed 1915, published 1918
Drypoint
37.3 x 54 cm (14 11/16 x 21 1/4 in.)
Publisher: Paul Cassirer, Berlin
Printer: probably Pan-Presse, Berlin
The Museum of Modern Art, New York. Purchase

10
The Grenade, 1915, published 1918
Drypoint
54 x 45 cm (21 1/4 x 17 11/16 in.)
Publisher: Paul Cassirer, Berlin
Printer: probably Pan-Presse, Berlin
The Museum of Modern Art, New York. Mary Ellen Meehan Fund, Johanna and Leslie J. Garfield Fund, and Frances Keech Fund

11
Portrait of Senior Medical Officer Prof. Dr. Philaletes Kuhn 1915
Pencil on paper
34.1 x 24.2 cm (13 7/16 x 9 15/16 in.)
Private Collection

12
Self-Portrait, Hand to Cheek, 1916
Drypoint
36.4 x 27.4 cm (14 5/16 x 10 13/16 in.)
The Museum of Modern Art, New York. Gift of Mr. and Mrs. Carroll Cartwright

13
Self-Portrait in Half Profile to the Left, 1917
Pencil on paper
41 x 31.5 cm (16 1/8 x 12 3/8 in.)
Staatliche Museen zu Berlin, Kupferstichkabinett. Bequest of Barbara Göpel (Donation of Erhard and Barbara Göpel)

14
Self-Portrait as Medical Orderly, 1915
Pencil on paper
36.2 x 25.3 cm (14 1/4 x 10 in.)
Private Collection

15
Self-Portrait, 1917
Pen and ink on paper
38.7 x 31.6 cm (15 1/4 x 12 1/2 in.)
The Art Institute of Chicago. Gift of Mr. and Mrs. Allan Frumkin

16
Seated Boy, 1918
Graphite on paper
50.4 x 32.9 cm (19 7/8 x 13 in.)
The Art Institute of Chicago. Gift of the Print and Drawing Club

17
The Defendants, 1916
Oil on canvas
47.5 x 65 cm (18 3/4 x 25 5/8 in.)
Kunsthalle Bremen

18
Landscape with Balloon, 1917
Oil on canvas
75.5 x 100.5 cm (29 $^{3}/_{4}$ x 39 $^{1}/_{2}$ in.)
Museum Ludwig, Cologne / Purchase 1954

19
Hallucination I, 1916
Pencil on paper
29.2 x 21.7 cm (11 $^{1}/_{2}$ x 8 $^{1}/_{2}$ in.)
Kunsthalle Mannheim

20
Adam and Eve, printed 1917, published 1918
Drypoint
46.8 x 35.9 cm (18 $^{7}/_{16}$ x 14 $^{1}/_{8}$ in.)
Publisher: J. B. Neumann, Berlin
The Museum of Modern Art, New York. Larry Aldrich Fund

21
Adam and Eve, 1917
Oil on canvas
79.8 x 56.7 cm (31 $^{3}/_{8}$ x 22 $^{3}/_{8}$ in.)
Neue Nationalgalerie, Staatliche Museen zu Berlin. Acquired with the support of the Ernst von Siemens Kunststiftung

22
Christ and the Sinner, 1917
Oil on canvas
149.2 x 126.7 cm (58 $^{3}/_{4}$ x 49 $^{7}/_{8}$ in.)
Saint Louis Art Museum. Bequest of Curt Valentin

23
Descent from the Cross, 1917
Oil on canvas
151.2 x 128.9 cm (59 $^{1}/_{2}$ x 50 $^{3}/_{4}$ in.)
The Museum of Modern Art, New York. Curt Valentin Bequest

24
Women's Bath, 1919
Oil on canvas
97.5 x 65 cm (38 $^{3}/_{8}$ x 25 $^{5}/_{8}$ in.)
Neue Nationalgalerie, Staatliche Museen zu Berlin. Acquired by the Federal State of Berlin in 1968

25
Self-Portrait, Plate 1, Faces portfolio, printed 1918, published 1919
Drypoint
45.1 x 35.6 cm (17 $^{3}/_{4}$ x 14 in.)
Publisher: Marées-Gesellschaft, R. Piper & Co., Munich
Printer: Franz Hanfstaengl, Munich
The Museum of Modern Art, New York. Abby Aldrich Rockefeller Fund

26
Family Scene (Beckmann Family), Plate 2, Faces portfolio, printed 1918, published 1919
Drypoint
45 x 37 cm (17 $^{11}/_{16}$ x 14 $^{9}/_{16}$ in.)
Publisher: Marées-Gesellschaft, R. Piper & Co., Munich
Printer: Franz Hanfstaengl, Munich
The Museum of Modern Art, New York. Abby Aldrich Rockefeller Fund

27
Madhouse, Plate 3, Faces portfolio, printed 1918, published 1919
Drypoint
37 x 36.7 cm (14 $^{9}/_{16}$ x 14 $^{7}/_{16}$ in.)
Publisher: Marées-Gesellschaft, R. Piper & Co., Munich
Printer: Franz Hanfstaengl, Munich
The Museum of Modern Art, New York. Purchase

28
Lovers I, Plate 4, Faces portfolio, printed 1916, published 1919
Drypoint
29.8 x 36.9 cm (11 $^{3}/_{4}$ x 14 $^{1}/_{2}$ in.)
Publisher: Marées-Gesellschaft, R. Piper & Co., Munich
Printer: Franz Hanfstaengl, Munich
The Museum of Modern Art, New York. Purchase

29
Lovers II, Plate 5, Faces portfolio, printed 1918, published 1919
Drypoint
29.8 x 37.2 cm (11 $^{3}/_{4}$ x 14 $^{5}/_{8}$ in.)
Publisher: Marées-Gesellschaft, R. Piper & Co., Munich
Printer: Franz Hanfstaengl, Munich
The Museum of Modern Art, New York. Abby Aldrich Rockefeller Fund

30
Main River Landscape, Plate 6, Faces portfolio, printed 1918, published 1919
Drypoint
37.3 x 36.6 cm (14 $^{11}/_{16}$ x 14 $^{7}/_{16}$ in.)
Publisher: Marées-Gesellschaft, R. Piper & Co., Munich
Printer: Franz Hanfstaengl, Munich
The Museum of Modern Art, New York. Abby Aldrich Rockefeller Fund

31
The Yawners, Plate 7, Faces portfolio, printed 1918, published 1919
Drypoint
45 x 36.9 cm (17 $^{11}/_{16}$ x 14 $^{1}/_{2}$ in.)
Publisher: Marées-Gesellschaft, R. Piper & Co., Munich
Printer: Franz Hanfstaengl, Munich
The Museum of Modern Art, New York. Abby Aldrich Rockefeller Fund

32
Theater, Plate 8, Faces portfolio, printed 1917, published 1919
Drypoint
24.1 x 32.7 cm (9 $^{1}/_{2}$ x 12 $^{7}/_{8}$ in.)
Publisher: Marées-Gesellschaft, R. Piper & Co., Munich
Printer: Franz Hanfstaengl, Munich
The Museum of Modern Art, New York. Purchase

33
Café Music, Plate 9, Faces portfolio, printed 1918, published 1919
Drypoint
44 x 37 cm (17 $^{5}/_{16}$ x 14 $^{9}/_{16}$ in.)
Publisher: Marées-Gesellschaft, R. Piper & Co., Munich
Printer: Franz Hanfstaengl, Munich
The Museum of Modern Art, New York. Abby Aldrich Rockefeller Fund

34
Evening (Self-Portrait with the Battenbergs), Plate 10, Faces portfolio, printed 1917, published 1919
Drypoint
30.4 x 24.1 cm (12 x 9 1/2 in.)
Publisher: Marées-Gesellschaft, R. Piper & Co., Munich
Printer: Franz Hanfstaengl, Munich
The Museum of Modern Art, New York. Abby Aldrich Rockefeller Fund

35
Descent from the Cross, Plate 11, Faces portfolio, printed 1918, published 1919
Drypoint
45 x 37 cm (17 11/16 x 14 9/16 in.)
Publisher: Marées-Gesellschaft, R. Piper & Co., Munich
Printer: Franz Hanfstaengl, Munich
The Museum of Modern Art, New York. Gift of Mrs. Bertha M. Slattery

36
Resurrection, Plate 12, Faces portfolio, printed 1918, published 1919
Drypoint
36.5 x 44.6 cm (14 3/8 x 17 9/16 in.)
Publisher: Marées-Gesellschaft, R. Piper & Co., Munich
Printer: Franz Hanfstaengl, Munich
The Museum of Modern Art, New York. Abby Aldrich Rockefeller Fund

37
Spring, Plate 13, Faces portfolio, printed 1917, published 1919
Drypoint
37.5 x 29 cm (14 3/4 x 11 7/16 in.)
Publisher: Marées-Gesellschaft, R. Piper & Co., Munich
Printer: Franz Hanfstaengl, Munich
The Museum of Modern Art, New York. Abby Aldrich Rockefeller Fund

38
Landscape with Balloon, Plate 14, Faces portfolio, printed 1918, published 1919
Drypoint
29.8 x 36.9 cm (11 3/4 x 14 1/2 in.)
Publisher: Marées-Gesellschaft, R. Piper & Co., Munich
Printer: Franz Hanfstaengl, Munich
The Museum of Modern Art, New York. Abby Aldrich Rockefeller Fund

39
Two Auto Officers, Plate 15, Faces portfolio, printed 1915, published 1919
Drypoint
18.2 x 22.6 cm (7 3/16 x 8 7/8 in.)
Publisher: Marées-Gesellschaft, R. Piper & Co., Munich
Printer: Franz Hanfstaengl, Munich
The Museum of Modern Art, New York. Abby Aldrich Rockefeller Fund

40
Playing Children, Plate 16, Faces portfolio, printed 1918, published 1919
Drypoint
37 x 36.9 cm (14 9/16 x 14 1/2 in.)
Publisher: Marées-Gesellschaft, R. Piper & Co., Munich
Printer: Franz Hanfstaengl, Munich
The Museum of Modern Art, New York. Purchase

41
Happy New Year 1917. Plate 17, Faces portfolio, printed 1917, published 1919
Drypoint
29.8 x 37.2 cm (11 3/4 x 14 5/8 in.)
Publisher: Marées-Gesellschaft, R. Piper & Co., Munich
Printer: Max Beckmann, Frankfurt
The Museum of Modern Art, New York. Gift of Victor S. Risenfeld

42
The Large Operation, Plate 18, Faces portfolio, printed ca. 1914, published 1919
Drypoint
37 x 52.2 cm (14 9/16 x 20 9/16 in.)
Publisher: Marées-Gesellschaft, R. Piper & Co., Munich
Printer: Franz Hanfstaengl, Munich
The Museum of Modern Art, New York. Abby Aldrich Rockefeller Fund

43
Self-Portrait with Stylus, Plate 19, Faces portfolio, 1919
Drypoint
44.8 x 37.1 cm (17 5/8 x 14 5/8 in.)
Publisher: Marées-Gesellschaft, R. Piper & Co., Munich
Printer: Franz Hanfstaengl, Munich
The Museum of Modern Art, New York. Gift of Edgar J. Kaufmann, Jr.

44
Self-Portrait, front cover, Hell portfolio, 1919
Lithograph
64.5 x 41.7 cm (24 15/16 x 16 7/16 in.)
Publisher: J. B. Neumann, Berlin
Printer: C. Naumann's Druckerei, Frankfurt am Main
The Museum of Modern Art, New York. Purchase

45
The Way Home, Plate 2, Hell portfolio, 1919
Lithograph
87.3 x 61.2 cm (34 3/8 x 24 1/8 in.)
Publisher: J. B. Neumann, Berlin
Printer: C. Naumann's Druckerei, Frankfurt am Main
The Museum of Modern Art, New York. Abby Aldrich Rockefeller Fund

46
The Street, Plate 3, Hell portfolio, 1919
Lithograph
87.3 x 61.2 cm (34 3/8 x 24 1/8 in.)
Publisher: J. B. Neumann, Berlin
Printer: C. Naumann's Druckerei, Frankfurt am Main
The Museum of Modern Art, New York. Larry Aldrich Fund

47
The Martyrdom, Plate 4, Hell portfolio, 1919
Lithograph
61.7 x 87.2 cm (24 5/16 x 34 5/16 in.)
Publisher: J. B. Neumann, Berlin
Printer: C. Naumann's Druckerei, Frankfurt am Main
The Museum of Modern Art, New York. Larry Aldrich Fund

48
Hunger, Plate 5, Hell portfolio, 1919
Lithograph
80.7 x 61.2 cm (31 3/4 x 24 1/8 in.)
Publisher: J. B. Neumann, Berlin
Printer: C. Naumann's Druckerei, Frankfurt am Main
The Museum of Modern Art, New York. Larry Aldrich Fund

49
The Ideologues, Plate 6, Hell portfolio, 1919
Lithograph
87 x 61.5 cm (34 1/4 x 24 3/16 in.)
Publisher: J. B. Neumann, Berlin
Printer: C. Naumann's Druckerei, Frankfurt am Main
The Museum of Modern Art, New York. Larry Aldrich Fund

50
Night, Plate 7, Hell portfolio, 1919
Lithograph
61.4 x 87.2 cm (24 3/16 x 34 5/16 in.)
Publisher: J. B. Neumann, Berlin
Printer: C. Naumann's Druckerei, Frankfurt am Main
The Museum of Modern Art, New York. Abby Aldrich Rockefeller Fund

51
Malepartus, Plate 8, Hell portfolio, 1919
Lithograph
87.5 x 61.3 cm (34 7/16 x 24 1/8 in.)
Publisher: J. B. Neumann, Berlin
Printer: C. Naumann's Druckerei, Frankfurt am Main
The Museum of Modern Art, New York. Larry Aldrich Fund

52
The Patriotic Song, Plate 9, Hell portfolio, 1919
Lithograph
87 x 61.1 cm (34 1/4 x 24 1/16 in.)
Publisher: J. B. Neumann, Berlin
Printer: C. Naumann's Druckerei, Frankfurt am Main
The Museum of Modern Art, New York. Larry Aldrich Fund

53
The Last Ones, Plate 10, Hell portfolio, 1919
Lithograph
86.8 x 61.2 cm (34 3/16 x 24 1/8 in.)
Publisher: J. B. Neumann, Berlin
Printer: C. Naumann's Druckerei, Frankfurt am Main
The Museum of Modern Art, New York. Larry Aldrich Fund

54
The Family, Plate 11, Hell portfolio, 1919
Lithograph
86.5 x 61 cm (34 1/16 x 24 in.)
Publisher: J. B. Neumann, Berlin
Printer: C. Naumann's Druckerei, Frankfurt am Main
The Museum of Modern Art, New York. Larry Aldrich Fund

55
Title page, City Night portfolio, 1920
Lithograph
30.8 x 25 cm (12 1/8 x 9 3/4 in.)
Saarlandmuseum, Saarbrücken

56
Drinking Song, Plate 1, City Night portfolio, 1920
Lithograph
30.8 x 24 cm (12 1/8 x 9 1/2 in.)
Saarlandmuseum, Saarbrücken

57
City Night, Plate 2, City Night portfolio, 1920
Lithograph
30.7 x 24.5 cm (12 1/8 x 9 5/8 in.)
Saarlandmuseum, Saarbrücken

58
Bitterness, Plate 3, City Night portfolio, 1920
Lithograph
30.6 x 24.5 cm (12 x 9 5/8 in.)
Saarlandmuseum, Saarbrücken

59
Suburban Morning, Plate 4, City Night portfolio, 1920
Lithograph
30.5 x 24.5 cm (12 x 9 5/8 in.)
Saarlandmuseum, Saarbrücken

60
Furnished Room, Plate 5, City Night portfolio, 1920
Lithograph
30.6 x 24.6 cm (12 x 9 5/8 in.)
Saarlandmuseum, Saarbrücken

61
The Sick One, Plate 6, City Night portfolio, 1920
Lithograph
30.6 x 24.4 cm (12 x 9 5/8 in.)
Saarlandmuseum, Saarbrücken

62
Beach Scene, ca. 1924
Pencil on paper
18.5 x 22.6 cm (7 1/4 x 8 7/8 in.)
Staatliche Museen zu Berlin, Kupferstichkabinett

63
In the Tram, 1922
Drypoint
29.8 x 43.8 cm (11 3/4 x 17 1/4 in.)
Museum of Fine Arts, Boston. Print Club Acquisition Fund

64
Self-Portrait, 1922
Woodcut
49.4 x 35 cm (19 7/16 x 13 3/4 in.)
Publisher: R. Piper & C., Munich
The Museum of Modern Art, New York. Given anonymously

65
Self-Portrait on Yellow Ground with Cigarette, 1923
Oil on canvas
60.2 x 40.3 cm (23 3/4 x 15 7/8 in.)
The Museum of Modern Art, New York.
Gift of Dr. and Mrs. F. H. Hirschland

66
Family Picture, 1920
Oil on canvas
65.1 x 100.9 cm (25 5/8 x 39 3/4 in.)
The Museum of Modern Art, New York.
Gift of Abby Aldrich Rockefeller

67
Carnival, 1920
Oil on canvas
186.4 x 91.8 cm (73 3/8 x 36 1/8 in.)
Tate. Purchased with assistance from the Art Fund and Friends of the Tate Gallery and Mercedes Benz (U.K.) Ltd. 1981

68
Carnival (design for painting), 1920
Ink on paper
25.8 x 16.8 cm (10 1/8 x 6 5/8 in.)
Staatliche Museen zu Berlin, Kupferstichkabinett. Bequest of Barbara Göpel (Donation of Erhard and Barbara Göpel)

69
Kasbek, 1923
Drypoint
64.5 x 35.9 cm (25 3/8 x 14 1/8 in.)
Sprengel Museum Hannover

70
Tamerlan, printed 1923, published 1924
Drypoint
57.7 x 45.5 cm (22 11/16 x 17 15/16 in.)
Publisher: Paul Cassirer, Berlin
The Museum of Modern Art, New York.
Larry Aldrich Fund

71
Dream I (Funeral Dirge), 1924
Drypoint
61.7 x 38.1 cm (24 5/16 x 15 in.)
Printer: Heinrich Wetteroth
Museum of Fine Arts, Boston.
Lee M. Friedman Fund

72
The Dream, 1921
Oil on canvas
181.9 x 91 cm (71 5/8 x 35 13/16 in.)
Saint Louis Art Museum,
Bequest of Morton D. May

73
The Trapeze, 1923
Oil on canvas
196.5 x 84.5 cm (77 3/8 x 33 1/8 in.)
Toledo Museum of Art. Purchased with funds from the Libbey Endowment, Gift of Edward Drummond Libbey

74
Landscape near Frankfurt (with Factory), 1922
Oil on canvas
66 x 100.97 cm (26 x 39 3/4 in.)
Rose Art Museum. Gift of Mr. and Mrs. Henry N. Abrams

75
Still-Life with Fish and Pinwheel, 1923
Oil on canvas
60.5 x 40.3 cm (23 7/8 x 15 15/16 in.)
Weisman Art Museum. Gift of Ione and Hudson Walker

76
Sleeping Woman, 1924
Oil on canvas
48 x 61 cm (18 7/8 x 24 in.)
Private Collection

77
Fridel Battenberg, 1917
Ink on paper
48.3 x 37.5 cm (19 x 14 3/4 in.)
Kunsthalle Mannheim

78
Portrait of Fridel Battenberg, 1917
Lithograph
35.1 x 25 cm (13 3/4 x 9 3/4 in.)
Kunsthalle Mannheim

79
Portrait of Reinhard Piper, 1920
Drypoint
46.2 x 29.1 cm (18 1/4 x 11 1/2 in.)
The Art Institute of Chicago.
Gift of Mr. Henry Schaefer-Simmern

80
Portrait of Reinhard Piper, 1922
Woodcut
42.2 x 29 cm (16 5/8 x 11 7/16 in.)
Publisher: R. Piper & Co., Munich
The Museum of Modern Art, New York.
Larry Aldrich Fund

81
Georg Swarzenski, ca. 1921
Crayon and graphite on paper
41.6 x 31.8 cm (16 5/16 x 12 1/2 in.)
Ackland Art Museum, University of North Carolina at Chapel Hill.
Ackland Fund

82
Portrait of Mrs. Marie Swarzenski, 1921
Woodcut
43.2 x 30.5 cm (17 x 12 in.)
The Yang Friedman Collection

83
Entertainment, ca. 1922
Pencil on paper
21.7 x 29 cm (8 1/2 x 11 3/8 in.)
Staatliche Museen zu Berlin,
Kupferstichkabinett

84
J. B. Neumann and Martha Stern, 1922
Lithograph
49.4 x 61.1 cm (19 7/16 x 24 1/16 in.)
Publisher: J. B. Neumann, berlin
The Museum of Modern Art, New York.
Abby Aldrich Rockefeller Fund

85
Königin Bar II, 1923
Drypoint
54.5 x 34.8 cm (21 7/16 x 13 11/16 in.)
Publisher: Verlag Jakob Hermelin, Ulm
Printer: Heinrich Wetteroth, Munich
The Museum of Modern Art, New York.
Gift of Mr. and Mrs. Eugene Victor Thaw

86
Portrait of J. B. Neumann, 1919
Drypoint
43.4 x 32.2 cm (17 1/8 x 12 11/16 in.)
The Art Institute of Chicago.
Gift of the Print and Drawing Club

87
Dancing Couple, 1922
Woodcut
37.4 x 25.2 cm (14 3/4 x 9 15/16 in.)
Publisher: R. Piper & Co., Munich
The Museum of Modern Art, New York.
Purchase

88
Paris Society, 1925/1931/1947
Oil on canvas
109.2 x 175.6 cm (43 x 69 1/8 in.)
Solomon R. Guggenheim Museum

89
Romanian Woman (Sketch for the Portrait of Mrs. Heiden), 1922
Pencil on paper
63.5 x 45.8 cm (24 x 18 in.)
Kunsthalle Bremen

90
Portrait of the Dancer Sent M'Ahesa, 1921
Lithograph
62.7 x 50.9 cm (24 5/8 x 20 in.)
Kunsthalle Mannheim

91
Self-Portrait in front of Red Curtain, 1923
Oil on canvas
122.9 x 59.2 cm (48 3/8 x 23 5/16 in.)
From a Private Collection

92
Portrait of Elsbet Götz, 1924
Oil on canvas
95.5 x 35.5 cm (37 5/8 x 14 in.)
Museum Behnhaus Drägerhaus

93
Portrait of Minna Beckmann-Tube, 1924
Oil on canvas
92.8 x 73 cm (36 1/2 x 28 3/4 in.)
Pinakothek der Moderne, Bayerische Staatsgemäldesammlungen,
Stiftung Günther Franke

94
Portrait of Irma Simon, 1924
Oil on canvas
122 x 60 cm (48 x 23 5/8 in.)
Private Collection

95
Landscape with Vesuvius, 1926
Oil on canvas
85.5 x 24.4 cm (33 5/8 x 9 5/8 in.)
Pinakothek der Moderne, Bayerische Staatsgemäldesammlungen

96
Portrait of La Duchessa "di Malvedi," 1926
Oil on canvas
66.5 x 27 cm (26 1/8 x 10 5/8 in.)
Pinakothek der Moderne, Bayerische Staatsgemäldesammlungen

97
Still-Life with Gramophone and Irises, 1924
Oil on canvas
114.3 x 55.6 cm (45 x 21 7/8 in.)
The Lewis Collection

98
Portrait of Quappi, 1925
Pencil on paper
48 x 32 cm (18 7/8 x 12 5/8 in.)
Staatliche Museen zu Berlin, Kupferstichkabinett, Bequest of Barbara Göpel (Donation of Erhard and Barbara Göpel)

99
Carnival in Naples, 1925
Brush and India ink, crayon and chalk on paper
110.5 x 69.5 cm (43 9/16 x 27 3/8 in.)
The Art Institute of Chicago.
Margaret Day Blake Collection

100
Italian Fantasy, 1925
Oil on canvas
127 x 23 cm (50 x 9 in.)
Kunsthalle Bielefeld

101
Galleria Umberto, 1925
Oil on canvas
113 x 50 cm (44 5/8 x 19 3/4 in.)
Private Collection

102
Lido, 1924
Oil on canvas
72.4 x 90.5 cm (28 1/2 x 35 5/8 in.)
Saint Louis Museum, Bequest of Morton D. May

103
Self-Portrait with White Cap, 1926
Oil on canvas
100 x 73.7 cm (39 3/8 x 27 3/4 in.)
Anonymous Lender

104
The Bark, 1926
Oil on canvas
180.3 x 90.2 cm (71 x 35 1/2 in.)
Courtesy of a Private Collection

SELECTED BIBLIOGRAPHY

Catalogue raisonnés and Bibliographies

Göpel, Erhard and Barbara Göpel. *Max Beckmann. Katalog der Gemälde*, 2 Vol. Bern: Kornfeld and Cie, 1976 (with Bibliography).

Hofmaier, James. *Max Beckmann. Catalogue raisonné of his Prints*, 2 Vol. Bern: Kornfeld, 1990.

Max Beckmann Bibliographie 1971–1993, ed. by Felix Billeter, Alina Dobrzecki and Christian Lenz. Munich, 1994.

Max Beckmann. Die Aquarelle und Pastelle. Werkverzeichnis der farbigen Arbeiten auf Papier, ed. by Mayen Beckmann, Siegfried Gohr and Max Hollein. Cologne: DuMont, 2006.

Max Beckmann. Die Skizzenbücher/The Sketchbooks, by Christiane Zeiller, 2 Vol. Ostfildern: Hatje Cantz, 2010.

Wiese, Stephan von. *Max Beckmanns zeichnerisches Werk 1903–1925*. Düsseldorf: Droste, 1978.

https://beckmann-gemaelde.org/

Exhibition catalogues (alphabetical/ chronological):

Max Beckmann, exh. cat. Frankfurter Kunstverein, in association with the Graphic Kabinett J. B. Neumann, Berlin, 1921.

Max Beckmann, exh. cat. Frankfurter Kunstverein, in association with Zinglers Kabinett, Frankfurt/M., 1924.

Max Beckmann, exh. cat. Artlover. J. B. Neumanns Bilderhefte, New Art Circle/Neue Kunstgemeinschaft, New York and Berlin, 1927.

Max Beckmann. Das gesammelte Werk. Gemälde, Graphik, Handzeichnungen aus den Jahren 1905 bis 1927, exh. cat. Städtische Kunsthalle, Mannheim, 1928.

Max Beckmann, exh. cat. Galerie Alfred Flechtheim, Berlin, 1928.

Max Beckmann. Gemälde aus den Jahren 1920–1928. Ill. index with preface by Wilhelm Hausenstein, exh. cat. Graphisches Kabinett Günther Franke, Munich, 1928.

Max Beckmann 1948, exh. cat. The City Art Museum, St. Louis, et al., 1948.

Max Beckmann zum Gedächtnis. 1884–1950, exh. cat. Haus der Kunst, Munich and Charlottenburger Schloß, Berlin, 1951.

Max Beckmann. Das Portrait, exh. cat. Badischer Kunstverein, Karlsruhe, 1963.

Max Beckmann, Text by Peter Selz, with contributions by Harold Joachim and Perry T. Rathbone, exh. cat. The Museum of Modern Art, New York, 1964–65.

Max Beckmann. Aquarelle und Zeichnungen 1903 bis 1950, ed. by Klaus Gallwitz, exh. cat. Kunsthalle Bielefeld; Kunsthalle Tübingen and Städtische Galerie im Städelschen Kunstinstitut, Frankfurt/M., 1977–78.

Max Beckmann. Radierungen, Lithographien, Holzschnitte, ed. by Ralph Jentsch, exh. cat. Kunstgalerie Esslingen, Munich and New York, 1981.

Max Beckmann. Die Triptychen im Städel, exh. cat. Städtische Galerie im Städelschen Kunstinstitut, Frankfurt/M., 1981.

Max Beckmann. Die frühen Bilder, exh. cat. Kunsthalle Bielefeld und Städtische Galerie im Städelschen Kunstinstitut, Frankfurt/M., 1982–83

Max Beckmann. Die Hölle, 1919, by Alexander Dückers, exh. cat. Kupferstichkabinett, Berlin, 1983.

Max Beckmann Frankfurt 1915–1933. Eine Ausstellung zum 100. Geburtstag, exh. cat. Städtische Galerie im Städelschen Kunstinstitut, Frankfurt/M., 1983–84.

Max Beckmann. Seine Themen – seine Zeit. Zum 100. Geburtstag des Künstlers, exh. cat. Kunsthalle, Bremen, 1984.

Max Beckmann. Graphik zum 100. Geburtstag, with contributions by Martin Gosebruch, Christian Lenz and Joachim Poeschke, exh. cat. Galerie der Stadt, Esslingen, 1984.

Max Beckmann, Josef-Haubrich-Kunsthalle, exh. cat. Cologne, 1984.

Max Beckmann. Graphik. Anläßlich der Ausstellung zum 100. Geburtstag, exh. cat. Museum der bildenden Künste, Leipzig, 1984.

Max Beckmann. Retrospektive, ed. by Clara Schulz-Hoffmann and Judith C. Weiss, exh. cat. Haus der Kunst, Munich; Nationalgalerie, Berlin; The St. Louis Art Museum, St. Louis and Los Angeles County Museum of Art, 1984–85.

Max Beckmann. Gesichter von Tag und Traum. Aus dem graphischen Werk von Max Beckmann (1884–1950), exh. cat. Graphiksammlung ETH Zürich, 1984.

Max Beckmann. Aus dem Menschenorchester. Graphische Zyklen um 1920, exh. cat. Kaiser Wilhelm Museum, Krefeld, 1985.

Max Beckmann Gemälde 1905–1950, ed. by Klaus Gallwitz, exh. cat. Museum der bildenden Künste, Leipzig and Städelsches Kunstinstitut, Frankfurt/M., 1990–91.

Max Beckmann Prints, exh. cat. The Museum of Modern Art, New York, 1992.

Max Beckmann Welt-Theater, Das graphische Werk 1901–1946, ed. by Jo-Anne Birnie Danzker and Amélie Ziersch, exh. cat. Villa Stuck, Munich, 1993.

Max Beckmann. Selbstbildnisse, exh. cat. Hamburger Kunsthalle and Staatsgalerie Moderner Kunst, Munich, 1993.

Max Beckmann. Weltbild und Existenz. Druckgraphik, exh. cat. Städtische Galerie, Albstadt, 1994.

Max Beckmann. Briefe an Reinhard Piper, exh. cat. Staatsgalerie Moderner Kunst, Munich, 1994.

Max Beckmann. Meisterwerke 1907–1950, ed. by Karin von Maur, exh. cat. Staatsgalerie, Stuttgart, 1994.

Max Beckmann, exh. cat. Galleria Nazionale d'Arte Moderna, Roma, 1996.

Max Beckmann. Die Nacht, ed. by Anette Kruszynski, exh. cat. Kunstsammlung Nordrhein-Westfalen, Düsseldorf, 1997.

Circus Beckmann, exh. cat. Sprengel Museum, Hannover, 1998.

Max Beckmann. Zeichnungen aus dem Nachlaß Mathilde Q. Beckmann, ed. by Herwig Gurtzsch, exh. cat. Museum der bildenden Künste, Leipzig 1998, Cologne, 1998.

Minna Beckmann-Tube, exh. cat. Staatsgalerie Moderner Kunst, Munich, 1998.

Max Beckmann. Landschaft als Fremde, exh. cat. Hamburger Kunsthalle; Kunsthalle, Bielefeld and Kunstforum, Wien, 1998–99.

Max Beckmann und Günther Franke, exh. cat. Staatsgalerie Moderner Kunst, Munich, 2000.

Max Beckmann. Selbstbildnisse. Zeichnung und Druckgraphik, exh. cat. Bayerische Staatsgemäldesammlungen and Neue Pinakothek, Munich and Herzog Anton Ulrich-Museum, Braunschweig, 2000–01.

Max Beckmann. Der Zeichner, exh. cat. Städtische Kunstsammlungen Galerie, Albstadt, 2001.

Spektakel des Lebens. Max Beckmann – Arbeiten auf Papier, ed. by Andrea Firmenich and Martina Padberg, exh. cat. Sinclair Haus, Bad Homburg; Folkwang Museum, Essen and Ulmer Museum, 2001–02.

"Ich kann wirklich ganz gut malen." Friedrich August von Kaulbach – Max Beckmann, ed. by Brigitte Salmen, exh. cat. Schloßmuseum, Murnau, 2002.

Max Beckmann. Lithographien, Kaltnadelradierungen, Holzschnitte, ed. by Sabine Fehlemann, with Edla Colsman, exh. cat. Von der Heydt-Museum, Wuppertal, 2002.

Max Beckmann. Un peintre dans l'histoire, exh. cat. Centre Pompidou, Paris, 2002–03.

Max Beckmann, ed. by Sean Rainbird, exh. cat. Tate Modern, London, 2003

Max Beckmann, ed. by Robert Storr, exh. cat. Museum of Modern Art, New York, 2003.

Max Beckmann. Menschen am Meer, exh. cat. Bucerius Kunst Forum, Hamburg, 2003–04, Ostfildern-Ruit: Hatje Cantz, 2003.

Max Beckmann in Baden-Baden. Gemälde, Skulpturen, Zeichnungen, exh. cat. Museum Frieder Burda, Baden-Baden and Museum für Neue Kunst, Städtische Museen Freiburg, 2005, Heidelberg: Kehrer, 2005.

Max Beckmann. Zeichnungen und Druckgraphik aus der Sammlung Hegewisch in der Hamburger Kunsthalle, exh. cat. Hamburger Kunsthalle, 2005, Bremen: H. M. Hauschild, 2005.

Max Beckmann. Druckgraphik 1914–1924, exh. cat. Staatliche Kunsthalle Karlsruhe, 2005, Heidelberg: Kehrer, 2005.

Max Beckmann. Traum des Lebens, ed. by Zentrum Paul Klee, Bern and Tilman Osterwold, exh. cat. Zentrum Paul Klee, Bern, 2006, Ostfildern: Hatje Cantz, 2006

Max Beckmann. Von Angesicht zu Angesicht, ed. by Susanne Petri and Hans-Werner Schmidt, exh. cat. Museum der Bildenden Künste, Leipzig, 2010–11, Ostfildern: Hatje Cantz, 2010.

"O mein Liebling ich werde so bös zu Dir sein" Quappi und Max Beckmann, exh. cat. Museum Wiesbaden, 2012.

Dix/Beckmann. Mythos Welt, ed. by Ulrike Lorenz et al., exh. cat. Kunsthalle Mannheim and Kunsthalle der Hypo-Kulturstiftung München, 2013–14, Munich: Hirmer, 2013.

Max Beckmann. Die Landschaften, ed. by Bernhard Mendes Bürgi and Nina Peter, exh. cat. Kunstmuseum Basel, 2015, Ostfildern: Hatje Cantz, 2015.

Max Beckmann. Kleine Stillleben, ed. by Cathrin Klingsöhr-Leroy and Nina Peter, exh. cat. Franz Marc Museum, Kochel a. See, 2013, Berlin and Munich: Deutscher Kunstverlag, 2013.

Max Beckmann. Die Stillleben, ed. by Karin Schick and Hubertus Gaßner, exh. cat. Hamburger Kunsthalle, 2014–15, Munich, et al.: Prestel, 2014.

Max Beckmann und Berlin, ed. by Thomas Köhler and Stefanie Heckmann, exh. cat. Berlinische Galerie, 2015–16, Bielefeld: Kerber, 2015.

Max Beckmann in New York, by Sabine Rewald, exh. cat. The Metropolitan Museum of Art, New York, 2016–17, New Haven and London: Yale University Press, 2016.

Max Beckmann. Weltheater, exh. cat. Kunsthalle Bremen and Museum Barbarini, Potsdam, 2017–18, Munich, et al.: Prestel, 2017.

Max Beckmann. Weiblich–Männlich, ed. by Karin Schick, exh. cat. Hamburger Kunsthalle, 2020, Munich, et al.: Prestel, 2020.

Städels Beckmann - Beckmanns Städel. Die Jahre in Frankfurt, exh. cat. Städel Museum, Frankfurt/M., 2020–21.

Max Beckmann. Departure, ed. by Oliver Kase et al., exh. cat. Pinakothek der Moderne, 2022–23, Ostfildern: Hatje Cantz, 2022.

Articles, Anthologies and Monographs (alphabetical/chronological):

Albert, Karl. "Philosophische Interpretationen zu Max Beckmanns Odysseus und Kalypso," in: *Zeitschrift für Ästhetik und Allgemeine Kunstwissenschaft*, Vol. XXIX, 1984: 99–126.

Anderson, Eleanor. "Max Beckmann's Carnival triptych," in: *Art Journal*, Vol. 24, 1965: 218–26.

Beall, Karen F. "Max Beckmann. Day and Dream," in: *The Quarterly Journal of the Library of Congress*, Vol. 27, 1970: 2–19.

Becker, Astrid. *Max Beckmann. Selbst und Weltbild in den Themen 'Caféhaus' und 'Tanz,'* Marburg: Tectum 2010.

Beckett, Sister Wendy. *Max Beckmann and the Self*, Munich and New York: Prestel, 1997.

Beckmann, Max. *Sichtbares und Unsichtbares*, ed. and with an afterword by Peter Beckmann, Introduction by Peter Selz, Stuttgart: Chr. Belser, 1965.

---. *Leben in Berlin. Tagebuch 1908/1909*, annotated and ed. by Hans Kinkel, Munich and Zürich: Piper, 1983.

---. *Briefe im Kriege 1914/1915*, collected by Minna Tube, Munich and Zürich: Piper, 1984.

---. *Frühe Tagebücher 1903/04 und 1912/13*, with memoirs by Minna Beckmann-Tube, annotated and ed. by Doris Schmidt, Munich and Zürich: Piper, 1985.

---. *Tagebücher 1940–1950*, compiled by Mathilde Q. Beckmann, ed. and with an afterword by Erhard Göpel, with a foreword by Friedhelm W. Fischer, Munich and Zürich: Piper, 1987.

---. *Die Realität der Träume in den Bildern. Schriften und Gespräche 1911 bis 1950*, ed. and with an afterword by Rudolf Pillep, Munich and Zürich: Piper, 1990.

---. *Briefe*, 3 Vol., ed. by Klaus Gallwitz, Uwe M. Schneede and Stephan von Wiese with the collaboration of Barbara Golz, Munich and Zürich: Piper, 1993–96.

---. *Self-Portrait in Words. Collected Writings and Statements, 1903–1950*, ed. and annotated by Barbara Copeland Buenger, Chicago and London: University Press, 1997.

Max Beckmann at the Saint Louis Art Museum. The Paintings, by Lynette Roth, Munich et al.: DelMonico Books/Prestel, 2015.

Max Beckmann. Der Zeichner, selection and introduction by Erhard Göpel, Munich: Piper, 1954.

Max Beckmann in der Pinakothek der Moderne, ed. by Felix Billeter, in collaboration with the Bayerischen Staatsgemäldesammlungen München, Ostfildern: Hatje Cantz, 2008.

Max Beckmann in Frankfurt, ed. by Klaus Gallwitz, Frankfurt/M.: Insel, 1984.

Max Beckmann Colloquium 1984, Sixth annual meeting of the art science section of the Association of Visual Artists of the GDR, edited protocol, Leipzig, 1984.

Max Beckmann Symposium, 15./16. Mai 1984, Joseph-Haubrich-Kunsthalle, Cologne, 1987.

Max Beckmann. Die Frankfurter Jahre, ed. by W.A. Nagel, text by Ewald Rathke, Hanau: Peters, 1991.

Beckmann, Mathilde Q. *Mein Leben mit Max Beckmann*, Munich and Zürich: Piper, 1985.

Beckmann, Peter. *Schwarz auf Weiss. Max Beckmann. Wege zur Wirklichkeit*, Stuttgart and Zürich: Piper, 1977.

---. *Max Beckmann. Leben und Werk*, Stuttgart and Zürich: Piper, 1982.

Max Beckmann. Vorträge 1996–1998, Munich, 2000.

Max Beckmann. Aufsätze, Munich, 2002.

Max Beckmann. Beiträge 2002, Munich, 2003.

Max Beckmann. Beiträge 2012, Munich, 2012.

Max Beckmann. Beiträge 2016, Munich, 2016.

Max Beckmann. Beiträge 2017, Munich, 2017.

Max Beckmann. Beiträge 2019, Munich, 2019.

Max Beckmann und J.B. Neumann. Der Künstler und sein Händler in Briefen und Dokumenten 1917–1950, ed. by Ursula Harter and Stephan von Wiese, Cologne: Walther König, 2011.

Max Beckmann und Thüringen. Eine Dokumentation Weimar 1900 – Erfurt 1937, ed. by Hans-Dieter Mück, Stuttgart and Frankfurt/M.: ARTeFACT, 1997.

Belting, Hans. *Max Beckmann. Die Tradition als Problem in der Kunst der Moderne*, Munich and Berlin: Deutscher Kunstverlag, 1984.

---. *Max Beckmann. Tradition as a Problem in Modern Art*, with a preface by Peter Selz, New York: Timken Publishers, 1989.

Bieber, Susanne. "Beckmann's Frankfurt Cityscapes: Concepts of Space," in: exh. cat. Beckmann/London, 2003: 73–9.

Blick auf Beckmann, Munich: Piper, 1962.

Brunner, Manfred. "Max Beckmann und der Kubismus. Ursachen des großen Stilumbruchs oder Anzeichen der Kunsterfahrung am Werden einer modernen Malerei," in: exh. cat. Beckmann/Cologne, 1984: 11–40.

Buch, Lilli. "Max Beckmann. Fußballspieler" (1929), in: *Das Kunstblatt*, Vol. 14, 1930: 148–50.

Buchheim, Lothar-Günther. *Max Beckmann*, Feldafing: Buchheim Verlag, 1959.

Buck, Matthias. "Max Beckmann und die gotischen Neger in der Hölle der Abstraktion," in: exh. cat. Beckmann/Albstadt, 1994: 24–35.

---. *Max Beckmann. Weltenbilder*, Phil. diss. Saarbrücken 1997 (unpublished).

Buenger, Barbara C. "Max Beckmann's Ideologues: Some Forgotten Faces," in: *Art Bulletin*, Vol. 71, 1989: 453–79.

---. "Max Beckmann in the First World War," in: *The Ideological Crisis of Expressionism. The Literary and Artistic War Colony in Belgium 1914–1918*, ed. by Rainer Rumold and O. K. Werckmeister, Columbia/South Caroline: Camden House, 1990: 237–79.

---. *Max Beckmann's Artistic Sources: The Artist's Relation to Older and Modern Traditions* (1979), Ann Arbor: UMI, 1997.

---. "Max Beckmann: 'Der Künstler im Staat,'" in: *Überbrückt. Ästhetische Moderne und Nationalsozialismus. Kunsthistoriker und Künstler 1925–1937*, ed. by Eugen Blume and Dieter Scholz, Köln: Walther König, 1999: 191–200.

---. "Das Italien Max Beckmanns und Wilhelm Worringers," in: Hannes Böhringer and Beate Söntgen, eds. *Wilhelm Worringers Kunstgeschichte*, Munich: Wilhelm Fink, 2002: 141–79.

---. "Some Portraits from the Weimar-Era in Frankfurt," in: Washton Long/Makela, eds., 2009: 165–98.

Chapeaurouge, Donat de. "Bilder von Max Beckmann, die bisher noch nicht auf zeitgenössische Ereignisse bezogen sind," in: *Wallraf-Richartz-Jahrbuch*, Vol. LIII, 1992: 209–22.

Clark, Margot Orthwein. "The many-layered imagery of Max Beckmann's 'Temptation' triptych," in: *Art Quarterly Detroit*, Vol. 1, 1978, No. 3: 244–64.

---. *Max Beckmann. Sources of Imagery in the Hermetic Tradition* (1975), Ann Arbor: UMI, 1997.

Clarke, Jay A. "Space as Metaphor: Beckmann and the Conflicts of Secessionist Style in Berlin," in: Washton Long/Makela, eds., 2009: 49–80.

Dückers, Alexander. "Vom Welttheater und der Sachlichkeit. Zu den Zeichnungen von Beckmann und Dix," in: *Aspekte deutscher Zeichenkunst*, Iris Lauterbach and Margaret Stuffmann, eds., Munich: Zentralinstitut für Kunstgeschichte, 2006: 175–84.

Die Bibliothek Max Beckmanns. Unterstreichungen, Kommentare, Notizen, Skizzen in seinen Büchern, Peter Beckmann and Joachim Schaffer, eds., Worms: Wernersche Verlagsanstalt, 1992.

Eberle, Matthias. *Max Beckmann. Die Nacht. Passion ohne Erlösung*, Frankfurt/M.: Fischer, 1984.

Engels, Christoph. "Auf der Suche nach einer 'deutschen Kunst': Max Beckmann in der Wilhelminischen Kunstkritik," Weimar: VDG, 1997.

Erpel, Fritz. "Rollenspiel für eine Utopie. Zu Beckmanns Selbstdarstellung," in: exh. cat. Beckmann/Cologne, 1984: 112–120.

---. *Max Beckmann. Leben im Werk. Die Selbstbildnisse*, Berlin/Ost: Henschel, 1985.

Fischer, Otto. "Die neueren Werke Max Beckmanns," in: *Museum der Gegenwart*, Vol. 1, 1930: 89–100.

Fischer, Friedhelm W. *Max Beckmann. Symbol und Weltbild. Grundriß zu einer Deutung des Gesamtwerkes*, Munich: Fink, 1972.

---. *Der Maler Max Beckmann*, Cologne: DuMont, 1990.

Fraenger, Wilhelm. "Max Beckmann. Der Traum. Ein Beitrag zur Physiognomik des Grotesken," in: Glaser, et al., 1924: 35–58.

Frosch, Beate. *Max Beckmann. Der Eisgang*, Städelsches Kunstinstitut, ed, by the Kulturstiftung der Länder, Frankfurt/M., 1994.

Gärtner, Peter J. *Der Traum von der Imagination des Raumes. Zu den Raumvorstellungen auf einigen ausgewählten Triptychen Max Beckmanns*, Weimar: VDG, 1996.

Gässler, Ewald. *Studien zum Frühwerk Max Beckmanns. Eine motivkundliche und ikonographische Untersuchung zur Kunst der Jahrhundertwende*, Phil. diss. Göttingen, 1974.

Gandelmann, Claude. "Max Beckmann's triptychs and the simultaneous stages of the 20s," in: *Art History*, Vol. 1, 1978: 472–83.

---. "Das Symbol der 'verkehrten Welt' im Werk Max Beckmanns," in: Max Beckmann, 1987: 9–17.

Glaser, Curt, et al. *Max Beckmann*, Munich: Piper, 1924.

Gohr, Siegfried. "Max Beckmann und Frankreich," in: *Wallraf-Richartz-Jahrbuch*, Vol. XLVII, 1986: 45–62.

---. *Max Beckmann. Motive. Einladung zur Werkbetrachtung*, Cologne: Wienand, 2019.

Gosebruch, Martin. *Mythos ohne Götterwelt*, Esslingen, 1984.

Güse, Ernst-Gerhard. *Das Frühwerk Max Beckmanns. Zur Thematik seiner Bilder aus den Jahren 1904–1914*, Frankfurt/M. and Bern: Lang, 1977.

Haxthausen, Charles Werner. "Der Erste Weltkrieg – Katalysator eines Neubeginns?," in: exh. cat. Beckmann/Munich, et al., 1984: 71–81.

---."'Das Gegenwärtige zeitlos machen und das Zeitlose gegenwärtig.' Max Beckmann zwischen Formalismus und Mythos," in: exh. cat. Beckmann/Düsseldorf, 1997: 35–52.

Hyman, Timothy. "Max Beckmann and the Neue Sachlichkeit," in: *Artscribe*, No. 15, 1978: 29–36.

Jähner, Horst. "Beckmann und das Signal der Auferstehung. Aspekte des Schaffens im Zeichen von Krieg und Revolution," in: *Beckmann-Colloquium 1984*: 42–55.

Jatho, Heinz. "Überlegungen zur Bildsemantik bei Max Beckmann," in: *Modernität und Tradition. Festschrift für Max Imdahl zum 60. Geburtstag*, Gottfried Boehm, ed., et al., Munich: Wilhelm Fink, 1985: 143–53.

---. *Max Beckmann. Schauspieler-Triptychon*, Frankfurt/M.: Insel, 1989.

---. "Das Werk Max Beckmanns als Bildersprache und Bilderschrift," in: *Die Kunst und die Situation des Menschen im 20. Jahrhundert. Symposion, Alfred Hagenlocher zum 75. Geburtstag*, Städtische Galerie Albstadt, 1989: 9–22.

Jedlicka, Gotthard. "Max Beckmann in seinen Selbstbildnissen," in: *Blick auf Beckmann 1962*: 111–31.

Kaiser, Stephan. *Max Beckmann*, Stuttgart: Emil Fink, 1962.

Karnatz, Sebastian. *Eine Szene im Theater der Unendlichkeit. Max Beckmanns Dramen und ihre Bedeutung für seine Bildrhetorik*, Göttingen: V&R unipress, 2011.

Kersting, Hannelore. Max Beckmann – das überschätzte Individuum, in: *Städel-Jahrbuch*, NF, Vol. 10, 1985: 261–76.

Kessler, Charles S. "Blindman's Buff. A triptych by Max Beckmann," in: *Gazette des Beaux-Arts*, Vol. LXXI, 110th Year, 1968: 127–28.

---. *Max Beckmann's Triptychs*, Cambridge/MA: The Belknap Press, 1970.

Kipphoff, Petra. *Max Beckmann. Der Maler als Schreiber*, Springe: zu Klampen 2021.

Kopp-Schmidt, Gabriele. "Max Beckmanns Illustrationen zur Novellensammlung 'Die Fürstin' von Kasimir Edschmid," in: *IDEA. Jahrbuch der Hamburger Kunsthalle*, Vol. 8, 1989: 175–95.

Lackner, Stephan. *Ich erinnere mich gut an Max Beckmann*, Mainz: Kupferberg, 1967.

---. "Das Welttheater des Malers Beckmann," in: exh. cat. Beckmann/Munich, 1993: 17–21.

Lang, Karen. "Max Beckmann's Inconceivable Modernism," in: Washton Long/Makela, eds., 2009: 80–101.

Lenz, Christian. "'Mann und Frau' im Werke von Max Beckmann," in: *Städel-Jahrbuch*, NF, Vol. 3, 1971: 213–37.

---. "Max Beckmanns *Synagoge*," in: *Städel-Jahrbuch*, NF, Vol. 4, 1973: 299–320.

---. "Max Beckmann. *Das Martyrium*," in: *Jahrbuch der Berliner Museen*, Vol. 16, 1974: 185–210.

---. *Max Beckmann und Italien*, Frankfurt/M.: Dt.-Ital. Vereinigung, 1976.

---. *Ewig wechselndes Welttheater*, Esslingen, 1984.

---. "'Ich habe gezeichnet, das sichert einen gegen Tod und die Gefahr.' Max Beckmann im Ersten Weltkrieg," in: *Gedanken zur Handzeichnung. Günter Busch zum 75. Geburtstag*, Bremen: Hauschild, 1992: 46–53.

---. "Kirchner-Meidner-Beckmann. Drei deutsche Künstler im Ersten Weltkrieg," in: *Kultur und Krieg. Die Rolle der Intellektuellen, Künstler und Schriftsteller im Ersten Weltkrieg*, Wolfgang J. Mommsen, ed. Munich: R. Oldenbourg, 1996: 171–78.

---. Max Beckmann und die Alten Meister. 'Eine ganz nette Reihe von Freunden,' Munich: Edition Braus, 2000.

---. *Max Beckmann*, Münster: Rhema, 2022.

Meier-Graefe, Julius. "Gesichter. Vorrede zu einer Mappe mit 19 Radierungen von Max Beckmann" (1919), in: *Blick auf Beckmann 1962*: 50–6.

Nentwig, Janina. "Eine Frage des Blickwinkels. Max Beckmann und die Neue Sachlichkeit," in: exh. cat. Beckmann 2015: 156–63.

Noll, Thomas. "'Adam und Eva' im Werk von Max Beckmann," in: *Jahrbuch der Berliner Museen*, NF, Vol. 43, 2001: 261–302.

---. "Max Beckmanns *Großes Stilleben mit Musikinstrumenten*. Zur Deutung des Gemäldes im Spiegel eines Bildgedichts oder: Der Künstler als Interpret seines Werkes," in: *Städel-Jahrbuch*, NF, Vol. 18, 2002: 271–96.

O'Brien-Twohig, Sarah. *Beckmann Carnival*, London: Tate, 1984.

---. "Die Hölle der Großstadt," in: exh. cat. Beckmann/Munich, et al. 1984: 93–112.

---. "Max Beckmann," in: exh. cat. London 1985/86: 436–40.

Olbrich, Harald. "Das Gemälde 'Junge Männer am Meer" im kunsthistorischen Umfeld," in: Beckmann/Cologne, 1984: 56–62.

Ottinger, Didier. *Beckmann en eaux troubles*, Paris: Centre Pompidou, 2001.

Peter, Nina. *Max Beckmann: Landschaften der zwanziger Jahre*, Frankfurt/M., et a.,: Peter Lang, 1993.

---. "The Painter at the Beach: Beckmann's Italian Paintings," in: exh. cat. Beckmann/London, 2003: 84–90.

Peters, Anne. "Das Kriegserlebnis bei Beckmann und Dix – Wendepunkt oder Neubeginn?," in: exh. cat. Beckmann/Albstadt, 1994: 36–54.

Peters, Olaf. "Max Beckmann, die Neue Sachlichkeit und das Problem des Werterelativismus in der Weimarer Republik," in: *Wallraf-Richartz-Jahrbuch*, Vol. 61, 2000: 237–61.

---. *Vom schwarzen Seiltänzer. Max Beckmann zwischen Weimarer Republik und Exil*, Berlin: Reimer, 2005.

---. "Max Beckmann – Neuerscheinungen zum Werk des Malers," in: *Kunstchronik*, Vol. 61, Issue 3, 2008: 117–27.

---. "Der Krieg und die Künstler. Ernst Ludwig Kirchner, Otto Dix und Max Beckmann im Selbstbildnis," in: *Nach 1914. Der Erste Weltkrieg in der europäischen Kultur*, ed. by Michael Braun, et al., Würzburg: Könighausen & Neumann, 2017: 337–59.

Pillep, Rudolf. "Max Beckmann und Politik. Aspekte," in: *Wissenschaftliche Zeitschrift der Humboldt-Universität zu Berlin. Gesellschafts- und Sprachwissenschaftliche Reihe*, Vol. 34, 1985: 137–44.

---. *Max Beckmann. Leben und Werk. Neue Forschungen*, Halle (Saale), 1992 (unpublished typescript).

Poeschke, Joachim. *Max Beckmann in seinen Selbstbildnissen*, Esslingen, 1984.

---. "'Meinen Stil zu gewinnen...Beckmann und Cézanne,'" in: Max Beckmann 2000: 9–22.

Rave, Paul Ortwin. "Max Beckmann. Bemerkungen zu der Geschichte seines Ruhmes," in: *Der Monat*, Vol. 4, 1952: 67–72.

Reifenberg, Benno. "Max Beckmann" (1921), in: *Blick auf Beckmann 1962*: 101–09.

---. "Der Zeichner Max Beckmann" (1954), in: *Blick auf Beckmann 1962*: 140–53.

Reimertz, Stephan. *Max Beckmann*, Reinbek: Rowohlt 1995.

---. *Max Beckmann und Minna Tube. Eine Liebe im Porträt*, Berlin: Rowohlt, 1996.

---. *Max Beckmann. Biographie*, Frankfurt/M.: Luchterhand, 2003.

Rother, Susanne. *Beckmann als Landschaftsmaler*, Munich: scaneg, 1990.

Schiff, Gert. "Max Beckmann: Die Ikonographie der Triptychen. Umrisse einer geplanten Arbeit," in: *Munuscula discipulorum. Kunsthistorische Studien, Hans Kauffmann zum 70. Geburtstag 1966*, Tilmann Buddensieg and Matthias Winner, ed. Berlin: Hessling, 1968: 265–85.

---. "Die neun vollendeten Triptychen von Max Beckmann," in: exh. cat. Beckmann/Frankfurt, 1981: 62–81.

Schmidt, Paul Ferdinand: "Max Beckmann," in: *Der Cicerone*, Vol. XI, 1919: 675–84.

Schneede, Uwe M. "Allegorien der Kunst. Zu einigen Triptychen von Max Beckmann," in: exh. cat. Beckmann, 1990–91: 37–45.

---. *Max Beckmann in der Hamburger Kunsthalle*, Stuttgart: Hatje Cantz, 1992.

---. *Max Beckmann. Der Maler seiner Zeit*, Munich: C.H. Beck, 2009.

---. *Max Beckmann*, Munich: C.H. Beck, 2011.

Schubert, Dietrich. "Die Beckmann-Marc-Kontroverse von 1912: 'Sachlichkeit' versus 'Innerer Klang'," in: *Expressionismus und Kulturkrise*, Bernd Hüppauf, ed. Heidelberg: Carl Winter, 1983: 207–44.

---. *Max Beckmann. Auferstehung und Erscheinung der Toten*, Worms: Werner, 1985.

---. *Max Beckmann. Vom Vietzker Strand zur Departure. Die Kristallisation seiner Werturteile und seine bildnerische Praxis 1904–1936*, Petersberg: Michael Imhof, 2021.

Schütz, Helmut G. *Sphinx Beckmann. Exemplarische Annäherungen an Max Beckmanns Kunst*, Munich: scaneg, 1997.

Schulze, Ingrid. "Über Traditionen von Tiersatire und 'Verkehrter Welt' und ihre Bedeutung für die Kunst des 20. Jahrhunderts, insbesondere für Max Beckmann," in: *Beiträge zur Burgenforschung. Hermann Waescher zum 100. Geburtstag*, Irene Roch, ed. Halle (Saale), 1990: 41–56.

---. "Zirkus, Karussell und Schaubude. Max Beckmanns Graphikmappe Der

Jahrmarkt von 1921 im Lichte literarischer und bildkünstlerischer Überlieferungen," in: *Weimarer Beiträge*, Vol. 37, 1991, Nr. 2: 196–212.

Schulz-Hoffmann, Carla. "Gitter, Fessel, Maske. Zum Problem der Unfreiheit im Werk von Max Beckmann," in: exh. cat. Beckmann/Munich et al., 1984: 15–52.

---. *Max Beckmann. Der Maler*, Munich: Bruckmann, 1991.

---. "Max Beckmann im 1. Weltkrieg – Die Bilder, die Briefe," in: Beckmann 2000: 49–61.

Schulz-Mons, Christoph. "Kirchner und Beckmann in Frankfurt," in: *Zeitschrift für Kunstgeschichte*, Vol. 43, 1980: 203–10.

---. "Zur Frage der Modernität des Frühwerks von Max Beckmann," in: exh. cat. Beckmann 1982–83: 137–45.

Schwarz, Birgit and Michael Viktor. *Dix und Beckmann. Stil als Option und Schicksal*, Mainz: von Zabern, 1996.

Seidel, Martin. "Kirchners 'Brücke'-Gemälde, ein Zeitungsphoto mit Max Beckmann und weitere Einflüsse," in: *Marburger Jahrbuch für Kunstgeschichte*, Vol. 25, 1998: 149–64.

Selz, Peter. "Max Beckmann 1933–1950. Zur Deutung der Triptychen," in: exh. cat. Beckmann/Frankfurt, 1981: 14–33.

---. *Max Beckmann. The Self-Portraits*, afterword by Nathan Oliveira, New York, 1992.

---. *Max Beckmann*, New York, London and Paris: Abbeville Press, 1996.

Simmen, Jeannot. "Max Beckmann. Schwebe-Sturz im Luftmeer," in: *Foedera Naturai. Klaus Heinrich zum 60. Geburtstag*, ed. by Hartmut Zinser, Friedrich Stentzler and Karl-Heinz Kohl, Würzburg: Königshausen & Neumann, 1989: 312–24.

Simon, Heinrich. "Max Beckmann," in: *Das Kunstblatt*, Vol. 3, 1919: 257–64.

---. *Max Beckmann*, Berlin and Leipzig: Klinkhardt & Biermann, 1930.

Soiné, Knut. "Das Mann-Frau-Verhältnis und das Fischsymbol. Zur Ikonographie Max Beckmanns und Bezüge zur zeitgenössischen Kunst," in: *kritische berichte*, Vol. 12, 1984: 42–67.

---. "Christus Beckmann? Zu Max Beckmanns *Selbstbildnis mit rotem Schal*," 1917, in: *Jahrbuch der Staatlichen Kunstsammlungen in Baden-Württemberg*, Vol. 39, 2002: 95–116.

Spieler, Reinhard. *Max Beckmann 1884–1950. Der Weg zum Mythos*, Cologne: Taschen 1994.

---. "Max Beckmann 'Versuchung,'" in: *Im Blickfeld. Jahrbuch der Hamburger Kunsthalle*, Vol. 1: Konstruktionen der Moderne, 1994: 61–88.

---. *Max Beckmann. Bildwelt und Weltbild in den Triptychen*, with a contribution from Hans Belting, Cologne: DuMont, 1998.

Tellini, Ute L. "Max Beckmann's 'Tribute' to Rosa Luxemburg," in: *Women's Art Journal*, Vol. 18, 1997–98: 22–6.

Washton Long, Rose Carol and Maria Makela, eds. *Of 'Truths Impossible to Put in Words'. Max Beckmann Contextualized*, Bern, et al.: Peter Lang, 2009.

Washton Long, Rose Carol. "Ambivalence: Personal and Politics. Beckmann's Print Portfolios, 1919–1924," in: Washton Long/ Makela, eds. 2009: 103–34.

Weisner, Uwe. "Der Wandelsweg. Zu einem Weg-Bilde Max Beckmanns in der Kieler Kunsthalle," in: *Nordelbingen*, Nr. 47, 1978: 80–92.

Werr, Barbara. "'Eine gute und ganz amusante Sache'. Max Beckmanns *Berliner Reise*," in: exh. cat. Beckmann 2015: 128–35.

Westheider, Ortrud. *Die Farbe Schwarz in der Malerei Max Beckmanns*, Berlin: Reimer 1995.

Wieg, Cornelia. *Max Beckmann seiner Liebsten. Ein Doppelporträt*, Ostfildern-Ruit: Hatje Cantz, 2011.

Wiese, Stephan von. "Die Welt – ein Inferno. Zu Beckmanns Zyklus 'Die Hölle,'" in: exh. cat. Beckmann 1983/84: 29–36.

---. "'Somnambulismus und Bewußtseinshelle.' Zu Max Beckmanns 'Auferstehung' (1916/18)," in: Max Beckmann 1987: 79–95.

---. "'Sogni contrastanti si mescolano di me.' Realità ed enigma nel dipinto 'Galleria Umberto' di Max Beckmann," in: exh. cat. Beckmann 1997: 41–8.

---. "'Zwiespältige Träume – laufen sie mir durcheinander'. Realität und Rätsel im Gemälde Galleria Umberto von Max Beckmann," in: *L'arte del disegno. Christel Thiem zum 3. Januar 1997*, Munich: Deutscher Kunstverlag, 1998: 196–206.

Wilkin, Karen. "Max Beckmann and the School of Paris," in: *New Criterion*, Vol. 17, 1999: 37–42.

Wolk, Joan. "Das 'Vanitas'-Motiv bei Max Beckmann und Jean Paul: Symbole der Unsterblichkeit und der Liebe," in: exh. cat. Beckmann 1983–84: 51–8.

Zeiller, Christiane: "'... wenn ich etwas vom Leben gefühlt habe, so steht es da drin.' Beobachtungen zur Gestik der Hände im Werk Max Beckmanns," in: *Festschrift für Christian Lenz. Von Duccio bis Beckmann*, ed. by Felix Billeter and Helga Gutbrod, Frankfurt/M.: Verlag Blick in die Welt, 1998: 169–82.

---. *Max Beckmann. Die frühen Jahre, 1899–1907*, Weimar: VDG, 2003.

Zenser, Hildegard. "Zu den Selbstbildnissen 1915–1930," in: exh. cat. Beckmann/Munich, et al. 1984: 53–70.

---. Max Beckmann. Selbstbildnisse, Munich: Schirmer Mosel, 1984.

INDEX

S

T

U

V

W

Z

PHOTOGRAPH AND COPYRIGHT CREDITS

We wish to thank the museums, galleries and individuals named in the captions of plates and text illustrations for supplying the photographic material in this publication.

Photograph credits

Ackland Art Museum: 190
akg-images: 38 (Berlinische Galerie), 259 (Buchheim Museum), 246 (Klassik Stiftung Weimar), 69 (Kunsthalle Bremen - Der Kunstverein in Bremen), 185, 203 (Museum Behnhaus Drägerhaus), 71 (Museum Ludwig), 74, 208, 123 bottom, 217 (Private Collection), 183 (Rose Art Museum), 14 (Stiftung Stadtmuseum Berlin), 184 (Weisman Art Museum)
Pfalzgalerie Kaiserslautern: 41 (Andreas Kusch © mpk)
ARTOTHEK: 56, 78, 114 top right, 198 (Kunsthalle Bremen – Die Kulturgutscanner), 200 (Kunsthalle Bremen - Lars Lohrisch), 182 (Christie's Images Ltd)
Art Resource, NY: 113 (Album / Museo del Prado, Madrid), 43, 67–68, 188, 195, 211 (The Art Institute of Chicago), 257 (bpk Bildagentur / Hamburger Kunsthalle, Private Collection / Elke Walford), front cover, 17 (bpk Bildagentur/Kunstsammlung Nordrhein-Westfalen/Walter Klein), 166, 192 (bpk Bildagentur / Kupferstichkabinett, Staatliche Museen zu Berlin / Volker-H. Schneider), 39, 75, 79 (bpk Bildagentur / Neue Nationalgalerie, Staatliche Museen zu Berlin / Jörg P. Anders), 170, 204, 206–207, 251 (bpk Bildagentur / Pinakothek der Moderne, Bayerische Staatsgemäldesammlungen), 26, 52, 175 (bpk Bildagentur / Sprengel Museum Hannover / Michael Herling / Aline Gwose), 159–165 (bpk Bildagentur / SSK / Raphael Maaß), 53, 112 left (bpk Bildagentur / Staatliche Museen zu Berlin, Kupferstichkabinett / Jörg P. Anders), 20, 49 (bpk Bildagentur / Städel Museum Frankfurt), 51, 54–55, 58–59, 61, 64, 73, 77, 81–99, 119 right, 122, 131–151, 168–169, 171, 177, 189, 193–194, 196 (© The Museum of Modern Art/Licensed by SCALA), 197 (The Solomon R. Guggenheim Museum), 173 (© Tate, London)
Bayerische Staatsgemäldesammlungen: 66, 102 (Margarita Platis)
Bridgeman Images: 209 (© Peter Willi), 215 (© Christie's Images)
Courtesy Galerie St. Etienne, New York: 205
Dietrich Schubert: 115, 124
Fritz Löffler: 123 top
Galleria Borghese, Rome: 253 right
Galleria dell'Accademia, Florence: 252
Germanisches Nationalmuseum, Nürnberg, ©Oliver Baker: 12, 36
Getty Images: 100 (Haeckel collection/ullstein bild), 244 (Topical Press Agency / Stringer)
Harvard Art Museums/ Busch-Reisinger Museum: 155
Holkham Hall, Norfolk: 25
Juan Trujillo: 201
Kunsthalle Bielefeld: 212 (Philippe Ottendörfer)
Kunsthalle Mannheim: 57, 72, 186, 187, 199
Kunst- und Museumsverein im Von der Heydt-Museum Wuppertal. Photo: Antje Zeis-Loi, Medienzentrum Wuppertal: 16 top, 117
Kunstsammlung Gera: 118 (Holger P. Saupe)
Kupferstichkabinett, Staatliche Museen zu Berlin (Dietmar Katz): 65, 174, 210
Kupferstich-Kabinett, Staatliche Kunstsammlungen Dresden: 114 bottom (Herbert Boswank)
Max Beckmann Archive, Bayerische Staatsgemäldesammlungen: 249 (© Bayerische Staatsgemäldesammlungen, Sibylle Forster)
Museum Folkwang Essen: 253 left
Museum of Fine Arts Boston: 167, 178
Pels-Leusden: 114 top left
© Staatsgalerie Stuttgart: 16 bottom, 21, 27, 116 left, 121
National Gallery of Art, Washington D.C.: 105, 107, 112 right
Tate Images: 6 (Paul Weller), 9
Saint Louis Art Museum: 23, 76, 179, 214
Sprengel Museum Hannover: 119 left (Döring and Lenz)
Toledo Museum of Art: 181
University of Colorado Boulder Libraries: 11
Universtitätsbibiliothek Erlangen: 111 (W. Hutt)
Von Wiese: 116 right

Copyright credits